41: *Afro-American Poets Since 1955,* edited by Trudier Harris and Thadious M. Davis (1985)

42: *American Writers for Children Before 1900,* edited by Glenn E. Estes (1985)

43: *American Newspaper Journalists, 1690-1872,* edited by Perry J. Ashley (1986)

44: *American Screenwriters,* Second Series, edited by Randall Clark, Robert E. Morsberger, and Stephen O. Lesser (1986)

45: *American Poets, 1880-1945,* First Series, edited by Peter Quartermain (1986)

46: *American Literary Publishing Houses, 1900-1980: Trade and Paperback,* edited by Peter Dzwonkoski (1986)

47: *American Historians, 1866-1912,* edited by Clyde N. Wilson (1986)

48: *American Poets, 1880-1945,* Second Series, edited by Peter Quartermain (1986)

49: *American Literary Publishing Houses, 1638-1899,* 2 parts, edited by Peter Dzwonkoski (1986)

50: *Afro-American Writers Before the Harlem Renaissance,* edited by Trudier Harris (1986)

51: *Afro-American Writers from the Harlem Renaissance to 1940,* edited by Trudier Harris (1987)

52: *American Writers for Children Since 1960: Fiction,* edited by Glenn E. Estes (1986)

53: *Canadian Writers Since 1960,* First Series, edited by W. H. New (1986)

54: *American Poets, 1880-1945,* Third Series, 2 parts, edited by Peter Quartermain (1987)

55: *Victorian Prose Writers Before 1867,* edited by William B. Thesing (1987)

56: *German Fiction Writers, 1914-1945,* edited by James Hardin (1987)

57: *Victorian Prose Writers After 1867,* edited by William B. Thesing (1987)

58: *Jacobean and Caroline Dramatists,* edited by Fredson Bowers (1987)

59: *American Literary Critics and Scholars, 1800-1850,* edited by John W. Rathbun and Monica M. Grecu (1987)

60: *Canadian Writers Since 1960,* Second Series, edited by W. H. New (1987)

61: *American Writers for Children Since 1960: Poets, Illustrators, and Nonfiction Authors,* edited by Glenn E. Estes (1987)

62: *Elizabethan Dramatists,* edited by Fredson Bowers (1987)

63: *Modern American Critics, 1920-1955,* edited by Gregory S. Jay (1988)

64: *American Literary Critics and Scholars, 1850-1880,* edited by John W. Rathbun and Monica M. Grecu (1988)

65: *French Novelists, 1900-1930,* edited by Catharine Savage Brosman (1988)

66: *German Fiction Writers, 1885-1913,* 2 parts, edited by James Hardin (1988)

67: *Modern American Critics Since 1955,* edited by Gregory S. Jay (1988)

68: *Canadian Writers, 1920-1959,* First Series, edited by W. H. New (1988)

69: *Contemporary German Fiction Writers,* First Series, edited by Wolfgang D. Elfe and James Hardin (1988)

70: *British Mystery Writers, 1860-1919,* edited by Bernard Benstock and Thomas F. Staley (1988)

71: *American Literary Critics and Scholars, 1880-1900,* edited by John W. Rathbun and Monica M. Grecu (1988)

72: *French Novelists, 1930-1960,* edited by Catharine Savage Brosman (1988)

73: *American Magazine Journalists, 1741-1850,* edited by Sam G. Riley (1988)

74: *American Short-Story Writers Before 1880,* edited by Bobby Ellen Kimbel, with the assistance of William E. Grant (1988)

75: *Contemporary German Fiction Writers,* Second Series, edited by Wolfgang D. Elfe and James Hardin (1988)

76: *Afro-American Writers, 1940-1955,* edited by Trudier Harris (1988)

77: *British Mystery Writers, 1920-1939,* edited by Bernard Benstock and Thomas F. Staley (1988)

78: *American Short-Story Writers, 1880-1910,* edited by Bobby Ellen Kimbel, with the assistance of William E. Grant (1988)

79: *American Magazine Journalists, 1850-1900,* edited by Sam G. Riley (1988)

(Continued on back endsheets)

Dictionary of Literary Biography® • Volume One Hundred Twenty-Three

Nineteenth-Century French Fiction Writers: Naturalism and Beyond, 1860-1900

Dictionary of Literary Biography® • Volume One Hundred Twenty-Three

Nineteenth-Century French Fiction Writers: Naturalism and Beyond, 1860-1900

Edited by
Catharine Savage Brosman
Tulane University

A Bruccoli Clark Layman Book
Gale Research Inc.
Detroit, London

10 9 8 7 6 5 4 3 2 1

Printed in the United States of America

Published simultaneously in the United Kingdom
by Gale Research International Limited
(An affiliated company of Gale Research Inc.)

The paper used in this publication meets the minimum requirements
of American National Standard for Information Sciences—Permanence
Paper for Printed Library Materials, ANSI Z39.48-1984. ∞™

Library of Congress Catalog Card Number 92-29415
ISBN 0-8103-7600-8

In memory of my parents and my cousin John

Contents

Plan of the Series

. . . Almost the most prodigious asset of a country, and perhaps its most precious possession, is its native literary product—when that product is fine and noble and enduring.

Mark Twain*

The advisory board, the editors, and the publisher of the *Dictionary of Literary Biography* are joined in endorsing Mark Twain's declaration. The literature of a nation provides an inexhaustible resource of permanent worth. We intend to make literature and its creators better understood and more accessible to students and the reading public, while satisfying the standards of teachers and scholars.

To meet these requirements, *literary biography* has been construed in terms of the author's achievement. The most important thing about a writer is his writing. Accordingly, the entries in *DLB* are career biographies, tracing the development of the author's canon and the evolution of his reputation.

The purpose of *DLB* is not only to provide reliable information in a convenient format but also to place the figures in the larger perspective of literary history and to offer appraisals of their accomplishments by qualified scholars.

The publication plan for *DLB* resulted from two years of preparation. The project was proposed to Bruccoli Clark by Frederick C. Ruffner, president of the Gale Research Company, in November 1975. After specimen entries were prepared and typeset, an advisory board was formed to refine the entry format and develop the series rationale. In meetings held during 1976, the publisher, series editors, and advisory board approved the scheme for a comprehensive biographical dictionary of persons who contributed to North American literature. Editorial work on the first volume began in January 1977, and it was published in 1978. In order to make *DLB* more than a reference tool and to compile volumes that individually have claim to status as literary history, it was decided to organize volumes by topic, period, or genre. Each of these freestanding volumes provides a biographical-bibliographical guide and overview for a particular area of literature. We are convinced that this organization—as opposed to a single alphabet method—constitutes a valuable innovation in the presentation of reference material. The volume plan necessarily requires many decisions for the placement and treatment of authors who might properly be included in two or three volumes. In some instances a major figure will be included in separate volumes, but with different entries emphasizing the aspect of his career appropriate to each volume. Ernest Hemingway, for example, is represented in *American Writers in Paris, 1920-1939* by an entry focusing on his expatriate apprenticeship; he is also in *American Novelists, 1910-1945* with an entry surveying his entire career. Each volume includes a cumulative index of the subject authors and articles. Comprehensive indexes to the entire series are planned.

With volume ten in 1982 it was decided to enlarge the scope of *DLB*. By the end of 1986 twenty-one volumes treating British literature had been published, and volumes for Commonwealth and Modern European literature were in progress. The series has been further augmented by the *DLB Yearbooks* (since 1981) which update published entries and add new entries to keep the *DLB* current with contemporary activity. There have also been *DLB Documentary Series* volumes which provide biographical and critical source materials for figures whose work is judged to have particular interest for students. One of these companion volumes is entirely devoted to Tennessee Williams.

We define literature as the *intellectual commerce of a nation:* not merely as belles lettres but as that ample and complex process by which ideas are generated, shaped, and transmitted. *DLB* entries are not limited to "creative writers" but extend to other figures who in their time and in their way influenced the mind of a people. Thus the series encompasses historians, journalists, publishers, and screenwriters. By this means

*From an unpublished section of Mark Twain's autobiography, copyright © by the Mark Twain Company

readers of *DLB* may be aided to perceive literature not as cult scripture in the keeping of intellectual high priests but firmly positioned at the center of a nation's life.

DLB includes the major writers appropriate to each volume and those standing in the ranks immediately behind them. Scholarly and critical counsel has been sought in deciding which minor figures to include and how full their entries should be. Wherever possible, useful references are made to figures who do not warrant separate entries.

Each *DLB* volume has a volume editor responsible for planning the volume, selecting the figures for inclusion, and assigning the entries. Volume editors are also responsible for preparing, where appropriate, appendices surveying the major periodicals and literary and intellectual movements for their volumes, as well as lists of further readings. Work on the series as a whole is coordinated at the Bruccoli Clark Layman editorial center in Columbia, South Carolina, where the editorial staff is responsible for accuracy of the published volumes.

One feature that distinguishes *DLB* is the illustration policy—its concern with the iconography of literature. Just as an author is influenced by his surroundings, so is the reader's understanding of the author enhanced by a knowledge of his environment. Therefore *DLB* volumes include not only drawings, paintings, and photographs of authors, often depicting them at various stages in their careers, but also illustrations of their families and places where they lived. Title pages are regularly reproduced in facsimile along with dust jackets for modern authors. The dust jackets are a special feature of *DLB* because they often document better than anything else the way in which an author's work was perceived in its own time. Specimens of the writers' manuscripts are included when feasible.

Samuel Johnson rightly decreed that "The chief glory of every people arises from its authors." The purpose of the *Dictionary of Literary Biography* is to compile literary history in the surest way available to us—by accurate and comprehensive treatment of the lives and work of those who contributed to it.

The *DLB* Advisory Board

Introduction

To many readers of literature, in both French- and English-speaking countries, the nineteenth century in France is preeminently the age of the novel. Although commentators have often proclaimed drama to be the dominant genre in France, principally because of the brilliant achievements of the great classical dramatists of the seventeenth century, the two centuries of writing that followed the Revolution of 1789 were most prominently marked by fiction. It is sometimes assumed even that French fiction is chiefly a creation of the nineteenth century. To be sure, in some ways, the Romantic and especially the realistic and naturalistic novels that flourished in the 1800s represent a break from eighteenth-century models, in both content and style. But it was the prerevolutionary authors—l'abbé Antoine-François Prévost, Denis Diderot, Pierre Carlet de Chamblain de Marivaux, Jean-Jacques Rousseau, and Choderlos de Laclos—who, through their craftsmanship and their use of the form to express individual emotions and evoke the social reality of their time, developed the novel into a major genre.

Jean-Paul Sartre observed in *Qu'est-ce que la littérature?* (1947; translated as *What Is Literature?*, 1949) that the eighteenth century was the first period in France in which writers were not subservient to a conservative institution—throne, aristocracy, church; rather, they acted as spokesmen for a developing, and literate, middle class with its concerns, to whom self-expression and self-examination, in both writing and politics, were becoming increasingly important. In *The Rise of the Novel* (1960), Ian Watt connected the appearance of the form in eighteenth-century England with the rise to prominence of the middle classes. Similarly, in France in the period of cultural transition between the death of Louis XIV in 1715—which brought to a tardy end the cultural hegemony of the previous century—and the 1800s, the novel flourished as literacy and readership expanded greatly among the bourgeoisie; it is estimated by Haydn Mason in *French Writers and Their Society, 1715-1800* (1982) that in the eighteenth century there were 250,000 people in France who could read. The middle class furnished not only readers but writers; with the exception of Charles-Louis de Secondat, Baron de Montesquieu, the major literary figures were self-made men from the middle classes. Doubtless the freedom offered by the novel and the story—a freedom deriving from the fact that there were no classical models—contributed to the popularity of these genres among writers and readers.

It can be argued, then, that the novel was a plausible choice for those who were to create a new literature after the fall of the ancien régime. In nineteenth-century France, nearly all the important literary figures chose the form as at least one of their genres, usually the major one. (The chief exceptions are the presymbolist and symbolist giants: Charles Baudelaire, Stéphane Mallarmé, and Arthur Rimbaud.) The literary landscape after 1800 is marked by monumental achievements in fiction by writers, some of whom themselves are monumental. Honoré de Balzac's title *La Comédie humaine* (1842-1855; translated, 1895-1900), with its suggestion of universality, fits well its creator's vast ambitions, energies, and visions, both artistic and social. Victor Hugo's first great novel, *Notre-Dame de Paris* (1831; translated, 1832), dominates Romantic fiction the way the cathedral dominates the city in his masterful reconstruction, and the way he himself dominated the 1800s in France, by his genius, his energies, and his massive literary production. Gustave Flaubert, the great mid-century realist who rejected romanticism, produced two weighty novels considered masterpieces—*Madame Bovary* (1857; translated, 1881) and *L'Education sentimentale* (1869; translated as *Sentimental Education*, 1898)—plus outstanding long stories. He also set the example of the writer so devoted to his art that all other considerations became secondary, and so obsessed with craft that he rewrote not just sentences and pages but entire works. As a master of fictional style and a technical innovator, he occupies a crucial position in French fiction, a position recognized by such figures as Henry James and Sartre, who paid him oblique homage in the form of a massive psychobiography. Emile Zola stands out in the second half of the century not only as the theoretician of naturalism and the author of a massive series of novels, *Les Rougon-Macquart* (1871-1893; translated as *The Rougon-Macquarts*, 1896-1900), whose aim was to chronicle an entire society, but also as a literary and social visionary and a heroic figure whose political convictions led him to leap into the battle that raged around the 1894 court-martial and ensuing conviction of Capt. Alfred Dreyfus for espionage.

To these towering figures, who created fictional worlds that, in the readers' minds, often rival or stand for the actual historical worlds in which they are set, one can add the name of Stendhal (Marie-Henri Beyle), the author of *Le Rouge et le noir* (1830; translated as *The Red and the Black*, 1913), underrated by readers and critics in his own time—Balzac being a striking exception—but considered since the late 1880s the premier psychologist among nineteenth-century novelists and one of the most acute students of social dynamics that France has produced. Prosper Mérimée, while not a literary giant, left a body of stories known throughout the world; Flaubert's pupil, Guy de Maupassant, less appreciated perhaps in his own country than abroad, stands out as a peerless practitioner of the short story. If one adds to this list such novelists as Edmond and Jules de Goncourt, George Sand, Alexandre Dumas *père*, Anatole France, and Jules Verne, as well as a score or so additional well-recognized writers of the century, such as Joris-Karl Huysmans and Alphonse Daudet, and if one considers the massive output of many on the list, one sees how dominant fiction was at this period in France and with what impressive results it was cultivated.

Throughout the late nineteenth century and part of the twentieth, the popularity of French fiction was demonstrated by many editions of collected works by major Romantic and realist authors—often dozens of volumes in each—in both the original language and translation. Toward the mid twentieth century, after the upheaval of one world war, then another, and with a deep cultural crisis reaching to the heart of literature, it might have appeared that, except for Stendhal, the giants of the previous century would lose their standing, to be replaced by the avant-garde artists of modernism, or the committed writers of the 1930s and 1940s, or, after 1950, those who cultivated the New Novel and the literature of the absurd. The novel itself was attacked by the poet Paul Valéry, for instance, and the surrealists, then the New Novelists, such as Alain Robbe-Grillet, who, while publishing books called novels, undermined methodically the aesthetic of representation on which the novel had rested since the eighteenth century. But recent decades have shown that to readers and critics alike nineteenth-century fiction retains great literary vitality. New editions of Stendhal, Balzac, Flaubert, and Zola—and of some less-known figures, such as Jules Vallès—find buyers among the general reading public in France. Similarly, both historical scholarship and critical inquiry on major figures and some lesser ones have flourished; indeed, renowned critics such as Roland Barthes, in *S/Z* (1970), and respected university scholars have shown the fecundity of postmodern critical positions with respect to authors so apparently tied to their age as Balzac and Flaubert. Moreover, some writers previously left in the critical shadows have been the subject of reassessments and new readings that bring out qualities previously underrated; among these writers, in the latter decades of the century, are Vallès and Rachilde.

The reasons for this ongoing interest in nineteenth-century fiction and the new critical approaches that have been taken toward it will be suggested by the essays that follow. It will be useful here to survey briefly the development of fiction in France and especially of the eighteenth-century background against which Romantic and realist fiction developed. The term *roman* (translated first as *romance*, then *novel*), which comes from Old French *romanz*, initially signified the vernacular tongue, then, from the twelfth century, a work, in prose or verse, in that tongue. Such examples as *Le Roman d'Alexandre* (twelfth century), Chrétien de Troyes's *Yvain* or *Le Chevalier au lion* (twelfth century; called a *roman courtois*, or courtly romance), the anonymous *Roman de Renart* (late twelfth century), and, somewhat later, the *Roman de la Rose* (thirteenth century), by Guillaume de Lorris and Jean de Meung, which Geoffrey Chaucer helped translate as the *Romaunt of the Rose* (fourteenth century), illustrate the wide variance in uses of the term, from narratives of adventures in the pseudo-antique mode and stories of chivalric quests, intended for a courtly audience, through a collection of satiric tales of animals, to the elaborate allegory spun around the image of the rose, which caught up the medieval imagination in the webs of Love and Jealousy.

With the replacement in the sixteenth century of nearly all medieval genres by ancient ones, when the Renaissance humanists gained wide access to and deliberately cultivated the forms of antiquity, the courtly romance nearly disappeared; but vestiges remained in the pastoral novel and the novel of adventures, which flourished in France in the seventeenth century following models by Italian and Spanish writers. Similarly, the popular tales that had appeared in the *Roman de Renart*, in the shorter medieval verse narratives called fabliaux, and in the *Cent nouvelles nouvelles* (fifteenth century; translated as *One Hundred Merrie and Delightsome Stories*, 1899) are not without connection to the *Heptaméron* (1558; translated, 1654) of Marguerite de Navarre (the sister of Francis I), who also borrowed from Italian models. While often mixed with fantasy or farce, the mimetic, or imitative, impulse so important to the modern novel of representation is found in many of these forms, whether in their concern for human psychology or the depiction of manners.

Until the latter part of the seventeenth century, however, there is little on the French literary landscape that can be called a novel in the modern sense, in which the marvelous and the artificial are replaced by a close and extensive study of the human heart, mores, or both. Samuel Richardson wrote that seventeenth-century French narratives "dealt so much in the marvelous and improbable, or were so unnaturally inflaming to the passions and so full of love and intrigue, that most of them seemed calculated to fire the imagination rather than inform the judgment." With *La Princesse de Clèves* (1678; translated, 1679), by Marie-Madeleine, Comtesse de La Fayette, the French psychological novel was born. Its judicious analysis of conflicting sentiments and motivations is not the only mode of the French novel—far from it—and especially not during the nineteenth century, but for many readers the type remains a major one, and such novels as Benjamin Constant's *Adolphe* (1816; translated, 1816) and Eugène Fromentin's *Dominique* (1863; translated, 1948) are close in spirit to Mme de La Fayette's masterpiece.

Georges May is one of several critics who have stressed the importance, for the development of fiction, of the claim to *truth* that began to characterize novels from the late 1600s on—a claim that provides some of the foundation for nineteenth-century realism. As Pierre-Daniel Huet noted in *De l'origine des romans* (On the Origin of Novels, 1670): "Novels are fictions of things that might have existed but did not." The eighteenth century, during which some three thousand novels were published in France, produced a wide variety of types. Such types as the epistolary novel and the novel in the form of memoirs, which had as a model the *Mémoires du Sieur de Pontis* (1676), by Louis de Pontis, laid claim, by their first-person voice and other features, to reality. "The word memoir," wrote Richard Steele, "is French for a novel." Dozens of writers, both men and women, exploited these forms, and, undeterred by what seems to modern taste the excessive length of the works, eighteenth-century readers devoured them.

At the same time, Voltaire (François-Marie Arouet le jeune) developed the philosophical tale, with *Zadig* (1747; translated, 1749) and *Candide* (1759; translated, 1864), and Diderot used, in addition to such types as the Oriental tale and the memoir-novel, his own creation, the dialogue form, as illustrated in *Le Neveu de Rameau* (1823; translated as *Rameau's Nephew*, 1897), *Jacques le Fataliste et son maître* (1796; translated as *James the Fatalist and His Master*, 1797), and "Ceci n'est pas un conte," whose title ("This Is Not a Story") and whose form—a dialogue with a reader-character—call into question in a thoroughly modern way its own form and raison d'être.

This development of the novel, which would be followed by an immense production in the next century (although Diderot's inventive forms would have few parallels until André Gide and other twentieth-century figures produced their own type of metafiction—a fiction that takes itself as its topic, investigating the ontology and epistemology of imaginative writing), took place against an intellectual and social background that deserves examination. Whereas philosophical and political thought in the eighteenth century—the first cultural period in France to give itself a name (l'Age des Lumières, or Age of Enlightenment)—was chiefly rationalistic, the arts were marked by two contradictory strains, reason and feeling. In the previous century Cartesian rationalism had given rise to or favored the scientific thought of the early modern period, but had not generally penetrated the area of political thought, where institutionalized authoritarianism in the form of absolute monarchy and church provided its own rationalism based on the authority of Scripture and tradition. After the death of Louis XIV and the ensuing Regency (1715-1723)—and despite the continued dominance of a nearly monolithic church and state—Cartesian reason was turned increasingly toward criticism of the principles of revealed religion and arbitrary royal power and their philosophical underpinnings. By their commanding intellects, Montesquieu, Voltaire, Diderot, and Rousseau all used critical reason to attack, in varying degrees, political and religious tyranny, ultimately with the implication that, since reason is universal, it alone should be the basis for society, in which all have an equal claim to authority.

Traceable through Montesquieu's *Lettres persanes* (1721; translated as *Persian Letters*, 1722) and *De l'esprit des lois* (1748; translated as *The Spirit of Laws*, 1750), Voltaire's *Lettres philosophiques* (1734; originally published in English as *Letters Concerning the English Nation*, 1733), and many other texts, as well as Rousseau's *Contrat social* (1762; translated as *The Social Contract*, 1893), surely one of the most influential political tracts of all time, the critical spirit found its culmination in the monumental *Encyclopédie* (1750-1780), assembled by Diderot, Jean Lerond d'Alembert, and others. While none of the philosophes just mentioned called for violent overthrow of the monarchy, the cumulative effect of their works, together with the example of the American Revolution, was to channel widespread social unrest and economic frustration into an uprising that resulted in the overthrow of the absolute monarchy and, eventually, regicide, and the establishment of government by popular assembly—a government that, tragically, produced not a stable constitutional republic but the Reign of Terror.

The sentimental strain in eighteenth-century literature and thought is not unrelated to the political developments just sketched. Sentimentalism was partly an import from England, through the fiction of Samuel Richardson, whose *Pamela* (1740-1741) and *Clarissa* (1747-1748) as translated by Pierre Letourneur were immensely popular. Richardson's focus on the virtue of ordinary men and women was paralleled in the novels of l'abbé Prévost and Marivaux and the fiction and plays of Diderot, among others. This appeal to the feelings of the common man and woman may well reflect readers' reaction against a long-dominant monarchy and aristocracy, whose splendid court life did not conceal the immense cost of recurrent warfare and widespread misery. The sentimental strain was also a response to the literary tyranny of a neoclassical literature that reflected the authority and concerns of the monarchy and followed too closely, for popular taste, the models of antiquity. One should not be surprised to see authors such as Diderot and Rousseau displaying in some areas a commanding critical reason, yet cultivating feeling and insisting that personal virtue, which comes from the heart, was superior—in practice and in principle—to nobility conveyed merely by birth and to morality imposed by authority. Sentimentalism was bolstered by critical reason inasmuch as the latter insisted on its own universality and a corresponding freedom of conscience. Both are the prerogative of the common man, as he was seen by poets and philosophers alike, and whose apotheosis in the Declaration of the Rights of Man (1789) was a political and philosophical revolution of major proportions.

In the artistic domain, sentimentalism produced scores of novels and a whole school of painting (genre painting, in which domestic subjects replaced the heroic ones appreciated by the aristocracy). An associated inspiration, which emphasized meditation in nature, led to a substantial, though now neglected, body of verse, such as that of Jean-François, Marquis de Saint-Lambert, inspired in part by the English poets Edward Young (*Night Thoughts* [1742-1745; translated, 1769]) and James Thomson (*The Seasons* [1726-1730; translated, 1769]). Rousseau's oeuvre provides the outstanding examples of these veins. His lengthy novel *Julie, ou La Nouvelle Héloïse* (1761; translated as *Julia, or the New Eloisa*, 1773) and his treatise on education, *Emile* (1762; translated, 1911), have domestic subjects, stress the value of the natural, and propose as the guiding principle of life a virtue based on individual conscience. Even more instructive than these fictional works are his *Confessions* (published in 1781 and 1788; translated, 1880) and *Rêveries du promeneur solitaire* (1782; translated as *Reveries of a Solitary*, 1927), both of which emphasize the uniqueness and importance of the self, the role of nature, the value of solitude, and natural religion (the belief that everyone can arrive at divine truth without revelation).

Defined sometimes as "freedom in art"—more precisely the throwing off of formal and rationalistic shackles and the proclamation of the individual, especially individual feeling—French romanticism, the last major Romantic movement in Europe, can be divided into two phases: preromanticism, lasting until about 1820, when the publication of Alphonse de Lamartine's *Méditations poétiques* signaled to the reading public at large that the new wave in literature had triumphed; and romanticism proper, when Romantic features triumphed in all major genres, the last being the drama, with the premiere of Hugo's play *Hernani* (1830). One can add perhaps a third phase, the decline of the movement in the 1840s, which was marked by the failure of Hugo's last Romantic drama, *Les Burgraves*, in 1843, five years before the Second Republic (1848-1851) replaced the Orléans monarchy, which had itself replaced the Bourbons after the "Trois Glorieuses" (Three Glorious Days) of the July Revolution in 1830.

The first wave of Romantic authors—François-René de Chateaubriand, Germaine de Staël, Etienne de Senancour—display in their novels and other prose a strong emphasis on the individual and feeling, fascination with the primitive and skepticism concerning social institutions and structures (a vogue that owed much to Rousseau), sometimes a taste for the medieval, and dithyrambic enthusiasm for nature. While their works frequently retain the expansiveness that marks most novels of the previous century, these authors show little concern for the forms and techniques of fiction as developed by their predecessors; their novels and tales are often more like meditations than stories. Following this first wave are other authors who may give similar importance to individual experience but whose romanticism, developed under the influence of Sir Walter Scott, turns toward historical re-creation or at least a striking local color—the sort that marks the fiction of Mérimée as much as the painting of Eugène Delacroix. Violence in action and extremes of emotion; striking contrasts in settings, characters, and images; melodramatic turns of plot; and a dynamic, emphatic prose mark the fiction of such writers as Alfred de Vigny, Hugo, Charles Nodier, and Mérimée. Some of these authors and others, including Théophile Gautier and Pétrus Borel, were also influenced by the English Gothic novel and the fantastic tales of E. T. A. Hoffmann, Novalis (Friedrich Leopold von Hardenberg), and Joseph von Eichendorff.

By some aspects of their works, Stendhal and Balzac belong to this second group of Romantic novelists who emphasize the violent and the colorful. Balzac's *Le Dernier Chouan* (1829; translated as *The Chouans*, 1889), set in the revolutionary period, includes highly picturesque characters and a melodramatic plot built on contrasts; Stendhal's *Chroniques italiennes* (1855) include tales of violence and passion. But these two masters may more properly be called Romantic realists, and as such are precursors not only of the mid-century realist movement but of its important offshoot, naturalism, with its emphasis upon social structures and processes. Stendhal's work, even at its most dramatic, is characterized by social criticism, directed at the France of the Restoration and the Orléans monarchy—ruling classes, church, and government. Moreover, like the later realists and naturalists, he was interested in causality and relied partly on documentation. His great novels are marked also by a psychological incisiveness that is rivaled by few works, and that made Friedrich Nietzsche consider the author of *Le Rouge et le noir* as one of his masters. Balzac, who similarly drew heavily on his observations and documentation, turned his genius to a fictional reconstruction and critique of his own period—a critique in which the Romantic impulses of the characters and melodramatic turns of plot are counterbalanced by thorough, probing studies of contemporary institutions, classes, and mores.

Except in the theater, there was no clear rupture between French romanticism and its sequels. Indeed, in poetry and in aesthetics generally, the movements that followed—beginning with the Parnassian poets, such as Gautier, Théodore de Banville, and Charles-Marie-René Leconte de Lisle, and the symbolists, through the early modernism of Marcel Proust and Gide and the surrealism of the 1920s and thereafter—can be considered direct developments of romanticism, the Parnassians and realists similarly emphasizing the concern for the exterior world that differentiated romanticism from classicism; the symbolists and surrealists, as well as many other modern authors, developing romanticism's concern with the irrational or suprarational.

In fact, to some degree modern French literature as a whole remains Romantic, prizing emotion above reason, the individual above society, spontaneity above reserve, nature above human constructs, and free forms above strict ones. One can nevertheless speak of the demise of the French Romantic movement as such, shortly before the middle of the century, and the rise of major literary reactions, which, in one way or another, all deserve the term *realist.*

As a literary movement, realism developed, parallel to a similar movement in painting, as the Industrial Revolution finally replaced, on a wide scale, the artisanry of the eighteenth century. It opened the way for the making of large fortunes by many in the middle classes and increased prosperity for many more and, concurrently, engendered the development of a large pool of urban labor, often grossly exploited, which would gradually lead to the creation of a French proletariat where, before, there had been only a peasantry and a class of artisans and shopkeepers. This increase in wealth and power for the upper bourgeoisie was favored by the Revolution of 1830, after conservative bourgeois elements intervened to place on the throne Louis-Philippe of the branch of Orléans (1830-1848). Sometimes called the "roi-parapluie" (umbrella king), he was the first king to wear "bourgeois" dress (a frock coat and trousers). The power of the property-owning middle classes was threatened briefly by the beginnings of the Second Republic (1848-1851), in which radical social revolutionaries played a role alongside liberals and moderates, until it turned violent in the famous "journées de juin" (June days), leading to another conservative reaction.

The transitional place of Stendhal and Balzac as Romantic realists, who took as their subject the social reality of their own time, has been noted above, but their work was bound up in crucial ways with Romantic conventions, including the cult of the individual and the belief in passion as the supreme justification and end of life. In the 1840s and 1850s, other writers, such as Jules Husson (Champfleury) and Henry Murger, encouraged by the doctrines of the painter Gustave Courbet—who in 1848 announced his intention of painting only ordinary scenes from modern life—began to insist that fiction must abandon Romantic conventions and render only observable reality. These authors concentrated on portraits of elements of the lower classes, who furnish much—though not all—of the subject matter of realist and naturalist fiction. In 1857, the same year that Flaubert's *Madame Bovary* appeared, Champfleury published articles collectively titled *Le Réalisme*, which served as a manifesto for the new aesthetic. The consolidation of realism took place against the ideological background of positivism as illustrated by Auguste Comte, a pragmatic philosophy according to which only material reality is knowable and which implies belief in the progressive amelioration of life through application of a materialist outlook and the scientific method to social problems.

While he did not accept the label of realist, Flaubert—for many, the supreme figure of the movement—was the first major writer to deny romanticism as part of an artistic platform, to set as a goal the depiction of the most banal reality imaginable, and to develop a method of composition and a style for rendering this reality that would envelop it, paradoxically, in artistic beauty. His rejection of romanticism was almost certainly a type of self-punishment; one way to interpret the famous phrase "Madame Bovary, c'est moi" (I am Madame Bovary) is to see it as a confession of Romantic impulses that would be visible throughout his career, as witness his flamboyant historical novel *Salammbô* (1862; translated, 1885)—impulses that were accompanied by an intense dislike for everything that was mean, ordinary, dull, and venal—in a word, everything that was bourgeois. Flaubert is thus preeminently, with Baudelaire, the mid-century writer opposed to his society, spiting and transcending it by making art from its evils and platitudes. For, in addition to depicting in *Madame Bovary* what the subtitle calls "mœurs de province" (provincial manners), he devoted *L'Education sentimentale* to a trajectory of failure and the disappointments of political liberalism under the Second Republic; and his masterly long story "Un Cœur simple" (1877; translated as "A Simple Heart," 1923) treats the commonest of lives—albeit with a tone of both pity and understanding.

His case is instructive: a bourgeois writing about the bourgeoisie, which he loathed, for an age dominated by middle-class tastes, values, and institutions, and whose most eminent representatives in turn loathed him; concerned in large measure with consolidating their power and maintaining social order against the threats of political and artistic radicalism, they did not wish to have their institutions denounced and their prejudices and private lives exposed. The result was that Flaubert was charged with offense to public morals for publishing *Madame Bovary*. Until tastes changed, the public, even a sophisticated one, would accept even less enthusiastically the naturalistic fiction of Zola, the Goncourt brothers, Huysmans, Maupassant, and others, attacked as being obsessed with the sordid and immoral and—in Zola's case—for adopting the deterministic scientism of the age.

Yet, as a style, realism gradually imposed itself in fiction and poetry (if one acknowledges that what Gautier stressed as the realist's concern for the outer world is translated into the impassive, descriptive verse of such Parnassian poets as Leconte de Lisle, Banville, José-Maria de Heredia, and Gautier himself). It even appeared in the theater, in sentimental or moralizing dramas by Alexandre Dumas *fils*, Henry Becque, and Eugène Brieux. At the same time, the disappointments of those who favored a radical revolution—disappointments that, in the early decades of the century, would have taken the form of the Romantic *mal du siècle* (the sickness of the century)—led either to increased disengagement—the attitude that Charles-Augustin Sainte-Beuve (referring to Vigny) called that of the "ivory tower"—or to violent hatred and alienation, producing the mid- and late-nineteenth-century phenomenon of the radically estranged, often vitriolic artist, illustrated by Flaubert, Baudelaire, Huysmans, Vallès, Philippe-Auguste, Comte de Villiers de l'Isle-Adam, and others.

Following the coup d'état of its president, Louis-Napoleon (Napoleon III), in December 1851, the Second Republic was replaced by the Second Empire (1852-1870), a paternalistic regime that was characterized at first by only a shadow of parliamentary government but in which gradually some power came to be exerted by the voters through elections and representative bodies. Louis-Napoleon's concern was to stabilize France, chiefly by modeling his new empire's institutions on those of the brilliant First Empire of his uncle, Napoleon I, which had redirected the fragmented energies of the Revolutionary years into undertakings and institutions that helped unite and strengthen France. A second aim was to enhance French prestige in Europe and in the colonial sphere—thus enhancing the emperor's own. His rule ushered in a period of prudery, conservatism, and, until its last years, repression of freedom of the press (although ways were found to circumvent censorship).

The Second Empire was ended by one of the most traumatic events of modern French history, the Franco-Prussian War (1870-1871). Louis-Napoleon, who was far from being the equal of his uncle, shared with the French as a whole the fear that the nation would be encircled by Prussian territories and influence, should Otto von Bismarck be successful in his support of the Prussian candidate for accession to the throne of Spain, Prince Leopold of Hohenzollern-Sigmaringen. This fear was all the stronger because of previous failures of French diplomatic and military undertakings, including the disastrous Mexican expedition. After diplomatic maneuverings, in which Bismarck manipulated successfully the king of Prussia as well as public opinion, France declared war on 19 July. A disorganized, badly commanded army led by marshals Achille Bazaine and Marie-Edmé-Patrice de MacMahon was quickly routed. MacMahon, accompanied by the emperor, was forced to surrender at Sedan (2 September 1870). The war, the defeat, and the occupation are major topics in novels and short stories by Zola, Maupassant, Daudet, Anatole France, Léon Bloy, and Maurice Barrès. After the emperor's abdication, a republic was proclaimed and a provisional government, the Government of National Defense, attempted to restore order; much of the country was occupied, Paris was besieged by the Prussians, and Bazaine's army also capitulated.

The winter of 1870-1871, during which the Parisians nearly starved, was one of the most severe of the period. It was followed by the proclamation of the Paris Commune in March 1871 and its eventual crushing by the forces of the government, which had withdrawn to Versailles. In May, France signed the Treaty of Frankfurt, which had been negotiated earlier, and by which it lost Alsace and most of Lorraine and was forced to pay a huge indemnity. National conflict had rarely been more acute in France; the nation was divided into adversarial factions formed variously by supporters and enemies of the Commune, Bonapartists, monarchists, moderate republicans, clerical conservatives, socialists, and more radical reformers, some of whom were associated with the International Working Men's Association (First International), founded in 1864. Reflections of these rifts are visible in the writing of the time, for instance, the novels of Vallès and Anatole France.

That the Third Republic—the longest-lasting of all modern French political regimes—could come into being and endure at all amid such enmities and political conflicts is little short of amazing. Until the accession to the papacy in 1878 of Leo XIII, who gradually introduced some liberalization, the Church withheld its support of the new republic, which, to instill patriotism and gain public support, looked instead to the national system of lay education first developed under Napoleon, now given an anticlerical tone by the laws passed in the 1880s under the leadership of Jules Ferry, a militant secularist in educational matters who became minister of education in 1879. The first decades of the republic were marked by sensational scandals and political crises. One of these was precipitated by Gen. Georges-Ernest Boulanger, a champion of revenge against Germany, who was supported by both monarchists and Bonapartists in his nearly successful coup d'état of 1889. Three years later the Panama Canal scandal, involving government figures in shady financial dealings, again shook the republic.

By the early years of the Third Republic, the real—in the sense of the quotidian—had become firmly entrenched as the primary subject for fiction. Art was to imitate life closely, as both Zola and the Goncourt brothers indicated incontrovertibly when they insisted upon visiting the sites that would be described in their novels, studying closely the human types they would portray, and taking detailed notes on everything from hospital procedures to butcher shops. The realist aesthetic that had been developed just two or three decades earlier had, furthermore, begun to evolve into the subtype known as naturalism, whose principal inventor and exponent was Zola (although the Goncourts disputed his claim to priority) and which was practiced also by Maupassant, Huysmans, the Goncourts themselves, and Daudet, to some degree.

Naturalism can be considered an exaggerated form of realism, incorporating the documentation just mentioned and stressing social process. In general, the naturalists' writings were characterized by emphasis on the sordid, or at least the details of the lives of those at the lowest social levels. These writers' concerns reflect the increased urban development in France (the population of Paris had nearly doubled between 1851 and 1870 through redrawing of boundaries and absolute growth), development of trade unions, expansion of the railroad system, and heavy industry's attraction of peasants to major urban areas. Moreover, as Zola understood it, naturalism approached what was beginning to be called sociology (the term, usually ascribed to Comte, would be given greater currency by Emile Durkheim)—that is, the scientific study of social phenomena. Under the influence of the scientism that marked much of the age—particularly that of Hippolyte Taine and Claude Bernard, the author of *Introduction à l'étude de la médecine expérimentale* (1865; translated as *An Introduction to the Study of Experimental Medicine*, 1927)—Zola came to believe not only in a two-edged scientific determinism—that of heredity and environment—but also in the capacity of literature to reproduce social experiments and thus identify social laws. Fortunately, much of his writing goes beyond the limits of this position, which by itself would lead only to formulaic fiction, one must suppose; his powerful imagination, the scope of his works, his style (long disdained but now recognized as having its own excellence), and his social conscience produce a fictional world whose characters, while they may illustrate the forces of social and biological laws, are also whole, impressive figures. In fact, in Zola's later works naturalism gives way to social idealism, based on the four principles of Fertility, Justice, Truth, and Work. His last novels illustrate the dialectic by which determinists often seek to escape, through imagining a social or political breakthrough, such as the Marxist ideal of the classless society, the laws to which they subscribe.

In opposition to Zola's scientism and the naturalists' emphasis upon material reality as the defining condition of human existence, there appeared in the last two decades of the century two major literary and artistic developments—symbolism and literary decadence. Baudelaire, the great transitional figure between romanticism and symbolism, had already denounced violently the reality of his own time and enunciated, in his criticism, prose poems (*Le Spleen de Paris* [1869; translated as *Poems in Prose*, 1909]), and his masterful *Les Fleurs du mal* (1857; translated as *Flowers of Evil*, 1909), an aesthetic of the antinatural, by which nature's elements would be transformed and moral categories inverted. His major successors of the next generation—Mallarmé, Rimbaud, Paul Verlaine—as well as lesser figures such as Jean Moréas, who identified themselves explicitly as symbolists, carried out in various directions the promises of Baudelairean aesthetics, as they denounced naturalism and all other mimetic literature (in Rimbaud's case, nearly the entirety of Western culture), cultivated the artificial, sought aesthetic values rather than social ones, and strove for metaphysical absolutes. None of these figures dealt in fiction, but symbolism did enter the novel, story, and drama in works by Villiers de l'Isle-Adam, Maurice Maeterlinck, and younger writers such as Gide.

The decadent spirit, which similarly put great emphasis on the artificial but without the symbolists' interest in poetics, dates from the 1880s, when the review *Décadent* appeared. The spirit was marked by a sense of futility, the rejection of anything ordinary or practical, a tone of languor, and a search for the ultrarefined. It is sometimes identified with Robert de Montesquiou (one of the models for Proust's character Charlus), Jean Lorrain, and other second- and third-rank writers, but is best embodied in the works of Huysmans, whose *A Rebours* (1884; translated as *Against the Grain*, 1922) constitutes a rigorous program of denial of the natural. Huysmans's career illustrates the late-nineteenth-century reaction not only against naturalism as a literary school (the aesthetic to which his early works are most closely allied) but also against scientism, which pervaded not only naturalist literature but much of the philosophy of the age; indeed, after having portrayed in detail the lives of prostitutes and the most depraved sexual maniacs, Huysmans was converted to Christianity. Yet he remained an aesthete, in his prose and his life, and under his pen language assumed a life of its own, as in the poetry of the symbolists, pointing to the linguistic crisis of the twentieth century, when, thanks to the work of Ferdinand de Saussure and his followers, it was recognized that language was arbitrary—merely a set of symbols—and thus the notion of sign became separated from the idea of the signified.

Other reactions to naturalism can be seen in the works of Anatole France and Daudet. Although the former did not denounce science, he, like certain other French intellectuals from the 1860s on, retained some skepticism about the claims of materialism to describe all reality. He was fascinated by the irrational and interested in the phenomenon of decadence, in his own time but especially during the period of postclassical Greece and the era around the birth of Christ. Yet, for all that, France was a rationalist, and his most characteristic works are marked by bemused, sometimes acerbic social satire (no one saw better than he through the maneuverings of government ministers and ecclesiastical authorities) and by various degrees of irony. As for Daudet, while works such as *Le Petit Chose* (1868; translated as *The Little Good-for-Nothing*, 1878) and his stories of the Franco-Prussian War show his affinity with the naturalists, he cultivated a humor that sets him apart from many of his contemporaries and is responsible for his longtime popularity among those who disliked the excesses of naturalism. To these writers should be added Verne, another author who eschewed the naturalist aesthetic, to launch instead the genre of modern science fiction.

Preoccupied with their status as fin-de-siècle figures (an instance where historical self-consciousness almost preceded the events themselves), the writers of the last decade of the century were witnesses also to one of the most turbulent periods of the Third Republic, marked by the Dreyfus Affair. After the court-martial and conviction of Dreyfus for espionage on behalf of Germany, it was alleged (and later proved) that the chief piece of evidence on which he was convicted, the famous bordereau found in a wastepaper basket, had been forged; rumors of corroborating forgeries and other acts of complicity also circulated. The army closed ranks to defend the conviction; monarchists, Bonapartists, clericals, and other enemies of the republic joined in support of the verdict with those who harbored anti-Jewish sentiments. On the other side, liberals and republicans of various persuasions gradually rallied to the cause of Dreyfus. Public opinion became inflamed; one of the most famous cartoons of the period, by Caran d'Ache, depicts, in a first panel, a dinner party, with the caption "Surtout! ne parlons pas de l'affaire Dreyfus" (Above all, let us not speak of the Dreyfus Affair); in the second panel, over a ruined dinner table, in a scene of utter disorder, the guests are tearing at each others' throats, with the caption "Ils en ont parlé" (They spoke about it). After the acquittal of one accomplice to the frame-up, the suicide of a high-ranking army officer, the circulation of public petitions for retrial, and Zola's famous open letter of 1898, entitled simply "J'accuse" (I Accuse), a new trial was held in 1899. Contrary to expectations, the verdict was still "guilty," but with extenuating circumstances, and the original sentence of life imprisonment on Devil's Island was reduced to ten years. Two weeks later Dreyfus was pardoned; only in 1906 was the original verdict fully overturned. The retrial of 1899 put the matter to rest in some senses, but the deep social divisions the case had revealed and exacerbated among political, intellectual, and artistic figures as well as the public at large left lasting scars. The heroes of one side were vilified by the other; Zola in particular was the subject of considerable persecution.

The political turbulence of the period was paralleled by many changes on the literary scene, and trends that cannot be grouped under a single label. Some careers came to an end, including those of Maupassant, who died in 1893, Edmond de Goncourt (1896), Verlaine (1896), and Mallarmé (1898); Zola's death came shortly thereafter, in 1902. Other careers were firmly established: Barrès achieved his first great success in 1897 with *Les Déracinés* (The Uprooted), and Paul Bourget experienced a decade of success as the premier psychological novelist of the time. New careers, whose importance would be measured only later, were begun, notably those of Paul Claudel, Gide, Proust, and Valéry. Symbolism, which as a named movement had existed only since the 1880s (although its roots go back farther), was under attack from various splinter groups and from two young and very gifted authors, Claudel and Gide, although its influence on them was lasting in some ways. The moralizing, conservative fiction of Bourget and Barrès was attacked by Gide and others even as it triumphed. Indeed, it appeared that neither didacticism nor the excesses of naturalism nor the hothouse atmosphere of late symbolism would satisfy the rising generation. The social questions that had preoccupied Zola somewhat earlier—conditions in the slums of Paris, the mines—would be replaced as literary topics first by the Dreyfus Affair and then by the urgent subjects of the separation of church and state, the international standing of France, and the all-important question of *revanchisme* (revenge against the German empire). Moreover, while such social questions remained current and would later be complemented by other political and social topics in the works of novelists who came to maturity shortly before World War I, the early years of the twentieth century, shaking off the yoke of fin-de-siècle aestheticism and decadence, would see the rise of a new literary eclecticism. Its most gifted figures, having assimilated the lessons of realism and symbolism, would go beyond the achievements of the nineteenth century and demonstrate in works such as Proust's *A la recherche du temps perdu* (1913-1927; translated as *Remembrance of Things Past*, 1922-1932) how mimetic and aesthetic values could be reconciled in a sweeping artistic vision.

—Catharine Savage Brosman

Acknowledgments

This book was produced by Bruccoli Clark Layman, Inc. Karen L. Rood is senior editor for the *Dictionary of Literary Biography* series. David Marshall James was the in-house editor.

Production coordinator is James W. Hipp. Projects manager is Charles D. Brower. Photography editors are Edward Scott and Timothy C. Lundy. Layout and graphics supervisor is Penney L. Haughton. Copyediting supervisor is Bill Adams. Typesetting supervisor is Kathleen M. Flanagan. Mary Scott Dye is editorial associate. Systems manager is George F. Dodge. The production staff includes Rowena Betts, Steve Borsanyi, Teresa Chaney, Patricia Coate, Rebecca Crawford, Margaret McGinty Cureton, Denise Edwards, Sarah A. Estes, Robert Fowler, Brenda A. Gillie, Bonita Graham, Avril E. Gregory, Jolyon M. Helterman, Ellen McCracken, Kathy Lawler Merlette, John Myrick, Pamela D. Norton, Thomas J. Pickett, Maxine K. Smalls, Deborah P. Stokes, Jennifer C. J. Turley, and Wilma Weant.

Walter W. Ross and Samuel Bruce did library research. They were assisted by the following librarians at the Thomas Cooper Library of the University of South Carolina: Jens Holley and the interlibrary-loan staff; reference librarians Gwen Baxter, Daniel Boice, Faye Chadwell, Cathy Eckman, Rhonda Felder, Gary Geer, Jackie Kinder, Laurie Preston, Jean Rhyne, Carol Tobin, Virginia Weathers, and Connie Widney; circulation-department head Thomas Marcil; and acquisitions-searching supervisor David Haggard.

Dictionary of Literary Biography® • Volume One Hundred Twenty-Three

Nineteenth-Century French Fiction Writers: Naturalism and Beyond, 1860-1900

Dictionary of Literary Biography

Maurice Barrès

(19 August 1862 - 5 December 1923)

Leonard R. Koos
Mary Washington College

SELECTED BOOKS: *Huit jours chez Monsieur Renan* (Paris: A. Dupret, 1888);

Sous l'œil des barbares (Paris: A. Lemerre, 1888); republished with "Un Examen des trois romans idéologiques" (Paris: Charpentier, 1895);

Un Homme libre (Paris: Perrin, 1889);

Le Jardin de Bérénice (Paris: Perrin, 1891);

L'Ennemi des lois (Paris: Perrin, 1893);

Du sang, de la volupté et de la mort (Paris: Charpentier & Fasquelle, 1894; revised edition, Paris: Fontemoing, 1903);

Les Déracinés (Paris: E. Fasquelle, 1897);

L'Appel au soldat (Paris: E. Fasquelle, 1900);

Scènes et doctrines du nationalisme (Paris: Juven, 1902);

Leurs figures (Paris: Juven, 1902);

Amori et dolori sacrum (Paris: Juven, 1903);

Les Amitiés françaises (Paris: Juven, 1903);

Au service de l'Allemagne (Paris: A. Fayard, 1905);

Discours prononcés dans la séance publique tenue par l'Académie Française pour la réception de Maurice Barrès (Paris: Firmin-Didot, 1907);

Colette Baudoche (Paris: Juven, 1909); translated by Frances Wilson Huard as *Colette Baudoche: The Story of a Young Girl of Metz* (New York: Doran, 1918); French edition republished with "Un Discours à Metz" (Paris: Nelson, 1919);

Le Greco (Paris: H. Fleury, 1911); republished as *Greco ou le secret de Tolède* (Paris: Emile-Paul, 1912);

La Colline inspirée (Paris: Emile-Paul, 1913); translated by Malcolm Cowley as *The Sacred Hill* (New York: Macauley, 1929);

Maurice Barrès (photograph by Nadar)

L'Ame française et la guerre, 12 volumes (Paris: Emile-Paul, 1915-1920); revised as *Chronique de la grande guerre*, 14 volumes (Paris: Plon-Nourrit, 1920-1924);

Les Traits éternels de la France (Paris: Emile-Paul, 1916); translated by Margaret W. B. Corwin as *The Undying Spirit of France* (New Haven: Yale University Press, 1917);

Les Diverses Familles spirituelles de la France (Paris: Emile-Paul, 1917); translated by Elisabeth Marbury as *The Faith of France: Studies in Spiritual Differences and Unity* (Boston: Houghton Mifflin, 1918);

Le Génie du Rhin (Paris: Plon-Nourrit, 1921);

Un Jardin sur l'Oronte (Paris: Plon-Nourrit, 1922);

Dante, Pascal et Renan (Paris: Plon-Nourrit, 1923);

Une Enquête aux pays du Levant (Paris: Plon-Nourrit, 1923);

Mes cahiers, 12 volumes (Paris: Plon, 1929-1938, 1949).

Collection: *L'Œuvre de Maurice Barrès*, 20 volumes, edited by Philippe Barrès (Paris: Au Club de l'Honnête Homme, 1965-1968).

OTHER: *Les Taches d'Encre*, edited by Barrès, nos. 1-4 (1884-1885);

Rachilde, *Monsieur Vénus*, preface by Barrès (Paris: Félix Brossier, 1889);

La Cocarde, edited by Barrès (September 1894 - March 1895);

Jean Lorrain, *La Petite Classe*, preface by Barrès (Paris: Ollendorff, 1895);

Stendhal, *Correspondance de Stendhal, 1800-1842*, preface by Barrès (Paris: C. Bosse, 1908);

Louis Ménard, *Rêveries d'un païen mystique*, preface by Barrès (Paris: A. Durel, 1909);

F.-A. Cazals and Gustave Le Rouge, *Les Derniers Jours de Paul Verlaine*, preface by Barrès (Paris: Mercure de France, 1911);

Mrs. Oliphant, *La Ville enchantée*, translated by Henri Bremond, introduction by Barrès (Paris: Emile-Paul, 1911);

Stanislas de Guaïta, *Essais de sciences maudites. Au seuil du Mystère*, preface by Barrès (Paris: Hector & Durville, 1915);

Charles Pèguy, *Œuvres complètes*, volume 2, introduction by Barrès (Paris: Editions de la Nouvelle Revue Française, 1920).

When the Parisian dadaists led by André Breton, Louis Aragon, and Tristan Tzara sought a figure from the cultural landscape to be the target of their infamous mock trial in the spring of 1921, their choice of Maurice Barrès as the embodiment of those literary and intellectual values they vowed to attack could not have been more appropriate. A member of the Académie Française since 1906, a member of the Chambre des Députés (from 1889 to 1893 as a Boulangist candidate from Nancy, then again from 1906 until his death in 1923 as a representative for the first arrondissement in Paris), an influential journalist in the wake of the Dreyfus Affair of the 1890s, and a noted essayist and novelist who played a significant role in the nationalist revival of the late nineteenth and early twentieth centuries, Maurice Barrès had become by the 1920s one of the major voices of the conservative cultural establishment, which would be incessantly questioned and ultimately rejected by the various strains of the emerging avant-garde. And yet, the trajectory that led to the consideration of Maurice Barrès as the paragon of nationalism, traditionalism, and Catholic spirituality was inaugurated in a completely different slant.

An essential element that informed Barrès's later voice of traditionalism can be located in the setting of his family origins: the Lorraine region of northeastern France. Born on 19 August 1862 to Auguste Barrès, an engineer and chemistry professor, and Claire (née Luxer) Barrès, the daughter of a well-established family from the Auvergne region, in the picturesque town of Charmes-sur-Moselle in the *département* of the Vosges, Maurice grew up in the shadow of an impressive genealogy that could be traced back to the Renaissance. Its most notable member before Maurice achieved fame as a writer and journalist was his paternal grandfather, Jean-François Barrès, who served as a soldier and battalion chief in the Napoleonic wars. Maurice's happy childhood was interrupted in 1867 when he contracted, and nearly died of, typhoid fever. During his long convalescence, his mother and his only other sibling, his sister Marie, would read to him for hours on end from books on the lives of famous men, from the adventure stories of Alexandre Dumas *père* and from what he would later cite as the most influential of these sickbed readings, the novels of Sir Walter Scott. Many critics have ascribed to his reading preferences during this period the origin of the hero worship that would characterize his nationalist and spiritual writings of the early twentieth century.

Among the most striking and memorable events of Barrès's childhood was the Franco-Prussian War (1870-1871) and the subsequent occupation of Lorraine by the Germans. As a youthful eyewitness to the disastrous French defeat, Maurice experienced the horrors of the war first-hand when he saw both his father and his paternal grandfather incarcerated by the occupying armies (his grandfather died while being held). The frail and oversensitive Maurice grew up in the somber and dispiriting atmosphere of the ruin and devastation resulting from the war, and his later thought and imagination, like that of many other members of the so-called generation of 1870, would be forever haunted by the tragic aura of the war and its aftermath. As early as 1884, Barrès wrote in his review *Taches d'Encre* (its title referred to the blot of ink from Barrès's pen that could be found on the cover of each copy): "Notre tâche spéciale à nous, jeunes hommes, c'est de reprendre la terre enlevée, de reconstituer l'idéal français" (Our own special task, young men, is to retake the stolen land and to restore the French ideal).

In 1872 Barrès attended school for the first time at the Nancy religious *collège*, La Malgrange. At the age of fourteen in 1876, he continued his education at the lycée in Nancy, where he would count among his friends Léon Sorg and Stanislas de Guaïta, whose later occultism in the 1890s would both fascinate and influence—but ultimately repel—Barrès. At the Nancy lycée Barrès was introduced to a world of thought that would significantly influence his writing for the next twenty years. His initial readings of Théophile Gautier, Gustave Flaubert, and Charles Baudelaire provided him with ideas and images that he reproduced and developed in his early works, most notably in his collection of essays *Du sang, de la volupté et de la mort* (Of Blood, Pleasure, and Death, 1894), which exemplifies late-nineteenth century Baudelairean aestheticism. Barrès's professor of philosophy at the Nancy lycée, Auguste Burdeau—on whose image Barrès later modeled the influential professor Bouteiller of his novel *Les Déracinés* (The Uprooted, 1897)—introduced the young man to thinkers who were beginning to animate the French intellectual scene, including Immanuel Kant and Arthur Schopenhauer.

Barrès's family had planned for him to take up a career in the legal profession, and in 1880 he began to study law. His interests, however, remained with the subjects that had captivated him at the Nancy lycée, literature and philosophy, and he soon began to contribute articles to the provincial review *Journal de Meurthe-et-Moselle*, then to the Parisian monthly *Jeune France*. The editor of *Jeune France*, who recognized in Barrès the potential of an important writer and thinker, showed some of his journalistic work to the novelist Anatole France and to the Parnassian poet Charles-René-Marie Leconte de Lisle. The latter advised Barrès to move to France's cultural and intellectual center, Paris, which he did in 1882; he subsequently became a member of Leconte de Lisle's Parnassian *cénacle*.

In the hothouse atmosphere of the Parisian literary scene during the 1880s, which was still dominated by naturalism, Barrès sought out the company of such writers as the eventual symbolist poet Jean Moréas, the dandy and poet Robert de Montesquiou (said to be the model for Joris-Karl Huysmans's decadent hero Des Esseintes as well as the inspiration for Marcel Proust's Charlus), and José-Maria de Heredia, all of whom were part of the most innovative, though marginalized, literary circles of the decade. Barrès continued to pen articles, but, not entirely content with the prospect of leaving his work's fate up to the decisions and whims of journal editors, he launched his own review in 1884, the *Taches d'Encre*. The review, with Barrès as its editor and sole contributor, was short-lived—it lasted for only four issues—but it proved to be an important stepping-stone in his career.

A *Taches d'Encre* article on Huysmans's novel *A rebours* (1884; translated as *Against the Grain*, 1922), often called the "bible of decadence," gained attention for the author, as it was one of the first critical accounts of the 1880s to view the emerging decadent aesthetic in a somewhat positive fashion. That article, "La Sensation en littérature: Les poètes suprêmes" (Sensation in Literature: The Supreme Poets), after treating such important writers as Baudelaire, Paul Verlaine, and Stéphane Mallarmé, concludes with a passage on the main character of *A rebours*, Des Esseintes, praising him as one of those minds who "poussent l'amour de l'unique jusqu'au culte du décadent" (push the love of the unique as far as the cult of the decadent). Barrès himself would produce his own version of the love of the unique by the end of the 1880s, a love that in great part depends on the rarefied and discriminating perspective that he rightly identified in the decadent aesthetic. *Taches d'Encre*, while not a financial or professional success, was a useful calling card for Barrès, permitting him entry into the elitist circles of the Parisian literati.

By 1888, after several years of regularly contributing articles and reviews to widely read Parisian reviews such as *Chroniques*, the *Presse*, and *Voltaire*, Barrès's attempt to make a name for himself in the French intellectual jungle was greatly boosted by the publication of two works: *Huit jours chez Monsieur Renan* (Eight Days at the House of Mr. Renan), an ironic, dilettantish pastiche of Ernest Renan's thought in the form of a se-

Medallion of Barrès by M. Delannoy (Collection of Philippe Barrès)

ries of imaginary dialogues; and the first novel of what would become Barrès's celebrated *Culte du moi* (Cult of the Ego) trilogy, *Sous l'œil des barbares* (Under the Eye of the Barbarians). Shortly after the appearance of the novel, Paul Bourget, a powerful and influential critic and writer in the late nineteenth century, penned an enthusiastic article on it and its author in the widely read *Journal des Débats*. With Bourget's article, Barrès became one of the luminaries of the French literary landscape, and the next two novels of the trilogy, *Un Homme libre* (A Free Man, 1889) and *Le Jardin de Bérénice* (The Garden of Bérénice, 1891), enjoyed an enormous success that secured the young writer's reputation as the theorist of a new current of thought, that of the cult of egoism.

The novels of the *Culte du moi* trilogy are very much the stylistic and intellectual products of the proto-avant-garde circles of decadence, symbolism, and aestheticism in the 1880s. Identified by their author as "metaphysical" and "ideological," the novels in the trilogy have a minimal plot, few and insubstantially drawn or developed characters, and a narrative whose abstractness challenges the most assiduous of readers. While critics generally label this trio of novels "psychological," these works certainly do not conform to the traditionally conceived image of the nineteenth-century psychological novels of, for example, Stendhal or Leo Tolstoy. They might be best described as cerebral. In fact, the very designation of "novel" when speaking of these works seems imprecise and unsatisfactory as a defining category. These works resemble more a series of philosophical musings on the nature of the world and the role of the investigative individual's consciousness in it. Their style, elliptical and ornately descriptive like that of *A rebours*, while adding to the difficulty of summarizing or analyzing the trilogy, becomes a barometer for the permutations that the ego will go through in the course of the three books, identified in Barrès's preface to the trilogy as "l'histoire des années d'apprentissage d'un moi" (the story of the years of apprenticeship of an ego).

In *Sous l'œil des barbares* the main character of the trilogy, Philippe, has recently finished his studies at a provincial college. In him, as with the young Barrès, can be identified the ongoing influences of the Romantics, Baudelaire, and Flaubert as well as that of German idealist philosophy. Philippe's education, however, has stifled in him the traditional organizing values of religion, nation, and ethics. And yet this newly entered world of ideas that demystifies the institutions of society ultimately proves itself to be deficient in providing any rule upon which Philippe can base his existence. Adrift in a sea of relative values (in later Barresian vocabulary, this state of existence is much more directly related to antinationalist, cosmopolitan culture and rests on the horticultural metaphor of being *déraciné* [uprooted]), Philippe, like so many other heroes and heroines of modern French literature, moves to Paris, where he begins his search for a system to be derived from that element of reality of whose existence he can be unquestionably sure: his own self. Barrès opposes the self or ego to the barbarians of the title, a term that refers not so much to the vulgar herd of philistines that threatens civilization, as in the decadent aesthetic's phantasmagoria of the hordes overrunning the late Roman Empire or as in Nietzschean philosophy's conception of the genealogy of morals, as to those who seek to exert an influence on the mind of the self: "Les Barbares, voilà le non-moi, c'est-à-dire tout ce qui peut nuire ou resister au Moi" (The Barbarians, they are the non-ego, that is to say all that can harm or resist the Ego).

Like the prescription of many thinkers of the late nineteenth century who witnessed the advent of mass society and the resulting crises that it presented for the individual, Barrès's temporary solution for Philippe comprises a retreat from society into the ivory-towered realm of self-knowledge through self-examination. While the external is never wholly rejected in the trilogy, in *Sous l'œil des barbares* and *Un Homme libre* it most often expresses itself in the form of the unpopulated space of history or legend (Lorraine, Venice) and remains a function of the inner search for transcendence (as many critics have pointed out, not unrelated to Johann Fichte's theory of knowledge as found in his tract *The Science of Knowledge* [1802]). And yet despite Philippe's enactment of his dream of a retreat into the undamaged, protective, and imaginative domain of pure ego, his readings of the accomplishments of others produce in him the longing for action. His conclusion that the inner and outer worlds must ultimately be reconciled in their separation, that the former cannot be and should not be translated into the latter, represents not so much a failure of the ego as an assertion of its uniqueness and his successful achievement of having gained control over it. At the end of the novel, Philippe's exercise in self-examination in the absence of the pernicious influence of the Barbarians has convinced him that his ego, which he unquestionably possesses, must be further disciplined, improved, and ultimately perfected.

The second novel of the trilogy, *Un Homme libre*, continues the metaphysical saga of Philippe as he makes plans to leave Paris in order to travel through France and Europe, all the while conducting further experiments of self-knowledge designed to strengthen his ego. Before setting out, he and his friend Simon, a kindred spirit in ego worship, have medical tests to verify that their bodies are healthy enough to engage in successive installments of the physically and mentally demanding program of the egoist. Despite the doctor's warning of the possibility of the development of serious and degenerating nervous disorders (this sort of development is the mainstay of decadent prose), Philippe and Simon, who share a similar perspective, vocabulary, and disdain for society, set off from Paris to share a small country house in a secluded area of the Lorraine region. As they leave the capital behind, their enthusiasm allows them to proclaim: "Nous nous étions débarrassés du siècle" (We had shaken off the century).

Philippe travels through his native Lorraine during his stay, visiting ancient towns and significant sights, such as the religious shrine dating from pagan times at Sion-Vaudrémont (the same shrine is the subject of his later historical work *La Colline inspirée* [1913; translated as *The Sacred Hill*, 1929]). Since, for Philippe in *Un Homme libre*, "l'homme idéal résumerait en soi l'univers" (the ideal man would summarize in himself the universe), his perspective turns to the sobering landscape of the region. Once prosperous, populous, and filled with glory and heroes, but now ravaged by the Franco-Prussian War, Lorraine seems haunted by these memories and becomes a point of identification for Philippe as he wonders whether the fate of his egoist program will parallel that of his native land: "Mais, Lorraine, j'ai touché ta limite, tu n'as pas abouti, tu t'es desséchée . . . tu m'as montré que j'appartenais à une race incapable de se réaliser. . . . Il faut que je me dissolve comme ma race" (But, Lorraine, I reached your limit, you did not end, you dried up . . . you showed me that I belonged to a race un-

Political cartoon depicting Barrès as a patriotic candidate for the Chambre des Députés, seeking revenge on Germany for the Franco-Prussian War

able to complete itself. . . . It is necessary that I dissolve myself like my race).

As Philippe and Simon continue their experiments in self-examination (this time based on Saint Ignatius of Loyola's *Spiritual Exercises*, although that author's method would be valorized over any potential religious value therein), the former frames the egoists' activities in melancholic and sentimental descriptions of the Lorraine countryside that already reveal the elements of his eventual traditionalism and nationalism as they relate to the native soil. Philippe, restless and desirous of making one final attempt to throw off the influence of origins, sets off alone to continue his journey south, drawn to Italy, the cradle of Latin civilization. In his anti-Germanic writings, such as the novel *Colette Baudoche* (1909; translated, 1918), Barrès later extolled France as the last bastion of that ancient Latin civilization. In Venice the hero of the novel finds the perfect setting for his dreams, imagination, feelings, and studies: "Enfin, je connus Venise. Je possédais tous mes documents pour dégager la loi de cette cité et m'y conformer" (Finally, I knew Venice. I possessed all of my documents in order to extricate the law of that city and to conform myself to it).

In that magnificent Adriatic setting and later in deserted, off-season Cannes on the Mediterranean coast in southern France, the isolated and very nearly sick ego of the narrator finally clears itself of its refusal of association with the so-called barbarians, those of the non-ego, and concocts a new rule of existence that includes contact with the non-ego as a part of the ego's own development: "Nous avons une partie de notre moi qui nous est commune à l'un et à l'autre. . . . Etranger au monde extérieur, étranger même à mon passé, étranger à mes instincts, connaissant seulement des émotions rapides que j'aurai choisies: véritablement Homme libre!" (We have a part of our ego that is common to both of us. . . . A stranger to the external world, a stranger even to my past, a stranger to my instincts, knowing only rapid emotions that I will have chosen: truly a Free Man!). Philippe's rule of existence acknowledges the dangerous excesses of his turn inward to solitude and self and admits that his physical and social inactivity have exacerbated appetites and desires that only an active life in society can fulfill. Confident of the mastery of his inner life that he has acquired from his cerebral exercises, Philippe no longer worries about the potentially contaminating influences of the barbarian minds and plans to reenter the world without renouncing the development and appreciation of his own ego.

In the final novel of the *Culte du moi* trilogy, *Le Jardin de Bérénice*, Philippe willingly engages in contact with society. After returning from his travels, he commits himself to a career in politics and is elected deputy. Philippe's choice of politics as a realm of redemption closely parallels Barrès's own increasing interest and involvement in the political arena. He later wrote in *Mes cahiers* (My Notebooks, 1929-1938, 1949): "Oui, j'ai failli être fou. Je ne sais plus ce qui me sauva. Si, je le sais: la politique. Pourquoi j'aime la Politique? D'abord, je lui dois la vie" (Yes, I almost was mad. I no longer know what saved me. Yes, I do know: politics. Why do I like Politics? First of all, I owe it my life).

In contrast to the restlessness of Philippe's inner life, which finally finds an acceptable external complement in the realm of political action, is the title character, Philippe's mistress. Bérénice, another native of Lorraine, is typical of the status of the Barresian woman. Ambiguous and mannequinlike, she spent her childhood playing in a fourteenth-century museum where her father was a caretaker, and her submission to and continuation of the traditions of her native soil provide a strong attraction for the young politician. Bérénice's presence in the novel—instinctive, unquestioning, and natural as she communes with the plants and animals in her garden—seems to be a pretext for her value as a symbol for the soul of the people, a collective unconscious of a regional or national group that emanates from a common heredity and tradition: "Ce n'était plus Bérénice que je voyais, mais l'âme populaire, âme religieuse, instinctive et comme cette petite fille, pleine d'un passé dont elle n'a pas conscience" (It was no longer Bérénice that I was seeing, but the popular soul, a religious and instinctive soul, and, like this little girl, full of a past of which she was not conscious).

Her appearance in this final novel of the trilogy produces a profound effect on Philippe, and the program of the ego's development becomes progressively conceived of in the context of the collective plane. Appropriating the example of Bérénice (whose idealization is fixed in representation by her death near the end of the novel) as the proof of a transcendent value will allow for this final shift away from an unengaged philosophy of egoism. By the end of *Le Jardin de Bérénice*, the cult of the ego is transformed into the first glimmerings of what will become the Barresian notion of nationalist culture.

In Barrès's works fiction and biography often inextricably mirror each other. The decisive turn in Philippe's course away from the solipsistic existence of the cult of the ego toward politics echoes to a great extent Barrès's own career in the 1880s and 1890s. His fashionable and nihilistic dilettantism of the *Taches d'Encre* and *Huit jours chez Monsieur Renan*, tempered by the *Culte du moi* trilogy, was significantly transformed by the Boulangist crisis of the late 1880s. Gen. Georges Boulanger, who led the ill-defined yet tremendously popular movement that sought to change the parliamentary government of the Third Republic into an authoritarian oligarchy, had a demagogic appeal for a variety of writers and thinkers, right and left, who, since the crushing French defeat in the Franco-Prussian War, dreamed of *revanche* (revenge).

So too for the young Barrès, who increasingly posited the importance of the values of tradition and nation, Boulanger represented the possibility of regeneration for the lost French power and glory. Animated by sentiments of anticlericalism, patriotism, antiparliamentarianism, and sometimes anti-Semitism (the most virulent anti-Semitic writer of the period, Edouard Drumont, whose pamphlet *La France juive* [Jewish France, 1888] remained influential in extreme rightist circles for decades, was one of Boulanger's strongest supporters), Boulangism presented a real threat to the power base of the Third Republic. Its popularity peaked in the legislative elections of 1889 (Barrès was elected to the Chambre des Députés at the age of twenty-five as a leftist Boulangist candidate from Nancy, a seat he held until 1893), but a suspected coup d'état plot caused the general to flee to the island of Jersey (in the interim he was convicted of treason in absentia).

While the support for Boulangism evaporated quickly in the period of his disgrace, and despite Boulanger's romantic suicide in Brussels on the tomb of his mistress in September 1891, Barrès's hero worship of the general remained steady. In his nonfictional account of this episode of French history and politics, *L'Appel au soldat* (The Call to the Soldier, 1900), he lionized Boulanger, who "convoquerait nos réserves d'énergie" (would summon our reserves of energy). His experience with Boulangism not only provided him with the aspirations of a political career, but also proved to reorient the form and content of his writing, which became dominated by political questions. His next work, *L'Ennemi des lois* (The Enemy of Laws, 1893), reduced the fictional and novelistic to a bare, less-than-pretextual minimum in its discussion of turn-of-the-century anarchism. His next trilogy, *Le Roman de l'énergie nationale* (The Romance of National Energy), includes *L'Appel au soldat* and *Leurs figures* (Their Faces, 1902), recounting respectively the years of Boulangism and the Panama Canal scandal of 1892, an account in which the literary is virtually absent. The first and most important work of the trilogy, the novel *Les Déracinés*, perhaps the most significant and influential work of Barrès's career, signals the emergence of his nationalist and traditionalist voice.

Les Déracinés, written during the growing storm of the Dreyfus Affair, was first published in serial form in the *Revue de Paris* in 1897, which may account for its episodic nature. Identified by critics as one of the first modern political and sociological novels, *Les Déracinés* marks a significant stylistic departure in Barrès's novelistic writing. This change depends in great part on a third-person narration that is stripped of the metaphysical vocabulary and discussions of the previous works, rendering the novel's perspective more direct, objective, and certainly more traditional in the context of nineteenth-century French literature.

The novel follows the progress of seven young Lorrainer men as they attempt to make careers for themselves in the Parisian metropolis after having received the *baccalauréat* in 1879 from the Nancy lycée. Although from differing social and economic backgrounds, the main characters have received the same education from the philosophy professor Paul Bouteiller, who, through the study of Kantian thought, has instilled in his students a passionate thirst for analysis based on that philosopher's critical method. Bouteiller is the paragon of the *déraciné*, "un produit pédagogique, un fils de la raison, étranger à nos habitudes traditionnelles, locales ou de famille, tout abstrait, et vraiment suspendu dans le vide" (a pedagogical product, a son of reason, a stranger to our traditional, local, or familial habits, completely abstract, and really suspended in the void).

Bouteiller is an important figure in the novel, not only for his later attempt to realize in the political realm his abstract theories, an attempt that ends in failure, but also for his status as an educator. Barrès's emerging traditionalism and nationalism became increasingly centered on the idea of education and its necessary role in the creation of a nationalist society, so much so that he originally titled his collection of journalistic articles *Scènes et doctrines du nationalisme* (Scenes and Doctrines of Nationalism, 1902), an influential text of the nationalist revival, "L'Education nationaliste" (Nationalist Education).

The education of the main characters of *Les Déracinés*, mirroring that of Philippe in the *Culte du moi* trilogy as well as Barrès's view of his own studies, has denaturalized their young minds to the extent that its relentlessly analytical method has uprooted them from their provincial heredity and traditions. Young, intelligent, and energetic, yet, like most Barresian heroes, not possessing an organizing principle or goal for their lives, the seven Lorrainers follow different paths in the cosmopolitan atmosphere of Parisian society, which the novel minutely chronicles (the form of the chronicle was increasingly employed by Barrès as his writing moved further away from the fictional or the literary). *Les Déracinés*, then, is presented as a chronicled indictment of the development of French society under the Third Republic—its culture, its educational system, its politics—which is sketched in opposition to the growing nationalist alternative.

Once in Paris, where they "vaguent dans le Quartier Latin.... libres comme des bêtes dans les bois" (wander in the Latin Quarter.... free like beasts in the woods), the seven provincials-turned-intellectuals, whose ambition leads them to be called "little Napoleons," set out to conquer Paris. Racadot and Mouchefrin, from socially and financially inferior backgrounds, might have led respectable lives had they remained in their native region, but they prove ill-equipped to handle the demands of the disorienting atmosphere of big-city life. They found a newspaper, but when political and financial disasters ensue, they turn to robbery and murder. Racadot is executed, and Mouchefrin, while spared the gallows, finishes out his days in abject poverty as a police informant.

Suret-Lefort and Renaudin, rendered cynical and insensitive by Parisian life, become respectively an influential newspaperman and a powerful lawyer; they demonstrate the catastrophic implications of uprootedness in their behavior as unscrupulous députés. Indeed, Barrès sees uprootedness as no longer an individual problem but one that dominates the collective and national plane. One of the most famous chapters of *Les Déracinés* is titled "La France dissociée et décérébrée" (Dissociated and Decerebrated France). The three remaining characters, Sturel, Roemerspracher, and Saint-Philin—all of whom are somewhat less driven to direct their energies toward creating careers for themselves, as their financial means are substantial enough to allow them to pursue paths of introspection and ideas—represent the optimistic types of the original group, Barrès's version of the future of France.

Sturel, who possesses a romantic imagination, becomes increasingly drawn to the sort of hero worship that characterizes Barrès's later writing and discovers in crowd activity surrounding the funeral of Victor Hugo in 1885 and the Boulangist movement of 1887-1889 a more significantly powerful and satisfying force than intellectual activity. Roemerspracher remains an intellectual and champions as an organizing principle Hippolyte Taine's historical evolutionist doctrine of the overriding importance of the influences of "la race, le milieu, et le moment" (race, surroundings, and time). Saint-Philin, the son of an aristocratic Lorraine family, ultimately abandons the denaturalizing life of the city and returns to his family's home in order to cultivate its land. The example that Barrès presents to the reader in the characters of Sturel (who is often seen as Barrès's alter ego), Roemerspracher, and Saint-Philin is meant to demonstrate his eventual contention that the degenerating process of uprootedness might well be reversible, as he later stated in *Mes cahiers*: "Ces jeunes gens, ces déracinés, le problème est maintenant de savoir s'ils prendront racine" (These young people, these uprooted, the problem is now to find out if they will take root).

In the evolution of Barrès's thought, *Les Déracinés* marks a significant moment in the acquisition of his traditionalist and nationalist voice, with its ultimate proposal of the idea of regionalism as an antidote to the socially etiolating influences of uprootedness. The Barresian conception of regionalism, from which would spring the possibility of an "énergie nationale," nearly always rests on the image of Lorraine, whose allegorical status allows for it to become the cornerstone for the articulation of nationalism that dominated his career in the twentieth century, as in the last trilogy of works, *Les Bastions de l'Est* (The Bastions of the East): *Au service de l'Allemagne* (In the Service of Germany, 1905), *Colette Baudoche*, the sole novel in the series, and *Le Génie du Rhin* (The Genius of the Rhine, 1921), all of which treat the question of the provinces of Alsace and Lorraine.

The importance of the native region for Barrès, which derives in part from Taine's doctrine of the influences of "la race, le milieu, et le

Caricature of Barrès by Axilette

moment," has many parallels among other late-nineteenth-century thinkers, insofar as it attempts a combination of historical, political, biological, medical, and literary discourses. Barrès came under the influence of a conservative neurophysiologist, Jules Soury, in the late 1890s, and the reorientation of Barrès's early nationalism toward the past reveals this new sway. France, in *Scènes et doctrines du nationalisme,* becomes a body: "Nulle conception de la France ne peut prévaloir, dans nos décisions, contre la France de chair et d'os" (No conception of France can prevail, in our decisions, against the France of flesh and bone).

Essential to Barrès's regionalism-cum-nationalism is a medico-organic determinism that becomes increasingly expressed in the "voix du sang" (voice of blood) that the land of one's ancestors produces in the race of one's descendants. The inscription of the image of the "voix du sang"—which appears elsewhere in late-nineteenth-century thought as an indirect representation linked to the fear of the then-incurable venereal disease syphilis and was transposed into political thought most often by anti-Semitic writers (this theme dominates chapter 10 of Adolf Hitler's *Mein Kampf* [1925-1927])—into Barrès's nationalist discourse transforms the horticultural metaphor of the French as uprooted into a physiological one that conceives of the French as a body. In *Scènes et doctrines du nationalisme,* Barrès renders the past medical: "La raison humaine est enchaînée de telle sorte que nous repassons tous dans les pas de nos prédécesseurs. . . . Nous sommes la continuité de nos parents. Cela est vrai anatomiquement" (Human reason is bound in such a way that we all pass again in the footsteps of our predecessors. . . . We are the continuity of our parents. That is anatomically true).

During the stormy years of the Dreyfus Affair in the late 1890s, Barrès's version of deterministic nationalism based on ideas culled from medicine and biology paralleled the rising tide of anticosmopolitanism, xenophobia, and anti-Semitism. The Jews, Barrès claimed in his journalistic prose of the period, were the quintessential *déracinés,* as they have no native land in France on which they can be the caretakers of the ancient spirit of their ancestors. Their foreignness was so complete in Barrès's estimation—as in *Les Déracinés* when Sturel mutters after having observed a family of Jewish-German immigrants in his native town of Neufchâteau, "Avec ceux-là, comment avoir un lien? Comment me trouver avec eux en communauté de sentiments?" (With them, how could I have a bond? How could I find myself with them in a community of feelings?)—that the possibility of assimilation, very much a debated issue in France since before the Revolution of 1789, was denied. Although Barrès's anti-Semitism became less pronounced in his later writing (particularly in the 1910s as a result of World War I), the xenophobic conception of the dangerous foreigners present in the body of the French nation remained an elemental aspect of his nationalism, its target shifting to the Germans (*Colette Baudoche* is the most striking example of this).

If for Barrès the 1880s had been a decade of apprenticeship in the ways of Parisian literary and political culture, the 1890s proved to be a period of newfound maturity in both the private and public spheres. In 1893 he married Paule Couche, the daughter of a French general, and in 1896 his only child, Philippe, was born. The death of Barrès's father in 1898 and that of his mother three years later cast a somber light on his personal life. His political career during the same period paralleled the worries of his private life. After his defeat in the legislative elections of 1893, Barrès lost again in 1896 and 1898. Some critics have pointed to his personal and public troubles as a partial explanation for the conservative turn in his writing during the 1890s. The decade saw one of the most divisive scandals to threaten the Third Republic, the Dreyfus Affair, an event that further polarized the French political spectrum and accelerated the nationalist revival.

Barrès, who had become increasingly involved in political activity since Boulangism, was editor of the antiparliamentarian journal the *Cocarde* (Cockade, a reference to a tricolor insignia) from 1894-1895 and became a vocal and staunch anti-Dreyfusard (the Dreyfusards represented internationalism, antimilitarism, and leftism). Although Barrès was allied during these years with various extremists on the right from whom he later distanced himself, he emerged from the crisis of the Dreyfus Affair an important, influential writer and political figure. He was elected to the Académie Française at the age of forty-four in 1906 and resecured a seat in the Chambre des Députés in the same year. Barrès's political career as a député and the formal recognition for his thought and work parallel the decline of the literary in his writing.

Colette Baudoche, the final panel of the *Bastions de l'Est* triptych, represents perhaps Barrès's

Frédéric Masson, Paul Bourget, and Barrès in 1910

most successful attempt at transposing the nationalist slogan of "la terre et les morts" (the land and the dead) into the literary. The novel recounts the story of Dr. Frederic Asmus and the young woman of Metz who comes to symbolize France in the course of the narrative. Colette, a poor, humble woman whose mother has taken Asmus as a boarder, proves irresistible to the young German professor. He forgets his German fiancée and begins to change, unbeknownst to himself, under the beguiling influence of Colette (his coworkers notice how he has become more French), but the young woman ultimately rejects her Pomeranian suitor's offer of marriage as the image of the dead soldiers of the Franco-Prussian War inspires her to assert her patriotism. Although alone, Colette, by virtue of her choice, has entered into the community of patriots.

In *Mes cahiers*, Barrès refers to the main character of the novel: "J'avais un peu la nostalgie de mon Asie intérieure tandis que j'écrivais Colette" (I had a little nostalgia for my interior Asia while I wrote Colette). This remark, coupled with Barrès's continued insistence on the native soil, presents an element that dominates the last phase of the author's literary writing, the historiographical *La Colline inspirée* and *Un Jardin sur l'Oronte* (A Garden on the Oronte, 1922), which recounts a thirteenth-century romance between a Syrian girl and a Crusader. In both of these works can be discerned the importance of a mystical space.

Throughout his career Barrès recognized the inspirational quality of the landscape, whether it be his native Lorraine, the Venice of *Un Homme libre*, the Toledo of his work on El Greco, the subjects of his travel writings (Italy, Spain, Greece, the Middle East), or the Alsace of *Au service de l'Allemagne*. In *La Colline inspirée*, which includes some of Barrès's most accomplished prose, the mystico-religious site is the shrine at Sion-Vaudrémont in the Lorraine region, which a group of priests at the beginning of the nineteenth century tried to transform into the object of a popular cult that took account of its pagan origins as well as its Catholic heritage. Barrès's romanticized version of the story of these priests, who were ultimately deemed heretics, valorizes the notion of place, which, in the case of Sion-Vaudrémont, is both mystical and religious: "Silence, les dieux sont ici" (Silence, the gods are here).

The idea of a mystical and spiritual place is an important part of Barrès's "orientalist" writings, such as *Un Jardin sur l'Oronte*. He had previously found occasion to represent the relationship of mystery and mysticism to the landscape of their origin in the character of Bérénice, in a Jewish mistress of Sturel in *Les Déracinés*, and in his study of the Middle East, *Une Enquête aux pays du Levant* (An Inquiry in the Levantine Countries, 1923), but nowhere in his writing is the power and seduction of his "interior Asia" more evident than in *Un Jardin sur l'Oronte*. When it first appeared, the novel caused a minor scandal, its diluted exoticism interpreted as a departure from the nationalist ideal that had dominated his work since the end of the nineteenth century. And yet, *Un Jardin sur l'Oronte* continues and develops an element that had nearly always been part of the Barresian perspective, that of place. In these final works Barrès transforms place into a spiritual source from which the individual, collective, national, and religious souls emanate.

Barrès's untimely death from a heart attack on 5 December 1923 brought to an end a career that can be appreciated as much for its quality as for its diversity and productivity. The monument of the writing of Barrès (for this was how he saw his work in the final years of his life) provided an important model of a rightist-engaged intellectual that conservative and fascist intellectuals of the decades following his death looked to and championed (certain critics, such as Zeev Sternhell and Robert Soucy, have gone so far as to consider Barrès a protofascist thinker, a position that might explain the diminution of interest in his work during the second half of the twentieth century). Despite the uncertain heritage of Barrès in the wake of twentieth-century politics, as the Parisian dadaists were correct in recognizing, his work profoundly shaped late nineteenth- and early twentieth-century social and literary thought.

Letters:

Barrès, Stanislas de Guaïta, and Léon Sorg, *Le Départ pour la vie* (Paris: Plon, 1961);

Henri Massis, *Barrès et nous, suivi d'une correspondance inédite, 1906-23* (Paris: Plon, 1962).

Bibliography:

Alphonse Zarach, *Bibliographie barrésienne, 1881-1948* (Paris: Presses Universitaires de France, 1951).

Biographies:

Pierre Moreau, *Maurice Barrès* (Paris: Le Sagittaire, 1946);

Jean-Marie Domenach, *Barrès, par lui-même* (Paris: Editions du Seuil, 1954);

Maurice Davanture, *La Jeunesse de Maurice Barrès (1862-1888)* (Paris: Champion, 1975).

References:

Marie-Claire Bancquart, *Les Ecrivains et l'histoire d'après Maurice Barrès, Léon Daudet, Anatole France, Charles Péguy* (Paris: Nizet, 1966);

Pierre de Boisdeffre, *Barrès parmi nous* (Paris: Drumont, 1952);

Denis W. Brogan, *French Personalities and Problems* (London: Hamish Hamilton, 1946);

Henri Clouard, *Bilan de Barrès* (Paris: Sequanna, 1943);

Michel Curtis, *Three Against the Third Republic: Sorel, Barrès and Maurras* (Princeton: Princeton University Press, 1959);

Elie Decahors, *Trois messages: Maurice Barrès, André Gide, François Mauriac* (Toulouse: Les Editions de l'Archer, 1939);

Charles Stewart Doty, *From Cultural Rebellion to Counterrevolution: The Politics of Maurice Barrès* (Athens: Ohio University Press, 1976);

Ida Frandon, *L'Orient de Maurice Barrès: Etude de genèse* (Geneva: Droz, 1952);

Paul Gaultier, *Les Maîtres de la presse française* (Paris: Payot, 1921);

André Gide, *Feuillets d'automne* (Paris: Mercure de France, 1949); translated by Elsie Pell as *Autumn Leaves* (New York: Philosophical Library, 1950);

Victor Giraud, *Les Maîtres de l'heure: Maurice Barrès* (Paris: Hachette, 1922);

Jean Godfrin, *Barrès mystique* (Neuchâtel: La Baconnière, 1962);

Anthony A. Greaves, *Maurice Barrès* (Boston: Twayne, 1978);

Albert Léon Guerard, *Five Masters of French Romance (Anatole France, Pierre Loti, Paul Bourget, Maurice Barrès, Romain Rolland)* (London: T. Fisher Unwin, 1916);

René Lalou, *Maurice Barrès* (Paris: Hachette, 1950);

Charles Maurras, *Maîtres et témoins de ma vie d'esprit* (Paris: Flammarion, 1954);

Henri de Montherlant, *Aux fontaines du désir* (Paris: Grasset, 1927);

Philip Ouston, *The Imagination of Maurice Barrès* (Toronto: University of Toronto Press, 1974);

Flora Emma Ross, *Goethe in Modern France, with Special Reference to Maurice Barrès, Paul Bourget and André Gide* (Urbana: University of Illinois Press, 1937);

Robert Soucy, *Fascism in France: The Case of Maurice Barrès* (Berkeley: University of California Press, 1972);

Zeev Sternhell, *Maurice Barrès et le nationalisme français* (Paris: Colin, 1972);

Albert Thibaudet, *La Vie de Maurice Barrès* (Paris: Gallimard, 1921).

Papers:

Barrès's manuscripts are at the Bibliothèque Nationale, Paris.

Léon Bloy

(11 July 1846 - 2 November 1917)

John E. Coombes
University of Essex

BOOKS: *Le Révélateur du globe* (Paris: Sauton, 1884);

Propos d'un entrepreneur de démolitions (Paris: Tresse, 1884);

Le Pal (Paris: Penin & Soirat, 1885); augmented as *Le Pal, suivi des Nouveaux propos d'un entrepreneur de démolitions* (Paris: Stock, 1925);

Le Désespéré (Paris: Soirat, 1886);

Un Brelan d'excommuniés: L'Enfant terrible, Le Fou, Le Lépreux (Paris: Savine, 1889);

Christophe Colomb devant les taureaux (Paris: Savine, 1890);

La Chevalière de la mort (Gand: Siffer, 1890);

Les Funérailles du naturalisme (Copenhagen: G. E. C. Gad, 1891);

Le Salut par les Juifs (Paris: Demay, 1892; revised edition, Paris: Victorion, 1906);

Sueur de sang (1870-1871) (Paris: Dentu, 1893);

Les Vendanges! (Paris, 1894);

Léon Bloy devant les cochons (Paris: Chamuel, 1894);

Histoires désobligeantes (Paris: Dentu, 1894);

Ici on assassine les grands hommes (Paris: Mercure de France, 1895);

La Femme pauvre (Paris: Mercure de France, 1897); translated by I. S. Collins as *The Woman Who Was Poor: A Contemporary Novel of the French Eighties* (New York: Sheed & Ward, 1939);

Le Mendiant ingrat (Brussels: Edmond Deman, 1898);

Le Fils de Louis XVI (Paris: Mercure de France, 1900);

Je m'accuse. . . . (Paris: Maison d'Art, 1900);

Exégèse des lieux communs (Paris: Mercure de France, 1902);

Les Dernières Colonnes de l'Eglise (Paris: Mercure de France, 1903);

Mon journal. Dix-sept mois en Danemark (Paris: Mercure de France, 1904);

Quatre ans de captivité à Cochons-sur-Marne (Paris: Mercure de France, 1905);

Belluaires et porchers (Paris: Stock, 1905);

Pages choisies (1884-1905) (Paris: Mercure de France, 1906);

L'Epopée byzantine et Gustave Schlumberger (Paris: Blaizot, 1906); republished as *Constantinople et Byzance* (Paris: Crès, 1917);

La Résurrection de Villiers de l'Isle-Adam (Paris: Blaizot, 1906);

Celle qui pleure N.D. de la Salette (Paris: Mercure de France, 1908);

L'Invendable (Paris: Mercure de France, 1909);

Le Sang du pauvre (Paris: Juven, 1909);

Le Vieux de la montagne (Paris: Mercure de France, 1911);

L'Ame de Napoléon (Paris: Mercure de France, 1912);

Léon Bloy in 1887

Sur la tombe de Huysmans (Paris: A. L. Laquerrière, 1913);
Le Pèlerin de l'absolu (Paris: Mercure de France, 1914);
Jeanne d'Arc et l'Allemagne (Paris: Crès, 1915);
Nous ne sommes pas en état de guerre (Paris: Maison du Livre, 1915);
Au seuil de l'Apocalypse (Paris: Mercure de France, 1916);
Méditations d'un solitaire en 1916 (Paris: Mercure de France, 1917);
Dans les ténèbres (Paris: Mercure de France, 1918);
La Porte des humbles (1915-1917) (Paris: Mercure de France, 1920);
Le Symbolisme de l'apparition (Paris: Lemercier, 1925);
Fragments inédits sur Barbey d'Aurevilly (La Rochelle: Cahiers Léon Bloy, 1927);
Inédits de Léon Bloy, introduction by René Martineau, with commentary by Joseph Bollery, Carton de Wiart, and Georges Rouzet (Montreal: Serge, 1945).

Editions and Collections: *Poèmes en prose* (Paris: Editions de la Grille, 1928);
Mon journal I (1896-1899) (Paris: Mercure de France, 1942);
Mon journal II (1899-1900) (Paris: Mercure de France, 1943);
Pilgrim of the Absolute, edited by Raïssa Maritain, with an introduction by Jacques Maritain (New York: Pantheon, 1947);
L'Œuvre complète de Léon Bloy, 8 volumes, edited by Joseph Bollery (Paris: F. Bernouard, 1947-1950);
She Who Weeps: Our Lady of La Salette. An Anthology of Léon Bloy's Writings on La Salette, translated and edited, with an introduction, by Emile La Douceur (Fresno, Cal.: Academy Library Guild, 1956);
Journal, 4 volumes, edited by Bollery (Paris: Mercure de France, 1956-1963);
Sur J.-K. Huysmans (Brussels: Editions Complexe, 1986).

OTHER: Jeanne Termier, *Derniers refuges*, preface by Bloy (Paris: Grasset, 1910);
Mélanie Calvat, *Vie de Mélanie, bergère de la Salette, écrite par elle-même en 1900*, introduction by Bloy (Paris: Mercure de France, 1912);
Pierre van der Meer de Walcheren, *Journal d'un converti*, introduction by Bloy (Paris: Crès, 1917).

Léon Bloy's undoubted eccentricity is of more than individual significance; his vituperative prose, whether fictional or nonfictional, merits consideration as more than a series of admittedly bizarre curiosities. The singularly uncharitable Christian polemic that constitutes the major part of his writing (and like those of all true sectarians, Bloy's attacks on others of his own faith are even more violent than those on atheists) is a significant element in the literary history of the *grands exaspérés*. This tendency, whose opposition to the dominant positivist rationality of the late nineteenth century had its literary origins in both the frenetic Catholic apologetics of Louis Veuillot and the quasi-nihilist irony of Gustave Flaubert's later works, was to be characterized principally in the writing of Bloy—and later that of Charles Péguy and Louis Céline—by a political ideology of extreme reaction (in varying combinations antirationalist, antidemocratic, and anti-Semitic). This ideology was articulated through a discourse that, in its implicit assertion of the supremacy of the revealed word—as opposed to the positivist supremacy of the fact—may be seen to have restricted affinities with certain aspects of modernism.

The external aspects of Léon Bloy's biography offer few features of interest, apart from the isolated monotony of its last forty or so years. From his birth in Périgueux on 11 July 1846 until he left home in 1863 to study art, unsuccessfully, in Paris, he lived in a household ideologically divided in a manner not unusual in nineteenth-century France: his father an atheist, his mother exhibiting strong mystical tendencies. In 1869 Bloy's acquaintance with Jules-Amédée Barbey d'Aurevilly (whose secretary he became for some time) brought him under the influence of irredentist Catholicism, and his study of the visionary Anna Katharina Emmerich led to his conversion to the church in 1870.

Bloy served as a volunteer in the Franco-Prussian War and later gave an account of his experiences in the short-story collection *Sueur de sang (1870-1871)* (Bloody Sweat [1870-1871], 1893); he subsequently worked as a journalist for the *Figaro* and *Gil Blas*, publishing his own weekly pamphlet, the *Pal*, in 1885. Henceforth, however, he withdrew increasingly into a life devoted to the polemics (collected in several volumes) of an idiosyncratic form of Catholicism (influenced after 1877 by Abbé Tardif de Moidrey, he was obsessed with the miracles of La Salette, which had allegedly occurred in the year of his birth, and which were influential to varying degrees on Joris-Karl Huysmans, Jacques Maritain, and Georges Rouault), and, in the very last years before his death on 2 November 1917, to vociferous bellicosity. His personal life throughout these years, spent, like that of Céline, in the drab landscape of the Paris suburbs, seems to have been unutterably unattractive, friendless, and joyless. Still more so, probably, were the lives of the two partners who predeceased him (Anne-Marie Roulé, the model for Véronique in his novel *Le Désespéré* [The Hopeless, 1886], an ex-prostitute ultimately incarcerated in Saint-Anne; and Berthe Dumont, who died of tetanus in 1885) and of the half-Danish Jeanne Molbech, whom he married in 1890, to say nothing of their four children, two of whom died of malnutrition.

However, as Roland Barthes has noted, the themes of money and poverty, around which Bloy's novels *Le Désespéré* and *La Femme pauvre* (1897; translated as *The Woman Who Was Poor*, 1939) are organized, are for Bloy not seen as historically motivated and conditioned—or indeed as motivating or conditioning—entities, but as unmediated, contingent facts. As such, they constitute the immutable solidities of the given world against which the flux of the writer's language pounds itself, perhaps, into exhaustion. Yet the dichotomy proposed in Bloy's work between established solidity and social power on the one hand and discursive flux, irony, vituperation, and spiritual assertion on the other has the ultimate effect of reinforcing that established and dominant position of nineteenth-century thought, to whose destruction his writing is ostensibly addressed. The division, cardinal to positivist thinking since Auguste Comte, between *le fait* (fact) and *l'inconnaissable* (the unknowable) is effectually and rigorously maintained.

One of the principal strategies of positivism for avoiding confrontation with its own contradictions has always been that of escape into taxonomy: the eternal deferment of the gratification of fulfilled significance through the absorption of method into categorization. A particularly brutal instance of such a taxonomy—both logically and socially brutal—is found in an anti-Semitic text completed relatively early in Bloy's writing career, *Le Salut par les Juifs* (Saving by the Jews, 1892).

In the violence of its vilification of "le Youtre moderne . . . le confluent de toutes les hideurs du monde" (the modern Yid . . . the mixture of all the world's horrors), the text even goes beyond other French anti-Semitic utterances of the period. Yet the significant difference between it and, say, Edouard Drumont's texts and similar previous writings is not one of degree but of kind. Bloy specifically attacks Drumont for limiting his concerns to an account of Jewish finance, for seeing the Jew as a specific rather than as a universal symbol. And it is true that Drumont's *La France juive* (Jewish France, 1885) can be characterized as little more than a series of anecdotal instances loosely grouped around a series of binary definitions of "Jews" and "Aryans"—a reflex of anti-Semitism as old, at least, as the Middle Ages.

To this Bloy opposes an argument at once more ambitious, and more premonitory of the horrors of the twentieth century. For Bloy, the Jews are disgusting, but this should not be seen in terms simply of binary opposition to their racial "superiors," since their disgusting inferiority is all part of God's plan of degradation and redemption: "Ils sont forcés par Dieu, invinciblement et surnaturellement forcés, d'accomplir les

Cover for the weekly pamphlet that Bloy published in 1885

abominables cochonneries dont ils ont besoin pour accréditer leur déshonneur d'*instruments de la Rédemption*" (They are forced by God, invincibly and supernaturally forced, to do the abominably foul deeds they need to in order to get their dishonor accredited as *instruments of His Redemption*).

Significantly, the fluidity of language as mediation between consciousness and the world becomes, when attributed to the Jews, a wild and sinister coruscation, "comme le malaise fantastique d'une flagellation gélatineuse" (like the fantastic discomfort of a sort of gelatinous flagellation). Their historical role becomes something at once subordinate to God's will and transcendent of binary categories—in this instance of hardness and softness—thus productive of a sense of formlessness: "(un) destin de fer qui . . . consistait . . . à préserver . . . la poignée de *boue* merveilleuse" ([an] iron destiny that . . . served . . . to preserve . . . a handful of wonderful *mud*). Clearly this central text offers the attempted absorption of a visceral and neurotic fear of the Other into a structure of metaphysical command at once universal and yet, by the same token, tenuous in the extreme.

The fears had already been obsessively articulated in *Le Désespéré*. The close resemblance of many elements in the novel to what is known of the details of Bloy's life serves to corroborate the traditional adage about truth being stranger than fiction. More significantly, obsessiveness is manifest in the very form of the text, a virtually disconnected episodic series: the funeral of the father of the protagonist, Marchenoir; Marchenoir's retreat to the Grande Chartreuse monastery; his life with the repentant whore turned *dévote*, Véronique, and her self-mutilation for his sake; and their shared religious fanaticism, leading in her case to madness and incarceration, in his to death and a kind of murky apotheosis.

The seriality of the text—on which continuity, such as it is, is conferred by Marchenoir's repeated threnodies, in which verbal ejaculations seem to do service for sexual ones, and strenuous rhetorical excoriation for more positive modes of affirmation—derives, quite evidently, from the initial rejection of the father, an anticlerical who apparently stands for a whole tradition of French rational logocentrism. That he is not part of an overall structure of Oedipal resolution is seen in the way in which Marchenoir—in the letter to a friend that, with its revelatory slip of tenses, begins the novel—identifies literary effect and parricide, and art and death. "Quand vous recevrez cette lettre, mon ami, j'aurai achevé de tuer mon père" (When you receive this letter, my friend, I shall finally have killed my father).

By comparison with the contradictions of Marchenoir's guilty detestation of his father and the France that he represents, "la Fille aînée de l'Eglise, devenue la salope du monde" (the eldest Daughter of the Church, now the world's slut)—and still more with his relations with the repentant whore Véronique—the sixty pages of the novel devoted to the ideologically positive elements of Marchenoir's stay in the Grande Chartreuse are as tedious, with their continual and unquestioning assertion of unremitting virtues, as the exhortatory passages of any Balzacian or socialist realist novel. The text itself seems to indicate this, its interminable account of regenerative piety interspersed with references to Véronique, whose tribulations dominate much of the rest of the book.

At one level Véronique, the whore turned *dévote*, variously perceived as "une chose à Marchenoir" (one of Marchenoir's possessions) and, more picturesquely, as "un encensoir toujours fumant devant Dieu" (a thurible perpetually smoking away before the Almighty), is a banal exemplification of Bloy's inability to break with the phallocentric and fundamentally unimaginative sexual fantasies of the nineteenth-century middle-class male, for whom woman had to be either angel or whore. (Significantly, for Bloy, just as the Jew could be incorporated into God's plan by a totalitarian strategy, so in the case of woman could both functions be combined in what is termed in *Belluaires et porchers* (Wild-Beast Tamers and Swineherds, 1905) "cet effarant Mystère de la Prostitution de la Femme" (this alarming Mystery of Female Prostitution).

The most memorable crisis in the story concerns Véronique's voluntary self-mutilation: out of concern for Marchenoir's continued lust for her (undiminished by her conversion from prostitution to religious devotion), she has all her teeth pulled—significantly by a Jew, seen simultaneously as verminous and mercenary, *and*, in an instance of truly totalitarian dialectic, as the unwitting instrument of the Divine Will. All this, unfortunately, serves only to make matters worse: her mutilations, and the odor of sanctity that surrounds them, transmit themselves to Marchenoir as "de suggestives incitations" (inflammatory suggestions) and provoke his lust still further. Finally—after Véronique's transformation from feared sex object into good cook, and her concomitant descent into total derangement—the situation is resolved by her incarceration in an asylum and Marchenoir's death.

The absurdity of this horror is self-evident; however, its unconscious black comedy is extremely revelatory. At one level the story indicates the role necessarily ascribed to women by male-dominated religion: as much by her present as by her past, Véronique is condemned to a situation of subordination and inefficacy; in no way is she to be allowed to transcend her role as object of desire or proselytization. Less apparently, but perhaps more significantly, Bloy's location of her struggle, within the ideology of religion, around her mouth and teeth may be seen as the projection of a pathologically violent male fear of woman and sexuality.

For plainly the mouth both is and is not a mouth. As the materializing organ of the word, it is hardly surprising—given Bloy's inchoate awareness of the complex relationship between language, power, and ideology—that it should engender, as it evidently does in Marchenoir, an insecurity Kierkegaardian in its intensity. But simultaneously the mouth is a vagina, the location of feminine sexual identity: in this case, for Bloy/Marchenoir (and it would be pointless to deny their homogeneity) very precisely *vagina dentata*, generative of obsessive fears of castration in the male. But in *Le Désespéré* the violent fear of castrating woman, once brutally displaced, is nonetheless transmitted into a successor fear of woman altogether as the wounded mouth, paradoxically, increasingly assumes the aspect of a "real" vulva (the seductive softness of its gentle outlines for Marchenoir is heavily stressed).

Bloy's account of Véronique is of more complexity than one that—in spite of itself—charts the successive stages in the destruction of a woman by the oppressive monolith of a totalitarian belief system. Initially submitting willingly to moral brutalization by Marchenoir, she interiorizes the submission to the extent—initially—of brutalizing herself physically, and (when the lustful Moloch of religious "purity" still refuses to be appeased) eventually by "going mad" and "putting herself away"—out of (Marchenoir's) harm's way.

Bloy's collection of grisly tales of universal violence and degeneracy in the Franco-Prussian War, *Sueur de sang*, includes at least one succinct and focused account of the operations of ideology that may be seen as complementary to the drama of Marchenoir and Véronique. In the first story of the collection, "L'Abyssinien," the eponymous central figure achieves dominant stature by rumor and repute; initially enigmatic and taciturn, he is gradually invested by his complaisant fellow soldiers with the characteristics of a monstrous psychopath. Their mythologization of his prowess at killing Prussians mirrors the ambivalence of the narrator's thwarted sexuality: "Mon Abyssinien avait à peu près le visage d'une très belle fille infiniment voluptueuse . . . il avait la concupiscence *exclusive* de l'égorgement" (My Abyssinian had more or less the face of a very lovely and infinitely voluptuous girl . . . with the sense of *exclusive* delight in cutting throats).

Yet such lucidity is uncharacteristic of the volume; more typical is the conclusion of the last story, "Une Femme franc-tireur" (A Female Guerrilla): "La guerre de 1870 est peut-être la seule où toutes les fautes furent commises par tout le monde sans exception, et *des deux côtés à la fois*"

Bloy with his daughters, Madeleine and Véronique, in June 1909

(The war of 1870 is maybe the only one in which every crime was perpetrated by absolutely everyone, on *both sides at once*). Here apocalyptic hyperbole suggests an apocalyptic distinction between the universal degeneracy of the present and the purity of the past. The reactionary implications of this threadbare appeal to confessional "authenticity" become apparent when one reads against it an earlier story, "Barbey d'Aurevilly espion prussien" (Barbey d'Aurevilly, Prussian Spy). Here positive values are plainly represented by the vulgar aristocratism of the eponymous author, whom Bloy greatly admired and who, having insulted a prostitute, is arrested by "la racaille plébiscitaire . . . de son quartier" (the enfranchised scum . . . of his district) as a spy, and rescued by some passing soldiers. Contempt for the people is offset by a residual faith in the force of the state—the effective corollary of the splenetic anarcho-individualism that inhabits so much of Bloy's writing.

Such spleen is perhaps a principal defining characteristic of Bloy's other collection of stories, *Histoires désobligeantes* (Offensive Histories, 1894). Insistent, moralizing rhetoric ensures that their grotesque inventiveness often dissolves into effective anticlimax. In social terms the ambiguity of the narrational distance from "the poor" leads to the establishment of a tenuous distinction between the "deserving" and the "criminal" poor, a distinction whose very questionability leads to its assertion with a virtually genocidal violence, as seen in "Une Recrue" (A Recruit): "Personnage débile qui eût pu être fauché d'un seul coup de poing décoché par un faible bras et trituré sous n'importe quel talon sans que la pitié la plus attentive s'en émût" (A degenerate character who could have been flattened by the single blow of a weakling's fist and ground under anyone's heel, without the most sensitive of souls bothering about it).

At their best these stories are nonetheless highly derivative. "Une Idée médiocre" (A Mediocre Idea) is, for instance, a moderately witty satire on progressive unanimistic ideas and attempts at communal living. Four young men resolve to live together, and when one of them marries, the others harass him for details of his sex life and pursue his wife until she takes a lover and escapes. All that distinguishes this from a Guy de Maupassant conte is the narrator's frenetic intervention, in this case to denounce "ces esclaves enchaînés de la sottise" (these bond slaves of stupidity). Perhaps more interestingly, "Terrible châtiment d'un dentiste" (Terrible Punishment of a Dentist) reads like a shortened version of Emile Zola's

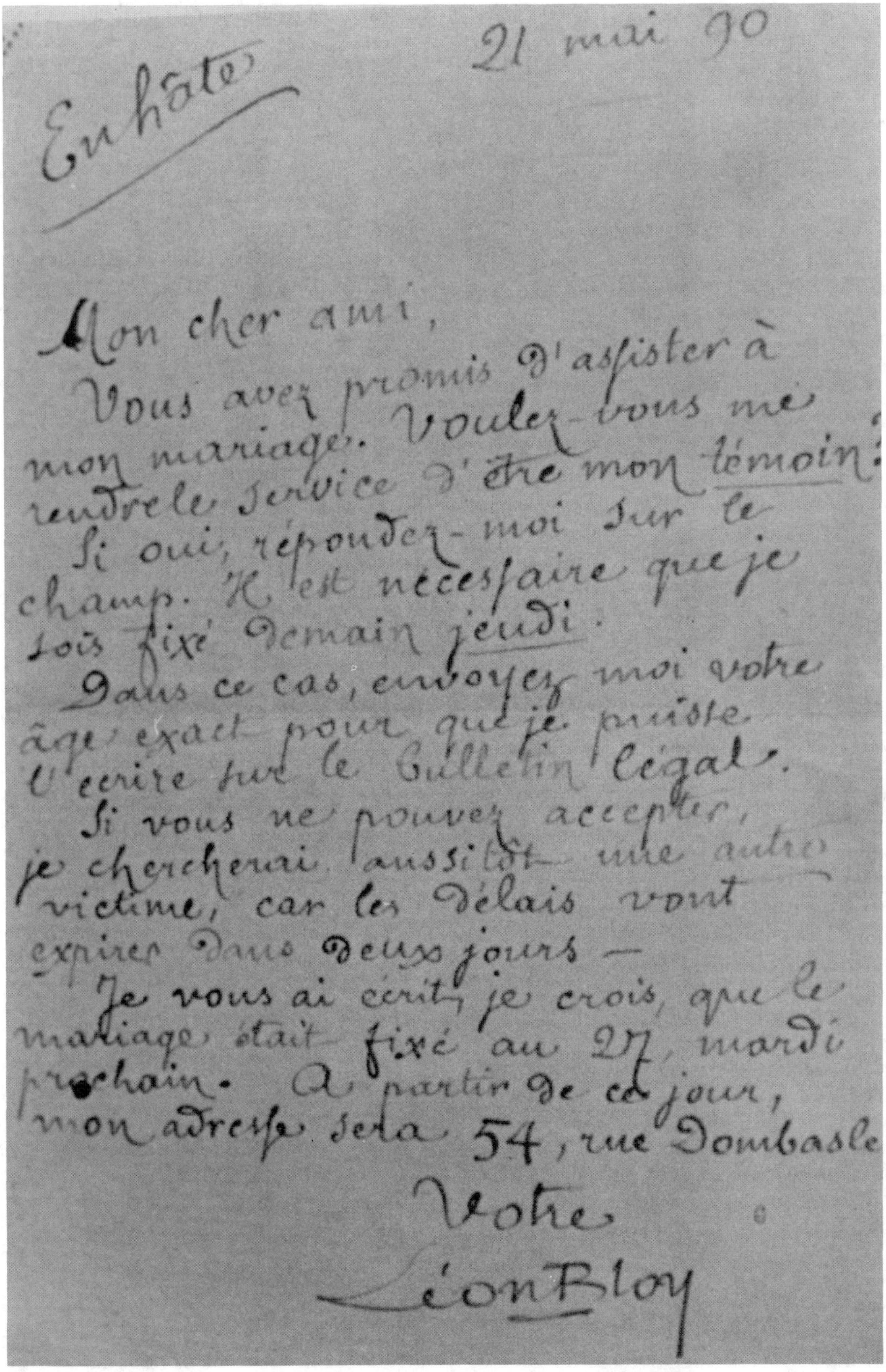

En hâte

21 mai 90

Mon cher ami,

Vous avez promis d'assister à mon mariage. Voulez-vous me rendre le service d'être mon témoin? Si oui, répondez-moi sur le champ. Il est nécessaire que je sois fixé demain jeudi.

Dans ce cas, envoyez moi votre âge exact pour que je puisse l'écrire sur le bulletin légal.

Si vous ne pouvez accepter, je chercherai aussitôt une autre victime, car les délais vont expirer dans deux jours —

Je vous ai écrit, je crois, que le mariage était fixé au 27, mardi prochain. A partir de ce jour, mon adresse sera 54, rue Dombasle

Votre

Léon Bloy

Letter from Bloy to Joris-Karl Huysmans, asking him to be a witness at Bloy's wedding (from Joseph Bollery, Léon Bloy, *volume 2, 1949)*

Thérèse Raquin (1867; translated, 1881) exaggerated *ad absurdum*. The incompetent dentist Gerbillon—his profession indicating a resurrection of the obsessional preoccupations of *Le Désespéré*—strangles his rival in love and, like his counterpart in the Zola text, is haunted by images of his victim. However, Zola's naturalism is supplanted by the horror of moralistic mysticism when Gerbillon's child is born both epileptic and with his victim's face.

For all its antinaturalist assertion, born out by the general tendency of its plot, that "les histoires vraisemblables ne méritent pas d'être racontées" (plausible stories are not worth telling), *La Femme pauvre* has marginal affinities with naturalism. For instance the assertion that its heroine, Clotilde, is "better" than the other girls of her milieu because her father was (almost certainly) an aristocrat is either an irritation or a parody of materialist genetics as simple snobbery; and the minute representation of vicious suburban feuding in the last sections of the book has an authentic feeling of naturalist claustrophobia. Against this, however, the novel is even more discursive than *Le Désespéré*, and its digressions—into racism, like that of Charles Maurras, medievalism, Richard Wagner, art, and Christianity (common to the Catholic novels of the period, notably those by Huysmans)—explicitly satisfied as giving purchase on the infinite: "Les bonnes gens qui n'aiment pas la *digression* ou qui regardent l'Infini comme un hors d'œuvre sont dévotement suppliées de ne pas lire ce chapitre" (The good folk who do not like *digressions* or who think of the Infinite as an hors d'oeuvre are piously requested not to read this chapter).

Between the digressions, however, an encounter occurs: Clotilde is forced by her degenerate father (a former Communard who has made some money, thus doubly damned) to pose for the painter Gacougnol, a fate worse than whoring, if not than death, for—in Bloy's, at this moment, intensely idealist epistemology, in which representation obliterates reality—models, unlike whores, displace the significance of holy images. The pious Gacougnol, however, allows Clotilde to keep her clothes on and installs her chastely in a pension. Bloy's two novels are interlinked episodically as she meets Marchenoir and, subsequently, Léopold, an illuminator and hermit whom she eventually marries. (The suggestion of the illuminator's superiority to the artist is strong at this point, as is that of the superior significance of the repeated decoration of universal and established truth to the puny possibilities of artistic innovation).

Their first child is already dead before the deaths of Gacougnol—killed by Clotilde's father—and Marchenoir. A second child, Lazare, is born to Clotilde and Léopold, who is going blind; and, as the reader anxiously awaits some bad news by way of contrast, the child conforms to his given name and dies unexpectedly. Clotilde and Léopold move to the suburbs, where they are persecuted by their rancorous neighbors, the Poulot family (this suburban conflict and the strategies employed to withstand it are undoubtedly the most intense, impressive part of the book). Eventually Mme Poulot, like Véronique and so many characters in French naturalist literature, is consigned to a padded cell in Sainte-Anne; Léopold dies saving spectators from a fire at the Opéra Comique; and Clotilde survives, divested of her few possessions, as a holy bag lady.

The temptation is especially strong in the case of this novel to reduce it to the status of a *sottisier* (collection of howlers) or, alternatively, to that of a roman à clef from which the lock has been removed. Of more significance and interest, however, is the way in which the text undermines its initial assumptions about the Divine Plan and man's place in it. At the outset these are voiced as what may be termed a form of ultrastructuralism, which recalls the all-encompassing, totalitarian philosophy of *Le Salut par les Juifs*. Here Chapuis, Clotilde's (step-) father, is at issue: "Sans Barabbas, point de Rédemption. Dieu n'aurait pas été *digne* de créer le monde, s'il avait oublié dans le néant l'immense Racaille qui devait un jour le crucifier" (Without Barabbas, no Redemption. God would not have been *worthy* to create the world, if he had left out in nothingness the enormous Scum who were, one day, to crucify him).

Yet against this, Bloy/Marchenoir, shortly before his death, unwittingly denounces the very basis of his moralistic and ultrastructuralist semiotic. Here there seems to be some awareness that, if everything is the signifier of God's system, then significance is fundamentally avoided: "Quand Jésus viendra, ceux d'entre nous qui 'veilleront' encore à la clarté d'une petite lampe, n'auront plus la force de se tourner vers sa Face, tellement ils seront attentifs à interroger les *Signes* qui ne peuvent pas donner la vie" (When Jesus comes, we who are still "waiting" by the light of a little lamp will no longer have the strength to turn toward his Countenance, being

Bloy, circa 1910

too preoccupied with interrogating those *Signs* that cannot give life).

In the absence of any resolution of this contradiction, the text is expended in expressions of more or less conventional political reaction. Clotilde mentally transforms 14 July into a religious festival, and Léopold's moral apotheosis is conveyed in terms that link anti-intellectualism and a dominance premonitory of clericofascism: "Il *croyait*, naturellement, spontanément, sans induction, comme tous les êtres faits pour commander" (He *believed*, naturally, spontaneously, without induction, like all those destined to command).

But that is not all: Clotilde's final exaltation seeks to transcend all categories of human thought and activity in a manner reminiscent of Juliana of Norwich ("All shall be well and all manner of things shall be well"): "Clotilde a aujourd'hui 48 ans, et ne paraît pas avoir moins d'un siècle.... Mais elle est plus belle qu'autrefois.... *Tout ce qui arrive est adorable*, dit-elle ordinairement" (Clotilde is 48, and looks at least 100.... But she is lovelier than ever.... *Everything that happens is adorable*, she is wont to say).

Credo quia impossible (I believe it because it is impossible). The maxim, emblematic of Bloy's discourse as a whole, seeks the absolute preemption of rational and critical endeavor, the immersion of the intellect in a totalized structure of contradiction and confusion. It has been subsequently seen, in the practices of fascism and its political allies, where such a path can lead.

Letters:

Lettres de jeunesse (1870-1893) (Paris: Edouard-Joseph, 1920);

Lettres à sa Fiancée (Paris: Stock, 1922); translated by Barbara Wall as *Letters to His Fiancée* (New York: Sheed & Ward, 1937);

Lettres à l'abbé Cornuau et au frère Dacien (Paris: Le Divan, 1926);

Lettres à Frédéric Brou et à Jean de la Laurencie (Paris: Bloud et Gay, 1927);

Lettres à Pierre Termier, suivies de Lettres à Jeanne Termier (Mme Jean Boussac) et à son mari (Paris: Stock, 1927);

Lettres à ses filleuls, Jacques Maritain et Pierre van der Meer de Walcheren (Paris: Stock, 1928);

Lettres à Georges Khnopff (Liège: Editions du Balancier, 1929);

Lettres à René Martineau (Paris: Editions de la Madeleine, 1933);

Drawing by Henry de Groux of Bloy on his deathbed (from Joseph Bollery, Léon Bloy, *volume 3, 1954)*

Lettres à Véronique (Paris: Desclée de Brouwer, 1933);

Lettres à Philippe Raoux (Paris: Desclée de Brouwer, 1937);

Correspondance Léon Bloy et Henri de Groux (Paris: Grasset, 1947);

Lettres intimes de Léon Bloy à sa femme et à ses filles (Paris: M. Astruc, 1952);

A son ami André Dupont. Lettres de Léon Bloy de 1904 à 1916 (Paris: M. Astruc, 1952);

Correspondance de Léon Bloy et Josef Florian (Lausanne: L'Age d'Homme, 1990).

Bibliographies:

Joseph Bollery and A.-L. Laquerrière, *Biblio-iconographie de Léon Bloy* (Paris: La Connaissance, 1935);

Giovanni Dotoli, *Situation des études bloyennes, suivie d'une bibliographie de 1950 à 1969* (Paris: Nizet, 1970).

Biographies:

Emile Baumann, *Mémoires* (Lyons: Nouvelle Edition, 1943);

Joseph Bollery, *Léon Bloy. Essai de biographie*, 3 volumes (Paris: Albin Michel, 1947-1954).

References:

Raymond Barbeau, "Le Secret de Léon Bloy, paraclétiste luciférienne," Ph.D. dissertation, University of Paris, 1955;

Jules-Amédée Barbey d'Aurevilly, *Lettres de Barbey d'Aurevilly à Léon Bloy* (Paris: Mercure de France, 1902);

Roland Barthes, "Bloy," in *Tableau de la littérature française de Madame de Staël à Rimbaud*, edited by Dominique Anry (Paris: Gallimard, 1974), pp. 412-416;

Albert Béguin, *Bloy. Mystique de la douleur* (Paris: Labergerie, 1948);

Béguin, *Léon Bloy, l'impatient* (Fribourg: Egloff, 1944); translated by Edith M. Riley as *Léon Bloy: A Study in Impatience* (London: Sheed & Ward, 1947);

André Billy, *Les Ecrivains de combat* (Paris: Œuvres Représentatives, 1932);

Joseph Bollery, *"Le Désespéré" de Léon Bloy. Histoire anecdotique, littéraire et bibliographique* (Paris: Malfère, 1937);

Bollery, *Genèse et composition de "La Femme pauvre"* (Paris: Lettres Modernes, 1969);

René-Louis Doyon, *Un Canulard mystique: Léon Bloy* (Paris: La Connaissance, 1939);

E. T. Dubois, *Portrait of Léon Bloy* (London & New York: Sheed & Ward, 1951);

Stanislas Fumet, *Mission de Léon Bloy* (Paris: Desclée de Brouwer, 1935);
Ruth E. Hager, *Léon Bloy et l'évolution du conte cruel: ses "Histoires désobligeantes"* (Paris: Klincksieck, 1967);
Rayner Heppenstall, *The Double Image: Mutations of Christian Mythology* (London: Secker & Warburg, 1947);
Heppenstall, *Léon Bloy* (Cambridge: Bowes & Bowes, 1953; New Haven: Yale University Press, 1954);
Hubot Juin, *Léon Bloy* (Paris: Editions du Vieux Colombier, 1957);
René Martineau, *Léon Bloy et "La Femme pauvre"* (Paris: Mercure de France, 1933);
Martineau, *Un Vivant et deux morts: Léon Bloy, Ernest Hello, Villiers de l'Isle-Adam* (Paris: Bibliothèque des Lettres Françaises, 1914);
Adolphe Retté, *Léon Bloy. Essai de critique équitable* (Paris: Bloud et Gay, 1923);
Bernard Sarrazin, *La Bible en éclats: L'imagination scriptuaire de Léon Bloy* (Paris: Desclée de Brouwer, 1977);
Ernest Seillière, *Léon Bloy. Psychologie d'un mystique* (Paris: Nouvelle Revue Critique, 1936);
Jacques Vier, *Léon Bloy ou le pont sur l'abîme* (Paris: Téqui, 1986).

Paul Bourget

(2 September 1852 - 25 December 1935)

Robert Lethbridge
Cambridge University

BOOKS: *La Vie inquiète* (Paris: Lemerre, 1875);
Edel (Paris: Lemerre, 1878);
Les Aveux (Paris: Lemerre, 1882);
Essais de psychologie contemporaine (Paris: Lemerre, 1883; revised and enlarged edition, Paris: Plon-Nourrit, 1901);
L'Irréparable. Deuxième amour. Profils perdus (Paris: Lemerre, 1884);
Cruelle énigme (Paris: Lemerre, 1885); translated by Julian Cray as *A Cruel Enigma* (London: Vizetelly, 1887);
Nouveaux essais de psychologie contemporaine (Paris: Lemerre, 1886);
Un Crime d'amour (Paris: Lemerre, 1886); translated as *A Love Crime* (London: Vizetelly, 1888);
Mensonges (Paris: Lemerre, 1887); translated as *Lies* (New York: Street & Smith, 1892); translation revised by G. F. Monkshood and Ernest Tristan as *Our Lady of Lies* (London: Greening, 1910);
André Cornélis (Paris: Lemerre, 1887); translated by Monkshood as *Andre Cornelis* (New York: Brentano, 1909);
Etudes et portraits, 2 volumes (Paris: Lemerre, 1889); includes *Sensations d'Oxford*, translated by M. C. Warrilow as *Some Impressions of Oxford* (London: Bell, 1901); French version revised, 3 volumes (Paris: Plon, 1906);
Le Disciple (Paris: Lemerre, 1889); translated as *The Disciple* (New York: Neely, 1898; London: Unwin, 1901);
Pastels. Dix portraits de femmes (Paris: Lemerre, 1889);
Un Cœur de femme (Paris: Lemerre, 1890); translated by Tristan as *A Woman's Heart* (New York: Brentano, 1890);
Physiologie de l'amour moderne (Paris: Lemerre, 1891);
Sensations d'Italie (Paris: Lemerre, 1891); translated by Mary Serrano as *Impressions of Italy* (New York: Cassell, 1892); translated by Lauretta Maitland as *The Glamour of Italy* (London: Matthews, 1923);
Nouveaux pastels. Dix portraits d'hommes (Paris: Lemerre, 1891); translated in part by Katharine Wormeley as *Pastels of Men*, first series (Boston: Robert Bros., 1891); second series

(Boston: Robert Bros., 1892); French version republished as *François Vernantes* (Paris: Plon-Nourrit, 1903);
La Terre promise (Paris: Lemerre, 1892);
Un Saint (New York: Huibland & Meyer, 1893; Paris: Lemerre, 1894);
Un Scrupule (New York: Amblard & Meyer / Paris: Lemerre, 1893);
Cosmopolis (Paris: Lemerre, 1893); translated by Cleveland Moffett (New York: Hurst, 1893);
Steeple-Chase. Maurice Ollivier (Paris: Lemerre, 1894);
Outre-mer. Notes sur l'Amérique, 2 volumes (Paris: Lemerre, 1895); translated as *Impressions of America* (New York: Scribner, 1895);
Une Idylle tragique, mœurs cosmopolites (Paris: Lemerre, 1896); translated as *A Tragic Idyll* (London: Dowmy / New York: Scribner, 1896);
Recommencements (Paris: Lemerre, 1897);
Voyageuses (Paris: Lemerre, 1897); translated by William Marchant as *Antigone; and Other Portraits of Women* (New York: Scribner, 1898);
Complications sentimentales (Paris: Lemerre, 1898);
La Duchesse bleue (Paris: Lemerre, 1898); translated by Tristan as *The Blue Duchess* (London: Greening, 1908; New York: Brentano, 1909);
Drames de famille (Paris: Plon-Nourrit, 1900);
Un Homme d'affaires (Paris: Plon-Nourrit, 1900);
Le Fantôme (Paris: Plon-Nourrit, 1901);
Monique (Paris: Plon, 1902);
L'Etape (Paris: Plon-Nourrit, 1902);
L'Eau profonde: Les pas dans les pas (Paris: Plon-Nourrit, 1903);
Un Divorce (Paris: Plon-Nourrit, 1904); translated as *A Divorce* (New York: Scribner, 1904);
Les Deux Sœurs; Le Cœur et le métier (Paris: Plon-Nourrit, 1905);
L'Emigré (Paris: Plon-Nourrit, 1907);
Les Détours du cœur (Paris: Plon-Nourrit, 1908);
La Dame qui a perdu son peintre (Paris: Plon-Nourrit, 1910);
L'Envers du décor (Paris: Plon-Nourrit, 1911);
Le Tribun. Chronique de 1911 (Paris: Plon-Nourrit, 1912);
Pages de critique et de doctrine, 2 volumes (Paris: Plon-Nourrit, 1912);
Le Démon de midi, 2 volumes (Paris: Plon-Nourrit, 1914);
Le Sens de la mort (Paris: Plon-Nourrit, 1915); translated by G. Frederic Lees as *The Night Cometh* (London: Chatto & Windus, 1916);
Lazarine (Paris: Plon-Nourrit, 1917);

Paul Bourget, circa 1889

Némésis (Paris: Plon-Nourrit, 1918);
Le Justicier (Paris: Plon-Nourrit, 1919);
Laurence Albani (Paris: Plon-Nourrit, 1919);
Anomalies (Paris: Plon-Nourrit, 1920);
Un Drame dans le monde (Paris: Plon-Nourrit, 1921);
Le Testament (Paris: Editions de la Guirlande, 1921);
L'Ecuyère (Paris: Plon-Nourrit, 1921);
Nouvelles pages de critique et de doctrine, 2 volumes (Paris: Plon-Nourrit, 1922);
La Geôle (Paris: Plon-Nourrit, 1923); translated by F. Mabel Robinson as *The Gaol* (London: Unwin, 1924);
Hélène (Saint-Félicien-en-Vivarais: Editions du Pigeonnier, 1923);
Le Roman des quatre, by Bourget, Mme Gérard d'Houville, Pierre Benoît, and Henri Duvernois (Paris: Plon-Nourrit, 1923);
La Leçon de Barrès (Paris: A la Cité des Livres, 1924);
De profundis clamavi (Lyons: Cercle Lyonnais du Livre, 1924);

Cœur pensif ne sait où il va (Paris: Plon-Nourrit, 1924);
Aux maisons de Barbey d'Aurevilly et de Balzac (Abbeville: Paillart, 1924);
Conflits intimes (Paris: Plon-Nourrit, 1925);
Le Danseur mondain (Paris: Plon-Nourrit, 1926);
Micheline et l'amour, by Bourget, Mme d'Houville, Benoît, and Duvernois (Paris: Plon-Nourrit, 1926);
Nos actes nous suivent (Paris: Plon-Nourrit, 1927);
Quelques témoignages (Paris: Plon, 1928);
Deux nouvelles: Le Scrupule de l'apostat; Confidences (Paris: Editions des Portiques, 1928);
Le Tapin (Paris: Plon, 1928);
Au service de l'ordre (Paris: Plon, 1929);
Sur la Toscane (Paris: Editions des Horizons de France, 1929);
On ne voit pas les cœurs (Paris: Plon, 1929).
Collection: *Œuvres complètes*, 9 volumes (Paris: Plon-Nourrit, 1899-1911)—unfinished project comprising major works up to 1904, substantially revised by Bourget.

PLAY PRODUCTIONS: *Mensonges*, by Bourget and Léopold Lacour, Paris, Théâtre du Vaudeville, 18 April 1889;
Un Divorce, by Bourget and André Cury, Paris, Théâtre du Vaudeville, 28 January 1908;
L'Emigré, Paris, Théâtre de la Renaissance, 9 October 1908;
La Barricade. Chronique de 1910, Paris, Théâtre du Vaudeville, 7 January 1910;
Le Tribun. Chronique de 1911, Paris, Théâtre du Vaudeville, 15 May 1911;
La Crise, by Bourget and André Beaunier, Paris, Théâtre de la Porte-Saint-Martin, 3 May 1912.

OTHER: Paul Scarron, *Le Roman comique*, preface by Bourget (Paris: Jouaust, 1880);
Jules-Amédée Barbey d'Aurevilly, *Mémoranda*, preface by Bourget (Paris: Rouveyre & Blond, 1883);
Léon Cladel, *Le Deuxième Mystère de l'Incarnation*, preface by Bourget (Paris: Rouveyre & Blond, 1883);
Stendhal, *Le Rouge et le noir*, preface by Bourget (Paris: Lemerre, 1886);
Frédéric Loliée, *Nos gens de lettres, leur vie intérieure, leurs rivalités, leur condition*, preface by Bourget (Paris: Calmann-Lévy, 1887);
A. Cerfberr and J. Christophe, *Répertoire de "La Comédie humaine,"* introduction by Bourget (Paris: Calmann-Lévy, 1887);
Benjamin Constant, *Adolphe*, preface by Bourget (Paris: Conquet, 1888);
Violet Paget, *Vernon Lee. Miss Brown*, translated by Robert de Cérisy, preface by Bourget (Paris: Calmann-Lévy, 1888);
René Maizeroy, *La Grande Bleue*, preface by Bourget (Paris: Plon, 1888);
Frédéric Bataille, *Poèmes du soir*, "sonnet-préface" by Bourget (Paris: Lemerre, 1889);
Albert Bataille, *Causes criminelles et mondaines de 1888*, preface by Bourget (Paris, 1889);
Paul Schafer, *Poésies intimes*, preface by Bourget (Paris: Lemerre, 1892);
François Bournand, *Nos sœurs de charité*, preface by Bourget (Tours, 1894);
Hugues Le Roux, *Gladys*, preface by Bourget (Paris: Calmann-Lévy, 1894);
"Lettre autobiographique," introduction to *Extraits choisis de Paul Bourget* (Boston: Ginn, 1894);
Jean de Forceville, *A côté*, preface by Bourget (Paris: Ollendorff, 1900);
Pierre Gérard, *L'Accalmie*, preface by Bourget (Paris: Editions du Livre de l'Auteur, 1902);
Georges Grappe, *J. H. Newman. Essai de psychologie religieuse*, preface by Bourget (Paris: Librairie des Saints-Pères, 1902);
Eugène Gilbert, *France et Belgique. Etudes littéraires*, preface by Bourget (Paris: Plon, 1905);
Contes choisis de Balzac, preface by Bourget (London: Dent, 1905);
R. P. Georges de Pascal, *Lettres sur l'histoire de France*, preface by Bourget (Paris: Nouvelle Librairie Nationale, 1908);
Jules Bois, *L'Humanité divine*, "sonnet-préface" by Bourget (Paris: Fasquelle, 1910);
Visions d'Autriche, section by Bourget (Paris: Grasset, 1911);
Eugène Melchior de Vogüé, *Pages choisies*, preface by Bourget (Paris: Plon, 1912);
Joseph Ferchat, *Le Roman de la famille française. Essai sur l'œuvre de M. Henry Bordeaux*, preface by Bourget (Paris: Plon, 1912);
Noël Bangor, *Les Deux Ivresses*, preface by Bourget (Paris: Perrin, 1913);
Paul Voivenel and Paul Martin, *La Guerre des gaz*, preface by Bourget (Paris: La Renaissance du Livre, 1919);
Gérard Bauër, *Sous les mers*, preface by Bourget (Paris: Edition Française, 1919);
Michel Salomon, *Portraits et paysages*, preface by Bourget (Paris: Perrin, 1920);

Bourget in 1877 (portrait by L. Tanzi; from Albert Feuillerat, Paul Bourget: Histoire d'un esprit sous la Troisième République, *1937)*

J. L. Faure, *L'Ame du chirurgien,* preface by Bourget (Paris: Crès, 1920);

Hector Reynaud, *Ames françaises,* preface by Bourget (Paris: Picard, 1922);

Paule Henry-Bordeaux, *Sur la route de Palmyre,* preface by Bourget (Paris: Plon, 1923);

Félicien Pascal, *Le Masque déchiré,* preface by Bourget (Paris: Flammarion, 1924);

Gaston Jollivet, *Souvenirs de la vie de plaisir sous le Second Empire,* "lettre-préface" by Bourget (Paris: Tallendier, 1927);

Rétif de la Bretonne, *La Vie de mon père,* preface by Bourget (Paris: Tallendier, 1929);

E. Sainte-Marie Perrin, *Images,* preface by Bourget (Paris: Plon, 1929).

Paul Bourget once enjoyed a reputation as the most brilliant French writer of his generation. He was not only prolific but also, in terms of official recognition, uniquely precocious. When he entered the Académie Française in 1895, he was the youngest novelist ever elected. By contrast, his present critical status excludes him even from the ranks of the second best. Not a single one of his hundred or so books remains in print; they lie unread on library shelves, barely dusted by attempts at scholarly rehabilitation undertaken since World War I. Even allowing for the fact that this has been the not-uncommon fate of Parisian intellectuals wrongly positioned in the Dreyfus Affair, Bourget's fall from grace has been indecently spectacular.

Charles-Joseph-Paul Bourget was born in Amiens on 2 September 1852, the son of Anne-Adèle Valentin and Justin Bourget. It was a heredity he would later invoke to account for unresolved contradictions informing his entire work. His mother's Lorraine origins were cited as being responsible for a poetic and philosophical outlook of Germanic persuasion superimposed on a French analytical tradition, while his father's career as a professor of mathematics explained the son's lifelong predilection for cerebral abstraction. Such a psychological self-portrait, provided by Bourget in his "Lettre autobiographique" (1894), has to be treated with caution, not least because access to his inner life has been restricted to perspectives fashioned by the writer himself. His private correspondence and diaries are locked away in family archives.

Frustrated biographers can thus only tendentiously confirm Bourget's problematic identity in the oblique mirrors of his fiction, notably in the figure of Robert Greslou in *Le Disciple* (1889; translated as *The Disciple,* 1898), who attributes his own split personality to an admixture of French and German ancestry. What has made this recuperative temptation virtually irresistible are the underlying assumptions of Bourget's critical and novelistic practice. For both contemporaries and invented characters are viewed through a highly deterministic grid; and that focus is shaped by the premise of what he termed "une dualité dans le moi" (a duality of the self).

It does not seem unduly speculative, however, to locate in his mother's death (1857) the source of a melancholy and an emotional insecurity inscribed in the title of *La Vie inquiète* (A Life of Anxiety, 1875). This collection of early poems is cast in a mode of regret; it speaks of the shadows in which a boy deprived of his mother at the age of five had lived his youth; and it prefigures the many tales of aching hearts that Bourget would make the privileged territory of his mature reflections. His father, at least, did not overextend the grieving process. He remarried only a year later and, whatever less tangible consequences there may have been, thereby fortuitously brought Bourget into contact with a decisive intellectual influence.

If his father's scientific vocation (consecrated by a chair at the Faculty of Science at Clermont-Ferrand in 1854) had encouraged filial ambitions as encyclopedic as an inventory of all the local insects, Bourget's new grandfather, Joseph-Alexandre Nicard, was a teacher of an altogether different cultural dimension. He introduced Bourget to the world of books, which, it has been argued, the latter never left. His literary apprenticeship was astonishing in its range, from the French classics to the Romantic poetry of Victor Hugo and Alfred de Musset. Bourget had learned to read at age three; two years later he was beginning to assimilate Shakespeare in translation; Greek and Latin were his grandfather's special field. It is significant that Bourget recalled the city of his childhood in an essay on Blaise Pascal (1923). For although the landscape of the Massif Central may have left its mark on the background to the botanical walks taken by the hero of *Le Disciple*, Bourget's years in Clermont-Ferrand were spent at a radical distance from open-air life. That is not to suggest he loved the classroom; in his *Sensations d'Oxford* (1889; translated as *Some Impressions of Oxford*, 1901), he took the opportunity to compare gilded English conditions with his own loathsome school days. But Bourget's bookish, introspective temper certainly is inseparable from an experience abnormally literary in conception and design.

This direction was reinforced in 1867, when his father was appointed dean of the Ecole préparatoire du Collège Sainte-Barbe in Paris. At one of the great Parisian schools, the lycée Louis-le-Grand, Bourget's dazzling achievements included being placed second in Latin in the Concours général of 1870. He also used the time to extend his reading to most of the literature of the period, although it was apparently his working through Honoré de Balzac's *Comédie humaine* (1842-1855; translated, 1895-1900) from beginning to end that fired his own literary ambitions. It would have been easier, after being placed top of the class list in his philosophy degree examinations in 1872, for Bourget to have pursued an academic career. Instead, and against the wishes of his father, he set himself up in the Latin Quarter as an aspiring writer.

Evidence of his initial penury and disappointments can be found in his narrative poem *Edel* (1878). During this apprenticeship Bourget regularly experimented with the short-story form. His work as a critic, however, was more properly formative. His first article, written under the pseudonym Pierre Pohl, was devoted to Benedict de Spinoza; as significant is the fact that it was published in the highbrow journal *Renaissance* (28 December 1872).

The next decade saw his byline in the most elitist reviews of the period, and his presence in the most prestigious salons associated with them. As drama critic, first for the *Globe* and then more permanently (from 1880 onward) for *Parlement*, Bourget was able to develop literary views by no means constrained by theatrical productions of the moment. Such a position also gave him the increased financial security to translate a latent fascination with distinction into a physical reality. His move to the Faubourg Saint-Germain in 1882 is not of purely incidental interest. It represented a literal movement to the heart of the high society that would provide the settings for his mature fiction as well as color Bourget's political stance for the rest of his life.

Nor is it possible to account for the pervasive authorial point of view that informs Bourget's novels without reference to his critical writing. He first came to public notice as a result of the penetrating analyses of the modern sensibility that he published in the *Nouvelle Revue* from November 1881 onward, which were collected in *Essais de psychologie contemporaine* (Essays in Contemporary Psychology, 1883) and in the complementary *Nouveaux essais de psychologie contemporaine* (New Essays in Contemporary Psychology, 1886). These deal with Charles Baudelaire, Ernest Renan, Gustave Flaubert, Hippolyte Taine, and Stendhal (volume one), and Alexandre Dumas *fils*, Charles-Marie-René Leconte de Lisle, Edmond and Jules de Goncourt, Ivan Turgenev, and Henri-Frédéric Amiel (volume two). But Bourget's articulated reflections and affinities insistently widen the perspectives afforded by these symptomatic case studies.

The range and the far-flung resonance of his essays can perhaps be gauged by the fact that, in 1885, the painter Berthe Morisot was copying out several passages of his chapter on the Goncourts that commented on the fragmentary nature of all visual experience; and this has since been directly related to her pictorial technique. The central thrust of Bourget's analysis remains that the Goncourts exemplified the self-conscious cultivation of the neurasthenia that formed the basis of the century's philosophical pessimism

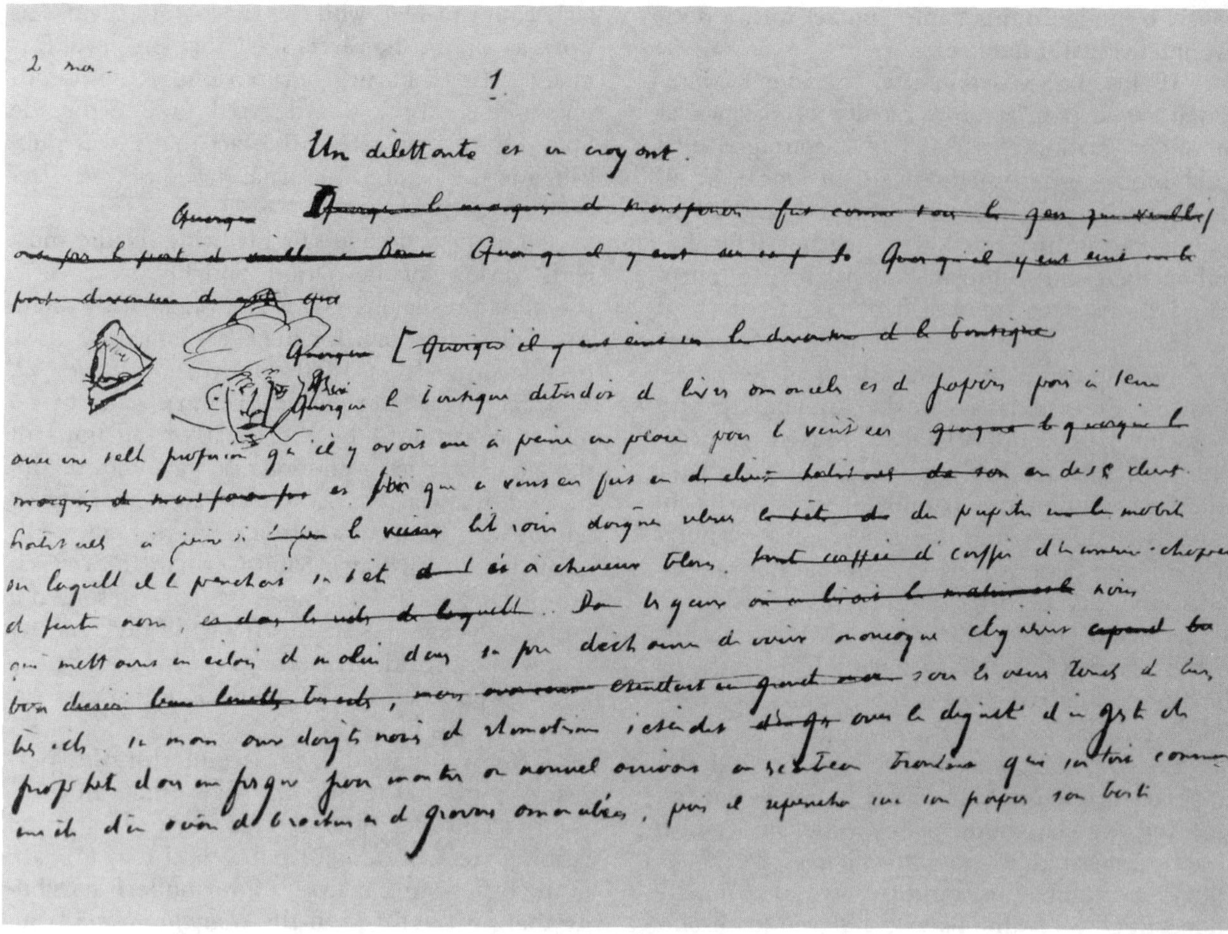
1

Un dilettante et un croyant.

Manuscript for the beginning of chapter 1 of Cosmopolis *(from Albert Feuillerat,* Paul Bourget: Histoire d'un esprit sous la Troisième République, *1937)*

and affective particularities. All the essays explore, in an unprecedented way, the specific links between the creative intelligence and emotional determinants. Bourget returned to these complicated equations from many subsequent critical platforms, whether in *Etudes et portraits* (Studies and Portraits, 1889) or in the prefaces he willingly supplied for the work of his admirers.

The success of the *Essais*, however, fed the long-held desire to reach a wider audience. In turning to the novel and applying to his fictional characters hypotheses similarly derived from advances in psychology, Bourget was immediately recognized as one of the most sophisticated exponents of the theory of the multiple personality. It is not in his writing alone, of course, that one can trace the progressive refinement of the idea that the self is not a fixed entity but rather the sum of the integrative processes of the mind's conscious and unconscious workings. Bourget's *Cruelle énigme* (1885; translated as *A Cruel Enigma*, 1887) and *Un Crime d'amour* (1886; translated as *A Love Crime*, 1888) nevertheless mark a date perceived as the moment when the complexity of individual psychology makes its appearance in the French novel. These works encouraged the critics of the day to define the psychological novel as a genre in its own right, and one moreover in the mainstream of a French tradition stretching from Marie-Madeleine Comtesse de La Fayette to Stendhal.

Bourget first made explicit the notion of the "duality of the self" in a letter to Taine about *L'Irréparable* (The Irremediable, 1884), a volume comprising two *nouvelles* and six short sketches under the heading of *Profils perdus* (Lost Profiles). *L'Irréparable* is a good example of the uneasy synthesis of Bourget's theoretical and fictional preoccupations. The narrative voice is transparently angled through an imaginary philosopher engaged in research into the subconscious realm at odds with overt behavior. To support his claims, he recounts the dismal fate of Noémie Hurtrel, a Jewish banker's daughter violated by a Don Juan figure whose advances she had unwittingly encouraged by playing the role of a cynical woman of the world. Although, during her convalescence in Cannes, she is offered a match consistent with her true and noble nature, Noémie is unable to repair the damage to her identity and commits a heavily symbolic suicide.

Cruelle énigme expands an analogous thesis in a less explicative form. The relationship between an innocent Hubert Liauran and his experienced mistress, Thérèse de Sauve, is plotted so as to provide a double focus on multiplicity. Thérèse's genuine love for Hubert is vitiated by the depraved sexuality that motivates her infidelity. But while her affair with a count leads her young lover to renounce his adoration, Hubert's idealism itself fails to survive the carnality to which his disillusion had driven him. The final reconciliation between the two is less a happy ending than a restatement of the enigmas of love and life amenable only to diagnosis. Where *Un Crime d'amour* differs, precisely, is in the remedial solutions now shadowing such moral dissolution. Hélène Chazel is seduced by Armand de Querne and emerges from her adultery on the slippery slope of promiscuous self-abasement. The novel ends with much remorse. The heroine forgives Armand's duplicity if not her own transgressions, while it is implied that he may find salvation in a return to his religious faith.

These texts establish the coordinates of much of Bourget's fiction. To detail each and every one of his investigations into female psychology would be to risk caricaturing repeated variations on the themes of Gustave Flaubert's *Madame Bovary* (1857; translated, 1881) forcibly updated by a quasi-clinical terminology. Indeed, Bourget was not indifferent to charges that his exploitation of technical vocabulary sometimes went too far. *Mensonges* (1887; most suggestively translated as *Our Lady of Lies*, 1910) seems deliberately restrained in this respect, however familiar the doubly adulterous destiny of its character Suzanne Moraines may appear. Bourget's undeniable success is surprising only if it is situated outside the context of a reading public weary of the materialist register of Emile Zola's naturalism. Nor is it by chance that his popularity was most evident in social circles whose members enjoyed sufficient leisure to indulge in introspection of the kind to which Bourget catered and that he also reflected. But that is not to adumbrate, as his instant detractors might, a readership of a facile disposition.

Those powerfully attracted to Bourget's novels included some of the most cultured and intelligent minds of the fin de siècle. One of them was Marcel Proust. One can relegate to the level of anecdote the curious irony whereby the elder writer introduced him to the model (Laure Hayman) for the future Odette de Crécy. Hayman then sent Proust, in October 1888, a copy of Bourget's story *Gladys Harvey* (which also transposes her personality) bound in flower-embroidered silk from one of her petticoats. Much more telling is that Proust's *Jean Santeuil* (1952; translated, 1955) is stylistically indebted to Bourget, and that, as one of Proust's boyhood masters, he contributed to the Bergotte of *A la recherche du temps perdu* (1913-1927; translated as *Remembrance of Things Past*, 1922-1932) rather more than an anagrammatic resemblance.

Gladys Harvey was subsequently reprinted as one of the ten sketches of women in *Pastels* (1889), a work notable for its lightness of touch. The same could not be said of the professorial *Physiologie de l'amour moderne* (Physiology of Modern Love, 1891), serialized between 1888 and 1891. Both books, however, added to Bourget's reputation as the supreme analyst of what he called, in the title of his 1890 novel, *Un Cœur de femme* (translated as *A Woman's Heart*, 1890).

It is not difficult to point to Bourget's major weaknesses as a novelist: an inability to leave unsaid the inner contradictions of his characters; psychological mechanisms demonstrated rather than observed; and authorial abstraction anticipating as well as concluding episodes unnecessarily framed by a theorist at work. It would nevertheless be a mistake to leave out of any final assessment the emotional vicissitudes he so patiently elaborates. While the increasingly didactic strain of his work gradually substitutes condemnation for understanding, Bourget's heroines are treated with a sympathy generated from within, neither patronizing nor patriarchal. His intuitions would be rehearsed throughout his career in countless descriptions of suffering, both inflicted and self-imposed, of erotic awakening, of opportunities missed, and of love's labors lost. Even as an expression of contemporary attitudes, they are more interesting than most of the nineteenth century's mysogynist record.

It remains a biographical mystery whether his insights had a source other than optical acuity. There is a notorious fictional portrait of Bourget in Guy de Maupassant's *Notre cœur* (1890; translated as *The Human Heart,* 1890), in which Lamarthe fails to seduce Mme de Burne notwithstanding his claim "connaître et analyser les femmes avec une pénétration infaillible et unique" (to know and analyze women with a singular and infallible penetration), an arrogance all the more cruelly debunked by this play on words. Bourget's elliptical scenes of sexual surrender certainly go beyond the purely derivative, and it does not seem coincidental that a mildly titillating voluptuousness is virtually eliminated from his fiction after his marriage to Minnie David on 21 August 1890.

The relative prominence of these concerns is underlined by the fact that only two of Bourget's novels in the 1880s are not organized as psychological studies of women. *André Cornélis* (1887; translated, 1909) is deliberately conceived as a modern *Hamlet* (circa 1601) and explores the eponymous hero's reaction to the discovery that Jacques Termonde had arranged his father's murder in order to marry the boy's adored mother. Bourget's transposition of some of Shakespeare's key scenes is of less significance than his remarkable assimilation of the psychosexual drama of *Hamlet.* From André's identification with his father's marital tribulations to his traumatic displacement within a structure of affective substitutions, the text foregrounds a scenario Oedipal in outline if not yet in name.

The novel traces at length André's suspicions and self-doubt, moving from a terrifying certainty of his mother's adultery to a recognition of the potentially monstrous implications of his imaginative constructions. Termonde's ultimate demise can be equated with the triumphant resolution of André's quest, sustained as it is by the heroic perseverance of the analytical intelligence. And it is in this self-conscious light that *André Cornélis* assumes its real importance. For, in his protagonist's "projet" to "fixer sur ces feuilles cette image de ma destinée que je ne regarde qu'avec trouble dans le miroir incertain de ma pensée" (project to imprint on these pages an image of myself that I can contemplate only with difficulty in the uncertain mirror of my mind), Bourget brings to his examination of an inner stage an implicit view of Hamlet as surrogate artist that is characteristic of symbolist interpretations.

Le Disciple develops such mirror images in a more patently allusive manner. At first sight Bourget's most famous novel is simply melodramatic. The "disciple" in question, Robert Greslou, is so subject to the intellectual influence of the dehumanized philosopher Adrien Sixte that he carries out an experiment on the feelings of a nobleman's daughter in whose household he is employed as a tutor. After seducing Charlotte, he unilaterally withdraws from their suicide pact and after she kills herself is accused of her apparent murder. While waiting for his trial he recounts to his mentor most of what constitutes the text of *Le Disciple.* Subsequently acquitted with Sixte's help, he is finally killed by Charlotte's vengeful brother.

Bourget in 1893, during an American tour

Yet this plot, even in its violent turns and sexual intrigue, is essentially allegorical, accommodating a far-reaching inquiry into the associated themes of freedom and responsibility. The novel's impact could be predicted as soon as it began to appear in installments in the *Nouvelle Revue* in September 1888. Its publication in volume form in June 1889 has been so widely acknowledged, both then and since, as a watershed in French cultural life that the reasons for its status are still debated by intellectual historians.

On a personal level it represented for Bourget a liquidation of some crucial allegiances. Of its autobiographical references, none could be identified more precisely than the Tainean silhouette of the corrupting Sixte. Taine himself was unsurprisingly wounded by this attack. Bourget had been one of his most fervent admirers ever since following his courses on Venetian art at the Ecole des Beaux-Arts in 1871. Taine had welcomed the struggling writer into his glittering salon on the boulevard Saint-Germain, where Bourget had made the acquaintance of Renan and Turgenev. Taine had taken an active interest in his work. And, in dedicating several of his books to him, Bourget had made a public gesture beyond an expression of gratitude for their personal friendship.

For Taine was also the mentor to an age. Among its dominant figures, Zola was by no means eccentric in having declared himself to be Taine's "humble disciple." Bourget's grandfather was yet another; he had been a colleague of both Emile Littré and the publisher Louis Hachette, two of the men largely responsible for disseminating a Tainean positivism founded on the premise that scientifically verifiable observation was the only legitimate instrumentation for understanding reality. Whether *Le Disciple* repudiates such an epistemology quite so uncompromisingly as it seemed at the time is now open to doubt. It can be argued that Bourget was not rejecting science as such, but rather a scientific ideology that had, in his view, subsumed metaphysics at the expense of the human spirit. But, in any case, contemporaries were right in discerning in the novel the fatal collapse of the positivist hegemony that had not been seriously probed for more than half a century.

Le Disciple speaks of a double analysis overlaid by authorial moralizing: Sixte is found guilty by Bourget, who judges himself through Greslou's confession. Charlotte's seduction and death, however, point to wider concerns than the nefarious consequences of sterile intellectualism. The sociological and the spiritual intersect in the destruction of aristocratic values at the hands of Greslou's morally alienated plebeian origins. And in this class-oriented mirror, what is held up for inspection is not an individual but a collective destiny; it is obviously less Bourget's development that is at stake than that of France. At the same time, nevertheless, he becomes its best-known spokesman, adopting the role of the bourgeoisie's moral conscience in his castigation of a secular ethic and loosened family ties.

If *Le Disciple* represents, in very many ways, the end of a chapter, there has been placed under it a more pejorative terminal line; it may grudgingly mark Bourget as a literary giant at the age of thirty-seven. But he is also seen as one whose potential for further intellectual growth was stunted by the hardening of his conservative beliefs and the institutional honors bestowed upon him. Bourget's career after 1889 is deemed unworthy of scholarly attention. There has never been a comprehensive study of the rest of his life and work, let alone any attempt to confront the massive editorial problems left behind by an author so given to republishing his texts after revising them.

Armand E. Singer would have one believe that Bourget entered his profession with his "ideological bags tightly packed." In fact he once espoused the kind of democratic ideals advocated by Hugo. He was on the staff of *Parlement*, which was left of the political center; he had lost his religious faith around 1867. Bourget's ultimate alignment with Catholic orthodoxy and the restoration of the monarchy thus was not achieved without considerable soul-searching and prevarication. Much of his writing in the decade after *Le Disciple* reflects a personal quest as much as a dogmatic point of departure.

Such existential searching finds its most literal expression in his prodigious travels. As soon as he became an independent adult, he went to Italy and Greece (1874); he made the first of many visits to England in 1880; and he went to Italy again, for an extended honeymoon, in 1890. No portrait of Bourget is complete without the radiant sensitivity of *Sensations d'Italie* (1891; translated as *Impressions of Italy*, 1892). His novel *La Terre promise* (The Promised Land, 1892) was finished in Rome and set in Palermo. In 1893 Bourget and his wife spent four months in the Holy Land, hoping in vain that such an immersion would overcome his theological uncertainties.

The more revealing consequence of all these contacts with foreign landscapes and cultural specificities can be found in *Cosmopolis* (1893; translated, 1893). At the center of an extraordinarily complex racial network, Catherine Steno (Venetian) catalyzes a drama of jealousy between her two lovers, Boleslas Gorka (Polish) and Lincoln Maitland (American). But this merely serves as a pretext for Bourget to assemble a cast of friends and relations almost perversely international in scope. Their petty rivalries and internecine strife are observed by the novelist Julien Dorsenne. Catherine's daughter becomes the tragic victim of his "impuissance d'aimer" (emotional impotence), and he will look to Catholicism as the only possible salvation. In this self-focusing negation of the life of the mind, few readers have ever hesitated to associate Dorsenne with the hero of *Le Disciple*; nor have they failed to point out how the novel prefigures Bourget's own formal return to the church in 1901. Where *Cosmopolis* reaches out beyond the writer's private doubts is in its analysis of a social decomposition paradoxically narrower, though politically far more contentious, than trans-European turpitude.

What holds *Cosmopolis* together is less its ingeniously linked subplots than a moral vision. Its characters are all as rootless as those in Maurice Barrès's *Les Déracinés* (The Uprooted, 1897), so cut off from their cultural origins and national values that they have forfeited their moral identity. With the wisdom of hindsight, the implications of this for the French nation-state can be traced right back through Bourget's writing, just as his travels abroad can be seen to be seldom unrelated to preoccupations closer to home. Exemplary in this respect are the eight months he spent in North America between August 1893 and April 1894, almost certainly the most extended visit made by any French author of the period. From eastern Canada to the Deep South, Bourget admired what he saw as the energy of a democratic New World.

His observations appeared in the *New York Herald*, owned by James Gordon Bennett, who had planned the trip, as well as in *Outre-mer* (1895; translated as *Impressions of America*, 1895). Ironically, they served only to reinforce his conviction that France's democratic revolutions were doomed to failure by virtue of being imposed on an ancient civilization. That conviction had been born in the aftermath of the Commune (1871), when Bourget had returned to Paris to witness a horrifying physical savagery incompatible with his lofty conception of human endeavor. It was inevitable that, in the Dreyfus Affair, Bourget should side with the forces defending traditional structures. From 1900 onward he was more closely involved with royalist politics, viewed as the last hope of a society characterized by its eroding class boundaries and disordered hierarchies.

In the preface to *La Terre promise*, Bourget spells out literature's corrective mission while perhaps being not unaware that he would be increasingly preaching only to the converted. Even the title of *L'Etape* (The Stage, 1902) warns against too rapid a social mobility. The moral exemplar is Jean Monneron, who manages to phase his advance, both through his love for the pious daughter of his philosophy teacher and by keeping in touch with the religion his father has rejected. The latter not only is an agnostic, but also has risen from peasantry to professoriat at a speed the folly of which is confirmed by an empty marriage and three dissolute children. *Un Divorce* (1904; translated as *A Divorce*, 1904) was Bourget's contribution to a topical debate, in the shape of imagined catastrophes lying in wait for those who, however justifiably, transgress the "loi naturelle" (natural law) of an indissoluble first marriage. *L'Emigré* (The Emigrant, 1907) is the third part of this trilogy devoted to the family's binding function, but here invoking an aristocratic model to set against the adulterating ravages of democratic practice. He adapted the last two of these novels for the stage in 1908.

World War I was hardly likely to induce a change of heart in a writer who had so consistently lamented the conflicting disasters of his time. Fortuitously, it also provides for his severest critics a completed pattern of absences from direct involvement in any of the major events he lived through: he had been sent away from Paris in 1870; he had gone to Italy during the most significant episodes of the Dreyfus Affair; now he was too old to fight. There is nevertheless something poignant, and certainly not cowardly, in the fact that, instead, this respected academician (well into his sixties) served in a military hospital, especially when it is remembered that, more than forty years earlier, he had abandoned the idea of training as a doctor because he was too high-strung to endure the physiological realities of suffering.

Le Sens de la mort (1915; translated as *The Night Cometh*, 1916) owes at least its setting to that brief experience. When Bourget returned to his writing, his nationalist sympathies could be synthesized with a vibrant patriotism. Only after the war could his marginalization be fully measured. He continued to publish both fiction and critical essays; their unswerving message remained out of step. His wife died in 1932. Bourget himself survived until 1935, dying on Christmas morning—not inappropriately perhaps, and at least spared

Bourget near the end of his life

the nightmare of Léon Blum's socialist government.

Since his death he has been almost as completely ignored as he was during his last years. He had wanted to be the Henry James of France. In a foreword to *Cruelle énigme*, he expressed the hope that James would find in that novel a reflection of their discussions in London the year before (1884), when they had agreed that all the laws of aesthetics were subordinate to the priority that fiction could best articulate: to render "une impression personnelle de la Vie" (a personal impression of Life). *L'Emigré* also was dedicated to James by "son admirateur et son ami" (his admirer and friend). Indeed, even allowing for the fact that few French writers have felt so intimate an affinity with the values of the English-speaking world, Bourget's admiration for James was unbounded.

This was not entirely reciprocated. James was sincere when he spoke privately of "remarkable qualities," but he also encouraged Bourget to curb his fondness for ratiocination. In a letter about *La Duchesse bleue* (1898; translated as *The Blue Duchess*, 1908), he wrote: "Your love of intellectual daylight, absolutely your pursuit of complexities, is an injury to the patches of ambiguity and the abysses of shadow which really are the clothing—or much of it—of the *effects* that constitute the material of our trade." And he was frankly appalled by what he saw as the erotic suggestiveness of the early novels.

That particular reaction is double-edged. It has the merit of balancing posterity's image of Bourget, established in the 1920s, as a rather dry and stuffy old man of letters. James recalled him as one of the most engaging conversationalists he had ever known. Other companions bear witness to an intelligence both witty and razor sharp. Alongside a complicated and withdrawn personality, there is also the Bourget of 1893: sitting on a yacht plying between Newport, Rhode Island (where he had been received by Edith Wharton), and Boston. Fizzing with new ideas from 1870 to 1890, he was also honest enough to recognize, in due course, his own anachronistic status.

His stilted prose now seems as dated as the salons he frequented and entranced. He was never able to overcome the paradox of being both a systematic thinker and a fashionable writer. In an 1881 letter Taine rightly pointed to Bourget's potential limitations as a novelist: "Vous êtes philosophe autant qu'artiste" (You are a philosopher as much as you are an artist). It can be suggested that the short-story form was his strongest fictional suit, simply because its constraints bore down on his tendency, as James put it, "to swim in the thick reflective element." On the other hand, his novels do have a power that his analytical rhetoric largely obscures. If one cuts through ideologically regressive conclusions and didactic plots, one can better appreciate how the destinies of his characters (some of them finely drawn) work themselves out with a compelling logic and a tragic force. At a quite different level, his doubling procedures, too obviously exploited to highlight social and moral oppositions, may enact an authorial drama as self-consciously as celebrated critical portraits of his contemporaries refract Bourget's own identity.

His historical importance is not in doubt. Before 1890 his name figured in many passionate debates. In 1876 he was subscribing to the decadent movement's strident call for "un renouveau poétique" (a poetic renewal). In the speculations of the 1880s about the future of the French novel, proliferated by theorists and practitioners alike, Bourget was repeatedly cited as the most prominent representative of an aesthetic antithetical to naturalism. Maupassant is only the best known of those who switched camps as a result of his influence.

Bourget's originality went further than moving the novel away from material conditions. He was the first French writer to include explicitly Freudian theories in his fiction. The great psychiatrist Dr. Ernest Dupré, whom he had known since 1905, was invited to check the vulgarized terminology in "Ma Maison de Saint-Cloud" (one of the stories in *Anomalies* [1920]), in which he also appears as Dr. Courriolles. In *Némésis* (1918), the "*trauma* affectif" to which the heroine succumbs after her husband's death is framed by a reference to "le Viennois Freud" well before the latter's *Introduction to Psychoanalysis* (1917) had become available in translation.

Nor does such a characteristic emphasis on an inner dynamic mean that the social contexts described by Bourget are redundant. With his multifarious interests and achievements, he was connected with the entire social and intellectual fabric of the period between the Second Empire and World War I. He was, and is, accused of restricting his own latter-day "Comédie humaine" to a stage occupied exclusively by an effete and parasitic class. The idle rich at play are indeed lined up to watch a Mediterranean regatta in *Une Idylle tragique* (1896; translated as *A Tragic Idyll*, 1896), or flit thoughtlessly through cosmopolitan liaisons. His novels are also peopled by bankers, statesmen, and thinkers, equally modeled on those he knew. And one can reconstruct, through both his fiction and his criticism, the preoccupations and the atmosphere of the Third Republic, rendered by Bourget with more sensitivity than most of his rivals.

It is very much to the point that Bourget's long career spans two centuries. In questioning the parameters of nineteenth-century realism, he creates a gap to be filled. Proust too would be concerned with integrating psychology and art, but he found a form in which to accommodate the imperatives of a rigorous analytical intelligence as well as an activating poetic design. Bourget, by contrast, has suffered the fate of most transitional figures: to be a point of reference, but never to fill the frame.

References:

Louis Auchincloss, "James and Bourget: The Artist and the Crank," in his *Reflections of a Jacobite* (Boston: Houghton Mifflin / London: Gollancz, 1961), pp. 127-137;

L.-J. Austin, *Paul Bourget: Sa vie et son œuvre jusqu'en 1889* (Paris: Droz, 1940);

Albert Autin, *"Le Disciple" de Paul Bourget* (Paris: Malfère, 1930);

Jean Calvet, *Le Renouveau catholique dans la littérature contemporaine* (Paris: Lanore, 1927);

Emilien Carassus, *Le Snobisme et les lettres françaises de Paul Bourget à Marcel Proust, 1884-1914* (Paris: Armand Colin, 1966);

Pierre Citti, *Contre la décadence: Histoire de l'imagination française dans le roman, 1890-1914* (Paris: Presses Universitaires de France, 1987);

Michel Crouzet, "La Mode, le moderne, le contemporain chez Paul Bourget: Une lecture des *Essais de psychologie contemporaine*,"

Saggi e Ricerce de Letteratura Francese, 26 (1987): 27-63;

Jérôme Demoulin, *La Famille française dans l'œuvre de Paul Bourget* (Le Puy: Mappus, 1939);

Gilles Dorion, *Présence de Paul Bourget au Canada* (Quebec: Presses de l'Université Laval, 1977);

Albert Feuillerat, *Paul Bourget: Histoire d'un esprit sous la Troisième République* (Paris: Plon, 1937);

Victor Giraud, *Paul Bourget: Essai de psychologie contemporaine. Avec une lettre autobiographique de l'auteur du "Disciple"* (Paris: Bloud & Gay, n.d. [1934]);

T. H. Goetz, "Paul Bourget's *Le Disciple* and the Text-Reader Relationship," *French Review*, 52 (October 1978): 56-61;

Henri Klerkx, *Paul Bourget et ses idées littéraires* (Nimègue-Utrecht: Dekker en van de Vegt, 1946);

Robert Lethbridge, "Bourget, Maupassant and *Hamlet*," *New Comparison*, 2 (1986): 58-68;

Michel Mansuy, *Un Moderne: Paul Bourget* (Paris: Les Belles Lettres, 1960);

Pierre Masson, *Le Disciple et l'insurgé: Roman et politique à la Belle Epoque* (Lyons: Presses Universitaires de Lyon, 1987);

I. D. McFarlane, "Paul Bourget: In Search of a Symbolist Aesthetic," *Australian Journal of French Studies*, 6 (1969): 376-409;

Anna L. Sebring, *La Pensée de Paul Bourget: L'exotisme (1852-1902)* (Grenoble: Didier & Richard, 1933);

Walter Todd Secor, *Paul Bourget and the Nouvelle* (New York: Columbia University Press, 1948);

Armand E. Singer, *Paul Bourget* (Boston: Twayne, 1976);

David Steel, "Les Débuts de la psychanalyse dans les lettres françaises, 1914-1922: Apollinaire, Cendrars, *Le Mercure de France, La Revue de l'Epoque*, Morand, Bourget, Lenormand," *Revue d'Histoire Littéraire de la France*, 79 (January-February 1979): 62-89;

Susan Rubin Suleiman, *Authoritarian Fictions: The Ideological Novel as a Literary Genre* (New York: Columbia University Press, 1983); published in French as *Le Roman à thèse ou l'autorité fictive* (Paris: Presses Universitaires de France, 1983);

Michael Tilby, "The Rewriting of a Mérimée Short Story. *La Double Méprise* and Bourget's *Un Crime d'amour*," *Studi Francesi*, 76 (January-April 1982): 44-53.

Papers:

Some of Bourget's correspondence is at the Bibliothèque Nationale, Paris.

Alphonse Daudet

(13 May 1840 - 16 December 1897)

Murray Sachs
Brandeis University

BOOKS: *Les Amoureuses* (Paris: Tardieu, 1858);

La Double Conversion (Paris: Poulet-Malassis et de Broise, 1861);

La Dernière Idole, drame en un acte, en prose, by Daudet and Ernest Lépine (Paris: M. Lévy, 1862);

Le Roman du Chaperon Rouge, scènes et fantaisies (Paris: M. Lévy, 1862);

Les Absents, opéra-comique en 1 acte (Paris: M. Lévy, 1865);

L'Œillet blanc, comédie en 1 acte, en prose, by Daudet and Lépine (Paris: M. Lévy, 1865);

Le Frère aîné, drame en un acte, by Daudet and Lépine (Paris: M. Lévy, 1868);

Le Petit Chose: Histoire d'un enfant (Paris: Hetzel, 1868); translated by Mary Neal Sherwood as *The Little Good-for-Nothing* (Boston: Estes & Lauriat, 1878);

Le Sacrifice, comédie en 3 actes (Paris: Lacroix, Verboeckhoven, 1869);

Lettres de mon moulin: Impressions et souvenirs (Paris: Hetzel, 1869; revised and enlarged edition, Paris: Lemerre, 1879); translated by Mary Carey as *Letters from My Mill* (London: Trübner, 1880);

Lettres à un absent, Paris, 1870-71 (Paris: Lemerre, 1871);

Lise Tavernier, drame en 5 actes et 7 tableaux (Paris: Dentu, 1872); translated by Henry C. Williams (New York: Hurst, 1890);

L'Arlésienne, pièce en 3 actes et 5 tableaux avec symphonies et chœurs de M. Georges Bizet (Paris: Lemerre, 1872); translated, with an introduction, by M. F. Sweetser as *The Girl of Arles* (Boston: Joseph Knight, 1894);

Aventures prodigieuses de Tartarin de Tarascon (Paris: Dentu, 1872); translated by C. Roland as *The New Don Quixote; or, The Wonderful Adventures of Tartarin de Tarascon* (Boston: W. F. Gill, 1875);

Contes du lundi (Paris: Lemerre, 1873; revised and enlarged edition, Paris: Charpentier, 1878); translated as *Monday Tales,* in a volume also including *Letters from My Mill* and *Letters to an Absent One* (Boston: Little, Brown, 1899);

Alphonse Daudet, circa 1866

Les Femmes d'artistes (Paris: Lemerre, 1874); translated by Laura Ensor as *Artists' Wives* (London & New York: Routledge, 1889);

Robert Helmont. Etudes et paysages (Paris: Dentu, 1874); translated by Ensor as *Robert Helmont. Diary of a Recluse, 1870-71* (London: Routledge, 1888; New York: Routledge, 1892);

Fromont jeune et Risler aîné, mœurs parisiennes (Paris: Charpentier, 1874); translated by Sherwood as *Sidonie* (Boston: Estes & Lauriat, 1877); original adapted as a drama by Daudet and Adolphe Belot (Paris: Calmann-Lévy, 1886);

Jack, mœurs contemporaines (Paris: Dentu, 1876); translated by Sherwood (Boston: Estes & Lauriat, 1877); original adapted as a drama by Daudet and Henri Lafontaine (Paris: Dentu, 1882);

Le Nabab, mœurs parisiennes (Paris: Charpentier, 1877); translated by Lucy H. Hooper as *The Nabob* (New York: Dodd, Mead, 1877); original adapted as a drama by Daudet and P.-E. Bonnier (Paris: Charpentier, 1881);

Le Char, opéra-comique en 1 acte, en vers libre, by Daudet and Paul Arène (Paris: Charpentier, 1878);

Les Rois en exil, roman parisien (Paris: Dentu, 1879); translated by Virginia Champlin as *Kings in Exile: A Novel of Parisian Life* (Chicago & New York: Rand McNally, 1879);

Numa Roumestan, mœurs parisiennes (Paris: Charpentier, 1881); translated by Mrs. J. Granville Layard as *Numa Roumestan; or, Joy Abroad and Grief at Home* (London: Vizetelly, 1884); original adapted as a drama (Paris: Lemerre, 1890);

L'Evangéliste, roman parisien (Paris: Dentu, 1883); translated by Sherwood as *L'Evangéliste: A Parisian Novel* (Philadelphia: T. B. Peterson, 1883);

Sapho, mœurs parisiennes (Paris: Charpentier, 1884); translated by Myron A. Cooney as *Sappho* (New York: Brookside Library, 1884); original adapted as a drama by Daudet and Belot (Paris: Charpentier et Fasquelle, 1893);

Tartarin sur les Alpes. Nouveaux exploits du héros tarasconnais (Paris: Calmann-Lévy, 1885); translated by Henry Frith as *Tartarin on the Alps* (New York & London: Routledge, 1887);

La Belle-Nivernaise, histoire d'un vieux bateau et de son équipage (Paris: Marpon-Flammarion, 1886); translated by Robert Routledge as *La Belle-Nivernaise; The Story of an Old Boat and Her Crew (and Other Stories)* (London: Routledge, 1887);

L'Immortel, mœurs parisiennes (Paris: Lemerre, 1888); translated by Arthur W. Verrall and Margaret de G. Verrall as *One of the "Forty"* (London: Swan Sonnenschein, 1888);

Trente ans de Paris, à travers ma vie et mes livres (Paris: Marpon et Flammarion, 1888); translated by Ensor as *Thirty Years of Paris and of My Literary Life* (London & New York: Routledge, 1888);

Souvenirs d'un homme de lettres (Paris: Marpon et Flammarion, 1888); translated by Ensor as *Recollections of a Literary Man* (London & New York: Routledge, 1889);

La Lutte pour la vie, pièce en 5 actes, 6 tableaux (Paris: Calmann-Lévy, 1890); translated as *The Struggle for Life, drama* (New York: Scribner's, 1889);

Port-Tarascon, dernières aventures de l'illustre Tartarin (Paris: Dentu, 1890); translated by Henry James as *Port Tarascon, The Last Adventures of the Illustrious Tartarin* (New York: Harper, 1891);

L'Obstacle, pièce en 4 actes (Paris: Marpon et Flammarion, 1891);

Rose et Ninette, mœurs du jour (Paris: Flammarion, 1892); translated by Mary J. Serrano as *Rose and Ninette; A Story of the Morals and Manners of the Day* (New York: Cassell, 1892);

La Menteuse, pièce en 3 actes, by Daudet and Léon Hennique (Paris: Flammarion, 1893);

Entre les frises et la rampe, petites études de la vie théâtrale (Paris: Dentu, 1894); translated by George Burnham Ives, with an introduction by James I. Ford, as *Between the Flies and the Footlights* in *The Works of Alphonse Daudet*, volume 16 (Boston: Little, Brown, 1899);

La Petite Paroisse, mœurs conjugales (Paris: Lemerre, 1895); translated by Ives, with an introduction by William P. Trent, as *The Little Parish Church* in *The Works of Alphonse Daudet*, volume 7 (Boston: Little, Brown, 1899);

L'Enterrement d'une étoile (Paris: Borel, 1896); reprinted as *La Fédor*, in *La Fédor, pages de la vie* (Paris: Flammarion, 1897); translated by Ives as *La Fédor* in *The Works of Alphonse Daudet*, volume 13 (Boston: Little, Brown, 1899);

Le Trésor d'Arlatan (Paris: Fasquelle, 1897); translated by Ives as *Arlatan's Treasure* in *The Works of Alphonse Daudet*, volume 13;

Soutien de famille, mœurs contemporaines (Paris: Fasquelle, 1898); translated by Levin Carnac as *The Head of the Family* (New York & London: Putnam's, 1898);

Notes sur la vie (Paris: Fasquelle, 1899); translated by Mary Hendee as *Notes on Life* in *The Works of Alphonse Daudet*, volume 23 (Boston: Little, Brown, 1900);

Premier voyage, premier mensonge, souvenirs de mon enfance (Paris: Flammarion, 1900); translated by Robert H. Sherard as *My First Voy-*

age, *My First Lie* (London: Digby, Long, 1901);

Pages inédites de critique dramatique, 1874-1880 (Paris: Flammarion, 1923);

La Doulou; La Vie: Extraits des carnets inédits de l'auteur (Paris: Fasquelle, 1931); translated by Milton Garvie, with commentary and notes by André Ebner, as *Suffering, 1887-95* (New Haven: Yale University Press, 1934).

Collections: *The Works of Alphonse Daudet*, 24 volumes (Boston: Little, Brown, 1898-1900);

Œuvres complètes d'Alphonse Daudet. Edition définitive précédée d'un essai de biographie littéraire par Henry Céard, 18 volumes (Paris: Houssiaux, 1899-1901);

Œuvres complètes illustrées. Edition ne varietur, 20 volumes (Paris: Librairie de France, 1929-1931).

PLAY PRODUCTIONS: *La Dernière Idole*, by Daudet and Ernest Lépine, Paris, Théâtre de l'Odéon, 4 February 1862;

Les Absents, music by Ferdinand Poise, Paris, Opéra-Comique, 26 October 1864;

L'Œillet blanc, by Daudet and Lépine, Paris, Théâtre-Français, 8 April 1865;

Le Frère aîné, by Daudet and Lépine, Paris, Théâtre du Vaudeville, 19 December 1867;

Le Sacrifice, Paris, Théâtre du Vaudeville, 11 February 1869;

Lise Tavernier, Paris, Théâtre de l'Ambigu, 29 January 1872;

L'Arlésienne, music by Georges Bizet, Paris, Théâtre du Vaudeville, 1 October 1872;

Fromont jeune et Risler aîné, by Daudet and Adolphe Belot, Paris, Théâtre du Vaudeville, 16 September 1876;

Le Char, by Daudet and Paul Arène, music by Emile Pessard, Paris, Opéra-Comique, 18 January 1878;

Le Nabab, by Daudet and P.-E. Bonnier, Paris, Théâtre du Vaudeville, 30 January 1880;

Jack, by Daudet and Henri Lafontaine, Paris, Théâtre de l'Odéon, 11 January 1881;

Sapho, by Daudet and Belot, Paris, Théâtre du Gymnase, 18 December 1885;

Numa Roumestan, Paris, Théâtre national de l'Odéon, 15 February 1887;

La Lutte pour la vie, Paris, Théâtre du Gymnase Dramatique, 30 October 1889;

L'Obstacle, music by Reynaldo Hahn, Paris, Théâtre du Gymnase, 27 December 1890;

La Menteuse, Paris, Théâtre du Gymnase, 4 February 1892.

OTHER: Arnold Mortier, *Les Soirées parisiennes de 1876*, preface by Daudet (Paris: Dentu, 1877);

Francis Poictevin, *La Robe du moine*, preface by Daudet (Paris: Sandoz et Thuillier, 1882);

Antoine Albalat, *L'Inassouvie*, preface by Daudet (Paris, 1882);

"Dialogue intime pour et contre Rousseau," in *J.-J. Rousseau jugé par les Français d'aujourd'hui* by John Grand-Carteret (Paris: Didier, Perrin, 1890), pp. 429-432;

Gabriel Montoya, *Chansons naïves et perverses*, preface by Daudet (Paris: Ollendorff, 1896);

Armand Charpentier, *L'Initiateur*, preface by Daudet (Paris: Ollendorff, 1897).

A century after his death, Alphonse Daudet has entered a familiar literary no-man's-land reserved for those unlucky authors who, once extremely popular, have declined in public favor to the point where the name is still very well known but the achievements that earned the fame are all but forgotten. Daudet has joined company with the likes of Guy de Maupassant, Rudyard Kipling, and Bret Harte, authors known, by name at least, to virtually every literate person, usually because of one or two short pieces that turn up so often in anthologies that the name is inescapable. Yet the great bulk of such an author's work is no longer read or studied, except by specialists, with the resulting paradox that the author is reduced to a household name about whom almost nothing is known anymore.

There are quite specific reasons, of course, that explain—partially at least—why Daudet's reputation has fallen victim to that oxymoronic fate of the familiarly obscure. For one thing, Daudet was a rather prolific author, but the handful of works that are still kept in print today are not only a tiny fraction of his total output, but are far from being representative of his strongest qualities. Those who have read only a few of his sparkling tales of Provence would hardly suspect the truth that he was a major novelist of Parisian manners. A second reason for his current obscurity is that he was an exceptionally private person who left to posterity no extensive collection of notebooks, diaries, or correspondence from which the public could satisfy its curiosity about him or his work, as it can about Gustave Flaubert, for instance, or about George Sand. Finally, there is the fact that Daudet's best-known works are celebrated for their charm and their human warmth, but not for their profundity. Those who do not

Daudet in his study

know his weightier and more provocative works find it all too easy to dismiss him as entertaining but trivial.

The fact of the matter is that Daudet was, to his contemporaries, a good deal more than "a fellow of infinite jest," like Hamlet's Yorick, or a regional author with a gift for amusing Parisians with the quaint foibles of his native Midi. Daudet was a major player on the literary scene at the height of his powers, during the 1870s and 1880s. He was not only popular with the general public, but respected and admired by his peers, including Flaubert, Emile Zola, Ivan Turgenev, Robert Louis Stevenson, George Meredith, and Henry James. He played a significant role, by example, in developing the novel of realism in France, while maintaining, within that aesthetic, a personal manner and voice in which his compassion for the disadvantaged of society was always manifest. So successful was he in developing his own distinctive brand of subjective realism that he was for a time in the late 1870s the most widely read French novelist outside of France, as well as a best-selling author at home. His career was so closely interwoven with all the significant literary movements of his time, and with most of its influential authors, that it is impossible to write an accurate history of French literature in the second half of the nineteenth century without taking account of Daudet's role and influence in that period.

Alphonse Daudet was born on 13 May 1840, in the Provençal city of Nîmes, the third son of Vincent Daudet, a silk merchant, and his wife, the former Adeline Reynaud, whose family was also in the silk business. Because the young Alphonse was a small and sickly baby, he was cared for by the family of his wet nurse and lived with them, in a village just outside Nîmes, for most of his first five years, rather than with his own family. One result of that arrangement was that Alphonse became fluent in Provençal, the language spoken in his foster home. Since his own parents did not approve of Provençal, the arrangement also created a certain distance between Alphonse and his own family, except for the warm and supportive relationship he always had with his brother Ernest, three years his senior, the sibling closest to him in age. Indeed, when Alphonse moved back permanently into his own family home at the age of five, he felt like a stranger, so somber and joyless had the atmosphere become, because his father's business was failing, which made Vincent anxious and preoccupied, and Adeline melancholy and withdrawn.

From that period of family financial problems came Alphonse's tendency to make frequent protective retreats into himself, and to prefer brooding solitude for lengthy spells, contrasting sharply with his normally gregarious and cheerful meridional temperament. When he was nine years old, the declining family fortunes forced a move northward to Lyons, and in that damp, dreary climate Alphonse's dual nature became even more accentuated. He felt humiliated in his new school because he had to wear coarse working-class clothing, which his classmates mocked. That circumstance became his excuse for spending entire days in solitary wanderings around the city rather than attending school. Yet his natural gregariousness and assiduousness continued to find expression, first by his excellence as a student when he did attend school, especially his enthusiasm for Latin and French composition; and second by his constant close companionship with Ernest during those years. In the society of others, it seemed he could be warm, sensitive, and articulate, but he experienced all too frequently the impulse to be by himself, and to observe the world from a safe distance.

Years later Daudet would record in his notebooks the Latin phrase *homo duplex* to describe what he perceived to be his dual nature and permanently divided self: the enthusiastic, compassionate participant in life, side by side with the detached, ironic observer of life. His most telling exemplification of his own ineradicably dual nature was the moment when, as a teenager, he saw his father react to the news that his oldest son, Henri, had died. Daudet insists that even as he himself took in the shocking and painful news of his brother's death, he could not help noticing that his father's outcry in reporting the news would be perfect in the theater for an actor who wished to convey grief convincingly. Daudet claimed to be disconcerted by this personal tendency to remain coolly observant even at moments of the strongest emotion, but he also recognized that it was an essential component of his literary calling.

Daudet's literary vocation had developed to such a degree during the family's Lyons period that at the age of sixteen he wrote a competent full-length historical novel, "Léo et Chrétienne Fleury," which the editor of the *Gazette de Lyon* agreed to publish; however, the newspaper collapsed before Daudet's work saw print. This event is proudly reported by Ernest, himself a writer, in a book he wrote a quarter century later about his relationship with his younger brother, *Mon frère et moi* (My Brother and Me, 1882). Ernest recalled that he was much impressed by this display of his brother's precocious talent and always regretted that the only manuscript of that early novel had somehow been lost by the newspaper editor who planned to publish it, and that the novel had thus never appeared.

By the time he wrote that early novel, Daudet's formal education was also coming to an end, for the family's fortunes had so declined that it could no longer afford to keep him in school. Using old connections, his family obtained for Alphonse a position as *pion*, or study assistant, in a secondary school at Alès, a town not far from Nîmes. He served in that position from May 1857 until November of that year, at which point he departed abruptly in order to accept Ernest's welcome invitation to join him in Paris, where he had recently gone in order to establish himself as a writer. The two brothers lived together and eked out a meager existence on Ernest's earnings over a period of many months, during which Alphonse attempted to get started on his own literary career. Within a year of his arrival in Paris, Alphonse succeeded in getting a small volume of poems published, which attracted one or two favorable notices and gave him the satisfied feeling, at the age of eighteen, that his literary career was well launched.

To his disappointment, however, *Les Amoureuses* (Women in Love, 1858) did not sell, and he needed a source of income in order to cease being a burden to his brother. When he was offered a sinecure as secretary to a prominent government official, he accepted gratefully, knowing he would have ample free time to establish himself in the literary world by means of journalism. The secretarial appointment lasted some five years until his patron died in 1865, and Alphonse diligently employed those years as an apprenticeship to the literary calling by publishing a stream of stories, poems, essays, and one-act plays in a variety of periodicals, and he gradually became known as a talented newcomer. Beginning in 1865 he began to earn his living solely by his pen and was soon embarked on three book-length projects: an autobiographical novel, *Le Petit Chose* (1868; translated as *The Little Good-for-Nothing*, 1878); a collection of short stories set in southern France, *Lettres de mon moulin* (1869; translated as *Letters from My Mill*, 1880); and a comic

Frédéric Mistral, Mme Eugène Giraud, and Daudet

novel about the meridional character, *Aventures prodigieuses de Tartarin de Tarascon* (1872; translated as *The New Don Quixote; or, The Wonderful Adventures of Tartarin de Tarascon*, 1875). With these projects, and his marriage in 1867, Daudet signaled to the literary world that his apprenticeship was over, and his career began in earnest.

These three volumes of Daudet's serious literary debut actually form a kind of trilogy. The bulk of the writing on all of them was done in a three-year period, 1866 to 1869; the heaviest emphasis in all of them is on his native region of the Midi and its special—and to his Parisian contemporaries, rather exotic—customs and characteristics; and there is an autobiographical underpinning to all three, including that highly personal tonal mixture of gentle, sympathetic warmth together with a certain detached, ironic mockery. The first volume in print, *Le Petit Chose*, was also Daudet's first published full-length novel. In 1868 it encountered only a modest commercial and artistic success, but its many subsequent editions have made it perhaps Daudet's most widely read work.

In spite of its generally recognized flaws—lack of unity, structural and psychological inconsistency, and a somewhat cloying sentimentality in certain scenes—the novel has endured mainly because of the authenticity of feeling it communicates about its gentle and long-suffering hero, Daniel Eyssette, a charming and talented would-be writer who fails to attain his ambition because of his own weaknesses of character. Since Daniel is unmistakably modeled on Daudet, the novel captures with great power and vividness the hopes and fears of a young man arriving in Paris and embarking on a literary career in an exciting but bewilderingly complex environment. These were the very feelings Daudet was experiencing at the time he wrote it. The book still has the remarkable capacity to move the reader both to laughter and to tears, in spite of its often awkward technique, because it draws so directly on the author's innermost feelings.

The emotional intensity of the novel was doubtless a product of the circumstances of composition. Daudet had gone back to the region of his birth in January 1866 for reasons of health as well as to escape the turmoil of his personal life. He settled into the deserted country home of a relative and lived in complete isolation for four feverish months as he set down the story of Daniel Eyssette. That he imagined his hero ruined by his fascination with an immoral siren of an actress, and forced in the end to abandon his literary ambitions and go into the porcelain business, suggests the somber frame of mind in which the author wrote the work. *Le Petit Chose* concludes with Daudet's projection of his worst fears for his own likely fate. That heartbreaking image of the failure of innocence is perhaps what has made this the most beloved, if not the most admired, of all Daudet's novels. Although plainly the work of a young and still inexperienced novelist, it has the ring of emotional truth.

Daudet carefully revised his feverishly composed first draft before allowing *Le Petit Chose* to appear in installments, and he revised it again before allowing it to come out as a book. Those revisions were the symbol of his newborn artistic conscience, and he applied the same technique to his second volume of that period, the celebrated collection of short stories *Lettres de mon moulin*. Most of the stories first appeared separately in periodicals from 1866 to 1868, but in preparation for their book publication, he carefully removed all telltale signs of the stories' journalistic origin and arranged them in a carefully thought-out order. His clear purpose was to make it a coherent composition and a book of enduring interest, unmarked by topical references. The stories portray the Provençal environment in which Daudet grew up with cordial sympathy, indulgent humor, and a gentle undercurrent of irony. Not surprisingly, several stories evoke themes similar to those of *Le Petit Chose*: the struggles and temptations of the young artist trying to get started, the perils of the innocent in a world full of morally and materially corrupt people, and the pain of unrequited love, failure, and defeat. The craftsmanship of these stories, the skill of the narration, and the charm of the style have made at least a half-dozen of them international favorites that still constitute one of Daudet's most potent claims to literary immortality.

The third volume of this early trilogy of successes, the comic novel *Tartarin de Tarascon*, had its origins in a short story Daudet wrote some five years before *Le Petit Chose* and *Lettres de mon moulin* were even begun. "Chapatin le tueur de lions" had appeared in the *Figaro* in June 1863. In 1869 he undertook a major revision and expansion of that early story and published the result in installments just before the outbreak of the Franco-Prussian War. The war forced postponement of its publication in book form, and Daudet undertook more polishing and refinement of the text. This volume was a more considerable success than either of the other two and is perhaps a better work of art, since it strikes a perfectly sustained balance between the endearing portrait of a lovable clown and the mocking account of the adventures of a fool and a braggart.

The hero, Tartarin, manages to be the embodiment of all the virtues and all the foibles of the meridional character and has thereby become Daudet's best-known creation. His name has become part of the French language, designating a universally recognizable type. If one adds that Tartarin is another version of Daudet's obsessive concern with the innocent figure repeatedly victimized by a world of temptresses and swindlers, one can see the common inspiration and outlook that unites these three very personal works with a strongly regional flavor. They succeeded in establishing Daudet, after a long, difficult apprenticeship, as a writer to be reckoned with on the French literary scene of the 1870s.

Daudet became a success as a writer by learning, through hard work, to present effectively to the public what he knew best: himself and his region. That is the meaning of his triumph at the end of the 1860s with *Le Petit Chose, Lettres de mon moulin*, and *Tartarin de Tarascon*. The Franco-Prussian War seems to have had the effect of maturing Daudet as a person after he had come of age as a writer. Because of a broken leg he did not serve in the early fighting in 1870, but by the time Paris was under siege, he had become a member of the National Guard. Those experiences brought out the thoughtful, serious observer in him to such an extent that Daudet actually produced four published volumes in three years' time, most of whose contents were observed vignettes or invented stories based on observations of Paris under siege. The collected pieces in *Lettres à un absent* (Letters to a Missing Person, 1871) and *Robert Helmont* (1874) were all journalistic items of little more than passing topical interest, and Daudet never allowed that material to be reprinted. He did not regard those volumes as part of his permanent oeuvre. The cases of *Contes du lundi* (1873; translated as *Monday Tales*, 1899) and *Les Femmes d'artistes* (1874; translated as *Artists' Wives*, 1889) were different. Material from both volumes was eventually included in the two revised and enlarged volumes of short stories he published at the end of the 1870s to represent all he felt worthy of surviving among his output as a short-story writer: *Lettres de mon moulin* and *Contes du lundi*.

However, short stories deriving from his observations of Paris and Parisians during the war have the great importance of marking a new shift in Daudet's aesthetics of fiction. The preoccupation with self and his exotic southern origins, and the lighthearted gaiety with which he had written about them, were giving way after the war to the keen, objective observer of life in Paris, who was both fascinated and appalled by modern urban existence. Perhaps because of the failure of his play *L'Arlésienne* (translated as *The Girl of Arles*, 1894) in 1872, Daudet had the idea of writing a play about the bustling life of the Marais section of Paris where he lived, because he thought it might be more meaningful, and therefore more appealing, to his audience, most of whom were Parisians. When he could not successfully shape the material into a drama, he turned it into a novel, *Fromont jeune et Risler aîné* (1874; translated as *Sidonie*, 1877), which was an immediate popular success, bringing Daudet more

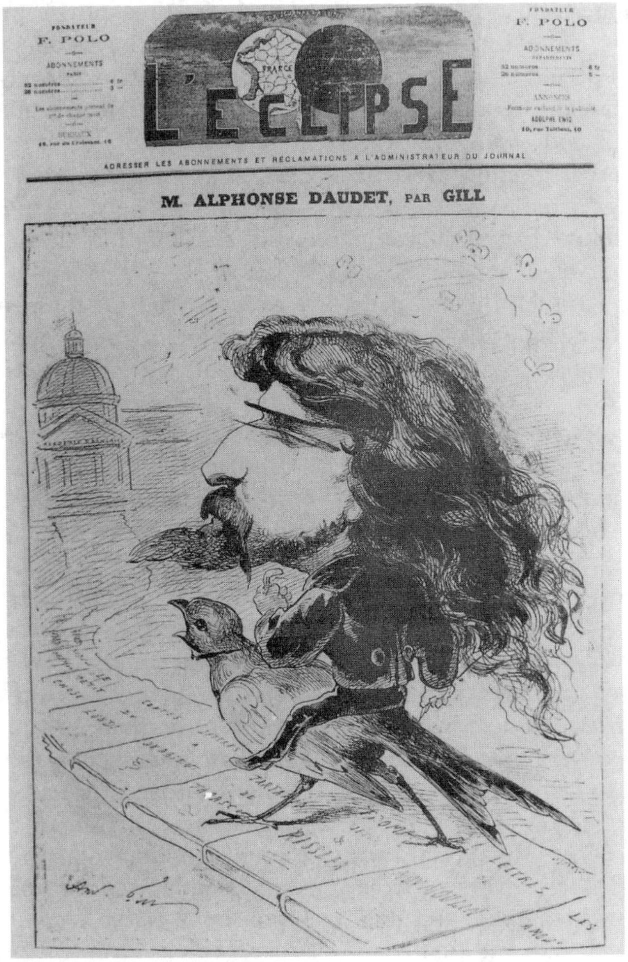

Caricature of Daudet by André Gill, depicting the author on a path of his books leading to the Académie Française

money than he had ever earned before, and so confirming him in his new literary direction as a novelist of realism.

Fromont jeune takes its title from the name of the business partnership that is the central focus of the novel's action. The plot mainly concerns the undermining of an honorable business enterprise by the ambitious scheming of Risler's wife, Sidonie, the product of a working-class neighborhood, who marries to raise her social status, and then ruthlessly pursues still greater wealth and power at her husband's emotional and moral expense. Rich in subplots, the novel has the overt purpose of showing the reader the variety of social classes and human types who inhabit Paris, and the corruptions—moral, ethical, and material—that flow from the overcrowded and competitive urban conditions. Paris is specifically implicated as the cause of many adulteries, suicides, and other forms of human misery. There are many powerful scenes and memorable characters, which explain the novel's extraordinary popularity in spite of its strongly depressing theme that the urban jungle is inherently destructive of family and social values.

Yet, new as this theme was for Daudet, it is worth observing that his fundamental cast of characters remains the same: figures of innocence and virtue, both male and female, are shown to be weak, ultimately victims of those who are motivated by selfish and evil objectives. Daudet's essentially pessimistic view of human nature remained intact when he became a novelist of realism. The setting and choice of theme in his fiction, presented with a finely balanced stance of objectivity, gave his work new life in 1874 and instantly placed him among the leading French novelists of his generation, Flaubert and Zola, who were the most renowned exponents of the aesthetics of realism at that time. Nor was Daudet's move to realism mere opportunism, an effort to accommodate his work to changing public taste. It was the natural result of his growing seriousness as an artist and his maturation as an observer of the human condition. No doubt he was also influenced by the regular discussions about literature he began to have in 1872 with Flaubert, Zola, Edmond de Goncourt, and Turgenev, who became his close friends.

In the decade that followed the publication of *Fromont jeune*, Daudet devoted himself to the cultivation of the novel of Parisian life and manners, choosing a different milieu each time. In 1876 he published a novel called *Jack* (translated, 1877), which tells the pathetic story of a young man neglected by his aristocratic but irresponsible and flighty mother, and who is thereby deprived of a proper education and forced to work in an iron foundry, which his frail health cannot endure, resulting in his early death, alone and indigent. There followed in quick succession *Le Nabab* (1877; translated as *The Nabob*, 1877), about a poor man from the provinces who makes a large fortune and tries to become a person of power and influence in Parisian society by means of the liberal use of his money, only to be fleeced by swindlers and driven into bankruptcy and disgrace; and *Les Rois en exil* (1879; translated as *Kings in Exile*, 1879), which evokes the special Parisian milieu of deposed monarchs living in exile, planning their return to power someday, and finding themselves deceived, exploited, and finally ruined by the sharp practices of Parisian entrepreneurs who prey on the vulnerable.

In subsequent novels he evoked the world of republican politics (*Numa Roumestan* [1881; translated, 1884]), the marginal world of religious fanatics (*L'Evangéliste*, [1883; translated, 1883]), and the bohemian world of artists and their mistresses (*Sapho* [1884; translated as *Sappho*, 1884]). The range of Daudet's thematic interests was exceptionally broad, and his productivity steady, during the phase of his novels of realism. His lasting achievement in that period was the creation of one of the most comprehensive portraits of Parisian society that exists for that era. Purely as social documentation, Daudet's novels from 1874 to 1884 are a mine of information. *Le Nabab* and *Sapho* also happen to be impressive works of art, well observed, well constructed, and wisely penetrating in their analyses of Parisian mores.

By the mid 1880s, however, Daudet's creative energy was showing clear signs of flagging, and the first symptoms of the debilitating illness that would eventually kill him began to appear and take their physical toll on him during the second half of the decade. From 1885 to 1890 he produced only three novels, two of them exploitative sequels to his celebrated comic novel *Tartarin de Tarascon*, and the other, *L'Immortel* (1888; translated as *One of the "Forty,"* 1888), a controversial depiction of the Académie Française and the politics surrounding elections to that august body of the forty "Immortals," as they were ironically called. None of these novels added substantially to his literary reputation or to his contribution to the study of Parisian manners and morals. Moreover, all three were marked by a new, slightly uncomfortable preachiness that undermined the stance of objectivity he had so carefully cultivated in the preceding decade.

That preachiness, compounded of starchy moralizing and saccharine sentimentality, seemed to have its origin in Daudet's remorse and feelings of guilt because of the harsh and relentless pessimism he had displayed in his realistic works. In his notebooks of the time, he speaks of his desire to become, through his writing, what he called *un marchand de bonheur* (a merchant of happiness), apparently as a way of atoning for the bleak view of human nature he had offered the public for so long. And indeed there is a benign and gentle, even compassionate, tone in the three novels he published after 1890, which closed his career as a novelist. Unhappily, these are also the weakest of his works, lacking in inspiration, insight, and even vital characters. All three are sentimental narratives in praise of the sanctity of marriage and the integrity of the family. The ugly underside of each is a critical representation of the social and economic factors that threaten the family: a recent French law reintroducing divorce, the selfish cynicism of a new Darwinian generation obsessed with the principle of the survival of the fittest, and the widespread breakdown of traditional moral values, opening the way for the ravages of infidelity, jealousy, and irresponsibility within the family circle, and of greed, rapacity, and fraud in business and politics, the ultimate consequences of which could be seen, Daudet thought, in the domestic turmoil of broken families and intergenerational hostility.

Thus, in all three novels of the 1890s—*Rose et Ninette* (1892; translated as *Rose and Ninette*, 1892), *La Petite Paroisse* (1895; translated as *The Little Parish Church*, 1899), and *Soutien de famille* (1898; translated as *The Head of the Family*, 1898)—Daudet graphically depicts instances of grave social disorder but always finds a way of restoring

Daudet and his wife, Julia, at Champrosay

happiness and harmony to the family circle in order to close on a positive, pointedly didactic note. The essential human drama of all his stories was still in evidence in his declining years: the innocent and the virtuous are always seduced, betrayed, or victimized by the ambitious and the unscrupulous. But the sad consequence of his "merchant of happiness" compulsion in those years was the distortion of his artistic integrity by what must be called maudlinism. The need to console his readers—and perhaps himself—seemed to overwhelm and displace the bleak but honest vision of human nature he had formed by dint of close, thoughtful observation. In all but two of his last works, Daudet transformed himself from a realist into a moralist.

The two exceptions, interestingly enough, were short stories on deeply personal themes, as though the Daudet of the 1860s and 1870s had suddenly and magically risen to the surface of his consciousness again and issued in two stunning works of art. Both stories are remembrances of Daudet's troubled, neurotic relationship with Marie Rieu, the volatile and tempestuous woman who had been his mistress during his apprenticeship years. In *La Fédor* (1897; translated, 1899), first published as *L'Enterrement d'une étoile* (The Burial of a Star, 1896), Daudet fictionalized Marie Rieu as an actress of renown who dies young. One of her lovers (clearly Daudet) attends her funeral and, in spite of himself, relives all the anguish of their relationship during the service. In *Le Trésor d'Arlatan* (1897; translated as *Arlatan's Treasure*, 1899), Daudet depicted, in fictional terms, his own attempt to escape from the painful love-hate relationship he had with Rieu by isolating himself in a deserted country house in Provence, only to find that she so haunted his consciousness that he could not exorcise her image from his imagination, even when she was far away. Both stories confront unblinkingly the morbid fascination Rieu exerted on Daudet, and they powerfully evoke his own helpless pain and suffering when in the toils of that uncontrollable passion. Both stories are simply and movingly told, with no trace of self-pity or self-justification, and testify to the survival of Daudet's literary artistry even amid the physical and moral wreckage of his illness-wracked last years.

In his fifty-seven years of life and forty years of active participation in the literary world, Daudet combined native talent and determination to build a solid literary monument, important in its own day and enduringly attractive to posterity. By his astute and perceptive observation of the world around him, and his uncanny ability to represent and articulate the fruit of his observations in memorable form and style, Daudet made himself into one of the most influential novelists of the second half of the nineteenth century, not only in France but in all of Europe and North and South America as well. Some of his work has not aged well, to be sure, and today seems a bit arch or contrived or sentimental. Yet anyone wishing to have an authentic sense of what life was like in Paris of the 1870s and 1880s could hardly do better than to read his impressive sequence of realistic novels beginning with *Fromont jeune* and ending with *Sapho*. As for artistic achievement, his most lasting claim to fame may well turn out to be his short stories, including those in the collections *Lettres de mon moulin* and *Contes du lundi*, and his last two tales, "La Fédor" and "Le Trésor d'Arlatan," plus some anthology pieces that are self-contained narratives embedded in such longer works as *Tartarin de Tarascon, Fromont jeune, Le Nabab*, and *Sapho*. Daudet's greatest natural gift was the sparkling and inventive art of the raconteur. Long after his realistic fiction has been forgotten, one suspects, the world will still be grateful to lend an ear to anyone who can tell a story as entrancingly as Daudet.

Daudet (photograph by Nadar)

Bibliographies:

Jules Brivois, *Essai de bibliographie des œuvres de Monsieur Alphonse Daudet, avec des fragments inédits* (Paris: Conquet, 1895);

Geoffrey E. Hare, *Alphonse Daudet: A Critical Bibliography*, 2 volumes (London: Grant & Cutler, 1978-1979).

Biographies:

Robert H. Sherard, *Alphonse Daudet: A Biographical and Critical Study* (London: Arnold, 1894);

Yvonne Martinet, *Alphonse Daudet (1840-1897). Sa vie et son œuvre. Mémoires et récits* (Gap: Imprimerie Louis-Jean, 1940);

Lucien Daudet, *Vie d'Alphonse Daudet* (Paris: Gallimard, 1941);

Georges Benoit-Guyod, *Alphonse Daudet, son temps, son œuvre* (Paris: Tallandier, 1947);

Grace V. Dobie, *Alphonse Daudet* (London: Nelson, 1949);

J.-H. Bornecque, *Les Années d'apprentissage d'Alphonse Daudet* (Paris: Nizet, 1951).

References:

Louis Auchincloss, "Early Reading and Alphonse Daudet," in his *Reflections of a Jacobite* (Boston: Houghton Mifflin / London: Gollancz, 1961);

Luc Badesco, "Les Débuts parisiens d'Alphonse Daudet: Légende et vérité," *Revue d'Histoire Littéraire de la France*, 63, no. 4 (October-December 1963): 581-618;

Marcel Bruyère, *La Jeunesse d'Alphonse Daudet* (Paris: Nouvelles Editions Latines, 1955);

Boyd G. Carter, "Alphonse Daudet and Darwinism," *Modern Language Quarterly*, 6, no. 1 (March 1945): 93-98;

Stirling Haig, "The Blue Illusion of Alphonse Daudet's *Fromont jeune et Risler aîné*," in his

The Madame Bovary Blues (Baton Rouge: Louisiana State University Press, 1987);

Louis Michel, *Le Langage méridional dans l'œuvre d'Alphonse Daudet* (Paris: Editions d'Artrey, 1961);

Sean O'Faolain, "Alphonse Daudet or the Interrupted Romantic," in his *The Short Story* (London: Collins, 1948; New York: Devin-Adair, 1951);

Alphonse V. Roche, *Alphonse Daudet* (Boston: Twayne, 1976);

Murray Sachs, *The Career of Alphonse Daudet: A Critical Study* (Cambridge, Mass.: Harvard University Press, 1965);

G. R. Saylor, *Alphonse Daudet as a Dramatist* (Philadelphia: University of Pennsylvania Press, 1940);

Emile Zola, "Alphonse Daudet," in his *Les Romanciers naturalistes* (Paris: Charpentier, 1881).

Papers:

Many of Daudet's manuscripts, notebooks, and letters are widely scattered in private collections, but a considerable collection of such autograph material is at La Vignasse museum, Saint-Alban-Auriolles, in the Ardèche region of France.

Edouard Dujardin

(10 November 1861 - 31 October 1949)

Terence Dawson
National University of Singapore

SELECTED BOOKS: *Les Fantasmagories 4: La vierge en fer* (Paris: Morellet, 1885);

Les Hantises (Paris: Léon Vanier, 1886);

A la gloire d'Antonia (Paris: Librairie de la Revue Indépendante, 1887);

Les Lauriers sont coupés (Paris: Librairie de la Revue Indépendante, 1888); translated by Stuart Gilbert as *We'll to the Woods No More* (Norfolk, Conn.: New Directions, 1938);

Litanies, mélopées pour chant et piano (Paris: Librairie de la Revue Indépendante, 1888);

Pour la vierge du roc ardent (Paris: Librairie de la Revue Indépendante, 1889);

Annuaire du duel, 1880-1889, as Ferréus (Paris: Perrin, 1891);

Antonia: Tragédie moderne en trois actes et en vers libres (Paris: Léon Vanier, 1891);

La Comédie des amours (Paris: Léon Vanier, 1891);

Deux suites anciennes: Poèmes (Tours: Deslis frères, 1891);

Le Chevalier du passé: Tragédie moderne, 2e partie de la Légende d'Antonia (Paris: Léon Vanier, 1892);

Réponse de la bergère au berger (Paris: Publications de la Revue Blanche, 1892);

La Fin d'Antonia: Tragédie moderne, 3e partie de la Légende d'Antonia (Paris: Léon Vanier, 1893);

L'Initiation au péché et à l'amour: Roman (Paris: Mercure de France, 1898);

Le Délassement du guerrier: Variations sur des motifs populaires; petits poèmes (Paris: Mercure de France, 1904);

La Source du fleuve chrétien: Historique critique du judaïsme ancien et du christianisme primitif, volume 1: *Le Judaïsme: Histoire du peuple juif depuis les origines jusqu'à saint Paul* (Paris: Mercure de France, 1906); translated by Joseph McCabe as *The Source of the Christian Tradition: A Critical History of Ancient Judaism* (London: Watts, 1911);

Les Prédécesseurs de Daniel: Recherches sur la trace de faits et d'idées datant de la fin du IIIe siècle avant notre ère et du commencement du second dans les prophéties d'Habacuc, Sophanies, Aggée, Zacharie et Malachie (Paris: Fischbacher, 1908);

Poésies: La Comédie des amours; Le Délassement du guerrier; Poésies anciennes (Paris: Mercure de France, 1913);

Edouard Dujardin, 1888 (drawing by Jacques-Emile Blanche; from the 1925 edition of Les Lauriers sont coupés)

De Stéphane Mallarmé au prophète Ezéchiel et Essai d'une théorie du réalisme symbolique, suivi d'un poème à la mémoire de Joseph Halévy (Paris: Mercure de France, 1919);

Les Epoux d'Heur-le-Port: Légende du temps présent (Paris: Les Cahiers Idéalistes, 1920);

Mari Magno: Poèmes 1917-1920 (Paris: Les Cahiers Idéalistes, 1921);

Les Premiers Poètes du vers libre: Etude historique et critique des commencements du symbolisme (Paris: Mercure de France, 1922);

Marthe et Marie: Légende dramatique (Paris: Les Cahiers Idéalistes, 1923);

Le Mystère du Dieu mort et réssuscité: Légende dramatique (Paris: A. Messein, 1924);

Le Retour des enfants prodigues: Poème dramatique (Paris: Les Cahiers Idéalistes, 1924);

Théâtre II: Les Argonautes: Marthe et Marie; Les Epoux-d'Heur-le-Port; Le Retour des enfants prodigues (Paris: Mercure de France, 1924);

Histoire ancienne du Dieu Jésus, I: Le Dieu Jésus: Essai sur les origines et la formation de la légende évangélique (Paris: A. Messein, 1927); abridged translation by A. Brodie Sanders of this work and *La Première Génération chrétienne* published as *Ancient History of the God Jesus* (London: Watts, 1938);

Demain ici ainsi la révolution (Paris: Delpeuch, 1928);

Le Monologue intérieur: Son apparition, ses origines, sa place dans l'œuvre de James Joyce et dans le roman contemporain (Paris: A. Messein, 1931);

Histoire ancienne du Dieu Jésus, II: Grandeur et décadence de la critique, sa rénovation: Le cas de l'abbé Turmel (Paris: A. Messein, 1931);

Le Retour éternel: Poèmes dramatiques (Sablons: Moly-Sabata, 1934);

Histoire ancienne du Dieu Jésus, III: La Première Génération chrétienne: Son destin révolutionnaire (Paris: A. Messein, 1935);

Mallarmé par un des siens (Paris: A. Messein, 1936);

Trois poèmes en prose mêlés de vers, 1886-1888 et 1892 (Paris: Les Cahiers Idéalistes et A. Messein, 1936);

De l'ancêtre mythique au chef moderne: Essai sur la formation et le développement des sociétés et l'exercice du commandement (Paris: Mercure de France, 1943);

Rencontres avec Houston Stewart Chamberlain: Souvenirs et correspondance (Paris: B. Grasset, 1943);

Histoire ancienne du Dieu Jésus, IV: L'Apôtre en face des apôtres (Paris: A. Messein, 1945).

PLAY PRODUCTIONS: *Antonia*, Paris, Théâtre d'Application, 20 April 1891;

Le Chevalier du passé, Paris, Théâtre Moderne, 17 June 1892;

La Fin d'Antonia, Paris, Théâtre Vaudeville, 14 June 1893;

Marthe et Marie, Paris, Théâtre Antoine, 31 May 1913;

Les Epoux d'Heur-le-Port, Paris, Comédie des Champs-Elysées, 3 June 1919;

Le Mystère du Dieu mort et réssuscité, Paris, Théâtre Antoine, 26 May 1923;

Le Retour des enfants prodigues, Paris, Comédie des Champs-Elysées, 9 February 1924;

Le Retour éternel, Paris, Théâtre de l'Atelier, June 1932.

OTHER: Jules Laforgue, *Les Derniers Vers*, edited by Dujardin (Paris, 1890);

Laforgue, *Poésies complètes*, edited by Dujardin (Paris, 1894);

Laforgue, *Suzanne de Callias*, preface by Dujardin (Paris: A. Messein, 1924).

SELECTED PERIODICAL PUBLICATIONS—UNCOLLECTED: "Richard Wagner et la poésie française contemporaine," *Revue de Genève*, 25 July 1886, pp. 252-266;
"Considérations sur l'art wagnérien," *Revue Wagnérienne*, 15 August 1887, pp. 153-188.

Edouard Dujardin is most often remembered as the author of *Les Lauriers sont coupés* (1888; translated as *We'll to the Woods No More*, 1938), a short novel that went virtually unnoticed until more than twenty-five years after its publication, when James Joyce told friends that its use of interior monologue had given him the idea for his own stream-of-consciousness technique. In spite of its original style, the work has aroused surprisingly little interest, and Dujardin's other works have fallen into almost total obscurity. And yet during the last fifteen years of the nineteenth century, he was widely recognized as one of the central figures of the symbolist movement. He experimented more or less successfully with every conceivable genre. He wrote two novels, a collection of short stories, eight plays, and three prose poems. He was among the first French poets to write vers libre. He founded the celebrated *Revue Wagnérienne*, was editor of the equally important *Revue Indépendante*, edited some half-dozen other literary and topical journals, was a literary critic of considerable insight, and, in the second half of his life, became a respected lecturer and authority on early Christianity and Judaism. His works reflect one of the most intriguing and original personalities of his time.

Edouard-Emile-Louis Dujardin was born near Blois, France, on 10 November 1861. When he was six, his parents moved to Rouen, where he attended the lycée Corneille and obtained the *prix d'excellence* at the end of four out of the six years he spent there. At seventeen he went to the lycée Louis-le-Grand in Paris to prepare for the Ecole Normale Supérieure, with the ultimate intention of becoming a teacher. He seems not to have taken his studies very seriously, preferring to spend his time enjoying the latest literary and musical works, with the inevitable result that three years later he failed to achieve the necessary grades. In 1881 he enrolled at the Conservatoire, apparently with the aim of making a career in music; his fellow students there included Claude Debussy and Paul Dukas.

He began to contribute music reviews to the weekly *Renaissance Musicale*, at first anonymously, and, from April 1882 onward, under his own name. In May of that year occurred what was probably the most decisive event of his life. He went to London to review Angelo Neumann's production of Richard Wagner's *The Ring of the Nibelung* (1857-1874), the first in a non-German-speaking country, and returned to Paris an ardent disciple of the German composer. A few months later he attended the premiere of Wagner's *Parsifal* in Bayreuth, Germany, which confirmed his enthusiasm. In 1884, while in Munich to see the *Ring*, he met Wagner's British-born son-in-law, Houston Stewart Chamberlain, and devised the idea of founding a French journal devoted to Wagner.

The first edition of the *Revue Wagnérienne*, with the title written in bold Gothic print, appeared on 8 February 1885. His greater interest in Wagner as poet and philosopher than as musician is the first significant key to his personality. His objective was not so much to foster the composer's work per se as to promulgate the aesthetic theories he understood to underly it. Although both influential and successful during its first two years, the journal gradually ran into financial difficulties, and the last number is dated 15 July 1888.

The other major influence on Dujardin during the 1880s was Stéphane Mallarmé, whose famous *mardis* in the rue de Rome he began to attend in the fall of 1884. His passionate interest in Mallarmé's poetic theories quickly enabled him to assume a central role in the literary circles of the day. The *Revue Indépendante*, which under Félix Fénéon had published some of the key poems of the emergent symbolist school, collapsed in April 1885. Dujardin, who was not yet twenty-five and had only a few months of editorial experience behind him, took it over and edited it from 1886 to 1889. He clearly had a talent for organization and managed to persuade many of the leading writers of the time, including Paul Verlaine, Jules Laforgue, Mallarmé, José Maria de Heredia, Auguste de Villiers de l'Isle-Adam, Paul Bourget, Anatole France, and Joris-Karl Huysmans to contribute to it, usually unpaid. It was, without doubt, the most important organ of the symbolist movement. Works that appeared under its imprint during his editorship include Laforgue's *Moralités légendaires* (1887; translated as *Six Moral Tales from Jules Laforgue*, 1928), the definitive edition of Mallarmé's *L'Après-midi d'un faune* (1876; translated, 1956), and the first collected edition of the latter's *Poésies* (1887).

Dujardin seized the opportunity to publish his own experiments in creative writing. *Les Hantises* (Obsessive Fears, 1886), which first appeared in the *Revue Indépendante* in 1886, is a remarkable collection of thirteen short stories, each of which is dedicated to a leading writer, painter, or other artist of the time. Their idealist aesthetic is encapsulated in the epigraph "Seule vit notre âme" (Only our soul is real), a phrase that he borrowed from an essay on Wagner by Teodor Wyzewa in the *Revue Wagnérienne* (October 1895). In "Le Dharana" (The Dharana), "Un Testament" (A Will), and "L'Apostolat" (The Disciple), a central protagonist's all-consuming obsession leads to his suicide or death by other means. Several stories deal with insanity. In "La Future Démence" (Future Madness), a young man discovers that his mother, whom he had thought dead, is in fact in a lunatic asylum. So afraid is he that madness might be hereditary that he ends by going insane. "Le Kabbaliste: La démence présente" (The Kabbalist: Present Madness) is about a lunatic who insists that, because he at least knows he is mad, he is in effect more sane than those who believe they are mentally well. The most important of the stories as far as Dujardin's subsequent development is concerned is "Histoire d'une journée" (The Story of a Day), which traces a day in the life of Maurice Dupont and which ends with the omniscient narrator's ironic comment on the hero's contentment with the external appearance of things and his own world of dreams: "Il se délectait de paraître; il jouissait de l'illusion" (He delighted in the semblance of things; he was excited by their illusory nature).

A la gloire d'Antonia (To the Glory of Antonia, 1887), a prose poem in eight parts of unequal length that alternate between poetic prose and free verse, initially appeared in the *Vogue* (August 1886). The first of several works that are centrally concerned with the representation of an idealized woman, it consists of descriptions of her as she is perceived by the narrator. Its language is at once sensuous and distant. As Kathleen M. McKilligan writes in *Edouard Dujardin: "Les Lauriers sont coupés" and the Interior Monologue* (1977), "It is as if we are seeing the action on a screen in the narrator's mind, where every irrelevant detail has been filtered out, leaving only the essence of his sensations." Perhaps the most curious feature of this prose poem is Dujardin's self-conscious idealism, the need to distinguish between dream and reality.

The way was prepared for *Les Lauriers sont coupés*, which first appeared in four monthly installments in the *Revue Indépendante* between May and August 1887. This slight novel (it is really a novella) traces six hours in the life of Daniel Prince, a law student, from sunset to midnight of an April evening. It has nine short sections. In the first the hero is walking in the street, thinking of a young chorus girl called Léa d'Arsay, with whom he is having a chaste affair. The second is set in a café; in the third he is on his way to his own home; in the next two he is at home; in the sixth he goes to her apartment; in the seventh section the reader is finally introduced to Léa, by which time one has already guessed that she is leading Prince by the nose. The climax of the novel is a drive in a carriage during which nothing happens. The novel contrasts the hero's adolescent dreams with moments of ironic lucidity, and although it ends with him resolving not to see her again, their parting words ("au revoir") suggest that he is still drawn to her: one thinks of Marcel Proust's Charles Swann.

Dujardin's present reputation rests on this work, largely because James Joyce happened to pick up a copy at a railway kiosk in 1903 and years later, while writing *Ulysses* (1922), sought another copy to reread. He candidly admitted that Dujardin had discovered the interior monologue before him. There is no reason to doubt Joyce's sincerity in this avowal. He clearly admired at least one aspect of this novel, and rightly so. Nothing quite like it had ever been written. It has of course been argued that no one really thinks in the clipped phrases that Dujardin employs; perhaps not, but this does not prevent the work from standing as the first major attempt to reproduce the dilatory nature of mental processes. In juxtaposing Prince's reflections with descriptions that are as neutral as those of a camera lens, Dujardin reinvented the language of fiction.

Prince describes his arrival at a friend's house in the opening pages: "Voici la maison où je dois entrer, où je trouverai quelqu'un; la maison; le vestibule; entrons" (Here is the house that I must enter, where I shall find someone; the house; the entrance; let us go in). The cadences of the phrases have an almost poetic intensity, urging the reader to question each part of the sentence. Why "must" he go in? Whom will he find? What kind of house is it? Is the entrance a portal to an initiation? Why does he use the first person plural?

In section 2 the way in which Prince's thoughts about the other customers in the café are mixed with his reflections about the dinner he is eating is a veritable tour de force. So too is the whole of section 6, in which the short clauses divided by semicolons take one deeper and deeper into Prince's fragile but obsessive mind. Although Joyce admitted his debt to this work, he considerably developed Dujardin's technique. Somewhat surprisingly, however, the influence of this slim volume on subsequent French writers from André Gide to the New Novelists has not been charted. The dry descriptions of Alain Robbe-Grillet's *La Jalousie* (1957; translated as *Jealousy*, 1959), for example, are clearly derived from the interior monologue of Daniel Prince.

Other works that initially appeared in the *Revue Indépendante* include *Litanies* (1888), a short collection of poems complete with piano accompaniment—the only piece of his music Dujardin ever published—and a further extended prose poem, *Pour la vierge du roc ardent* (For the Virgin of the Burning Rock, 1889), a development of his earlier invocation of Antonia. But the *Revue* began to lose money, and Dujardin was soon forced to give it over to another publisher.

Dujardin's private life during these years remains something of a mystery. On 18 November 1886 he married a young woman named Germaine, with Mallarmé and the painter Jean Raffaëlli as witnesses. It was a virtually secret affair, and although he had a son by her, none of his friends seems to have met his wife. It apparently was an unhappy marriage, and the couple probably did not live together for very long. Following the collapse of the *Revue*, Dujardin's life seems to have been peculiarly unsettled, a situation alleviated only by his having inherited some money about this time. It is known that he proposed to Mallarmé's daughter, Geneviève, but nothing came of it. He began to frequent the artists, dancers, and singers who were to be found around Montmartre, in particular Henri de Toul ouse-Lautrec, Yvette Guilbert, and Jane Avril. He became something of a dandy, and in 1891 he published pseudonymously the 290-page *Annuaire du duel, 1880-1889*, a description of various affairs of honor. Just what occasioned this extraordinary work is still unclear.

Of more interest is his excursion into symbolist theater. His first play, *Antonia*, was performed in 1891 at the Théâtre d'Application, with Dujardin acting the male lead and students from the drama course at the Conservatoire in the other parts. The two main characters are called simply L'Amant (The Lover) and L'Amante (The Beloved). The plot is slight and revolves around The Beloved's fall through infidelity. The following year he hired the Théâtre Moderne and mounted a lavish production of a continuation called *Le Chevalier du passé* (The Knight of the Past), to which he invited *le Tout-Paris*. It begins with a courtesan weeping at her fate, which, not surprisingly, caused the audience to burst into laughter during the first act. Unabashed, Dujardin went on and asked the spectators to be more courteous. The play continued with the title hero appearing and "rescuing" the woman from her ways. *La Fin d'Antonia* (The End of Antonia, 1893) completed the trilogy, but it fared little better with the critics. Even Dujardin's friends and supporters had to admit that the play was not entirely successful.

Few symbolist dramas have stood the test of time. It is difficult today to recapture the appeal they had at the end of the nineteenth century. What distinguishes Dujardin's work from similar plays of the time is its overt indebtedness to Wagner. The timelessness of the setting, the bare minimum of plot, the slowness of the action, and the intensity of the dialogue, together with several overt references (for example, flower girls called the Floramyes), all remind one of Wagner. Dujardin's trilogy is a libretto that never found its score. One is reminded that *Pelléas et Mélisande* (1892) is better known today as an opera by Debussy, even as tone poems by Jean Sibelius and Arnold Schönberg, than as a play by Maurice Maeterlinck.

About this time Dujardin appears to have lost most of his money, either as a result of poor theatrical investments or unsuccessful gambling. He always avoided speaking of how he made his living in the fifteen years between 1893 and 1908. The most likely hypothesis is that he did a great deal of editorial work for different newspapers. It is known that he was involved with at least three periodicals at this time: *Fin de Siècle* (which was often involved in legal proceedings for obscenity), the *Journée*, and the *Eclair*. But he once described two of his later plays, *Les Epoux d'Heur-le-Port* (The Couple from Heur-le-Port, 1920) and *Marthe et Marie* (1923), as being autobiographical, and it is not impossible that he also made money in speculating on business ventures

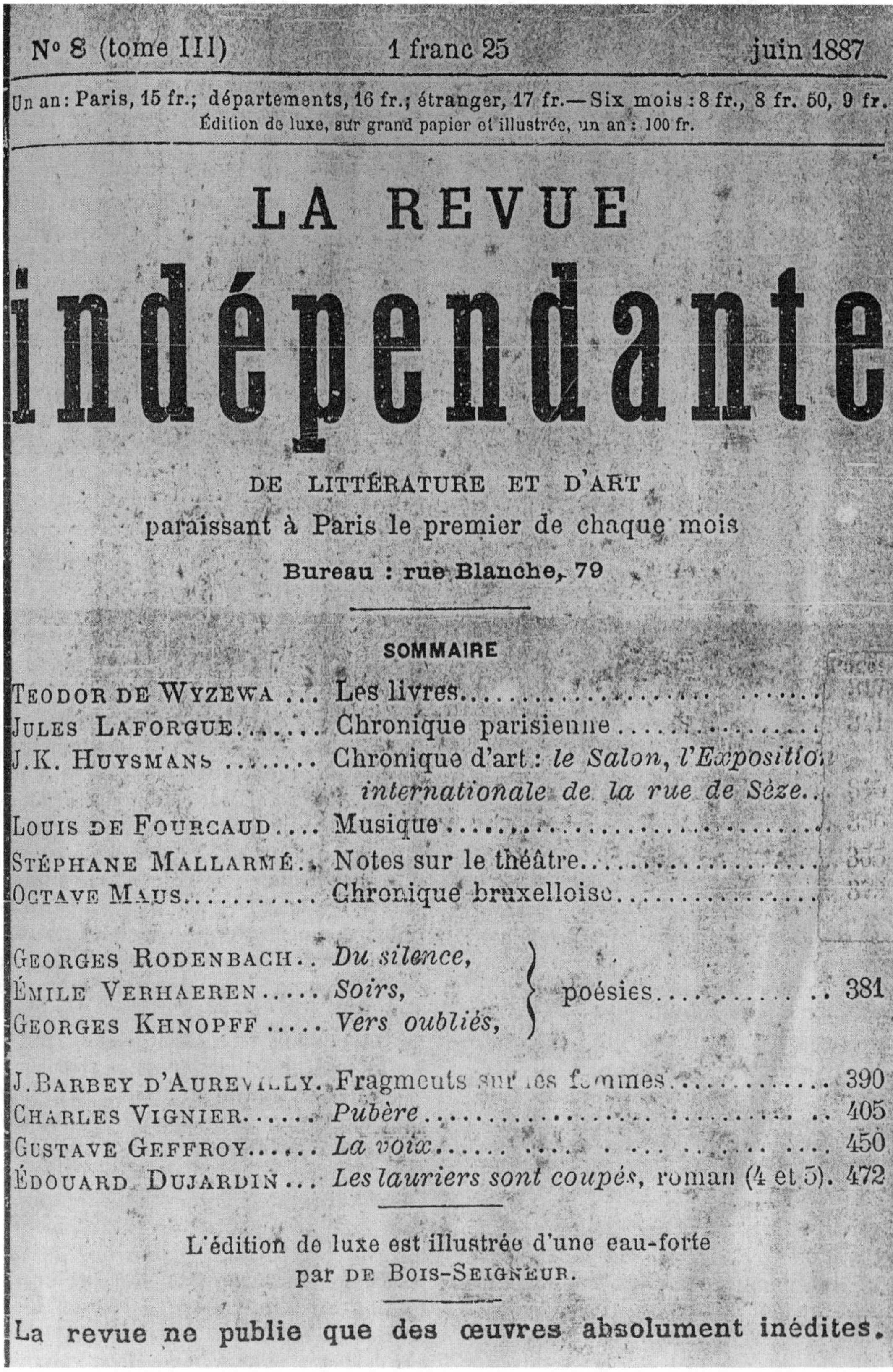

N° 8 (tome III) 1 franc 25 juin 1887

Un an : Paris, 15 fr. ; départements, 16 fr. ; étranger, 17 fr. — Six mois : 8 fr., 8 fr. 50, 9 fr.
Édition de luxe, sur grand papier et illustrée, un an : 100 fr.

LA REVUE indépendante

DE LITTÉRATURE ET D'ART
paraissant à Paris le premier de chaque mois

Bureau : rue Blanche, 79

SOMMAIRE

L'édition de luxe est illustrée d'une eau-forte
par de Bois-Seigneur.

La revue ne publie que des œuvres absolument inédites.

Cover for an issue of one of the journals that Dujardin edited, which includes two installments of his best-known novel in overseas colonies, as does the hero of *Les Epoux*.

After some five years of silence, a second novel appeared in 1898. The hero of *L'Initiation au péché et à l'amour* (The Initiation into Sin and Love) is Marcelin Desruyssarts. The first part of the novel charts the various early influences upon him until he is sixteen. The second deals with his emotional life during his student years in Paris. Too shy and awkward to be able to cement a relationship with any young woman of his own class, he is gradually drawn to prostitutes. In the third part he returns to his family home and resolves to turn over a new leaf. No sooner has he done so than an old friend leads him back to his old ways. He leaves for Paris, where he sets out to seduce a married woman.

In the preface to the 1925 edition of *L'Initiation*, Dujardin was astute enough to acknowledge that the "pseudo-Christian" dualism (sin/love) on which it is based had less intrinsic interest than its psychological implications. He even stated that he had discovered the Oedipus complex before Sigmund Freud, and the claim is not altogether empty. The work provides a striking picture of the fragility of adolescence. Marcelin's veneration of his dead mother, whose "sacrifice" for him (she died in childbirth) he can never forget, his resentment of and hostility toward his father, and his difficulty in establishing relationships during adolescence offer a vivid depiction of the neuroses charted by Freud a few years later. The novel's general relevance, in symbolic terms, is made explicit by Marcelin's final retort to the friend who upbraids him: "Que veux-tu? . . . Pas la taille d'un ascète, encore que bien dégoûté d'être un jouisseur. . . . Comme les autres, tout simplement, un pauvre bougre qui vit la vie" (What do you expect?. . . I'm not made to be a monk, even if I am thoroughly disgusted by my sensual appetites. . . . Like everyone else, I'm just an ordinary chap trying to live his life). Dujardin has been criticized for reverting in this novel to a more conventional narrative technique. The style, however, is entirely appropriate to its subject. For example, the hero's visit to his cousins and attendance at the provincial wedding festivities, where he is almost seduced by the young woman whom he is detailed to look after, are more effective for being described objectively. They also provide a delightfully witty picture of bourgeois and provincial mores at the turn of the century. There can be no doubt about the influence of this *récit* on other writers of the time, including Gide.

Dujardin wrote no more novels. He seems to have been divorced about 1904, and this same year saw him returning to literary activity. He published a short volume of poetry, *Le Délassement du guerrier* (The Warrior's Relaxation, 1904), a title that sums up the collection's overall mood of self-conscious meditation, and, together with Rémy de Gourmont, founded the *Revue des Idées*, a journal of "culture générale" intended as a forum for both sciences and arts. Somehow he managed to acquire a luxurious summer house at Val Changis, near Fontainebleau, which he designed himself with the help of a friend, Louis Anquetin, and here he entertained many visitors, including George Moore, Paul Fort, Dukas, Laurent Tailhade, and Aristide Marie. But he was no longer the same dandy he had been ten years earlier.

He gradually developed an interest in early Christianity, and in his early forties he began to attend a course on the history of religion at the Ecole Pratique des Hautes Etudes. He even learned biblical Hebrew. In 1906 he received his diploma for a thesis, *Les Prédécesseurs de Daniel* (The Predecessors of Daniel), which he published two years later. He also found time to begin a long-term project, *Histoire critique du judaïsme ancien et du christianisme primitif* (A Critical History of Ancient Judaism and Primitive Christianity), the first volume of which was *La Source du fleuve chrétien* (1906; translated as *The Source of the Christian Tradition*, 1911).

After this burst of activity, the following years were surprisingly unproductive. One can assume that he continued working on *Histoire critique*, but the subsequent volumes did not appear. And yet he must have been devoting considerable time to studies in this field, for in 1913 he was appointed to lecture on the history of religions at the Ecole des Hautes Etudes, which he continued to do until 1922. In the introduction to his collected poetry, *Poésies* (1913), he describes its content, together with *La Légende d'Antonia*, as constituting his complete poetic work, which suggests that he intended to devote the rest of his life to the study of early Christianity.

But he was reckoning without World War I, whose atrocities caused him to write poems on the senselessness of war. In 1917 he founded a monthly journal, *Cahiers Idéalistes*, as a mouthpiece for those who were opposed to the war for pacifist or other ideological reasons. This monthly inevitably brought him into conflict with the censors. Many of the poems that he wanted to include had to be withdrawn, and blank pages were a feature of many of its early issues. Even after the Treaty of Versailles, to which he was opposed, he tried to keep the journal going. *Les Epoux d'Heur-le-Port,* which was performed in 1919, was published by the *Cahiers Idéalistes* the following year. His collected war poems appeared as *Mari Magno* (1921), and the first of his religious dramas, *Marthe et Marie,* which was performed the year before the war broke out, was finally published in 1923. But even retitling the journal as the *Cahiers Idéalistes Français* could not arouse greater interest in it, and only by writing most of the articles himself was he able to keep it going until 1926.

During the war another facet of his talent came to light. His first extended piece of literary criticism, with the paradoxical title *De Stéphane Mallarmé au prophète Ezéchiel et Essai d'une théorie du réalisme symbolique* (From Stéphane Mallarmé to the Prophet Ezekiel, with an Essay on the Theory of Symbolic Realism), appeared in 1919. Its basic argument is that a writer must discover a precise formulation for his experience of reality if he is to escape from the dead metaphors of the past and so assert his own voice. His key example is of course Mallarmé, and his analysis of the role of metaphor, rhetoric, and vers libre in symbolist writing is undoubtedly perceptive. The second part of the monograph is taken up with illustrating how classical Greek, and particularly biblical Hebrew, are languages that encourage not metaphor, but a physical, sensual description of experienced reality, and hence represent ideal poetic languages. The Bible, he concludes, is literature. The study ends with an extraordinary prose poem to Joseph Halévy, his professor of Hebrew at the Ecole des Hautes Etudes; its last section is a re-creation of Halévy's deathbed advice to him.

The following year Dujardin was invited to give a short series of lectures at the Sorbonne on the major symbolist poets, and to his credit he recognized the preeminence of Mallarmé, Verlaine, and Arthur Rimbaud. This turned his thoughts to vers libre, and two years later he published another short monograph, *Les Premiers Poètes du vers libre* (The First Poets of Free Verse), whose sharp critical distinctions between *vers régulier, vers libéré,* and vers libre still provide a basis for academic debate. Dujardin was not modest: he frequently alludes to his own works and is at pains to claim that he was among the very first to use vers libre.

This work appeared the same year that *Ulysses* was published in Paris, and Joyce's admiration of Dujardin's first novel, which resulted in its being republished in 1925 with a preface by Valéry Larbaud, raised his reputation for a short while. But the truth is that he had lost touch both with the mood of the country and with new literary trends. Neither of his religious plays of this period, *Le Mystère du Dieu mort et ressuscité* (The Mystery of the God Who Died and Was Resurrected, 1924), which consists of an imaginative account of how the cult of Christianity spread through the Mediterranean world, or *Le Retour des enfants prodigues* (The Return of the Prodigal Children, 1924), which he produced privately, was successful.

Undeterred, he began a long-term project, *Histoire ancienne du Dieu Jésus* (The Early History of the God Jesus), the first volume of which appeared in 1927. In *Le Dieu Jésus: Essai sur les origines et la formation de la légende évangélique* (The God Jesus, An Essay on the Origins and Development of the Evangelical Legend), he argues that Jesus was not so much a historical person as a spiritual being whose origins go back not to Judaism but to prehistoric mystery religions. It is not an altogether original argument—the end of the nineteenth century had seen a flurry of interest in the gnostic aspect of Christianity—but the conviction with which Dujardin argues his position and the elegance of his style make it a study of more than passing interest. Unfortunately, claims such as the identification of Jesus with Baal, or that David worshiped Jesus before being converted to Yahwism, served only to marginalize Dujardin further, making him an even more dubious figure in the eyes of the church and giving him a reputation for crankiness among his literary friends.

Nevertheless, he continued with his plan, bringing out a second volume four years later. *Grandeur et décadence de la critique* (Greatness and Decadence of Biblical Scholarship, 1931), which consists of an analysis of the Pauline epistles, was designed to question orthodox Catholic theology, but it went almost unnoticed. A third volume, *La Première Génération chrétienne* (The First Generation of Christians, 1935), contends that Christianity was born not of the events recounted in the Gospels, but of a vision of Christ seen by Peter on Golgotha, and that the purpose of early Christianity was to reawaken men to a sense of their original brotherhood. In this sense, Dujardin argues, Christianity is revolutionary; he even likens its emergence to the revolutions of 1789 and 1917. It is his most original work, one that seeks an answer not to the historical question "Who was Christ?" but to the much more interesting sociopsychological question "Why did the early Christians come to believe what they did?" This kind of religious polemic has dated badly, but the abridged English translation of volumes one and three, *Ancient History of the God Jesus* (1938), is evidence of the considerable interest it aroused at the time.

Ever since his early enthusiasm for Wagner, Dujardin had been an ardent Germanophile. During the 1930s National Socialism was on the rise in Germany, and he openly admired it. Although history was soon to reveal its dangers, Dujardin was unrepentant. He firmly believed that civilization had become decadent and that only Germany was capable of reinvigorating it. His study of leadership, *De l'ancêtre mythique au chef moderne* (From Our Mythic Ancestors to the Modern Leader, 1943), does not actually name Adolf Hitler, but the implications are clear. Today, of course, it makes embarrassing reading. However, it would be too simplistic just to regret this as an aberration. It is as central to Dujardin's thought as perhaps any of his other works. It reveals yet another aspect of the idealist philosophy that he had espoused since the symbolist period more than a half century earlier. His last two works consolidate the two major trends in his life. *Rencontres avec Houston Stewart Chamberlain* (Meetings with Houston Stewart Chamberlain, 1943) is a montage of annotated letters tracing not only the evolution of a friendship, but also Dujardin's admiration for both Wagner and Germany. Unfortunately, the final volume of *Histoire ancienne du Dieu Jésus, L'Apôtre en face des apôtres* (The Apostle Confronted by the Apostles, 1945) is a sadly hurried conclusion to his extraordinary study of the origins of Christianity.

Dujardin died in Paris on 31 October 1949. His tragedy was that he had long outlived his time. Symbolism and literary idealism were already a thing of the past by the turn of the century, and he never fully realized this. Moreover, for all his interest in sociology, Dujardin never had any understanding of the realities of social processes. To do him justice one must allow one's imagination to leap beyond the literal. Like a great many writers and other artists of his time, Dujardin was obsessed by the imaginal, by the

Dujardin in 1924 (painting by Jacques-Emile Blanche; from the 1925 edition of Les Lauriers sont coupés)

realm of images that everyone mistakes for reality. His insistence that the world that one unwittingly creates with the imagination is more real than so-called reality—that it is indeed the only reality one can ever know—belongs to a major trend of European modernism that has still not been sufficiently investigated. One needs to read his works, even those given a social setting, as an expression of timeless concerns and archetypal interactions. When they are approached as such, one can assess better his achievement. Dujardin's work developed from a consideration of the purely personal concerns of adolescence to an exploration of the most powerful archetype of Western civilization.

In the same way as Benjamin Constant's later works throw considerable light on his only novel, *Adolphe* (1816; translated, 1816), so Dujardin's later studies help one to see what he was trying to achieve in his poetry, plays, and prose fictions. Although his poetry has not survived as well as that of some of his peers, its place in the history of French symbolism is nonetheless assured. His symbolist dramas are unlikely to be frequently performed, but they can still be read as essays in spiritual impressionism. And his two novels, which so well capture the obsessive and dilatory nature of adolescent fantasy, deserve to stand between Eugène Fromentin's *Dominique* (1863; translated, 1932) and Alain-Fournier's *Le Grand Meaulnes* (1913; translated as *The Wanderer*, 1928). They represent a major contribution to an established subgenre. It is time that Dujardin be allowed to emerge from the long shadows cast by Mallarmé and Joyce. He had the courage to experiment and personality enough to be original. His works have considerable intrinsic merit and deserve to be better known.

Bibliography:

Hector Talvert and Joseph Place, *Bibliographie des auteurs modernes de langue française, 1801-1927*, volume 4 (Paris: Chronique des Lettres Françaises, 1933), pp. 403-408.

References:

Theodor W. Alexander and Beatrice W. Alexander, "Schnitzler's *Leutnant Gustl* and Dujardin's *Les Lauriers sont coupés*," *Modern Austrian Literature*, 2, no. 2 (1969): 7-15;

Liisa Dahl, "A Comment on Similarities Between Edouard Dujardin's *monologue intérieur* and James Joyce's Interior Monologue," *Neuphilologische Mitteilungen* 72 (1972): 45-54;

C. D. King, "Edouard Dujardin and the Genesis of the Inner Monologue," *French Studies*, 9, no. 2 (1955): 101-115;

King, "Edouard Dujardin, Inner Monologue and the Stream of Consciousness," *French Studies*, 7, no. 2 (1953): 116-128;

Gabriel Marcel, "*Les Lauriers sont coupés*, par Edouard Dujardin," *Nouvelle Revue Française*, 24, no. 2 (1925): 240-242;

Kathleen M. McKilligan, *Edouard Dujardin: "Les Lauriers sont coupés" and the Interior Monologue* (Hull: University of Hull, 1977);

McKilligan, "Theory and Practice in French Wagnerian Drama: Edouard Dujardin and *La Légende d'Antonia*," *Comparative Drama*, 13, no. 4 (1979-1980): 283-299;

McKilligan, "The Trials and Tribulations of a Symbolist Editor: Edouard Dujardin and the *Revue Indépendante*," *Nottingham French Studies*, 20, no. 2 (1981): 37-50;

Clive Scott, "Edouard Dujardin," in his *Vers Libre: The Emergence of Free Verse in France, 1886-1914* (Oxford: Clarendon, 1990), pp. 145-154;

Bernard C. Swift, "Edouard Dujardin: Central Consciousness in the 'Poetic' Novel," in his "The Real and the Ideal in French Symbolist Prose-Fiction, 1884-1895," Ph.D. dissertation, University of Aberdeen (1971), pp. 144-205;

Frida Weissman, "Edouard Dujardin, le monologue intérieur et Racine," *Revue d'Histoire Littéraire de la France*, 74, no. 3 (May-June 1974): 489-494.

Anatole France
(François-Anatole Thibault)
(16 April 1844 - 12 October 1924)

Catharine Savage Brosman
Tulane University

SELECTED BOOKS: *La Légende de Sainte Radegonde, reine de France* (Paris: France Libraire, 1859);

Alfred de Vigny (Paris: Bachelin-Deflorenne, 1868; revised edition, Paris: C. Aveline, 1923); translated by J. Lewis May and Alfred Allinson in *Marguerite and Count Morin, Deputy, together with Alfred de Vigny and The Path of Glory* (London: John Lane/Bodley Head, 1927);

Les Poèmes dorés (Paris: Alphonse Lemerre, 1873);

Jean Racine (Paris: Alphonse Lemerre, 1874);

Le Livre du bibliophile (Paris: Alphonse Lemerre, 1874);

Racine et Nicole: La querelle des imaginaires (Paris: J. Charavay, 1875);

Les Poèmes de Jules Breton (Paris: J. Charavay aîné, 1875);

Les Noces corinthiennes (Paris: Alphonse Lemerre, 1876);

Jocaste et le Chat maigre (Paris: C. Lévy, 1879); translated by Agnes Farley as *Jocasta and the Famished Cat* (London & New York: John Lane, 1912);

Le Crime de Sylvestre Bonnard, membre de l'Institut (Paris: Calmann-Lévy, 1881); translated by Lafcadio Hearn as *The Crime of Sylvestre Bonnard* (New York: Boni & Liveright, 1890);

Les Désirs de Jean Servien (Paris: Alphonse Lemerre, 1882); translated by Allinson as *The Aspirations of Jean Servien* (London & New York: John Lane, 1912);

Abeille (Paris: Charavay frères, 1883); translated by Peter Wright as *Bee, the Princess of the Dwarfs* (London: Dent / New York: Dutton, 1912);

Le Livre de mon ami (Paris: Calmann-Lévy, 1885); translated by May as *My Friend's Book* (London & New York: John Lane, 1913);

Nos enfants: Scènes de la ville et des champs (Paris: Hachette, 1887); translated as *Our Children: Scenes from the Country and the Town* (New York: Duffield, 1917);

Anatole France, 1893 (photograph by Nadar)

La Vie littéraire, 4 volumes (Paris: Calmann-Lévy, 1888-1892); translated by A. W. Evans as *On Life and Letters*, first series (London & New York: John Lane, 1911); second series translated by Evans (London & New York: John Lane, 1922); third series translated by D. B. Stewart (London & New York: John

Lane, 1922); fourth series translated by Bernard Miall (London: John Lane/Bodley Head / New York: Dodd, Mead, 1924); volume 5 of original (Paris: Calmann-Lévy, 1950);

Balthasar (Paris: Calmann-Lévy, 1889); translated by Mrs. John Lane (London & New York: John Lane, 1909);

Notice historique sur Vivant Denon (Paris: P. Rouquette et fils, 1890);

Thaïs (Paris: Calmann-Lévy, 1890; revised, 1920); translated by A. D. Hall (Chicago: N. C. Smith, 1891);

L'Etui de nacre (Paris: Calmann-Lévy, 1892; revised, 1923); translated by Henri Pène Du Bois as *Tales from a Mother-of-Pearl Casket* (New York: G. H. Richmond, 1896);

L'Elvire de Lamartine: Notes sur M. and Mme Charles (Paris: H. Champion, 1893);

La Rôtisserie de la reine Pédauque (Paris: Calmann-Lévy, 1893; revised, 1921); translated by Jos. A. V. Stritzko as *The Queen Pedauque* (New York: Boni & Liveright, 1923);

Les Opinions de M. Jérôme Coignard (Paris: Calmann-Lévy, 1893; revised, 1925); translated by Mrs. Wilfrid Jackson as *The Opinions of Jérôme Coignard* (London & New York: John Lane, 1913);

Le Lys rouge (Paris: Calmann-Lévy, 1894; revised, 1921); translated as *The Red Lily* (New York: Brentano's, Macaulay, 1898);

Le Jardin d'Epicure (Paris: Calmann-Lévy, 1894?; revised, 1922); translated by Allinson as *The Gardens of Epicurus* (London & New York: John Lane, 1908);

Le Puits de Sainte Claire (Paris: Calmann-Lévy, 1895); translated by Allinson as *The Well of Santa Clara* (Paris: Charles Carrington, 1903); partially republished in *The Human Tragedy* (London & New York: John Lane, 1917);

Poésies: Les Poèmes dorés; Idylles et légendes; Les Noces corinthiennes (Paris: A. Lemerre, 1896);

Séance de l'Académie française du 24 décembre 1896. Discours de réception d'Anatole France (Paris: Calmann-Lévy, 1897);

L'Orme du mail (Paris: Calmann-Lévy, 1897; revised, 1923); translated by M. P. Willcocks as *The Elm-tree on the Mall; A Chronicle of Our Own Times* (London & New York: John Lane, 1910);

Le Mannequin d'osier (Paris: Calmann-Lévy, 1897; revised, 1924); translated by Willcocks as *The Wicker-Work Woman* (London & New York: John Lane, 1910);

Au petit bonheur (Paris: Pierre Dauze, 1898); translated as *One Can But Try* (London: John Lane, 1925);

La Leçon bien apprise (Paris, 1898);

L'Anneau d'améthyste (Paris: Calmann-Lévy, 1899); translated by B. Drillien as *The Amethyst Ring* (London & New York: John Lane, 1919);

Pierre Nozière (Paris: A. Lemerre, 1899); translated by May (London & New York: John Lane, 1916);

Filles et garçons: Scènes de la ville et des champs (Paris: Hachette, 1900?); translated as *Girls and Boys: Scenes from the Country and the Town* (New York: Duffield, 1913);

Clio (Paris: Calmann-Lévy, 1900); translated by Winifred Stephens (London: John Lane / New York: Dodd, Mead, 1922);

Jean Gutenberg (Paris: E. Pelletan, 1900);

L'Affaire Crainquebille (Paris: E. Pelletan, 1901); translated by Stephens in *Crainquebille, Putois, Riquet and Other Profitable Tales* (London: John Lane, 1915);

Monsieur Bergeret à Paris (Paris: Calmann-Lévy, 1901); translated by Drillien as *Monsieur Bergeret in Paris* (London & New York: John Lane, 1921);

Funérailles d'Emile Zola (Paris: E. Pelletan, 1902);

Opinions sociales (Paris: G. Bellais, 1902);

Crainquebille: Pièce en trois tableaux (Paris: Calmann-Lévy, 1903); translated by Barrett H. Clark as *Crainquebille* (New York: Samuel French, 1915); translated by Stephens (New York: Dodd, Mead, 1925);

Discours prononcé à l'inauguration de la statue d'Ernest Renan à Tréguier (Paris: Calmann-Lévy, 1903);

Histoire comique (Paris: Calmann-Lévy, 1903; enlarged, 1930); translated by Charles E. Roche as *A Mummer's Tale* (New York: Dodd, Mead, 1908);

Le Parti noir (Paris: Société Nouvelle de Librairie et d'Edition, 1903);

L'Eglise et la république (Paris: E. Pelletan, 1904);

Sur la pierre blanche (Paris: Calmann-Lévy, 1905); translated by Roche as *The White Stone* (London & New York: John Lane, 1910);

Vers les temps meilleurs (Paris: E. Pelletan, 1906); translated by May as *The Unrisen Dawn* (London: John Lane / New York: Dodd, Mead, 1928); original enlarged as *Vers les temps meilleurs: Trente ans de vie sociale*, 3 volumes, edit-

Léontine Arman de Caillavet, circa 1883. Her affair with France lasted twenty-five years.

ed by Claude Aveline (Paris: Emile-Paul, 1949); revised edition, 4 volumes (Paris: Cercle du Bibliophile, 1970);

Les Contes de Jacques Tournebroche (Paris: Calmann-Lévy, 1908); translated by Allinson as *The Merrie Tales of Jacques Tournebroche* (London: John Lane / New York: Dodd, Mead, 1909);

Vie de Jeanne d'Arc, 2 volumes (Paris: Calmann-Lévy, 1908); translated by Stephens as *Joan of Arc* (London & New York: John Lane, 1908);

La Descente de Marbode aux enfers (Paris, 1908);

L'Ile des pingouins (Paris: Calmann-Lévy, 1908); translated as *Penguin Island* (New York: Grosset & Dunlap, 1909);

Le Tombeau de Molière (Paris: Imprimerie Nationale, 1908);

Rabelais (Paris: Calmann-Lévy, 1909); translated by Ernest Boyd (New York: Holt, 1929);

Les Sept Femmes de la Barbe-Bleue et autres contes merveilleux (Paris: Calmann-Lévy, 1909); translated by Stewart as *The Seven Wives of Bluebeard and Other Marvellous Tales* (London & New York: John Lane, 1920);

L'Uruguay et ses progrès (Montevideo: Tipografía y Litografía Oriental, 1909);

Aux étudiants (Paris: E. Pelletan, 1910);

Deux discours sur Tolstoï (Paris: "L'Emancipatrice," 1911);

Les Dieux ont soif (New York: Macmillan, 1912; Paris: Calmann-Lévy, 1912?); translated by Allinson as *The Gods Are Athirst* (London & New York: John Lane, 1913);

La Comédie de celui qui épousa une femme muette (Abbeville: F. Paillart / Paris: Calmann-Lévy, Edouard Champion, 1912); translated by Curtis Hidden Page as *The Man Who Married a Dumb Wife* (New York: John Lane, 1915);

Le Génie latin (Paris: A. Lemerre, 1913; revised edition, Paris: Calmann-Lévy, 1917); translated by Wilfrid S. Jackson as *The Latin Genius* (London: John Lane, 1924);

La Révolte des anges (Paris: Calmann-Lévy, 1914); translated by Mrs. Wilfrid Jackson as *The Revolt of the Angels* (London & New York: John Lane, 1914);

Sur la voie glorieuse (Paris: E. Champion, 1915; enlarged, 1915); translated by Allinson as *The*

Path of Glory (London & New York: John Lane, 1916);
Ce que disent nos morts (Paris: R. Helleu, 1916);
Le Crime de Sylvestre Bonnard [stage version] (Paris: Calmann-Lévy, 1918);
Le Petit Pierre (Paris: Calmann-Lévy, 1918; revised, 1928); translated by May as *Little Pierre* (London & New York: John Lane, 1920);
Marguerite (Paris: A. Coq, 1920); translated by May (London & New York: John Lane, 1921);
Stendhal (Abbeville: F. Paillart, 1920); translated by May (London, 1926);
Histoire contemporaine, 4 volumes (Paris: Calmann-Lévy, 1920-1921)—comprises volume 1: *L'Orme du mail*; volume 2: *Le Mannequin d'osier*; volume 3: *L'Anneau d'améthyste*; volume 4: *Monsieur Bergeret à Paris*;
Le Comte Morin député (Paris: Chez Mornay, 1921); translated by May as *Count Morin, Deputy* (London: John Lane, 1921);
Les Matinées de la Villa Saïd: Propos d'Anatole France, edited by Paul Gsell (Paris: Grasset, 1921); translated by Boyd as *The Opinions of Anatole France* (New York: Knopf, 1922);
Le Miracle de la pie (Paris: F. Ferroud, 1921);
La Vie en fleur (Paris: Calmann-Lévy, 1922); translated by May as *The Bloom of Life* (New York: Dodd, Mead, 1923);
Le Chanteur de Kymé (Paris: Ferroud, 1923);
Frère Joconde (Paris: A. Ferroud/J. Ferroud, 1923);
Mademoiselle Roxane (Paris: F. Ferroud, 1923);
Dernières pages inédites d'Anatole France, edited by Michel Corday (Paris: Calmann-Lévy, 1925);
Les Noces corinthiennes: Poème dramatique en trois parties (Paris: A. Ferroud/F. Ferroud, 1926); translated by Wilfrid Jackson and Emilie Jackson in *The Bride of Corinth* (London: John Lane / New York: Dodd, Mead, 1924);
Prefaces, Introductions, and Other Uncollected Papers by Anatole France, translated by May (London: John Lane, 1927; New York: Dodd, Mead, 1928);
Itinéraire de Paris à Buenos-Ayres (Paris: G. Gres et Cie, 1927);
Le Café Procope (Paris: Au dépens d'un amateur, 1928);
Le Château de Vaux-le-Vicomte (Paris: Calmann-Lévy, 1933); translated by Stephens in *Clio and The Château de Vaux-le-Vicomte* (London: John Lane, 1923).

Collections: *The Works of Anatole France in an English Translation*, 36 volumes, edited by Frederick Chapman, James Lewis May, and Bernard Miall (London & New York: John Lane, 1909-1926);
The Works, 30 volumes (New York: G. Wells, 1918-1924);
Œuvres complètes illustrées, 25 volumes, edited by Claude Aveline and Léon Carias (Paris: Calmann-Lévy, 1925-1935);
Works, 10 volumes (New York: Wise, 1930);
Œuvres complètes, 29 volumes, edited by Jacques Suffel (Geneva: Edito Service, 1968-1971);
Œuvres, 2 volumes to date, edited by Marie-Claire Bancquart (Paris: Gallimard, Bibliothèque de la Pléiade, 1984-).

PLAY PRODUCTIONS: *Le Lys rouge*, Paris, Théâtre du Vaudeville, 25 February 1899;
Les Noces corinthiennes, Paris, Théâtre de l'Odéon, 30 January 1902;
Crainquebille, Paris, Théâtre de la Renaissance, 28 March 1903;
Le Mannequin d'osier, Paris, Théâtre de la Renaissance, 22 March 1904;
Au petit bonheur, Paris, Théâtre de la Renaissance, 2 February 1906;
La Comédie de celui qui épousa une femme muette, Paris, Café Voltaire, 21 March 1912;
Les Noces corinthiennes (opera), music by Henri Busser, Paris, Opéra-Comique, 10 May 1922.

OTHER: *Les Œuvres de J.-B. P. Molière*, with a life of Molière, variants, and glossary by France (Paris: Alphonse Lemerre, 1876);
Bernardin de St.-Pierre, *Paul et Virginie*, notice and notes by France (Paris: Alphonse Lemerre, 1877);
Xavier de Maistre, *Voyage autour de ma chambre*, notice by France (Paris: Alphonse Lemerre, 1877);
Marquis de Sade, *Dorci ou la bizarrerie du sort*, notice by France (Paris: Charavay frères, 1881);
Mme de La Fayette, *L'Histoire d'Henriette d'Angleterre*, preface by France (Paris: Charavay, 1882);
Jean de La Fontaine, *Fables*, notice and notes by France (Paris: Alphonse Lemerre, 1883);
Mme de La Fayette, *La Princesse de Clèves*, preface by France (Paris: Conquet, 1889);
Marcel Proust, *Les Plaisirs et les jours*, preface by France (Paris: Calmann-Lévy, 1896);
Emile Combes, *Une Campagne laïque (1902-1903)*, preface by France (Paris: H. Simonis Empis, 1904);

Charles Rappoport, *Jean Jaurès, l'homme, le penseur, le socialiste,* preface by France (Paris: Rouvière, 1915);

Hommage à l'Arménie, text by France (Paris: E. Leroux, 1919);

Paul Louis Couchoud, *Japanese Impressions,* translated by Frances Rumsey, preface by France (London & New York: John Lane, 1921);

"Le Mobilier en bois de rose," attributed to France, *Revue France-Hongrie,* 71 (November 1961): 63-80; 72 (December 1961): 37-64.

In 1927 poet Paul Valéry delivered his *discours de réception,* or initial speech, to the Académie Française after being elected two years earlier to fill the seat of Anatole France, who had died in October 1924. Remembering and resenting the fact that, in 1875, as an editorial reader for the third series of the famous poetry anthologies entitled *Le Parnasse contemporain,* France had excluded Stéphane Mallarmé's hermetic but very beautiful *L'Après-midi d'un faune* (1876; translated, 1956), Valéry, while following the convention according to which the new academician pays homage to his predecessor, damned France with somewhat ambiguous, if not faint, praise, suggesting in particular that his grace, clarity, and ease of style disguised superficiality of content; moreover, while affecting to speak of him, Valéry avoided all mention of his name. In 1924, on the occasion of France's death, the surrealists—Louis Aragon, André Breton, Pierre Drieu La Rochelle, Paul Eluard, and others—disseminated a pamphlet against him, called "Un Cadavre" (A Corpse), in which they denounced the values he represented—skepticism, irony, French wit—and accused him, in essence, of having been a walking corpse. In 1916 André Gide had already remarked that France's work, while elegant and subtle, was "sans inquiétude" (without anxiety), meaning that he is too clear, too easily understood, never disturbing his readers—the contrary of the ideal that Gide set for himself and, implicitly, for others.

These judgments illustrate how, by the mid 1920s, Anatole France's position as a literary master was already slipping, although biographical studies began to appear in that decade, and his works had been translated into at least a dozen languages, including Esperanto, and were still widely popular. English-speaking readers could buy his works in a series published by John Lane, and several translations appeared in the Modern Library series, with introductions by such literary notables as James Branch Cabell and Lafcadio Hearn. Despite the pronouncements of Gide and the surrealists, few at that time must have divined that, some decades later, France's reputation would plummet, reaching its nadir after mid century. The reasons for this decline are now apparent. Although France lived nearly a quarter of the way through the new century, his aesthetic was that of the previous century, foreign to the modernism that marked the prose of the new age. In poetry, after French symbolism had triumphed with Mallarmé and reached its most classic phase in the work of Valéry, and surrealism had imposed itself on younger writers as a radical movement, France's own poetic values,

Drawing of France on the cover of the journal that included a tribute by Paul Verlaine

formed under Parnassian masters, appeared entirely passé. As a social critic, to the proponents of *littérature engagée* (committed literature) and left-wing activism between the wars and beyond, his criticisms of dominant social institutions and the conservative thought behind them seemed timid; in 1924 the Communist Henri Barbusse, in his magazine *Clarté,* urged his followers to keep their distance from the Master.

Moreover, France's brand of intellectual skepticism and Epicureanism has not set well generally with readers and critics of the mid and late twentieth century, as the humanism of the Enlightenment, to which he remained faithful, has been called into question, and the moderate literary values of ornamental beauty in form and critical reason in substance have been widely discarded in favor of radical positions, both literary and political—formalism, anarchism, Marxism, militant Catholicism. As Breton put it, "L'attitude réaliste, inspirée du positivisme, de Saint-Thomas à Anatole France, m'a bien l'air hostile à tout essor intellectuel et moral" (The realistic attitude, inspired by positivism, from Saint Thomas to Anatole France, seems to me hostile to all intellectual and moral development).

Although some substantial critical works, including university theses, appeared on France up to and through the 1960s, for nearly a score of years thereafter no major scholarship was devoted to him, and his works disappeared from anthologies and school syllabi. Thanks in great part to the scholarly efforts of Marie-Claire Bancquart, the 1980s saw a modest resurgence of work on him, with her biography, *Anatole France: Un sceptique passionné* (Anatole France: A Passionate Skeptic, 1984), and her thoroughly annotated edition, now in progress, of his major works in Gallimard's Bibliothèque de la Pléiade. Even so, current critics, suspicious of any work that appeals to reason and still widely influenced by deconstructionism, which calls into question the possibility of literary meaning, have not yet returned to his work to discover its hidden subversiveness and thus its modernity, as they have for Honoré de Balzac and Gustave Flaubert; and France thus remains marginalized in the present literary canon. Almost surely, however, there will be discerning readers who will discover in France's brilliant prose windows onto the violent and turbulent world of nineteenth-century Europe that gave rise to the twentieth century.

For France was not merely the superficial observer, the Epicurean, the facile writer for which he has been taken. He said of himself that he was too bold for his own time but later would appear timid—surely the fate of moderates and evolutionaries, as opposed to revolutionaries. In the French tradition, at least, to adopt reason, with a goodly dose of skepticism, as a guide to living and thinking is thoroughly honorable and far from mindless: Michel Eyquem de Montaigne, Voltaire, and Denis Diderot illustrate how searching the rationalist position can be. Furthermore, in an age when scientific positivism, especially in the Darwinian form, was received doctrine for many thinkers and writers, France, although eschewing religious dogma, was nearly as suspicious of the dogmatic claims of science, at least in its most reductionist form, and in his works he made ample room for human feeling and intuition as well as freedom. To the contention that "l'homme est fait pour comprendre" (man is created to understand), Balthasar, in the story of the same name, replies, "Il est fait pour aimer" (He is made for love). In fact France seems to suggest that sentiment becomes all the more important as developments in knowledge indicate that one can never be sure of anything.

From this intellectual position, and using talents that his contemporaries recognized as extraordinary, France produced a body of literature that is truly sui generis. His fiction is not entirely distant from the realist current, especially in works such as *Les Désirs de Jean Servien* (1882; translated as *The Aspirations of Jean Servien,* 1912) and *Le Lys rouge* (1894; translated as *The Red Lily,* 1898), but he eschewed the naturalist current of realism because of its preoccupation with the sordid and its scientific pretensions. (He was also singularly lacking in admiration for the naturalist writers—Edmond and Jules de Goncourt, who had treated him with condescension, and Emile Zola, whose novel *La Terre* [translated as *The Soil,* 1888] he criticized in 1887 but whom, however, he later learned to appreciate at his just worth.) Alongside elements of naturalism, France's work displays a noticeable vein of sentimentalism, which certainly attracted many readers. He also has much in common with the decadents of the last two decades of the century, cultivating, like Maurice Barrès, Joris-Karl Huysmans, and Pierre Louÿs, a sensuous prose and often choosing his topics from the legends or history of periods in which old worlds were ending—in particular, the late Hellenic period and the transitional time between pagan and Christian Rome. Irony, that marker of modern literature, is rarely far below the surface in his prose, but it is less the deep self-doubt and self-hatred visible in the works of Charles Baudelaire and Flaubert or the existentialist irony of Søren Kierkegaard and Albert Camus than a cultural irony—the understanding that all customs and all history are subject to revision, and that human perspective is necessarily limited, subjective.

François-Anatole Thibault was born in Paris on 16 April 1844, also the birth year of the poet Paul Verlaine. His father, François-Noël Thibault, had become a bookseller and minor publisher after having learned to read, it would appear, only as an adult, in the service of his military (and, later, civil) patron, Count Henri de La Bédoyère. Following the custom of the Anjou region from which he came, Noël Thibault had shortened his first name to "France"; he then called his bookshop "France-Thibault," and by 1844 his imprint was simply "Noël France" or "France." Anatole himself, while baptized under the name Thibault, was sometimes known as "Anatole France" as early as grammar school. His choice of name under which to write and indeed to live as an adult should hence be considered only a half-pseudonym. Anatole's mother, née Antoinette Galas, had married Noël France in 1840, having been widowed sometime before. She was the illegitimate offspring of a miller's daughter, who married shortly after Antoinette's birth, was widowed, and remarried; the second stepfather, Jean-Pierre Dufour, an apparently charming but ne'er-do-well figure, remained, until his death in 1865, a drain on his immediate family and then on the family of his son-in-law, Noël. Despite the financial burden imposed for decades on the Thibault household by him and his impoverished wife, Anatole perceived his eccentricities as charming; in his writings they appear in various fictional guises, including that of Tudesco in *Les Désirs de Jean Servien.*

Anatole grew up surrounded by books, and his early life was molded by the atmosphere of his father's shop on the quay overlooking the Seine. To it writers repaired frequently to exchange ideas, as in the coffeehouses of the previous century. At the age of eight Anatole composed for his mother a collection of thoughts and maxims. He also began for her a translation of Virgil's first eclogue, complete with notes and a preface explaining the circumstances in which the poet was led to celebrate Augustus in verse. At ten he thought that nothing in life was more beautiful than correcting proofs. Even if he later came to recognize the inadequacies of his autodidactic father's learning, books formed Anatole's mind, and he would always remain not quite a bookish man but a learned one, a devourer (as well as a copious producer) of the printed page, embracing both classics and moderns and accumulating a vast store of knowledge. In an entirely different way from Mallarmé, France is a preeminent example of the late-nineteenth-century *homme de lettres,* one who lived by and for books and for whom humanistic learning was essential to life.

Noël was not, however, the boy's favorite parent. Without conceiving for his father the black hatred Stendhal felt toward his, Anatole experienced, it would seem, considerable alienation from Noël. "En toutes choses, d'instinct, je m'opposais à lui" (I was opposed to him in everything, instinctively). Noël's royalist loyalties led his son to adopt republican sympathies very early, before he had given much thought to politics; and it is perhaps as a reaction against his father that he refused to adopt the same livelihood, insisting instead, over paternal objections, upon pursuing a writer's career. Certainly Anatole was closer to his mother and, as her only child, was showered with affection. This relationship is painted with tenderness in the autobiographical *Le Livre de mon ami* (1885; translated as *My Friend's Book,* 1913), in which Noël is transformed into a doctor but Antoinette appears much as she apparently was. It has been pointed out that this tender, intimate relationship between son and mother is a foreshadowing of that depicted by one of France's emulators, Marcel Proust, who almost surely found in *Le Livre de mon ami* encouragement for his own study of a close mother-son relationship and who, at least at the outset of his career, was much influenced by France's prose style (the model, it is generally believed, for that of the fictitious writer Bergotte in Proust's *Du côté de chez Swann* [1913; translated as *Swann's Way,* 1922]).

Anatole's father and mother were both traditionalists; the mother attended Mass regularly. Anatole was probably sensitive to the beauty of services, for aesthetic appreciation of the liturgy is expressed by characters who are his spokesmen, but he may have lost his faith early, as his hero Jean Servien loses it, after the disappointment of his First Communion. In any case, as an adult France can in no way be considered a believer, and his rejection of the church, its dogmas, and its influence is aggressive enough to be termed anticlericalism.

Another source of resentment for the boy, besides the paternal figure, was the Collège Saint-Stanislas, to which he was sent in 1855 after two years at the Institution Sainte-Marie. While the priests were not unkind, nor indifferent to belles lettres—several had humanistic leanings, and the director even wrote edifying dramas—Anatole did not flourish under their discipline; his performance received praise and prizes only rarely, when he was taken with the topic of his lessons. Moreover, he felt very much at a disadvantage with respect to the other boys, nearly all from much wealthier and socially prominent households. His humiliation at having to carry an old portfolio of his father's instead of a proper bookbag is recorded in *Le Livre de mon ami.* A certain awkwardness in his personality, sometimes called obsequiousness, noticeable until he achieved renown as a writer, can perhaps be traced to the feeling of inferiority that marked his childhood.

Anatole left Saint-Stanislas in 1862, presumably to study independently. Upon receiving his baccalaureate somewhat tardily in 1864, he began earning money from various publishers, including a friend of his father, Jacques Charavay, and embarked on his own writing career via journalism (especially in bibliophilic publications) and poetry. A short stint as a proctor in a lycée did not turn out well, if one is to believe its fictional transposition in *Les Désirs de Jean Servien.* Finding a position with Alphonse Lemerre improved France's fortunes considerably, for Lemerre shortly made him a reader for *Le Parnasse contemporain,* in the second series of which France's own poetry was included. At that stage it would have appeared that the young writer would become chiefly a poet, modeling his work on that of the older Parnassians, especially Charles-Marie-René Leconte de Lisle, known for his impassive, chiseled verse (a reaction against the excesses of Romantic self-expression) and his cult of antiquity.

France had been writing verse since childhood; in 1864 he succeeded in passing off lines by his own hand as work by André Chénier, a poet of the revolutionary period. Indeed, France's early poetry stands up well in comparison to that of other writers of the mid nineteenth century, a fact that speaks to his considerable talents. James Lewis May, the author of an early biography of the writer, asserted that "the Anatole France who will outlive the rest . . . is France the poet." However, the explosion and disintegration of poetic forms in the twentieth century and the resurgence of a poetry of explicit self-expression have rendered Parnassian poetic values almost antiquarian. To be noted in France's verse is a strong personal tone, despite Parnassian objectivity, as well as themes and motifs to which he returned later, such as the figure of Thaïs.

Much of his poetry was nourished by personal experience, especially the anguish of unrequited love. From his adolescence he had been singularly unsuccessful with women, from the sisters of family acquaintances to Nina de Callias, a bluestocking, and the actress Elise Devoyod, for whom he harbored for years a frustrated passion. The figure of the actress is one of the constants of his *imaginaire.* In real life, when he was past sixty, he had a liaison with a performer touring with the Comédie Française; and actresses appear in several of his works, notably *Histoire comique* (1903; translated as *A Mummer's Tale,* 1908), inspired by the memoirs of Mlle Clairon, a celebrated eighteenth-century actress.

As France was developing as a poet and publishing verse in collections and newspapers, he turned to criticism. His 1868 book on Alfred de Vigny is the first product of his rich critical vein. While somewhat derivative and now thoroughly outdated, the book was for its time a sensitive, if rambling, study of the only would-be impassive and stoic among the Romantics, the poet for whom the phrase "ivory tower" was coined by Charles-Augustin Sainte-Beuve. The book is a tentative instance of the critical style France would later perfect and make famous in his many prefaces and regular columns of literary and cultural criticism in the *Univers Illustré* (1883-1896), the *Temps* (1886-1893), the *Echo de Paris* (1892-1899), and the *Figaro* (1899-1901). What he wished to do as a critic can be understood from his celebrated formula defining a critic's function as that of recounting "les aventures de son âme au milieu des chefs-d'œuvre" (the adventures of one's soul amid masterpieces). His style was labeled "impressionist" by the then-authoritative critic Ferdinand Brunetière, who intended the term pejoratively because he believed in objective standards for literary judgment and scorned all those who, like France, thought all aesthetic appreciation was subjective and one might as well acknowledge it. Modern critics, of course, have sided with France.

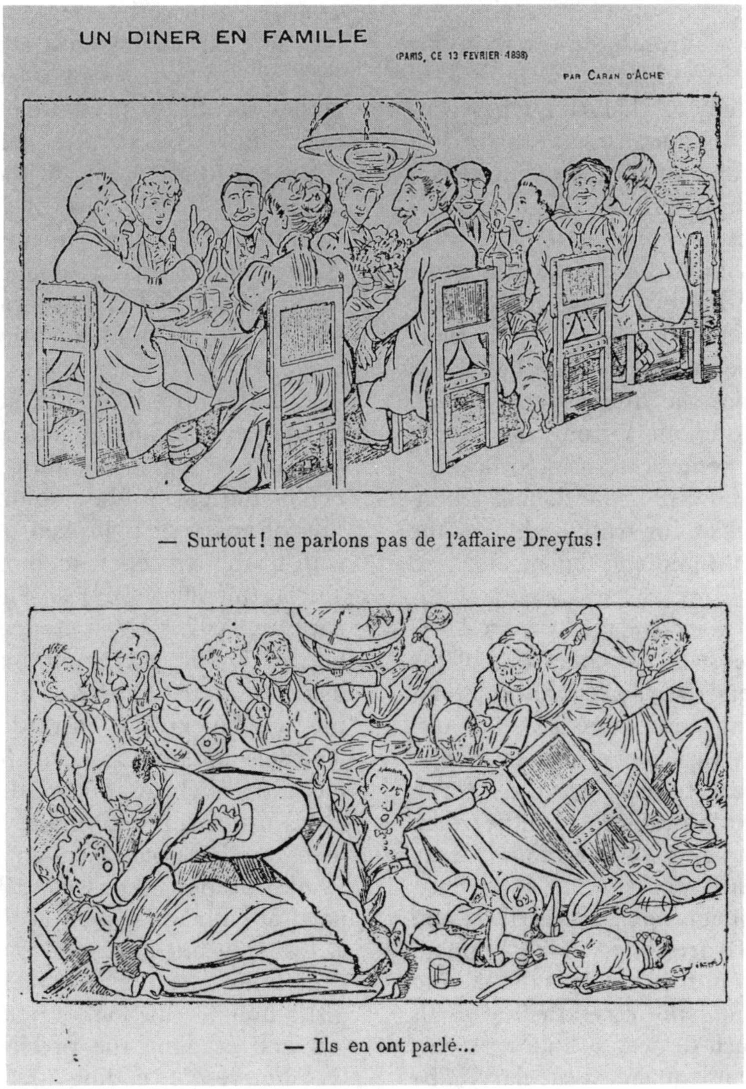

"A Family Dinner," the best-known cartoon of the Dreyfus Affair, which appeared in the Figaro, *14 February 1898 (drawing by Caran d'Ache). The caption for the first panel is "Above all, let us not speak of the Dreyfus Affair!" The caption for the second panel is "They spoke about it."*

By the mid 1870s France had not yet published any fiction, but he was well known in several Parisian literary circles, such as the salon of Leconte de Lisle and the group of writers, including Guy de Maupassant, who gathered at the "Dîners du Pot-au-Feu." To augment his small writing income (mostly from prefaces, encyclopedia articles, and ghost work for Lemerre), which left him dependent often upon his parents for lodging, he finally obtained employment in 1876 at the library of the Senate, after having sought a position ten years before. In 1877 he married Valérie Guérin de Sauville, thirteen years younger than he, in what was at least a half-arranged match. The union produced one daughter, Suzanne (born in 1881), on whom France long doted. But France and Valérie apparently had little in common besides their daughter, and the marriage was not a happy one. It was dissolved by divorce in 1893.

France's first published fiction, *Jocaste,* appeared in 1878 in magazine form, like most of his other fiction, then was collected with *Le Chat maigre* (translated together as *Jocasta and the Famished Cat,* 1912) the following year. Whereas many writers begin by publishing early novels, usually autobiographical, that are weak in craft, substance, or both, France's first published fiction is a mature and nonsubjective work in which the command of language and composition are impressive, the character portraits vigorous and perceptive, and the plot designed for the maximum effect on nineteenth-century readers craving sensation. While short, the novel has more than one vein: it is realistic in its emphasis on the role of money and the creation of character types worthy of Balzac; it is Romantic in its portrait of mute, idealized love and of the powerful effects of unexpressed feelings; it is Gothic in its mystery elements (a deformed and vaguely threatening servant slowly poisons his master and then murders a crafty old forger); and it is melodramatic in the fate of its characters (the heroine hangs herself, and the man who loved her, René Longuemare, welcomes the disease that will kill him). Even France's trademark irony and skepticism are not lacking. René professes a radical scientism that is nearly nihilistic, questioning all enterprises and possibilities for truth—while at the same time harboring a timid and tender idealized love.

The title *Le Chat maigre* refers to a Latin Quarter bar where most of the characters of the story meet—characters to whom France, in his 1879 preface, refers as "fous" (lunatics). The disquieting eccentricities that mark certain characters in *Jocaste* reappear here in harmless form, and the tone is generally humorous, rather than tragic. In a tradition well established since Henry Murger and other early realists, the author depicts a Left Bank bohemia of poets, artists, and ne'er-do-wells, to which are added a Haitian politician and his son. The author's style is directed in part toward heightening the eccentricities of his characters through such devices as antithesis, sarcasm, juxtaposition, and quaint vocabulary. The following is a morning scene in the lodgings of a tutor whose opinion of himself is in exact inverse proportion to his worth: "L'homme supérieur, réveillé en sursaut, avait enfourché à la hâte un pantalon crotté d'une boue très ancienne qui s'écaillait. Un jour verdâtre, épuisé par de nombreux ricochets, filtrait péniblement à travers les vitres sales" (The superior man, awakened in a start, had hastily pulled on trousers dirtied with very old mud that was coming off in flakes. A greenish light, exhausted by numerous bends, filtered with difficulty through the dirty panes). Despite this scene of misery, the ending of the story, which brings together the young Creole and the girl he has worshiped and leaves the rest of *la bohème* to its incorrigible ways, imparts a sense of human freedom, rather than fatality.

The same is true for France's next fiction, *Le Crime de Sylvestre Bonnard* (1881; translated as *The Crime of Sylvestre Bonnard,* 1890), which was awarded a prize by the Académie Française and was long one of his most admired books. It consists of two sections of unequal length, tied together only by the presence of the eponymous narrator. But the character of the latter is quite sufficient to give unity to the text. France's hero is, as the second part of the title indicates, a "membre de l'Institut" (member of the French Institute, with its five academies). A retired professor and book and manuscript collector, he resembles his creator in his timidity and his love of old texts.

In the first section he sends a Christmas gift of firewood, including "une vraie bûche de Noël" (a real Yule log), to a young couple living in misery in the garret above him. Otherwise his routine of research is broken only by conversations with his housekeeper, memories of visits to Uncle Victor (modeled on Jean-Pierre Dufour), and a trip to Sicily to visit a dealer from whom he hopes to buy a coveted manuscript. When he learns that the dealer, who had promised him the parchment, has instead given it to his son, who sells antiques in Paris, Bonnard is both furious and acutely disappointed. His travels are, however, made more pleasant by three encounters with a charming Parisian and her husband, Prince Trépof, a collector. Back in Paris, Bonnard attends an auction at which the manuscript is for sale, but he cannot outbid an anonymous competitor. At the year's end, he receives as a gift a hollow Yule log, overflowing with fresh violets and cradling the precious manuscript. This O. Henryesque ending has been made possible by Princess Trépof, who is none other than the woman in the garret, widowed and remarried into wealth; having learned in Sicily of Bonnard's disappointment, she has repaid her benefactor generously, with the added drama of surprise.

This sentimental ending fits the character of Bonnard—good-hearted, easily moved, unfit for practical life. In the second section of the book, he again exercises charity, this time toward Jeanne, the orphaned granddaughter of a woman he had once loved, with whose family his own had quarreled, thus preventing their marriage. His efforts to protect the girl and favor her education lead to involvements with a dishonest notary and a mean-spirited, frustrated, calculating headmistress, who attempts to maneuver Bonnard into marriage and, when she fails, turns her ire on the girl. The description of the school and schoolmistress and the episode in which Bonnard successfully spirits Jeanne away are both

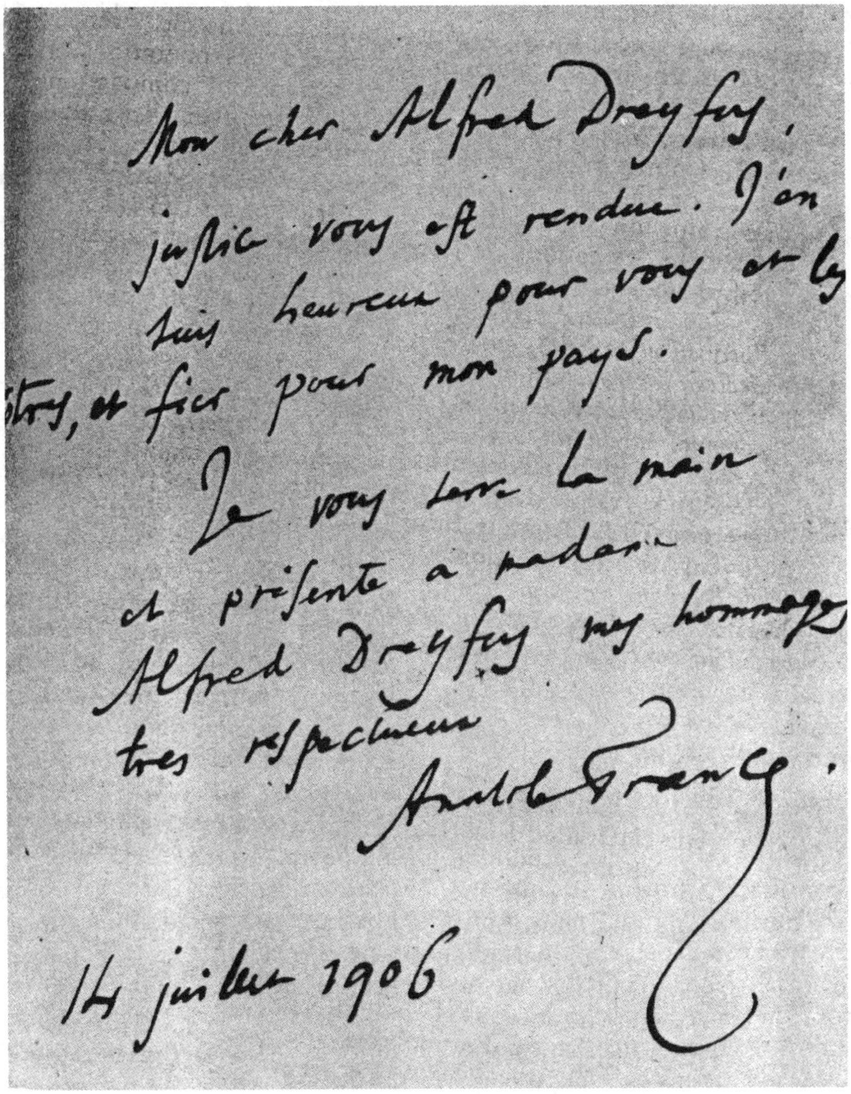

Mon cher Alfred Dreyfus,

justice vous est rendue. J'en
suis heureux pour vous et les
tres, et fier pour mon pays.

Je vous serre la main
et présente à madame
Alfred Dreyfus mes hommages
très respectueux

Anatole France.

14 juillet 1906

Letter from France to Capt. Alfred Dreyfus, congratulating him on the overturning of the guilty verdict he received twelve years earlier (from Jacques Suffel, Anatole France par lui-même, *1963)*

charming and suspenseful, for, although one feels that the basic goodness of the hero and his protégée must triumph, human malice and the cruelty of fate form a thematic undercurrent to Bonnard's humanism.

Bonnard subsequently sees to it that Jeanne receives her due in all respects—the completion of her education and, finally, a suitor, a young scholar whose initial desire to visit Bonnard is singularly accrued by acquaintance with Jeanne. The hero's "crime" occurs at this juncture. It is not, as one might think, having helped Jeanne escape from school; rather, Bonnard, who has promised to sell his library in order to give her a dowry, "steals" books from those to be sold—books with which he cannot bear to part. No matter; Jeanne is duly and happily married, and, in his last years, Bonnard retires to the country, where he can observe not only the young couple's happiness but also the beauty of nature, whose truths he so long forsook.

Les Désirs de Jean Servien, which is semiautobiographical, apparently offered an outlet for some of France's bitterness and resentment concerning his youth, and certainly allowed him to set forth his views on some contemporary social issues. Published in 1882, it was, according to his preface, composed ten years before, and thus in some ways may be considered a youthful Bildungsroman; but he shortened and otherwise revised it considerably before publication. Of all his novels, it comes closest to naturalism, despite the author's own term for it: *roman d'analyse.* Some of its themes can be found also in Alphonse Daudet's *Le Petit Chose* (1868; translated as *The Little Good-for-Nothing,* 1878) and in *Le Bachelier* (The Graduate, 1881), by Jules Vallès.

France's hero, Jean, is clearly close to the author in many ways. But Jean's mother dies when he is small, leaving a void from which France himself did not suffer, and the father, a hard-toiling bookbinder, is more a slave to his labor and less erudite than Noël France. The boy suffers from the misery in which he lives with his father and aunt, and is sensitive to his plebeian status; but he shows no great gifts and has none of the energy of Stendhal's Julien Sorel. His sometime tutor, the boastful drunkard Baron Tudesco, is a farcical character whose appearances always bode ill for the Serviens' pocketbook, and finally for Jean's life. Although Jean receives his baccalaureate, he has no prospects; he is without a useful trade, and society offers few positions for those with liberal educations. Much of the time he does nothing but go to the theater with money filched from his aunt. (One notes that Noël complained in 1868 that his son just scribbled and was accomplishing nothing.) A job as a school proctor humiliates Jean; he is shortly fired anyway, because he cannot keep order. Sometime before, Jean has become enamored of an actress. He writes to her, follows her, and finally, having waited for her at her house, confronts her and kisses her hand in a passionate gesture. Recognizing that he is just a mooning schoolboy, she dismisses him, though not unkindly. He falls into despair, and his love turns bitter.

The hero's private drama, which is recounted with insight and sensitivity, although he is quite ordinary, becomes part of a larger drama during the Commune, which followed the Franco-Prussian War. The novelist's own views on the Second Empire and its violent ending are pertinent in this connection. As a youth, Anatole France had espoused republicanism, a position that opposed him not only to his father but also to the current government. He had, however, none of the revolutionary or anarchist in him, and until past middle age chose not to involve himself in political causes. Carter Jefferson quite rightly entitled the first chapter of his book on the writer's politics "The Conservative." During the last years of Napoleon III's reign, when there was considerable liberalizing of laws governing freedom of association and the press, Anatole became less hostile to the empire, which, he recognized, had wide popular support. After the defeat at Sedan in 1870, he served briefly as a reserve soldier, posted in Paris only. The consequences of the war, especially the bloody Paris Commune (March-May 1871), during which he managed to escape, thanks to a forged passport, seemed to him disastrous. It was both the sign and the cause of chaos; it represented the triumph of irrationality over a rational social order.

Jean Servien's attitude is different: he nourishes hatred for the empire and joins those who hope to overthrow it and establish a popular socialist government; the Commune, then, represents realization of his political dream. He has not forgotten the actress, however. Discovering one evening that she is the mistress of Bargemont, a corpulent bureaucrat from the Ministry of Finances who had been, briefly, his protector, he falls ill from the shock. Later, meeting Tudesco, who has become a colonel of the Commune, he confesses his misfortunes in love. Tudesco, thanks to his drunkenness, imagines that Jean is enamored of Bargemont's wife, and steals her portrait for him. When Jean goes to ask for an explanation, he is arrested by Communard guards as a spy of the Versaillais (the army and the Government of National Defense). He is imprisoned, released, but seized again and, ironically, shot by a vigilante-type *citoyenne* as a personal act of vengeance against the hated bourgeoisie.

Jean's story is thus an indictment of the Commune for its violence and anarchy, as well as of an uncaring society that finds little use for the youths to whom it grants a liberal education, and of women, whose venality seems unlimited. It is a somber picture of personal and social failure. In contrast, the main section of France's next semiautobiographical work, *Le Livre de mon ami,* is an idealized portrait of himself as a child, under the guise of Pierre Nozière. (The second section, "Le Livre de Suzanne," depicts not his own childhood but his daughter's.) Inspired, he writes, by a meditation on Dante's line "Nel mezzo del cammin di nostra vita" (In the middle of our life's road), the narrator looks back with tender and bemused eyes on his mother, father, family friends, even an idealized first love (for an older woman).

Unlike *Les Désirs de Jean Servien,* the work purports to be reminiscences, and early biographers leaned heavily on the text as if it were an unmediated account of France's childhood. However, the work and its sequels, *Pierre Nozière*

(1899; translated, 1916), *Le Petit Pierre* (1918; translated as *Little Pierre,* 1920), and *La Vie en fleur* (1922; translated as *The Bloom of Life,* 1923), doubtless represent considerable retouching of the truth. Long a favorite with readers for its charm, indulgence, and what one can now call an almost Proustian sensitivity to the Parisian setting as well as to the feelings of childhood, *Le Livre de mon ami* lacks the critical dimension that, since Gide's *Si le grain ne meurt* (1920-1921; translated as *If It Die . . .,* 1935) and other twentieth-century autobiographies, readers now expect; moreover, the whole problematics of memory and recounting the self are missing. But the work is not entirely without irony: while the narrator paints himself as a new René, for instance, he immediately undermines the portrait by admitting that, in his time, the Romantic despair of François-René de Chateaubriand's hero was worn out, and that, instead of calling on the north winds or burying himself in a cloister, he simply was very unhappy but took his baccalaureate degree. In the midst of narrative passages, France shows his talent for the nice formula, the perceptive observation. For example, when the adolescent hero has just humiliated himself unspeakably by replying "Yes, sir" to a woman whose beauty mesmerizes him, France writes: "Puisque la terre ne s'entrouvrit pas en ce moment pour m'engloutir, c'est que la nature est indifférente aux vœux les plus ardents des hommes" (If the earth didn't open up then to swallow me up, it is because nature is indifferent to the most ardent wishes of men).

The title story of France's first collection of tales, *Balthasar* (1889; translated, 1909), which drew together pieces previously published in magazines, introduced into his prose a note visible in his early poetry and shortly to become important in his work—Orientalism. His is of a particular type. The Romantic writers and painters earlier in the century had cultivated what they called the Orient, mostly Egypt (made popular by Napoleon's expedition) and other areas of the Near East, including other parts of North Africa after the French conquest of Algiers in 1830; but these artists were preoccupied with the exoticism of their own time. France's Orientalism, like that of some mid-century writers such as Flaubert and Louis Ménard, includes a historical dimension. He displays particular interest in late Hellenic civilization, Egypt, and the Levant at the time of Christ, which appeared to him, accurately, as a period of change with tremendous historical implications.

He characteristically draws on the Bible, historical texts such as the writings of Flavius Josephus, and hagiography, especially Jacques de Voragine's (Iacopo da Varezze) *La Légende dorée* (published first in Latin as *Legenda aurea,* circa 1474; translated as *The Golden Legend,* 1483), as well as his own imagination. Under his pen, much of the material on which he embroiders acquires an almost mythic character, revealing, under the disguise of history and legend, some of the truths that readers of the late nineteenth century, devoted in large part to the ideal of progress, were not entirely ready to acknowledge: both the disruptive and the creative power of sexuality, the violence in human character, the death of empires, and the power and persistence of religious belief, including superstition. By his taste for the Hellenic and medieval periods, France can be considered an heir both of the Romantics, with their Christian mythology, and of the Parnassians, at least Leconte de Lisle, with his interest in antiquity and his pessimism. But France is also a forerunner of those twentieth-century authors who have had recourse to myth as an alternative to realism in fiction.

Most of the other stories of the collection, and many of France's later tales, deal either with biblical and legendary material, such as "Laeta Acilia," concerning Mary Magdalene, one of France's favorite biblical figures, and "La Fille de Lilith," or with parapsychological and fantastic elements. The taste for the occult and the fantastic, which seems incongruous in a skeptic such as France, was deeply ingrained. He was, as Bancquart puts it, "seduced" by Gnostic sciences. This interest bespeaks his kinship with the Romantics, especially some lesser-known figures, and with a host of late-nineteenth-century writers, some of whom are now almost forgotten but whose works fascinated many of their contemporaries. It was the era of the Theosophists, the revival of Rosicrucianism, and other manifestations of the resurgence of occultism and Gnostic mysticism, which had been a subcurrent, during the Enlightenment, in the works of Louis-Claude de St.-Martin, and which, through Emanuel Swedenborg, had influenced Balzac and Baudelaire.

One of the main figures in nineteenth-century occultism was the author of *La Clef des grands mystères* (The Key to the Great Mysteries, 1861), Alphonse-Louis Constant, who took the name Eliphas Lévi. In the 1880s and 1890s Joséphin Péladan (who called himself the Sâr), Stanislas de Guaïta, and Gérard Encuasse (called

France at home (photograph by Paul Boyer)

Papus) actively promoted occultism; its influence can be seen in the prose of Joris-Karl Huysmans, Philippe-Auguste de Villiers de l'Isle-Adam, and, later, Guillaume Apollinaire. France, who appears to be the heir less of rationalist and serene Greece than of its turbulent sequels, developed a keen interest in the Mediterranean cauldron of cultures and cults in which Christianity had been forged, and in competing sects such as Mithraism. He was also interested in biblical Apocrypha, both Jewish and Christian. In another vein, the final story of *Balthasar,* the novella *Abeille* (translated as *Bee, the Princess of the Dwarfs,* 1912), which had been published separately in 1883, is a medieval fairy tale suitable, he says, for those who are neither reasonable nor serious—that is, true children of whatever age. It and other texts by France, including passages in *Le Crime de Sylvestre Bonnard,* compose a considerable corpus of writing suitable for children, which would warrant study.

Thaïs (1890; translated, 1891), which France originally called a philosophical tale after the manner of Voltaire, is his first full-length work marked by Orientalism. Set to music in 1894 by Jules Massenet, with a libretto by Louis Gallet, it became a successful opera. Based on legend, it was inspired in part by marionette performances in Paris in 1888, which led the author to investigate a corpus of hagiographic puppet plays dating from the tenth century. This source complemented his other readings in hagiography and a long-term interest in the courtesan Thaïs, whom he had treated in an early poem.

The novel, divided into three parts, concerns a beautiful and successful courtesan of Alexandria, whom the hermit monk Paphnuce, leaving his desert cell, undertakes in the first part to convert. The prose is sensuous, the visual element powerful. France's anticlericalism sprang in part from the church's denunciation of the pleasures of the flesh, pleasures that he accepted in the purest Enlightenment tradition as being perfectly natural and thus good. In *Thaïs* the flesh takes keen revenge on those who would deny it. Until the end, Paphnuce is blind to the attraction of Thaïs for him, blind to his own motivations and demons, who, unlike those that beset the saint in Flaubert's *La Tentation de Saint Antoine* (1874; translated as *The Temptation of Saint Anthony,* 1895), an obvious point of comparison, are entirely internal. Throughout, the author suggests the connection between religious and erotic ecstasy, as well as the power of human pride disguised by pious motives. The monk becomes even more obsessed with Thaïs when he learns that a friend, Nicias, was once her lover.

The middle section, after tracing the heroine's life, presents a lengthy banquet scene in Alexandria, clearly modeled on Plato's symposium. The form of the philosophical dialogue is used to good effect to convey a range of philosophical opinions (Stoicism, Epicureanism) among intellectuals who reject religion in the name of nature and the senses, and who discuss such topics as the reason for creation, evil, free will, and death. At the close of this section, Paphnuce seems to have triumphed: Thaïs consents to renounce her life of pleasure and bury herself among the female monks of the desert. However, he remains obsessed by her. In the last section, a period of extreme asceticism atop a pillar only torments him with further temptations. The stylite ultimately recognizes that he has been the dupe of God, who led him to deny the only true good, sensual love. Too late, he goes to reclaim Thaïs from her hermitage; she is dying, honored as a holy woman.

The wheel of fate, whose turning brings Thaïs to the end—holiness— that Paphnuce had sought for himself, can be given both an ancient and a modern interpretation. Venus has had her revenge, as the monk's friend Nicias, a hedonist, had warned him; the constants of human destiny, which the Athenian Greeks had identified and whose later Hellenic development is explored in the symposium, have prevailed over the efforts of Christianity to deny and counteract this destiny. In modern terms the libido has burst through the hypocritical and repressive consciousness of Paphnuce, who has lied to himself so thoroughly and so methodically that he has denied his true self.

E. M. Forster cited *Thaïs* for its hourglass construction, by which the destinies of the two main characters join briefly only at the center, then diverge again in opposite directions. One can admire it even more for its imposition, by means of a lush style, of a worldview both alien to the modern period and yet psychologically provocative, in which, despite the edifying ending of the courtesan, France's anticlericalism grounds itself not on rationalist impatience with absurdities but on the understanding of the human self. The violent denunciation of the book by a Jesuit priest, Father Brucker, in the periodical *Etudes* may have sprung from his recognition that in Anatole France the church was facing not just another anticlerical rationalist but an enemy who, going beyond the doctrines of scientism, proposed for human beings a total fulfillment of the potentialities of the self that could not be countenanced by a church preaching sacrifice and self-denial. The Jesuit's attack also reflected the fact that the novel was a notable success. The church was not to change its position: in 1922 all of France's work was placed on the Index.

The defense of human desire expressed in *Thaïs* is particularly significant in view of France's personal life. In 1883 he had begun frequenting the salon of Léontine Arman de Caillavet, a lively and intelligent Jewish woman who had converted to Christianity, whose husband, Albert Arman, had assumed the particle *de* and his mother's maiden name. At first the relationship between France and Léontine was that of guest and hostess, and the writer became known as the lion of her gatherings; but by 1888 they were lovers. Not surprisingly, France's marriage, long unsatisfactory, deteriorated even further. (Reflections of it can be found in *Le Mannequin d'osier* [1897; translated as *The Wicker-Work Woman,* 1910].) In 1892, after an especially savage domestic quarrel in which his wife insulted him deliberately, France, in dressing gown and slippers, seized his writing materials, walked out of the room and the apartment, and went to a hotel; he never again resided with her. Some time later he moved to an apartment. Thenceforth the center of his activities was Mme Arman's residence.

Appearances were always maintained: although he had his room upstairs, it is said that for her receptions he entered through the front door, like the other guests; but he lunched and dined and spent nearly all day there, and it was well known that the two shared an intimate relationship. Léontine was still married and would remain so until her death in 1910. Albert took no visible umbrage at his wife's involvement with the by-then famous writer, and the three traveled together. Although the husband was complacent, the son, Gaston, who became a successful playwright in collaboration with Robert de Flers, was disturbed by his mother's conduct. Mme Arman became freer when in 1893—the same year Valérie and Anatole were divorced—Gaston married Jeanne Pouquet, a friend of Proust (and considered one of the models for Gilberte Swann). France and Mme Arman accompanied the young married couple on a wedding trip to Italy.

Even though they seemed well matched, for several years the affair between Mme Arman and France was a stormy one, marked by quarrels

France in his later years

and reconciliations; each was jealous especially of the other's past. But they established a close intellectual companionship. She spurred him on to writing—sometimes to do a full-length work, sometimes a short piece; it was doubtless she who urged him to compose the preface for *Les Plaisirs et les jours* (1896; translated as *Pleasures and Days,* 1957), the first book by Proust. Although his muse's urgings may at times have been despotic, France seemed to thrive under them, and she gave him more confidence in himself than had Valérie, always hostile to his career; even public adulation was not as inspiring to him as Léontine's presence. On occasions she wrote a column or so for him. But it is excessive to maintain that she composed whole works.

The late 1880s and 1890s were thus marked for France by a turbulent but ultimately very propitious sentimental life. It was also a period of success. His books and columns were widely appreciated, and he was making money. In 1890 he resigned from his librarian's position at the Senate, a stopgap duty for which he had never had much enthusiasm. In 1894 he bought a private townhouse, 5 Villa Saïd. Two years later, after he had satirized the institution in *Les Opinions de M. Jérôme Coignard* (1893; translated as *The Opinions of Jérôme Coignard,* 1913), he was elected to the Académie Française, to the seat vacated by the death of Ferdinand de Lesseps. The decade was saddened for him, however, by the death of one of his intellectual masters, Ernest Renan, in 1892. The author of *Vie de Jésus* (1863), an attempt to recount the life of Christ according to the principles of scientific historiography as the mid nineteenth century understood them, had been widely appreciated for his prose style as well as his eight-volume history of Christianity; France looked upon him as one of the towering intellects of the period.

The last decade of the century was noteworthy also for France's initial involvement in political matters. Conservative by temperament, fond of order, yet Voltairean in his hatred of fanaticism and obscurantism, France had maintained for years what was, under the Second Empire and in the early years of the Third Republic, a course of moderation. His fear of anarchy, nourished by his experiences in the Commune and his vast reading concerning the French Revolution, had made him particularly wary of anarchism and, what was to him nearly the same thing, socialism. This is visible in some of the short stories in *L'Etui de nacre* (1892; translated as *Tales from a Mother-of-Pearl Casket,* 1896)—reprinted from a long periodical publication entitled "Les Autels de la peur" (The Altars of Fear; published in *Journal des Débats,* 1884)—which show in a very unfavorable light the brutality and lawlessness of the Jacobins during the Reign of Terror. In 1888 France was vaguely interested by the rise to power of the nationalist general Georges-Ernest Boulanger, but denounced him when it became clear that he represented a threat to constitutional government.

The Dreyfus Affair was to change Anatole France permanently. In 1894, when Capt. Alfred Dreyfus was convicted of treason and subsequently condemned to deportation to Devil's Island, the public had no reason to doubt the justice of the sentence, but in the following years evidence emerged that cast doubt on the captain's guilt as well as the propriety of the government's conduct in the matter. In a November

1897 interview, France said he could not approve of the verdict, since he had not been able to examine the evidence. After Zola published his famous open letter, "J'accuse," in the *Aurore* (13 January 1898) and was charged with defamation, France signed the "Pétition des intellectuels" in his support the next day and then testified at his trial. When in 1898 Zola was suspended from the Legion of Honor, France, who had been named to the society in 1884, refused to wear his decoration, and in 1900 he ceased attending Académie Française meetings because of the coolness colleagues showed him as a result of the affair. France pronounced an impassioned eulogy at Zola's funeral in 1902.

For the remainder of his career he would remain a left-leaning liberal, associated on and off with the Socialist party, which he supported in a public speech in 1904 and to whose paper, the *Humanité,* he contributed. His socialism was, however, very undogmatic, inspired much less by economic theory than by his observations on the failures of the Third Republic, dominated by a wealthy oligarchy. In the quarrel and subsequent split within the party, he followed Jean Jaurès rather than the intransigent Jules Guesde. His socialism was also an expression of his humanist's concern for individuals, visible from the beginning of his career, and in no way represented a radical conversion. In 1921 it was announced that he had joined the Communist party, but he withdrew his support the next year.

Some of France's best-known prose was published in the last ten years of the century. One vein he was then pursuing can be called his eighteenth-century mode. *La Rôtisserie de la reine Pédauque* (translated as *The Queen Pedauque,* 1923) and *Les Opinions de M. Jérôme Coignard,* both published in 1893, feature a fictional style and structure that recall the picaresque novels, philosophical tales, and rambling novels of ideas and conversation of the previous century; and the characters are right out of the period. One of France's most appreciated works, *La Rôtisserie* is a rich and thematically complex tale that weaves together three thematic strands. The first is the skepticism of the Enlightenment, the sort associated with Voltaire but visible also in works by such figures as Diderot and Pierre Bayle, whose *Dictionnaire historique et critique* (1697) helped initiate the struggle against superstition that characterized the period after Louis XIV's death. The second strand is orthodox church doctrine in its most fundamental form, which the author mocks and which does not come off very well on moral grounds, but which is not entirely discredited, especially in comparison to crude popular superstition.

The third strand is occultism, which plays a major role. It too is patently mocked, but France reveals considerable interest in it despite his own disbelief. Moreover, since he is suspicious of dogma of any sort, including dogmatic scientism, both occultism and religion benefit from the skeptic's recognition that perhaps, after all, one should not rule out certain phenomena simply because one cannot understand them, and from the psychologist's awareness that irrational beliefs may spring from the soul. As Jérôme Coignard says in his *Opinions,* "Il semble que les vieilles erreurs soient moins fâcheuses que les nouvelles, et que, puisque nous devons nous tromper, le meilleur est de s'en tenir aux illusions émoussées" (It seems that old errors are less harmful than new ones, and, since we must necessarily deceive ourselves, the best thing is to stay with well-worn illusions).

France drew on a wealth of sources for *La Rôtisserie,* although his text is certainly not just a compilation of previous writings. In her Pléiade edition commentaries, Bancquart has identified various models and sources, including Gnostic texts, *The Arabian Nights,* some eighteenth-century tales and novels, and the life of Montfaucon de Villars, a seventeenth-century priest of whom Voltaire wrote that he was "killed by Sylphs." The novel takes its title from a Paris cookshop where the young Jacques Ménétrier helps his father by turning the spit—hence his sobriquet, Tournebroche. The story is presented as having been written in the second half of the eighteenth century by Jacques, who narrates the adventures of his youth around 1730 in the company of his tutor, Jérôme Coignard, a priest who is given to the delights of the flesh and whose fortunes have declined; later they are joined by M. d'Astarac, an alchemist and occultist. The loose structure of the work allows for digressions and reporting of many sayings of Coignard and d'Astarac, but the plot is not merely episodic: France knots its threads successfully to bring about a dramatic denouement.

Coignard represents skepticism (which he imparts to the candid Jacques) in all matters save doctrine, for despite his moral failings, he remains faithful to the core of church dogma, through the mechanism of *credo quia absurdum* (a position France mocks but considers no worse than the efforts of reason to prove the existence of God). In worldly matters the priest is a prudent and perspicacious counselor. D'Astarac is the opposite; persuaded that he can overcome the limitations of reason and the senses, he tries to fabricate diamonds, pursues the invisible (in the form of sylphs and salamanders), and conducts other magical experiments. He engages Jacques and Coignard to come to his estate outside Paris to assist him in interpreting Greek Gnostic texts while he works with Egyptian hieroglyphs. His illuminism is contagious: Jacques almost brings himself to believe in otherworldly beings and comes close to expecting the beautiful salamander that d'Astarac has promised him. What Jacques meets, however, is no spirit but a very real young woman, Jahel, the niece (and probably mistress) of old Mosaïde, a Jew who lives on the property in order to help d'Astarac with Cabalistic texts. A projection, perhaps, of some of the author's images of woman—from his disappointment with the actress, his unfortunate experience with Valérie, and his jealous liaison with Mme Arman—she resembles also many eighteenth-century heroines in her faithlessness and talent for troublemaking.

Jacques and Coignard become embroiled in a farcical scrape in Paris involving Catherine, a luscious creature Jacques had coveted long before, one of her lovers, and the older "protector" at whose house the group is engaged in revelry during his absence. After the protector's sudden return, there is a scuffle, during which Coignard kills a servant. Jacques, Coignard, and the lover are forced to flee summarily, while Catherine, like l'abbé Antoine-François Prévost's Manon Lescaut, will be shipped off to Louisiana. The three men take temporary refuge on d'Astarac's estate and then head by coach for a hideaway near Lyons, taking with them what they believe to be one of d'Astarac's valuable diamonds and Jahel, who has meanwhile deserted Jacques for the new arrival, Catherine's former lover. On the road their carriage is wrecked when Coignard utters a magic word, "Agla." As they are preparing to spend the night in a solitary spot, Coignard is brutally attacked by Mosaïde, who has pursued them from Paris in a jealous rage. But d'Astarac, who has accompanied him, says it was not Mosaïde who wounded Coignard but the spirits, because he had revealed the secrets of the elves.

Coignard dies an edifying death, his sins remitted, according to a local priest, by his repentance in extremis. Sometime thereafter Jacques returns to Paris and finds work at the bookshop of St. Catherine, where he is comfortable with his candor and erudition. While going to visit d'Astarac, he learns that Mosaïde has drowned, and he sees the château burning—the result, doubtless, of an experiment gone awry, with the alchemist himself perched on the flaming rooftop, calling out that he is rising on the wings of fire.

The main characters are all memorable. By his erudition, his frank admission of his shortcomings, his vitality, and his appeal to reason, Coignard, who seems very close to his creator, endears himself to both Jacques and the reader. D'Astarac is impressive by his very lunacy; while mocking occultism and showing the power and danger of fanaticism, the novelist creates a character who is at once frightening and charming, with even a few grains of wisdom. Jacques, a brother to Voltaire's Candide, appeals by his thirst for knowledge as well as his very uninhibited attitude toward young women. The rational and the irrational exist side by side not only thematically but in the development of the plot—as if France wanted to acknowledge, as Voltaire had done in *Zadig* (1747; translated, 1749), the inscrutability of human destiny—and in the reader's reactions.

At the beginning of the sequel, *Les Opinions de M. Jérôme Coignard*, the narrator explains that he found the manuscript of *La Rôtisserie de la reine Pédauque* in a Montparnasse bookstall; he has published it and now is adding a second text composed by Jacques, discovered at the same time. France thus evokes the "found manuscript" trope frequent in novels of the eighteenth century. This second work clearly reflects the author's liking for Coignard, who, in early drafts of *La Rôtisserie,* played a less significant role than in the final version and here becomes France's spokesman—"le plus sage des moralistes, une sorte de mélange merveilleux d'Epicure et de saint François d'Assise" (the wisest of moralists, a sort of marvelous mixture of Epicurus and Saint Francis of Assisi). The topics on which he discourses are nineteenth-century political and cultural issues, thinly disguised under a cloak of eighteenth-century references—on the model of Enlightenment texts in which Oriental characters and settings are subterfuges for authorial criticism of the present. Readers had no trouble, for instance, in seeing reflections of the Panama Scandal of the 1880s, in which de Lesseps had been implicated, in "L'Affaire du Mississipi," ostensibly concerning the John Law financial scandal (in con-

Portrait of France by Eugène Carrière (from Jacques Suffel, Anatole France par lui-même, *1963)*

nection with land in Louisiana) at the beginning of the eighteenth century.

The work consists of a series of conversations between the abbé Coignard and Jacques Tournebroche, chiefly on the topic of government. Parallels between the ancien régime of Louis XV and the republic 150 or so years later come readily to mind, as when, in the case of a woman who has testified against government corruption, the priest argues that *raison d'état* cannot justify dishonesty (and this was written before the Dreyfus Affair broke). Even more striking is the political philosophy underlying Coignard's remarks. It is antirevolutionary because it refutes the Rousseauist principle (never so named except in the preface) according to which human beings are perfectible creatures and a government of virtue can be attained. Writing from the perspective of more than a century after the Revolution, France knows that those who had wished to usher in the reign of virtue had brought instead the Reign of Terror, and that the lofty ideals of the Enlightenment are still far from being realized: injustice and inequity prevail in society, obscurantism dominates men's minds, and so-called civilized nations wage war as frequently and brutally as barbarians. He thus has his abbé argue that changing the form of government would do little to improve conditions; the next government may be worse than the last, and government by the many holds out more possibilities for mediocrity and abuse than government by one. If there is to be progress, it will be imperceptible. Meanwhile, ministers are all venal and incompetent, and instead of virtue, wealth and honors reign; the only good thing that can be said is that ministers play a minor role in the development of human history, which France identifies as the product of vast forces rather than the action of a few individuals. Under such circumstances true freedom is as yet impossible in the body politic; it should be sought, rather, in the self, in a soul freed from ignorance, superstition, and the vanities of the world.

Le Lys rouge, one of France's best-constructed novels, is written in a totally different vein, that of psychological and social realism. It demonstrates that, contrary to his own view and that of critics such as May, who said that he was by nature a creator of contes, he had a sense of the novel also. In his tales and episodic fictions, he could afford to let his fancy wander, but he knew also how to structure a work so as to make plot and psychology coincide. Almost Jamesian in parts, *Le Lys rouge* is a study in love and jealousy. It is also a portrait of society; like Stendhal before him and Proust afterward, France excels at making social mechanisms not only the background but an agent of personal development.

Thérèse Martin-Bellème is a sensitive and intelligent woman married to a politically ambitious man, who gives her wide latitude in her private life as long as she adheres to proprieties. Their Parisian salon brings together a diverse gathering of social, artistic, and political figures. She is also, as she says, a sensual woman; but while in the late nineteenth century a French novelist could, without shocking the public as Zola did with *Nana* (1880; translated, 1880), allow himself, as France does here, to refer openly to sexual desire and satisfaction among the upper classes, there is no detailed description of erotic scenes. When Thérèse's lover, Le Ménil, prolongs a hunting trip in the country, she decides to accept the invitation of her English friend, Miss Bell, a Pre-Raphaelite poetess, to visit her villa in Florence. Much of the action thus takes place in Italy, where natural beauty competes with some of the most exquisite products of the human eye and hand.

In this setting, where nearly every prospect delights the eye—excepting cemeteries and other reminders of decay—Thérèse is courted by an artist, Dechartre (to whom the author attributed much of himself). Finally yielding, reluctantly, to his importunate suit, she then finds herself falling in love with him. The scenes of their passionate idyll are overlaid with references to art but also to unhappiness. Unfortunately, Le Ménil, receiving no reply to his letters and anxious to retrieve the woman he had nearly taken for granted, arrives in Florence. Each lover discovers the existence of the other and feels betrayed. Back in Paris, where her husband needs her help in promoting his election, Thérèse tries to cut her ties with Le Ménil, but he pursues her. Dechartre, already jealous of her past, suspects, wrongly, that Thérèse and Le Ménil are still lovers. His physical and mental sufferings are such that he must break with her; love has ended in its own destruction. During a scene at the opera (Charles-François Gounod's *Faust*) near the novel's end, Thérèse injures her hand on the red lily pin he had designed for her as a sign of their Florentine love, and the blood drips onto her bosom.

The character portraits—including those of the eccentric Miss Bell and her unscrupulous suitor, Prince Albertinelli, and the half-mystic, half-calculating poet Coulette (modeled partly on Verlaine in his last years)—match those by other masters of the French novel. Similarly, the social comedy and workings of a salon where contacts are made and political maneuvers prepared—scenes in which contemporary readers recognized figures and circumstances of their time—are handled with great skill. France excels chiefly, however, at depicting love, with its various modes and phases, especially the impossible desire for total possession of the beloved. While the language, symbolism, and other aspects of the fictional codes are highly marked by their time, such nineteenth-century conventions do not invalidate the work as a keen study of desire and unhappiness.

The reader of *Thaïs, Balthasar,* and some of the most famous tales by France, including "Le Jongleur de Notre-Dame" ("Our Lady's Juggler," first published in the *Gaulois,* 10 May 1890) and "Le Procurateur de Judée" ("The Procurator of Judea," first published in the *Temps,* 25 December 1891), collected in *L'Etui de nacre* along with other stories based on saints' legends, might conclude that he was incurably attracted to the past, precisely because it is unverifiable and thus can give free rein to the imagination. But in the four novels grouped together as *Histoire contemporaine* (1920-1921), which constitute a third major current in his fiction of the 1890s, France revealed himself to be a keen, witty, inventive, and accurate painter (sometimes a caricaturist) of the mores, society, and politics of his own time. It is even appropriate to rank him not far from Proust for his depiction of the social and political mechanisms and currents that dominated the Third Republic just before the end of the century. Visible already in *Le Lys rouge,* France's skills as a social novelist are illustrated on a much wider scale in these four volumes, which are filled with references to their time.

In *L'Orme du mail* (1897; translated as *The Elm-tree on the Mall,* 1910), first published serially, like so much of France's fiction, the novelist deals with two major opposing forces of the period: the church, which, until the law of separation of the following decade (1905), was still an established and protected religion; and the republic itself, built to some degree on the strictly secular principles of the Revolution and including virulently anticlerical elements. The situation is complicated by the new papal order of *ralliement* (that is, the expedient recognition of the legitimacy of the French republic), which the novelist satirizes. Despite a structure that lets some plot threads simply dangle, the work has unity, due to the author's piercing social satire and the convincing tones and phrasing by which he renders the speech and thoughts of the characters, major and minor. Deft turns of the plot mirror the machinations of the church and the unvisionary Third Republic, the very image of government by intrigue.

The main plot centers around who will be named bishop of Tourcoing. The competing candidates and the archbishop are so well individualized by their speech, appearance, and thoughts that, as Jacques Suffel notes in *Anatole France par lui-même* (1954), they rival the priests of Stendhal and Balzac. Their unctuousness nearly drips off the page; but through their self-righteousness their scheming and ambitious ways are as clearly visible as those of their lay counterparts, the politicians who support one candidate or another according to their own—or their wives'—purposes. In the background is the insoluble conflict between an established church that remains royalist in both its pronouncements and sympathies and a republic that is anticlerical through historical reference and has a pathological fear of restoration. An additional focus of the novelist's attention is Jewish influence in French society and the role of Jews as brokers of both wealth and power. In a nation where Edouard Drumont's inflammatory tract *La France juive* (Jewish France, 1886) had enjoyed widespread favor, the depiction of Jewish politicians involved in naming a bishop was not merely a nice irony. In counterpoint to this main plot and its associated intrigues are others, chiefly the story of M. Bergeret. Like Sylvestre Bonnard, he seems dear to the author's heart. A modest professor married to a haughty and somewhat shrewish wife, he is only an observer, not a maker, of political and ecclesiastical intrigue; but, as a Voltairean and a man of intellectual parts, neither fanatical nor venal, he can play the role of listener and *raisonneur*.

The same characters and intrigues are pursued in *Le Mannequin d'osier,* likewise published in 1897, but politics plays a minor role compared to M. Bergeret's continuing story. It is essentially a domestic drama, rendered without bathos, with wry humor. The main character is portrayed in his triple role of husband, professor, and voice of civic reason. He exercises the latter function often in the setting of the local bookshop and in walks with friends, as he comments on mores and politics, repeating some of Coignard's (that is, the author's) views. As a professor he is not seen at the university but rather at home, with his favorite pupil, M. Roux. Here, as in the works featuring Sylvestre Bonnard and Jérôme Coignard, the author is clearly interested in the master-disciple relationship. In this case it takes a melodramatic turn: the professor comes home unexpectedly to find his wife and M. Roux joined in embrace. If his first reaction is predictable and uncivilized—namely, the impulse to kill them—his next, following immediately upon the first, is to leave the room and hurl to the courtyard below the effigy of his wife, in the form of her wicker dressmaker's model (a gesture France himself had performed in rage), which has long stood in his study.

To put the whole thing out of mind and reassert his rights as master of the house, the professor henceforth denies Mme Bergeret's existence, neither conversing nor having any other commerce with her. Public opinion sides with her (her friends deny the rumors of an affair and see her as victimized by her eccentric spouse, and even those who are aware of M. Roux's assiduities tend to blame Bergeret, since cuckolds are always ridiculous); but M. Bergeret philosophically ignores the mockery and spends his time either with his books (the classics, always France's favorites) or with his friends. By the end he succeeds in driving his wife to return to her mother. This drama is not entirely unrelated to the political concerns that appear occasionally, for the conflict between the spouses obliquely reflects that between the conservative aristocracy and upper bourgeoisie and their republican opponents.

In *L'Anneau d'améthyste* (1899; translated as *The Amethyst Ring,* 1919), the bishop is finally named, thanks in part to pressure from three different women—two of whom are Jewish, and all of whom are involved in illicit affairs—who, for varying reasons, none disinterested, urge the government to choose the abbé Guitrel. The crafty Guitrel has been helping his own cause since the first volume of the series, particularly by seeing to it that a huge debt owed by his rival is publicized and by prudently taking the public position that religious orders in the diocese to which he aspires should, for the sake of the republic, be kept

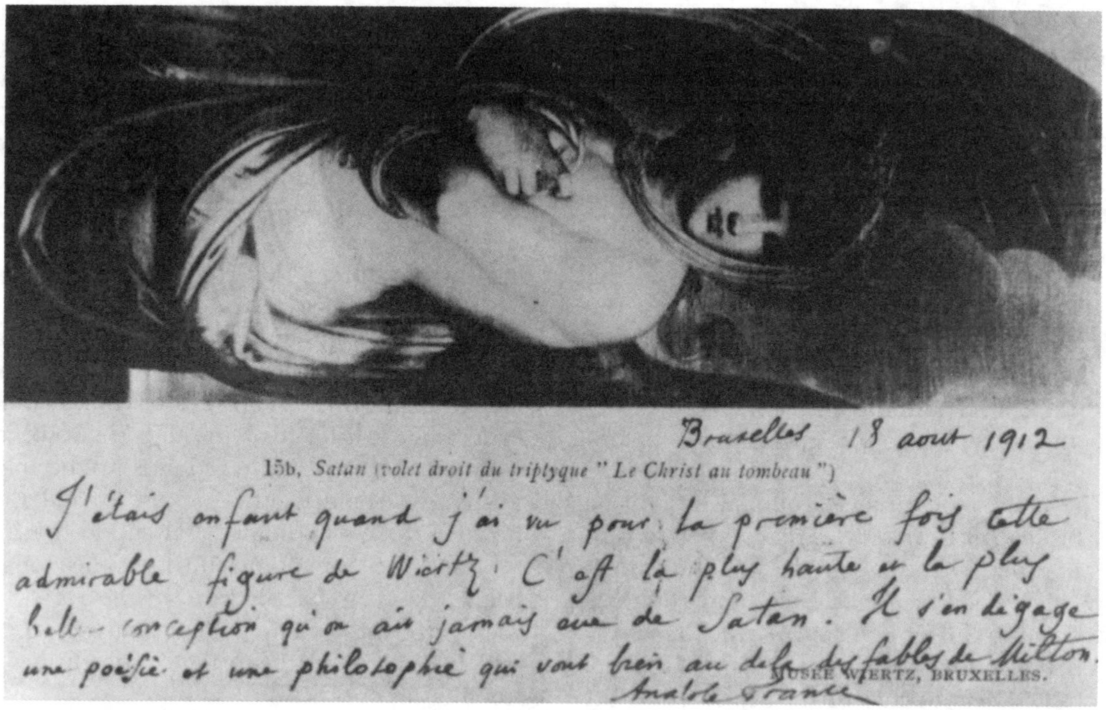

Postcard to Jules Coüet on which France discusses this painting of Satan in the Musée Wiertz, Brussels (from Jacques Suffel, Anatole France par lui-même, *1963)*

divided, hence weak, through continuation of the burdensome tax arrangements to which they are subject. As the book concludes, the new bishop's first official act is to declare that, given the unjust tax burden—from which, according to papal decree, the church should be exempt—the congregations of the diocese have joined together to refuse henceforth to comply.

In the background is the Dreyfus Affair. What, in the novelist's view, made the original judicial error possible and so hard to rectify is implicit throughout the social analysis of the first three volumes of *Histoire contemporaine,* although the series was planned before the affair broke. The aristocracy and upper bourgeoisie, who as a caste wield dominant power in the Third Republic—although some of their members are royalist—are anti-Semitic, proarmy, and prochurch. The characters' reactions are entirely predictable: the politicians and churchmen say that to doubt the verdict of the military court or call for revision is nothing less than treason, and point out that charges of judicial error come from Freemasons and Jews. M. Bergeret, on the contrary, whose critical intelligence is turned more and more toward contemporary events and who is far from optimistic about human conduct and institutions, argues that seven judges may indeed have been in error.

Monsieur Bergeret à Paris (1901; translated as *Monsieur Bergeret in Paris,* 1921) is a novel of politics, but not quite a political novel because the political vision is never called into question and never itself dramatized. The plot is concerned chiefly with *how* a partisan program can be carried out in practice, rather than with the relationship between individual experience and political life. Moreover, there is little change in the political understanding of the characters, and the title character undergoes almost no evolution. If he appears as a thoroughgoing socialist partway through the book, discoursing on collective ownership and human solidarity, it is not the result of some personal drama, but rather the logical consequence of views adumbrated earlier, especially concerning the Dreyfus Affair, still a burning issue in this volume. M. Bergeret, now a professor at the Sorbonne, again takes the position that since it was the government that committed errors, to accuse Dreyfusards of attacking and sabotaging the army and the nation is unjust; they are merely trying to rectify errors. Opposed to this minority position is the view of those who through conviction or self-interest affirm Captain Dreyfus's guilt and call his supporters subversive.

The strange political alliances created by the affair, related to the deep division between republicans and monarchists that marked the entire century, will surprise no one familiar with party politics in France. In the major plot—unrelated to the activities of M. Bergeret, who is again more of an observer than a player—a staunch royalist activist runs for election and wins as a nationalist, endorsed eventually by republicans and socialists, whom he despises. Much is made also of the alliances between old aristocrats, often impoverished, and wealthy Jewish families, who adopt anti-Semitic positions in order to secure their social standing. The mobility of French society at the time, which Proust would later analyze brilliantly and incisively, is well suggested, especially in connection with the Dreyfus Affair.

The structure of the novel is not entirely satisfying: its plots are not well interwoven and it ends without real closure. But the portraits are skillfully done and the conversations lively. In addition, the themes are played out in multiple registers, including a sixteenth-century fable that the novelist introduces through *mise en abyme* (interior reproduction of stories or motifs). What is most important about this last volume and the series as a whole is the connection established, implicitly and explicitly, between fundamental flaws in the French social and institutional fabric and outward political dramas such as the Dreyfus Affair. "L'Affaire a révélé le mal dont notre belle société est atteinte comme le vaccin de Koch accuse dans un organisme les lésions de la tuberculose" (The affair has revealed the moral evil with which our fine society is afflicted, as the Koch vaccine indicates tubercular lesions). In this series, France proved himself to be, with Stendhal, Balzac, and Zola, one of the major sociologists in nineteenth-century French fiction. The best-known among his remaining works are similarly devoted to the criticism of a society that he saw, increasingly, as oppressive, unjust, obscurantist, and dangerously benighted.

The first decade of the new century was marked for France by both personal achievement and emotional distress. Two of his major works, *L'Ile des pingouins* (translated as *Penguin Island,* 1909) and *Vie de Jeanne d'Arc* (translated as *Joan of Arc,* 1908), were both published in 1908, and many other books, articles, and prefaces appeared. Some of his works were presented on the Parisian stage. His literary fame increased, along with his political notoriety. To the conservatives, he was persona non grata. He published in

France at his wedding to Emma Laprévotte, 11 October 1920

Charles Péguy's *Cahiers de la Quinzaine* and wrote the preface to *Une Campagne laïque* (1904), in which the politician Emile Combes recounted his efforts to pass the separation law that bears his name.

For some years France had traveled frequently in Europe and enjoyed lengthy stays at the country properties of friends such as the novelist Gyp (Countess of Martel) and of course the Arman de Caillavets. After 1900 his travels became even more frequent: he made sometimes extended stays in Rome, London, Switzerland, Austria, Greece, Turkey, and elsewhere, and took several cruises. On most of these trips, Mme de

Caillavet accompanied him. In 1909 he visited South America to give lectures on François Rabelais. He was accompanied by his friend Pierre Calmettes and his secretary, Jean-Jacques Brousson, who was dismissed during the visit and subsequently published an unflattering and unreliable account of the master's trip.

France's private life was again turbulent. The marriage of his daughter, Suzanne, in 1901 to Henri Mollin was followed by her scandalous liaison with a young student, Michel Psichari, Renan's grandson. The marriage ended in divorce in 1905, and later she married Psichari, after the birth of their son Lucien. France refused, however, to attend the wedding, and he and Suzanne thenceforth remained estranged.

While traveling in South America in 1909, France had an affair with an actress, Jeanne Brindeau; this was not the first occasion on which he had been unfaithful to Léontine (their relationship had deteriorated and she had agreed to the South American voyage partly because a temporary separation seemed desirable), but, unlike others, this liaison was broadcast in the scandal sheets of Paris. Upon returning to Paris he found that Mme de Caillavet, who had attempted suicide, was gravely ill; he then broke off the affair with Jeanne. Léontine died in January 1910. Sometime the same year he began an affair with Emma Laprévotte, who had traveled with them as Léontine's chambermaid and by December Emma was living at Villa Saïd. This arrangement did not prevent his engaging in other liaisons, notably with an American woman, Laura MacAdoo Gagey, who committed suicide in 1911. France finally married Emma in 1920.

Sur la pierre blanche (1905; translated as *The White Stone,* 1910) is concerned with both the knowability of the historical process and the possibility of achieving an ideal society—topics that must be connected in any rational theory of history. The story is set in Rome, where visiting archaeologists gather in the Forum to discuss the past, present, and future. The past and future are evoked by embedded tales read aloud by their authors; France was fond of frame narratives, although he did not always exploit their possible irony. The first tale is set in the Roman Empire during the first century A.D. Questions of cultural change and the unforeseeability of the future are raised when—like Pontius Pilate in France's story "Le Procurateur de Judée," who does not remember Jesus—Seneca's brother Gallion, the Roman proconsul in Corinth, misunderstands the implications of the new religion that the apostle Paul, Stephen, and others preach, although he is interested in questions concerning the gods and is cognizant of the spread of Jewish monotheism. In ironic contrast to the disdain Gallion shows for the new religion, which, he says, will not replace the cult of Jupiter, is the supposition that the *pax romana* of the Empire, over which Nero is about to reign, will endure indefinitely (he is called "l'espoir du monde" [the hope of the world]). The conclusion is that human beings are enclosed within cultural solipsism and cannot identify historical process.

The second tale (in the form of a dream) deals with a socialist utopia of 2270, which France, avoiding determinism, presents as only one of the possible developments of the present. All means of production are owned by the state, men and women dress in unisex clothes and the traditional division of labor between the sexes is blurred, and religions have multiplied so that no one dominates. Yet individualism remains, particularly since art is widely cultivated, and the state is not markedly oppressive. Unlike most authors of utopias, however, France acknowledges both social and individual flaws in even this rational society. Anarchism persists; there is illegal dealing; and the constants of the human condition—illness, unhappiness—remain, for human beings are animals and not very reasonable ones at that. France sees the end of history not as some rational synthesis but rather as a process of both social and biological evolution, in which the human species will ultimately be replaced by another.

Doubtless the most famous of France's books in North America, *L'Ile des pingouins* is a cutting satire of his nation, in the form of a historical fable. The author's wit spares virtually nothing and no one. It is not subtle, either: perhaps he had concluded that satiric niceties would be ineffective for people capable, for instance, of stampeding in the streets to join in fanatical pursuit of Zola when he tried to defend Dreyfus. In most readers' memories, the fable is preeminently the history of the Dreyfus Affair, transposed into the "Affair of the Eighty Thousand Bales of Hay," but this is only part of the matter.

In early medieval times, the myopic Saint Maël baptizes by mistake some penguins, having taken them for men. A heavenly council decides that they must be turned into human beings, since the virtue of baptism with which they have been graced would otherwise be fruitless, and that would be contrary to Christian theology.

France near the end of his life

The novelist, speaking as a historian who has researched the matter, undertakes to recount their history, from the time of the metamorphosis and the miraculous hauling of their island to the Breton coasts (hence a Celtic flavor in the early sections), to the Renaissance, the Enlightenment (passed over very quickly), and the Revolution, thence to the present. Indeed, he even recounts what he calls future time, which he foresees with frightening lucidity. (One has only to consider his depiction of the polluted, barren, skyscraper-dominated city of fifteen million, and his vision of a great tree of smoke that rises above the city when the energies of radiation are released.)

It becomes increasingly clear that the penguins stand for the French. The author's satire is directed chiefly against nationalism and superstition, including what passes for Christian hagiography; both, he shows, easily invite fanaticism and lead to persecutions and other abuses. "Qui dit voisins dit ennemis" (To say neighbors is to say enemies), he writes. He criticizes the very idea of divine omnipotence and omniscience, mocking God's "aveugle clairvoyance" (blind lucidity). He is also concerned with tearing away the pious veil that clothes French history. The medieval period, he shows, was characterized by brutality, by which private property and aristocratic privilege were established. (His depiction of the origin of private property is almost Rousseauist.) Other critical remarks concern topics as varied as the idea of French racial purity, American imperialism, the role of the press, and modern-style architecture in "Alca" (that is, Paris).

The themes of superstition, nationalism, the aristocracy, and anti-Semitism are brought together in the affair of the bales of hay. Partisans of the army (still smarting, one would suppose, from a defeat like the 1870 defeat of France by Prussia), anti-Jewish nationalists, royalists anxious to restore the monarchy so that their own privileges may be restored, and ecclesiastics, never reconciled to the republic, are allies against a handful who think that justice has miscarried. The invented controversy follows very closely the real one, and contemporary readers had no difficulty identifying the historical figures called Greatauk, Pyrot, Maubec, and so on. Zola appears as Colomban and France himself as Bidault-Coquille.

Throughout the section on the affair, as in the pages on the great penguin revolution (that is, 1789) and the section that explains the outbreak of a great war (which would actually occur six years later), the author jabs constantly at French politics, satirizing the governments of fanaticism, militarism, and intrigue that had plagued his nation for more than a century. He does not suggest that these social vices are the result of flawed institutions; rather, the institutions derive from and mirror human viciousness. Religion and morality are but a hypocritical cloak; in reality, men are brutes. Clearly, France's view of life had not mellowed after he passed sixty; thanks to the Dreyfus Affair and other signs of what he took to be institutionalized injustice and inequity throughout European society, he had fallen into a deep pessimism, which the satires of *L'Ile des pingouins,* despite their incisive wit, appealing to the reader's intelligence, only underline instead of offsetting.

L'Ile des pingouins is related to *Sur la pierre blanche* through its examination of the past and predictions of the future. Whereas the prophetic tale in *Sur la pierre blanche* evokes a rational and successful (if, to present readers, somewhat fanciful) new society, the image of the future in the penguin fable is somber. The book does hold, however, some possibilities for the amelioration of society. For instance, a character who obviously speaks for the author argues for different relationships between men and women, including a new sexual morality. These views, which many current readers will find forward-looking, stand in contrast to the morality of the double standard, still countenanced at the time not only by the church but by such supposedly racy novelists as Marcel Prévost, whose *Les Demi-Vierges* (1894; translated as *The Demi-Virgins,* 1895) extols chastity for women while granting to men the privilege of unlimited sexual adventures.

As a study in the Middle Ages, superstition, and nationalism, *L'Ile des pingouins* should be read also in the context of France's history of Joan of Arc, published earlier the same year. The study was well received in almost no quarter, and the author was probably pleased some months later to offer to his detractors a parody of hagiography in his penguin fable. France had been interested for years in the Maid of Orléans and had worked intermittently since 1875 on what turned out to be two massive volumes. He was not alone: after the seminal work on her by Jules Michelet, which read the Middle Ages in Romantic terms, Maurice Barrès, Léon Bloy, and Péguy all wrote on the girl from Lorraine. Since 1871 and the loss of the eastern provinces, interest in her had increased, and during World War I the figure of Joan would play an important role in patriotic iconography and rhetoric.

When France wrote on her, she was not yet a saint, however; declared Venerable in 1894, she was on the point of being pronounced Blessed (1909) before reaching full canonization in 1920. He took issue with the church conservatives, who interpreted her story in miraculous terms. While concerned to preserve her status as a national heroine, he explained her "voices" and other behavior in rational terms, and indulged his anticlericalism by attacking the church that was responsible for her death. His views are not wholly consistent, however; the task of giving a coherent, nonreductionist explanation was beyond him, given the lacunae in knowledge concerning the period when Joan lived.

After Mme de Caillavet's death in 1910, the writer's existence was filled with activity, although—or perhaps because—he felt her loss very keenly. He continued his travels, visiting Algeria and, in 1913, taking his seventeenth, and last, trip to Italy. He knew well and corresponded with many of the famous—the sculptor Auguste Rodin; the socialist Jaurès; the actor Sacha Guitry; the writer Barrès—and he met once or twice some others, including Bernard Shaw, Albert Einstein, and Valéry. His support for liberal causes was constantly solicited, and he so often answered the appeal that his activity in this decade, joined to his intervention in various causes in the previous ten years, justifies calling him one of the first *écrivains engagés,* or committed writers, of the twentieth century.

France's last major fictional works, *Les Dieux ont soif* (1912; translated as *The Gods Are Athirst,* 1913) and *La Révolte des anges* (1914; translated as *The Revolt of the Angels,* 1914), are, like many of his books, novels of ideas, although not *romans à thèse* in which characters are manipulated in patterns intended to demonstrate the dominant thesis. *Les Dieux ont soif* is a novel of the Terror of 1793, when the principles of liberty, fraternity, and equality, which had been recognized as politically fundamental through the Revolution four years before, were perverted to legitimize one of the most repressive regimes in modern history. The novelist had long been interested in the Revolution; *L'Etui de nacre* contains stories concerning the period extracted from a periodical publication, "Les Autels de la peur." Although after 1900 he stated frequently his confidence that a better society could be established and war eliminated in Europe through political and economic reform, this reformist creed was only grafted onto and did not replace his long-held belief that ideals are not sufficient to improve mankind, and especially that power held by the masses leads to anarchy and violence. In *Les Dieux ont soif,* the hero, Evariste Gamelin, whose devotion to the republic and its principle of popular sovereignty is unmatched, and who is by nature a generous and honorable person, becomes one of the butchers of the Terror, voting with self-righteous conviction for the execution of his neighbor, his brother-in-law, and countless others.

France lets the reader see the Revolution through Gamelin's eyes (there are long passages of quoted reflections): the heroism of Jean Marat, Maximilien de Robespierre, and other Jacobins; the treachery of the moderate Girondists; and the terrible threat to liberty and survival posed by the alliance of European powers determined to overthrow the young republic. In these matters, as throughout the novel, the author follows facts closely. But the reader sees Gamelin also through the novelist's eyes (by means of authorial commentary, criticisms offered by other characters, and plot development). The Terrorists are possessed by an idea, which usurps traditional morality, feeling, and rational thought; no better than the tyrants and inquisitors they replaced, they are of the breed the author dreaded most, fanatics.

Opposed to their fanaticism is the tolerance of Brotteaux, the neighbor who is denounced because of a chance involvement with a royalist sympathizer and then condemned by Gamelin. A reader of Lucretius and a spokesman for the author, he illustrates the best of the eighteenth-century philosophes' thought: stoical by nature,

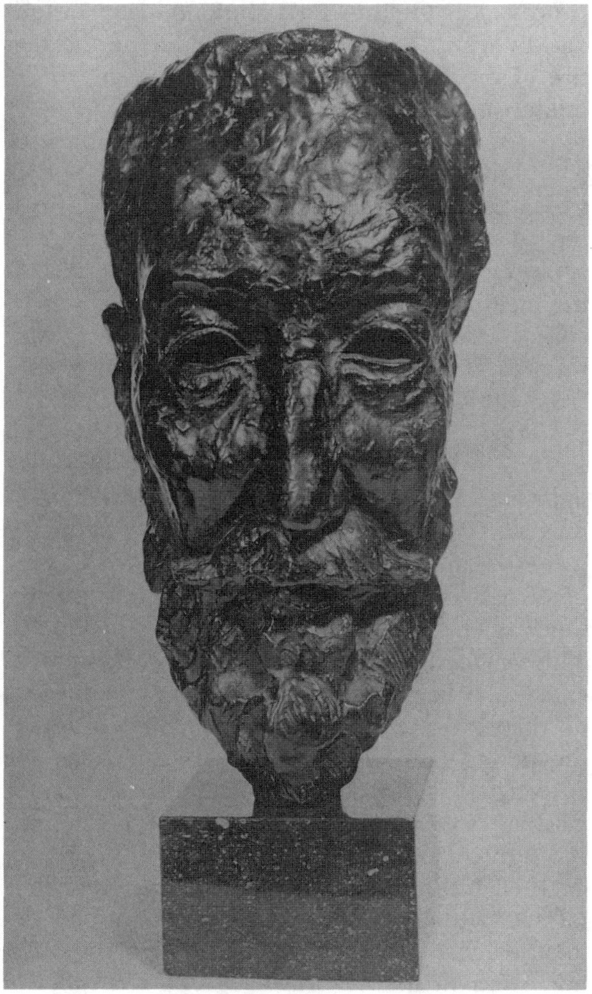

Portrait bust of France by Alfred Huettenbach, made at the time of the author's Nobel Prize award in 1921

he accepts with equanimity the changes in his fortunes; virtuous and moral, although he is an atheist, he willingly assists others. When he is condemned, he accepts his end with dignity, while realizing the price of the life he is losing. As a clerical counterpart to Brotteaux, France introduces the abbé Longuemare, a persecuted priest who is his friend, although he is just as devoted to his Christian faith as Brotteaux is to Lucretian philosophy; it is a measure of France's own tolerance and pity that he makes the abbé die with as great a dignity as his friend.

Gamelin's end—upon the guillotine to which he had sent many—brings together poetic and historical justice, since it reflects the fate of the principal Jacobin leaders, a fate that illustrates the author's conviction that persecutions and injustice beget further persecutions. The novel also contains intimations of the synthetic process, identified by Karl Marx and later historians, by which the excesses of the Terror and failure of the republic led, through reaction, to the militarism of Napoleon and the empire.

La Révolte des anges, France's last novel, of which sixty thousand copies were sold within six weeks, is a whimsical fable on very serious matters. A sort of mock epic set in modern France, it is partly a satire of French mores, politics (including the opposing strains of monarchism and anarchism), class structure, religion, and, not least, women. It is also a retelling of Western history from the Greeks and Romans through the Middle Ages, Renaissance, and modern times. Finally, it is an attack on the Judeo-Christian religious tradition through mockery of sacred teachings and God, or Yahweh, himself. The attack was especially timely, in the author's eyes, in view of what has come to be called the Catholic Renaissance of the early part of the century in France. This included noteworthy conversions among writers such as Péguy and Francis Jammes (Paul Claudel had already returned to the faith in 1886); the period also witnessed various manifestations of religious militancy—the militarism of Ernest Psichari, Georges Bernanos's call to arms under the sign of Joan of Arc, the ministry of Charles de Foucault in the heart of Africa, and the nationalistic Catholicism of the Action Française movement of Charles Maurras. The Catholic press did not overlook the offensiveness of *La Révolte des anges*: one review was entitled "Un Possédé de Belzébuth," a clear indication of the view that the novelist was possessed by the devil.

Indeed, France's novel will offend deeply any pious reader who might proceed far enough to see that God is called merely a petty Demiurge, the local and very limited, but tyrannical, deity of a few primitive Syrian tribes; but it will delight those who appreciate the Enlightenment tradition of biblical and doctrinal criticism by its reductio ad absurdum and arguments appealing to natural law. For it is nature that is the author's great model: natural substance, natural law, and natural impulses are the only truth, and morality is merely an artifice arrived at and prolonged by custom, for the purposes of social utility. The novel illustrates some of the best features of the author's style and characteristic topics and motifs: for instance, the superb private library in which early events take place; the references to the eighteenth century, partly through chapter titles that evoke novels of the period; the emphasis on the Greek ideals of harmony and reason; and criticisms of the vanity of women—but of men too. Throughout, the style is witty and fresh, the plot inventive; the author shows a tolerant understanding of human foibles, as well as human possibilities. The work constitutes a remarkable feat for a man of seventy years; while its mixture of fantasy and social criticism has led critics to compare it to Gide's *Les Caves du Vatican* (translated as *The Vatican Swindle,* 1925), which appeared the same year, by its vitality it also bears comparison with his witty farewell to fiction, *Thésée* (1946; translated as *Theseus,* 1948).

The cosmogony and theology of Dante and John Milton and the universal history of Jacques-Bénigne Bossuet are the author's negative models, as he ridicules their vision of the divine and human drama. He gives free rein to anticlericalism, mocking the account of creation and the fall in Genesis, the Mosaic law, the doctrine of redemption, and criticizing the imposition of the new religion in the Roman Empire, the establishment of a state church, monasticism, obscurantism, the Reformation (Martin Luther and John Calvin are worse than the popes), and the emotional religion of the Romantics. His fallen angels—for it is they who have turned against God, descended to live in France among men, and taken on very human features—expound the truth about the universe and the Divinity himself and, like Prometheus, propose to assist men, whom they pity. But they also plot a new rebellion against Heaven—one which they hope will succeed, thanks to new tactics, where Lucifer failed.

When, after very earthly peripeteia, the angels are ready for the offensive, they consult with Lucifer, who resides in a comfortable Hades where the shades pass the time of day in the sort of intellectual discourse the author loved. Taking the matter under advisement, he then has a prophetic dream that enacts what will happen if Heaven is besieged and God is overthrown: God will then be exiled to Hell, a new and admirable victim, and Satan will assume all the divine prerogatives and reign just as tyrannically as Yahweh. Thanks to this warning, which shows what France thought of political power, the angels decline to pursue their plan. The fable ends without apology for its irreverence and anthropomorphism, and the novelist leaves his reader with a fraternal sense of the physical world, which is the field of human possibility.

The Great War confirmed predictions France had made in *Les Opinions de M. Jérôme Coignard* and *L'Ile des pingouins* concerning the dangers of industrialized warfare. In September 1914, after he had made a public statement concerning the possibility of friendship with Germany after the conflict, he was hounded by printed and anonymous accusations of treason—including an attack by Maurras of the Action Française—and calls for punishment. He then asked—at the age of seventy—to be drafted for military service. Pronounced unfit, he left Paris with Emma for a country property, La Béchellerie, which he purchased two years later. Thenceforth he was very cautious about making pronouncements that could be taken as unpatriotic.

In 1917 Michel Psichari was killed at the front, and the next year Suzanne died of Spanish influenza. Three years later, when Mme France (who had remarried) died, Anatole was declared the guardian of his only grandson, Lucien. After the war he made some famous pacifist statements that are probably truer to his convictions than the patriotic positions he had taken in wartime writings. His prestige was tremendous; as Bancquart notes, he was endowed, in the eyes of many, with a sort of "sacerdoce antisacerdotal" (antipriestly priestly authority). In 1919 he received an honorary doctorate from the University of Athens, and in 1921 he was awarded the Nobel Prize for literature. For his eightieth birthday, an official celebration was held in Paris, attended by representatives from all over the world, and after his death on 12 October 1924 he was granted a national funeral.

To those who would argue that France's current reputation accurately represents his worth, one can reply that his work illustrates, in a pleasing style, some of the traits generally admired as most Gallic, as if his mind were in harmony with his name: urbanity, wit, taste, craftsmanship, perspicacity, and rationalism. Not without reason was he called "The Master," both in his own time and often in the large body of criticism that appeared after his death. But few, if any, authors who live to occupy a pontifical position avoid the pitfalls fame brings; as their skills decline, their art rarely meets their own earlier standards and still less frequently the demands created by changing tastes and artistic evolution. Even as France reached fame in his own nation and elsewhere as one of the foremost authors of his time (the first collection of his *Pages choisies*, or selected texts, was published in 1898), Gide and others were ready to point out the serious limitations of his achievement.

Indeed, his work presents no great synthesis. He came too late, and was perhaps temperamentally unsuited, for the great, creative, utopistic imagination of the French Revolution and some of the Romantics, and he was prejudiced, partly because of his experience in the Commune, against its positivist avatars in the late nineteenth century; so that, despite his adoption of liberal views when he was past middle age, his modes of writing and his *imaginaire* were set and he was unable to go beyond his essentially critical spirit. As for visions of destruction and cataclysm, like those that mark many authors who followed him, he was prophet enough to see what risks the twentieth century would run but not enough to imagine fully the moral and spiritual consequences. In short, by the measures of the emerging twentieth century, and even more so by present ones, France may seem to come up short, his humor and workmanship more ornamental than substantive, his insights superficial—his art like the flitting of the bee in Jean de La Fontaine's sixteenth epistle, the "chose légère" (light thing) who goes "de fleur en fleur et d'objet en objet" (from flower to flower and object to object).

Yet to see him as only superficial or a bourgeois dilettante would be shortsighted. At the risk of alienating friends and readers, he embraced the major liberal cause of the end of the century, and in his social novels he attempted to show the flaws in French thought and institutions that made possible the miscarriage of justice for Dreyfus. Like Voltaire, he was determined to instruct in his writings—indeed to chastise—as well as to please; he was a relentless *moraliste.* His work is like the new *In Praise of Folly* (the reference is to the work by Desiderius Erasmus, first published in 1511) that he envisaged, "qui semblera frivole à la frivolité mais où les sages reconnaîtront la sagesse prudemment cachée" (which will seem frivolous to the frivolous but in which the wise will recognize wisdom prudently hidden). In opposition to the scientism of many of his contemporaries, he argued that the apparent progress of science was illusory, since the horizons of the infinite unknown merely retreat, and that too much reliance on the intellect was dangerous. Many of his pages on such subjects as forms of government, belief versus skepticism, happiness, the needs of the body, and so on shine with truth. He belongs thus to a major tradition in French literature and thought that, mutatis mutandis, is visible, and respected, in later writers

France on his deathbed

such as Camus and Gide himself.

As for the *inquiétude* or anxiety that Gide found missing, it was not entirely absent. In France's writings, reason is constantly struggling with the unreasonable, with the mystery that mocks the very reason with which one identifies it, and with the inadequacy of language: "On ne dit rien dans un livre de ce qu'on voudrait dire. S'exprimer, c'est impossible" (One says nothing in a book of what one would like to say. It is impossible to express oneself). Perhaps that is why the abbé Coignard expresses the wish that, like Candide, he had retreated to an enclosed orchard, a garden, rather than devoting himself to studies, which leave a taste of sadness and bitterness. Anatole France lived long enough to see that the twentieth century would bear out his skepticism: although the abbé said that the future was a useful place for building dreams, as in utopia, it was not a brave new world that the new century brought to fruition, but destruction: "Les armées augmentent sans cesse en force et en nombre. Les peuples entiers y seront un jour engouffrés" (Armies are ceaselessly growing in strength and numbers. Whole peoples will one day be engulfed by them). With such a prospect, France cultivated the garden of belles lettres and of the mind, for his own pleasure and that of countless readers.

Letters:

Lettres inédites d'Anatole France à Jacques Lion, edited by Marie-Claire Bancquart (Paris: Société Anatole France, 1965);

Lettres inédites d'Anatole France à Paul-Louis Couchoud et à sa femme (Paris: Société Anatole France, 1968);

Lettres inédites d'Anatole France à Paul Grunebaum-Ballin (Paris: Société Anatole France, 1971);

Lettres intimes, edited by Jacques Suffel (Paris: Nizet, 1984).

Biographies:

Lewis Piaget Shanks, *Anatole France* (New York: Harper, 1919; revised, 1932);

James Lewis May, *Anatole France* (New York: Dodd, Mead, 1924);

Nicolas Ségur, *Conversations avec Anatole France* (Paris: Fasquelle, 1925); translated by May as *Conversations with Anatole France* (London: John Lane / New York: Dodd, Mead, 1926);

Jeanne-Maurice Pouquet, *Le Salon de Madame de Caillavet* (Paris: Hachette, 1926);
Ségur, *Dernières conversations avec Anatole France* (Paris: Fasquelle, 1927); translated by May as *The Opinions of Anatole France* (London: John Lane / New York: Dodd, Mead, 1928);
Pierre Calmettes, *La Grande Passion d'Anatole France* (Paris: Seheur, 1929);
Jacob Alexrad, *Anatole France: A Life Without Illusions* (New York & London: Harper, 1944);
Léon Carias, *Les Carnets intimes d'Anatole France* (Paris: Emile-Paul, 1946);
Jacques Suffel, *Anatole France* (Paris: Editions du Myrte, 1946);
David Tylden-Wright, *Anatole France* (New York: Walker, 1967);
Géraldi Leroy, ed., *Les Ecrivains et l'Affaire Dreyfus* (Paris: Presses Universitaires de France, 1983);
Marie-Claire Bancquart, *Anatole France: Un sceptique passionné* (Paris: Calmann-Lévy, 1984).

References:

Marie-Claire Bancquart, *Anatole France, polémiste* (Paris: Nizet, 1962);
Bancquart, *Les Ecrivains et l'histoire d'après Maurice Barrès, Léon Bloy, Anatole France, Charles Péguy* (Paris: Nizet, 1966);
Jean-Jacques Brousson, *L'Itinéraire de Paris à Buenos-Ayres* (Paris: Cres, 1927);
Haakon Chevalier, *The Ironic Temper: Anatole France and His Time* (New York: Oxford University Press, 1932);
Europe, no. 32 (December 1954): 3-67 [group of articles on France];
Carter Jefferson, *Anatole France: The Politics of Skepticism* (New Brunswick, N.J.: Rutgers University Press, 1965);
Jean Levaillant, *Essai sur l'évolution intellectuelle d'Anatole France* (Paris: Armand Colin, 1965);
Le Lys Rouge (Paris: Société Anatole France, 1933-1965, 1969-);
Jean Sareil, *Anatole France et Voltaire* (Geneva: Droz, 1961);
Jacques Suffel, *Anatole France par lui-même* (Paris: Editions du Seuil, 1954);
André Vandegans, *Anatole France: Les années de formation* (Paris: Nizet, 1954);
Reino Virtanen, *Anatole France* (New York: Twayne, 1968);
Loring Baker Walton, *Anatole France and the Greek World* (Durham, N.C.: Duke University Press, 1950).

Papers:

Many of France's manuscripts, including correspondence and notebooks, are at the Bibliothèque Nationale and the Bibliothèque Historique de la Ville de Paris. Others are held in private collections.

Eugène Fromentin

(24 October 1820 - 27 August 1876)

John A. Fleming
University of Toronto

SELECTED BOOKS: *Un Eté dans le Sahara* (Paris: Michel Lévy, 1857);

Une Année dans le Sahel (Paris: Michel Lévy, 1859);

Dominique (Paris: Hachette, 1863); translated by V. I. Longman (London: Gerald Howe, 1932); translated by Edward Marsh (London: Cresset, 1948);

Les Maîtres d'autrefois: Belgique; Hollande (Paris: Plon, 1876); translated by Mary C. Robbins as *The Old Masters of Belgium and Holland* (Boston & New York: Houghton, Mifflin, 1882); translated by Andrew Boyle, with an introduction and notes by H. Gerson, as *The Masters of Past Time* (London: Phaidon, 1948);

Voyage en Egypte, edited, with an introduction, by Jean-Marie Carré (Paris: Fernand Aubier, 1935);

Gustave Drouineau, by Fromentin and Emile Beltrémieux, edited, with an introduction, by Barbara Wright (Paris: Minard, 1969);

Etude sur l' "Ahasvérus" d'Edgar Quinet, by Fromentin and Paul Bataillard, edited by Wright and Terence Mellors (Geneva: Droz, 1982).

Edition and Collection: *Œuvres complètes*, edited by Guy Sagnes (Paris: Gallimard, Bibliothèque de la Pléiade, 1984);

Dominique, Eugène Fromentin, edited by Pierre Barbéris (Paris: Flammarion, 1987).

Eugène Fromentin (portrait by Ricard; from J. W. Batchelor and Philippe Garcin, eds., "Dominique": Morceaux choisis, *1969)*

Although Eugène Fromentin published only one novel, his place among the important writers of the nineteenth century has been secured by the continuing popularity of that work. By the early years of this century, more than thirty printings of *Dominique* (1863; translated, 1932) had appeared, clear evidence of the novel's reception by Fromentin's contemporaries. That number now exceeds one hundred.

Dominique belongs in part to the tradition of the "intimate" confessional novel, in which the narrator recounts the sentimental adventures of his younger self as seen and judged through the eyes of the present. Sometimes apologetic, sometimes critical, almost always nostalgic, such narrators give a very personal and usually tendentious tone to their story. Within this context *Dominique* falls chronologically and thematically between François-René de Chateaubriand's *René* (1805; translated, 1813) or Benjamin Constant's *Adolphe* (1816; translated, 1816) and Alain-Fournier's *Le Grand Meaulnes* (1913; translated as *The Wanderer*, 1928). In other ways Fromentin's novel reaches further back into the psychological classicism of the seventeenth century in the manner of Marie-

Madeleine, Comtesse de La Fayette's *La Princesse de Clèves* (1678; translated as *The Princess of Cleves*, 1679) and forward, as one can now see, toward the increasing formalism of the *nouveau roman*.

The editors of successive editions of *Dominique* have brought to the apparent conventionality of this text their own readings and interpretations of its meaning. These range from the confrontation of classicism with romanticism to the notion of a historical and political novel in which the values of the ancien régime are a kind of subtext against which the Industrial Revolution and the lingering ideals of romanticism play out the emerging conflicts of the modern world. Perhaps the key to the importance and the success of *Dominique* lies in this very ambivalence of meaning and in Fromentin's unconscious anticipation of many of the technical and theoretical preoccupations of twentieth-century art forms. Each generation of readers has found its own sense above and beyond the sentimental adventure of thwarted love and renunciation.

Eugène-Samuel-Auguste Fromentin was born in La Rochelle on 24 October 1820, the son of a successful doctor, Toussaint Fromentin-Dupeux, and Jenny Billotte Fromentin-Dupeux, daughter of a secretary of the Naval Service in Rochefort and regional councillor in La Rochelle. His elder brother, Charles, born in 1818, became a doctor like their father while Eugène, after abortive beginnings in law, and against the wishes of his father, pursued an uncertain and often difficult career as a painter, still dependent upon financial support from his family until he was more than thirty. The family's summer house at Saint-Maurice, a few miles from La Rochelle on the road to La Pallice, where residence stretched from June to November, was to play an essential role throughout Fromentin's life. It was there that the final, rewritten version of *Dominique* was completed, and it was there that he died on 27 August 1876.

Fromentin lived most of his adult life in Paris. Summer and autumn were spent at Saint-Maurice. Except for brief visits beyond the capital to friends and fellow artists, and his several formative trips to North Africa, he was by nature a stay-at-home, disinclined to travel except in the cause of art.

Fromentin excelled as a student at the Collège de La Rochelle and finished his "classe de huitième" with a prize in history in 1830. Eight years later a report in the *Charente-Inférieure* (30 August 1838) records that he was received *bachelier* at the head of the class. Instead of proceeding directly to university studies, Fromentin spent the ensuing year at home writing poetry and verse translations of classical and foreign authors, a young man à la mode in La Rochelle. In 1839 he began studies in law in Paris, completing his *baccalauréat en droit* (first diploma in law) in 1841 and his *licence* (second diploma in law) in 1843.

During these years Fromentin continued to write poetry and collaborated on a variety of other literary projects. He established friendships with Paul Bataillard and Emile Beltrémieux from La Rochelle, and in 1842 he met Armand du Mesnil, who would become a lifelong friend and mentor. Because he was already actively engaged in painting at this time, his failure to pass the examination for a doctorate in law in 1844 prompted him to abandon his studies and shift to art as his chief occupation. In that same year Jenny Léocadie Chessé, whom Fromentin had known and fallen in love with as a schoolboy of fourteen before her marriage to Emile Béraud in 1834, died of cancer and was buried at Saint-Maurice, where the two families had lived as neighbors throughout his childhood. Four years older than Fromentin, she was to be the model for Madeleine in *Dominique*, although recent evidence suggests that unlike the relationship of Dominique and Madeleine, their liaison was not platonic. The correspondence of the two lovers, intermittently separated by their families and circumstances, was reportedly destroyed during her funeral.

In 1845 Fromentin entered the studio of the landscape painter Louis Cabat for three months as part of his more general literary and painterly activity. This commitment, expressed in a letter to his mother, drew him further into the sphere of painters and painting: "Je suis peintre, je le crois, je le sens, on me l'affirme; pourquoi, mon Dieu! me contraindre à n'être pas ce que je puis être" (I am a painter, I believe it, I feel it, people tell me so; why for Heaven's sake! should I be prevented from being what I can be). His contacts and friendships with painters such as Albert Aubert and Charles Labbé continued to grow without excluding an ongoing interest in literature.

Fromentin's first trip to Algeria, from March to April 1846, with his friends du Mesnil and Labbé set forever his course as a painter and sowed the seeds of his first two published works, *Un Eté dans le Sahara* (A Summer in the Sahara,

1857) and *Une Année dans le Sahel* (A Year in the Sahel, 1859). A year later Fromentin exhibited his first paintings in the Salon and made a second trip to Algeria, again with Labbé, which lasted from September 1847 until May 1848. This second visit provided much of the material for *Une Année dans le Sahel*. However, at that time painting, not writing, was his priority. Five paintings of Algerian subjects were shown in the Salon of 1849, but despite the sale of several, Fromentin was still financially dependent upon his parents.

In May 1852 Fromentin married Marie Cavellet de Beaumont, granddaughter of du Mesnil's mother, who lived with the du Mesnil family more as sister to Armand than niece. The young couple left six months later for what would be Fromentin's third and final visit to Algeria, which lasted until October 1853. They returned not to Paris but to Saint-Maurice. Their only child, Marguerite, was born at Lafond. Fromentin had just completed his first book-length manuscript, based upon the North African experience, *Un Eté dans le Sahara*, published in serial form in the *Revue de Paris* (June-December 1854). By this time he was also working on *Une Année dans le Sahel* as well as continuing to paint and to participate in the annual Salon.

Fromentin had contacts with Gustave Moreau, indeed borrowed his studio for a time when Moreau was in Italy in 1859. Théophile Gautier and George Sand published articles about his work, Gautier in the *Artiste* (1857), Sand in the *Presse* (1857). Having returned to Paris in 1857, Fromentin was more in the public eye than ever before. His paintings in the Salon of 1859 drew favorable critical reviews from Gautier and Charles Baudelaire. Despite illness, he completed *Une Année dans le Sahel*, which appeared in the *Revue des Deux Mondes* (November-December 1858). Probably begun in October 1859, work on *Dominique* would continue until serial publication in the *Revue des Deux Mondes* (April-May 1862) and publication in volume form.

This literary activity, often painfully accomplished, did not diminish his output as a painter. Six canvases by Fromentin were shown in the Salon of 1861. His reputation as both an artist and a writer was now well established. A long correspondence with Sand followed the publication of *Dominique*; Charles-Augustin Sainte-Beuve published an article on his three books in the *Constitutionnel* (1864); the state acquired one of his paintings, *La Curée, ou Chasse au faucon en Algérie* (The Kill, or Falcon Hunt in Algeria, 1863), for ten thousand francs.

The early 1860s were Fromentin's most successful years, but as the 1870s approached, both his personal and professional life deteriorated. His father died on 19 December 1867, and his candidacy for the Académie des Beaux-Arts failed, although he did become an "officier de la Légion d'Honneur" in 1869. Meanwhile, Fromentin's attempts at renewing his art centered in Orientalism and were for the most part badly received. His mythological painting for the Salon of 1868, *Centaures et centauresses s'exerçant à tirer à l'arc* (Centaurs and Centauresses Practicing with Bow and Arrow), was publicly deprecated. Sickness and a certain physical and mental fatigue appear to have overtaken Fromentin during these years. Brief trips to Egypt, for the opening of the Suez Canal, and to Venice, while undertaken in his usual spirit of serious endeavor, brought few concrete results. Although he participated as a jury member for the Salons and served on a commission for reforms in the fine arts, his efforts at personal intellectual renewal were unproductive, and his own judgment of his work and its worth was increasingly severe.

Two very different and more positive events came in 1873 and 1874: the marriage on 12 August 1873 of his daughter Marguerite to Alexandre Billotte, eldest son of his uncle Alexandre; and in the professional sphere, a reedition (1874) in separate volumes of his two books on North Africa, with a preface in which he sets out a kind of aesthetic program. In July 1875, after a winter of sickness and discouragement, and at the urging of his old friend du Mesnil, Fromentin traveled to Belgium and Holland to see firsthand the works by the old masters of the north. This trip of less than a month was to result in his final publication during his lifetime, *Les Maîtres d'autrefois* (1876; translated as *The Old Masters of Belgium and Holland*, 1882), perhaps the finest, most subtle piece of historical art criticism produced in nineteenth-century France.

He returned to Saint-Maurice on 30 July, where he wrote and revised his text into the autumn. It was published in the *Revue des Deux Mondes* (January-March 1876) and appeared as a book in June. As he was working on the proofs for a second edition of *Dominique* in the summer of 1876, Fromentin fell ill, shortly after arriving for his annual sojourn at Saint-Maurice on 19 August. He died on 27 August of an "anthrax charbonneux" (malignant tumor) before du Mesnil and others could be summoned. He was buried in the cemetery at Saint-Maurice.

Fromentin's first published literary works, apart from the occasional poetry and translations of his youth, are the two travel narratives, both closely tied to his career as a painter as well as to the ambivalence and difficulty that accompanied this choice. His first voyage to Algeria in the spring of 1846, with neither the knowledge nor the consent of his family, set his direction as a painter and led to the two longer trips to Algeria, which gave him the materials upon which he drew almost exclusively for the rest of his life. *Un Eté dans le Sahara* and *Une Année dans le Sahel,* which recorded the experiences, impressions, and souvenirs of these excursions into exotic landscapes and another culture, became in the end essential not only to his reputation as an Orientalist but to his claims as a talented writer as well. Although other authors of the time also combined literary and artistic gifts, the two were nowhere more intimately reciprocal than in the case of Fromentin. The importance of sensibility as exercised through the filter of memory, which was to become a mark of his technique as a painter, informs in much the same way the narrator's reconstitution of his past in *Dominique.*

Fromentin was acutely aware of the complementary and necessary nature of these two activities as he pursued a dual career. In the 1874 preface to the reedition of his two travel texts—so apparently conventional within a historical and generic context, so unconventional in attitude and presentation—he develops a kind of aesthetic credo based on psychological self-analysis: "Le seul intérêt qu'à mes yeux ils n'aient pas perdu, celui qui les rattache à ma vie présente, c'est une certaine manière de voir, de sentir et d'exprimer qui m'est personnelle et n'a pas cessé d'être mienne" (The only interest in my view that they have not lost, what links them to my present life, is a certain way of seeing, of feeling, and of expressing things, which is a part of me and has not ceased to be mine).

A statement of similar tone was made much earlier in a letter to Sand (19 April 1862) while he was working on *Dominique*: "M'émouvoir encore avec des souvenirs . . . et exprimer sous forme de livre une bonne partie de moi, la meilleure, qui ne trouvera jamais place dans des tableaux" (To feel again through memory . . . and to express in written form a large part of myself, the best of me, that which will never find a place in my paintings). The North African adventure and the more intimate, personal experience of his adolescent love for his young neighbor, although entirely different in nature, would both require literary rather than plastic form if certain qualities of sensation and feeling were to be recreated.

Conscious of his inexperience as a painter when confronted with the North African landscape and its peoples, yet filled with "le désir impatient de le reproduire n'importe comment" (the impatient desire to represent it [his visit] by whatever means), Fromentin recorded many of his impressions and reactions during his trips to Algeria: "C'est alors que l'insuffisance de mon métier me conseilla, comme expédient, d'en chercher un autre, et que la difficulté de peindre avec le pinceau me fit essayer de la plume" (It was then that the inadequacy of my means as a painter suggested to me, as an expedient, that I look for other ways, and that the difficulty of representation with a brush made me try the pen).

Un Eté dans le Sahara, which is presented in one-way epistolary form—the letters are sent to an imaginary recipient but no answering voice is transcribed—recounts the progress of Fromentin's vocation as a painter. Determined to turn the search for the Sahara and the essence of the North African experience into an affirmation of his calling, Fromentin chose a narrative form to give shape and continuity, and intellectual and affective structure, to the painterly and fundamentally static subject of his observations. This too, like his paintings, was a retrospective project in which memory served to filter and refine the materials of brute experience.

The image of quest that some critics have found in *Un Eté dans le Sahara* records the assimilation of a subject and a theme, the assumption of a vocation, which will eventually bring both success and impasse to the artist, for Fromentin's achievements as an Orientalist were to fix him in that role forever in the public eye, and inhibit his own search for renewal during his mature years as a painter. Fromentin's third and final trip to Algeria was no longer a voyage of discovery, but one of consolidation and reflection. The title of the text to be drawn mainly from this period—*Une Année dans le Sahel*—reflects the more static form of the content, although several anecdotes were added at the suggestion of du Mesnil to give it some narrative interest.

The choice of the epistolary form for these two travel volumes is significant. It creates from

Self-portrait of Fromentin in 1843 (from S. A. Rhodes, ed., Dominique, *1930)*

the beginning a first-person voice, as in *Dominique*, which is located in the subject matter it conveys. The letter by its very nature concretizes separation and another space, while the formal fragmentation of the text constitutes at the same time a material and narrative chronology. Sometimes dated, sometimes located, letters—however disparate in subject or separated in space and time—convey a sense of structure and unified perspective. The physical linearity of words and the sequential inevitability of letters supplied Fromentin with a predetermined coherence for experiences, both visual and emotional, which was not so readily to hand in plastic form.

The North African adventure was external and intellectual, and it engaged the artistic ambitions and sensibilities of Fromentin in a material and perceptual way that provided a subject matter essentially visual and separate, a kind of geographic and cultural "elsewhere," very distinct from his own origins and personality. In *Dominique* the adventure is sentimental and strikes closer to home. The tale of Dominique's frustrated love and renunciation has psychological and human dimensions not to be found in the depiction of local color and the exoticism of desert spaces. At the same time the interior landscapes of *Dominique* resemble in quality and manner, if not in subject, the written transpositions of the impressions provoked by the desert and its inhabitants in *Un Eté dans le Sahara* and *Une Année dans le Sahel.*

Fromentin's youthful promise to himself to tell one day the story of his love for Jenny Léocadie Chessé was to be as difficult to keep as his beginnings as a painter had been difficult. Under pressure from his publisher to fulfill an earlier commitment to provide a text for the *Revue des Deux Mondes*, Fromentin tried, apparently without inclination or inspiration, to recount this story fifteen years later. Because he was dissatisfied with his first efforts, it was only at the urging of du Mesnil that he finally rewrote the entire text of the novel, as he proclaimed in a letter to Gaston Romieux: "J'ai récrit d'entrain, en deux mois, sans m'arrêter, depuis la première ligne jusqu'à la dernière, un volume qui ne ressemble pas plus au premier que la nuit ne ressemble au jour" (I have briskly rewritten, in two months, without stopping, from the first line to the last, a volume that resembles the first no more than night resembles day).

Whatever merit there may be in the novel as autobiographical fiction, whatever pleasure can be found in a key to characters and events, *Dominique* remains a classical psychological study of thwarted or mistaken love, like *La Princesse de Clèves* or *Le Grand Meaulnes*, in which the particulars of the anecdote embrace a more general human experience of love and innocence lost in a multitude of ways. One of the reasons for the continuing appeal of *Dominique* through more than a hundred reprints and editions lies in the representation of the state of mind, of the diffuse but powerful emotion created by a nostalgia for lost happiness and lost possibilities. There is a bitter pleasure in misfortune—a particular kind of sensibility growing out of romanticism and the passage of time—that forms one of the principal strains in Marcel Proust's work as well. But while memory in Proust re-creates the past in its physical and sensuous integrity, in Fromentin's work it blurs the edges of past experience, forever lost, as it enhances the emotional content.

Guy Sagnes, in the Pléiade edition of the *Œuvres complètes* (1984), provides a psychological and thematic interpretation of *Dominique* that describes the novel as the expression of a personality and a tradition, without reducing the complexity and the originality of the text to the usual clichés about either of these elements. For Sagnes this story of a young man's impossible love is reconstituted by a "mémoire spéciale et infaillible" (special and infallible memory) that transposes and represents not so much the sentimental adventure as the sensations and emotions provoked by it, fixed in the memory and possessed of all the regrets and uncertainties of the "might have been." According to Sagnes, the purely introspective nature of the experience, its qualities of lost happiness, solitude, and reflection, are indifferent to historical period and external events. Pierre Barbéris, in a 1987 edition of the work, takes a very different view and sees behind the romantic anecdote a historical chronology and a political dimension that give substance to the personal and psychological content.

Beyond these and other explanations of the continuing popularity of *Dominique* may be found prefigurations of subjects and methods of representation that have attracted the growing interest of readers, writers, and artists in the twentieth century. Dominique stands at the end of a long line of Romantic heroes as the "man of failure" and anticipates thereby the "classic" modern protagonist, the antihero. More important still perhaps, one discovers in the themes and techniques of his discourse many of the preoccupations of modern art: the planimetric nature of landscape and canvas, the geometry of artificial spaces, the abstractions hidden within natural forms, the negative syntax and images of absence, and the emptiness and zero latitude that underlie representation. *Dominique* may still be read partly because of the universally human experience with which it deals, but also because it coincides with a certain modern sensibility and because it possesses technical dimensions that test the ongoing questions of artistic representation.

Dominique is an apparently conventional and realistic text that employs the usual confessional device of the narrator who looks back and recounts his past until it rejoins the present in which he and his listener/reader find themselves. His story is equally conventional in its superficial biographical content. As an adolescent, Dominique has fallen in love with a young woman, Madeleine, a year or so older than he, who marries an older man in what seems an arranged marriage. Only at the moment of the marriage does young Dominique realize, too late, that he loves Madeleine. Time itself has conspired against him: too young to assess properly his emotions, too young to enter into the game of love. Time and retrospection will continue to shape his fate, for time is the medium of narration and absence in *Dominique*, as space is the dimension of presence and of painting.

Much of the ensuing action recalls Dominique's efforts to suppress his love for Madeleine, his occasional lapses and outbursts of desire, and his eventual renunciation when Madeleine herself is about to succumb to these pressures. Two friends counsel him and, through the example of their own lives, propose very different solutions to Dominique's moral dilemma in this bourgeois adaptation of the classical confrontation between passion and duty. Olivier, the school friend and cynical young dandy, leads a frivolous, detached, and idle life of pleasure, which ends eventually in his suicide manqué and his withdrawal from society. Augustin, Dominique's young tutor and lifelong mentor, represents a life of impoverished struggle and honest endeavor as a writer, minor functionary, and politician. Madeleine's sister Julie, in her unrequited

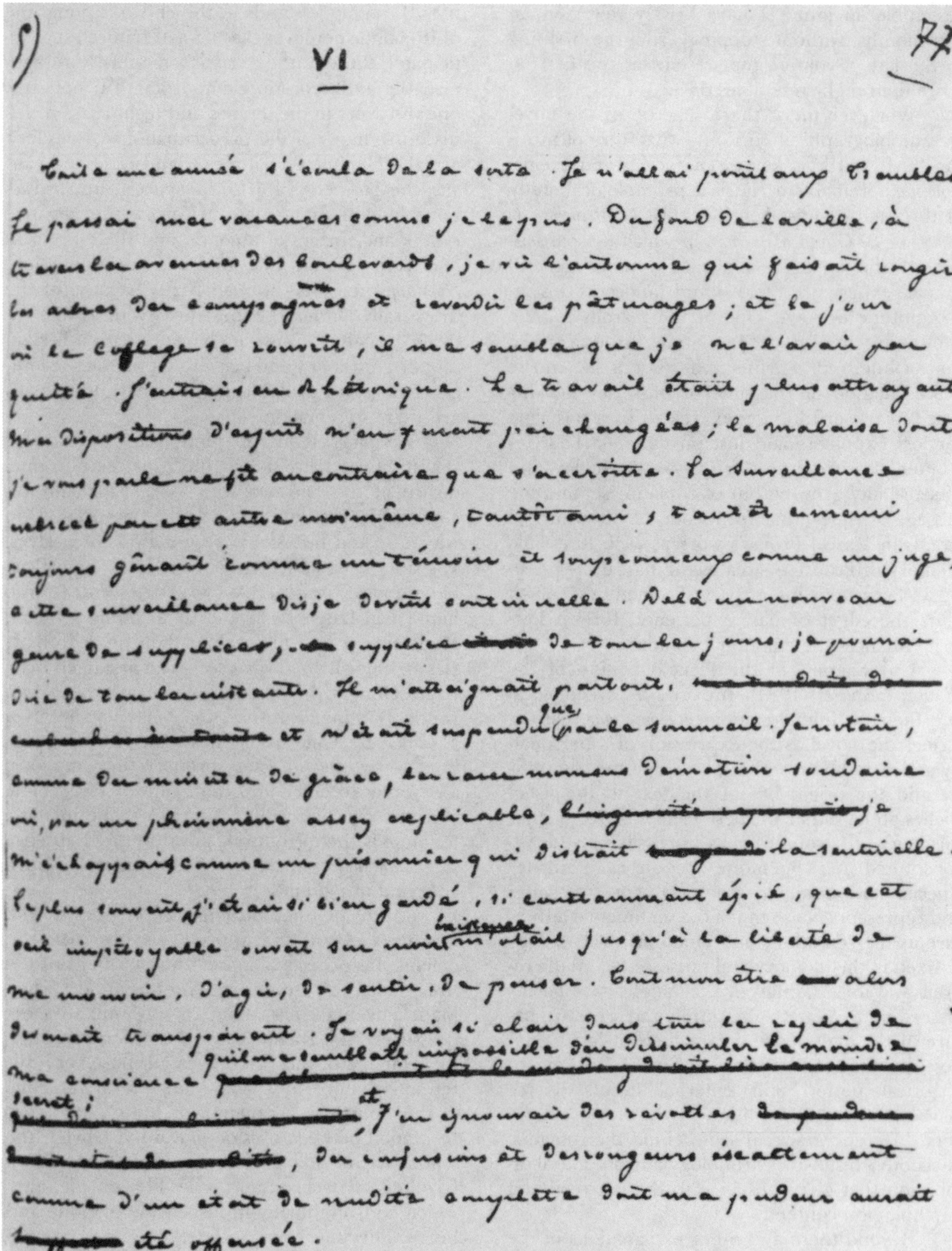

5) 77

VI

Toute une année s'écoula de la sorte. Je n'allai point aux Trembles. Je passai mes vacances comme je le pus. Du fond de la ville, à travers les avenues des boulevards, je vis l'automne qui faisait rougir les arbres des campagnes et reverdir les pâturages; et le jour où le collège se rouvrit, il me sembla que je ne l'avais pas quitté. J'entrais en rhétorique. Le travail était plus attrayant; mes dispositions d'esprit n'en furent pas changées; le malaise dont je vous parle ne fit au contraire que s'accroître. La surveillance exercée par cet autre moi-même, tantôt ami, tantôt ennemi, toujours gênant comme un témoin et soupçonneux comme un juge, cette surveillance dis-je devint continuelle. De là un nouveau genre de supplices, supplice de tous les jours, je pourrais dire de tous les instants. Il m'atteignait partout, et n'était suspendu que par le sommeil. Je n'eus, comme des minutes de grâce, les rares moments d'inattention soudaine où, par un phénomène assez explicable, je m'échappais comme un prisonnier qui distrait la sentinelle. Le plus souvent j'étais si bien gardé, si constamment épié, que cet œil impitoyable ouvert sur moi m'ôtait jusqu'à la liberté de me mouvoir, d'agir, de sentir, de penser. Tout mon être alors devenait transparent. Je voyais si clair dans tous les replis de ma conscience qu'il me semblait impossible d'en dissimuler le moindre secret; et j'en éprouvais des révoltes, des confusions et des rougeurs exactement comme d'un état de nudité complète dont ma pudeur aurait été offensée.

Page from the manuscript for Dominique *(Collection of Eric Dahl)* love for Olivier, plays a lesser role as a counterpoint to Dominique's impossible although reciprocated love.

The conclusion to Dominique's sentimental adventure is presented in the opening lines of the novel in a series of negative and paradoxical statements that creates an immediate psychological and thematic ambiguity. Dominique is now married, the father of two children, and a gentleman farmer occupied with his estates, as well as mayor of the local village, and his initial words seem to belie the suppression of his desire and his happy resignation to the life of a country squire: "Certainement je n'ai pas à me plaindre . . . car, Dieu merci, je ne suis plus rien, à supposer que j'aie jamais été quelque chose" (Certainly I have no reason to complain . . . for, thank Heavens, I am no longer anything, if indeed I ever were).

As Dominique reaches back in memory to retell the story of his youth and fateful encounter with Madeleine to his anonymous interlocutor, the events of his life unfold within this frame of negative and absent beings. At the same time, however, the reader's attention is diverted to some extent from the usual referential indicators in the fictional world to the purely visual constituents of the text by Dominique's insistence upon ciphers, codes, and the visual aspects of the written word. As the painter constructs his representation with colors and contours, so Fromentin the writer seems preoccupied with the raw materials of the text, the alphabet, the lexicon, and the typographical materiality of the printed page. The very act of writing—and the use of ciphers as encoded memoirs ("mémoires chiffrés") or mnemonic devices—becomes a kind of parallel subject and structure bridging the gap between the fictive adventure or referent world of *Dominique* and the physical materials of language used to represent it.

Dominique tells his story in the library of his ancestral home, Les Trembles, whose walls are covered with dates, initials, and hieroglyphs of all kinds, the encoded symbols of his youth that he now confronts, in particular those two elementary geometric forms, the triangle and the circle, which constitute his personal cipher as well as the beginning (A—alpha) and end (O—omega) of the alphabet. This scene is the most sustained manifestation of the essential structure and content of *Dominique*. The protagonist's life appears as a code inscribed in the physical decor of the room, as it is in the text before the reader. Here in the library the two Dominiques confront one another and set off the dynamic of the narration. Like the books themselves, the labeled boxes, the mountains of paper, the old desk spotted with ink and rutted with the marks of a knife, and the map of the globe represent both an absent experience and a catalogue of codes and materials: natural language, numbers, hieroglyphs, paper, ink, wood and glass, pen and stylus ("canif "). These are the raw materials of the writer's craft, the analogues of the painter's canvas, pigments, and brush.

Among these cryptic elements one in particular stands out: "Une figure géométrique élémentaire. Au-dessous, la même figure était reproduite, mais avec un ou deux traits de plus qui en modifiaient le sens sans en changer le principe, et la figure arrivait ainsi, et en se répétant avec des modifications nouvelles, à des significations singulières qui impliquaient le triangle ou le cercle originel, mais avec des résultats tout différents" (An elementary geometric figure. Below, the same figure was reproduced, but with one or two additional elements that modified its meaning without changing its principle, and the figure assumed in this way, and through repetition with further modifications, singular meanings that implied the triangle or the primordial circle, but with very different results). The anonymous narrator finds in the various glyphs and inscriptions a mute register of the phases of development and struggle in Dominique's life, "plus significatif dans sa mnémotechnie confuse que beaucoup de mémoires écrits" (more significant in its confused mnemonics than many written memoirs).

The triangle and the circle associated with the events in Dominique's life and the alphabetical and structural arrangement of the names can scarcely escape the reader's notice. The structural superposition of beginning and end created by the framing device is given further concrete existence by the superposition of the first and last words of the text, the title, and Augustin. The confrontation in the library of Dominique's past and present selves (his desire, and his abnegation as taught by Augustin) can be figured by facing *D*s (ᗡD), suggestive of the omega of the story. The beginning of the text does indeed follow the end of it, and the secret of the equation A = Ω lies in the relationship of the two Dominiques. The reader's eye must penetrate the ciphers ("chiffres") of the character and the alphabet, as his mind must pierce the manifest content of the words, for

Dominique's declarations are continuously ambivalent or paradoxical.

As the framing device integrates the "real" world of the first narrator with the space and time of Dominique's narration, so must the ciphers, signs, and words inscribed upon the library walls, and the page in front of the reader, replace or represent an absent reality of thing or experience, the function of the text (and Dominique's discourse) being to show the reader what is *not* present. *Dominique* is a self-conscious text presented as an encoded representation to be deciphered on the level of both event (content) and discourse (code). The negatives and the paradoxical affirmations of negative quantities that dominate the opening lines and recur throughout have both personal and psychological resonances for the protagonist, and a formal and problematical significance akin to the experimentations with figure, space, and representation of modern art. The opening pages then set up the dialectic of affirmation through (ab)negation, which will "dominate" the text. Similarly the text will render visible and readable the absent past and the insubstantial present on the level of object and experience, as well as the analogous nature of its own operations.

The natural world and its phenomena are also used to represent the archetypal and psychological content of the novel through an interplay of images, Christian and pagan, and through an identification of the human body with the anatomy of the natural world. The text of *Dominique* treats its content as a code made concrete in the graphemes of its own existence. Landscape, vegetation, and birds become ciphers in a psychic language that imitates the alphabet of words. This old idea is expressed discursively in *Une Année dans le Sahel*: "Le monde extérieur est comme un dictionnaire; c'est un livre rempli de répétitions et de synonymes" (The external world is like a dictionary; it is a book filled with repetitions and synonyms).

The anonymous narrator first meets Dominique one autumn day in the vineyards of the region he is visiting. Dominique is hunting with his two dogs. The decor (the vineyard of the Lord—*dominus*) and the players (Dominique and the dogs) suggest the Latin locus *domini canes* (the hounds of God), that is to say, the Dominicans, for whom renunciation and contemplation are as central as they are in Dominique's present life. Similarly the pagan rituals that invest the peasant celebrations of the grape harvest are bacchic in nature, and as the young people dance to the wild sound of bagpipes or dream in their beds of "contredanses" (country dances; contravention), the scarcely sublimated elements of desire and transgression introduce the other side of Dominique's experience, his past.

Fromentin near the end of his life (drawing by A. Gilbens; from S. A. Rhodes, ed., Dominique, *1930)*

Thus the framing scenes establish the representational characteristics of the text through letter form, intertext, and the image of the world as book upon and through whose physical materials the record of man is inscribed. The principle of the narration is contained in the proper names of the characters, more specifically their ciphers, which generate and summarize both structure and action. "Je ne suis plus rien" (I am no longer anything), says Dominique, echoing the cipher (O, Ω) that embodies his existence in time and space. Within space, "il s'éloignait aussi peu que possible du cercle étroit de cette existence active et cachée qui ne mesurait pas une lieue de rayon" (he strayed as little as possible from the narrow circle of this active and hidden existence that measured scarcely a league in radius). Within time, "l'hiver arrivait; le cercle de l'année se refermait sur lui" (winter would come, bringing the circle of the year to a close again).

At the same time the circle of omega created by the vis-à-vis of Dominique's past and present selves also contains Augustin's cipher in the implied grapheme of the protagonist's initial: D = delta = Δ. In effect Dominique's cipher is both circle and triangle. The meaning as well as the form of the inscription on the library walls is now intelligible. The circle and the triangle are not exclusive, but integral to the same "figure géométrique élémentaire." Madeleine's cipher, the double delta, identifies her absent and occulted love with Dominique's double self. In this way the ciphers of the characters—or rather the text, to take the word in both its senses—constitute a formal arrangement of the letters of the alphabet related to the structure and operations of the text as discourse and as story.

Fromentin excelled in Greek and Latin as a schoolboy, and, whether he consciously structured his text in these specific ways or not, the many explicit references in the novel to ciphers, numbers, and codes of one sort or another support an interpretation of *Dominique* that recalls as well the careful transpositions of sensuous perception—the languages of painting and text—that preoccupied him throughout his life. The intervention of time and memory in the process of artistic creation was necessary to the distillation of perceptual and emotional experience and the encoding of that experience in another medium. The trajectory between the two allowed for the internalization of the "object" and a change of perspective in which the consequences of perception displaced the percept itself.

Fromentin's 1875 trip to Belgium and Holland to study the great Flemish and Dutch masters, in particular Peter Paul Rubens and Rembrandt van Rijn, resulted in the publication of his last book, *Les Maîtres d'autrefois*. It was as though some sort of physical displacement were necessary to his creative urge, as if study in the field were requisite to the high seriousness that lay behind all his work. The reasons for this final trip are not clear. Perhaps poor health, from which he had suffered all his life, a need to find new ideas and fresh strength, or some sentimental impasse gave him the initial impulse. But it was du Mesnil once again who encouraged him to go.

Although art criticism and reviews of the Salons had been an institution in France for more than a century, *Les Maîtres d'autrefois* represented both a broader, more theoretical approach to the analysis of a tradition and a more profound technical and evaluative method. Because Fromentin was a practicing painter who had struggled laboriously with the techniques of his craft, whose knowledge of composition, color, and space had been hard won, he was able to bring to the evaluation of the masters of the past a personal understanding of their achievements. His analysis of these common problems in *Un Eté dans le Sahara* and *Une Année dans le Sahel* provided the critical language necessary to the exposition of this experience. On the other hand, his criticism of certain contemporary painters, such as Edouard Manet, reflected his own prudence and conservatism, perhaps his own pessimism, which played some part, no doubt, in his mixed but largely negative reaction to the revolution in artistic techniques of the day.

Chapters on Rubens and Rembrandt, as well as Jacob van Ruysdael, Jan and Hubert van Eyck, and Hans Memling, provide a central dynamic to the work, in which the detailed analysis of individual paintings leads to an evaluation of the personalities they reveal. In its method and manner of presentation, *Les Maîtres d'autrefois* resembles the introspective qualities of *Dominique*. Sagnes suggests that the literary characteristics of this final text reveal Fromentin as a writer more than a painter, despite his subject. It had been thirteen years since the publication of *Dominique*. Although the notes taken during Fromentin's 1862 visit to the Ile de Ré, his "Programme de critique" begun in 1864, and his "Carnet de voyage en Egypte" of 1869 had not been successfully concluded or published, *Les Maîtres d'autrefois* was quickly written at Saint-Maurice during the summer of 1875, and its publication in the *Revue des Deux Mondes* (January-March 1876) and then as a book took less than a year from inception to completion.

As a painter and a writer Fromentin's work was based upon the qualities of experience, whether visual or sentimental, rather than a narrative content of subject or anecdote. The thematic materials of romanticism and the exotic interests of Orientalism were of concern to him in their effects upon his own experience rather than in their intrinsic and independent existences. The literary currents and fashionable subjects of his time occur as elements necessary to the definition and expression of his own internal adventure. This is why all of Fromentin's work is retrospective in both nature and technique, dependent upon the creative power of memory to sort and enhance in personal terms the sensations and feelings provoked by the experience of the past.

Letters:

Eugène Fromentin, Lettres de jeunesse, biography and notes by Pierre Blanchon (Paris: Plon, 1909);

Eugène Fromentin, Correspondance et fragments inédits, biography and notes by Blanchon (Paris: Plon, 1912);

Gustave Moreau et Eugène Fromentin, Documents inédits, edited, with an introduction, by Barbara Wright and Pierre Moisy (La Rochelle: Quartier Latin, 1972).

Bibliography:

Barbara Wright, *Eugène Fromentin: A Bibliography* (London: Grant & Cutler, 1973).

Biography:

Louis Gonse, *Eugène Fromentin, peintre et écrivain* (Paris: Quantin, 1881).

References:

Anne-Marie Christin, *Fromentin conteur d'espace: Essai sur l'œuvre algerienne* (Paris: Sycomore, 1982);

Colloque Eugène Fromentin (Lille: Université de Lille, 1979);

John A. Fleming, "Representational A, B, C's: Cipher and Structure in *Dominique*," *Romanic Review,* 77, no. 2 (March 1986): 116-124;

Claude Herzfeld, *"Dominique" de Fromentin, thèmes et structure* (Paris: Nizet, 1977);

Jean-Pierre Lafouge, *Etude sur l'orientalisme d'Eugène Fromentin dans ses récits algériens* (Paris: Peter Lang, 1988);

Emanuel J. Mickel, *Eugène Fromentin* (Boston: Twayne, 1981);

James Thompson and Barbara Wright, *Les Orientalistes. La Vie et l'œuvre d'Eugène Fromentin* (Paris: ACR, 1987).

Papers:

Fromentin's papers are in the possession of his descendants in La Rochelle. A second manuscript version of *Les Maîtres d'autrefois* is in the municipal library at Versailles.

Joseph-Arthur de Gobineau

(14 July 1816 - 13 October 1882)

E. J. Richards
Tulane University

BOOKS: *Les Adieux de Don Juan, poème dramatique* (Paris: Jules Labitte, 1844);

La Chronique rimée de Jean Chouan et de ses compagnons (Paris & Leipzig: Franck, 1846);

Le Prisonnier chanceux (Paris: Louis Chlendowski, 1847); translated by F. M. Atkinson as *The Lucky Prisoner* (London: Heinemann / New York: Doubleday, Page, 1926); translated by William A. Drake as *Lucky Prisoner* (New York: Brentano's, 1930);

Nicolas Belavoir (Paris: E. Proux, 1847);

Ternove (Brussels: Librairie de Tarride, 1848);

Essai sur l'inégalité des races humaines, 4 volumes (Paris: Firmin-Didot / Hanover: Rumpler, 1853-1855); first half translated by Josiah Clark Nott and Henry Hotz as *The Moral and Intellectual Diversity of the Races* (Philadelphia: Lippincott, 1856); first half translated by Adrian Collins as *The Inequality of Human Races* (New York: Putnam's, 1915);

Lectures des textes cunéiformes (Paris: Firmin-Didot, 1858);

Trois ans en Asie (de 1855 à 1858) (Paris: Hachette, 1859);

Voyage à Terre-Neuve (Paris: Hachette, 1861);

Traité des écritures cunéiformes (Paris: Firmin-Didot, 1861);

Les Religions et les philosophies dans l'Asie centrale (Paris: Didier, 1865);

L'Abbaye de Typhaines (Paris: E. Maillet, 1867); translated by Charles D. Meigs as *The Rose of Typhaines: A Tale of the Commune in the Twelfth Century* (Philadelphia: Claxton, Bemsen & Haffelfinger, 1872);

Histoire des Perses, 2 volumes (Paris: Plon-Nourrit, 1869);

L'Aproessa, poésies (Paris: E. Maillet, 1869);

Souvenirs de voyage (Paris: Plon, 1874); translated by Henry Longan Stuart as *The Crimson Handkerchief and Other Stories* (New York: Putnam's, 1927);

Les Pléiades (Stockholm: Jos. Muller / Paris: Plon, 1874); translated by J. F. Scanlan as *The Pleiads* (New York: Knopf, 1928); translated by Douglas Parmée as *The Sons of Kings* (London & New York: Oxford University Press, 1966);

Joseph-Arthur de Gobineau as a young man

Catalogue d'une collection d'intailles asiatiques (Paris: Didier, 1874);

Amadis, poème (Paris: Librairie des Bibliophiles, 1876);

Nouvelles asiatiques (Paris: Didier, 1876); translated as *Romances of the East* (New York: Appleton, 1878); translated by Helen Morgenthau Fox as *Five Oriental Tales* (New York: Viking, 1925); translated by James Lewis May as *Tales of Asia* (London: G. Bles, 1947);

La Renaissance, scènes historiques (Paris: Plon, 1877); translated by Oscar Levy as *The Renaissance* (London: Heinemann, 1913);

Histoire d'Ottar Jarl, pirate norvégien, conquérant du pays de Bray, en Normandie, et de sa descendance (Paris: Didier, 1879);

Alexandre le Macédonien, tragédie en cinq actes, in *Nachgelassene Schriften von Grafen Gobineau* (Strasbourg: Trübner, 1902);

Deux études sur la Grèce moderne: Capodistras, Le Royaume des Hellènes (Paris: Plon, 1905);

La Troisième République française et ce qu'elle vaut (Strasbourg: Trübner / Paris: Plon, 1907);

Adélaïde, edited by André de Hevesy (Paris: Nouvelle Revue Française, 1914);

Ce qui est arrivé à la France en 1870, edited by Ludwig Schemann (Strasbourg: Trübner, 1918);

Mademoiselle Irnois (Paris: Nouvelle Revue Française, 1920); translated and edited by Annette Smith and David Smith as *"Mademoiselle Irnois" and Other Stories* (Berkeley: University of California Press, 1988);

Scaramouche (Paris: Léon Pichon, 1922);

La Fleur d'or (Paris: Grasset, 1923); translated by Pen Ray Redman as *The Golden Flower* (New York: Putnam's, 1924);

Stendhal, edited by Charles Simon (Paris: Editions du Stendhal-Club, 1926);

Etudes critiques (1844-1848). Balzac, Alfred de Musset, Théophile Gautier, Henri Heine, Jules Janin, Sainte-Beuve (Paris: Simon Kra, 1927);

Ce qui se passe en Asie, suivi de L'Instinct révolutionnaire en France (Paris: Editions des Cahiers Libres, 1928);

Mémoire sur diverses manifestations de la vie individuelle, edited by A. B. Duff (Paris: Desclée de Brouwer, 1935);

Les Conseils de Rabelais, nouvelle inédite, edited by Duff (Paris: Mercure de France, 1962);

Poemi inediti di Arthur de Gobineau, edited by Paola Berselli Ambri (Florence: Olshki, 1965);

Etudes critiques (1842-1847), edited by Roger Béziau (Paris: Klincksieck, 1984).

Collection: *Œuvres*, 3 volumes, edited by Jean Gaulmier (Paris: Gallimard, Bibliothèque de la Pléiade, 1983).

Although Joseph-Arthur de Gobineau is best known for his *Essai sur l'inégalité des races humaines* (Essay on the Inequality of Human Races, 1853-1855; first half translated as *The Moral and Intellectual Diversity of the Races*, 1856), he was a prolific writer of novels, novellas, and verse and an indefatigable correspondent. His enormous body of fictional work and letters (many of which are still unpublished and whose importance can be gauged by such addressees as Alexis de Tocqueville, Prosper Mérimée, Alexander von Humboldt, Albert Sorel, George Sand, Cornélie Renan, and Cosima Wagner) places his historical, critical, and ethnographic writings in a different light. One critic suggested that if Gobineau had continued to devote himself to literary criticism, typified by the essays on contemporary writers that he composed during the 1840s, he would have been one of the most distinguished French literary critics of the mid-nineteenth century. Mérimée twice asked Gobineau whether he had several natures, several individualities, or several nationalities that would explain the wide range of his writings. In fact, Gobineau's work exhibits a consistency and a continuity that are nothing short of remarkable and that require careful scrutiny.

A brief survey of Gobineau's life helps to situate his writings in their original historical and cultural contexts, a step that illuminates their other striking feature—their thematic monotony. One biographer surmised that the four classes of humanity that Gobineau set forth in *Les Pléiades* (1874; translated as *The Pleiads*, 1928)—*imbéciles, drôles, brutes, fils de roi* (imbeciles, comic types, brutes, king's sons)—describe the members of his own family. The author was born on 14 July 1816—a date that, with his antidemocratic bent, he found supremely ironic—in Ville d'Avray, near Paris. His father, Louis de Gobineau, was an army officer with strong royalist leanings; his mother, Anne-Louise Magdeleine de Gercy, the daughter of a royal tax official and a Creole woman from Santo Domingo, was a lady-in-waiting to Pauline Bonaparte and subsequently published both a sentimental novel, *Marguerite d'Alby* (1821), and her own memoirs, *Une Vie de femme, liée aux événements de l'époque* (A Woman's Life, Tied to the Events of the Time, 1835). This royalist/Bonapartist marriage was unhappy from the outset. Arthur was the first child, followed by two daughters, only one of whom, Caroline, survived childhood, later becoming a nun, and with whom Gobineau maintained an active correspondence. As a child his health was fragile, and he was instructed at home by a young tutor, Charles de la Coindière, who became his mother's lover and for whom she left her husband in 1830, taking her children and settling in Biel, Switzerland.

At the school in Biel, Gobineau received thorough instruction in German and Latin, and his interest in the Orient seems in part to date from the influence of his schooling there. The mixture of Orientalism, pan-Germanism, medievalism, and Italianism in Gobineau's writings betrays the specific influence of German romanticism (often misunderstood) and the use of temporal, spatial, or national alterity to hold a mirror up to France. Much like Germaine de Staël, who used the portrayal of Germany to criticize France, Gobineau wrote of exotic places as a foil in order to elaborate his own sense of identity. His literary "imperialism" aims not so much at the conquest of foreign lands as at self-mastery. For this same reason, psychological interpretations that claim that Gobineau's racist theories arose as a reaction to an unhappy family situation are inadequate—although Gobineau's letters to his father clearly reveal a deeply troubled young man and many of his later writings attempt, in classic compensatory fashion, to compose a family saga reaching back to the Middle Ages and Renaissance—since they ignore the more immediate, widespread contamination of literary culture by factitious images of other nations, cultures, and times. Much of the literary output of Gobineau's youth (and old age, as well), dominated as it is by a *rêve de dépaysement* (yearning for exotic places and times), was composed at a time when, as Alphonse de Lamartine noted, France was bored.

In 1832 Gobineau rejoined his father in Brittany and prepared unsuccessfully for a military career at Saint-Cyr. After this time his contacts with his mother became more and more distant. Because of a variety of crimes, his mother was in and out of prison much of the rest of her life. Although he generally despised his father, he initially shared his father's royalist sentiments, and when he went to Paris in October 1835—at the heyday of the July Monarchy, of the reign of Louis-Philippe, the Citizen King—he frequented aristocratic circles and took the title of "count," to which he had no legitimate claim. Indeed, as Maxime Du Camp, a friend of Gobineau's at this time, later noted, "il avait la folie de la noblesse" (he was nobility-crazy). At this time he earned his living by minor clerical jobs with a gas company and the postal service and received a small pension from his uncle. Not unlike Honoré de Balzac's Rastignac, he was ambitious and looking for his entrée into Parisian society. At the same time, Gobineau's hatred of Paris and all it represented—bourgeois mediocrity, physical degeneracy, materialism, equality, liberalism, democracy, socialism—dates from this period.

His greatest promoter at this time was the countess de Serre, the widow of a former minister of Louis XVIII, who introduced him to many of the most important royalists in France. Beginning in January 1836 Gobineau attended classes in Persian held at the Collège de France, although his mastery of this language remained at best imperfect. In March 1840 he also became part of a small literary clique, "La Sérénissime Société des Scelti, ou Cousins d'Isis" (The Most Serene Society of the Elect, or the Cousins of Isis; modeled on E. T. A. Hoffmann's *Die Serapions-Brüder* [1819-1821]), whose members included Du Camp, Paul de Molènes, and Hercule and Gaston de Serre. Hercule remained one of Gobineau's closest friends and, like Gobineau, also became a diplomat. The ideals of the Scelti were threefold, Gobineau wrote to his sister: "l'ambition, l'indépendance d'esprit, les idées aristocratiques" (ambition, independence of mind, aristocratic ideas). These ideals inform Gobineau's entire literary production.

In 1840 Gobineau published his first short *roman-feuilleton* (serialized potboiler romance), *Le Mariage d'un prince*, in the journal *France*. In 1841 he published an article on Capo d'Istria in the *Revue des Deux Mondes*, in which he attacked modern forms of philo-Hellenism for viewing the modern Greeks as the descendants of the ancient Greeks. Starting in 1842 he helped to organize two royalist journals, the *Unité* and the *Quotidienne*, though with the death of the duc d'Orléans in July 1842 he gradually moved away from a royalist position. In one of his contributions, Gobineau argued against Edgar Quinet's article "De la teutomanie" (*Revue des Deux Mondes*, 15 December 1842), which dismissed the journalistic celebration of German sentimentality, blond bonhomie, and prudish humility and decried the moribund state of German philosophy and literature. Instead, Gobineau invoked the image of the Germanic Aryan, fierce in defense of freedom and independence, the true representative of nobility. Ironically, Gobineau even cited Heinrich Heine's *Deutschland: Ein Wintermärchen* (1844) in support of his ideas, though Heine's critique of Germany there coincided perfectly with Quinet's position.

This and other pieces of the period anticipate Gobineau's later reflections on the state of

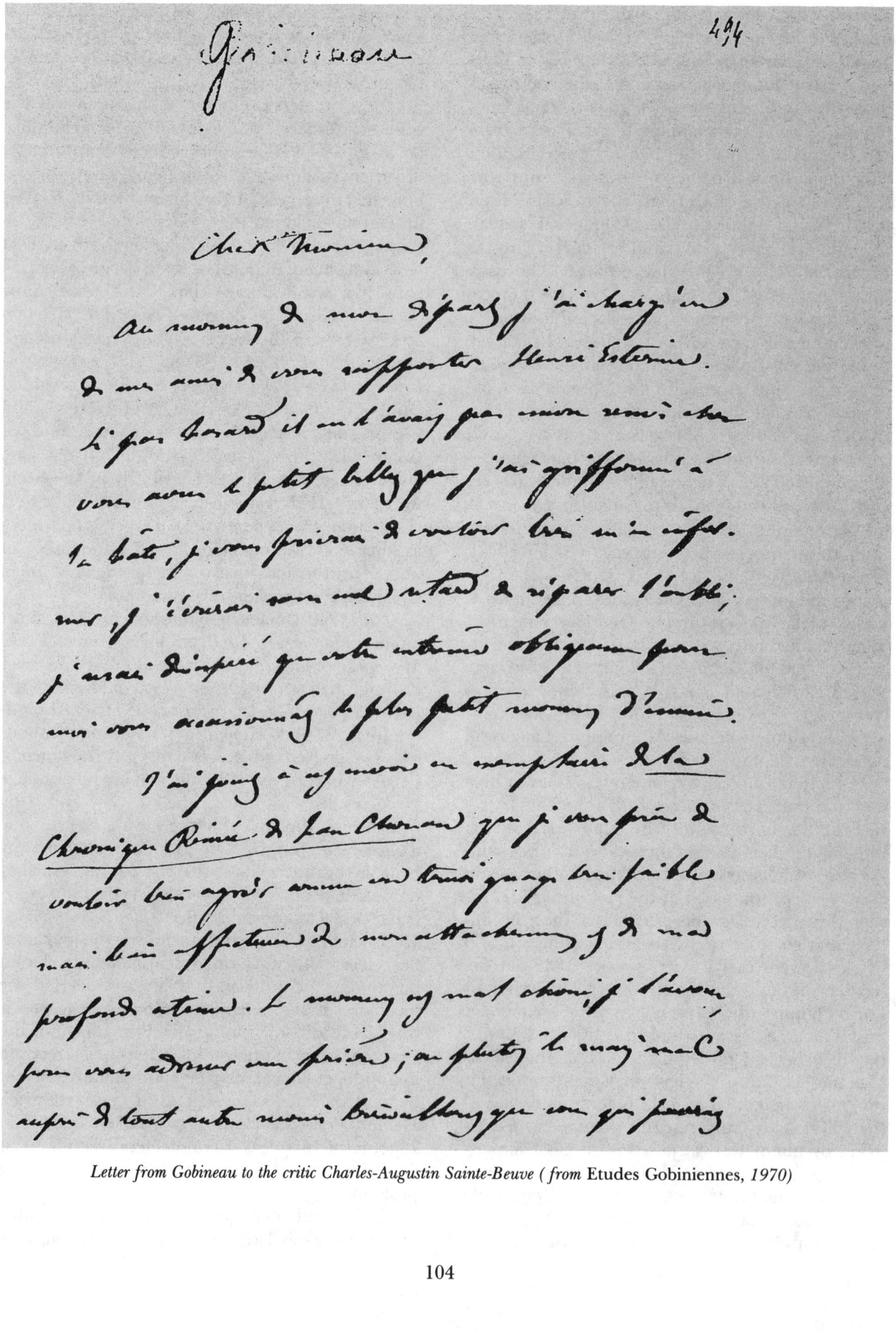

Gobineau 494

Cher Monsieur,

Au moment de mon départ j'ai chargé un de mes amis de vous rapporter Henri Estienne. Si par hasard il ne l'avait pas encore remis chez vous avec le petit billet que j'ai griffonné à la hâte, je vous prierai de vouloir bien me le [illegible]. mais je [illegible] sans nul retard à réparer l'oubli; j'aurais du regret que cette extrême obligeance pour moi vous occasionnât le plus petit moment d'ennui.

J'ai joint à ce mois un exemplaire de la Chronique Rimée de Jean Chouan que je vous prie de vouloir bien agréer comme un témoignage bien faible mais bien affectueux de mon attachement et de ma profonde estime. Le moment est mal choisi, je l'avoue, pour vous adresser une prière; au plutôt le [illegible] auprès de tout autre moins bienveillant que vous qui pourriez

Letter from Gobineau to the critic Charles-Augustin Sainte-Beuve (from Etudes Gobiniennes, *1970)*

modern European culture. This period also saw the composition of essays devoted to literary criticism, including one devoted to Stendhal, published in *Commerce* (January 1845), and one from the *Revue Nouvelle* (May 1845) with the striking title, "Une Littérature nouvelle est-elle possible?" (Is A New Literature Possible?). At the same time Gobineau was writing and publishing these serious essays, he was engaged in publishing several *romans-feuilletons* in the tradition of Eugène Sue, a genre that epitomized the literary tastes of the July Monarchy. Indeed, Charles-Augustin Sainte-Beuve, among others, singled out the *roman-feuilleton* as a symptom of the literary depravity of the age. It is impossible to reconcile these compositions with Gobineau's scorn of the masses and his elitism, with his yearning for a "new literature," though he attempted to defend the *roman-feuilleton*.

On 15 April 1843 Gobineau was introduced to Tocqueville. (It is not clear whether he owed this introduction to Charles de Rémusat or to the painter Ary Scheffer. Scheffer had introduced Gobineau both to his own future wife and to Ernest Renan.) Gobineau's friendship with Tocqueville dramatically changed the course of the young man's career. Tocqueville commissioned Gobineau on behalf of the Académie des Sciences Morales to investigate "l'état des doctrines morales au XIXe siècle et . . . leurs applications à la politique et à l'administration" (the state of moral doctrines in the nineteenth century and . . . their applications to politics and administration). In his examination of morality, Gobineau concentrated on the influence of Christianity in spreading the ideals of equal rights to the goods of this world for all, and on the duty of the haves to provide for the have-nots, both of which he condemned. Gobineau instead proposed a rehabilitation of the flesh in reaction to Christianity's historical emphasis on the spirit.

Although Tocqueville sharply disagreed with Gobineau—the two represented political opposites—he maintained an active interest in the younger man's career, and Gobineau contributed articles to the journal *Commerce*, which Tocqueville directed. When Tocqueville was named foreign minister on 2 June 1849, he appointed Gobineau to be his *chef de cabinet* (chief of staff). Gobineau's professional qualification for this position stemmed from his extensive (if uncritical) knowledge of contemporary German culture as illustrated in his journalistic writings throughout the 1840s, particularly the polemic against Quinet. When Tocqueville left office only a few months later, on 31 October 1849, he sent Gobineau as a legate to Bern, an appointment that marked the beginning of Gobineau's diplomatic career, which would take him to many world capitals.

In the meantime, on 10 September 1846, Gobineau married Clémence-Gabrielle Monnerot, a Creole from Martinique. The circumstances surrounding the marriage are unclear. The first of two daughters, Diane, was born in 1848; the second, Christine, in 1857. Until his appointment to Tocqueville's staff, Gobineau dashed off a series of articles, poems, plays, and novels to feed his family. The pressure under which he was forced to work took a severe toll on his health. It also explains the hasty, if sometimes felicitous, turn of phrase so characteristic of Gobineau's style, so much the opposite of the polished style of Gustave Flaubert, whose meticulous attention to everyday events and "turpitude" disgusted Gobineau, and whose complex irony contrasts markedly with the oft-touted but heavy-handed irony Gobineau cultivated. In 1846 he published *Les Aventures de Jean de la Tour-Miracle, surnommé le Prisonnier chanceux* in serial form in the *Quotidienne*. It was retitled *Le Prisonnier chanceux* (translated as *The Lucky Prisoner*, 1926) when it appeared in book form in 1847. During that year alone Gobineau published *Mademoiselle Irnois* in serial form in the *National*, *Ternove* in serial form in the *Journal des Débats*, and *Nicolas Belavoir* in volume form, and he completed *L'Abbaye de Typhaines*, published in serial form in the *Union* (1849).

After entering the diplomatic corps, Gobineau concentrated completely on social and historical subjects, and yet his literary output hardly flagged. He turned his interest to what he called in February 1851 "un gros livre que je fais sur les races humaines" (a big book that I am writing on human races), which emerged logically from his earlier writings on morality. Gobineau sent the first two completed volumes of *Essai sur l'inégalité des races humaines* to the publisher Firmin-Didot in June 1852. The rapidity of their composition was again characteristic of a trait underlying Gobineau's entire career, that of a *polyscribator*: his nonfictional writings on race and the Near East sprang from the pen of an amateur, not from the careful research of an ethnologist or Orientalist. The *Essai* had barely appeared when Gobineau learned that his work was being translated into English by Josiah Clark Nott and

Henry Hotz in order to combat abolitionist claims, *faire une machine de guerre contre les négrophiles* (to build a war machine against the Negrophiles), as Gobineau put it in a letter to the Austrian diplomat Anton, Baron Prokesch von Osten (whom the author had met in Frankfurt in 1854 when Prokesch von Osten was president of the Diet).

However, Gobineau was particularly disturbed by this partial version of his work, since the third and fourth volumes of the *Essai* hardly favored the cause of the slaveholder, and he wrote to Tocqueville, "Les Américains croient que je les encourage à assommer leur nègres, me portent aux nues pour cela, mais ne veulent pas traduire la partie du livre qui les concerne" (The Americans believe that I am encouraging them to slaughter their Negroes and lionize me for this, but they do not want to translate the part of the book that concerns them). Gobineau detested the United States for its democracy and teeming masses, and was glad never to have been sent on a diplomatic mission to Washington.

His diplomatic assignments, however, did take him to Frankfurt (1854), Teheran (1855-1858, 1861-1863), Newfoundland (1859), Athens (1865-1868), Rio de Janeiro (1869-1870), and Stockholm (1872-1876). He took advantage of his postings in Persia to gain closer acquaintance with the Oriental culture that had fascinated him as a youth, attempting to become "more Persian than the Persians." During this period he undertook an idiosyncratic explanation of cuneiform, published as a treatise, *Lectures des textes cunéiformes* (1858), which experts rejected out of hand. He also wrote a long work on religions and philosophies of central Asia, which was poorly received. During the Franco-Prussian War, Gobineau served as the magistrate in his village of Tyre when it was occupied and helped assist in the negotiations with the Germans following the end of the war. He was an eyewitness to the Paris Commune, spending time in Versailles and Paris during the spring of 1871. In February 1871 he began to write *Les Pléiades*, considered his best novel, and his lasting literary fame is founded on this and two other works from this late period: *Nouvelles asiatiques* (1876; translated as *Romances of the East*, 1878) and *La Renaissance, scènes historiques* (1877; translated as *The Renaissance*, 1913).

In 1876 Gobineau met Richard Wagner in Rome. Wagner explained that he had immediately been taken by the thin old man who denounced Miguel de Cervantes for having made fun of Don Quixote. Following his retirement in 1877, Gobineau devoted himself wholeheartedly to sculpture, an interest that he had begun to cultivate during his assignment to Athens. He enjoyed only minimal success in this new endeavor. While posted to Stockholm, he had met the wife of the Italian minister there, the countess Mathilde de la Tour. His romantic—but platonic—attachment to her led to the disruption of his marriage. She represented to Gobineau love in its purest, most absolute form, the same kind of love that his earlier novelistic works had explored. He spent the remainder of his life in her company, dividing his time between France and Rome. It was on his way to Rome that Gobineau died, alone, on 13 October 1882 in Turin, where he was buried. Following his death Mme de la Tour devoted her energies to his memory, collecting his papers and books, and working with Ludwig Schemann, a close associate of Wagner, to found the Gobineau Vereinigung, whose members included Paul Bourget, Max Müller, and Ernst Curtius.

A survey of Gobineau's major works will help to demonstrate that in many respects he essentially repeated the same story over again and again. His models were Balzac, Stendhal, Sand, Alexandre Dumas *père*, and Sir Walter Scott, and his novels bring no formal innovation to the genre itself. The specific literary-historical context of Gobineau's work turns on the controversy over the *roman-feuilleton* during the last years of the July Monarchy. In 1839 Sainte-Beuve launched his celebrated attack on the contemporary commercialization of literature (*la littérature industrielle*): "L'argent, l'argent, on ne saurait dire combien il est vraiment le nerf et le dieu de la littérature aujourd'hui" (Money, money, one cannot say how it is truly the nerve and god of literature today). In this new twist of the *querelle des anciens et des modernes*, Sainte-Beuve's opponents took up the cause of the tastes of the July Monarchy.

Gobineau at this early point in his career defended both Sand and Stendhal. In the *Revue Nouvelle* (May 1845) he announced, "Je ne vois rien qui se puisse comparer à certaines descriptions, à des volumes entiers de George Sand" (I see nothing that can be compared to certain descriptions, to entire volumes of George Sand). Stendhal earned special praise from Gobineau, who called *La Chartreuse de Parme* (1839; translated as *The Charterhouse of Parma*, 1925) "peut-être un des romans les plus remarquables de

Caricature of Gobineau from Le Charivari, *27 January 1870*

cette époque-là" (perhaps one of the most remarkable novels of that period). Underlying this affirmation of contemporary literature lay a firmly rooted optimism and vitalism: Gobineau wrote in 1844, "Je ne suis pas de ceux qui méprisent leur époque" (I am not one of those who despise their age)—a position he reversed completely twelve years later in a letter to Tocqueville (29 November 1856): "Je suis de ceux qui méprisent" (I am one of those who despise). Tocqueville observed to Gobineau shortly after the publication of the *Essai*, "Soit naturel, soit conséquence des luttes pénibles auxquelles votre jeunesse s'est courageusement livrée, vous vous êtes habitué à vivre du mépris que vous inspire l'humanité en général et en particulier votre pays" (Either because of your nature or as a result of the painful struggles to which your youth courageously devoted itself, you have become accustomed to live on the scorn that humanity in general, and your country in particular, inspires in you).

Gobineau's cultural pessimism, a hallmark of his mature work, seems to contradict this early optimism. Less charitably, one might note that one of Gobineau's protectors, Rémusat, had come out firmly in favor of the literary tastes of the age at the time Gobineau denied scorning his period. Gobineau had criticized Balzac for making concessions to the tastes of the age, but instead of rejecting the genre, Gobineau insisted that he wanted to bring order to "l'invasion des barbares dans les domaines littéraires" (the barbarian invasion of literary domains), as though the moderns were contributing new energy to an otherwise moribund, bloodless tradition. Underlying Gobineau's literary criticism is the firm belief, typical of the Romantics, in the organic tie between literature and its environment. His social theories reflect a similar belief in organicity and determinism. What links the young and the mature Gobineau, moreover, is the consistent adherence to vitalism. His remarks from 1844 proclaim the coming triumph of liberty and progress and a simultaneously moribund culture: "On croit au triomphe de la liberté, au perfectionnement de la race humaine; on chante les splendeurs de l'industrie, à laquelle on prédit d'étonnantes victoires; mais, d'un commun aveu, la littérature est morte" (People believe in the triumph of freedom, in the perfectibility of the human race; people celebrate the splendors of industry for which astounding victories are predicted; but, as is commonly accepted, literature is dead). Although Gobineau came to relinquish his optimism, he never abandoned his vitalism, which then in an inverted form reemerged in his racial theories. Precisely this vitalist element played a crucial role in Gobineau's fortune in the early twentieth century.

Thematically, Gobineau's earlier novels are historical romances dominated by adventure, and in this regard the debt to Dumas *père* seems clear. Dumas's highly successful *Les Trois Mousquetaires* (1844; translated as *The Three Musketeers,* 1846) and *Le Comte de Monte-Cristo* (1844-1845; translated as *The Count of Monte-Cristo,* 1846) form the backdrop for Gobineau's experiments, and the rapid plot developments of Dumas may explain what sympathetic critics term Gobineau's dynamic style and what less sympathetic readers denounce as the mark of rushed composition. The historical nostalgia of these works is all the more striking, since they were all written on the eve of the revolution of 1848. For all his attempts to head off the barbarians at the gates of the literary republic, there may be some doubt whether Gobineau's early novels—*Le Prisonnier chanceux, Mademoiselle Irnois, Ternove,* and *Nicolas Belavoir*— do not open the gates further.

Le Prisonnier chanceux recounts the story of a young Catholic noble, Jean de la Tour-Miracle, during the wars of religion. Jean's godmother is none other than Diane de Poitiers (and the novel's description of Diane's sumptuous Renaissance court at Anet anticipates Gobineau's celebration of the Italian Renaissance). Jean is in love with a girl whose low social class of course precludes marriage. Jean, entrusted with a necklace for Diane, arrives at Anet and in a complicated turn of events is accused of having murdered the Duc de Guise. The plot thickens, but Jean eventually escapes and is able to marry his first choice.

In *Ternove,* Gobineau combines a love story (reminiscent of Sand's *Le Meunier d'Angibault* [1845; translated as *The Miller of Angibault,* 1863]) with a historical romance, based largely on the experiences of Gobineau's own father during the Hundred Days. In the midst of the description of the Bourbons' retreat Gobineau inserts the story of Ternove, son of a noble murdered during the Revolution, who falls in love with Marguerite, his uncle's own daughter from his marriage with the daughter of a miller. The conflict in the novel centers on Ternove's desire to be adopted by the Marquis de Marvejols and his wife, who would hardly accept Marguerite as a daughter-in-law. In the end Ternove abandons his social ambitions in order to marry Marguerite, despite his fear that marriage will mean an end to this *grande passion* and lead to "cet attachement tendre et doux, bonheur négatif, pis-aller misérable qui n'a jamais suffi aux âmes vives" (that tender and sweet attachment, negative happiness, miserable last resort that never satisfied lively souls). The major formal problem of this work is the clumsy combination of two plots, a problem similar to the one that Gobineau would skillfully resolve in *Les Pléiades.*

In *L'Abbaye de Typhaines,* Gobineau again combines history and romance. He wrote his sister that this novel was the first of his books to which he attributed any importance. He takes as the historical setting the rise of the communes during the twelfth century, a subject popularized by Augustin Thierry in his *Lettres sur l'histoire de la France pour servir à l'étude de cette histoire* (Letters on the History of France to Serve Its Study, 1827). Gobineau's description of the commune of Typhaines is closely based on Thierry's account of the commune of Vézelay. The crusader Philippe de Cornhaut returns home to learn that his father has given his patrimony to the church. Before Philippe can resolve this problem, he must defend the local abbey from the revolting villagers, though the abbey eventually falls and Philippe is taken prisoner by the bourgeois Simon. The romantic complications—which presage similar difficulties in *Les Pléiades*—begin: Philippe's fiancée, Mahaut Cornhouiller, is unable to rescue him because her liege lord, the Duc de Nevers, himself wishes to seize the abbey's lands and even sends two knights to aid the commune. Philippe is rescued by a monk assisted by none other than Damerones, the daughter of the bourgeois Simon. Romance must cross class lines. The abbey, however, is restored to the church, and the commune quashed. Mahaut, jealous of Damerones, dismisses Philippe, who returns to the Holy Land. Damerones enters a convent. The implications of this novel for Gobineau's understanding of love and history seem obvious, though it must be stressed that his medievalism comes straight from Scott's *Ivanhoe* (1819), a book he praised in his letters to Pedro II, Emperor of Brazil, for its *magnificence du paysage* (magnificence of the landscape). (Significantly, André Malraux singled out the description of landscapes in the novel as its most interesting feature.) Gobineau's Middle Ages are neither Catholic nor Latin, but utterly pagan, heroic, and Germanic.

Essai sur l'inégalité des races humaines posits three separate races—white, black, and yellow—with innate permanent differences. Genetic mixing of traits has led to a degeneration that has destroyed irreparably humanity's original racial purity. Gobineau stressed that Aryan purity had been lost: "La famille ariane, et, à plus forte raison, le reste de la famille blanche, avait cessé d'être absolument pure à l'époque où naquit le Christ" (The Aryan family, and, for even stronger reasons, the rest of the white family, had ceased to be absolutely pure at the time Christ was born). Gobineau's racial theories, including his claim for the original superiority of the white race, are not original: many of the ideas can be traced directly to Immanuel Kant's *Anthropologie in pragmatischer Hinsicht* (1798; translated as *Anthropology from a Pragmatic Point of View*, 1974). Georg Wilhelm Friedrich Hegel's historical writings, particularly those discounting blacks, are certainly in Gobineau's mind as well, especially since Gobineau's panorama reverses in an unwitting parody Hegel's universal historical perspective. For Hegel, pure *Geist* becomes progressively more manifest in human history. For Gobineau, one can substitute pure blood for pure spirit and speak of the progressive disappearance of pure blood in human history.

The first volume sets forth a series of claims denying historical progress and human perfectibility, positing the intellectual inequality of the races, but sketching out in positive terms the respective character traits of the three great races. The next volumes outline the characters of various historical civilizations, tracing the gradual decline of racial purity over time and space. Much of what Gobineau asserts is based on the contradictory claim that "l'histoire n'existe que chez les nations blanches" (history exists only among the white nations), since his own work portrays encounters among all the races. Annette Smith and David Smith have wisely put the significance of the *Essai* in context: "It is a somber *epic* on the origins and history of mankind, prompted, like all fiction, by its author's psychic needs. Raised on a Legitimist myth, bypassed by the bourgeois monarchy of his time, disgusted by the spectacle of the 1848 Revolution, and tormented by his own origins, Gobineau saved his sanity by finding the world sick, even moribund." It must be stressed again that the content of Gobineau's racist analysis was not original. It dramatizes racial clichés in a deeply pessimistic vein that turns on the impossibility of regaining racial purity. This historical tragedy, though, becomes all the more acute because some scattered privileged individuals still preserve the original noble virtues of the Aryans, and these are the *fils de roi*, Gobineau's version of Stendhal's "happy few."

Not surprisingly, *Les Pléiades* recapitulates many of the themes of Gobineau's earlier work. It concerns an aristocratic individual and reveals once again Gobineau's scorn for bourgeois democracy. In the course of their self-discovery, the protagonists learn their true nobility and come to form a human constellation, whence the title. Three young men meet by chance on the island Bella in Lake Como: the Englishman Wilfred Nore, just returned from Baghdad, where he had separated from Harriet Coxe, a woman several years his senior who had turned down his marriage proposal; the German Conrad Lanze, a sculptor from the small principality of Burbach, on his way to Italy following an involvement with the Polish Countess Tonska, the mistress of Jean-Théodore, the Prince of Woerbeck-Burbach; and the Frenchman Louis Laudon, running from an entanglement, his with Lucie de Gennevilliers. Each of these protagonists undergoes a process of suffering and self-discovery provoked by love: Nore, diverted briefly by his attraction for another woman, Liliane, finds true love with Harriet; following a series of intrigues, Lanze and the Countess Tonska find that they really are in love; Laudon chooses renunciation; and Jean-Théodore, after great suffering, finds true love with his cousin Aurore Pamina, and his marriage to her concludes the novel.

These four major plots are set off by four subplots involving other possible couples, including Jean-Théodore and Tonska, and Nore and Liliane, among others. Michael Riffaterre considers this balance of plot and subplot a major formal breakthrough for the novel, a kind of point-counterpoint structure (though it seems clumsy by comparison with the "comices agricoles" chapter in *Madame Bovary* [1857; translated, 1881]). The novel's form has been called open (yet hardly comparable to Denis Diderot's *Jacques le Fataliste et son maître* [1796; translated as *James the Fatalist and His Master,* 1797]), and indeed Gobineau interrupts the narrative frequently to quote letters and diaries or to digress on a wide range of topics. Such digressions may be a mark of the "literary" character of the work, according to Russian formalist criteria, but Gobineau's technique here is more reminiscent of the thirteenth-century *Roman de la Rose* than of Laurence Sterne's *Tristram Shandy* (1760-1767). The tone of conversation tends to be stilted and wooden, and characters, rather than being nuanced, as some recent critics would claim after examining Gobineau's models, often conform to the most hackneyed national stereotypes: Wilfred epitomizes the determination of the Aryan; Harriet, the ideal strength of the "Saxon" woman; and Tonska, the fiery, passionate "Slav." The "French" characters of the work, such as Laudon, who ends up dedicating himself to science, seem unable to love.

These national images are deliberate and conform to the philosophical message of the entire novel: the celebration of energy, vitality, and will in the service of absolute love—all traits that Gobineau had considered Aryan par excellence. Indeed, Jean Cocteau welcomed the elitist mentality behind *Les Pléiades* and the cult of the *fils de roi*: "Ce roman sublime enseigne que le destin travaille dans une zone où nos signes d'intelligence cessent de signifier" (This sublime novel teaches that destiny operates in a zone where our signs of intelligence cease to signify). Cocteau's remarks, chilling in their endorsement of irrationality, go straight to the heart of Gobineau's elitist ideal and help explain why Gobineau's works enjoyed so much popularity among those in the twentieth century all too ready to abandon reason in the name of some higher, intuitive truth shared only by "the happy few."

Even though Gobineau claims to have corrected *Les Pléiades* seven times (three times more than he did any of his other books, he added), the work lacks rigor. Gobineau, unlike Flaubert, includes useless detail. The first sentence of the novel is a false start: "Il était six heures du soir à peu près, peut-être six et demie" (It was around six o'clock in the evening, maybe six-thirty). Why modify the time with "à peu près" and then add as an afterthought "peut-être six et demie"? When the novel ends with the news of the convenient death of Jean-Théodore's wife, he reads in the telegram that the Princess Mother had suffered a stroke at ten and had died at six. The incredulous reader, recalling the opening, could ask, "Did she have the stroke around ten and then die maybe at six-thirty?" This gratuitous use of detail points to Gobineau's ongoing debt to the *roman-feuilleton.*

Critics are divided regarding the novel's formal qualities: the contemporary reaction was limited at best. The editors of the Pléiade edition of Gobineau's works strain in trying to establish the novel's original importance. Even Gobineau's daughter Diane von Guldencrone noted to her father after reading *Les Pléiades,* "Je ne le croyais pas si romanesque" (I did not think it was very novelistic). Jules-Amédée Barbey d'Aurevilly, writing in the *Constitutionnel* (18 May 1874), severely criticized the novel. He detected an underlying misanthropy and noted that if Gobineau wanted to give his readers history, it should at least be lived history. He found the conclusion unsatisfying because he thought the work had more than one subject, and severely faulted it for its false and contrived ending that confuses the social implications of the novel: "La fade bergerie qui du reste, n'y est pas la seule, et qui est la conclusion de son roman, cette berquinade amoureuse et transie d'un *roi épousant une bergère,* d'un homme à qui l'auteur avait d'abord accordé de la force d'esprit et de caractère et qui devient le *pastor fido* d'une fillette, de pasteur de peuple que Dieu l'avait fait, n'est pas non plus la seule conclusion de ce roman qui en a plusieurs, parce qu'il a plusieurs sujets" (The insipid pastoral, which, moreover, is not the only one found there, and which constitutes the conclusion of his novel, this amorous and chilled sentimental romance of *a king marrying a shepherdess,* of a man to whom the author first bestowed force of mind and character who becomes the *faithful pastor* of a maid,

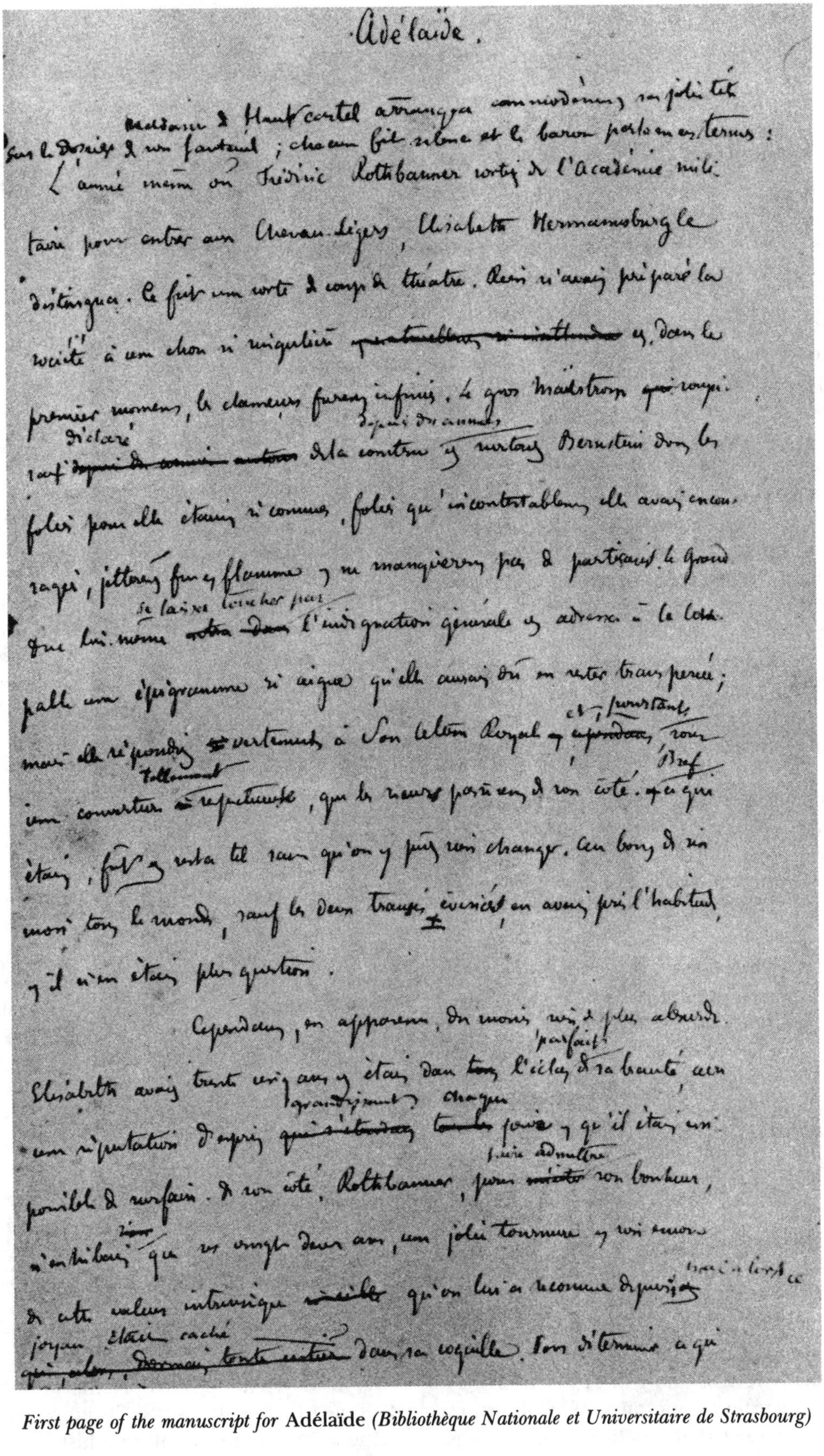
Adélaïde.

First page of the manuscript for Adélaïde *(Bibliothèque Nationale et Universitaire de Strasbourg)* after having been the shepherd of people, as God had made him, is also not the only conclusion of this novel, which has several, just as it has several subjects). Barbey d'Aurevilly essentially recognized *Les Pléiades* for the spin-off of a *roman-feuilleton* that it is. Although the novel's later defenders, beginning with Cocteau, might wish to champion its elitism, they must recognize the paradox that its origins lie in kitsch. For Gobineau love was the preeminent passion; as he wrote in 1877 to Philipp von Eulenburg in a burst of banality, "Die Liebe geht allem vor—dann kommt die Arbeit—und weiter gibt es nichts" (Love precedes everything—then comes work—and there is nothing else).

The debate over the novel's form has continued ever since its appearance. For Arnold H. Rowbotham it was a *roman à tiroirs* (episodic novel) with little formal unity, as Gobineau struggled to juggle the parallel narratives; for Riffaterre, it represented a fugue—a comparison that cannot hide, however, disharmonies in the original composition. Alain (Emile Chartier) placed Gobineau in the tradition of Voltaire, the Voltaire who married Orient and Occident in his fiction (although Gobineau objected to the implied equality among nations that the moralists cherished), and of Stendhal. "Leur style n'est point de tout parlé" (Theirs is not at all a spoken style). Many recent critics emphasize instead the dynamic, oral nature of Gobineau's style and tie it to his reputation as a consummate raconteur. As early as 1905 Jacques Morland, writing in the *Mercure de France*, noted: "Dans ses œuvres d'ordre plus strictement littéraire,—souvenirs de voyages, nouvelles, roman,—il compose à peine, il écrit vite" (In his more strictly literary works—travelogues, novellas, novel—he barely composes, he writes fast), and he termed Gobineau's overall style *bavard* (chatty).

The novel's success, however, appears linked to extraliterary developments. Gobineau was the first to connect the novel to his theories of race, as he wrote to Sorel (1 May 1874): "Mon livre des *Races* est ce que j'ai fait de mieux et il faut que cela soit comme cela, car les *Pléiades* en sortent" (My book on the Races is what I have done best, and it is necessary that this be so, for the *Pléiades* emerges from it). This thematic dovetailing between the *Essai* and *Les Pléiades* brings out once again the monotony of Gobineau's works but also shows that his historical writings are in fact veiled fictions.

Shortly after the publication of *Les Pléiades*, Gobineau published two collections of novellas, the first set in the Orient, *Nouvelles asiatiques*, and the other in Italy, *La Renaissance, scènes historiques*. Both provided further illustration of his historical theories and became his most popular works. In *Nouvelles asiatiques*, Gobineau intends to demonstrate the fundamental differences of the Asiatic mind, the *variétés de l'esprit asiatique*. The eighteenth-century moralists were wrong, he argues, for "les hommes ne sont nulle part les mêmes" (men are nowhere the same). The most famous story of the collection, "La Danseuse de Shamakha" ("The Dancer of Shamakha"), is programmatic in its depiction of the survival of Aryan virtues in a savage Caucasian woman's scorn for a degenerate compatriot. *La Renaissance* brings together five biographical sketches of Girolamo Savonarola, Cesare Borgia, Julius II, Leo X, and Michelangelo. Their genius, grandeur, energy, and thirst for power—in short, their megalomania—explain their importance for Gobineau, all traits reminiscent of the *fils de roi* in *Les Pléiades*. *La Renaissance* illustrates again the continuity of Gobineau's work, for although it was written late in his life, Gobineau had spoken as early as 1841 of the attraction exerted on him by the "strong men" of the Renaissance. He wrote that he had been fascinated by "l'histoire des capitaines italiens du XVIe siècle" (the story of Italian captains in the sixteenth century): "J'ai été toujours raffolé des *condottieri*. J'ai déjà marqué dans ma pensée Piccinino, Strozzi, Sforza, Trivulzio, Jean de Médécis et surtout le trois fois illustre César de Valentinois si calomnié de nos jours et des siens" (I was always infatuated by the *condottieri*. I already noted in my mind Piccinino, Strozzi, Sforza, Trivulzio, Giovanni de' Medici [Pope Leo X] and especially the thrice illustrious Cesare Borgia, Duke of Valentinois, so slandered in our time and his). Although *La Renaissance* enjoyed distinct popularity in Germany around the turn of the century, it was something of an anomaly, especially when one considers that it appeared in the same year as Zola's *L'Assommoir* (translated, 1879).

In 1879 Gobineau crowned his novelistic achievements with *Histoire d'Ottar Jarl*, in which—again turning to family history, as in *Ternove* from thirty-two years before—he retold his family history, dating from the ninth century. Gobineau argued that "si l'histoire générale était bâtie sur un grand nombre d'histoires de familles particulières, elle y gagnerait en profondeur et en largeur comme en vérité" (if history in general were seen as the history of particular families, it would gain in depth, breadth, and truth).

The lasting significance of Gobineau's work has long been in dispute. On 12 March 1875 Gobineau wrote to his friend Pedro II, "Ce ne sont pas les auteurs qui font les chefs-d'œuvre mais le temps, les circonstances, les causes extérieures auxquelles on ne peut rien" (Authors do not create masterpieces, but rather the times, the circumstances, the exterior causes that one can do nothing about). The overall tendency has been to deduce the meaning of Gobineau's work from its reception after his death—a virtual necessity given the small numbers of readers it attracted during his lifetime. (Most of his poetry, mercifully, remained unpublished until 1965.) The gradual rehabilitation of his work stemmed from the efforts of the Gobineau Vereinigung in Germany. Its members, heavily influenced by Wagner, obsessively sought to shore up the political legitimacy of the Wilhelmine Reich by creating a mythic German past. Gobineau the legitimist of French royalty appealed to the legitimist yearnings of German Wilhelmine imperialists who overlooked his firm belief that a restoration of past Aryan glory was impossible. It is no coincidence that Von Eulenburg, one of Wilhelm II's closest advisers—who at the age of twenty-eight had met Gobineau in Stockholm—was a moving force in the Gobineau revival, along with Hans Paul von Wolzogen, editor of the *Bayreuther Blätter*, a Wagnerian expert and advocate of Germanic Christianity (*Deutschchristentum*—the marriage of Teutonic and Christian myth in Wagner's *Parsifal* [1882], for example).

In a striking turn the French rehabilitation of Gobineau gained new strength after World War I. On the one hand, he appealed to the irrational, vitalist tendencies among Expressionists in the early 1920s. In 1923, under the editorship of René Arcos, the journal *Europe* devoted an entire number to Gobineau. Except for a balanced essay by Romain Rolland, the articles there are overwhelmingly positive: Elie Faure, whose biography of Napoleon celebrates all of the virtues associated with *fils de roi*, is lavish in his praise. Writing in French, the German Expressionist Kasimir Edschmid is equally positive. On the other hand, Gobineau attracted French intellectuals interested, for a variety of reasons, in German culture. Jacques Rivière, editor of the *Nouvelle Revue Française*, was also the author of the notorious but influential anti-German tract *L'Allemand* (1918), and many of the most important articles from the 1920s treating Gobineau appeared in the *Nouvelle Revue Française*. Indeed, in 1934 the *Nouvelle Revue Française* dedicated an entire issue to him, including many articles openly celebrating his elitism. The inclusion in this special issue of Warren C. Kincaid's survey of Gobineau's influence in the United States and Scandinavia—which enthusiastically welcomes the introduction of national quotas to govern immigration into the United States—raises serious questions about its editorial intent.

Gobineau's writings are illustrative of how pervasive and uncritical racial and national myths had become in the wake of the Romantics. They offer a cautionary note that literary culture is never innocent, even in celebrating a fictional past. The ongoing challenge of Gobineau's writings was best expressed in 1923 by Rolland, and his remarks still bear repeating: "Comme au temps de Tocqueville et Gobineau, l'opposition s'affirme entre les hommes d'hier, les vieux humanitaires, les libéraux impénitents, qui s'obstinent à croire au progrès, et les hommes nouveaux qui ont une rancune cachée contre la liberté et le mépris d'une humanité qui les a trop déçus. . . . Cette jeunesse d'aujourd'hui—(et ceux, parmi les aînés, qu'elle entraîne),—retrouveront sans peine, dans le comte de Gobineau, le même dédain avoué du progrès, du libéralisme, de '*l'opium humanitaire*,' des idéaux démocratiques,—la même vision tragique et hautaine de la bataille des races,—le même choix volontaire du pouvoir absolu dans l'Etat et l'Eglise, ici-bas et là-haut" (As in the time of Tocqueville and Gobineau, the opposition has solidified between the men of yesterday, the old humanitarians, the unrepentant liberals, who stubbornly believe in progress, and the new men who have a hidden rancor against freedom and a scorn for a humanity that has disappointed them too much. . . . The youth of today—[and those older ones that it drags along with it]—will find with no trouble in the Count de Gobineau the same avowed scorn for progress, for liberalism, for that "*humanitarian opium*," for democratic ideals—the same tragic and haughty vision of the struggle of the races—the same voluntary selection of absolute power in the State and Church, here below and in heaven above).

Letters:

"Une Correspondance inédite de Gobineau et Prosper Mérimée," edited by Ludwig Sche-

Gobineau in his later years (portrait from Michael D. Biddiss, Father of Racist Ideology: The Social and Political Thought of Count Gobineau, *1970)*

mann, *Revue des Deux Mondes,* 72 (1902): 721-752, 836-861;

Briefwechsel Gobineaus mit Adelbert von Keller, edited by Schemann (Strasbourg: Trübner, 1911);

Lettres inédites de Gobineau à M. Adolphe Franck et à sa famille, edited by René Worms (Paris: Giard et Brière, 1916);

Correspondance entre le comte de Gobineau et le comte de Prokesch-Osten (1854-1876), edited by Clément Serpeille de Gobineau (Paris: Plon, 1933);

Lettres à deux Athéniennes (1868-1881), edited by N. Mela (Paris: Grasset, 1938);

Don Pedro II e o Conde de Gobineau, Correspondencias ineditas, edited by Georges Raederstoerffer (Sao Paolo: Companha Editora Nacional, 1938);

"Sept lettres du comte Arthur de Gobineau à sa sœur," edited by A. B. Duff, *Revue de Littérature Comparée,* 23 (1949): 541-561;

"Lettres à Diane de Gobineau (1861-1863)," edited by Jean Mistler, *Revue de Paris* (1950): 10-21;

Lettres persanes, edited by Duff (Paris: Boivin, 1952);

Ecrit de Perse, Treize lettres à sa sœur, edited by Duff (Paris: Mercure de France, 1957);

Comte de Gobineau-Mère Bénédicte de Gobineau (1872-1882), 2 volumes, edited by Duff (Paris: Mercure de France, 1958);

Correspondance d'Alexis de Tocqueville et d'Arthur de Gobineau, 2 volumes, edited by Maurice Degros (Paris: Gallimard, 1959);

Lettres brésiliennes, edited by Marie-Louise Concasty (Paris: Société des Bibliophiles de France, 1968);

Lettre à Ernest Renan, 10 janvier 1857, edited by François d'Argent (Paris: Editions à l'Ecart, 1986);

Lettres à la princesse Toquée, edited by Duff (Paris: Editions du Seuil, 1988).

Biographies:

Eugen Kretzer, *Joseph-Arthur Graf von Gobineau, Sein Leben und sein Werk* (Leipzig: Hermann Seemann, 1902);

Robert Dreyfus, *La Vie et les prophéties du comte de Gobineau* (Paris: Cahiers de la Quinzaine, 1905);

Cosima Wagner, *Graf Arthur Gobineau, Ein Erinnerungsbild aus Wahnfried* (Stuttgart: Frommann, 1907);

Ludwig Schemann, *Gobineau, Eine Biographie*, 2 volumes (Strasbourg: Trübner, 1913-1916);

Schemann, *Quellen und Untersuchungen zum Leben Gobineaus*, volume 1 (Strasbourg: Trübner, 1914); volume 2 (Leipzig: Walter de Crayter, 1919);

Maurice Lange, *Le Comte Arthur de Gobineau, étude biographique et critique* (Strasbourg: Istra, 1924);

Jean Boissel, *Gobineau, un Don Quichotte tragique* (Paris: Hachette, 1981).

References:

Alain (Emile Chartier), "Gobineau romanesque," *Nouvelle Revue Française*, 42 (1934): 198-209; republished in his *Humanités* (Paris: Presses Universitaires de France, 1960), pp. 75-88;

Paola Ambri Berselli, "*Les Pléiades* di Gobineau," *Convivium*, 32 (1964): 41-74;

Fernand Baldensperger, "France et Suède: De Descartes à Gobineau," *Revue de Paris*, 140, no. 3 (1917): 625-640;

Jules-Amédée Barbey d'Aurevilly, "Le Comte de Gobineau, *La Renaissance*," in his *Les Œuvres et les hommes, XIX*[e] *siècle: Les historiens* (Paris: Quantin, 1888), pp. 67-82;

Barbey d'Aurevilly, "*Les Pléiades*," in his *Voyageurs et romanciers* (Paris: Lemerre, 1908), pp. 251-267;

André Bellessort, "Gobineau l'Européen," in his *Les Intellectuels et l'avènement de la Troisième République* (Paris: Grasset, 1931), pp. 161-187;

Roger Béziau, *Les Débuts littéraires de Gobineau, Première époque (1835-1846)*, 3 volumes (Lille: Atelier national de reproduction des thèses, 1982);

Michael D. Biddiss, *Father of Racist Ideology: The Social and Political Thought of Count Gobineau* (London: Weidenfeld & Nicolson, 1970);

Jean Boissel, *Gobineau, l'Orient et l'Iran*, volume 1: *Prolégomènes et essai d'analyse* (Paris: Klincksieck, 1973);

Abel Bonnard, "Gobineau," *Nouvelle Revue Française*, 42 (1934): 179-184;

Marcel Brion, *Gobineau* (Marseilles: Cahiers du Sud, 1928);

Janine Buenzod, *La Formation de la pensée de Gobineau et "l'Essai sur l'inégalité des races humaines"* (Paris: Nizet, 1967);

Gustave Charlier, "Gobineau et le romantisme," *Revue de l'Université de Bruxelles* (February 1924): 3-24; republished in his *De Montaigne à Verlaine: Nouveaux problèmes d'histoire littéraire* (Brussels: La Renaissance du Livre, 1957), pp. 173-196;

Jean Cocteau, "Eloge des *Pléiades*," *Nouvelle Revue Française*, 42 (1934): 194-197;

Paul Colin, "L'Ame de Gobineau," *Europe*, 3 (October 1923): 27-34;

Andrée Combris, *La Philosophie des races du comte de Gobineau et sa portée actuelle* (Paris: Alcan, 1937);

Marie-Louise Concasty, "A propos des *Pléiades*," *Etudes Gobiniennes* (1970): 243-253;

Claude Digeon, *La Crise allemande de la pensée française, 1870-1914* (Paris: Presses Universitaires de France, 1959);

Robert Dreyfus, "Gobineau, qui est-ce?. . . ," *Nouvelle Revue Française*, 42 (1934): 161-168;

Kasimir Edschmid, "Gobineau," *Europe*, 3 (October 1923): 41-58;

Hassan El Nouty, "Gobineau et l'Asie," *Cahiers de l'Association Internationale des Etudes Françaises*, 13 (1961): 25-40;

Elie Faure, "Destin de Gobineau," *Nouvelle Revue Française*, 42 (1934): 245-249;

Faure, "Gobineau et le problème des races," *Europe*, 3 (October 1923): 41-58;

Bernard Faÿ, "Le Comte de Gobineau, critique littéraire," *Revue Européenne*, new series 2 (1928): 405-409;

Faÿ, "Les Légendes du Comte de Gobineau," *Nouvelle Revue Française*, 42 (1934): 169-178;

Ramon Fernandez, "*Nicolas Belavoir*," *Nouvelle Revue Française*, 29 (1927): 398-399;

Friedrich Fritz, *Studien über Gobineau* (Leipzig: Avenarius, 1906);

Jean Gaulmier, "Gobineau et George Sand," *Zeitschrift für französische Sprache und Literatur,* 76 (1966): 99-107;

Gaulmier, *Gobineau et sa fortune littéraire* (Saint-Médard en Jalles près Bordeaux: Guy Ducros, 1971);

Gaulmier, "Un Mythe: La science orientaliste de Gobineau," *Australian Journal of French Studies,* 1 (1964): 58-70;

Gaulmier, *Spectre de Gobineau* (Paris: Pauvert, 1965);

René Guise, "Aux sources de l'italianisme de Gobineau," *Revue de Littérature Comparée,* 40 (1966): 362-373;

Edouard-Félix Guyon, "Tocqueville et Gobineau d'après leur correspondance," *Revue d'Histoire Diplomatique,* 86 (1972): 54-76;

André de Hevesy, "Sur le comte de Gobineau," *Nouvelle Revue Française,* 9 (1913): 852-863;

Jean Hytier, "Gobineau, peintre de l'Orient," *Revue des Vivants,* 7 (1933): 657-670;

Herbert Juin, "Un Grand Poète romantique," in Gobineau's *Essai sur l'inégalité des races humaines* (Paris: Pierre Belfond, 1967), pp. vii-xxiv;

Hermann, Graf von Keyserling, "Réflexions sur Gobineau," *Nouvelle Revue Française,* 42 (1934): 240-244;

Warren C. Kincaid, "L'Influence de l'œuvre scientifique du Comte de Gobineau en Amérique et en Scandinavie," *Nouvelle Revue Française,* 42 (1934): 257-264;

Jacques de Lacretelle, "*Adélaïde, Mademoiselle Irnoise,*" *Nouvelle Revue Française,* 23 (1924): 372-375;

Lacretelle, "Gobineau romancier: *Les Pléiades,*" *Europe,* 3 (October 1923): 87-95;

Lacretelle, *Quatre études sur Gobineau* (Liège: A la Lampe d'Aladdin, 1926);

G.-V. de Laponge, " 'La Fin du monde civilisé' (Gobineau)," *Europe,* 3 (October 1923): 59-67;

Eugen Lerch, "Der Rassenwahn, Von Gobineau zur UNESCO-Erklärung," *Der Monat,* 26 (November 1950): 157-174;

Jean Louverné, "Gobineau sinologue," *Nouvelle Revue Française,* 42 (1934): 233-239;

André Malraux, "*L'Abbaye de Typhaines,*" *Nouvelle Revue Française,* 19 (1922): 97-98;

Vladimir Minorsky, "Les Itinéraires parallèles: Gobineau et Loti en Perse," *Europe,* 3 (October 1923): 99-126;

Pierre Moreau, "*Les Pléiades* ou Le poème du Moi," *Etudes Gobiniennes,* 3 (1968/1969): 169-182;

Jacques Morland, "Gobineau romancier (*Les Pléiades*)," *Mercure de France,* 55 (1905): 5-21;

Jean Prévost, "Le Comte de Gobineau et l'amour," *Nouvelle Revue Française,* 42 (1934): 210-214;

Pierre-Louis Rey, *L'Univers romanesque de Gobineau* (Paris: Gallimard, 1981);

Louis Reynaud, *L'Influence allemande en France au XVIIIe siècle et au XIXe siècle* (Paris: Hachette, 1922);

Michael Riffaterre, *Le Style des "Pléiades" de Gobineau* (New York: Columbia University Press, 1957);

Romain Rolland, "Le Conflit de deux générations: Tocqueville et Gobineau," *Europe,* 3 (October 1923): 68-80;

Arnold H. Rowbotham, *The Literary Works of Count Gobineau* (Paris: Champion, 1929);

Guido Saba, "Gobineau, *Mademoiselle Irnois* e Vigny," *Studi Francesi,* 8 (1964): 229-238;

Ludwig Schemann, *Gobineaus Rassenwerk, Aktenstücke und Betrachtungen zur Geschichte und Kritik des "Essai sur l'inégalité des races humaines"* (Stuttgart: Frommann, 1910);

Schemann, *Die Rasse in den Geisteswissenschaft, Studien zur Geschichte des Rassengedankens* (Munich: J. F. Lehmann, 1928-1931);

Ernest Seillière, "Un Différend littéraire entre la France et l'Allemagne, *Les Scènes historiques de la Renaissance* par le Comte de Gobineau," *Revue Germanique,* 4 (1908): 15-39;

Seillière, *Mysticisme et domination* (Paris: Alcan, 1913);

Seillière, *La Philosophie de l'impérialisme, Le comte de Gobineau et l'aryanisme historique* (Paris: Plon, 1903);

Seillière, "La Philosophie religieuse de Gobineau," *Nouvelle Revue Française,* 42 (1934): 229-232;

Clément Serpeille de Gobineau, "Le Gobinisme et la pensée moderne," *Europe,* 3 (October 1923): 35-40;

Serpeille de Gobineau, "Le Gobinisme et la politique moderne," *Nouvelle Revue Française,* 42 (1934): 250-256;

Gerald M. Spring, *The Vitalism of Count de Gobineau* (New York: Institute of French Studies, 1932);

Rudolf Streidl, *Gobineau in der französischen Kritik* (Würzburg: R. Mayr, 1935);

Louis Tenenbaum, "Love in the Prose Fiction of Gobineau," *Modern Language Quarterly,* 18 (June 1957): 107-112;

André Thérive, "Gobineau poète," in his *Du siècle romantique* (Paris: La Nouvelle Revue Critique, 1927);

Albert Thibaudet, "Tocqueville et Gobineau," *Nouvelle Revue Française*, 42 (1934): 215-222;

Louis Thomas, *Arthur de Gobineau, inventeur du racisme* (Paris: Mercure de France, 1941);

Rebecca M. Valette, *Arthur de Gobineau and the Short Story* (Chapel Hill: University of North Carolina Press, 1969);

Charles Vildrac, "Sur les *Nouvelles asiatiques*," *Europe*, 3 (October 1923): 87-98;

E. J. Young, *Gobineau und der Rassismus, Eine Kritik der anthropologischen Geschichtstheorie* (Meisenheim am Glan: A. Hain, 1968).

Papers:

Gobineau's correspondence and manuscripts are located at the Bibliothèque Nationale et Universitaire, Strasbourg; the Bibliothèque Nationale, Paris; the Bibliothèque Municipale, Bordeaux; and the Universitätsbibliothek, Freiburg im Breisgau. His diplomatic dispatches are located at the Archives du Ministère des Affaires Etrangères, Quay d'Orsay.

Edmond de Goncourt
(26 May 1822 - 16 July 1896)

Jules de Goncourt
(17 December 1830 - 20 June 1870)

B. F. Bart
University of Pittsburgh

SELECTED BOOKS: *En 18 . .*, by Edmond and Jules de Goncourt (Paris: Dumineray, 1851); revised as *Un Premier Livre. En 18 . .* (Brussels: Kistemaeckers, 1884);

Histoire de la société française pendant la Révolution, by Edmond and Jules de Goncourt (Paris: Dentu, 1854);

Une Voiture de masques, by Edmond and Jules de Goncourt (Paris: Dentu, 1856); republished as *Quelques créatures de ce temps* (Paris: Charpentier, 1876);

Sophie Arnould, d'après sa correspondance et ses mémoires inédits, by Edmond and Jules de Goncourt (Paris: Poulet-Malassis et de Broise, 1857);

Portraits intimes du XVIIIe *siècle*, by Edmond and Jules de Goncourt (Paris: Dentu, 1857);

Histoire de Marie-Antoinette, by Edmond and Jules de Goncourt (Paris: Firmin-Didot, 1858); enlarged as *Histoire de Marie-Antoinette, revue et augmentée de documents inédits et de pièces tirées des archives de l'Empire* (Paris: Firmin-Didot, 1859);

L'Art du XVIIIe *siècle*, 12 brochures, by Edmond and Jules de Goncourt (Paris: Dentu, 1860-1875); republished in 3 volumes (Paris: Charpentier, 1894-1895); translated by R. Ironside as *French XVIIIth Century Painters* (New York: Phaidon, 1948);

Les Hommes de lettres, by Edmond and Jules de Goncourt (Paris: Dentu, 1860); republished as *Charles Demailly, 2*^e^ *édition des Hommes de lettres* (Paris: Librairie Internationale, 1868);

Les Maîtresses de Louis XV, 2 volumes, by Edmond and Jules de Goncourt (Paris: Firmin-Didot, 1860); translated as *The Confidantes of a King: The Mistresses of Louis XV* (London: Foulis, 1907); original revised and enlarged in 3 volumes (Paris: Rosny aîné, 1927-1934)—comprises *Madame de Pompadour*; *La Du Barry*; *La Duchesse de Châteauroux et ses sœurs*;

Sœur Philomène, by Edmond and Jules de Goncourt (Paris: Bourdilliat, 1861); translated as *Sister Philomene* (New York: Street & Smith, 1891);

La Femme au XVIIIe *siècle*, by Edmond and Jules de Goncourt (Paris: Firmin-Didot, 1862); translated by Jacques Leclerc and Ralph Roeder as *The Woman of the XVIIIth Century* (New York: Minton & Balch, 1927);

Renée Mauperin, by Edmond and Jules de Goncourt (Paris: Charpentier, 1864); translated,

Edmond and Jules de Goncourt, circa 1855 (photograph by Nadar)

with an introduction, by James Fitzmaurice-Kelly (London, 1902);

Germinie Lacerteux, by Edmond and Jules de Goncourt (Paris: Charpentier, 1864); translated by Ernest Boyd (New York, 1922); translated by J. Griffith as *Germinie* (New York: Grove / London: Weidenfeld & Nicolson, 1955);

Henriette Maréchal, by Edmond and Jules de Goncourt (Paris: Lacroix, Verboeckhoven, 1866);

Idées et sensations, by Edmond and Jules de Goncourt (Paris: Lacroix, Verboeckhoven, 1866);

Manette Salomon, 2 volumes, by Edmond and Jules de Goncourt (Paris: Lacroix, Verboeckhoven, 1867);

Madame Gervaisais, by Edmond and Jules de Goncourt (Paris: Lacroix, Verboeckhoven, 1869);

Gavarni, l'homme et l'œuvre, by Edmond and Jules de Goncourt (Paris: Plon, 1873);

La Patrie en danger, by Edmond and Jules de Goncourt (Paris: Dentu, 1873);

La Fille Elisa, by Edmond de Goncourt (Paris: Charpentier, 1877);

Les Frères Zemganno, by Edmond de Goncourt (Paris: Charpentier, 1879); translated as *The Zemganno Brothers* (New York: Munro, 1879);

La Maison d'un artiste, by Edmond de Goncourt (Paris: Charpentier, 1881);

La Saint-Huberty, d'après sa correspondance et ses papiers de famille, by Edmond de Goncourt (Paris: Dentu, 1882);

La Faustin, by Edmond de Goncourt (Paris: Charpentier, 1882);

Chérie, by Edmond de Goncourt (Paris: Charpentier, 1884);

Journal des Goncourt. Mémoires de la vie littéraire, 9 volumes, by Edmond and Jules de Goncourt (Paris: Charpentier, 1887-1896);

Germinie Lacerteux, pièce en 10 tableaux, by Edmond de Goncourt (Paris: Charpentier, 1889);

Mademoiselle Clairon, d'après ses correspondances et les rapports de police du temps, by Edmond de Goncourt (Paris: Charpentier, 1890);

L'Art japonais du XVIIIe siècle: Outamaro, le peintre des maisons vertes, by Edmond de Goncourt (Paris: Charpentier, 1891);

La Guimard d'après les registres des Menus-plaisirs, de la bibliothèque de l'Opéra, by Edmond de Goncourt (Paris: Charpentier, 1893);

L'Italie d'hier, notes de voyages, 1855-56, entremêlées des croquis de Jules de Goncourt jetées sur le carnet de voyage, by Edmond and Jules de Goncourt (Paris: Charpentier et Fasquelle, 1894);

Manette Salomon, pièce en neuf tableaux, by Edmond de Goncourt (Paris: Charpentier et Fasquelle, 1896);

L'Art japonais du XVIIIe siècle: Hokousaï, by Edmond de Goncourt (Paris: Charpentier, 1896).

Edition: *Le Journal d'Edmond et Jules de Goncourt*, 22 volumes, edited by Robert Ricatte (Monaco: Imprimerie Nationale, 1956-1959); edited and translated, with an introduction, by Lewis Galantière as *The Goncourt Journals (1851-1870)* (Garden City, N.Y.: Doubleday, 1958).

Edmond and Jules de Goncourt, brothers and lifelong, intimate friends, played a role of considerable importance in the development of French culture, and especially the novel, in the second half of the nineteenth century. By the time they entered adulthood, romanticism was already waning in the arts and letters and in cultural life; the brothers shared in the elaboration of attitudes, approaches, and artistic and literary techniques that gradually acquired recognition during their lifetimes. While romanticism has certainly never died and the Goncourts subscribed to Romantic doctrines—for instance, their belief in the elite status of the artist—they were important forces in developing newer doctrines. They shared with their contemporaries Charles Baudelaire and Gustave Flaubert the conviction that words, properly used, could capture most of what it is to be human, including those aspects of humanity that may not be readily perceived in behavior but that can be investigated and portrayed through literature. They came to believe also that science and the scientific attitude (scientism) held further keys to unlock the gates to understanding; their works helped to open the way for the new literary school of naturalism, which was to dominate French fiction for some years. They were thus close in spirit to many of the great creative people and movements of their age in France. After receiving a comfortable inheritance in 1848, the brothers led the lives they desired of connoisseurs and dilettantes and became historians of art and taste as well as novelists.

Like many other authors of their period, the Goncourts felt that the writer must live in a state of repose and must avoid entangling himself in the world about him—the attitude to which the critic Charles-Augustin Sainte-Beuve gave the label "ivory tower." At one moment they even sold their evening clothes so as not to be tempted to go out into society. They lived together, sharing an apartment, then a house, and all their tastes till the premature death of Jules in 1870 at the age of thirty-nine. Their aristocratic birth, their relative wealth, their refined culture, and their writings placed them among the arbiters of taste of their period and gave their views weight with many of their contemporaries, perhaps even beyond what later generations have been willing to accord them.

Indeed, part of the difficulty the historian of French literature encounters in discussing the Goncourts is that, although they certainly overestimated their own talents, their work does have merit, but their taste fits only their own period. Later developments in style and subject matter have led critics to deal harshly with their cherished views on the novel and literature in general. Yet, though their work does not have the transcendent value they tended to believe it had, they are nevertheless important milestones in the development of French nineteenth-century culture, and, if one discounts slightly their own claims, one may readily see their central roles.

Except for brief trips the Goncourts lived almost all their adult lives in Paris, where they knew everyone of cultural importance: the court of Emperor Louis-Napoleon, the salon of his cousin, Princess Mathilde, and the worlds of artists and writers, of actresses and courtesans, who were such an important feature of social life in Paris from 1850 on. They wisely abandoned an early desire to be professional artists. To be sure, Jules did have a minor talent as a printmaker, but his important work lay elsewhere. Turning from sketching, painting, and printmaking, they moved to writing detailed and learned publications on eighteenth-century art and women of note, then on history itself; finally they interspersed these with novels and plays. In all cases their method was the same; therefore, to some extent one must consider most of their productions—including those in art, history, and the theater—in order to understand their novels. In each domain they sought a careful accumulation of available data and then the elaboration of a structure that would link their materials together. Hence brief studies, longer art and historical monographs, and finally the novels are all built on the same approach, which they perfected throughout their lifetimes.

Today, the importance of the Goncourts' works lies in the literary interest the brothers had in neuropathic personalities not unlike their own, in their turning to the lower classes for their subjects, in their role in bringing Japanese art to the attention of artists and the public in western Europe, and in a special concern with style that, though not widely imitated, was part of the movement to make style a central concern. In this last regard they were akin to Flaubert and Baudelaire and to the group in England around the renowned critic Walter Pater and Oscar Wilde that referred to its members as aesthetes.

Although the Goncourt brothers were very conscious of their noble background and the prerogatives they felt it gave them, in reality their title goes back less than a century before their births, to 1786. Their father's family had been mostly functionaries and bureaucrats, though their father himself had had a military career under Napoleon. Moving to Paris from their native Lorraine, the family was at first quite poor. Nevertheless, the mother loved antiques and started Edmond on a long career of collecting them, a habit that was to be crucial to his intellectual development. By 1848, with both their parents dead, the brothers decided to abandon earning a living and turned instead to painting. (How they afforded all they did on what one may suppose their income to have been remains a problem that has not been elucidated.) While their talents in the arts were not great, their efforts gave them insight into how paintings were actually produced and a firsthand acquaintance with the bohemian artistic circles of Paris in their day. They were to draw on both in their novels.

Leaving Paris in the autumn of 1848, the brothers traveled together through southern France and on to Algeria. During the trip, like so many other novelists who would become members of the realist and naturalist schools, they began writing descriptions of the scenes before them. Flaubert and, in America, William Dean Howells began their careers as writers in exactly this fashion, an excellent schooling in how to handle words to evoke life. Returning to Paris in the spring of 1849, the Goncourts settled quietly at 24, rue St.-Georges, where they remained for twenty years. By then their interest had turned to writing plays, a love they never abandoned, but their ventures were all ill fated, as were most of those of their contemporaries, especially the other naturalists. Many of the Goncourts' early works were refused by theater directors.

By 1850 their lives were devoted exclusively to art and literature, and particularly to the development of a style they called "l'écriture artiste" (artistic writing), which sought to reproduce in the reader as much as possible of the hypersensitive reactions the brothers had to the world about them. The first work of the Goncourts, *En 18 . .* (1851), a rather weak novel, unfortunately came out on the day of the coup d'état that made Louis-Napoleon emperor of France. They had had to pay for its publication themselves, a fate they were to have for many years. The book disappeared into the vortex of the political news around the start of the new empire. Only some sixty copies were sold, and it was not an important work, although Edmond did, many years later, publish a revised edition (1884). But it did nothing to gain them the fame they so desired. Several attempts to write plays were no more successful. By this time Jules had contracted syphilis; the brothers' health was never solid.

In the early 1850s the Goncourts wrote articles for various periodicals. None is important, but the activity let them come to know the world of journalism, the subject of their more successful novel *Les Hommes de lettres* (Men of Letters, 1860; republished as *Charles Demailly*, 1868). During the 1850s they enjoyed the life of the boulevards and bohemian milieus. Before long they knew most of the important writers and critics of their day. In addition to the artist Gavarni, the most important were the reigning critic Sainte-Beuve, Théophile Gautier, and, later, Emile Zola, about all of whom they felt a certain ambivalence. As their circle widened, they also came to know important historians and cultural critics, including Ernest Renan and Hippolyte Taine.

In 1854 the first of their major historical studies on the eighteenth century appeared, *Histoire de la société française pendant la Révolution* (History of French Society during the Revolution), for which again they had to pay publication expenses themselves. Although it did not have any public success, it was based on reliable data that they painstakingly sought out and presented

Edmond and Jules de Goncourt, 1853 (portrait by Gavarni; from Robert Baldick, ed., Pages from the Goncourt Journal, *1978)*

in an orderly form, despite the difficulty of getting at archival materials at this time. (There was, for instance, as yet no catalogue of the Bibliothèque Nationale in Paris.) While the brothers did not invent the historical study of social customs, at any rate they did give it great impetus in their works on the eighteenth century. They knew they were on solid ground and steadily appended footnote references to their archival and other sources. Their works in this vein are pleasant to read, but for present-day tastes they consist too much of archival bits that the brothers threaded together to make a story. In contrast, by this time Taine was already bringing to fruition his own understanding of a scientific history built on a philosophical basis. The Goncourts are perhaps more delightful to read, but they are less nourishing.

In the autumn of 1855 the brothers set out on a trip to Italy; it lasted until the following May and provided material for a novel set in Rome (*Madame Gervaisais* [1869]). In 1894 Edmond published most of their notes under the title *L'Italie d'hier* (The Italy of Yesterday). Meanwhile, since they were enjoying writing and planned to continue, they envisaged monographs on subjects drawn from eighteenth-century France, combining archival documents with connecting prose and dealing with social figures and artists. Their *Histoire de Marie-Antoinette* (1858, with a second and better edition in 1859) marks their transition to a major figure whose full life was, in and of itself, important. Their account, eminently readable, is written from a clearly marked point of view favorable to their subject and seeks to arouse the reader's sympathy for the ill-fated queen.

The organization of *Marie-Antoinette* is more unified than were the Goncourts' earlier attempts at writing history and thereby constitutes an advance toward the structural techniques they would need for their novels. In its successful unifying of disparate elements, the work gave them practice in resolving one of their chief difficulties, both in their earlier works and in those that came after, including the novels: the problem of assembling materials so as to produce a coherent, satisfying, and convincing work. Here, as opposed to some of their earlier and later books, they succeeded admirably, and *Marie-Antoinette* can be read with some of the same pleasure that is aroused by a successfully written novel.

The brothers' next study, *L'Art du XVIII*[e] *siècle* (1860-1875; translated as *French XVIIIth Century Painters*, 1948), allowed them to turn more directly to the history of art, which had already furnished them with useful details in their earlier work. Its publication was an important moment in the development of French taste: Antoine Watteau was, for instance, largely unknown till the Goncourts brought out his quintessential importance. Theirs was the first history of this painter to contain the results of reliable research.

The Goncourts came to know more women, a matter of considerable importance in the development of these misogynistic bachelors. The reader today cannot but conclude that they did not understand very much about women; their portraits of them suffer from this ignorance, and yet they often sought to portray female characters. They were not romantics in this regard: one day they canvased their recollections carefully and could not recall a single love affair that either of them had had that had lasted more than a week. They sought women of lower classes, with little education, who could add gaiety and a natural charm to their own somewhat limited masculine domain. The woman they wanted would charm them, they felt, like an agreeable animal, but she must absolutely not try to be their equal. This sharp and regrettable limitation in their understanding was to weaken their works as they turned to fiction. In the same building with them lived the actress Suzanne Lagier, friend and passing mistress of many of their friends. What made their views even more limiting was that they indulged themselves in various quasi-sadistic imaginings. Improbable as it may seem, they shared a mistress, whose life they drew on in several of their works.

By the late 1850s the Goncourts had perfected their "écriture artiste." Many of their perceptions could have been shared only by people with the neurotic psyches of the Goncourts, who could not stand noise, whose taste was so exquisite that much in their surroundings and many people in them made them acutely uncomfortable or, alternatively, opened pleasurable experiences closed to others. Nevertheless it was their hope and belief that they could put these reactions into words so that others, less sensitive than they, could also experience them. Their style depends upon the refinement of their French vocabulary and the unexpected turns of their French phrasings to render exactly what they were feeling, through the rhythm of their sentences, by their movement, and by unusual alliances of words. Unfortunately this makes "l'écriture artiste" almost untranslatable into any other language.

In "l'écriture artiste" a description should not merely give the reader the sense of, for instance, the landscape or the building in which the scene is taking place; it should also stand in its own right as a piece of artistic writing to be valued in and for itself. Often the Goncourts' prose is highly effective, and the brothers were properly proud of the results of their efforts. Nevertheless two difficulties arise. The first is simple enough: such a description, to be savored word by word, may risk slowing down the development of the novel, which is presumably the principal enjoyment of the reader. Their intense attention to adjectives, with dozens of them for some nouns, can be overwhelming. A more serious weakness arises from the Goncourts' mode of composition. They would decide what the content of the next pages should be, then they retired to their own desks and each wrote a draft. These two drafts were then combined to produce the final result. The risk was that each author would find quite enough descriptive material on his own; when it was combined with what the other had produced, the result could be a passage seriously overburdened with words.

A few lines from *Charles Demailly* suggest both the excellence and some of the defects of their style. The hero and a friend have gone to the opera and are observing the boxes: "Sur le repoussoir de leur fond *rouge*, des cravates *blanches*, des visages *rougis* par la chaleur, le triangle *blanc* des chemises d'hommes, des chapeaux *noirs*, des habits *noirs*; des ombres de femmes *noires*, des paires de gants *blancs*" (Against the *red* background of the boxes, were the *white* ties, faces *reddened* by the heat, the *white* triangle of the men's shirts, *black* evening clothes, *black* shadows of the women, pairs of *white* gloves [emphasis added]). This quotation constitutes five lines from a paragraph that goes on in similar style for more than twenty lines. The novel can pick up again only with a gasp from the reader.

By 1858 the Goncourts, their "écriture artiste" perfected, deemed they were ready to write another novel. *En 18 . .* was now behind them. Moreover, their techniques for writing historical works could readily translate into writing novels. For the Goncourts the book would be only a variant on their previous framework. History, they felt, was an accurate account of what had been; the novel would be a similar account of what was. In it they would invent a principal character, for whom they often drew heavily on people they knew and themselves, so as to be sure of their material. For the surrounding circumstances and characters of *Charles Demailly*, they could draw on their personal knowledge and supplement that by such research as needed. The Goncourts' *Journal* (1887-1896) makes this clear by listing the models for the characters in this novel. This approach, while useful and perhaps constructive, can unintentionally produce a disjointed work, as the characters may adhere too strictly to their sources to make it possible to fuse the fictional elements into a totality. On both counts, however, their practices seemed to them to guarantee the validity of what they presented.

Charles Demailly, which warrants examination in some detail, portrays the contemporary world of the small newspaper. Such ephemeral publications sold well at the time because they were filled with juicy scandals and vented the personal hatreds of the journalists involved. Significantly, the Goncourts titled their imaginary paper the *Scandale* and commented at length about how this sort of publication had lowered the literary level of France. Unfortunately, the degree of rage that the brothers felt against this milieu so severely colors their novel as to leave them with almost no agreeable character, except their hero, among the many journalists portrayed. The Goncourts found them disagreeable, and so do readers.

To make it worse the period had witnessed the outbreak of a wildly successful formula for joking, "la blague," which the Goncourts were not alone in condemning. It involved aggressive attacks that consisted of heaping ridicule on the victim; little remained sacred, and the reader tends to be as revolted by the depiction of this conduct as the Goncourts apparently were. The world of low-life journalism is not a pleasant subject for a novel, and some readers have wondered whether the Goncourts were able actually to present accurately what this world really was. Is the observer not a part of what he observes and presents?

The composition of the book was extremely difficult for the Goncourts. At first they wrote it as a play, but they could not find a theater director who would accept it. They then reworked it into a novel. Its original title, *Les Hommes de lettres*, failed to emphasize adequately Charles Demailly, their hero and only likable character, who dominates the second half of the book. In 1868 they wisely changed the title to *Charles Demailly*. While the two interests, Charles and his milieu, are interrelated (the hero is a journalist), they do not fuse fully. The reader follows one of them and then, separately, the other. The novel displays both the excellences and the flaws inherent in the methods of the Goncourts, flaws that recurred each time they published.

The example of Honoré de Balzac and their own inexperience perhaps led them to feel they needed a vast cast of characters, to most of whom, one after another, they introduce the reader in the opening pages. One is forty pages into the novel before Charles Demailly himself is presented. Against this mass of second-raters, Demailly is a delightful change; but the reader's mood is perhaps already soured. His is the story of a neurotic man of talent and noble nature who is destroyed by a miserable wife. Woman, they write here, is the error of man. Charles's early death foreshadows that of Jules himself a decade later (although that did not result from his mistreatment by a woman).

Unfortunately, as the Goncourts knew, Balzac had written successfully on this subject only a few decades before, and the situation in journalism had not changed enough, although there had been deterioration in professional behavior, to make a new novel on the subject easily convincing. They were thus confronting one of the greatest geniuses of French literature on his own terrain; comparisons could only be unfavorable.

Demailly is the neurotic, incredibly sensitive result of overcivilization. He has an acute perception of everything and of life itself; it is almost painful to him, where others would notice nothing. That is, he is an amalgam of the two brothers, as all their later principal characters would also be. Though the brothers explicitly wanted characters who were raised to the level of types, Flaubert, who personally liked the Goncourts very much, believed that the writer could not be a proper subject for fiction: he was too particu-

Jules de Goncourt, 1857 (watercolor sketch by Edmond de Goncourt; from M. A. Belloc and M. Shedlock, eds., Edmond and Jules de Goncourt, *volume 1, 1895)*

lar, too individualized, to stand in for humanity in general.

To be successful, a novel, at least as understood by nineteenth-century readers, needs in some way to be a unified, integrated whole. Although *Charles Demailly* is replete with excellent examples of "l'écriture artiste" and all sorts of characters and scenes drawn from different moments, it is not coherent. It was largely ill received, which hurt the brothers profoundly. The portrait of Demailly's mistress turned wife, Marthe, was part of the problem. The Goncourts were convinced that they were describing a typical woman, whose imperfections were inherent in her sex. In a long digression they write that women are marked by an automatic rebellion against anyone who counters their slightest wishes. To the Goncourts—if one is to judge by this passage—combativeness is the very proof of women's existence, and caprice, the way they exercise their will. Because they are persistent, they will always win their battles with men. It is not a flattering portrait nor one likely to win the assent of many female readers.

The passage where these statements occur appears in some dozen pages of the novel that come, one is told, from Charles's diary. When one returns to the text of the third-person narrator, one has lost sight of the main plot. This compositional flaw is a recurrent one in too many of the Goncourts' novels. This work is also marred by excessively long conversations that degenerate into exchanges of monologues between characters. When the novel does focus at last on Charles (and one is nearing the hundredth page), one learns that he is writing the definitive study of the bourgeoisie, "the world built on plutocracy," a work in which Demailly wishes to depict the psychological drama of the social catastrophes he will paint. This drama of the bourgeoisie is behind many of the Goncourts' novels. In order to work more fully on his study, Charles withdraws from the *Scandale*, where his erstwhile friends take advantage of his leaving in order to attack him ferociously. He is duly warned but is too noble hearted to reply. The attack is led by his supposed friend Nichette, a particularly disagreeable member of the team at the journal.

The editor eggs them on, hoping to get free copy from each, once the battle is engaged.

When Charles's book comes out, he meets his erstwhile friends at a café. He cannot but notice that no one says a word to him of his book, but it does sell. Charles meets and later marries a beautiful young actress, Marthe. He decides to write a play in which she will have the leading role. But they cannot really talk together, for that is not within her range; yet she has what Charles and the Goncourts deemed the perfect virtues of a woman. She listens, she chatters, she smiles; they make love. But when Marthe orders a dress that is three times their income and he remonstrates with her, she sulks. When Nichette attacks him in the *Scandale* he shocks Marthe by not replying, considering that silence is all that Nichette merits. She is pained and, as time passes, comes to wonder about Charles's talent, particularly as concerns the play he has written for her. Not suspecting how much she is wounding him, she tells him that he should take a collaborator and suggests the name of an idiot.

Charles takes to listening to his wife more carefully and discovers the real nullity of her mind. The Goncourts note that modern novels all play to their female readers' fantasies by giving them the idea that their marriages should incarnate passion. But, they note, novels (other than *Charles Demailly*) do not portray what their counterparts, the husbands, may find lacking in their wives. And to whom can these husbands turn? To no one. The Goncourts' comments are in part a response to the complaints of the wife in Flaubert's *Madame Bovary* (1857; translated, 1881). The authors speculate on the way in which an actress's role (and specifically Marthe's) can gradually spill over into her life. It can result, they affirm, in the development of a whole second nature, as with Marthe. The phenomenon would recur in Edmond's *La Faustin* (1882).

Charles's health begins to decline as a consequence of his conflict with Marthe. They go to take the waters at a new spa, where Charles talks with the doctor, a most intelligent man who is exploring the influence of psychological factors on the body. The Goncourts are convincing in detailing Charles's troubles as his difficulties with Marthe increasingly undermine his health. She takes to excusing his behavior on the grounds of his nerves, telling him so, however, at every turn.

The two take up boating, and for six pages the action stops completely as the Goncourts describe the river scenes. The brothers would have held that these pages had their own value, in and for themselves. But that can be true only for the reader who by now does not care to find out quickly what happens between this unhappy wife and husband. When the story line returns to them, Marthe takes to torturing Charles with her complaints of boredom. Despite the Goncourts' earlier claim that the husband can turn to no one at these difficult times, Charles writes of his anguish to an old friend: he has discovered, he says, that his wife has no heart and is stupid to boot. She is at ease only with inferiors, and that is a role Charles cannot play with her.

Demailly becomes aware that his mind is giving way; he cannot concentrate on anything serious. He learns that Marthe is complaining about him to his old acquaintances at the *Scandale*, then that she, to whom he gives all the money she needs, tells others that he leaves her penniless, so that she must borrow to meet her expenses. He tells her that she is dishonoring him by such lies. Then Marthe announces that she does not wish to play the lead role in his play, and their apparent friend Nichette arranges for another actress to replace her. Marthe is furious, and a glacial cold enters the marriage. She now confides that she and Nichette are almost in love. Charles begs her to stop torturing him with jealousy, but Marthe brushes him off and flings in his face the declaration that, while he loves her, she does not love him. Eventually he drives her from the house. She leaves, throwing at him: "J'ai ton nom, c'est toujours ça" (But after all, I will still have your name).

Nichette and Marthe arrange an act of vengeance for her, which will offset the former's feeling of inferiority to Charles. She gives him a packet of letters Charles has written her, in which among other things he makes fun of his acquaintances at the *Scandale*. In a complex arrangement Nichette manages to persuade Charles erroneously that the letters have been published in the newspaper. When it all blows up, Nichette explains to Marthe that he never cared for her and was only using her against Charles. As for the latter, he falls to the ground, thunderstruck. He has been mortally hurt; his mind will never recover. He sells his furniture, rents an apartment, and prepares to die. One night, while out walking, he discovers that his wife is playing a role in a worthless drama. His mind goes completely.

Though the novel is fundamentally crippled by its defects of structure and certain weaknesses of "l'écriture artiste," one can still read it with

Edmond de Goncourt, 1860 (engraving by Walker & Boutall after a portrait by Jules de Goncourt; from M. A. Belloc and M. Shedlock, eds., Edmond and Jules de Goncourt, *volume 1, 1895)*

not inconsiderable pleasure after the initial pages on the milieu at the *Scandale*. And the ending is sufficiently believable to be deeply sad. Nonetheless, the public did not like the novel, and it was not reprinted for nine years. It was another in the long series of failures the Goncourts had to undergo. After further historical publications on major women of the eighteenth century, the brothers returned to fiction with *Sœur Philomène* (1861; translated as *Sister Philomene*, 1891), an account of a nun who serves in a hospital. The story begins with her childhood. An orphan who lives only briefly with a kind aunt, Philomène is soon placed in an orphanage and is brought up by nuns. The change breaks her spirit, and she lives only for the days when her aunt might visit her. Her native sensitivity, of the sort that characterizes all the Goncourt heroes and heroines, develops early and reflects the creators' delight in their own nervous sensitivities.

Philomène becomes extremely devout and is the joy of the good sisters who run the convent. The character of her religion reflects her nervous temperament; she is filled with tremors and is, as it were, in love with God. She feels herself called to serve him; her first communion is a moment of ecstasy. She begins to show what a later age would widely call hysteria. Her face loses its healthy coloring; she begins to think of death. Concurrently but vaguely, the idea of marriage begins to present itself to her as well.

As Philomène is becoming visibly ill, the sisters fear for her health and arrange for her to go back to her aunt. But finding that she can give outlet to her need to feel love only toward Jesus Christ, she determines to enter the religious life. Before her novitiate is finished, she is sent to serve in a hospital. (At very great cost to their nerves, the Goncourts visited a hospital so as to describe it from life.) At this point in the novel the plot is interrupted so that the Goncourts can report on this environment and portray the hospital interns; one returns to Philomène only after some fifteen pages. By then attention has been seriously diverted from the heroine.

Philomène continues to be excessively sensitive; she gives herself entirely to seeking to lessen the suffering of the patients under her care. She finds that this gives a specific charm to her life, which is now entirely limited to the hospital. One intern in particular is especially close to her; she talks with him daily. He seeks in vain to shake her faith, but the reader may sense that the Goncourts were here discussing a matter they could not understand from within. They were self-proclaimed atheists, a position that would also be reflected in *Madame Gervaisais*. Instead of letting herself be convinced by the intern, Philomène advances to the moment of pronouncing her final vows despite the sarcasm of her friend, who seeks to undermine her faith by drawing her attention to all the suffering that God apparently permits about her.

Gradually the affection linking the intern and the sister becomes obvious to others. The intern, egged on by his fellows, follows the sister into an empty room and tries to force a kiss on her; she slaps him. To relieve the stresses of his medical post, he turns to alcohol. The Goncourts study his slow transition from seeking excitement in spirits to rejoicing instead in a sort of torpor. The account of this development is delicately handled, but attention is once again distracted from the heroine.

As the intern sinks into his addiction, the sister finds herself less wholly involved in her work at the hospital, less consumed with caring for her patients. Mortified over what she is obliged to recognize as her growing passion for the intern, she seeks every means to dominate her body. But then her beloved deliberately cuts his finger and lets the wound become infected from a patient. As the novel ends, Sister Philomène comes almost secretly by night and takes a lock of his hair while he lies dying.

The novel has much to recommend it, but its two subjects—religion and the affection linking the intern and the nun—tend to cancel each other out instead of reinforcing each other. The novel initially sold poorly, although a new edition in 1876 was more successful. The great director André Antoine briefly staged a dramatized version in 1887, but, like the works of most of the other naturalists who turned to the theater, *Sœur Philomène* was not a great success as a play. Returning to their studies of the eighteenth century, the brothers began work on *La Femme au XVIIIe siècle* (1862; translated as *The Woman of the XVIIIth Century*, 1927). They searched avidly for documents to make the work more vivid. It had been their thought to produce a study in four parts; it was never completed.

The Goncourts' next novel, *Renée Mauperin* (1864; translated, 1902), was a return to the portrayal of the society in which the brothers lived, and many of the characters were again drawn from people they knew. *Renée Mauperin* is an analysis of the contemporary bourgeoisie which Charles Demailly had castigated. The brothers did not like contemporary youth any more than they did the world of journalism portrayed in their earlier novel. The heroine, herself a likable young woman, has the cordiality and the loyalty of a young man, traits that suggest the ambivalent attitude of the Goncourts toward women. In contrast, her brother, Henri, a distant, calculating person who, in some senses, has never been young, lacks almost all likable qualities as he coldly pursues his advantages. The Goncourts portrayed in the brother and sister what they deemed to be the result of the upbringing of young people of the upper bourgeoisie during the previous thirty years.

The story line, neither melodramatic nor a primary aspect of the work, served mostly to let the Goncourts display their dislike of their period. The novel is much less stuffed with details than their earlier ones, but this unfortunately leads to a lack of diversity for the reader. Hence the success the authors had was once again minimal. Many of their close friends even avoided speaking of it to them on its appearance, a situation in which the Goncourts had already placed Charles Demailly. The brothers were in despair over this reaction, though most reviewers were at least moderately favorable.

The Goncourts began work on a play, *Henriette Maréchal* (1866), but set it aside when a subject for a new novel, *Germinie Lacerteux* (1864; translated, 1922), presented itself in an unexpected fashion. For some fifteen years their devoted servant Rose had tended them like children, even tucking them into bed at night. She gave every appearance of being the ultimately faithful servant, a view they held until her death. After her burial it came out to their dismay that she had in fact been seriously depraved, a hopeless nymphomaniac, an alcoholic beyond control, robbing them at intervals to pay for her vices. They believed that Rose's story would be an excellent vehicle for their nuanced prose.

The Goncourts prepared their material with their usual care. They visited the low dives frequented by the model of their Germinie, where they must have constituted most incongruous guests. They read extensively about hysteria (at that date still ill understood) and made trips about the outskirts of Paris to find the right areas in which to locate Germinie's walks in the country. This preparation was integral to their work in view of their conviction that art should be true, whereas they felt earlier authors had prettied up such subjects. (The question of what may be considered "true" was not as complex in their day as it has now been for some time.)

What truths were appropriate for fiction and other art forms was, however, a major question on the French literary scene, one integral to the development and critical reception of naturalism, the type of social realism that Zola named and soon was to claim as his own. In the 1860s some of the details of the brothers' subject, Germinie's depraved life, were, according to most readers, quite simply unacceptable in a novel, although today they might seem almost ordinary and would become so in France in a few years after the appearance of *Germinie Lacerteux*. The French reading public of 1865 under the moralistic Second Empire was not ready for so tawdry a topic; and the Goncourts were not necessarily the best authors to undertake to treat it, however much they felt protected by their basis in fact. (A dozen years later Zola would mine the same vein of "the people" in his hugely successful novel *L'Assommoir* [1877; translated, 1879].)

As French literature moved forward from realism, *Germinie Lacerteux* was probably the first novel in the new style. Zola's claim to priority is understandable, for he succeeded in imposing the new strain on literature, whereas *Germinie Lacerteux* infuriated and alienated many readers by its subject and details. But the Goncourts never forgave Zola for his boasts of priority. The brothers considered their novel a work with the accuracy of science and the truth of history, the two reigning beliefs of the age that was dawning. The doctrine is known as scientism, today a set of beliefs long in serious decline. That the novel is not and cannot be science and that the "truth" of history is often not a good basis for literature were two considerations the Goncourts and the naturalists who followed would generally have rejected.

The Goncourts had further problems in addition to that of public disapproval of their topic. As their earlier works had demonstrated, they had always had great difficulty understanding and depicting women convincingly in any context. And a woman willing to risk everything for sex was to prove very challenging for them to portray. Oddly, they also felt that an author who could handle the matter had to be an aristocrat, which, fortunately, they were. The subject was certainly an exotic one for them, one from which perhaps they hoped to have enough distance to see objectively. Ironically, the Goncourts had been present, day by day, with Rose (Germinie) and had never suspected anything at all; yet they felt themselves keen students of human nature. Despite these handicaps, they produced a novel that is certainly their best-known work and perhaps their most significant one.

Germinie, at the start of the novel, has long worked as a servant in the house of an old maid. This may later provoke some skepticism in the reader: if it was in fact possible for two aging bachelors not to notice the conduct of their Rose (including two pregnancies), it seems nearly inconceivable that a woman, and especially an older woman, would notice nothing of the behavior in which Germinie is supposed to indulge. But that is how the Goncourts wished to tell their story. Germinie, seeking someone who understands her, first turns to religion and the confessional, where she feels sure to be understood. But when her confessor sees that Germinie, unbeknownst to herself, has fallen in love with him, he turns her over to another priest. She abandons the church, keeping only a certain aura in her memory.

Germinie now falls in love with Jupillon, the young son of a neighbor; mother and son are modeled on people the Goncourts knew, a fact that, they felt, would guarantee the validity of their portrayal. Thoughts of him fill her entirely, yet at the start she does not wish it to become a physical relationship. It does not long remain platonic, however, and she feels renewed and fortified by her passion. The boy's mother sees in this attachment a means to make money out of Germinie, who will buy her mistress's provisions in the mother's store. It is Germinie's ill fortune that Jupillon becomes her master, for in fact he scorns women. For him the whole affair is an obscenity; he finds Germinie unbearable, ridiculous, and comic in her devotion to him. He takes to avoiding her; to find him she goes to public dance halls where she knows he may be. Whereas until now she has had the respect that servants of wealthy masters or mistresses tend to receive, as her liaison with Jupillon becomes known in the neighborhood she meets with scorn and contempt for her conduct. Yet it only leads her to hold onto her liaison more desperately.

Then Germinie becomes pregnant. This fills her with joy, though she has no money to buy clothes for her child-to-be. Shortly after the child's birth, the infant falls ill and dies. Then her lover's number comes up in the military draft. At that time it was possible to avoid being called up by making a large payment to the state. Borrowing on every hand, Germinie amasses the sum needed; she knows she will be dogged by her debt for the rest of her days. Like almost all Goncourt heroes and heroines, Germinie has an excessively sensitive nervous organization. She alternates between moments of deep melancholy and hyperactivity as she contemplates what her life has become. She takes to drinking heavily, seeking forgetfulness in alcohol: it protects her from an existence that she no longer has the courage to face.

The Goncourts describe her state with minute, delicate touches. But the reader is left wondering whether it is plausible that such a character should hide successfully her addiction from a woman who is her mistress (as opposed to a man), for she is constantly at least partially drunk and detached from everything about her. To be sure, the brothers themselves had lived closely with Rose, but can that be a sufficient guarantee for the reader of a work of fiction? It can be only a question, but the reader may well ask it. It is, the Goncourts wrote, a miracle that she performs. The reader must accept this or deny the fabric of the book. Her behavior with her mistress is, they affirm, not hypocrisy but devotion to her, which keeps up her strength.

But Germinie's degradation begins to be visible in her whole person. In order to buy the complicity of the superintendent of the apartment and his wife, Germinie begins bringing them delicacies left over from her mistress's table. The various shopkeepers who sell her provisions find they can give her spoiled, underweight food, knowing that she will not dare complain lest they inform on her. And her physical desire for her lover becomes an obsession that lasts through her waking hours. He takes to asking for presents, which she gladly buys for him. She even steals from her mistress to meet his demands.

When a robbery occurs in her building, there are many who suspect Germinie and threaten to tell her mistress of her debts. The idea of suicide begins to loom in her imagination. She takes up with a drunken bum and makes herself his slave. She waits long hours outside his house, hoping for his return, and she begins to have hallucinations. She indulges in wild debauches with her new lover, but as time passes and his behavior with her becomes repulsive, they separate. She then picks up any man she can find on the street. She even seeks to renew her affair with her first lover, begging him to beat her.

Germinie's overt behavior changes so much that her mistress cannot but at least wonder at her, but Germinie is stout in her denials and keeps the woman from discovering her horrible secret. At last her alcoholism engenders a physical decline so serious that she has to be transported to a hospital. Shortly, she dies there. And then, as with Rose, Germinie's whole secret existence comes out as her debtors seek to recover their money. Her mistress is at first furious with her dead servant, hating her for her duplicities. But with time she recalls all those moments when Germinie had seemed (as she now realizes) on the verge of confessing. Understanding replaces hatred, and she comes to forgive. She even goes to the cemetery at Montmartre, where she finds that Germinie's grave lacks even a cross with her name; she has slipped into the undifferentiated mass of the dead. It is, the Goncourts wrote in their last pages, as though the earth had no more room for her body than it had had for her heart.

Germinie Lacerteux is surely one of the Goncourts' two or three best-written works. This time their heroine has a fully three-dimensional character that imposes its existence on readers. They succeeded in giving literary life to the concrete reality they had known. Despite the improbability inherent in the plot, Germinie is very much alive for the reader as the brothers analyze her successive states with understanding; she moves the reader at all times. Yet the Goncourts treated this topic without the veils to which readers were accustomed, although under pressure they made some cuts in their manuscript. By an odd twist, the brothers had become naturalists (before the word existed)—that is, mercilesss painters of human degradation—and yet sympathetic to their subject at the same time, a most unusual position for partisans of this school. Zola was one of the few reviewers who appreciated and praised the novel.

In August 1862 the brothers came to know Princess Mathilde, cousin of the emperor and one of the principal figures of the Second Empire. She had read their *Marie-Antoinette* and would soon read *Germinie Lacerteux* (which she dis-

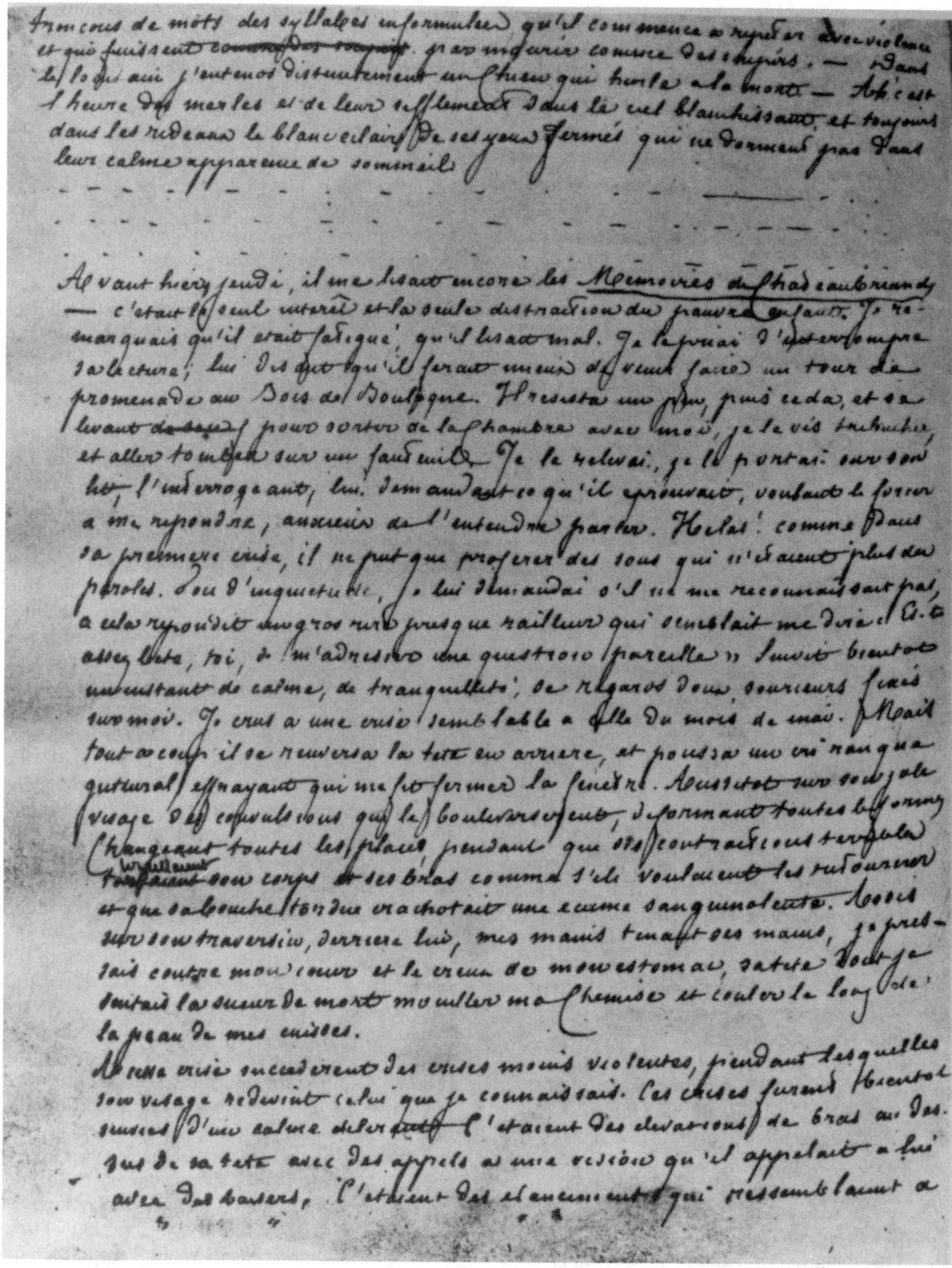
fragments de mots, des syllabes informulées qu'il commence à répéter avec violence et qui finissent par des injures comme des soupirs. — Dans le silence j'entends distinctement un chien qui hurle à la mort. — Ah! c'est l'heure des merles et de leur sifflement dans le ciel blanchissant, et toujours dans les rideaux le blanc éclair de ses yeux fermés qui ne dorment pas dans leur calme apparence de sommeil.

- - - - - - - - - - - - - - - - -

Avant hier jeudi, il me lisait encore les Mémoires de Chateaubriand — c'était le seul intérêt et la seule distraction du pauvre enfant. Je remarquais qu'il était fatigué, qu'il lisait mal. Je le priai d'interrompre sa lecture, lui disant qu'il ferait mieux de venir faire un tour de promenade au Bois de Boulogne. Il résista un peu, puis céda, et se levant pour sortir de la chambre avec moi, je le vis trébucher, et aller tomber sur un fauteuil. Je le relevai, je le portai sur son lit, l'interrogeant, lui demandant ce qu'il éprouvait, voulant le forcer à me répondre, anxieux de l'entendre parler. Hélas! comme dans sa première crise, il ne put que proférer des sons qui n'étaient plus des paroles. Fou d'inquiétude, je lui demandai s'il ne me reconnaissait pas, à cela répondit un gros rire presque railleur qui semblait me dire « Es-tu assez bête, toi, de m'adresser une question pareille » Suivit bientôt un instant de calme, de tranquillité, de regards doux, souriants fixés sur moi. Je crus à une crise semblable à celle du mois de mai. Mais tout à coup il se renversa la tête en arrière, et poussa un cri rauque guttural effrayant qui me fit fermer la fenêtre. Aussitôt sur son joli visage des convulsions qui le bouleversèrent, déformant toutes les formes, changeant toutes les places, pendant que des contractions nerveuses tordaient son corps et ses bras comme s'il voulait les retourner et que sa bouche tordue crachotait une écume sanguinolente. Assis sur son traversin, derrière lui, mes mains tenant ses mains, je pressais contre mon cœur et le creux de mon estomac sa tête, je sentais la sueur de mort mouiller ma chemise et couler le long de la peau de mes cuisses.

A cette crise succédèrent des crises moins violentes, pendant lesquelles son visage redevint celui que je connaissais. Ces crises furent bientôt suivies d'un calme délirant. C'étaient des élévations de bras au dessus de sa tête avec des appels à une vision qu'il appelait à lui avec des baisers. C'étaient des élancements qui ressemblaient à

Journal entry in which Edmond de Goncourt recorded the fatal illness of his brother, Jules (Bibliothèque Nationale)

liked). She had a much-sought-after salon where she received the leading lights of the day, including writers and artists, in the tradition of the eighteenth-century French salons. The Goncourts and she became fast friends when she decided to adopt them for her circle, although they found it too bourgeois for their tastes. Through the princess they met her cousin, Louis-Napoleon, and his son Prince Napoleon.

After finishing the novel based on their servant's life, the Goncourts completed their interrupted play *Henriette Maréchal*. After many uncertainties it was accepted for the prestigious Comédie Française, the great government-backed theater. Although the princess had not liked it, she used her influence to get it past government censorship. The plot is familiar: a triangle involving a mother and daughter who are rivals for the same man. It is not a major work, but it raised a storm of furor among much of the public, that is, those elements resolutely opposed to the Bonapartist government. They disliked the play before they had even seen it because of the official protection they believed had led to its acceptance. Student protesters flocked to the opening night; when there was difficulty seating all of them, it added to their irritation. The hall was in eruption before the end of the first act. The second act is not strong, and the shouts continued. No one could hear the third act. In order to mollify the audiences, the brothers made several cuts, but all in vain. When the play was revived in 1885, it was better received, but on the whole it did not fare better with the public than the other naturalist plays. The lack of success was a further deep disappointment for the brothers.

The Goncourts then turned to a portrayal of the world of artists in mid-nineteenth-century France. *Manette Salomon* (1867) featured a topic they had first thought of treating as early as 1850. As with the world of journalists in *Charles Demailly*, the brothers were on a terrain they knew well and loathed cordially. Their dislike shows in their novel and weakens it. But the depiction of artistic life in France at midcentury is surprisingly good, as many of the issues of the day in the arts are clearly raised. However, the Goncourts appreciated no art that developed after the reign of Louis-Philippe (1848). They disliked the painter Gustave Courbet, who came to prominence in the late 1840s and whose enemies were the first to coin the term *realism* to describe a style of which they disapproved. And the Goncourts had no idea that the lighter tonalities of the Impressionists were the wave of the future. For Edouard Manet they had only scorn. These limitations are especially noticeable in the novel, as their hero is a painter who specializes in landscapes. As so often in their works, most of the characters are shown only from the outside. The brothers visited an art studio, read on aesthetics and on species of chickens (which appear in the novel), and on anti-Semitism (which is central).

As with their examination of journalists, this novel suffers from having two focuses, the world of artists and the characters. Like *Charles Demailly*, it also displays the devastation that they felt a woman could work on a talented lover. For the Goncourts, women were still superlatively dangerous, of mediocre intelligence, and slaves of their nerves and temperaments. They drive their men down until madness takes over. At the end of this novel, the hero dies insane.

Unfortunately, in order to set the scene of the art world adequately, the Goncourts held back the introduction of their heroine, Manette Salomon, until the book was half over. Weakening it still further is the basic, pervasive anti-Semitism of the brothers, whose heroine is Jewish. Additionally, the dual focus of the novel again leaves the reader disoriented; loss of interest may follow. The book becomes a succession of loosely constructed tableaux, interesting largely for the discussions of art. Manette comes onstage too late really to capture the reader's interest, and her role is then so devastating that one dislikes her intensely. Finally, there are the long, often exquisite landscape scenes done in "l'écriture artiste," but when the topic that they are interrupting is painting, they may move from an account of the surrounding landscape into an equally detailed and delicate account of the landscape on the hero-artist's canvas; this may produce monotony as well as disorientation for the reader. Some contemporary interest was aroused by the Goncourts' giving to their characters the real names of the models, but that proved only a passing attraction. The novel was hardly discussed by reviewers; this indifference still further discouraged the brothers.

Their next novel, *Madame Gervaisais*, has no real plot—if by that is meant a series of actions—but is instead a nuanced and fascinating presentation of the development of a woman's soul as she evolves from an eighteenth-century deism to Christian mysticism. In writing the book the Goncourts checked their own atheism and distaste for religion, but both come through nevertheless. They did show considerable understanding of their heroine, however, which makes for the interest of the book, though this could not win over Catholic readers, who would almost certainly be irritated by the anticlerical tone.

Mme Gervaisais is by temperament sad. She cannot defend herself against a feeling of melancholy as evening falls; she is, in this manner, a typical Goncourt chief character. She has come to Rome to help fight off tuberculosis and to take care of her young handicapped son, Pierre-Charles, to whom she devotes herself. His birth was difficult; brain injuries have partially and permanently incapacitated him. He learns to speak only late and imperfectly. Mme Gervaisais intends to remain in Rome for a lengthy period. The Goncourts place her in a comfortable apartment close to the Spanish Steps, near which they themselves found a place while they were taking notes for the novel. The lovely, laughing light of Mme Gervaisais's apartment and the gay atmosphere of the rooms provide that satisfaction which, the Goncourts affirm, sickly, nervous temperaments can find in a sympathetic lodging. She responds ecstatically to the beautiful flowers of Rome. She is astonished at the heightening of her impressions since she settled in the city. While descriptions of her reactions and of what provokes them slow the novel markedly, to the reader who knows Rome, the Goncourts' "écriture artiste" offers special pleasures; their nuanced perceptions revive the unique feeling that all who know the city will recognize and love.

As one comes to know Mme Gervaisais, one learns her favorite readings, an austere list of books for a beautiful woman of thirty-seven: the Scottish philosophers, such as Dugald Stewart (widely read among European intellectuals at this time); Immanuel Kant; and the French popularizer Théodore Jouffroy. Her readings suggest the woman who, the Goncourts state, was typical of a small group of ladies under the reign of Louis-Philippe (1830-1848). She is intelligent, born serious, and has carried out serious studies. She has grown up almost without companions of her own age, passing her time in reading, music, and painting. Typical of the generation that was educated on the philosophic system of Victor Cousin, which was dominant at that period in France, she seeks her reference points in his creed—a quasi-religious one—of the Beautiful, the True, and the Good. One day shortly after her arrival in Rome, she watches the vast spectacle of a solemn Christian procession through the city. It bothers her deeply, and she wonders to herself if religion really demands so much spectacle.

At intervals as she travels about Rome, Mme Gervaisais stops in one or another of the churches, seeking not a religious experience but a place of tranquillity and peace. Easter Week, however, upsets her sensitivities and irritates her. Originally she responded with delight to the art of pagan Rome, but with time it seems to her to celebrate the body alone by representing only strength, power, health, and physical beauty. As she remembers the bloody life of the Romans, without pity and built on slavery, she finds herself turning more toward Christianity, whose followers believe in the brotherhood of man. Slowly she begins to open herself to religion, and the Goncourts describe the nuances of this process with loving delicacy. She takes to going to the great church of the Gesù, the mother church of the Jesuits. Gradually her pride in her intelligence begins to lessen; she becomes more open to spiritual sensations and values. She is moving, say the Goncourts, toward a rational Catholicism that would ideally combine her intelligence and spirituality.

On this path Mme Gervaisais senses her own revolt against this denial of her critical mind and, as a reaction, strives to make her conversion a work of her intelligence. She finds a Jesuit confessor to guide her. He struggles to make her more docile to his teachings, to bend her reason before his instruction. This is so contrary to all her previous life that she often revolts. She longs then for a more rigid director and finds one accustomed to the pride of well-educated people seeking religion. He recognizes that it is her intelligence that is holding her back. Coming to fear that her absorbing love for her poor son may be an obstacle to her faith, she seeks to detach herself from him. She also succeeds, under the same tutelage of her confessor, in stifling her enjoyment of nature. She begins to feel moments of religious ecstasy. Here, however, the reader senses in their writing that the brothers had no personal knowledge of piety and religious enthusiasm.

Mme Gervaisais slowly succumbs to the tuberculosis that brought her to Rome in the first place, a process the Goncourts carefully documented through medical research. Her illness markedly furthers her aspiration toward the supernatural aspects of her spirituality. She moves imperceptibly to unity with God. But it is not to

Edmond de Goncourt near the end of his life

be easy, and her moments of ecstasy become more infrequent. At this point her confessor tells her that she must wholly abandon her love for her child: Christ had ordered those who would follow him to abandon all, including family. This breaks the child's heart. But she comes to realize that she has in fact abandoned all earthly affections; her humanity has been stifled. She has lost even her desire to live and impatiently anticipates the moment of her death, though resigned to awaiting the moment God will choose. Her brother, deeply alarmed, arrives in Rome and attempts to revive her interest in life. He arranges for her a meeting with the pope, but she dies as she is entering the audience chamber. As she falls prone, Pierre-Charles is able for the first time to articulate "ma mère" (Mother).

The tone of the novel is sufficiently anticlerical and antireligious to bother many readers, although the full text is less baldly so than this summary may suggest. But the portraits of Rome, based on the brothers' long and loving visits to the city, are highly successful. The book of course annoyed Catholic reviewers and sold badly. It was the last of the brothers' collaborations.

As the Second Empire was nearing its end, the Goncourts mistakenly attempted to return to the theater with *La Patrie en danger* (The Nation in Danger, published in 1873). It was another failure, despite the topicality of the subject, which was born of the widespread French fears of Prussia, whose maneuverings brought on the Franco-Prussian War in 1870. The Goncourts also finished their study of Gavarni, the well-known lithographer whose close friend they had been since 1852; they owned hundreds of his prints. Edmond felt, certainly erroneously, that the nineteenth century in France had been dominated by Gavarni and Balzac. But, despite this distorted view, the Goncourts' *Gavarni* (1873) is so good that even though it lacks illustrations, it is immensely readable. The brothers were completely at ease with their topic.

They were at work on this book when Jules fell fatally ill. His death came as the result of a brain lesion, after five days of unconsciousness, on 20 June 1870. A lifetime of close friendship and collaboration thus came to an end. He had long been sickly and had always been unable to stand noise. He declined for months preceding his death. As the end neared, his mental faculties began to weaken, as did his aristocratic sense of self. Some sounds became impossible for him to pronounce, and he began to forget places and names. He found it hard to concentrate and eventually lost interest in everything. Edmond contemplated killing Jules and then himself but found he could not bring himself to carry out the project. However, he took notes on everything until the funeral cortege reached the cemetery. The ending of *Charles Demailly* turned out to be prophetic. Edmond felt that it was the anguish of his life as a writer that killed Jules, but the true cause, more mundane, was probably syphilis, contracted some two decades before. Jules's death was an immense blow to Edmond, whose friends thereafter often referred to him as "The Widow." They rallied round to try to help him. Ironically, he and Jules had just purchased a new house at Auteuil, in the suburbs of Paris, hoping to find it quieter than their longtime residence on rue St.-Georges. But their purchase was ill-advised for a pair seeking quiet and tranquillity: it was near a railroad station.

The relationship of the two brothers had been so close that critics have tried in vain to determine what part each played in writing their collaborative novels. Their whole lives had been shared: their pleasures, their work, their disappointments, and their temperaments. There were differences, however. Jules was more outgoing, with a prompt wit and fancy. Edmond was less brilliant, colder, taciturn, and even introverted. Both were good-looking, but Jules was much more drawn to women than Edmond, and they to him.

After long months of literary sterility, Edmond returned alone to writing on 23 February 1871, picking up a subject—prostitution—that had earlier interested him and Jules. The result was the novel *La Fille Elisa* (The Prostitute Elisa, 1877). Its inspiration goes back to a visit that the brothers had made to a women's prison in 1862. In his preface Edmond was at pains to establish that this was not a work of pornography (and it is not), but rather a novel in the lineage of *Germinie Lacerteux.*

As always, Edmond carefully amassed documentation and made use of information provided by his (and Jules's) mistress, Maria, who was (as Elisa was to be) the daughter of a midwife and had also been a prostitute. He produced a sympathetic and sad portrait of the prostitute Elisa, which he finished only after several long delays, at the end of 1876. It had a reasonable success, and, despite Edmond's fears, the censors offered no problems. The book features a lengthy attack on the regime of silence imposed on women in certain French penitentiaries. Edmond found madness a not uncommon result, though other contemporaries do not report it.

Edmond's next project was a biographical study, *La Faustin,* the result of an idea the two brothers had had earlier. Edmond called it a novel, but the work is based fairly closely on the life of the great nineteenth-century French actress Rachel and probably should not be considered fiction. The book, though not a major one in the Goncourts' oeuvre, caused considerable discussion when it came out, finally, in 1882. As always, the portrait was based on as careful and thorough documentation as possible. Edmond wished to examine the case of an illustrious actress, a subject that neither he nor Jules had treated directly but that the two brothers had adumbrated in *Charles Demailly.* He was interested in the ways in which his heroine's imagination spilled over into her existence as well as into her roles. His publisher, Charpentier, put up advertising posters all over Paris, which much embarrassed Edmond. The book sold reasonably well and was widely discussed, evidence at last of his growing popularity.

Edmond's final venture into imaginative literature was *Les Frères Zemganno* (1879; translated as *The Zemganno Brothers,* 1879). It recounts the lives of two acrobats who spend all their time perfecting circus tricks to be performed in tandem. It mirrors touchingly the affection of the Goncourt brothers for each other. Under the transparent mask of the Zemgannos perfecting acrobatic tricks, the reader watches the Goncourt brothers collaborate on their books. Or, to be more precise, the reader studies the nuances of their characters as they lived, together, for their work. The older acrobat is the embodiment of strength; the younger, of grace. The novel succeeds best in its subjective analysis of experience.

After finishing *Les Frères Zemganno,* Edmond felt that he no longer had the powers to write another imaginative work. He therefore turned to writing *La Maison d'un artiste* (The House of an Artist, 1881), an account of the books, prints, and artistic treasures that he and Jules had collected over the decades, which were now pleasantly displayed in the house at Auteuil.

For his next book Edmond turned to the private papers, which he had long owned, of the famous late-eighteenth-century singer La Saint-Huberty. To these, over the years, he had added further documents concerning her that he had been able to purchase. He determined to write her biography, and, as had been his wont, he consulted public archives on her as well. The result, *La Saint-Huberty* (1882), was a typical Goncourt work, filled with those private details that, in the Goncourts' view, brought their historical subjects to life. Goncourt then turned to an idea he had mentioned in the preface to *La Faustin,* in which he had asked his female readers to send him their private recollections of their own experiences as they moved from childhood into womanhood. He was, he realized, like most men in not really knowing much about young women. Many of his women readers did take up his invitation and wrote him of their trials and tribulations as they moved through adolescence into womanhood. Edmond later said that his purpose in the projected work was to suggest how a young woman might recount her life if she were talking to a friend. He found that adolescence led young women to an excess of ethical sensitivity, which caused them to suffer from neurological disturbances as they became fixed upon their illusions.

Edmond began writing this work, *Chérie,* in 1880, but it did not appear until 1884. He did not intend it to be a novel, but rather a book of pure analysis in which fiction gives way to what he considered to be psychological fact. His discussions of the character of his heroine and her sensations are penetrating. And some of the descriptions are of real places that Edmond visited. He was, as always, seeking to base his account on facts. The work had a modest success. This happy development might have furthered the erroneous feeling Edmond had that "l'écriture artiste" was finally triumphing, especially as he had included in *Chérie* a manifesto on the style that he and his brother had used. But many of his critics were in fact hostile, nor is the work today considered major. Indeed, by the mid 1880s naturalism itself, increasingly under attack from the symbolists and other writers, had almost had its day.

Beginning in 1885 Edmond took to receiving his guests in "le Grenier" (the attic) of his house at Auteuil—a successor to the Sunday afternoons on which Flaubert, now dead, had received his friends. Edmond's group belonged largely to a generation after his own, as few of those his age were still alive. Somehow the public learned of a project that originated in part from these meetings. The brothers, largely at Edmond's instigation, had amassed a large and valuable art collection. In addition, they owned the house at Auteuil. Since there were no heirs to whom Edmond could leave his estate, he conceived the idea of establishing a trust to support an academy whose funds would come from the sale of that estate, to which would be added royalties from his and Jules's books. For fourteen years the funds were to accumulate. Then ten people were to be announced as members of the Académie Goncourt; there would be enough money to keep these ten from financial problems for the rest of their lives. The projected academy would, among other purposes, serve to keep the names of the Goncourts alive.

Regrettably word got out, and many people offered conjectures as to who the lucky ten were to be; such speculation led to uncomfortable situations. The academy was created in 1900, and, among other activities, ever since it has awarded an annual prize for the best work of fiction published during the previous year—a prize greatly coveted, since it usually ensures high sales figures. The annual furor as the academy meets in December to award the prize has indeed served to keep the Goncourt name alive till this day.

Another of Edmond's projects also became known when it was carelessly revealed that he and Jules had made it their custom to write in a journal almost every night, a practice that Edmond had continued. Whenever it was useful, the brothers had turned to the *Journal* to pillage pages for their work at hand. While this practice gave immediacy to passages in their fiction and other works by presenting what the brothers had felt at a given time, it risked leading to further fragmentation in the novels into which they introduced such passages. For the unity of the novel could easily disappear in the midst of bits that had nothing to do with the main plot development.

It had been Edmond's intention to keep the many volumes of the *Journal* under seal for twenty years after his death, but his devoted friend Alphonse Daudet persuaded him to allow partial publication in his lifetime. Daudet was right in believing that many people would read the *Journal* avidly. What neither he nor Edmond foresaw was that some readers would be irritated by what Edmond and Jules had written about them; and Edmond failed to catch and delete all the tactless passages from this first, partial publication (1887-1896). The brothers had delighted in recording biting remarks, adverse criticism, and dislikes revealed by the people they knew. Here on paper were the opinions of these people, appearing in the cold light of print with none of the conviviality of a pleasant dinner at which the observations were offered, for instance, and which might, at least sometimes, have made the tone less unpleasant.

Edmond found many of his acquaintances furious, others dismayed or anxious at the thought of what else might be in the *Journal.* Princess Mathilde begged not to be quoted thenceforth, as did many others whom he had cited not only in passing. Quite simply, if some of it is entertaining to read today, this is in part because the tone of the *Journal* is often nasty. The *Journal* was finally published fully from 1956 to 1959, some sixty years after Edmond's death. It is a mine of gossipy information. There are passages that throw light on what the brothers sought to do in literature, but for the most part little information on how they composed their books.

In the early pages of the *Journal,* Edmond and Jules did, however, explain how they com-

Bust of Edmond de Goncourt in 1890 by Lenoir

posed it, yet their explanation remains puzzling. It was, as Edmond affirmed, the account of their lives, which were so similar in every way that, as he said, the work could be considered the production of a single person. The Goncourts state that they wrote it up more or less day by day, and this may well be the case. But the manuscript is almost all in Jules's hand during his lifetime. When this is coupled with the fact that there are almost no erasures or words crossed out, it becomes possible to suppose that this is a copy of what they first wrote out and then perfected, but such is not certain. It seems unlikely that Jules wrote all of the first part, though Edmond of course wrote what follows Jules's death.

If to some extent the composition must remain an enigma, it does seem clear that the reports are fairly accurate. Corroborating evidence suggests that most of the time remarks attributed to people the Goncourts knew correspond to what these people probably said, albeit colored by the brothers' slightly malevolent attitudes. Abridgments have been published, and they often make better reading than the complete text, which, for many pages at a time, consists of jeremiads and complaints about the incomprehension of contemporaries and the bad taste of the public. It should be noted that Marcel Proust paid homage to the Goncourts by introducing into *Le Temps retrouvé* (1927; translated as *The Past Recaptured*, 1932) a seven-page pastiche of the *Journal*, in which the style is imitated to perfection; but Proust also uses the passage as a pretext for his narrator to denounce literature, given the superficiality it seems to have under the Goncourts' pen.

Edmond's last years were warmed by friendships, particularly those of Daudet and his wife—an author who published under the pseudonym Karl Steen—with whom he became close friends beginning in 1874. They were all fond of each other, and one senses in the younger couple a real love for the aging Edmond and a desire to make his life more filled with affection and happier than it would have been without them. Edmond's health, though better than Jules's, had never been good. He suffered from nervous ailments, his digestion was weak, and he could never tolerate noise. He also had frequent bouts of liver trouble.

In his final decade Edmond's approach to literature no longer met with much opposition. Despite the rise of symbolism and its attacks on the naturalist aesthetic, the brothers' novels fitted in more easily than when they first were published and appeared less revolutionary, more within the accepted canons of literature. The Goncourts had become part of the mainstream as readers had become accustomed to subjects they had previously not thought fit for novels and as they had seen how much further other authors, such as Zola, were willing to push what was acceptable. Goncourt began republishing previous works that had passed unnoticed, or had been severely criticized, when they first appeared. These new editions continued for some decades after his death, testimony to the enduring aspects of the Goncourts' writings.

Edmond also made repeated efforts to get his works on the stage. But an 1888 play based on *Germinie Lacerteux* met with a mixed reception, a disappointment that he had not foreseen, since the novel had come gradually to be accepted after its initial shock effect had been smoothed over by time. He also supervised similar efforts to turn his other works into plays, none of which was successful. The problem with these and other naturalist plays is probably that the naturalists saw character as a reaction to surroundings; that is, they had a deterministic view of the world. This can be, and often is, interesting in a novel, but onstage it makes for wooden characters who fail to draw the audience into their orbit.

Edmond continued his interest in writing about art. He and Jules had both responded warmly to what works of Japanese art were available in the Parisian print shops of their day; they had built an interesting collection of these and other prints. Their interest stimulated many of their friends to be more open to Japanese art, so very new to European viewers at this time. As Edmond's life was drawing to an end, he published two monographs, *Outamaro* (1891) and *Hokousaï* (1896), on these masters in the Japanese tradition. The brothers' taste does not at this remove seem very sure, but this was almost inevitable, given the newness of the aesthetic for Europeans and the relative paucity of prints and studies to help them form their opinions. In any case, both of Edmond's books are important milestones in the history of French taste and the acceptance of Japanese art in the West.

Further monographs on famous actresses closed out Edmond's work and his life, finally that of a grand old man of letters, although, given the changes in taste and the rise of important new figures such as Maurice Barrés as well as the prestige of the master poet Stéphane Mallarmé, he was less than influential with upcoming writers, including the symbolists and the young novelists, such as André Gide, who would be close students of human psychology. While it was true that, thanks to Mallarmé, Barrès, Joris-Karl Huysmans, the young Gide, and others, style had advanced far beyond "l'écriture artiste," Edmond seems not to have realized the importance of this development. Happily, the public acceptance he had long awaited was granted him, and his group of younger friends, orchestrated by the Daudets and others, furnished him with a more serene old age.

Biographies:

Alidor Delzant, *Les Goncourt* (Paris: Charpentier, 1889);

François Forca, *Edmond et Jules de Goncourt* (Paris: Albin Michel, 1941);

André Billy, *The Goncourt Brothers*, translated by Margaret Shaw (New York: Horizon, 1960);

Wanda Bannour, *Edmond et Jules de Goncourt, ou le génie androgyne* (Paris: Persona, 1985).

References:

David Baguley, *Naturalist Fiction: The Entropic Vision* (Cambridge: Cambridge University Press, 1990);

B. F. Bart, "World Views into Style: The Goncourt Brothers and Proust at the Opera," *Nineteenth-Century French Studies*, 15 (1986): 174-188;

Jean-Jacques Brochier, "Les Frères Goncourt, le journal d'un demi-siècle," *Magazine Littéraire*, 269 (September 1989): 19-69;

Enzo Caramaschi, "Actualité des Goncourt," *Francofonia*, 10 (Fall 1990): 74-143;

Caramaschi, *Réalisme et impressionisme dans l'œuvre des Goncourt* (Pisa: Goliardici, 1971);

Caramaschi, "La Révolution dans les mœurs," *Francofonia*, 9 (Fall 1989): 67-90;

Therese Dolan, "Musée Goncourt: Manette Salomon and the Nude," *Nineteenth-Century French Studies*, 18 (Fall-Winter 1989-1990): 173-185;

Richard B. Grant, *The Goncourt Brothers* (New York: Twayne, 1972);
Raymond Pouillart, *Le Romantisme III: 1869-1896* (Paris: Arthaud, 1968);
Robert Ricatte, *La Création romanesque chez les Goncourt, 1851-1870* (Paris: Colin, 1953);
Ricatte, *La Genèse de "La Fille Elisa"* (Paris: Presses Universitaires de France, 1960);
Ernest Seillière, *Les Goncourt moralistes* (Paris: NRC, n.d.);
Stephen Ullmann, "New Patterns of Sentence-structure in the Goncourts," in his *Style in the French Novel* (Cambridge: Cambridge University Press, 1957);
Roger L. Williams, *The Horror of Life* (Chicago: University of Chicago Press, 1980).

Joris-Karl Huysmans (Charles-Marie-Georges Huysmans)

(5 February 1848 - 12 May 1907)

Roy Jay Nelson
University of Michigan

BOOKS: *Le Drageoir à épices* (Paris: Dentu, 1874); republished as *Le Drageoir aux épices* (Paris: Librairie Générale, 1875); translated by Samuel Putnam as *Dish of Spices*, in his *Down Stream* (Chicago: Covici, 1927), pp. 187-261;

Marthe, histoire d'une fille (Brussels: Gay, 1876); translated by Putnam as *Marthe*, in *Down Stream*, pp. 5-114;

Sac au dos (Brussels: Félix Callewaert, 1878); republished in *Les Soirées de Médan* (Paris: Charpentier, 1880); translated by L. G. Meyer as "Sac au dos," in *Short Story Classics*, edited by William Patten (New York: B. F. Collier & Son, 1907), pp. 1515-1555;

Les Sœurs Vatard (Paris: Charpentier, 1879); translated by James C. Babcock as *The Vatard Sisters* (Lexington: University Press of Kentucky, 1983);

Croquis parisiens (Paris: Vaton, 1880); translated by Richard Griffiths as *Parisian Sketches* (London: Fortune Press, 1962);

En ménage (Paris: Charpentier, 1881); translated by J. W. G. Sandiford-Pellé as *Living Together* (London: Fortune Press, 1969);

Pierrot sceptique, by Huysmans and Léon Hennique (Paris: Rouveyre, 1881);

A vau-l'eau (Brussels: Kistemaeckers, 1882); translated by Putnam as *Down Stream*, in *Down Stream*, pp. 115-185;

L'Art moderne (Paris: Charpentier, 1883);

A rebours (Paris: Charpentier, 1884); translated by John Howard as *Against the Grain* (New York: Lieber & Lewis, 1922); translated by Robert Baldick as *Against Nature* (London: Penguin, 1959);

En rade (Paris: Tresse et Stock, 1887);

Un Dilemme (Paris: Tresse et Stock, 1887);

Certains (Paris: Tresse et Stock, 1889); three of these essays translated by Putnam as "Gustave Moreau," "Degas," and "Félicien Rops," in *Down Stream*, pp. 271-275, 276-281, 282-315;

Les Vieux Quartiers de Paris; La Bièvre (Paris: Genonceaux, 1890);

Là-bas (Paris: Tresse et Stock, 1891); translated by Keene Wallis as *Down There* (New York: Boni, 1924); translated by Wallis as *Là-bas* (New York: Dover, 1972);

En route (Paris: Tresse et Stock, 1895); translated by Kegan Paul (London: Kegan Paul, Trench, Trübner, 1896);

La Cathédrale (Paris: Stock, 1898); translated by Clara Bell as *The Cathedral* (New York: New Amsterdam, 1898);

La Bièvre et Saint-Séverin (Paris: Stock, 1898);

La Magie en Poitou: Gilles de Rais (Ligugé: "Le Pays Poitevin," 1899);

La Bièvre; Les Gobelins; Saint-Séverin (Paris: Société de Propagation des Livres d'Art, 1901);

Joris-Karl Huysmans, 1881

Sainte Lydwine de Schiedam (Paris: Stock, 1901); translated by Agnes Hastings as *St. Lydwine of Schiedam* (London: Kegan Paul, 1923);

De tout (Paris: Stock, 1902);

Esquisse biographique sur Don Bosco (Paris, 1902);

L'Oblat (Paris: Stock, 1903); translated by E. Perceval as *The Oblate* (London: Kegan Paul, 1924);

Trois primitifs (Paris: Librairie Léon Vanier, A. Messein, 1905);

Le Quartier Notre-Dame (Paris: Librairie de la Collection des Dix, Romagnol, 1905);

Les Foules de Lourdes (Paris: Stock, 1906); translated by W. H. Mitchell as *Crowds of Lourdes* (London: Burns, Oates, 1906);

Trois églises et trois primitifs (Paris: Plon-Nourrit, 1908);

Là-haut ou Notre-Dame de la Salette, edited by Pierre Cogny, with an introduction by Artine Artinian and Pierre Cogny and notes by Pierre Lambert (Tournai: Casterman, 1965); edited by Michèle Barrière (Nancy: Presses Universitaires de Nancy, 1988).

Collection: *Œuvres complètes de J.-K. Huysmans*, 23 volumes, with an introduction and notes by Lucien Descaves (Paris: Crès, 1928-1934).

SELECTED PERIODICAL PUBLICATION—UNCOLLECTED: "J. K. Huysmans," as A. Meunier, *Les Hommes d'Aujourd'hui*, 6, no. 263 (1885): 1-4.

OTHER: Théodore Hannon, *Rimes de joie*, preface by Huysmans (Brussels: Kistemaeckers, 1881);

Remy de Gourmont, *Le Latin mystique*, preface by Huysmans (Paris: Mercure de France, 1892);

Jules Bois, *Le Satanisme et la magie*, preface by Huysmans (Paris: Flammarion, 1895);

Abbé Henri Dutilliet, *Petit catéchisme liturgique*, preface by Huysmans (Paris: J. Bricon, 1895);

F.-A. Cazals, *Paul Verlaine, ses portraits*, preface by Huysmans (Paris: Bibliothèque de l'Association, 1896);

Abbé J.-C. Broussolle, *La Jeunesse du Pérugin et les origines de l'Ecole ombrienne*, preface by Huysmans (Paris: Lecène-Oudin, 1901);

Paul Verlaine, *Poésies religieuses*, preface by Huysmans (Paris: Messein, 1904).

The work of Joris-Karl Huysmans, novelist, essayist, and art critic, provides one of the clearest examples of the transformation of popular philosophy and literary art that took place near the turn of the century. He is one of those rare prose writers who have situated themselves and their work squarely on the cusp of a moment of literary change, when ways of looking at and representing the world are being transformed, in life as in art. And so one can follow in his writing a startling evolution, bridging the apparent gap between the social realism of late-nineteenth-century French naturalism and the highly subjective fiction of the early twentieth century, in the works of novelists such as André Gide and Marcel Proust. In no other writer can be seen so clearly the path French fiction took to get from Emile Zola to Proust. The change involves both a transformation of perception, from the objectivist pretensions of Zola and the other naturalists to a more self-centered fiction, and a change in the very function of language—as Pierre Cogny said, "de l'écriture à l'Ecriture" (from writing to Writing)—from writing to scripture. Huysmans's literary subjects evolved from naturalistic portrayals of the economically deprived to decadent and horrifyingly satanic topics, and finally to the treatment of Christian themes. His life itself paralleled this extraordinary development.

Born just about a month before the revolution that finally deposed the monarchy in France and raised shock waves across Europe, Huysmans was the son of Elisabeth-Malvina Badin, a French schoolteacher, and Victor-Godfried-Jan Huysmans, a painter, printer, and lithographer from Breda in the Netherlands, who had settled in Paris, painting and preparing miniature illustrations for prayer books. Godfried and Malvina had been married in 1845, when he was thirty and she, nineteen. Their son was born at their home in the rue Suger and was baptized Charles-Marie-Georges the next day, in the Saint-Séverin church in the Latin Quarter. Indeed, much of Huysmans's life was spent within walking distance of Saint-Séverin; growing up, he lived in the rue Saint-Sulpice and the rue de Sèvres.

His childhood seems to have been on the whole rather dreary. Although he enjoyed occasional romping in the Luxembourg Gardens with other children, he appears to have been somewhat sickly, spending a great deal of time at home. He did visit some of his father's relatives who lived in Dutch and Belgian convents, a lugubrious and impressive atmosphere that cannot have failed to affect the boy's sensibilities.

But other events were to impress him still more. In June 1856 Godfried died, leaving the eight-year-old and his mother to grieve. Deeply affected, Huysmans carefully kept three of his father's paintings: a self-portrait, a portrait of Malvina, and a copy of *The Monk* by Francisco de Zurbarán. The latter was in his bedroom when he died in 1907.

Malvina hastened to stabilize her financial situation. First she and her son moved in with her parents, who occupied rather somber quarters in the rue de Sèvres. The building that housed them had once been a monastery, and the monks' high-ceilinged cells had been connected by doorways to form cavernous apartments along wide corridors. Huysmans recalled in *De tout* (On Anything and Everything, 1902) how cold the tile floors of the second-story apartment became in winter, and how the family huddled around the fireplace, with a screen behind them, to keep warm. Malvina found work in a department store and packed her son off to a boarding school in the rue du Bac known as the Institution Hortus. Thus, within about four months' time, Huysmans lost his father and was separated from his mother. His sense of abandonment must have grown as he was obliged, at age eight, to live away from home, eat foul school food, and suffer the bullying of the discipline monitors, with no recourse to parental comforting, except on Sundays.

What finally intensified his sense of separation, however, was his mother's rapid remarriage. Early in 1857, less than a year after Godfried's death, Malvina wed Jules Og, whose money assured her financial security. He invested in a bookbindery on the ground floor of the rue de Sèvres apartment block where Malvina's parents lived, a business that provided not only a regular income but furnished Huysmans with memories that he would use in his naturalist novel *Les Sœurs Vatard* (1879; translated as *The Vatard Sisters*, 1983). Malvina's marriage to Og lasted until his death in 1867 and produced two daughters, whom she apparently preferred to her son. If Huysmans felt some bitterness about this, it was reflected only in a general silence with respect to his mother in all his publications, and perhaps in a certain degree of misogyny that critics have discovered in his work. He seems indeed to have felt a stronger affinity for his father. His adopted name, "Joris-Karl," is surely intended as a Dutch version of his French given names "Georges" and "Charles," recalling his father's origins. And it was more than a pen name: his intimates in adult life all knew him as "J.-K."

He made a few friendships at the Institution Hortus, but when he entered secondary school in 1862 at the lycée Saint-Louis, he remained quite alone, largely because he was a scholarship student; his government grant marked him as a poor boy, a target for teasing and class discrimination. But despite mistreatment by classmates and monitors, he maintained an above-average academic record. And he was learning other things, too: at age sixteen he sought out and received sexual initiation from a prostitute, who apparently took not only his virginity and her pay, but also his precious bottle of cologne.

By the time he was seventeen, Huysmans had had enough of high school, and he had gained sufficient self-confidence to refuse to go back to class. Thenceforth one of the teachers from Saint-Louis was hired to tutor him at home, and with these private lessons he earned his *baccalauréat* (diploma) by passing the requisite examinations in 1866. In April of the same year, the young man took a job that was to help support him for many years, a civil-service position in the Ministry of the Interior, looking after welfare cases. Ostensibly the income was intended to see him through law school, and he did enroll that fall, although the law was not his primary interest. Instead he was to be found in the Latin Quarter cafés, talking literature into the wee hours of the night. Still, he passed his first-level law examination in 1867.

But another interest marked the end of his studies: he had fallen in love with an actress from the show at the old Bobino nightclub. Like a typical stage-door Johnny, he left her flowers and (ironic) poems. Using the name of a contact in the magazine business, he posed as a journalist and thus actually got past the door to meet and interview the one he had worshiped from afar. His blandishments were effective. Having moved out of the family apartment in the rue de Sèvres, he set up housekeeping with the actress, who surrounded him with something resembling a stable, homelike atmosphere. According to Robert Baldick, his primary biographer, he sought from her refined lovemaking techniques, complete with eye shadow and black corsets. This fascination with camouflage of the natural flesh is echoed in Huysmans's fiction by a pronounced preference for things artificial and an apparent fear of nature, which can dominate orderly reason through instinct, and which decrees that all things organic must at last decay and die. But the nightclub soubrette was apparently less than refined; indeed, she was downright slovenly, leaving the ironing board up in the living room and the laundry strewn about. And his dreams of an artificial paradise were soon utterly shattered by the voice of nature: the actress became pregnant—and not by Huysmans. The baby was born and brought home to the tiny flat, where its very puking, piddling naturalness, together with all the disorder that a baby in cramped quarters implies, revolted the young civil servant to the depths of his being. Fortunately, perhaps, for Huysmans, the actress soon disappeared from his life, taking the baby with her.

In July 1870 Huysmans was called to the colors (sixth battalion of the Mobile Guard) to face the invading Prussians. Wild drinking in Paris, departure by cattle car to the staging point in Châlons-sur-Marne, where nothing was ready to receive them, and a week with no straw for the tents and unsanitary food and water all left Huysmans weakened and a prey for dysentery. When his unit set off for the front, he found himself left behind in the infirmary. Indeed, he spent the entire war in military hospitals rather than on the so-called field of honor. Before the Prussian onslaught he was evacuated to Rheims, then Paris, Arras, Rouen, and finally Evreux. There he enjoyed the company of a patient named Anselme, and of Sister Angèle, who nursed (and spoiled) him. He also participated in an illicit escapade outside the hospital grounds. But to put any distance between himself and the clinic, he needed legal intervention; with the help of a barrister friend, he finally succeeded in obtaining sick leave beginning 8 September 1870. And home he went to Paris, just in time for the Prussian siege of the city. There, amid the intermittent shellings and bombardments, the food shortages, and the crime that flourished in the darkened streets, Huysmans's life began to merge with his fiction.

A nearly impenetrable barrier stands between real life and linguistic accounts thereof. Biographical yarns can state the facts of a life; however, lives are not made up of facts but of wordless personal perceptions and interactions. Transforming these to words is an act of translation—and thus inevitably a betrayal—of the real stuff of living. Furthermore, biographies and autobiographies must be read; since readers understand words only on the basis of their own sensory knowledge, how can uniquely personal experience be transmitted to others? Still, bound by denotation and grammar, words do provide a governed realm, with relatively stable and quite artificial rules. Perhaps language was then for Joris-Karl, partly through its betrayal of the "real," the very substance of an artificial paradise, a haven from the unpredictable bombardment of nature, which is life.

In the chaos of Paris under siege, Huysmans began to take notes, to keep a running account of his experience for a novel to be entitled "La Faim" (Hunger). Although it was never published (and the manuscript was destroyed shortly before his death), it directed his mind toward the relationship between life and language, an activity that would soon bear fruit.

Having been mustered out of the army, he returned to his modest job at the Interior Ministry, only to flee to Versailles with the government as the popular uprising of the Commune engulfed Paris. Then, after the brutal military repression of the rebellion, he returned to the city with the ministry. He spent hours in the Louvre, engrossed in the painting of the Dutch masters.

He also spent time writing, beginning the first draft of a never-completed war memoir called "Chant du départ" (Departure Song) and the manuscript of a romantic play in verse, grandly titled "La Comédie humaine" (The Human Comedy).

But Huysmans's first publication was to be a collection of vignettes, which have been compared with some justification to Charles Baudelaire's prose poems. The venture began inauspiciously. After receiving more than a few rejections, he turned to his mother for help, for Mme Og had inherited the bookbindery in the rue de Sèvres and had contacts in the publishing world. She directed her son to an editor of children's books, P.-J. Hetzel, who provided Huysmans with his most stinging rejection: he told him that he was totally lacking in talent and promise, that his style was atrocious, and that he was attempting an insurgency in literature akin to the political uprising of the Commune. After that, Huysmans saw no way out but to publish the vignettes at his own expense, under the title *Le Drageoir à épices* (1874; translated as *Dish of Spices*, 1927). After favorable reviews it was soon republished by a paying editor, with the virtually identical title *Le Drageoir aux épices* (1875). This collection of prose poems and astutely observed little scenes is not the fictionalized autobiography that was to become Huysmans's stock-in-trade, but rather a mirror held up to the writer. Huysmans called them "un choix de bric-à-brac" (a selection of bric-à-brac), yet in the choice of subjects and the clever play of erudite language, one can discover (or invent) the mind behind it all, as if in a mirror.

While he continued to work on his abortive novel about the siege of Paris, Huysmans carried on a brief affair with a working girl in the dressmaking industry, doubtless Anna Meunier, who would later become his steady partner. On 4 May 1876 his mother died, leaving him the bindery in the rue de Sèvres and his two half sisters to support. He had moved back into an apartment over the bindery, and he now began taking a more than casual hand in management. He seems to have had little difficulty providing for the misses Og until they were able to provide for themselves.

Apparently still fighting the temptation to fictionalize his own life, he laid his siege novel aside and undertook a story in the naturalist vein, a real slice of (someone else's) life, which would show, through an ostensibly scientific study of the "facts," the workings of determinism. This interest in so-called objective fiction seems to have had two sources. First, he admired Edmond and Jules de Goncourt, whose *Germinie Lacerteux* (1864; translated, 1922) depicted the inevitable downward slide of a nymphomaniac servant girl. Then too, Henry Céard, a fellow writer and close friend, was also in contact with Zola, who would soon draw J.-K. into the inner circle of naturalist writers. Huysmans chose the subject for his fictional sociology carefully: his text would document the life of a prostitute. He called it *Marthe, histoire d'une fille* (1876; translated as *Marthe*, 1927), a title bound to arouse interest, despite the absence of seriously erotic material. The novel was well under way when Huysmans learned that Edmond de Goncourt had undertaken a virtually identical project, a novel called *La Fille Elisa* (Elisa the Whore, 1877). From then on it was a race to see who would publish the first fictitious "prostitute's life" in French letters. Huysmans finished his first draft in July 1876 and had his book in press a month later in Brussels, thus avoiding potential hassles with censorship in France. *Marthe* was in the stores by 1 October 1876; Goncourt's novel did not appear until March 1877, although it did so in Paris, and with a section on the brutalizing effects of Elisa's time in prison. (*Marthe* was not published in France until 1879.) Despite Huysmans's "objective" presentation, his story obviously draws upon his experience with the actress from the club Bobino: fictionalized reality remains at work, subverting Huysmans's "real" fiction.

Nonetheless, with the help of Céard's introduction, J.-K. was moving into the little group of naturalists of which Zola was the patriarch and theorist. His primary disciples, in addition to Céard and Huysmans, were Paul Alexis, Léon Hennique, and Guy de Maupassant. This group of five met regularly in Zola's apartment in the rue Saint-Georges, and they became known as the Médan group, after the location of Zola's country home, where they spent an occasional summer Sunday together. They defended Zola's work in the press, and their credo, as laid down by Zola, was depiction of reality; if one wished, in a novel, to describe a wholesale food market at 5:00 A.M., one must go to such a market at that hour and take notes. And reality was determined, according to the master, by the inexorable laws of cause and effect, heredity and environment directing the outcome of all human events. The novelist's

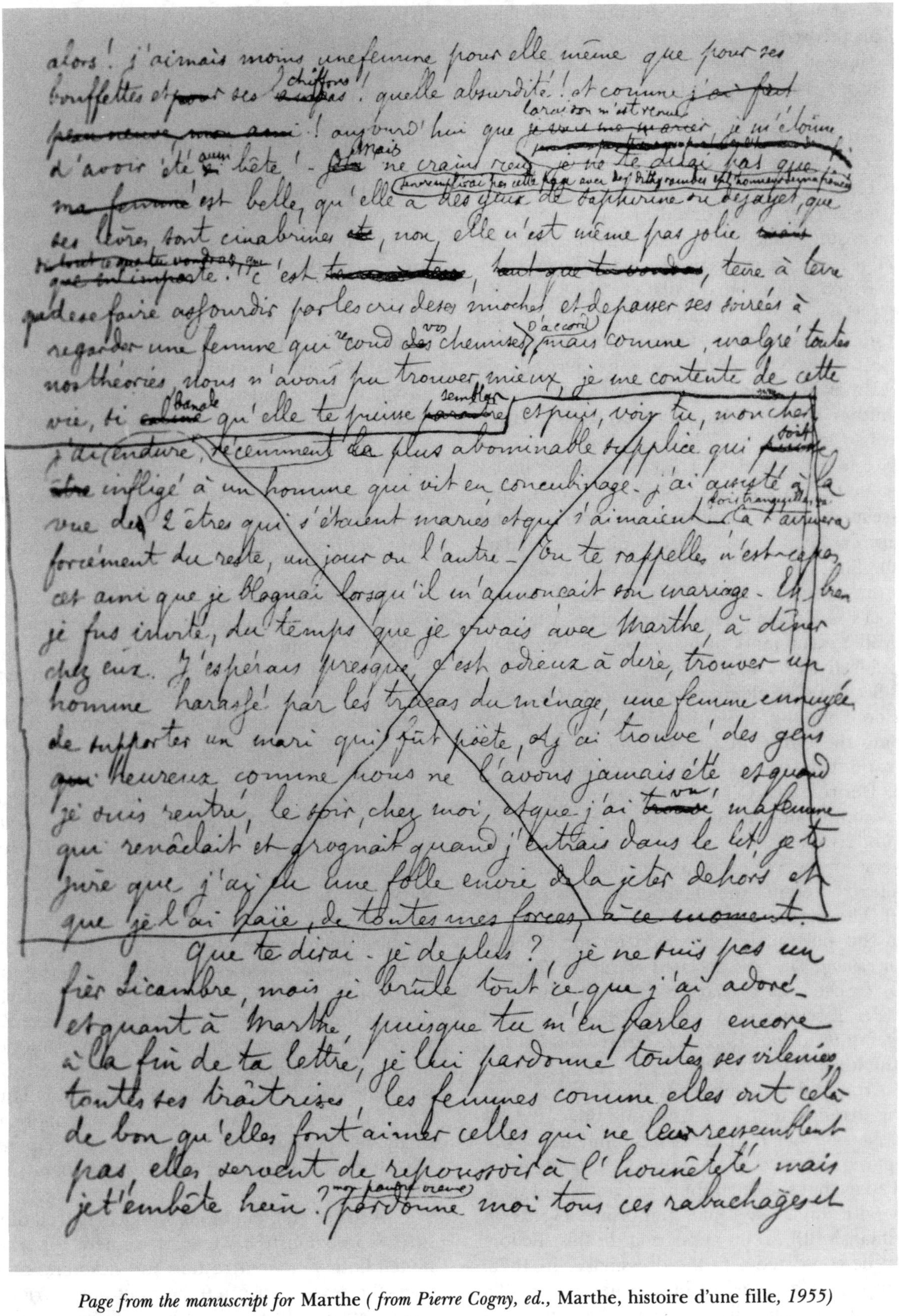

alors ! j'aimais moins une femme pour elle même que pour ses bouffettes et ses chiffons ! quelle absurdité ! et comme [illegible] ! aujourd'hui que l'occasion m'est venue [illegible] je m'étonne d'avoir été aussi bête ! — Mais ne crains rien, je ne te dirai pas que [illegible] est belle, qu'elle a des yeux de saphirine ou de jayet, que ses lèvres sont cinabrines, non, elle n'est même pas jolie [illegible] c'est [illegible], terre à terre de se faire assourdir par les cris de ses mioches et de passer ses soirées à regarder une femme qui coud vos chemises, d'accord, mais comme, malgré toutes nos théories, nous n'avons pu trouver mieux, je me contente de cette vie, si banale qu'elle te puisse sembler et puis, vois-tu, mon cher j'ai enduré récemment le plus abominable supplice qui soit infligé à un homme qui vit en concubinage. j'ai assisté à la vue des 2 êtres qui s'étaient mariés et qui s'aimaient — ça t'arrivera forcément du reste, un jour ou l'autre — tu te rappelles n'est-ce pas cet ami que je blaguai lorsqu'il m'annonçait son mariage. Eh bien je fus invité, du temps que je vivais avec Marthe, à dîner chez eux. J'espérais presque, c'est odieux à dire, trouver un homme harassé par les tracas du ménage, une femme ennuyée de supporter un mari qui fût poète, et j'ai trouvé des gens heureux comme nous ne l'avons jamais été et quand je suis rentré, le soir, chez moi, et que j'ai vu ma femme qui renâclait et grognait quand j'entrais dans le lit, je te jure que j'ai eu une folle envie de la jeter dehors et que je l'ai haïe, de toutes mes forces, à ce moment.

Que te dirai-je de plus ? je ne suis pas un fier Sicambre, mais je brûle tout ce que j'ai adoré — et quant à Marthe, puisque tu m'en parles encore à la fin de ta lettre, je lui pardonne toutes ses vilenies, toutes ses traîtrises, les femmes comme elles ont cela de bon qu'elles font aimer celles qui ne leur ressemblent pas, elles servent de repoussoir à l'honnêteté mais je t'embête hein ? pardonne-moi tous ces rabâchages et

Page from the manuscript for Marthe *(from Pierre Cogny, ed.,* Marthe, histoire d'une fille, *1955)*

stance was to be, above all, scientific and objective; on this score *Marthe* came in for some criticism, since its language mingled poetic and erudite terms with street slang in a most idiosyncratic manner.

Although he was seldom able to live up to the credo, Huysmans had great intellectual respect for it and undertook two additional "objective" texts. First he reworked his old army memoirs as a story called *Sac au dos* (1878; translated, 1907), a nostalgic reference to the military knapsack, which might be translated "Your Old Kit Bag." Here it is virtually impossible to tell whether one is reading autobiography or fiction, so completely is the autobiography masked; yet one cannot help but envision a live and imaginative author lurking behind the narrator's *I*. Huysmans had this text published serially in France in 1879, and he reworked it for publication under the same title in a famous collection of naturalist, war-related stories published by Zola and his group, *Les Soirées de Médan* (Evenings in Médan, 1880). That he was able to get personal memoirs into this "official" naturalist publication headed by Zola's "L'Attaque du moulin" ("The Attack on the Mill") was a mark of his success in concealing the subjectivity of his account.

Secondly, exploiting his personal experience with bookbinding, he wrote *Les Sœurs Vatard*, describing the effects of poverty and hard manual labor on two sisters from the Parisian underclass, Désirée and Céline. This seemingly objective account nonetheless lets very subjective sexual undertones shine through, and one oddly perverse or perverted character named Cyprien Tibaille represents the degenerate artist in the novel. There was enough of Huysmans's subjectivity in this portrait for the character to resurface in *En ménage* (1881; translated as *Living Together*, 1969); he even shares characteristics with the decadent des Esseintes of *A rebours* (1884; translated as *Against the Grain*, 1922). *Les Sœurs Vatard* is still not the ideal naturalist text.

Around 1877 Huysmans developed a long-lasting arrangement with Anna Meunier. By this time she had her own dress shop and was a single parent to two daughters. J.-K. and Anna lived apart, but she often spent weekends and vacations with him. As usual, important events in Huysmans's life kept appearing in his fiction. When he consorted with the dressmaker in 1872, she appeared destined to be the heroine of "La Faim"; when she disappeared, the projected novel did too. Now Meunier became the prototype for another character, Jeanne, the second mistress of André Jayant in *En ménage*: Baldick even turned up a copy of the novel dedicated to "Jeanne—Anna Meunier."

Jayant is a young writer who marries to provide himself with the comforts of life—someone to cook, sew, and handle other menial tasks about the house. His bride provides flawless service in these areas, but she has a flaw in another that Jayant did not expect: she is sexually unfaithful. So he then tries living alone, but he cannot find a restaurant to make his favorite sauce just right, nor can he cope with lost buttons and the other petty annoyances of life. He tries living with one woman and then another, but each has proclivities he finds disturbing. This jaded treatment of the old "can't-live-with-'em-can't-live-without-'em" theme provides through Jayant a glimpse of Huysmans's view of his own material self, including his severe chronic dyspepsia; Cyprien Tibaille, here Jayant's friend and confidant, represents the artist's original, creative psyche.

In 1882 Huysmans published a similar life-into-fiction story originally entitled "Jean Folantin." It recounts the misadventures of a dyspeptic, lonely, unmarried civil servant (Huysmans was still working daily from 11:00 A.M. to 5:00 P.M. at the Interior Ministry) as he struggles with the everyday hassles of living. His satisfaction with life seems to go inevitably downhill, and at Zola's suggestion the title *A vau-l'eau* (translated as *Down Stream*, 1927) was chosen for the text at the last moment. This expression, which Huysmans had used to describe the destiny of his imaginary prostitute Marthe, well represents his entropic view of the material world: everything physical degenerates, disintegrates, or decays, including human bodies. Nature's universal prescription is a one-way trip to the tomb, marked by small annoyances and painful surprises. Zola read Folantin as a kind of Everyman, a modern antihero in whom humanity in general (or rather the male half thereof) can find itself. To Huysmans, however, this was assuredly one more pathetic self-portrait, one more cry for help in a life that was becoming increasingly painful to him.

A major element of Huysmans's hatred of nature was obviously his fear of women, for whom he felt both violent attraction and sickening repulsion, the sexual act often forming but a brief respite between lust and disgust. These feelings surely disturbed him. He did establish with

Portrait of Huysmans by Odilon Redon (from Pierre Brunel and André Guyaux, eds., Huysmans, *1985)*

Meunier an almost conjugal life (her children called him Papa Georges), but even that was soon turned to pain with the onset of Anna's mortal malady; headaches and weakness were her early symptoms, followed by shooting pains: she was gradually dying of a degenerative brain disease, possibly general paresis. This must have contributed as well to Huysmans's vision of women as corrupt and decaying beings—all too natural in mind and body. The misogyny apparent in his works thus doubtless reflects a personal horror, based on the fear of his own condition, of which women reminded him. Not surprisingly he began to experience frightening periods of impotency. With Théodore Hannon, his Belgian editor and fellow writer (Huysmans had come to know him well while putting the finishing touches on *Marthe* in Brussels, when they had together visited museums in the daytime and brothels by night), he maintained a sometimes sexy (and sexist) correspondence; to him he wrote in February 1878, "Quant aux délices culières, je baisse de plus en plus. Je tourne au ramolissement des aines le plus complet. Je rêvasse à revêtir ma déesse de costumes étranges pour me pimenter un brin" (As for the vaginal delights, I'm going from bad to worse. I'm developing a total softening of the crotch. I dream of dressing my goddess in bizarre costumes, to stimulate myself a mite). At this point for Huysmans, even (or especially) sex demanded the odd, the unnatural.

Despite these problems, during this period Huysmans was writing highly subjective art criticism, covering the 1879 Salon for the newspaper *Voltaire* and the Salon of 1880 for the *Réforme*. His review of the independents' own exhibition, held in 1880, is an important analysis of impressionism, and his warm appreciation of this burgeoning movement has of course been validated by history. His admiration for the work of Gustave Moreau and of Odilon Redon (whom he later came to know quite well) bespeaks his appreciation of highly original painting with antinatural themes. His art criticism of this period was collected in a volume, *L'Art moderne* (Modern Art, 1883). In 1880 he published a new set of prose poems and vignettes reminiscent of *Le Drageoir*, entitled *Croquis parisiens* (translated as *Parisian Sketches*, 1962).

Huysmans's writings were by then bringing him fame. He was recognized in literary circles; he met Gustave Flaubert, whom he had admired from afar, and he was in correspondence with Stéphane Mallarmé, the intellectual leader of the symbolist poets. He came to the aid of Paul Verlaine when the lyric poet consumed too much of his liquid assets in the form of absinthe. He helped as well the impoverished decadent novelist and dramatist Auguste de Villiers de l'Isle-Adam, and, at times, the less grateful, flamboyantly bitter Catholic writer Léon Bloy. While he remained in contact with Zola, he was enjoying it less. The master still believed in documenting the scenes in his novels, but he felt less and less inclined to do the legwork himself. The disciples were often dispatched to the four corners of Paris to note the details of whatever it was that Zola planned to describe. With his writing and his job at the ministry, Huysmans had little time for such labors, and he prepared to break with the naturalist group.

But there were obviously more deep-seated differences between Huysmans and Zola. For Joris-Karl, Zola's naturalism was too exclusively materialistic to be true. For there was much more to life than material nature, than the body as the plaything of environment and heredity. Huysmans perceived a spiritual side to life, human yet "artificial" and antinatural. He therefore set about to write a study of this spirit at work, a psychological novel about an individual in crisis, rather than the pseudosociology Huysmans perceived as constituting naturalist writing. He hoped this new direction might revitalize naturalism, which in his opinion was otherwise condemned to repeat itself in an endless materialistic formula, always mingling hereditary "flaws" and environmental factors (usually including sex) to produce an inevitable decline in the characters.

The product of Huysmans's effort was *A rebours*, his masterwork and the standard defining example of French decadent fiction. It is the tale of an effete nobleman, Jean des Esseintes, the ultimate scion of an inbred and degenerating family. Driven to raw-nerved distraction by human foibles and the material imperfections of life in Paris, he goes into reclusion in a suburban retreat, where he builds an antinatural life for himself. He lives by night and sees no one; the servants slip in during the daytime, while he sleeps, to clean and to leave him prepared meals.

The novel is essentially a series of disconnected chapters, each devoted to a phase of the elegant depravity of des Esseintes's existence: the interior decoration of his refuge (for example, his dining room is a fake ship's cabin; his bedroom, a paradoxically luxurious monk's cell), his favorite readings (his appreciation of the dark side of symbolist poetry, from Baudelaire to Mallarmé, aroused the interest of the general public in those poets), his taste in nineteenth-century painting (similar to Huysmans's own), his preference for locomotives over women (at least as aesthetic objects), his selection of houseplants (species chosen because of special inbreeding that makes them appear artificial), his nightmares (one is so fully described and so lifelike that it is hard to believe Huysmans did not dream it himself), his aborted trip to London (loitering near the Saint-Lazare station, waiting for his train, he experiences enough British atmosphere—fog, Englishmen, English food—to make further travel unnecessary), and so on.

The story line itself is simple: driven to reclusion by hypersensitivity and neurotic fears, des Esseintes concocts an antinatural life to eliminate his neuroses, but instead it worsens his condition, with psychosomatic side effects—notably severe chronic dyspepsia (nature's revenge!). His doctor then orders him back to Paris and a more normal life; he leaves his refined retreat with a startling prayer on his lips: "Seigneur, prenez pitié du chrétien qui doute" (Lord, have pity on the Christian who doubts). A human mind, with its love of the order and predictability to be found only in the artificial, is here set up in opposition to the random chaos of physical nature. But where order is imposed upon it, nature dies, destroying the function of the order, if not killing the mind that created it. Des Esseintes had, for example, gilded and bejeweled the shell of a tortoise he had bought to enliven the tones of the carpets on which it crawled; transformed thus to a decorative object, the tortoise promptly died. Leading a rigidly antinatural life in his seclusion, des Esseintes is similarly on his way to death there.

The essence of decadence here lies in the advocacy as inevitable of a perverse mental paradox: that human beings are bound to admire what they hate and destroy what they love. For example, one must cherish nature, which is life itself, although it defines everyone as frail and mortal; likewise, one cannot be sincerely blasphemous or sacrilegious unless one believes in the religion one would strive to subvert. Huysmans and des Esseintes obviously share the same dialectic in their lust/disgust relationship to women (although it must be noted that des Esseintes, doubtless in Huysmans's name, advocates full rights for women to abortion, as an artificial control over one natural process). The novel shows des Esseintes to have had some homosexual experience, and Baldick presents reasons for believing that Huysmans, perhaps horrified at himself, had tested those waters as well.

But the struggle between nature and artifice is more than thematic. In *A rebours*, Huysmans deploys in full strength his enormous and precise vocabulary—poetic, lyrical, technical, biological—with extraordinary refinement and acumen. For not only is he painting des Esseintes's retreat, but he is forging an artificial lexical domain for the mind of the reader (and his own) to inhabit. In the nineteenth century the meanings of words, which had previously seemed divinely decreed, were, like the existence of God, being called into question. What had seemed absolute began to appear quite relative—to content, to syntax, to the reader's own experience. Through such changing perceptions the apparent chaos of material entropy was invading language itself, and referentiality was becoming unhinged. Like Edgar Allan Poe, Mallarmé was struggling in poetry to give a purer sense to "les mots de la tribu" (the words of the tribe), and Huysmans's startling language in *A rebours* seeks, if not pure poetry, at least a purely artificial prose, in which for a time one can escape the fluctuations of the natural lexicon and daily syntax. For avoidance of the natural is not really a matter of physical but of mental flight, and language is the steed. Huysmans was among the first to explore the ways in which this new perception of language could be managed for the purpose of creating a linguistic artificial paradise.

While some critics were scandalized by the psychotic morbidity of des Esseintes's preoccupations, the text seems to have pleased many others and reached a relatively wide audience. Zola was predictably displeased, however, and he criticized Huysmans for leading the naturalist movement astray. But from then on, Huysmans was to follow his own path: his "naturalist" years were effectively over.

He published a little autobiographical text (under the pseudonym A. Meunier!) in *Les Hommes d'Aujourd'hui* series in 1885. It declared, with insight and a little false mockery, that Tibaille, Jayant, Folantin, and des Esseintes were all avatars of Huysmans himself, only set in different situations. He was to attempt one more fictional self before settling on his permanent artificial identity. The name of this new self-projection was Jacques Marles, and he appeared as the hero of *En rade* (1887); the title may be considered an example of a kind of linguistic artificiality, for it implies both security (it means "in the harbor") and abandonment (as a slang expression, it means "in the lurch"). In 1885 and 1886 J.-K. and Anna had spent the summers at Jutigny, in a dilapidated castle called the Château de Lourps, which Huysmans had used as des Esseintes's birthplace. Jacques Marles spends a summer vacation in the same place, fleeing the trauma of Parisian existence for the supposed joys of a secluded country life. Of course there is no joy; the tumbledown château is a perfect torture chamber of discomfort, country life is one sickening natural event after another (for example, the birth of a calf), and the humble farm folk are stupid bumpkins. Once again physical flight is not the answer to the decadent dilemma. The only flight that works in this situation is psychological: the narrative occasionally escapes into dream sequences, which can lead nowhere (except to other fictions—in these dreams one finds a bell tower that readers of *Là-bas* will also visit).

At this juncture of his career Huysmans, perhaps repressively, published a more objective novelette, *Un Dilemme* (A Dilemma, 1887), a mordant satire of bourgeois greed, in which a father, whose son has just died, succeeds in depriving the son's poor, pregnant girlfriend of any inheritance—thus driving her to a pauper's grave. In *Certains* (Certain [Artists], 1889), Huysmans grouped much of his art criticism written since *L'Art moderne*. It contains studies on Moreau (much admired by des Esseintes), Edgar Degas, and James Whistler; there is also a major description and analysis of Félicien Rops's salacious and sadistic prints. Beneath the surface the strain of his neurotic fears was obviously beginning to take its toll on the writer's mental equilibrium.

Early in 1890 he wrote to Arij Prins, a young Dutch novelist and friend, "Je suis plongé dans des courses, à la recherche d'un prêtre

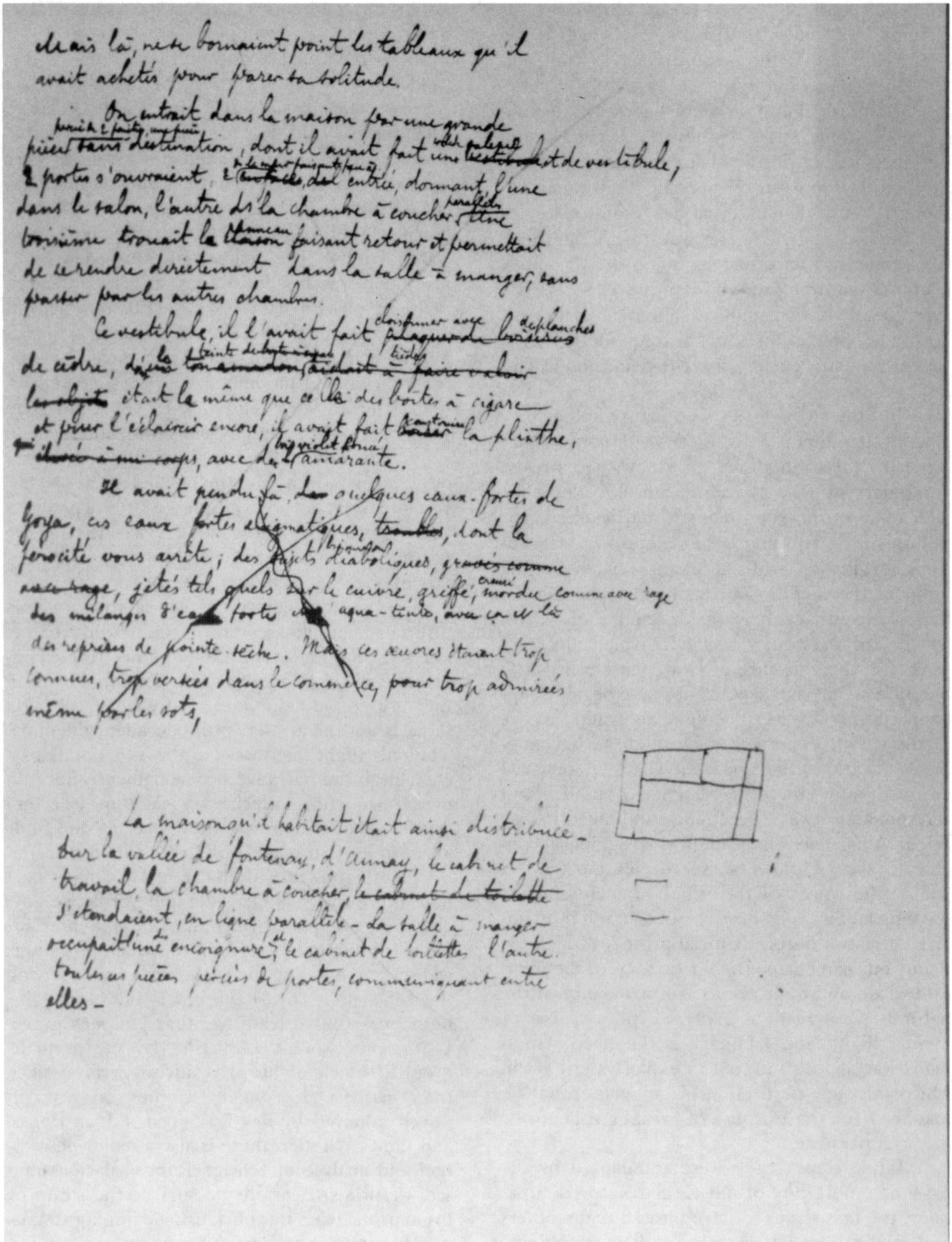
Mais là, ne se bornaient point les tableaux qu'il avait achetés pour parer sa solitude.

On entrait dans la maison par une grande pièce ~~sans destination~~, dont il avait fait une sorte de vestibule, 2 portes s'ouvraient, dans l'entrée, donnant, l'une dans le salon, l'autre ds la chambre à coucher, une troisième trouvait la ... faisant retour et permettait de se rendre directement dans la salle à manger, sans passer par les autres chambres.

Ce vestibule, il l'avait fait cloisonner avec des planches de cèdre, ... était la même que celle des boîtes à cigare et pour l'éclaircir encore, il avait fait ... la plinthe, ..., avec de l'amarante.

Il avait pendu là, quelques eaux-fortes de Goya, ces eaux fortes énigmatiques, ..., dont la férocité vous arrête; des sujets diaboliques, ... jetés tels quels sur le cuivre, griffé, mordu comme avec rage des mélanges d'eau forte ... aqua-tinta, avec çà et là des reprises de pointe sèche. Mais ces oeuvres étant trop connues, trop versées dans le commerce, pour trop admirées même par les sots,

La maison qu'il habitait était ainsi distribuée sur la vallée de Fontenay, d'Aunay, le cabinet de travail, la chambre à coucher, ~~le cabinet de toilette~~ s'étendaient en ligne parallèle - la salle à manger occupait une encoignure, le cabinet de toilette l'autre. toutes ces pièces percées de portes, communiquant entre elles -

Page from the manuscript for A rebours *(from Pierre Brunel and André Guyaux, eds.,* Huysmans, *1985)*

démoniaque et sodomite qui dit la messe noire. J'en ai besoin pour mon livre. J'ai dû pénétrer dans le monde des occultistes pour tout cela—quels jobards et quels fripons!" (I'm running hither and yon looking for a demoniac, sodomite priest who performs black masses. I need him for my book. I've had to insinuate myself into the occultists' world for all this—what dupes, what scoundrels!). This book, *Là-bas* (1891; translated as *Down There*, 1924), was to bring old preoccupations to the surface in a remarkable way. Inspiration for the novel ostensibly began in 1888, when Huysmans took a summer trip to Germany, largely to visit museums for a piece on German art that he never published. While there, he was particularly struck by one painting, Matthias Grünewald's *Crucifixion*, in the museum at Kassel. It depicted in naturalistic detail the ugly face of death—Christ's brutally torn body, his oozing wounds, upon the Cross. Yet precisely through the realistic suffering the miraculous spirituality of the Victim was made manifest, with that of the Virgin and the disciples grouped around to mourn. The very excessiveness of Christ's pain seemed to Huysmans to transfigure him, without halos or other symbols: the author had his first glimpse of what he was to call, in *Là-bas*, "supranaturalism" or "spiritualistic naturalism." It now seemed possible to him, through the naturalists' techniques of documentation and realistic detail that he still respected, to go beyond the natural and the material: to show the human soul.

Huysmans's life at the same time was a confrontation with gruesome reality. Meunier's painful illness was a constant reminder of nature's cruelty. His friends were dying: among them Jules-Amédée Barbey d'Aurevilly, who died of old age and an internal hemorrhage in 1889, and Villiers de l'Isle-Adam, who slowly expired the same year of stomach cancer (J.-K. was involved in Villiers's grotesque marriage in extremis to his housekeeper, arranged to legitimize his son).

In his personal torment Huysmans set about to document the manifestations of spiritual forces in the real world. *Là-bas* may well have begun as a documented study of a medieval figure, Gilles de Rais (or "de Retz"), one model for Bluebeard, who fought piously and nobly with Joan of Arc, then became a kidnapper, torturer, and slaughterer of children in his castle at Tiffauges; he was tried and executed in 1440. This historical character's child killings are described in intimate, gory detail in the text. But the novel really became the story of the research Huysmans undertook in order to write it, with the central character, Durtal, at last a mere transparent stand-in for Huysmans himself: if autobiography and fiction had merged before, they were thenceforth inextricably blended in his work.

In order to understand the horrible deeds of Gilles de Rais, Durtal (and Huysmans) studied the occult, the black arts, the Black Mass. Huysmans was already in contact with "Berthe" de Courrière, through the writer Remy de Gourmont, who seems to have played the role of her agent and lover. She believed in black magic and beguiled the decadent novelist with tales of her paranormal experiences. He met as well Henriette Maillat, who had previously seduced Bloy, it appears, and now had a brief, bizarre affair with Huysmans; she is one of the models for Hyacinthe Chantelouve in *Là-bas*. J.-K. also contacted Stanislas de Guaïta, a founding member of the modern French Order of the Rosy Cross (Rosicrucians); Sâr Joséphin Péladan, a onetime bank teller who claimed to be descended from the Chaldean Magi; Michel de Lézinier, an expert on alchemy; and many others. His research may also have included attendance at a Black Mass (an orgiastic ritual narrated in nauseating and erotic detail in *Là-bas*), where he claimed to have spied a Belgian priest, the abbé Louis Van Haecke, who became the prototype of Canon Docre in the novel. And he was in direct contact with the "abbé" Joseph-Antoine Boullan, who provided reams of documentation on the black arts in nineteenth-century France. Boullan was apparently an exquisitely evil ex-cleric, no stranger to prisons, who advocated all forms of sexual intercourse as acts of worship, and who, according to Baldick, confessed to having slain his own illegitimate child, born of a complicitous nun, on the altar after Mass. The novel describes Durtal's research, parallel to Huysmans's, and his findings. They both discover that Satanism is alive and flourishing in nineteenth-century France, just as it was in the times of Gilles de Rais: a durable spiritual force observable and documentable in real phenomena.

Huysmans created in this work another artificial realm by the power of words. For *Là-bas*, whose subject matter is often abhorrent, as art is nonetheless highly original, since the categories of imagination and reality, of fiction and nonfiction, are called into question by its very form. It is a major milestone in the evolution of French prose fiction.

Cover for the autobiographical sketch that Huysmans wrote under the pseudonym A. Meunier

While the novel received good press, it had three unpleasant consequences for its author. First, Bloy, from whom Huysmans had apparently been gradually separating himself, launched violently vituperative attacks on the work, calling into question its originality. Thenceforth, Bloy was as venomously hateful to J.-K. as he was to many others. When he questioned the originality of *Là-bas*, however, he was putting his finger on a central point: it was of course not "original," since Huysmans had previously "lived" its plot. The second consequence is a case in point. Maillat and a friend of hers recognized in the letters of Hyacinthe Chantelouve (the character in the book who has Durtal admitted to a Black Mass) mere copies of actual letters Maillat had written to Huysmans; J.-K.'s realism was of a dangerous sort, and blackmail appears to have reared its ugly head. Fortunately for him, Huysmans had been connected at the ministry with the Sûreté (French secret police) since 1876; when Maillat and her friend discovered that detectives were asking probing questions about them, they disappeared from Huysmans's life. Finally, the Rosicrucians were predictably disturbed at Huysmans's close contacts with Boullan, whose housekeeper and right-hand woman, Julie Thibault, was later to perform these functions for Joris-Karl. And so for years afterward Huysmans felt that spells were being cast upon him, that he was a victim of evil magic because of his perilous research, and he could be found, from time to time, pathetically huddled inside a chalk circle scrawled upon his floor, presumably to ward off the Rosicrucians' hellish vibrations.

And so began a strange and literary conversion. From the occult horror of *Là-bas* arose a vision of a new field of research: the beauty and grandeur of the Christian religion, its mysteries and rites, and the ancient majesty of its art, architecture, and music. Could there be a more powerful force in the combat against nature than Christianity, with its moral discipline, its miraculous conquest of natural laws, its aesthetic domination of time and space in its monasteries, churches, and cathedrals? Huysmans immediately sent Durtal (and himself) off on this new voyage of discovery and undertook, with equal intellectual curiosity, a "white book" called "Là-haut" (Up There) to mirror the "black" *Là-bas*.

He started by going to the identical sources. It was "Berthe" de Courrière who sent him to Abbé Arthur Mugnier, who was to become his spiritual guide and friend. And in July 1891, as he visited Boullan in Lyons, the ex-priest encouraged him to make a pilgrimage to the shrine of Our Lady of La Salette, above the timberline in the nearby mountains, an experience that touched him deeply. He was also admitted to the Grande Chartreuse monastery, where he stayed over briefly, sleeping in a monk's cell, before returning to Lyons. The light was dawning: might not a monastery be the superior refuge, far better than those he had depicted in *A rebours* and *En rade*?

But his sexual desire continued unabated, and, with Anna now gravely ill, he returned to houses of prostitution, where a certain Fernande caught his fancy for a time. He also explored some of the poorer sections of Paris, on which he wrote descriptive pieces: *La Bièvre* (The Bièvre, 1890) and *Saint-Séverin* (published with *La Bièvre* in 1898). The Bièvre is an ugly stream, flowing into Paris from the south, winding through the town in culverts, and, thoroughly polluted, ending in the city sewers. Huysmans gaily followed its course through unpleasant neighborhoods, describing as he went. He made a stop in a little chapel in the rue d'Ebre (Christmas 1890), but his life was still guided by a murky underground current.

His "white book," now called *Là-haut ou Notre-Dame de la Salette* (1965), remained in manuscript form. It included an account of the pilgrimage to La Salette and the text of the apocalyptic vision called "le secret de Mélanie" (Melanie's secret), and it expressed interest in the Blessed Lydwine of medieval Holland. It also recounted Durtal's conversations on faith with sage ecclesiastics and others, his discoveries, his meditations, and the remarkable beginnings of his conversion. But Huysmans never published it, for his life itself was changing: as he had become Durtal to investigate Satanism, now Durtal, converted to Christianity, became Huysmans. Durtal's life in the verbal world of *Là-bas* had created living fears in a real Huysmans; likewise, Durtal's discovery of the Christian mysteries gave birth to actual belief in the flesh-and-blood author. After all, belief in the devil and in the Good Lord are both expressions of the supernatural: either could express rebellion against nature.

It has always been difficult to make good literature from good sentiments, and the novelist-autobiographer withheld his first attempt at it from publication. On his deathbed, he ordered the manuscripts of *Là-haut ou Notre-Dame de la Salette* burned, along with his early, unpublished novel on the siege of Paris. A secretary, however, apparently with an eye to personal profit, spared *Là-haut* from the flames. It was at last published in 1965, together with the so-called "Journal of *En route*," consisting of extracts from his correspondence of the period and notes from his "carnet vert" (green notebook), a sort of diary of the early 1890s—excellent documentation of Durtal-Huysmans's conversion. A second, "critical" edition of *Là-haut*, based on two manuscripts, appeared in 1988.

Obediently, Huysmans followed Durtal to the altar. On 12 July 1892 he entered upon a retreat in the Trappist monastery at Igny. In these most austere of monastic surroundings, where monks live under a vow of silence, Huysmans made his confession and communed: he had entered the household of faith. Shortly after leaving the monastery, he returned (on 25 July) to Lyons for a visit with Boullan. It was to be his last; the thaumaturge died in January 1893, in Huysmans's thinking as the result of Rosicrucian spells. Afterward Julie Thibault came to serve as Huysmans's housekeeper—performing her strange rituals still—in the rue de Sèvres apartment. Meunier became so seriously ill that she was a danger to herself; when she knocked over a lamp and nearly set her apartment ablaze, Huysmans reluctantly had her interned in a home for the insane, where he visited her faithfully each week until she died in 1895.

On 3 September 1893 Huysmans was dubbed Chevalier de la Légion d'Honneur, an honor granted, however, for his twenty-seven years of devoted service at the Ministry of the Inte-

Meeting of the Académie Goncourt in 1903: (seated) Joseph-Henri Rosny, Huysmans, Léon Hennique; (standing) Elémir Bourges, Séraphin-Justin Rosny, Gustave Geffroy, Lucien Descaves, Léon Daudet

rior rather than for his writing. Undaunted, the author was at work on a new version of Durtal's conversion, *En route* (1895; translated, 1896). Copying out extensive passages from the text of *Là-haut*, Huysmans cast them in a new framework, to form an essentially actionless, plotless "novel," in which Durtal, through conversation and meditation, enters upon the Christian life. Characters from *Là-haut*, such as the abbé Gévresin (perhaps inspired as much by Boullan as by Mugnier) and Madame Bavoil (who seems to resemble Thibault), reappear. As he had fictionalized his life in *Là-bas*, with *En route* he realized the fiction, leading both character and author to the foot of the Cross.

Because of the originality of its relatively actionless structure, Paul Valéry was to express great admiration for *En route*, and a more recent scholarly committee was to name it among the best novels of the nineteenth century. The work was a popular success as well and quickly sold out several editions. But the clergy was less pleased; some members of the secular arm, unfavorably compared with monks in the text, cast doubt on Huysmans's conversion and seemed to suspect him of crass, commercial publicity-seeking. The author's colorful language, which he never abandoned, surely did little to endear *En route* to the clergy; he described Charles Gounod's church music, for example, as "ces fonts à l'eau de bidet" (fonts of bidet water), and as "onanisme musical" (musical onanism).

Still, Huysmans was convinced that his own conversion could serve as a model for others, and there is some evidence that it did. He therefore began a second religious novel, structured around Chartres cathedral, that would reveal the beauty and deeper meaning of Christian art and architecture. Although he never moved to Chartres while he was studying the cathedral for the novel (Durtal, this time separating himself a bit from his author, takes up residence there), he spent much time in the edifice researching his subject. Baldick relates that on 25 December 1896, as he was leaving after prayers in the cathedral, a letter was handed to him from Catharina Alberdingk Thijm, a Dutch writer who had given her fortune to charity upon reading *En route*. She had addressed the missive to Huysmans in care of Chartres cathedral, to be delivered Christmas morning, although she had no earthly reason to believe he would be there; its

M

Vous êtes prié d'assister aux Convoi, Service et Enterrement de

Monsieur Joris Karl Huysmans,

Homme de Lettres,

Président de l'Académie des Goncourt,

Officier de la Légion d'Honneur,

décédé le 12 Mai 1907, muni des Sacrements de l'Église, en son domicile, Rue Saint-Placide N° 31, à l'âge de 59 ans;

Qui se feront le Mercredi 15 courant, à 10 heures très précises, en l'Église Notre-Dame des Champs, sa paroisse.

De Profundis.

On se réunira à la Maison Mortuaire.

De la part de Mademoiselle Juliette Og, de Monsieur et Madame Albert Marois, ses sœurs et beau-frère; de Mesdemoiselles Suzanne et Germaine Marois, ses nièces; de Madame Veuve Armand Colin; de Monsieur et Madame Paul Badin; de Monsieur et Madame Paul Gout, de Monsieur et Madame Max Leclerc et leurs enfants, de Monsieur et Madame Victor Bérard et leurs enfants, de Messieurs André et Marcel Badin; de Monsieur et Madame Maurice Boverat et leurs enfants, de Monsieur et Madame Albert Chevalet et leurs enfants, de Madame Veuve Alavoine et ses enfants, ses cousins, cousines, petits-cousins, petites-cousines, et de ses amis.

L'Inhumation aura lieu au Cimetière Montparnasse.

Administration Spéciale des Funérailles, 70 Rue des Saints-Pères.. Maison Henri de Borniol.

Invitation to Huysmans's funeral, the wording for which was dictated by the author before his death from cancer (from Brian R. Banks, The Image of Huysmans, *1990)* "miraculous" delivery revivified her faith.

Research for the book on Chartres continued over several years; still, like *En route,* the final version contained lengthy passages salvaged directly from the *Là-haut* manuscripts. When Huysmans published it in 1898, *La Cathédrale* (translated as *The Cathedral,* 1898) was an even greater success than its predecessor; indeed, despite its less-than-sensational subject (it has served as a tourist guide to Chartres), its initial sale was the best of all of Huysmans's works. Continuing debates in the press over the sincerity of his conversion doubtless boosted sales. Some members of the clergy even asked that the work be placed on the *Index Prohibitorum,* but that action was never taken.

The fact was that Huysmans was fighting the good fight to lead a Christian life, although the demon of lust was exceptionally difficult for him to conquer throughout most of the rest of his life. Temptations remained, the primary ones being, apparently, the Spanish countess de Galoez, who came to him because of her interest in the occult and who allegedly sought to seduce him so as to rescue him from the monks, and Henriette du Fresnel, the attractive young daughter of a nobleman. Baldick writes that Henriette, who shared his faith, sat at J.-K.'s feet declaring her love, and that she refused to give up her suit despite the author's entreaties. He encouraged her to enter a convent, which she finally did after an abortive first attempt, which ended when she returned to the writer's doorstep.

After *La Cathédrale,* Huysmans turned to hagiography, relating what to many was an exemplary Christian life in *Sainte Lydwine de Schiedam* (1901; translated as *St. Lydwine of Schiedam,* 1923). Lydwine, born in 1380 in Huysmans's ancestral homeland, was not canonically a saint, but only "blessed." Huysmans's biography tells the story of a girl who made a vow of perpetual virginity. Pursued by suitors, she resisted temptation; but to avoid further distress, she prayed to be ugly. Her prayers were amply answered, as she was granted all sorts of hideous diseases and afflictions, over which Huysmans's naturalistic pen lingers. She is said to have achieved the capacity to perform miracles; at any rate, her biographer apparently believed in the redemptive efficacy of suffering: by the doctrine of substitution, saintly persons can suffer to redeem others, and Lydwine was, for Huysmans, saintly in this sense.

He too was beginning to know physical suffering. In the spring of 1900 his dental problems began, adding serious pain to the discomforts of his long-standing rheumatism and dyspepsia. He had teeth extracted, but to no avail: the pain grew constantly worse. This was doubtless the onset of the cancer of the jaw from which he would die seven years later.

His attempts to flee the petty annoyances of Parisian society, like his characters des Esseintes and Jacques Marles, continued. But then he had a grandiose idea: it would be nice to take refuge in a monastery, nicer still to found a monastery where Christian writers and artists could live in community. He investigated several possibilities for the creation of such a religious retreat, but all fell through for lack of a suitable site, or for lack of committed volunteers. But he made personal retreats to monasteries. One of these was to the Benedictine house at Ligugé, where he came closest to realizing his dream.

He had already severed ties to Paris, retiring from his job at the ministry in 1898 with the honorary title of bureau chief. And he had promised the public a third Christian novel, to complete *En route* and *La Cathédrale. L'Oblat* (1903; translated as *The Oblate,* 1924) describes the life of an oblate, a member of a Catholic religious community living under somewhat flexible rules. With fiction again dictating life, he undertook to become an oblate himself at Ligugé, and he had a home, Notre-Dame House, built on the monastery grounds. He moved in about July 1899 and underwent the first ceremony of oblation in March 1900. Notre-Dame House was large enough for others, although no fellow writers joined him there. Instead his fast friends M. and Mme Léon Leclaire, a middle-class couple with whom he had been on intimate terms since 1896 and who had helped him financially to build it, moved in with him for a time.

There he composed *Sainte Lydwine,* and there he edited a collection of his journalistic pieces from over the years under the title *De tout.* Its subjects are as heterogeneous as its title suggests; it contains writings on "everything" his life touched, from his mother's rue de Sèvres flat to Notre-Dame House. He also researched *L'Oblat* while at Ligugé. But like all of his other real and imagined retreats, the idyll was not to last: the French laws on the separation of church and state took effect in 1901, and many "jointly owned" properties reverted to the state, not the church—Ligugé among them. The monks were forced to leave, and a desolate Huysmans returned alone, shortly after taking his final vows

Huysmans near the end of his life

as an oblate, to face the unpleasantness of apartment life in Paris. His second hagiographic work, *Esquisse biographique sur Don Bosco* (Don Bosco, A Biographical Sketch, 1902), was perhaps the least successful of his writings.

L'Oblat, finally published in 1903, told of Durtal's stay at Val des Saints (Ligugé). It details the meaning and beauties of the Catholic liturgy, evoking the Virgin's redemptive suffering. Huysmans also prepared his famous "Préface écrite vingt ans après le roman" (Preface written twenty years after the novel) for the 1903 edition of *A rebours*. This tells of his desire to escape the constraints of the materialistic naturalist novel, and of Zola's somber disapproval of his revolutionary approach to fiction. He also quoted from Barbey d'Aurevilly's original review of *A rebours*: "Après un tel livre, il ne reste plus à l'auteur qu'à choisir entre la bouche d'un pistolet ou les pieds de la croix" (After a book like this, the author has nothing left but to choose between the mouth of a pistol and the foot of the cross). And Huysmans added, "C'est fait" (The choice is made).

He presided at the first official banquet of the Académie Goncourt on 26 February 1903. Then he was off to visit the Leclaires, who had taken up residence in Lourdes. It was the first of two visits he made there. Huysmans was apparently fascinated by the grotto of "miracles," but he was appalled by the tawdry, circuslike atmosphere of the town and the sanctuary.

After further tooth extractions, he took another museum trip, this time to Strasbourg, Colmar, Basel, Freiburg, Frankfurt am Main, Cologne, Brussels, and Antwerp. His explorations led to the composition of *Trois primitifs* (Three Primitives, 1905), containing some forceful passages on the Grünewald paintings in the Colmar museum and notes on the collections in Frankfurt.

By the summer of 1905 his neck was swollen by cancer, and the tumor had closed one of his eyes. An operation on the eye improved his sight but did nothing to ease the pain. The cigarettes he had smoked all his life, in brothels and in monasteries, were still with him. His cancerous jaw and neck made eating a painful task, and he grew rapidly weaker, often confined to bed. Even treatments with the new X-ray technology failed to halt his tumor's atrocious progress. In these conditions, working with a secretary, he composed *Les Foules de Lourdes* (1906; translated as *Crowds of*

This photograph, circa 1898, accompanied Huysmans's obituary in the periodical Illustration

Lourdes, 1906). Writing in the first person—Durtal had at last disappeared—he described therein the horrid afflictions of those who came to pray, and he recounted the rites of the grotto. He affirmed that he had seen no cures there, but that he had observed great faith. And so he claimed to believe in miracles, although he could authenticate none.

In January 1907 Huysmans was named Officier de la Légion d'Honneur for his literary achievements. A final operation on his neck prolonged his life and his agony. Extraction of most of his remaining teeth was exceptionally painful, as the anesthetic wore off before the end of the surgery. His excruciating death had begun.

He ordered destruction of his unpublished manuscripts. He composed the invitations to his own funeral. He received Communion almost daily. When he died at age fifty-nine on 12 May 1907, a requiem was sung for him at Notre-Dame des Champs in Paris, his final parish church, and he was entombed in Montparnasse Cemetery, near Meunier's grave. The last of his works that he intended for publication, *Trois églises* (Three Churches), treating the symbolism of Notre-Dame de Paris, the medieval art and spirit of Saint-Germain de l'Auxerrois, and the history of Saint Merry, appeared in 1908, together with a reedition of *Trois primitifs*.

All of his attempts at flight had failed, except for his escape into words. Huysmans's writings, virtually all of them lexical transmogrifications of his own mental states, evolved as the literary life of his period did, revealing how the crisis of referentiality undermined the pseudorealism of the naturalist school. Still, he sought to transpose the truth values of naturalistic detachment into the realms of psychological aestheticism, where he "discovered" Freudian dreams along with Sigmund Freud and involuntary memory well before Proust (*A rebours*). He attempted to plumb the psychological depths of evil, where Baudelaire had preceded him, and moved easily, symmetrically, from there into the new Catholic renaissance, the rebirth of faith that marked turn-of-the-century France. There he forms the link between Bloy and Verlaine of his own generation and Francis Jammes, Paul Claudel, Charles Péguy, Jacques Maritain, and others of the next. His personal revolution, spiritual and literary, mirrors that of his age.

Letters:

Lettres inédites à Emile Zola, edited by Pierre Lambert, with an introduction by Pierre Cogny (Geneva: Droz, 1953);

Lettres inédites à Edmond de Goncourt, edited by Lambert, with an introduction by Cogny (Paris: Nizet, 1956);

Lettres inédites à Camille Lemonnier, edited by Gustave Vanwelkenhuyzen (Geneva: Droz, 1957);

Lettres inédites à Jules Destrée, edited by Vanwelkenhuyzen (Geneva: Droz, 1967);

Lettres inédites à Arij Prins, edited by Louis Gillet (Geneva: Droz, 1977);

Lettres. Correspondance à trois: Léon Bloy, J.-K. Huysmans, Villiers de l'Isle-Adam, edited by Daniel Habrekorn (Vanves: Editions Thot, 1980);

Lettres à Théodore Hannon (1876-1886), edited by Cogny and Christian Berg (Saint-Cyr-sur-Loire: Christian Pirot, 1985);

The Road from Decadence: From Brothel to Cloister. Selected Letters of J.-K. Huysmans, selected, edited, and translated by Barbara Beaumont (London: Athlone, 1989).

Bibliography:

George A. Cevasko, *J.-K. Huysmans: A Reference Guide* (Boston: G. K. Hall, 1980).

Biography:

Robert Baldick, *The Life of J.-K. Huysmans* (Oxford: Clarendon, 1955).

References:

Ruth B. Antosh, *Reality and Illusion in the Novels of J.-K. Huysmans* (Amsterdam: Rodopi, 1986);

Philippe Audouin, *J.-K. Huysmans* (Paris: Henri Veyrier, 1985);

Maurice M. Belval, *Des ténèbres à la lumière: Etapes de la pensée mystique de J.-K. Huysmans* (Paris: Maisonneuve et Larose, 1968);

Bulletin de la Société J.-K. Huysmans (Paris: Chez Durtal, 1928-);

Per Buvik, *La Luxure et la pureté: Essai sur l'œuvre de J.-K. Huysmans* (Oslo: Solum Forlag A/S, 1989);

Cahiers de l'Herne, issue on Huysmans, edited by Pierre Brunel and André Guyaux (Paris: Editions de l'Herne, 1985);

Pierre Cogny, *J.-K. Huysmans à la recherche de l'Unité* (Paris: Nizet, 1953);

Cogny, *J.-K. Huysmans, de l'écriture à l'Ecriture* (Paris: Editions TEQUI, 1987);

Marcel Cressot, *La Phrase et le vocabulaire de J.-K. Huysmans* (Paris: E. Droz, 1938);

Pie Duployé, *Huysmans* (Paris & Bruges: Desclée de Brouwer, 1968);

Havelock Ellis, "Huysmans," in his *Affirmations* (London: Walter Scott, 1898), pp. 158-211;

John D. Erickson, "Huysmans's *Là-bas*: A Metaphor of Search," *French Review*, 43 (February 1970): 418-425;

Françoise Gaillard, "*A rebours*: Une écriture de la crise," *Revue des Sciences Humaines*, 43, nos. 170-171 (1978): 111-122;

Gustave Guiches, *Le Banquet* (Paris: Editions Spes, 1926);

André Guyaux, Christian Heck, and Robert Koop, eds., *Huysmans, une esthétique de la décadence. Actes du Colloque de Bâle, Mulhouse et Colmar des 5, 6, et 7 septembre 1984* (Geneva & Paris: Slatkine, 1987);

Charles Maingon, *L'Univers artistique de J.-K. Huysmans* (Paris: Nizet, 1977);

Roy Jay Nelson, "Track and Sidetrack," in his *Causality and Narrative in French Fiction from Zola to Robbe-Grillet* (Columbus: Ohio State University Press, 1990), pp. 103-121;

Madeleine Y. Ortoleva, *Joris-Karl Huysmans, romancier du salut* (Sherbrooke, Quebec: Editions Naaman, 1981);

George Ross Ridge, "The Decadent: A Metaphysical Hero," in his *The Hero in French Decadent Literature* (Athens: University of Georgia Press, 1961), pp. 48-66;

Ridge, *Joris-Karl Huysmans* (New York: Twayne, 1968);

Arthur Symons, "Huysmans as a Symbolist," in his *The Symbolist Movement in Literature* (London: Heinemann, 1899), pp. 141-150;

Ruth Plaut Weinreb, "Structural Techniques in *A rebours*," *French Review*, 49 (December 1975): 222-233.

Papers:

Huysmans's papers are at the Bibliothèque de l'Arsenal, Paris; at the Bibliothèque Nationale, Paris; and in private collections.

Pierre Loti
(Louis-Marie-Julien Viaud)

(14 January 1850 - 10 June 1923)

Alec G. Hargreaves
Loughborough University, England

SELECTED BOOKS: *Aziyadé. Stamboul 1876-1877. Extrait des notes et lettres d'un lieutenant de la marine anglaise, entré au service de la Turquie le 10 mai 1876, tué sous les murs de Kars, le 27 octobre 1877*, anonymous (Paris: Calmann-Lévy, 1879); translated by Marjorie Laurie as *Constantinople (Aziyadé)* (New York: Frederick A. Stokes / London: T. Werner Laurie, 1927);

Le Mariage de Loti—Rarahu (Paris: Calmann-Lévy, 1880); translated by Clara Bell as *Rarahu; or, The Marriage of Loti* (New York: W. S. Gottsberger, 1890);

Le Roman d'un spahi (Paris: Calmann-Lévy, 1881); translated by G. F. Monkshood and E. Tristan as *The Romance of a Spahi* (London: Greening / New York: Brentano, 1881);

Fleurs d'ennui (Paris: Calmann-Lévy, 1882);

Mon Frère Yves (Paris: Calmann-Lévy, 1883); translated by Mary P. Fletcher as *My Brother Yves* (London: Vizetelly, 1884);

Pêcheur d'Islande (Paris: Calmann-Lévy, 1886); translated by Clara Cadiot as *An Iceland Fisherman* (London: J. & R. Maxwell, 1887);

Propos d'exil (Paris: Calmann-Lévy, 1887); translated by Bell as *From Lands of Exile* (New York: W. S. Gottsberger, 1888);

Madame Chrysanthème (Paris: Calmann-Lévy, 1887); translated by Laura Ensor (Paris: Guillaume, 1889);

Japoneries d'automne (Paris: Calmann-Lévy, 1889);

Au Maroc (Paris: Calmann-Lévy, 1890); translated by E. P. Robins as *Into Morocco* (New York: Welch, Fracker, 1890);

Le Roman d'un enfant (Paris: Calmann-Lévy, 1890); translated by Mary L. Watkins as *The Romance of a Child* (Chicago & New York: Rand McNally, 1891);

Le Livre de la pitié et de la mort (Paris: Calmann-Lévy, 1891); translated by T. P. O'Connor as *The Book of Pity and Death* (London: Cassell, 1892);

Pierre Loti in his naval lieutenant's uniform

Fantôme d'Orient (Paris: Calmann-Lévy, 1892); translated by J. E. Gordon as *A Phantom from the East* (London: T. Fisher Unwin, 1892);

Discours de réception à l'Académie Française (Paris: Firmin-Didot, 1892; revised edition, Paris: Calmann-Lévy, 1892);

L'Exilée (Paris: Calmann-Lévy, 1893); translated by Fred Rothwell as *Carmen Sylva, and Sketches from the Orient* (New York: Macmillan, 1912);

Matelot (Paris: Alphonse Lemerre, 1893); translated by Robins as *Jean Berny, Sailor* (New York: Cassell, 1893);

Le Désert (Paris: Calmann-Lévy, 1895);

Jérusalem (Paris: Calmann-Lévy, 1895); translated by W. P. Baines (London: T. Werner Laurie, 1915);

La Galilée (Paris: Calmann-Lévy, 1896);

Ramuntcho (Paris: Calmann-Lévy, 1897); translated by Henri Pène du Bois (New York: R. F. Fenno, 1897);

Figures et choses qui passaient (Paris: Calmann-Lévy, 1898); translated as *Impressions* (Westminster: Constable, 1898);

Judith Renaudin (Paris: Calmann-Lévy, 1898);

Reflets sur la sombre route (Paris: Calmann-Lévy, 1899); translated by Rothwell as *On Life's By-Ways* (London: G. Bell & Sons, 1914);

Les Derniers Jours de Pékin (Paris: Calmann-Lévy, 1902); translated by Myrta L. Jones as *The Last Days of Peking* (Boston: Little, Brown, 1902);

L'Inde (sans les Anglais) (Paris: Calmann-Lévy, 1903); translated by George A. F. Inman as *India* (London: T. Werner Laurie / New York: James Pott, 1906);

Vers Ispahan (Paris: Calmann-Lévy, 1904);

La Troisième Jeunesse de Madame Prune (Paris: Calmann-Lévy, 1905); translated by S. R. C. Plimsoll as *Madame Prune* (New York: Stokes, 1905);

Les Désenchantées, roman des harems turcs contemporains (Paris: Calmann-Lévy, 1906); translated by Bell as *Disenchanted* (London: Macmillan, 1906);

La Mort de Philae (Paris: Calmann-Lévy, 1908); translated by Baines as *Egypt* (London: T. Werner Laurie / New York: Duffield, 1909);

Discours prononcés dans la séance publique tenue par l'Académie Française pour la réception de M. Jean Aicard (Paris: Firmin-Didot, 1909);

Le Château de la Belle-au-bois dormant (Paris: Calmann-Lévy, 1910);

La Fille du ciel, by Loti and Judith Gautier (Paris: Calmann-Lévy, 1911); translated by Ruth Helen Davis as *The Daughter of Heaven* (London: Constable / New York: Duffield, 1912);

Un Pèlerin d'Angkor (Paris: Calmann-Lévy, 1912); translated by Baines as *Siam* (London: T. Werner Laurie, 1913);

Turquie agonisante (Paris: Calmann-Lévy, 1913; revised and enlarged, 1913); translated by Bedwin Sands as *Turkey in Agony* (London: African Times & Orient Review, 1913);

La Hyène enragée (Paris: Calmann-Lévy, 1916); translated by Laurie as *War* (London: T. Werner Laurie, 1917);

Quelques aspects du vertige mondial (Paris: Flammarion, 1917);

L'Horreur allemande (Paris: Calmann-Lévy, 1918);

Prime jeunesse (Paris: Calmann-Lévy, 1919);

La Mort de notre chère France en Orient (Paris: Calmann-Lévy, 1920);

Suprêmes visions d'Orient; fragments de journal intime (Paris: Calmann-Lévy, 1921);

Un Jeune Officier pauvre, edited by Samuel Loti-Viaud (Paris: Calmann-Lévy, 1923); translated by Rose Ellen Stein as *Notes of My Youth* (London: Heinemann / Garden City, N.Y.: Doubleday, Page, 1924);

Journal intime, 1878-1881, edited by Loti-Viaud (Paris: Calmann-Lévy, 1925);

Journal intime, 1882-1885, edited by Loti-Viaud (Paris: Calmann-Lévy, 1929);

Journal intime de Pierre Loti à Tahiti (Papeete, Tahiti: Société des Etudes Océaniennes de Papeete, 1934).

Editions and Collections: *Œuvres complètes*, 11 volumes (Paris: Calmann-Lévy, 1893-1911);

Cent dessins de Pierre Loti (Tours: Arrault, 1947);

Pierre Loti, correspondant et dessinateur, 1872-1889, edited by C. W. Bird (Paris: P. André, 1948).

PLAY PRODUCTIONS: *Pêcheur d'Islande*, Paris, Grand Théâtre, 1893;

Judith Renaudin, Paris, Théâtre Antoine, 1898;

Ramuntcho, Paris, Théâtre de l'Odéon, 1908;

La Fille du ciel, by Loti and Judith Gautier, New York, Century Theatre, 12 October 1912.

OTHER: Marc de Chandplaix, *Louloute (mœurs parisiennes)*, "lettre" by Loti (Paris: Ollendorff, 1885);

Pierre Maël, *La Double Vue suivi de Djina*, "lettre-préface" by Loti (Paris: Frinzine, 1886);

Emile Roustan, *Le Roman d'un marin*, "lettre" by Loti (Paris: Calmann-Lévy, 1888);

René Maizeroy, *La Grande Bleue*, preface by Loti (Paris: Plon, 1888);

L. de Kadoré, *En Sêvre: Notes de voyage*, preface by Loti (Niort: Clouzot, 1889);

Carmen Sylva, *Qui frappe?*, translated from the German by Robert Sheffer, preface by Loti (Paris: Calmann-Lévy, 1890);

Loti as a young man (painting by Lévy d'Hurmer; from Edmund B. D'Auvergne, Pierre Loti: The Romance of a Great Writer, *1926)*

Napoléon Adrien Marx, *Sub Jove*, preface by Loti (Paris: Dentu, 1890);
Georges Gourdon, *Le Sang de France*, preface by Loti (Paris: Albert Savine, 1891);
Yann Nibor, *Chansons et récits de mer*, preface by Loti (Paris: Flammarion, 1893);
Baron Robert de Heïmann, *A cheval de Varsovie à Constantinople*, preface by Loti (Paris: Ollendorff, 1893);
Alexandre d'Arc, *La Steppe*, preface by Loti (Paris: Calmann-Lévy, 1893);
Arthur Chassériau, *Deuil de fils*, preface by Loti (Paris: Ollendorff, 1893);
Comtesse de Gidrol, *Cyprès et roses*, preface by Loti (Paris: Sauvaitre, 1893);
Maurice Loir, *La Marine française*, "lettre-préface" by Loti (Paris: Hachette, 1893);
A. Coffinières de Nordeck, *Essais sur les phénomènes cosmogoniques*, "lettre" by Loti (Paris: Berger-Levrault, 1893);
Charles Lallemand, *Le Caire*, preface by Loti (Algiers: Gervais-Courtellemont, 1894);
Xavier de Cardaillac, *Fontarabie*, "lettre-préface" by Loti (Bordeaux: Gounouilhou, 1896);
Jean Dargène, *Le Feu à Formose*, preface by Loti (Paris: Havard, 1897);
Paule Faure, *André Kerner*, preface by Loti (Paris: Ollendorff, 1897);
Marx, *Nos cols bleus*, preface by Loti (Paris: Ollendorff, 1898);
Comtesse Diane, *Les Glanes de la vie*, preface by Loti (Paris: Ollendorff, 1898);
Jules Michelet, *La Mer*, foreword by Loti (Paris: Calmann-Lévy, 1898);
Emile Duboc, *Trente-cinq mois de campagne en Chine et au Tonkin*, preface by Loti (Paris: Librairie d'Education de la Jeunesse, 1898);
Chassériau, *Du côté de chez nous*, preface by Loti (Paris: Ollendorff, 1899);
Emile Vedel, *Lumières d'Orient*, preface by Loti (Paris: Ollendorff, 1901);
William Shakespeare, *King Lear*, translated by Loti and Vedel (Paris: Calmann-Lévy, 1904);
Vice-Amiral Eugène de Jonquières, *Poésies d'un marin*, preface by Loti (Paris: Calmann-Lévy, 1911);
Justin Massé, *Les Deux Rives*, "lettre-préface" by Loti (Paris: Grasset, 1912);

Henri Saladin and René Mesguich, *Le Yali des Keupruli à Anatoli-Hissar*, preface by Loti (Paris: Société des Amis de Stamboul, 1915);

André Dreux, *La Bibliothèque des aveugles*, preface by Loti (Paris: Association Valentin Haüy, 1917);

Izzet-Mélyh, *Sermed*, "lettre-préface" by Loti (Paris & Geneva: Atar, 1919.

Pierre Loti was the most popular travel writer of his day. From the lands he visited during his career as a naval officer, which took him to virtually every corner of the globe, he quarried a large body of novels, short stories, and travelogues. The exotic decors for which he is best remembered belong to what is known today as the Third World. In Loti's day they were frontier lands over which rival European powers competed for supremacy. His works are in fact directly contemporary with what historians have called the age of imperialism, which, in the final decades of the nineteenth century and the early years of the twentieth, brought most of Africa, together with large parts of Asia and Oceania, under European control. An undercurrent of anticolonialism runs through many of Loti's writings, though his position was in some respects more ambiguous than has often been thought. Toward the end of his life he engaged in a series of polemics in defense of the faltering Ottoman Empire, whose territories were the target of European designs.

His powers as a political analyst and ideologue were limited, however. At the core of his writings was a twin preoccupation with sensory stimulation on the one hand and a dread of death on the other. In his native France or far afield, he sought to surround himself with beautiful sights and loved ones in whose presence he could take pleasure. Loti's willingness to don exotic costumes, his close relationships with male friends, and his apparent intimacy with women the world over raised complex questions about his sexual orientation. By creating within the walls of his home in Rochefort a compendium of architectural styles drawn from radically contrasting civilizations, he earned a reputation as something of a crank. While his sentimental musings on human mortality met with ridicule in some quarters, they also helped to win for him a large and faithful readership among women in particular.

With the advent of mass travel in the twentieth century, his books lost much of their appeal, for the distant places into which he had initiated his readers became increasingly accessible to ordinary tourists. Yet he has continued to attract scholarly studies. Among the most informative of these is the biography by Alain Quella-Villéger, *Pierre Loti l'incompris* (1986), together with *Pierre Loti l'enchanteur* (1988), a sumptuously illustrated record of Loti's life and times produced by Christian Genet and Daniel Hervé. Moreover, his powers as a stylist remain considerable. Lesley Blanch's biography, *Pierre Loti: Portrait of an Escapist* (1983), shows that Loti's romantic qualities can still cast their spell, and in recent years publishers have again found a ready market for inexpensive paperback editions of his best-known works.

In broad terms three main phases may be distinguished in his career as a writer. In most of his early books, Loti's travel descriptions are interwoven with at least a semblance of fictional characters and structured plots. As Lucien Duplessy observed, however, "Les romans de Loti appartiennent à peine au genre. Leur fil intérieur, ce n'est pas l'action, mais tout simplement la personnalité de l'auteur" (Loti's novels can hardly be classed as novels at all. Their inner unity resides not in the pattern of events but quite simply in the personality of the author). From the late 1880s onward, Loti played to his strengths by focusing essentially on highly personalized travel narratives and miscellaneous autobiographical writings, returning to the novel form proper only occasionally. By the time he retired from the navy in 1910, his traveling days were numbered, and in this final phase of his career polemical writings came to the fore. Here too his personal experiences in Turkey, rather than abstract principles or political ideology, lay at the heart of what he wrote.

Loti, whose real name was Louis-Marie-Julien Viaud, was born on 14 January 1850 in Rochefort, a port in southwest France on the Charente River a few miles inland from the Bay of Biscay. He was the son of Jean-Théodore Viaud, an official in the local town hall, and Nadine Viaud, née Texier. Loti's early years and family roots have been usefully documented by Odette Valence and the author's son, Samuel Pierre-Loti-Viaud. Four elements in particular stand out. First, there were on both sides of Loti's family strong connections with the sea, which helped to pave the way for his naval career. Second, his mother came from a staunchly Protestant family, and her beliefs were a pervading influence at home. Nadine's father, Philippe

When he was a sublieutenant in the French navy, Loti usually wore the enlisted men's uniform on leave because it allowed him more freedom

Texier, was a naval administrator on the Isle of Oléron, at the mouth of the Charente River, where the Huguenot ancestors of his wife, Henriette Renaudin, had resettled after a period of exile during the persecution of Protestants in France. On marrying Henriette, Texier converted to Protestantism, and Loti's father did the same when he married Nadine. By the time he reached adulthood, Loti's own religious faith was lost, but he retained a lifelong nostalgia for the promises of an afterlife about which he had read in the Bible. The religious aspects of his work have been explored by Per G. Ekström and Marie-Jean Hublard.

A third early feature of particular significance was that Loti was surrounded by a family that was relatively advanced in years, whose members showered upon him the special love reserved for the youngest member of the household. His mother and father were both more than forty when he was born, while his sister Marie and brother Gustave, who were nineteen and twelve respectively, were almost old enough to be his parents. The household also included his maternal grandmother, Henriette, her sister Clarisse and her aunt Rosalie. In later life he would frequently look back on these early years as a kind of lost paradise.

The near-idyllic circumstances of his early years in Rochefort and the surrounding countryside were, however, shattered by a fourth factor: the financial ruin of his father after he was accused of embezzling municipal funds in 1866. Although he was later cleared of the charges, Jean-Théodore lost his job and died a few years later. The family's financial difficulties made it necessary for Loti to begin training for a career without delay. Casting aside her reservations, his mother agreed to let him enter the navy. In the fall of 1866, he began a year's study at the Lycée Napoléon (now known as the Lycée Henri IV), at the end of which he qualified for entry into the Ecole Navale, France's most prestigious naval college.

In October 1867 he enrolled as a cadet aboard the training ship *Borda*, which was permanently anchored at Brest. His first real taste of life at sea came in 1868 aboard the *Bougainville*, which was used for exercises off the French coast. The following year, as a second-class midshipman aboard the *Jean-Bart*, he sailed for the first time into foreign waters. Within a matter of months, he visited Tenerife, Gibraltar, Algiers, Syracuse, Smyrna, Port Said, Malta, New York, and Halifax. For the next forty years, he would sail the oceans and traverse the continents with similar zest until being forcibly retired from the navy on the grounds of his age in 1910.

Haunted by the financial plight of his family, Loti decided to earn extra cash from his travels by making drawings for publication in popular French magazines such as *Illustration* and the *Monde Illustré*. The first of these drawings, based on a voyage that had taken him to South America, the Pacific Ocean, and the West Coast of the United States, appeared in *Illustration* in 1872, accompanied by notes that he had provided to make the illustrations more salable. It was not until 1880, however, that he succeeded in clearing the family's debts. He was able to do this as a result of switching the main thrust of his creative energies from drawing into writing. The shift came during a lull in his travels, between 1877 and 1883, when he was based mainly in home waters. During this period his earliest books were written.

Loti's first novel, *Aziyadé* (1879; translated as *Constantinople (Aziyadé)*, 1927), was based on a tour of duty that the author had recently completed in the eastern Mediterranean during one of the many crises that shook the Turkish-ruled Ottoman Empire in the closing decades of the nineteenth century. The unwieldy title of the original edition is *Aziyadé. Stamboul 1876-1877. Extrait des notes et lettres d'un lieutenant de la marine anglaise, entré au service de la Turquie le 10 mai 1876, tué sous les murs de Kars, le 27 octobre 1877*, a reflection of the book's diverse and unevenly integrated ingredients.

Aziyadé is a young Circassian woman who becomes the lover of the protagonist and principal narrator, an English naval officer nicknamed Loti. He, as was the author, is stationed first in Salonika and later in Istanbul during the crisis in relations between Turkey and the European powers that culminated in the war of 1877-1878 between Russia and Turkey. The reference in the title to the circumstances of his death reflects the pro-Turkish sentiments engendered in the protagonist by his stay in Istanbul. The political backdrop is, however, less important than his romance with Aziyadé, which is in turn a peg on which to hang the descriptions of exotic locations for which the author was to become famous. The topographical importance of Istanbul is underlined by placing its name directly after that of Aziyadé, whose favors served as the gateway through which Loti conceived the lifelong love of Islamic civilization that would mark the author's subsequent works.

There are many rough edges in the novel. As the original title indicates, it is made up of a miscellany of notes and letters. These were drawn for the most part from the author's own correspondence and above all from his private journal, which was to serve as the primary source for virtually all his later works. The refashioning of those materials into a structured fictional whole was quite perfunctory in places. Loti's strengths as a writer lay in passages of lyrical descriptions rather than in intricate plots or complex narrative strategies, and he would later recognize this by all but abandoning the novel form in favor of travelogues. There remained, however, an important sense in which he was still engaged in a fictional enterprise, for the self that he projected in his travel sketches and other openly autobiographical narratives was in part a mythical creation. The romantic, virile, yet mawkish qualities of his public persona amounted to a highly selective and often inflated version of his private life.

Aziyadé, like the other young women around whom most of Loti's early narratives ostensibly revolve, is ambiguous in several respects. Is his allegiance to Turkey and the affection with which he will later speak of many other lands anything more than a transposition of Loti's erotic attachment to certain of their female inhabitants? If he really loves Aziyadé and those with whom similar relationships are described in other texts, how can he sail off and leave them with little more than a parade of sentimentality whenever it is time for his ship to depart? Are these women really the devoted and selfless lovers that the author would have us believe? A cynical Edmond de Goncourt suggested a different interpretation: "Loti n'a fait au fond que chanter, tout le long de ses œuvres, les prostituées qui *font le trottoir* sous les cocotiers" (At root, throughout his works, Loti has simply been singing odes to prostitutes *plying their trade* beneath the palm trees).

Where Aziyadé herself was concerned, Edmond de Goncourt was among those who gave currency to persistent rumors that the real-life model on which she was based was in fact a man. While dismissing these claims, Keith G. Millward and Alain Quella-Villéger have shown that parts of the manuscript deleted before publication provide powerful evidence of homosexual tendencies within the author and his fictional alter ego. Roland Barthes has indeed argued that veiled homosexuality is the fundamental theme of the novel. While Aziyadé does appear to have been based at least in part on a female model whose real name was Hakidjé, it is hard to believe that a woman belonging to the harem of a Muslim noble could enjoy the freedom of movement attributed to Loti's lover. It seems more likely that she was of more humble origins.

Loti's second novel, *Le Mariage de Loti—Rarahu* (1880; translated as *Rarahu; or, The Marriage of Loti,* 1890), was originally to appear under the title "Rarahu" in 1879. Just before it came out, Juliette Adam asked the publisher, Calmann-Lévy, for permission to serialize the novel in the *Nouvelle Revue,* which she had recently founded. Calmann-Lévy delayed publication of the book until after the serialized text had appeared in the *Nouvelle Revue* in early 1880 under the title *Le Mariage de Loti.* When the book went on sale later that year, the new title superseded "Rarahu," which appeared simply as a subtitle; in later editions it was dropped altogether.

Rarahu is the name of Aziyadé's counterpart in a mixture of romance and travelogue similar in spirit and structure to Loti's first novel, but set this time in Polynesia. It is based on the Pacific voyage that the author made in 1872. Tahiti in particular had fascinated Loti ever since his elder brother, Gustave, had sent back to the Viaud family in Rochefort magical descriptions of the island while serving there as a naval surgeon from 1859 to 1861. Loti's search for Gustave's Tahitian lover and the children born from their liaison is one of the elements incorporated into the novel. As in *Aziyadé* the narrator-protagonist bemoans the destruction of an ancient culture under the impact of Western imperialism, but his main energies are reserved for lyrical celebrations of Tahiti's natural beauty, with the largely fictional relationship with Rarahu serving as a prop for sentimental effusions and mild eroticism tinged with an undercurrent of moral trepidation over the pleasures of the flesh.

Le Mariage de Loti is perhaps most famous for its opening passage, which describes how Loti is given his nickname—said to be derived from a Tahitian flower—during a ceremony held in the sweetly perfumed gardens of the island's monarch, Queen Pomaré. The sensuousness of the night air is contrasted with the wintry climate of Europe, thus establishing from the outset the idyllic image for which Tahiti has become a byword in the West. Unlike *Aziyadé,* which had passed almost unnoticed, *Le Mariage de Loti* immediately attracted a wide readership, and Loti rapidly became something of a celebrity. It also marked the beginning of his collaboration with Adam, in whose review many of his subequent works were serialized prior to their publication in book form.

Le Roman d'un spahi (1881; translated as *The Romance of a Spahi,* 1881) drew on a posting that had taken Loti to West Africa a little more than a year after his Pacific voyage. In Senegal he fell in love with the wife of one of the senior members of the French settler community, who left him heartbroken after a brief but passionate affair. The novel does not deal directly with this affair, instead focusing on a fictional relationship between the protagonist, a French army conscript named Jean Peyral, and an African girl, Fatou-gaye. Her sexual charms ensnare Peyral into prolonging his stay in Senegal, where he perishes in a battle against one of the many African potentates who at the time had yet to submit to French rule. As in Loti's previous novels, one finds interwoven with the love story extensive topographical descriptions laced with anxious broodings over the inevitability of death.

Fleurs d'ennui (Flowers of Gloom, 1882) is a collection of short stories based for the most part on brief visits that the author made to Algeria and the Adriatic in 1880. The title story takes the form of an exchange of letters between Loti and Plumkett, a nickname given to a naval friend, Lucien-Hervé Jousselin, who in real life read and corrected many of the author's early works. In his letters Loti expounds on the anxieties resulting from his loss of religious faith, recalls the simple delights of his childhood, and suggests that a substitute for both may be found amid the hard-living but God-fearing seafarers of Brittany, with whom he had come into close contact while based at various ports in northwest France. Included within this correspondence is "Les Trois Dames de la Kasbah" (Three Ladies from the Casbah), a humorous tale of Breton and Basque sailors who spend a drunken and licentious evening in the

Loti (right) with Samuel, a Turkish boatman who became enamored of Loti when he was stationed at Salonika in 1876

Arab quarter of Algiers. "Pasquala Ivanovitch" recounts a brief romance between Loti and a seemingly innocent peasant girl in Herzegovina. Some of the more sordid realities behind the sugary images presented in stories such as this are plain to see in "Suleïma," whose eponymous heroine is a sixteen-year-old prostitute in the Algerian port of Oran.

Loti's close friendship with a Breton sailor, Pierre Le Cor, provided the substance of his next novel, *Mon Frère Yves* (1883; translated as *My Brother Yves*, 1884), the first of several books initially serialized in the *Revue des Deux Mondes*. Le Cor's slightly fictionalized counterpart, Yves Kermadec, embodies the mixture of rustic simplicity, physical strength, high spirits, and religious faith for which Loti admired the seafaring folk of Brittany. Yves's weakness for drink, which threatens both his marriage and his career in the navy, is the Achilles' heel from which Loti, his friend and superior, attempts to save him.

Strictly speaking, Yves's officer friend is identified in the text simply as Pierre, but as he narrates the story, he is conventionally identified with the author, who was by now publishing his books under the nom de plume Pierre Loti. *Aziyadé* had originally been published anonymously, while *Le Mariage de Loti* was attributed simply to "l'auteur d'Aziyadé" (the author of *Aziyadé*) when it first appeared. In both volumes the real name of the protagonist, who goes under the nickname Loti, is given as Harry Grant, who is presented as an English naval officer. In *Le Roman d'un spahi*, as in all his subsequent books, the author's name was given as Pierre Loti. Although the author does not figure as a character in *Le Roman d'un spahi*, the name Pierre Loti is used by both the author and the narrator-protagonist in most of Loti's later books, where, apart from a slightly untidy transition in *Fleurs d'ennui*, this apparently unitary persona is clearly of French nationality. References to his earlier experiences in

Polynesia and Turkey leave no doubt that this is the same Loti originally encountered in the pages of *Aziyadé* and *Le Mariage de Loti*. The supposedly English protagonist who dies at the end of Loti's first book was thus effectively resuscitated under his true national colors for a literary career spanning more than forty years.

Hardly had this literary persona crystallized in the unitary author-narrator of *Mon Frère Yves* than Loti found his candor as a writer threatening to end his naval career. In May 1883 he was posted to Indochina, where the French were seeking to impose a protectorate on Emperor Tu-Duc of Annam (central Vietnam), whose dependencies included Tonkin (northern Vietnam). Three months later Loti watched as the French fleet bombarded and then captured the coastal forts of Tuan-An, close to Tu-Duc's residence in the imperial city of Hué. From his ship Loti could see hundreds of cornered and virtually defenseless Annamite troops mowed down by the French. Some of the sailors involved in the ground operations described to him shortly afterward how, in an emotional frenzy, they had massacred many of the wounded Annamites.

Splicing together his own observations with those of his sailor friends, Loti wrote a powerful account of the operation for the *Figaro*, where the first three installments appeared in September and October 1883. Publication was then halted because of the domestic and international outcry provoked by Loti's gruesome descriptions of the seemingly wanton carnage in which some of the French troops had engaged. When the government announced that it was recalling Loti from the Far East, his naval career appeared to be in the balance.

By the time he reached France in early 1884, the storm had blown over. No disciplinary action was taken against him, and he returned to the Far East the following year, visiting Japan as well as Indochina. Far from souring his career, the Hué incident generated valuable publicity for the young author. It also helped to create the myth of Loti's anticolonialism. Because his articles in the *Figaro* were seized upon by opponents of French expansionism, who argued that France's colonial ambitions were being pursued with unacceptable brutality, many have assumed that Loti was an uncompromising opponent of colonialism.

Yet, as Loti pointed out in letters to friends in France, his account of the operation at Hué had been written in admiration of the sailors involved. He had indeed glossed over his own purely passive role, narrating events from an affective viewpoint so close to that of the sailors that a casual reader might well have assumed that the author himself had been a direct participant in the ground fighting. In his correspondence he repeatedly spoke of his desire to share in the excitement of expansionist military campaigns. In *Propos d'exil* (1887; translated as *From Lands of Exile*, 1888), a collection of reportages and short stories based on his Far Eastern postings, Loti recounts with great relish how, after Tu-Duc's surrender, he was sent ashore to secure the formal submission to French rule of Tourane, a coastal town better known in contemporary times as Da Nang.

Loti's reputation as an anticolonialist rests on two main pillars. The first of these consists of his frequent laments over the French lives lost in colonial missions. This obsession undoubtedly sprang from the fate of Gustave, who had died in 1865 while returning home in bad health from Cochin China (southern Vietnam), where he had been assisting in the establishment of French rule. It is also true that Loti admired certain non-European civilizations and wished to protect them from Western influences. His protective instincts were, however, highly selective. His fierce defense of Islamic lands had no counterpart where Asiatic peoples were concerned. After his retirement from the navy, when he was free from the constraints of military discipline, he spoke harshly of the government ministers who, he said, had wasted French lives in colonial conquests, but said virtually nothing of the sufferings inflicted on the indigenous peoples of Indochina and other French colonies.

Loti's anticolonialism appears never to have been strong enough to make him worry about his personal involvement in overseas expansion as an officer in the French navy. On the contrary, in his published writings he constantly magnified his military prowess, and when he was forcibly retired in 1898 under a new policy designed to rejuvenate the officer corps, he fought the decision tooth and nail. Having succeeded in having himself reinstated, he was delighted to return to the Far East, this time as part of the expeditionary force dispatched by the Western powers to Peking in response to the Boxer Rebellion.

Loti's antipathy for Asiatic peoples was clear from his earliest writings on the region, collected in *Propos d'exil*, *Madame Chrysanthème* (1887; translated, 1889), and *Japoneries d'automne* (Autumnal

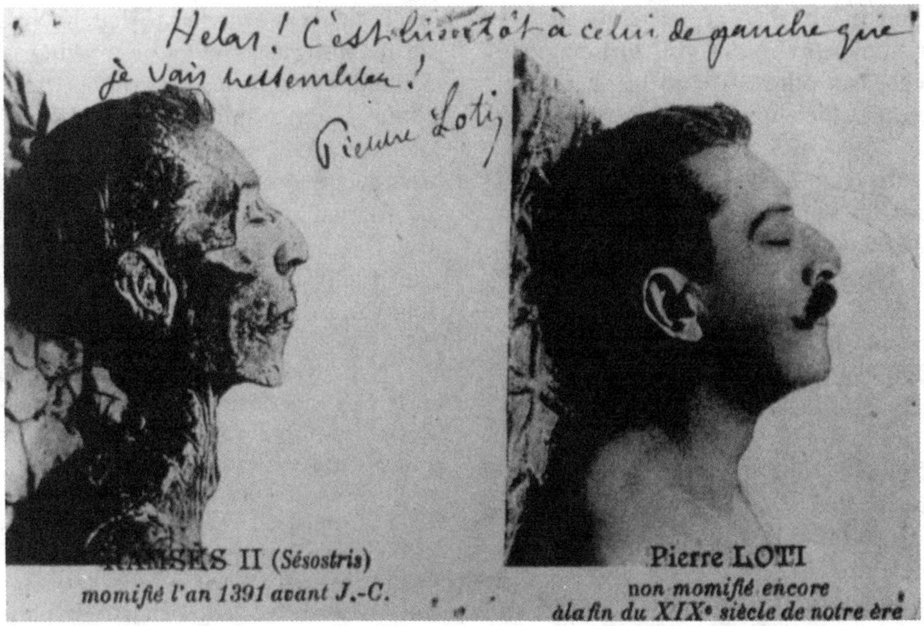
II (Sésostris)
momifié l'an 1391 avant J.-C.
Pierre LOTI
non momifié encore
àla fin du XIXe siècle de notre ère

Postcard designed by Loti, comparing his profile with that of the mummified Ramses II. Loti believed that he had been the Egyptian pharaoh in a past life.

Japanese Pieces, 1889). In *Madame Chrysanthème*, which is set in Japan, he goes through the motions of the basic formula employed in most of his novels, a romance between a visiting seaman (usually, as in this instance, Loti himself) and a local woman. However, Loti fails to muster even a semblance of passion for the woman he calls Madame Chrysanthemum and cannot resist heaping ridicule on her and the Japanese people as a whole. A similar element of mockery is never far below the surface of the travel sketches collected in *Japoneries d'automne*.

During his second tour of duty to the Far East, in 1885, Loti gave much more serious attention to the manuscript of what was to become his most admired and widely read novel, *Pêcheur d'Islande* (1886; translated as *An Iceland Fisherman*, 1887). Like *Mon Frère Yves* it features a cast of Breton seafarers, but as Henry James observed, the most powerful aspect of the novel is its depiction of the sea itself. The changing moods of the sea—becalmed and mysterious, stormy and destructive—dominate the lives of the simple fishermen who earn their living in Europe's northern waters. The sea becomes in this way a symbol of man's dependence on and struggle against nature, which is at once bountiful and all-consuming. Along with James, Jules Lemaître was among those who greeted the novel as a masterpiece.

On 20 October 1886, shortly after the publication of *Pêcheur d'Islande*, Loti married Jeanne Blanche Franc de Ferrière. Over the years the author had suffered several rebuffs in his attempts to find a wife. On returning to France from the Far East in early 1886, he was introduced to Jeanne by an aunt, Nelly Lieutier, who had made it her business to seek out a suitable partner for him. Jeanne came from a wealthy Protestant family in the Bordeaux area. Outwardly, her marriage to Loti seemed to suit all concerned, but Loti was soon complaining privately that it was an empty union. Once Jeanne had assuaged Loti's desire to see his flesh perpetuated beyond his death in the shape of a son, Samuel, born in 1889, the couple rapidly drifted apart, though the marriage was never formally dissolved. In all his published works, she was referred to only once. As Sacha Guitry observed, "L'homme était marié, l'officier l'était moins—Loti ne l'était pas" (While the man was married, the naval officer appeared less so—and Loti not at all).

Only a year after his marriage, Loti traveled to Istanbul in search of Hakidjé, the Oriental lover on whom Aziyadé had been modeled. In his melancholy account of the visit, *Fantôme d'Orient* (1892; translated as *A Phantom from the East*, 1892), Loti retained Aziyadé's fictional name while acknowledging that many of the other elements of disguise adopted in his first book were no longer necessary. Aziyadé, it transpired, had died in his absence, a victim, he implied, of a broken heart. Loti's visit to her grave is above all seen as a pilgrimage to his own past, the transience of which dominates his emotions and thoughts.

Loti's visit to Istanbul was made while returning to France from Romania, where he had been the guest of Queen Elizabeth, who under the pseudonym of Carmen Sylva had recently translated *Pêcheur d'Islande* into Romanian. Loti's impressions of his stay in Bucharest and of his subsequent meetings with Carmen Sylva in Venice were published in *L'Exilée* (1893; translated as *Carmen Sylva, and Sketches from the Orient,* 1912). Their tone of gushing obsequiousness typifies the stance adopted by Loti whenever he wrote of his dealings with royal or aristocratic personages. Beneath the respect that this conveys for those of elevated social rank lies the underlying message that to have merited these audiences Loti, too, must be a person of very special qualities. A similar element of self-aggrandizement is often visible in his relationships with those at the opposite end of the social scale. The humble seamen and seemingly helpless females who enable him to strike paternalistic and patriarchal poses minister to Loti's unremitting sense of his own self-importance.

Similar gratification came from the Parisian salons to which his success as a writer gave him access. Throughout his life Loti cultivated the great and the famous, from actresses such as Sarah Bernhardt to writers such as Alphonse Daudet to aristocratic ladies such as Comtesse Diane (Marie Suin de Beausacq) and Princess Bibescu of Romania. The contacts he made in this way were of considerable assistance in his election to the Académie Française in 1891, much to the irritation of Emile Zola, whose own candidacy for the seat was unsuccessful.

In *Discours de réception à l'Académie Française* (Inaugural Speech to the French Academy, 1892), Loti included an uncompromising critique of naturalism, the brand of social realism pioneered by Zola, which he accused of focusing unduly on the most sordid aspects of contemporary life. It would indeed be difficult to find a literary school more antipathetic than naturalism to Loti's deepest creative instincts. His romantic idealizations of distant lands untouched by industrialization were poles apart from the naturalists' preoccupation with the tough realities of urban life in France. Their cultivation of a seemingly impersonal mode of narration was also wholly at odds with the fundamentally lyrical posture adopted by Loti. Acknowledging that he had no interest in inventing characters or weaving plots, Loti described himself as a writer who "n'a su que chanter son admiration épouvantée devant l'immensité changeante du monde, ou jeter son cri de révolte ou de détresse devant la mort" (has been capable only of singing his awestruck admiration for the infinite variety of the world, or his anguish and abhorrence in the face of death). Loti told the Academy:

> Les vrais poètes—dans le sens le plus libre et le plus général de ce mot—naissent avec deux ou trois chansons qu'il leur faut à tout prix chanter, mais qui sont toujours les mêmes; qu'importe, du reste, s'ils les chantent chaque fois avec tout leur cœur! ... Les vrais écrivains n'ont qu'au début de légères variations ... sous l'influence des lectures premières; ensuite ils se retrouvent eux-mêmes; ils le deviennent de plus en plus, et restent ce qu'ils sont, sans souci des critiques, des insultes, ni des modes qui changent.

> (A true poet—in the loosest and most general sense of the word—is born with just two or three melodies that he feels utterly compelled to sing, and that never really change; nor does it matter, provided he sings them with all his heart! ... A true writer varies only a little at the beginning of his career ... under the influence of his early reading; he soon finds his real self, focuses on this more and more, and remains faithful to it regardless of any criticisms, insults, or changes of fashion.)

While questionable as a general guide to critical analysis, these remarks constitute in effect a literary self-portrait of Loti. They show a growing awareness on his part of where his true center of gravity lay as a writer. In his early works he borrowed from Romantic authors such as George Gordon, Lord Byron and Alfred de Musset and cobbled together miscellaneous characters and fictional events in order to embroider what at root was his own intensely personal response to the people and places encountered during his travels. By the end of the 1880s, he was increasingly inclined to kick away these props, all but eliminating from his works the sustained depiction of any characters other than himself.

After *Pêcheur d'Islande,* Loti wrote only a handful of books that could be properly classed as novels. Despite its title, *Le Roman d'un enfant* (1890; translated as *The Romance of a Child,* 1891) is in fact an autobiographical volume recounting, albeit in a romanticized way, the author's child-

Loti at home, among his Middle-Eastern furnishings

hood and adolescence. *Au Maroc* (1890; translated as *Into Morocco,* 1890) presents an undisguised travelogue based on a visit that Loti made to Morocco in 1889. *Le Livre de la pitié et de la mort* (1891; translated as *The Book of Pity and Death,* 1892) is a collection of occasional writings, only a few of which could be tentatively described as short stories. Similar collections of travel sketches, autobiographical musings, and other short narratives were assembled in *Figures et choses qui passaient* (1898; translated as *Impressions,* 1898), *Reflets sur la sombre route* (1899; translated as *On Life's By-Ways,* 1914), and *Le Château de la Belle-au-bois dormant* (The Sleeping Beauty's Castle, 1910). Some of his least autobiographical writings were the plays *Judith Renaudin* (1898), evoking his Huguenot ancestors, and *La Fille du ciel* (1911; translated as *The Daughter of Heaven,* 1912), a historical drama set in China written in collaboration with Judith Gautier.

Matelot (1893; translated as *Jean Berny, Sailor,* 1893) does possess sufficient elements of plot and characterization to be classed as a novel. It mixes aspects of the author's youth with memories of his brother Gustave and elements drawn from one of Loti's many sailor friends, Léo Thémèze, to produce the story of Jean Berny, a middle-class lad who dies in the Far East after enlisting in the navy in order to support his family following its financial ruin. Apart from *Les Désenchantées, roman des harems turcs contemporains* (1906; translated as *Disenchanted,* 1906), which was conceived in extremely unusual circumstances, *Ramuntcho* (1897; translated, 1897) was effectively the last of Loti's novels. The eponymous hero and his friends are Basque smugglers based on young men befriended by Loti while stationed near Hendaye during much of the 1890s. Their virility, rustic simplicity, and profound religious faith enabled Loti to replicate much of the formula adopted in his earlier Breton cycle of novels, but in a new locale, the Basque country of southwest France, which had its own distinctive landscapes and traditions.

While Loti's works continued to draw on personal experiences in areas of France that he knew well, his main sources of inspiration remained overseas. In place of the semifictional love affairs with local women depicted in his early works, the author now began to emphasize the notion of a spiritual quest as a counterbalance to his anxieties over the inevitability of death. Thus in 1894 he visited the Holy Land, bringing back a trilogy of works, *Le Désert* (The Desert, 1895), *Jérusalem* (1895; translated, 1915), and *La Galilée* (Galilee, 1896). Instead of proceeding directly to Palestine, Loti began his journey by traveling through the Arabian Petraean desert, ostensibly in order to prepare himself better for his pilgrimage to Jerusalem. However, this itinerary may in part have been calculated to generate additional literary material.

The first volume of the trilogy, which is devoted to Loti's trek across the desert, does indeed smack of somewhat contrived sentiments in places, and the same may be felt where some of the scenes in *Jérusalem* are concerned. The journey to Palestine enables Loti to put on yet another performance of his well-worn spiritual anguish; there is little evidence of serious theological inquiry. Even the English critic Sir Edmund Gosse, who declared himself to be "always among the bewitched" when it came to Loti's writings, found his patience wearing thin over the affectation and repetitiveness displayed in the third volume, *La Galilée*.

A less pretentious note is struck in *L'Inde (sans les Anglais)* (1903; translated as *India*, 1906) and *Vers Ispahan* (Bound for Isfahan, 1904), which describe Loti's travels in India and Persia from 1899 to 1900. They are among the most sumptuous of his travelogues. *Les Derniers Jours de Pékin* (1902; translated as *The Last Days of Peking*, 1902), is Loti's account of the period he spent in China from 1900 to 1901 as part of the armed forces protecting Western interests following the suppression of the Boxer Rebellion. It combines gruesome descriptions of the carnage of war with dazzling evocations of Peking's previously hidden treasures, then thrown open for the first time to Western eyes. Excursions to Japan and Korea interwoven by Loti with this tour of duty in China are described in *La Troisième Jeunesse de Madame Prune* (1905; translated as *Madame Prune*, 1905), which is every bit as shallow in its perceptions and perfunctory in its structure as the author's earlier books on Japan. *Un Pèlerin d'Angkor* (1912; translated as *Siam*, 1913), in which Loti describes a visit to the ancient Cambodian temples at Angkor Wat, is a more finely crafted piece of writing.

From 1903 to 1905 Loti was stationed in Istanbul. This was to be the scene of his last novel, *Les Désenchantées*, which is notable principally as one of the greatest literary hoaxes of all time. During his stay Loti was contacted by three young women who pleaded with him to write a novel about their plight, which they said was typical of the condition in which modern Turkish women found themselves. Thinly disguising himself and his informants, the author duly recounted their secret meetings and seemingly firsthand tales of the desperation experienced by westernized women anxious to throw off the patriarchal attitudes prevalent among Turkish men. Shortly after Loti's death in 1923, the leading member of the trio revealed that Loti had in fact been hoaxed. The woman who had presented herself to the author under the name of Leyla and who, in *Les Désenchantées*, appears as Djénane, was not, as she claimed, Turkish, nor was she sequestered in an Oriental harem. She was in fact a French journalist, Marie Léra, who wrote under the pen name of Marc Hélys.

The gullibility with which Loti had fallen for her ruse reflected the precision with which Hélys and her accomplices had pinpointed and played upon his foibles. The author was not at root sympathetic to their modernizing ethos, but he was unable to resist the romantic appeal of the secret meetings proposed by the trio, who in this respect modeled themselves directly on his earlier writings. In addition, their ready-made intrigue provided Loti with a convenient pretext for another book about his beloved Istanbul while relieving him of the tiresome business of inventing fictional characters and events. In this way the ease with which the author was manipulated clearly revealed his imaginative deficiencies.

His creative energies were by then undoubtedly on the wane. *La Mort de Philae* (1908; translated as *Egypt*, 1909) presents a somewhat jaundiced account of a 1907 visit to Egypt, where Loti was constantly irritated at having to rub shoulders with other tourists. Apart from *Un Pèlerin d'Angkor*, which describes his earlier journey through Cambodia, it was virtually the last of his full-length travelogues. The texts collected in *Suprêmes visions d'Orient* (Final Visions of the Ori-

Loti as a captain of the French navy

ent, 1921), based mainly on visits to Turkey in 1910 and 1913, were only partially prepared for publication by the author; his son, Samuel Loti-Viaud, also included in the volume some unrevised passages taken directly from Loti's journal.

The final phase of Loti's career was marked by an unexpected shift into polemical writings. Their primary impetus came from his dismay over the political decline of Turkey on the eve of World War I and the dismembering of the Ottoman Empire in the immediate aftermath of the conflict. His fierce defense of the Turks and his conviction that France should try to block the ambitions of other powers such as Great Britain were articulated in newspaper and magazine articles collected in *Turquie agonisante* (1913; translated as *Turkey in Agony*, 1913) and *La Mort de notre chère France en Orient* (The End of Our Beloved France in the Orient, 1920). During World War I, he also lent his weight to France's anti-German propaganda machine in the writings collected in *La Hyène enragée* (1916; translated as *War*, 1917), *Quelques aspects du vertige mondial* (Aspects of the World in Turmoil, 1917), and *L'Horreur allemande* (German Horrors, 1918).

After the war he published a further volume of autobiography, *Prime jeunesse* (The Prime of My Youth, 1919), which picked up from where *Le Roman d'un enfant* had left off, and, with the assistance of his son, *Un Jeune Officier pauvre* (1923; translated as *Notes of My Youth*, 1924), a collection of letters and notes dating from his early years in the navy. In failing health Loti was decorated with the Legion of Honor in 1921. When he died two years later, he was given a state funeral. Following his death several volumes containing further extracts from his journal were published, as well as two volumes of correspondence and some of the many drawings that he made during his travels. Extracts from Loti's journal and other previously unpublished writings have also appeared in the periodicals published by associations dedicated to his memory: *Bulletin de l'Association Internationale des Amis de Pierre Loti* (1933-1935, 1950-1951), *Cahiers Pierre Loti* (1952-1979), and *Revue Pierre Loti* (1980-1988).

Letters:

Lettres de Pierre Loti à Mme Juliette Adam (1880-1922) (Paris: Plon-Nourrit, 1924);

Correspondance inédite (1865-1904), edited by Nadine Duvignau and Nicolas Serban (Paris: Calmann-Lévy, 1929).

Biographies:

Nicolas Serban, *Pierre Loti: Sa vie et son œuvre* (Paris: Presses Françaises, 1924);

Edmund B. D'Auvergne, *Pierre Loti: The Romance of a Great Writer* (London: Werner Laurie, 1926);

Raymonde Lefêvre, *La Vie inquiète de Pierre Loti* (Paris: Société Française d'Editions Littéraires et Techniques, 1934);

Pierre Brodin, *Loti* (Montreal: Parizeau, 1945);

Lesley Blanch, *Pierre Loti: Portrait of an Escapist* (London: Collins, 1983); also published as *Pierre Loti: The Legendary Romantic* (New York: Harcourt Brace Jovanovich, 1983);

Alain Quella-Villéger, *Pierre Loti l'incompris* (Paris: Presses de la Renaissance, 1986);

Christian Genet and Daniel Hervé, *Pierre Loti l'enchanteur* (Gémozac: La Caillerie, 1988).

References:

Roland Barthes, "Le Nom d'Aziyadé," *Critique*, 28 (February 1972): 103-117;

Pierre Briquet, *Pierre Loti et l'Orient* (Neuchâtel: Editions de la Braconnière, 1945);

Lucien Duplessy, "Pierre Loti a-t-il fait des romans?," *Grande Revue*, 29 (December 1925): 219-240;

Per G. Ekström, *Evasions et désespérances de Pierre Loti* (Gothenburg: Gumperts, 1953);

Pierre Flottes, *Le Drame intérieur de Pierre Loti* (Paris: Le Courrier Littéraire, 1937);

Edmond and Jules de Goncourt, *Journal: Mémoires de la vie littéraire*, volumes 3 & 4 (Paris: Fasquelle et Flammarion, 1956);

Edmund Gosse, "Pierre Loti," in his *French Profiles* (London: Heinemann, 1913), pp. 199-232;

Albert Guerard, "Pierre Loti," in his *Five Masters of French Romance* (London: Unwin, 1916), pp. 135-171;

Sacha Guitry, "La Maison de Loti," *Revue des Deux Mondes*, 1 October 1931, pp. 592-596;

Alec G. Hargreaves, *The Colonial Experience in French Fiction: A Study of Pierre Loti, Ernest Psichari and Pierre Mille* (London: Macmillan / Atlantic Highlands, N.J.: Humanities Press, 1981);

Marc Hélys (Marie Léra), *Le Secret des "Désenchantées" révélé par celle qui fut Djénane* (Paris: Perrin, 1924);

Marie-Jean Hublard, *L'Attitude religieuse de Pierre Loti* (Fribourg: Imprimerie St-Paul, 1945);

Henry James, "Pierre Loti," *Fortnightly Review*, 1 May 1888, pp. 647-664;

Jules Lemaître, "Romanciers contemporains: Pierre Loti," *Revue Bleue*, 18 September 1886, pp. 360-366;

Michael G. Lerner, *Pierre Loti* (Boston: Twayne, 1974);

François Le Targat, *A la recherche de Pierre Loti* (Paris: Seghers, 1974);

Mercure de Flandre, issue on Loti, 10 (January-February 1931);

Keith G. Millward, *L'Œuvre de Pierre Loti et l'esprit "fin de siècle"* (Paris: Nizet, 1955);

Prisme, issue on Loti, no. 18 (Winter 1980-1981);

La Revue Maritime, Pierre Loti 1850-1923 (Paris: Les Grandes Editions Françaises, 1950);

Irene L. Szyliowicz, *Pierre Loti and the Oriental Woman* (New York: St. Martin's Press, 1988);

Robert de Traz, *Pierre Loti* (Paris: Hachette, 1948);

Odette Valence and Samuel Pierre-Loti-Viaud, *La Famille de Pierre Loti ou l'éducation passionnée* (Paris: Calmann-Lévy, 1940);

Clive Wake, *The Novels of Pierre Loti* (The Hague & Paris: Mouton, 1974).

Papers:

The complete manuscript of Loti's *Journal intime*, much of which remains unpublished, is held, along with other manuscripts and extensive unpublished correspondence, in the collection of Pierre and Jacques Pierre-Loti-Viaud in Sceaux, a suburb of Paris. Manuscripts and correspondence are also held at the Bibliothèque Nationale in Paris and the Maison de Pierre Loti in Rochefort.

Pierre Louÿs
(Pierre Louis)

(10 December 1870 - 4 June 1925)

Catharine Savage Brosman
Tulane University

SELECTED BOOKS: *Astarté* (Paris: Librairie de l'Art Indépendant, 1891 [1892]);

Chrysis ou la cérémonie matinale (Paris: Librairie de l'Art Indépendant, 1893);

Lêda (Paris: Librairie de l'Art Indépendant, 1893); republished in *Le Crépuscule des nymphes* (Paris: Editions Montaigne, 1925); translated in *Leda, A New Pleasure* (New York: Privately printed, 1920);

Ariane ou le chemin de la paix éternelle (Paris: Librairie de l'Art Indépendant, 1894); republished in *Le Crépuscule des nymphes*;

La Maison sur le Nil ou les apparences de la vertu (Paris: Librairie de l'Art Indépendant, 1894); republished in *Le Crépuscule des nymphes*;

Scènes de la vie des courtisanes (Paris: Librairie de l'Art Indépendant, 1894);

Danaë ou le malheur (Paris: Mercure de France, 1895); republished in *Le Crépuscule des nymphes*;

Les Chansons de Bilitis (Paris: Librairie de l'Art Indépendant, 1895 [1894]; enlarged, 1898); translated by Horace Manchester Brown as *The Songs of Bilitis* (London: Privately printed for the Aldus Society, 1904);

Aphrodite: Mœurs antiques (Paris: Mercure de France, 1895; enlarged edition, Paris: Librairie Illustrée-J. Tallandier, 1902; enlarged edition, Paris: Privately printed, 1938); translated by Sydney Reynolds as *Aphrodite: A Novel of Ancient Manners* (Paris: L. Borel, 1900);

Byblis changée en fontaine (Paris: Borel, 1898); republished in *Le Crépuscule des nymphes*; translated by Mitchell S. Buck in *Leda, A New Pleasure* (New York: Privately printed, 1920);

La Femme et le pantin: Roman espagnol (Paris: Mercure de France, 1898); translated by G. F. Monkshood as *Woman and Puppet* (London & Glasgow: Collins' Clear-type Press / New York: Brentano's, 1908);

Pierre Louÿs, circa 1895

Une Volupté nouvelle (Paris: Borel, 1899); translated in *Leda, A New Pleasure* (New York: Privately printed, 1920);

Les Aventures du Roi Pausole (Paris: Charpentier-Fasquelle, 1901); translated as *The Adventures of King Pausole* (Philadelphia: Privately printed for the Pierre Louÿs Society, 1926);

L'Homme de pourpre (Paris: Librairie Borel, 1901); translated as "The Artist Victorious" in *The Collected Tales of Pierre Louÿs* (N.p.: Privately printed, 1930);

Sanguines (Paris: Charpentier-Fasquelle, 1903); partially translated by E. H. Pfeiffer as *At the Setting of the Sun* in *Ten Minute Plays*, edited by P. Loving (New York, 1923); translated by James Cleugh (London: Willy-nilly Press, 1932);

Une Enigme littéraire: L'Auteur des 'XV Joyes de Mariage' (Paris, 1903);

Archipel (Paris: Charpentier-Fasquelle, 1906);

Les Trois Roses de Marie-Anne (Paris: Librairie des Amateurs F. Ferroud, 1909);

Contes choisis (Paris: Arthème Fayard, 1911);

La Femme et le pantin, en quatre actes et cinq tableaux, by Louÿs and Pierre Frondaie (Paris: Librairie des Annales Politiques et Littéraires, 1911);

Isthi (Paris: Librairies-Imprimeries Réunies, 1916);

Poétique (Paris: Georges Crès, 1917);

Le Crépuscule des nymphes (Paris: Editions Montaigne, 1925); translated as *The Twilight of the Nymphs* (New York: Privately printed for the Pierre Louÿs Society, 1927);

Quatorze images: Proses inédites de Pierre Louÿs (Paris: Briant-Robert, 1925);

Quelques vers inédits de Pierre Louÿs (Paris: L. Stiquel, 1925);

Journal inédit (Paris: Editions Excelsior, 1926);

Poésies (Paris: Georges Crès, 1926);

Trois filles de leur mère (N.p.: Privately printed, 1926); translated as *The She-Devils* (Paris: Ophelia Press, 1958);

Histoire du roi Gonzalve et des douze princesses (Paris: Privately printed, 1927[?]);

Pages choisies (Paris: Editions Montaigne, 1927);

Psyché, suivi de la Fin de Psyché par Claude Farrère (Paris: Albin Michel, 1927); translated by Buck in *The Collected Works of Pierre Louÿs* (New York: Liveright, 1932);

Madalou: Poème inédit de Pierre Louÿs (Paris: Briant-Robert, 1927);

Catalogue de la bibliothèque de feu M. Pierre Louÿs (Paris: Bosse, 1927);

Poésies nouvelles (Paris: Editions Montaigne, 1928);

Contes antiques (Paris: Editions du Bois Sacré, 1929);

Contes choisis (Paris: Georges Crès, 1929);

Les Chansons de Bilitis inédites (Mytilène [?], 1929);

Journal intime 1882-1891 (Paris: Editions Montaigne, 1929);

Catalogue des livres anciens et modernes (Paris: L. Giraud-Badin, 1930);

Manuel de civilité pour les petites filles à l'usage des maisons d'éducation (N.p., 1930[?]);

Les Chansons secrètes de Bilitis (Paris: Marcel Lubineau, 1931);

Pibrac: Quatrains érotiques (London, 1933);

La Femme: Trente-neuf poèmes érotiques inédits (Mytilène: A l'Enseigne de Bilitis, 1937 [1938]);

Broutilles, suivi de Le Problème Corneille-Molière vu par Pierre Louÿs, edited by Frédéric Lachèvre (Paris: Privately printed, 1938);

Douze douzaines de dialogues, ou Petites scènes amoureuses (N.p., n.d.);

Etudes sur des livres anciens (Paris: E. de Boccard, 1947);

Dialogues de courtisanes (Paris: Eurédif, 1976).

Editions and Collections: *Œuvres* (Paris: Mercure de France, 1896-1906);

Œuvres complètes, 13 volumes (Paris: Editions Montaigne, 1929-1931);

The Collected Tales of Pierre Louÿs (N.p.: Privately printed, 1930);

The Collected Works of Pierre Louÿs, translated by Mitchell S. Buck and James Cleugh (New York: Liveright, 1932);

Les Poëmes de Pierre Louÿs, 2 volumes, edited by Yves-Gérard Le Dantec (Paris: Albin Michel, 1945);

Collected Works (New York: Shakespeare House, 1951);

Les Chansons de Bilitis; Pervigilium mortis, edited by Jean-Paul Goujon (Paris: Gallimard, 1990).

TRANSLATIONS: Meleager, *Poésies*, translated by Louÿs (Paris: Librairie de l'Art Indépendant, 1893);

"Sonnet: A Letter written in prose poetry by Mr. Oscar Wilde to a friend, and translated into rhymed poetry by a poet of no importance," translated by Louÿs, in *The Spirit Lamp* (Oxford, 1893);

Lucianus Samosatensis, *Mimes des courtisanes*, translated by Louÿs (Paris: Mercure de France, 1899; enlarged edition, Paris: Editions Montaigne, 1927);

Samosatensis, *Cyprian Masques*, translated by Louÿs, retranslated by Ruby Melvill (Paris: Fortune Press, 1929[?]).

OTHER: Pierre de Ronsard, *Les Amours de Marie*, with a life of Marie Dupin by Louÿs (Paris: Mercure de France, 1897).

Pierre Louÿs might appear to belong more to the twentieth century than the nineteenth, since most of his adulthood was spent in the former. One year younger than his classmate and sometime friend André Gide, who is rightly considered one of the great modernists in France, Louÿs lived almost a quarter-century into the

1900s. In fact, however, he is preeminently an author of the last decade of the previous century. All three of the novels he finished and published in his lifetime appeared by 1901. Most of his stories and poetry, including the celebrated *Chansons de Bilitis* (1895; translated as *The Songs of Bilitis*, 1904), also were in print by the beginning of the new century. Moreover, his aesthetic is characteristic of that period, more so than of the new age of modernism, which developed in France just before and just after World War I. He has much in common with the French Parnassian poets, the English Pre-Raphaelites, whom he admired, and the French Decadents. In short, his work constitutes more a brilliant achievement of the fin de siècle than a transition to a new age.

Pierre-Félix Louis was born in Ghent, Belgium, on 10 December 1870 to Pierre-Philippe Louis, a lawyer, then fifty-eight years old, and his wife, née Claire Céline Maldan. Fleeing Champagne to escape the German armies, which were approaching from the east and subsequently laid siege to Paris, the couple had fled first to Normandy, then to Lille, finally to Belgium, where their second son was born. Pierre and his older brother Paul were Pierre-Philippe's second family. A first marriage, which had ended with his wife's death, had produced a daughter and a son, Georges (born in 1847). Claude Farrère, to whom Louÿs acted as mentor and friend, suggested in *Mon ami Pierre Louÿs* (1953) that the writer's real father was not Pierre-Philippe but this half brother Georges. Whatever the truth—and there is no clear evidence to support the hypothesis—Louÿs always felt distant from his father, and, especially after the latter's death in 1889, Georges, a career diplomat, served as a parental figure. The death of Louÿs's mother in 1879, followed by Paul's death from tuberculosis, made the need for such a supportive parental figure acute.

In 1882 Pierre was enrolled in the Ecole Alsacienne in Paris, where he remained until transferring to the lycée Janson-de-Sailly for his final year in 1888. During most of these lycée years he lived in Georges's apartment. He was a very gifted student and showed early aptitudes for composition and literature. Two authors whose work exercised a major influence on his developing talents were Victor Hugo and Charles-Marie-René Leconte de Lisle; the value given by the latter to the Greek classics proved to be an enduring example, for much of Louÿs's work has a Greek setting, which he chose not just for its exotic appeal but because he was convinced that the Greek ethic was superior by far to the later European one. At the Ecole Alsacienne from 1887 to 1888, Pierre met Gide, with whom he struck up an immediate and very close friendship, which was to play an important role in the personal and literary lives of each until, in 1895, after repeated and bitter quarrels, they finally ceased seeing each other. Despite resemblances between them—both semiorphans early in their lives, sensitive, sickly, committed to a literary career, in love with formal beauty—their relationship could not have endured indefinitely, for Pierre not only was wholly, and very actively, heterosexual but was even hostile to male homosexuality. When, after having been on very close terms with Oscar Wilde, he broke with him in 1893, it was because he discovered during a visit to London the nature of the relationship between Wilde and Lord Alfred Douglas. Gide did not openly practice pederasty at the time of his friendship with Louÿs, but the role homosexuality plays in his work would probably have alerted Louÿs later to Gide's sexual interests and brought about estrangement.

Little magazines were the outlet for Louÿs's first literary production. With Gide and others he founded in 1889 *Potache-revue* (Schoolboy magazine), for which he wrote the editorial introduction and some pastiches of poets, including Paul Verlaine. In the introduction—a sort of manifesto—he called for a rejection of Parnassian poetry because of its emphasis on rules, especially its use of rhyme; but he himself used rhyme virtually throughout his verse, and his aesthetic ideal remained always very close to the Parnassian goal of creating beautiful objets d'art in poetry. This short-lived magazine was followed by others, including the *Conque*, which he edited, and the *Centaure*, to which he contributed. In 1890, the year after he took his baccalaureate degree, a poem called "L'Effloraison" appeared in the *Revue d'Aujourd'hui*, edited by Tola Dorian and Rodolphe Darzens, over the signature "Pierre Louys"—the first time the young author had replaced the *i* of his surname with what the French call "Greek *i*" (the spelling had, however, appeared in his diary as early as 1888). Two months later he told Gide that he was adding the diaeresis. The effect—including the final, pronounced *s*—was to underline the author's penchant for things Greek.

Meanwhile, in Montpellier, Louÿs had made the acquaintance of an unknown poet, Paul

Valéry, just slightly younger than he. Their friendship would last until the former's death, and Louÿs may have been responsible for having verse by Valéry included in *Poètes d'aujourd'hui* (1900), edited by Paul Léautaud and Adolphe van Bever. He may also have encouraged Valéry to work on what became *La Jeune Parque* (1917; translated as *The Young Fate*, 1917). When Louÿs learned that Valéry had wanted to entitle the poem "Psyché" but had given it up upon learning that Louÿs was working on a book by that name (his one posthumous novel), Louÿs offered him the title, but the offer was declined. One of the bases for their friendship was their mutual admiration for Stéphane Mallarmé, whose Tuesday receptions in his rue de Rome apartment Louÿs attended, starting in 1890. (Another salon he frequented was that of the poet José-Maria de Heredia, whose chiseled and hammered sonnets, often on ancient subjects, appealed to the young man's cult of formal beauty.)

From the beginning of his career, Louÿs conceived of art as the supreme ideal. He held it in such esteem that he was loath to consider writing as a livelihood. This view was shared by Mallarmé and others, but Louÿs went farther than most. Not only was he willing to pay for the publication of his early books; he desired very small printings, insisting that such was the only way of preserving the integrity of art and preventing its becoming an object of mass consumption. He also refused repeatedly most offers he received to contribute regular columns to newspapers, an arrangement that could have been very lucrative. Unlike Gide and Marcel Proust, he had little personal fortune; his inheritance from his father was easily spent in a few years. Throughout his life he would have serious, sometimes almost insuperable financial difficulties, which occasioned great worries and doubtless contributed to his physical deterioration as well as his lack of productivity.

He worried also about his health itself, fearing that, like his brother, he might succumb to tuberculosis. He seemed convinced that he would not live long. The sense of urgency that he felt as a consequence may have led to his accumulation of love affairs, his cult of the beautiful, and, paradoxically, sleepless nights and abuse of tobacco and drugs, which exacerbated his health problems. The same fear of early death may explain a presiding note in his work: a Greek sense of the brevity, fragility, and beauty of life.

After taking his baccalaureate, Louÿs enrolled in the Sorbonne, with the goal of obtaining a *licence*, which might prepare him for a profession. Unfortunately, no career interested him except that of writer, and, while studying (especially languages), he spent much of his time with literature. He was also fond of music, particularly that of Richard Wagner, around whom a veritable cult had grown up in France, as evidenced in the *Revue Wagnérienne*, founded by Téodor de Wyzewa and Edouard Dujardin. Louÿs was such an aficionado that he traveled to Bayreuth on several occasions, where he listened to repeated performances of *Parsifal* (1882). He later became a very close friend of Claude Debussy, before the latter attained renown; the composer set some of his songs to music.

Despite restricted funds Louÿs also managed to travel; throughout the 1890s he would make long sojourns abroad. One of his first trips was to the monastery of the Grande Chartreuse in Dauphiné, a retreat intended to heighten less his religious spirituality (for he had very little or none) than his aesthetic sense and his powers of concentration. His favorite regions were, however, Mediterranean countries: Spain, where he traveled frequently and which serves as the setting for *La Femme et le pantin* (1898; translated as *Woman and Puppet*, 1908); Algeria; and Egypt. He sought there relief from the Parisian climate, which his less than robust constitution did not endure well; he also found inspiration, partly thanks to the same local color that had enchanted Gustave Flaubert, Eugène Delacroix, Guy de Maupassant, and other predecessors, partly—like Gide—through coming into contact with an entirely different set of sexual standards.

His first trip to Algeria, in 1894, was occasioned by hearing Gide (whom Louÿs was visiting in Switzerland) tell about an Oulad Naïl prostitute he had met in Biskra the previous winter. The girl, Meriem ben Atala, who appears in Gide's autobiography *Si le grain ne meurt* (1920-1921; translated as *If It Die . . .* 1935), had been a participant in his effort at sexual emancipation and normalization. Louÿs was so taken by the description of her that he changed his travel plans and, accompanied by their mutual friend Ferdinand Hérold, left for North Africa. Arab society favored both erotic and literary expansion; some of *Les Chansons de Bilitis* was written in Constantine, inspired by Meriem.

From his adolescence Louÿs had frequented prostitutes. His first extended romance, with a young woman from a good family, Marie Chardon, might have resulted in marriage, except that, when he failed his *licence* examination in 1892, he broke off the match, realizing that, in such circumstances, marriage with her would be impossible. His next major involvement was with Marie de Heredia, whom he met in her father's salon in 1890 and with whom he gradually fell in love. The sentiment was probably reciprocal, but in the summer of 1895 she married the poet Henri de Régnier. Louÿs was devastated. In the winter of 1897, while recovering from illness in Algeria, he met Zohra ben Brahim, with whom he was taken sufficiently to bring her back to Paris and install her in his apartment. With interruptions the liaison lasted for two years.

Louÿs's first volume was a slim collection of poems, *Astarté* (1891). The rhymed verses, mostly sonnets, are laden with fin-de-siècle traits: ethereal atmosphere, faint sensations, a delicately nuanced coloring ("mauve," "azur"), names of flowers and jewels, rich rhymes, and frequent alliteration. The poet's remarkable craftsmanship helps offset, however, the précieux tone and atmosphere. This collection was shortly to be followed by other verse and prose.

Very early the writer's predilection for erotic subjects manifested itself, for instance, in his second *plaquette*, *Chrysis ou la cérémonie matinale* (Chrysis or the Morning Ritual, 1893), which became the first chapter in *Aphrodite* (1895; translated, 1900). A substantial body of later prose and poetry in this vein makes him one of the major erotic writers of the fin de siècle. Louÿs, who had scolded Gide for his prudery vis-à-vis women without recognizing its source and implications, shared none of the puritanism and hypocrisy that he identified in the Third Republic. He insisted that his position was one of neither amorality nor immorality, however.

Rather, he wished to offer a different morality, the creative eroticism of the Greeks, acknowledging that sensuality and intellectual development are a whole: "J'ai chanté d'un cœur ardent et pur le divin amour d'où nous sommes nés, alors qu'il était sans souillure, sans honte et sans péché. Je me suis efforcé, oubliant dix-huit siècles barbares, hypocrites et laids, de remonter de la mare à la source, de revenir pieusement à la beauté originelle ... et de consacrer avec enthousiasme, au sanctuaire de la vraie foi, nos cœurs toujours entraînés par l'immortelle Aphrodite" (I have sung with an ardent and pure heart the divine love from which we are born, at the time it was unsullied, shameless, and without sin. I tried, forgetting eighteen hypocritical, barbarous, and ugly centuries, to go back from the pond to the spring, to return piously to original beauty ... and to consecrate enthusiastically, in the sanctuary of true faith, our hearts still inspired by immortal Aphrodite). His interest in sexuality led him, in articles published in 1900, to make a plea for greater freedom for women and a different attitude toward marriage; he argued notably that removing some of the legal obstacles toward marriage and lifting the stigma attached to unmarried mothers would help offset the declining French birthrate, which was a matter of widespread concern.

Most of Louÿs's erotic works are of the same aesthetic order as his other writing, the beauty of the language and the exquisite descriptions acting to offset what might otherwise be offensive to those readers who do not share his attitude. But this embellishment of sensual acts must not be misinterpreted; it is not a disguise, or what François, Duc de La Rochefoucauld, referred to in a famous maxim as "the homage that vice pays to virtue." "L'amour n'a pas besoin d'être épuré par le sentiment pour être pur, ni d'être transfiguré par l'art pour être beau" (Love does not need to be purified to be pure, nor to be transfigured by art to be beautiful). There is, nonetheless, an obvious impulse in his prose and verse to make not only the language but sexual acts themselves beautiful, treated as grave and exquisite rituals, and to see the body, with or without artificial adornments, as an object of beauty. In light of this impulse, it is difficult to believe that another corpus of erotica attributed to him, including *Dialogues de courtisanes* (1976) and *Manuel de civilité pour les petites filles* (1930[?]) is really his; one theory is that some of these texts were forged by a former secretary after the writer's death.

Les Chansons de Bilitis develops a special strain in Louÿsian erotica, lesbian love. What drew the writer to the theme has not been clarified. Unlike Proust, he did not apparently use it as a cover under which to write about male inversion; nor is there evidence that his close women friends were attracted to lesbianism. Jean-Paul Goujon suggests in his edition of *Les Chansons de Bilitis* that lesbians expressed for Louÿs the essence of femininity. The poet, who had already translated from the Greek the verses of Meleager, labeled the *chansons* "translations" and prefaced them with a "vie de Bilitis" recounting the life of the supposed poetess Bilitis. This was, however, a hoax, since the poems were composed by

Group picture from the Ecole Alsacienne, circa 1888. On the extreme left, André Gide is standing, his hands on Louÿs's shoulders.

him, on Greek models. Many readers and even a professor of Greek archaeology were taken in by the mystification. This hoax probably hurt Louÿs in later years, when he attempted in vain to interest publishers in the results of some entirely genuine scholarly investigations he had done concerning, among other things, the possible authorship by Pierre Corneille of some plays attributed to Molière. Like his erotic writing as a whole, the emphasis on lesbian love in the *Chansons de Bilitis* and elsewhere is connected to the writer's general concern for moral and intellectual freedom. Despite their differences Louÿs shared with Gide the conviction that moral standards should be challenged and barriers broken down if the potential of human beings was to be fulfilled in European society as it had been at the height of Greek civilization. One aspiring writer who was attracted by Louÿs's stand was Colette, who referred to the examples set by *Aphrodite* and *Les Chansons de Bilitis*.

The subtitle of *Aphrodite, Mœurs antiques* (ancient manners), points to what the author indicated in the preface as his chief aim: the depiction of life and mores in the Greek world (specifically, in Alexandria in the last century before the Christian era). The portrait is not, however, intended as neutral; it is directed toward glorifying Greek sensuality, a sensuality that, Louÿs argues, is "la condition mystérieuse, mais nécessaire et créatrice, du développement intellectuel" (the mysterious but necessary and creative condition of intellectual development). As he announces in the preface—in an obvious reference to Anatole France's *Thaïs* (1890; translated, 1891)—the heroine does not convert; the aim is glorification of pagan morality, in contrast with "la tradition israélite" in its Christian form, and especially with the moral ideas of Geneva (that is, Protestantism). It is less France's novel with which Louÿs's should be contrasted, however, than such writings as those of the Marquis de Sade and Jules-Amédée Barbey d'Aurevilly, whose premise is that sexual pleasure is closely associated with the sense of sin and danger.

The heroine, Chrysis, is an Alexandrine courtesan from Galilee who lives freely and splendidly. (The author's choice to make her Jewish probably reflects the supposition that Jewish women were more passionate than Gentiles.) She is not alone in her vocation, as Louÿs calls it: over the city presides Aphrodite, to whom a large temple is consecrated amid sacred gardens inhabited by some of the many who have devoted themselves to the goddess. The heroine's rites of washing and adornment and her sexual pursuits (including lesbian ones) are emphasized, as is the constant search for pleasure in the city.

The main story line is based partly, according to Mitchell S. Buck, on a passage from Athenaeus. It concerns the relationship of Chrysis with the queen's sculptor and lover, Démétrios, who, handsome and desired by every woman, desires little until he sees Chrysis. She, who is at the disposal of all, refuses to give herself to him. This choice, which Louÿs does not elucidate fully, supports the traditional image of the capricious, demanding woman—an image that reappears in *La Femme et le pantin*. It also introduces into the story, probably despite the author, the implication that even Alexandrine sensuality must, for psychological reasons, deny itself; that is, one must go beyond desire, and the keener the desire, the more significant the denial. Chrysis sets three conditions on which she will accept Démétrios: he must get for her the silver mirror of Bacchis (a rival courtesan), the comb of the high priestess, and the pearl necklace from the temple statue of Aphrodite. To demand them is to demand crime. The sculptor, who could have any other woman, is victim enough of passion—a passion that resembles nineteenth-century models more than Greek ones—to steal the mirror from Bacchis's house, kill the priestess for her comb, and desecrate the statue.

Démétrios is successful in avoiding detection as the author of the crimes. Bacchis discovers the theft during a banquet (or rather, an orgy) given to celebrate the imminent freeing of her most beautiful slave, the dark Aphrodisia. Instead of being freed, however, the slave is falsely denounced by a servant girl as responsible for the theft and is immediately crucified, in a scene that will hardly inspire in most readers admiration for ancient manners. The populace later discovers the other two sacrilegious deeds. Strangely, once Démétrios has obtained the three objects, he undergoes a change of heart that leads him to refuse from Chrysis the very gift for which the crimes had paid—as if an obstacle to the fulfillment of desire were necessary; or, better, because desire has *already* been fulfilled, through the process of achieving it (he tells Chrysis he has possessed her in a dream). When the courtesan, not accustomed to being denied, becomes the pleader, he imposes a condition of his own, which she agrees to meet before knowing it: she must wear the stolen ornaments before the crowd.

When she consents to do so she is choosing death. She does not acknowledge a desire to die young and beautiful, in full possession of what gives her self-identity; but one may suppose such a desire as a motivation, given its role in the short story "Escale en rade de Nemours" ("A Landing from the Roadstead of Nemours") in *Sanguines* (1903; translated, 1932). Démétrios says that he will visit her in prison, where, she supposes, they will be joined in a climactic paroxysm of fulfillment. "Quelle fin bienheureuse.... Quel incomparable destin" (What a happy end.... What an incomparable fate). The connection between Eros and Thanatos, which Louÿs had seen acted out in Wagnerian opera and which, according to Denis de Rougemont in *L'Amour et l'occident* (1939; translated as *Love in the Western World*, 1956), is not Greek but a Western European phenomenon, originating in Provençal and Celtic sources, here imposes itself on the ancient view by which, Louÿs argues, sexuality was viewed as profoundly natural and associated with life, not death. Before she is captured, Chrysis achieves a kind of apotheosis as, adorned with only a veil and the goddess's pearls, she climbs to the summit of the great Alexandrine lighthouse, where the crowd hails her as Aphrodite. But, ironically, by the time Démétrios arrives at her prison cell at dawn, she has already drunk the hemlock to which she has been condemned, and there can be no passionate embrace. He returns later to mold the hardening limbs and body in clay, on which he will later model a marble statue: art, in fin-de-siècle fashion, replaces life.

Aphrodite is by far the most popular work by Louÿs. Reprinted in many editions, often illustrated, and frequently translated, it sold only modestly at first, both despite and because of the somewhat scandalous subject matter; but when the generally conservative poet François Coppée published his eulogistic review, sales rose rapidly, and some fifty thousand copies were sold by the end of the year. The author was put off by such success, which did not fit his image of the writer in the ivory tower; but of course the royalties were extremely helpful to him. The novel belongs to its period in more than a few ways. By its emphasis on Greek motifs and pre-Christian values and mores, it prolongs the interest in Hellenism fostered by such writers and scholars as Leconte de Lisle, Louis Ménard, and Anatole France; by its somewhat savage and exotic romanticism, it displays kinship with *Salammbô* (1862;

translated, 1885) and *La Tentation de Saint Antoine* (1874; translated as *The Temptation of Saint Anthony,* 1895) of Flaubert; its emphasis on love and death makes it Wagnerian and pre-Freudian; and its hedonism shows the kinship of Louÿs with Gide and other writers of the 1890s who were determined to reject the fleshless hothouse atmosphere of symbolism as well as the Christian moral code.

The title of Luis Buñuel's 1977 film based on *La Femme et le pantin, Cet obscur objet du désir* (That Dark Object of Desire), points to the psychological, perhaps even metaphysical, problem that the novel brings alive: desire—sexual desire in this instance—the more powerful for being irrational. French writers had treated the theme of uncontrollable passion from *Tristan et Iseut* through the Romantics; the tragedies of Jean Racine are unexcelled as studies in the enslavement created by passion that knows no bounds. In most works belonging to this tradition, however—especially in lyric poetry of the troubadours—the beloved is either truly worthy of devotion or perceived as worthy. Beginning with Charles Baudelaire in the mid nineteenth century and extending through Proust, the theme of passion has generally assumed the form of the enslavement of a superior lover to an inferior beloved. Such is the case in *La Femme et le pantin*; the pejorative word "puppet" referring to the hero should not obscure the fact that he is a man of culture, integrity, and generosity, whereas his antagonist is shallow and venal, if clever, with all the cruelty of la Belle Dame sans merci.

Louÿs composed the novel in two periods of intense writing after a stay in Seville in 1896. Ever since Prosper Mérimée's *Carmen* (1847; translated, 1878), Spain had been associated in French eyes with the fiercest temperaments and most spontaneous, if brutal, acts of passion. The work is constructed as a frame story, with the inner and outer narratives joined by theme and the presence of the identical woman. In the outer narrative, André Stévenol, a Frenchman who is in Seville for the carnival, meets an attractive woman who flirts with him discreetly and gives him an assignation out of town. Before going to the appointment, André runs into a friend, Don Mateo Diaz, a man of forty, who is wealthy and cultivated. When Mateo learns the identity of the woman André is going to meet, he warns him unambiguously against her. To give force to his warning, he relates his own story of suffering at the hands of the same Concha Pérez.

Conchita, a child when Mateo first meets her, is supremely a femme fatale. This is because she is what Baudelaire called the *femme naturelle,* in whom nature is untouched by morality or conscience. Seductive by instinct, she kindles Mateo's desire, then retreats to a posture of virtuous virgin or even victim, and slips away; then, when it suits her, the comedy begins again. She is interested in money, of course, and he gives her vast sums, only to see her once more disappear. But, as he depicts her retrospectively, she is also sadistic, torturing him for the pleasure of it, or perhaps—a social critic might say—as a way of denying the social structures and circumstances that make her, a woman of no means, dependent upon those who have wealth and power, and force her to turn love into a commodity. Sadism is not the only brutal strain in her character. Like Anatole France in the same period and Guillaume Apollinaire not long after, Louÿs was interested in the phenomenon described by Leopold von Sacher-Masoch as well as that named for Sade. After Conchita has achieved what seems to be the epitome of mockery and torture of Don Mateo, she suddenly reverses her stance and throws herself at him passionately. For a short while he possesses the woman who has teased him mercilessly. But she can give herself to him only in his anger, preferably after physical violence; hence she is driven to commit infidelities and other acts that arouse his ire. Finally, when an innocent girl is hurt by Conchita's violence, Mateo has the strength to leave her.

Neither the embedded story nor the frame narrative quite ends here. In an epilogue that offers, as its title says, the moral to the story, André takes leave of his host, but follows—by chance?—the road where Conchita had agreed to meet him. Although it is much past the appointed time, she is there. The next day she is heard giving orders to her maid to pack her trunks; she is leaving for Paris. That men are attracted to what will destroy them, and perhaps precisely for that reason, is demonstrated not just by André's choice but by Mateo's final act: the novel ends with a note he has written—after recounting his story—begging Concha to return.

The novel has been widely appreciated; an early admirer was the British critic Edmund Gosse. As suggested by the multiple film versions—before Buñuel's, it was adapted for the screen in 1920, with Geraldine Farrar as Conchita; Josef von Sternberg used it as the basis for *The Devil Is a Woman* (1935), with Marlene

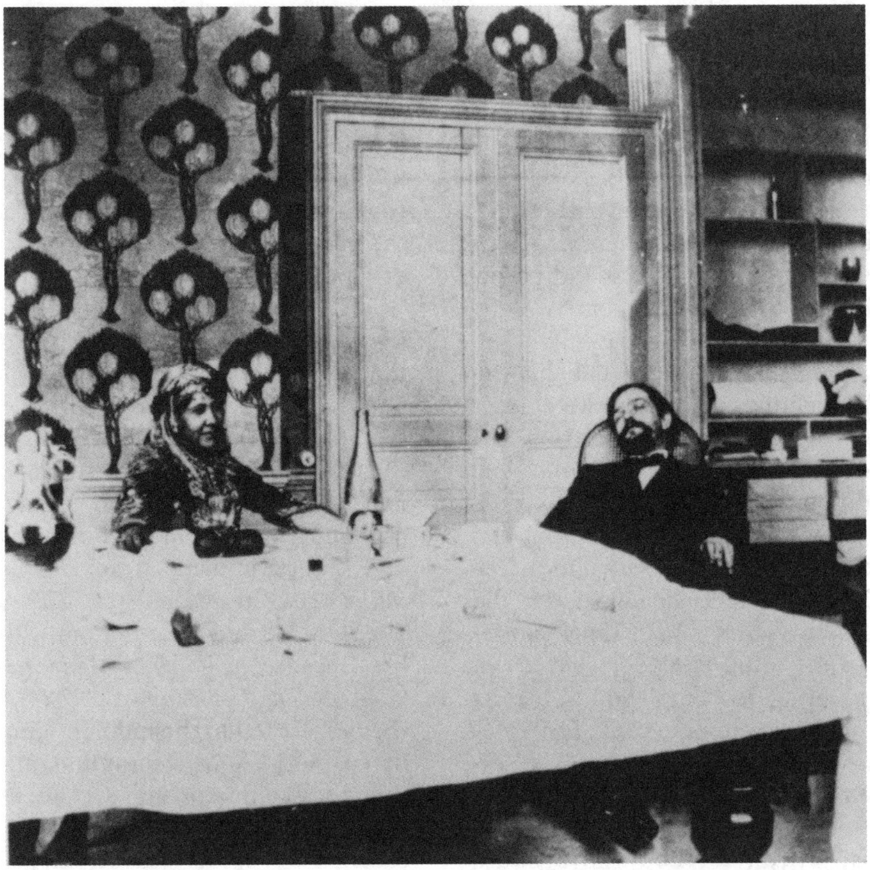

Zohra ben Brahim, Louÿs's Algerian mistress, with Claude Debussy in Louÿs's apartment, 1897

Dietrich; and Julien Duvivier made a French version in 1958—*La Femme et le pantin* is singularly appealing to audiences in a period when will is devalued and the irrational, especially the libido, is considered either more authentic or more powerful than reason. Of Louÿs's three finished full-length works, it is not only the finest, because of its craftsmanship, insights, and power, but also the one most deserving the term *novel* used in the modern sense, for, through its Spanish exoticism, it shows a subjectivity wrestling with a psychological dilemma that it both sees through and is powerless to resolve.

In the fall of 1897 Louÿs began with Marie de Régnier the most passionate love affair of his life. It inspired the unfinished novel *Psyché* and the exquisite poems "Psyché" and "Pervigilium mortis" (the first initially published in the review *Lettres* [15 May 1907], the second in volume 13 of *Œuvres complètes* [1931]), lyrical masterpieces in which, despite some traces of late symbolist vocabulary, a pure and vibrant personal sentiment is expressed. The relationship was not without strains and crises: he continued to travel extensively, and, in particular, even before the liaison began, Marie was jealous of Zohra; that is doubtless why Louÿs shipped the Algerian girl back to North Africa in December. A first rupture between Marie and Louÿs took place in May 1898, after he learned that during his absence she had had an affair with his friend Jean de Tinan. She also was expecting a child; later she told Louÿs that the boy was his, not Tinan's. Their relationship was renewed in the fall of 1898, after the child's birth, and continued even during Louÿs's subsequent marriage, but finally ended in 1901.

In 1898, the same year he both ended and resumed the liaison with Marie, he fell in love with the sister of a friend; marriage was discussed. Simultaneously, Marie's younger sister, Louise, was strongly attracted to him; and Zohra had returned to Paris. He obviously was not concerned with, or did not succeed in, keeping his personal life simple. In 1899, after another sojourn in North Africa with Zohra, he returned—still accompanied by her—and proposed to Louise. The marriage ended in divorce in 1913; immediately thereupon Louise married Gilbert de Voisins, a close friend of her former husband.

Marriage did not bring stability into Louÿs's life. Throughout their years together the couple lived from hand to mouth, always short of cash, borrowing from her father and Pierre's brother Georges, sometimes living with her parents because they could not pay their own rent. Louÿs had very expensive tastes in art objects and particularly books, which he collected for some twenty-five years, amassing a library of some twenty thousand volumes. He boasted later that his investment in rare volumes had paid well, since they had greatly appreciated, but during the years when he assembled most of the collection, he was often riddled with debts. He also experienced difficulty in writing; long periods of inactivity were followed by frenzied efforts, doubtless deleterious to his health, to meet deadlines. He did manage, however, to write some short stories shortly before and after 1900, collected in *Sanguines*, and to bring to completion a project he called his "roman philosophique," *Les Aventures du Roi Pausole* (1901; translated as *The Adventures of King Pausole*, 1926). First written, at Heredia's suggestion, for a newspaper, the *Journal*, the text was difficult for Louÿs to produce on command and dissatisfied him as it appeared, but it was edited only slightly for publication as a book.

The generic label fits the work well, if one remembers the eighteenth-century term *conte philosophique*, or philosophical tale; for Pausole's adventures and their treatment are close to certain works of fiction by Voltaire and Denis Diderot. Like them, Louÿs depicts a fictitious country, which both resembles and differs from the France of his time, that is, serves at once as critique and utopistic model. Despite its geographic proximity to France, the kingdom includes an Oriental-style harem, like that in many eighteenth-century tales. The plot of the novel is episodic, complicated to excess, with the barest claim to verisimilitude, and farcical, despite some serious subject matter. The philosophical lesson itself is not without connection to prerevolutionary tales, since it is an argument for freedom—of the libertarian variety—whose benefits for both the collectivity and individuals are demonstrated in the course of the action. The tone and diction of the story, with its chapter titles beginning "Où . . . " ("Wherein . . . "), its obsolescent "Ci finit l'aventure . . . " (which has the flavor of "Here finisheth the adventure"), and its explicit moral and instructions for interpretation are reminiscent of fiction from the eighteenth century. Even the controlled licentiousness of the story recalls the philosophes' use of the licentious or even pornographic tale to make a political or social point, or to suggest, as Louÿs does, that morality in the narrow sense must be called into question so that the moral question in the wider sense can be properly posed.

The young hero, Giglio, or Gilles, as the king calls his favorite page, is a manipulator like the valets of Italian comedy and Molière's farces, and reminds one also of Pierre de Beaumarchais's Chérubin; he also shares with Stendhal's favorite heroes physical charm, energy, and resourcefulness, and even anticipates the charming adolescent heroes of Gide—capricious and seductive, like Lafcadio in *Les Caves du Vatican* (1914; translated as *The Vatican Swindle*, 1925), or devoted to freedom within social order, like Bernard in *Les Faux-Monnayeurs* (1925; translated as *The Counterfeiters*, 1927). In short, he is the perfect foil to the indolent king Pausole, dominated by the spirit of routine, and even more to the chief counselor and Grand Eunuch, Taxis, a Huguenot imported from France, whose lack of charm and somber accoutrement match his dour disposition and tedious moralizing.

The plot turns on the escape of Pausole's young daughter, Aline, seduced by a dancer—a girl *en travesti* (disguised as a man)—and the king's efforts to bring her back. The author's predilection for sapphic love reappears as the two girls engage in a love affair depicted as delightful but very physical. Since in Pausole's kingdom the only principle is that of the Abbaye de Thélème in Rabelais's *Gargantua* (1534; translated, 1653), "Fay ce que vouldras" (Do what thou wilst)—assuming that one's neighbor is not thereby harmed—Aline's escapade is entirely moral. Alas, the king cannot respect in his own palace the law of freedom he so generously decrees for others, and thus, with his counselor's encouragement, is determined to bring Aline to her senses. How he is converted to his own principle is the rest of the story. In the course of his mock-epic efforts to retrieve her, the king experiences for himself a wealth of adventure, mostly sexual; Aline discovers that she prefers Giglio to her young woman lover; the latter finds a new companion; and many lose their virginity. At the conclusion Taxis is dismissed, freedom is declared in the harem, and all is well. The novelist said himself that he preferred King Pausole's adventures—one of the least personal of his books, at least in appearance—to all his others, perhaps because he felt he had succeeded thereby in irritating figures such as René Bérenger, called "Père la Pudeur" (Father Prudery), a promoter of the laws against moral offenses.

Louÿs had worked with short fiction from the outset of his career, if one includes among fiction the mostly mythological tales that appeared, one by one, in *plaquettes*, starting with *Lêda* in 1893. The five such tales that appeared separately were supposed, with two others, to compose a *heptaméron*, or group of seven stories, joined by a common frame setting. (The final stories exist only in fragments.) Finally, in 1925 the stories were collected as *Le Crépuscule des nymphes* (translated as *The Twilight of the Nymphs*, 1927). The mythological topics are rendered in a prose sometimes approaching poetry. Louÿs makes no attempt to modernize the topics, unlike such authors as Jean Anouilh, Jean Cocteau, and Gide, who in the 1920s and beyond clothed Greek legends in modern psychology and sometimes even modern dress. There is little eroticism. The very ornamental, almost oppressive language, laden with names of places and figures for which a very Greek orthography is used (for example, Bakkhos), usually conveys a rather thin story line, such as the transformation of Byblis into a spring.

Louÿs's own sensibility is sometimes perceptible through the Greek manner. *Lêda*, which is dedicated to Gide and resembles somewhat his *Traité du Narcisse* (1891; translated as *Narcissus*, 1953), proposes an idealistic view of the symbol, derived probably from meditation on the symbolist aesthetic as well as mythology. Forms, he says, hide the invisible. "Il ne faut jamais expliquer les symboles. . . . Celui qui a figuré le symbole y a caché une vérité, mais il ne faut pas qu'il la manifeste, ou alors pourquoi le symboliser?" (One must never explain symbols. . . . He who has created the symbol has hidden truth in it, but he must not manifest it, or otherwise, why should he symbolize it?). In *Ariane* (1894) it is said that the law of love is for the lover to be abandoned—a phrase that foreshadows *Psyché*. *La Maison sur le Nil* (1894; translated as *The House Upon the Nile*, 1927) summarizes late-nineteenth-century aestheticism and the author's own view by asserting that "la seule règle de vie qui semble légitime, c'est le souci de la beauté" (the only rule of life that seems legitimate is the concern for beauty).

The stories that comprise *Sanguines*, some of which had been previously published and which were later collected with others in the *Œuvres Complètes* (1929-1931) as contes, are closer to the modern short story than are the Greek tales, although the styles range considerably and Louÿs ignores the principles of verisimilitude and persuasiveness that Maupassant and other realists had illustrated so well. The collection was published in a large printing—an unusual decision for the author—and forty-two hundred copies were sold the first day. The title, which means red-ocher pencil, or a drawing done with such a pencil, suggests blood (*sang*), hence passion and violence; it also suggests sketches, situations not fleshed out. A few of the stories are in a light vein, including the brief Greek pastoral "Dialogue au soleil couchant" (translated as *At the Setting of the Sun*), "L'Aventure de Mme Esquollier," and "Une Volupté nouvelle" (translated as *A New Pleasure*). In the latter story, Callistô, a Greek woman deceased some eighteen hundred years ago who has revived from her sarcophagus in the Louvre, visits the narrator and inquires what wonderful new pleasures the modern world has invented. She is scornful upon learning that pleasure—especially love—has not been enriched. The narrator—who is close here to his creator—acknowledges that all science fundamentally goes back to the Greeks. Finally, when he casually offers her a cigarette, she discovers a delight unknown to antiquity.

Most of the other stories stress the brutality of life. In "Escale en rade de Nemours"—a frame narrative—a Moroccan stabs his wife, who has escaped with her lover; she dies in a paroxysm of passion and triumph. In "La Fausse Esther," which is presented via the old "found manuscript" device, the heroine's Balzacian name—Esther van Gobseck—leads her first to meet the great novelist, then to doubt her self-identity, finally to assume the character and life of her homonym in Honoré de Balzac's works. "La Persienne" (The Shutter) is the narrative of a woman who never married because as a girl, she witnessed an atrocious scene of rape, during which she was covered with the blood of the assailant, killed by the victim more or less by chance. In "L'In-plano" (the title refers to a volume of large format), a Spanish saint who has come to life from the pages of a hagiography reveals to an innocent girl what her life will be like—what all life is like: unhappiness, grief, pain, death.

The most arresting story, "L'Homme de pourpre" (translated as *The Artist Victorious*), concerns a Greek sculptor, Parrhasios, whose tale is related years later by his friend (in an outer narrative) as an example of the artist who puts himself above moral law. Parrhasios, successful and revered, buys a slave—a Greek physician, captured in war—to serve as a model for his painting of Prometheus. Attaching him to a boulder, where his limbs are nearly torn asunder, the artist orders him to cry aloud, the better to create the reality from which to paint. Although the slave, proud and rebellious, dies inopportunely, Parrhasios finishes the painting. Meanwhile a mob has come to demand vengeance for his having purchased and kept in subjection a fellow Greek; but when Parrhasios displays the painting, hostility turns to awe and acclamations of praise. Is the artist above moral and social law? The question is not answered explicitly. Many writers in the 1890s wrote as if it were so, but Louÿs, pagan as he was, showed in this story that he was not wholly an immoralist.

The novel *Psyché*, conceived, according to the author, in 1900 or 1901, was composed in several stages and published posthumously in 1927. Farrère, to whom Louÿs had previously read the early part, affirmed that he saw the final chapters in 1912. Another acquaintance maintained that the manuscript he saw in 1917 was unfinished and that the author intimated he would not complete it. Louÿs chose not to publish the work, whether because he was not satisfied with it, or indeed had not finished it, or, plausibly, because it was exceptionally personal. After his death only an incomplete manuscript was found. When it was published, Farrère added a summary of the conclusion as Louÿs had apparently indicated it. It is both an anomaly in Louÿs's writing and a splendid representative of a type of sentimental idealism dating from the Romantic period. The eroticism that marked earlier works, whether creative, as in the pseudo-Greek lyrics and parts of *Aphrodite*, or destructive, as in *La Femme et le pantin*, here is redefined, so that it stands for the gift of the whole self, body and mind.

The structure of the novel, built on a crescendo followed by a decrescendo, illustrates the problem Gide identified in *L'Immoraliste* (1902; translated as *The Immoralist*, 1930) by asking, "Que serait le récit du bonheur?" (What would the story of happiness be like?). The heroine, Psyché Vannetty—whose name, first used by Louÿs in one of his Meleager translations, contrasting with the earlier title *Aphrodite*, suggests the sort of love to be portrayed—is a young woman whose arranged marriage has been a failure (the husband has conveniently but inexplicably disappeared). In a burst of romantic passion, the hero, Aimery Jouvelle, who knows her only casually, declares his love and proposes a relationship that will be worthy, he claims, of them both. She struggles with religious and social scruples—her reputation, she says, is all she has—but yields despite herself. (The plot bears considerable resemblance to Balzac's novella *La Femme abandonnée* [1832; translated as *The Deserted Mistress*, 1897]). The lovers' idyll takes place on a Breton estate, which includes a private forest, Gothic ruins, and a tower, which Aimery explicitly associates with the Sleeping Beauty theme and in which he first possesses Psyché. The heroine reacts like a proper woman of the nineteenth century, with Christian morality always at her back; yet she is brought to acknowledge that the senses can convey the gift of the soul. In a very different register from his Greek works, Louÿs appears to be concerned to go beyond Christian and Cartesian mind-body dualism, while confronting the psychological realities created by such dualism.

The lovers' union of selves would seem to be perfect. But, according to Romantic idealism itself, such perfection cannot endure in a world in which, as Baudelaire put it, action is not the sister of dream. When Psyché reads one evening, by the light of a symbolic lamp, the beautiful lines Aimery has left on her dresser (lines that were published as "Psyché" after bearing other titles and now form the fourth part of "Pervigilium mortis"), she senses the future—which is change—implicit in the tribute to the present and realizes thus before he does that Aimery will desert her. Practical reasons for such sentimental alteration are scarcely needed, since the drama is psychological. As Louÿs had already written in *Danaë ou le malheur* (Danaë or the Misfortune, 1895), "Il ne faut jamais parler du bonheur. Celui qui parle de sa joie l'abandonne mot par mot" (One must not speak of happiness. He who speaks of his joy abandons it word by word). But, according to Farrère, Louÿs did plan to recount the manner in which Aimery abandons the heroine. The inevitable return of the lovers to Paris was to be both a symptom and a cause for change; moreover, Aimery's former mistress—an exotic Creole who looks and lives like an odalisque—was to revive his love by leaving France. Psyché's despair would lead her to return

Painting of Louÿs and Henri de Régnier by Jacques-Emile Blanche (from Claude Martin, André Gide par lui-même, *1970)*

to the estate, deserted and frozen in winter, and die there in the wind and snow. One may speculate that recounting the end of the affair, in which readers recognize elements of his experience with Marie de Régnier, was especially painful for Louÿs, and it may have been at that point that the work was abandoned or pages destroyed; the melodramatic ending is not drawn from life, but Aimery's falling out of love may well have been.

Incomplete as it is, *Psyché* warrants recognition as an outstanding example of the psychological novel, wherein the obstacles to happiness are those of human life itself. It recalls the subtle dramas of renunciation in Mme de La Fayette's fiction and some of Gide's, and the passion of Racine's tragedies (the language has Racinian overtones). Despite what now seem like artifices and implausibilities, the novel illustrates well the modern duality of the self, a division not between body and spirit but between creative and destructive impulses; in that way it belongs in the same group with its predecessors that are so different otherwise, *Aphrodite* and *La Femme et le pantin.*

Louÿs's career after the publication of *Sanguines* offers a striking example of an artist's decline. After that date he produced only a few poems and stories, a collection of articles, *Archipel* (Archipelago, 1906), a few scholarly essays, and the essay *Poétique* (1917). Ironically, his name was kept before the literary public through several reprintings of his major works and dramatic and operatic adaptations: *Aphrodite* was set to music by several composers, Ricardo Zandonai composed a *Conchita* in 1911, and Arthur Honegger created *Le Roi Pausole* in 1930. With what was clearly an exceptional literary talent, Louÿs was not able to fulfill his potential. One may speculate about some of the reasons for this failure; others are evident. He had not renounced his aesthete's view of the role of the artist, and continued to refuse most offers to publish in newspapers and magazines. The absence of any fruitful relationship with an audience may be a hidden factor in his lack of productivity. His health, hence his energies, declined markedly; he suffered, or thought he suffered, from nervous exhaustion and neurasthenia, and had recourse to alcohol and cocaine. The state of his finances made travel difficult; he took his last major trip in 1901 and left France after that for only neighboring spots—not the places where he had previously sought inspiration. While some friendships lasted, others were ended, notably that with Debussy; and Georges Louis, always his brother's greatest friend and often a source of financial support, died in 1917. The past seemed to acquire increasing importance for him, hence his cult of books and his scholarly work, pursued despite worsening eyesight. In his last years his habits were practically Proustian, including endemic illness, sequestration, and a nocturnal mode of life; but, unlike Proust, he could not be productive under such conditions.

Moreover, his marriage was not successful. Although at times he showed great devotion to Louise, as when severe hemorrhaging nearly killed her in 1900, there were constant strains, both financial and sentimental. H. P. Clive has pointed out that, apparently, he never wrote anything for her. Yet the divorce in 1913 was very painful for him. Shortly thereafter he began a liaison with the actress Jeanne Montaud (Moriane of the stage). It was followed by an affair with Claudine Rolland, which lasted for several years, with interruptions. Claudine was later replaced with her half-sister Aline Steenackers, by whom Louÿs had a son, born in 1920. A second child, a daughter, was born in 1923; and later that year Louÿs and Aline were married. It is reported that on 3 June 1925 the writer wept as he listened to recordings of Johann Sebastian Bach and Wolfgang Amadeus Mozart. The following day he died, shortly before the birth of his third child on 8 June.

Louÿs has a secure reputation as a minor literary figure of the 1890s who was connected to Mallarmé, Heredia, Gide, Valéry, Debussy, and others. He has a similarly secure position as the author of artistically wrought but licentious works that present a Greek view of erotic morality in contradistinction to a Christian one and contributed to the reaction against the excesses of the symbolist aesthetic. These are his most frequently translated works (there are versions in more than seven languages, including Esperanto). What should be recognized is that, beyond his role on the literary scene—which has given rise to a preponderance of biographical and literary-historical studies of Louÿs—and beyond the sensual appeal of the pseudo-Greek works, whose lyricism and flavor of antiquity are often striking but which do not convey the breadth of the author's sensibility, there is a varied corpus of strong writing, particularly in *La Femme et le pantin* and *Psyché*, which has not achieved the recognition it deserves. The first critical edition of the former, with a preface by Michel Delon, and of *Les Chansons de Bilitis* and *Pervigilium mortis*, with new material (both published by Gallimard), may assist in a reevaluation of his achievement.

Bibliographies:

Bibliographie du roman érotique au XIXe siècle . . . de 1800 à nos jours, volume 2 (Paris: Georges Fourdrinier, 1930), pp. 175-177;

Hector Talvart and Joseph Place, *Bibliographie des auteurs modernes de langue française (1801-1953)*, volume 12 (Paris: Chronique des Lettres Françaises, 1954), pp. 317-356;

Douglas W. Alden and Richard A. Brooks, *A Critical Bibliography of French Literature*, volume 6: *The Twentieth Century* (Syracuse: Syracuse University Press, 1979), pp. 836-844.

Letters:

"Quelques lettres de Pierre Louÿs à André Gide," *Nouvelle Revue Française*, 33 (1929): 640-649, 782-799;

Paul Iseler, *Les Débuts d'André Gide vus par Pierre Louÿs, avec une lettre d'André Gide à l'auteur et de nombreuses lettres inédites de Pierre Louÿs à André Gide* (Paris: Le Sagittaire, 1937);

Claude Debussy and Pierre Louÿs, *Correspondance (1893-1904)* (Paris: Corti, 1945).

Biographies:

Claude Farrère, *Mon Ami Pierre Louÿs* (Paris: Domat, 1953);

H. P. Clive, "Pierre Louÿs and Oscar Wilde: A Chronicle of Their Friendship," *Revue de Littérature Comparée*, 43 (1969): 353-384;

Robert Fleury, *Pierre Louÿs et Gilbert de Voisins: Une curieuse amitié* (Paris: Tête de Feuilles, 1973);

Clive, "Notes on *La Conque* and on the Early Friendship of Pierre Louÿs and Paul Valéry," *Studi Francesi*, no. 52 (1974): 94-103;

Clive, *Pierre Louÿs (1870-1925): A Biography* (Oxford: Clarendon, 1978);

Gordon Millan, *Pierre Louÿs ou le culte de l'amitié* (Aix-en-Provence: Pandora, 1979);

Musidora, *Souvenirs sur Pierre Louÿs* (Paris: A l'Ecart, 1984);

Paul-Ursin Dumont, *Pierre Louÿs: L'hermite du hameau* (Vendôme: Libraidisque, 1985);
Jean-Paul Goujon, *Pierre Louÿs: Une vie secrète (1870-1925)* (Paris: Seghers/Jean-Jacques Pauvert, 1988).

References:

Bulletin de l'Association des Amis de Pierre Louÿs (1977-);
Albert Gier, "Die Karikatur des Skeptikers: Anatole France in *Aphrodite* von Pierre Louÿs," *Archiv*, 221, no. 2 (1984): 286-296;
Jean-Paul Goujon, "Pierre Louÿs et Wagner (avec 6 lettres inédites)," *Littératures*, 18 (Spring 1988): 151-170;
Yves-Gérard Le Dantec, "Pierre Louÿs et la genèse du *Pervigilium mortis*," *Mercure de France*, 45, no. 876 (15 December 1934): 516-537;
Bertrand Mathieu, "Le Motif lunaire dans le 'Pervigilium Mortis' de Pierre Louÿs," *Littératures*, 12 (Spring 1985): 107-117;
John Neubauer, *The Fin-de-Siècle Culture of Adolescence* (New Haven: Yale University Press, 1992);
Felicitas Olef-Krafft, "*Aphrodite* (Pierre Louÿs) und die zeitgenössischen Kunsttheorien," in *Aspekte der Literatur des "Fin de siècle" in der Romania*, edited by Angelika Corbineau-Hoffmann and Albert Gier (Tübingen: Niemeyer, 1983);
Paul Souday, "Literary Career of Pierre Louÿs," *New York Times Book Review*, 28 June 1925, p. 18.

Papers:

Louÿs's papers, including manuscripts of published works and an extensive correspondence, are scattered in many private collections. His papers are also located at the Bibliothèque Littéraire Jacques Doucet, Paris; the Bibliothèque de l'Arsenal, Paris; the Bibliothèque Nationale, Paris; Syracuse University Library; and the Harry Ransom Humanities Research Center, University of Texas, Austin.

Guy de Maupassant

(5 August 1850 - 6 July 1893)

Mary Donaldson-Evans
University of Delaware

BOOKS: *Des vers* (Paris: Charpentier, 1880);
La Maison Tellier (Paris: Havard, 1881);
Mademoiselle Fifi (Brussels: Kistemaeckers, 1882);
Une Vie (Paris: Havard, 1883); translated as *A Woman's Life* (London: Vizetelly, 1885);
Contes de la bécasse (Paris: Rouveyre et G. Blond, 1883);
Clair de lune (Paris: Monnier, 1883);
Miss Harriet (Paris: Havard, 1884);
Les Sœurs Rondoli (Paris: Ollendorff, 1884);
Yvette (Paris: Havard, 1884);
Au soleil (Paris: Havard, 1884); translated as *African Wanderings* (Akron, Ohio: St. Dunstan Society, 1903);
Contes du jour et de la nuit (Paris: Havard, 1885);
Bel-Ami (Paris: Havard, 1885); translated (Chicago: Laird & Lee, 1891);
Monsieur Parent (Paris: Ollendorff, 1885);
Toine (Paris: Marpon et Flammarion, 1886);
La Petite Roque (Paris: Havard, 1886);
Mont-Oriol (Paris: Havard, 1887); translated (New York: Belford, 1891);
Le Horla (Paris: Ollendorff, 1887);
Pierre et Jean (Paris: Ollendorff, 1888); translated by Albert Smith as *The Two Brothers* (Philadelphia: Lippincott, 1889);
Sur l'eau (Paris: Marpon et Flammarion, 1888); translated by Laura Ensor as *Afloat* (London: G. Routledge & Sons, 1889);
Le Rosier de Madame Husson (Paris: Quantin, 1888);
Fort comme la mort (Paris: Ollendorff, 1889); translated by Teofilo E. Comba as *Strong As Death* (London & Philadelphia: Drexel Biddle, 1899);
La Main gauche (Paris: Ollendorff, 1889);
L'Inutile Beauté (Paris: Havard, 1890);
Notre cœur (Paris: Ollendorff, 1890); translated by Alexina Loranger Donovan as *The Human Heart* (Chicago: Laird & Lee, 1890);
La Vie errante (Paris: Ollendorff, 1890); translated as *In Vagabondia* (Akron, Ohio: St. Dunstan Society, 1903);

Guy de Maupassant, 1888 (photograph by Nadar)

La Paix du ménage (Paris: Ollendorff, 1893); translated by Jean Heard as *Peace at Home—at any Price*, in *Poet Lore*, 47, no. 3 (1941): 195-234;
Le Père Milon (Paris: Ollendorff, 1899);
Le Colporteur (Paris: Ollendorff, 1900);
Les Dimanches d'un bourgeois de Paris (Paris: Ollendorff, 1901);
A la feuille de rose: Maison turque (Paris, 1945).
Editions and Collections: *Contes et nouvelles* (Paris: Charpentier, 1885);

The Life Work of Henri René Guy de Maupassant, preface by Paul Bourget, introduction by Robert Arnot (Akron, Ohio: St. Dunstan Society, 1903);

Œuvres complètes de Guy de Maupassant, 29 volumes (Paris: Conard, 1907-1910);

The Collected Novels and Stories of Guy de Maupassant, translated and edited by Ernest Boyd (New York: Knopf, 1922);

Œuvres complètes illustrées de Guy de Maupassant, 15 volumes, edited by René Dumesnil (Paris: Librairie de France, 1934-1938);

The Complete Short Stories of Guy de Maupassant, edited by Artine Artinian (New York: Hanover House, 1955);

Maupassant journaliste et chroniqueur, edited by Gérard Delaisement (Paris: Albin Michel, 1956);

Romans, edited by Albert-Marie Schmidt (Paris: Albin Michel, 1959);

Œuvres complètes, 16 volumes, edited by Gilbert Sigaux (Paris: Rencontre, 1961-1962);

Œuvres complètes, 17 volumes, preface by Pascal Pia, chronology and bibliography by Sigaux (Paris: Cercle du Bibliophile, 1969-1971);

Contes et nouvelles, 2 volumes, edited by Louis Forestier (Paris: Gallimard, Bibliothèque de la Pléiade, 1974-1979);

Chroniques, 3 volumes, edited by Hubert Juin (Paris: Union Générale d'Editions, 1980);

Romans, edited by Forestier (Paris: Gallimard, Bibliothèque de la Pléiade, 1987).

PLAY PRODUCTIONS: *A la feuille de rose. Maison turque*, by Maupassant and Robert Pinchon, Paris, Becker's studio, May 1877;

Histoire du vieux temps, Paris, Théâtre-Français, 19 February 1879;

Musotte, Paris, Théâtre du Gymnase, 4 March 1891;

La Paix du ménage, Paris, Comédie-Française, 6 March 1891.

OTHER: "Boule de Suif," in *Les Soirées de Médan* (Paris: Charpentier, 1880).

Acknowledged throughout the world as one of the masters of the short story, Guy de Maupassant was also the author of a collection of poetry, a volume of plays, six novels, three travel journals, and many chronicles. However, he clearly excelled in the short-story form, and the remarkable ease with which he manipulated this genre can be measured by the fact that he produced some three hundred short stories in the single decade from 1880 to 1890, a period during which he also produced most of his other works. Maupassant himself would have preferred fame as a novelist, and his publications chronology confirms a growing obsession with the longer form: five of his six novels were published during the second half of the decade. Indeed, he doubtless would have benefited from greater critical attention had he cultivated the novel even more. Even his most ardent admirers feel compelled to temper their accolades with disparaging remarks about the short-story form, echoing the sentiments of Jules Lemaître, who considered Maupassant "un écrivain à peu près irréprochable dans un genre qui ne l'est pas" (an almost irreproachable writer in a literary form that is not irreproachable).

At least partly because of this unfortunate prejudice, Maupassant usually has not been ranked with the most illustrious of France's nineteenth-century prose writers—Stendhal, Honoré de Balzac, Gustave Flaubert, and Emile Zola—although one could easily defend the claim that he is France's best-known author outside France. His short fiction has been compared to that of Ivan Turgenev and Anton Chekhov, Edgar Allan Poe and Henry James. Among the authors outside of France who were influenced by him are Rudyard Kipling, August Strindberg, Joseph Conrad, William Sydney Porter (O. Henry), Somerset Maugham, William Saroyan, and Gabriele D'Annunzio. Although various labels have been affixed to him ("realist," "naturalist"), he steadfastly refused identification with any literary movement. Nourished by his reading of Arthur Schopenhauer and tutored in the writer's art by Flaubert, Maupassant took as his primary goal the realistic portrayal of everyday life. He wrote about what he knew best: the peasants of his native Normandy, the war of 1870, the lives of government employees and of Parisian high society, and his own fears and hallucinations.

Both during his lifetime and throughout the twentieth century, writers and critics have been unanimous in their praise of Maupassant. His mentor Flaubert, who died just as his disciple's career was being launched, had high hopes for him, and his faith was not unfounded. Such luminaries as Leo Tolstoy and Anatole France also recognized his genius. His stories were seen as masterpieces of economy and clarity, classical in their formal simplicity, uncommonly varied in their themes, and keenly evocative in their descriptions. His originality was believed to lie not in his subjects (in fact, Maupassant himself avowed readily that he lacked inspiration and found the seeds for his narratives in anecdotes recounted by friends or in newspapers) but in his style. His sobriety of expression, his masterful control, and his remarkable ability to suggest character with one deft stroke of the pen—a single phrase, a couple of well-chosen verbs—have been considered particularly noteworthy.

However, many early critics found his dispassionate narration, devoid of commentary or judgment, deeply troubling, and they were quick to criticize what they saw as a lack of moral fiber on the part of the author. James, in *Partial Portraits* (1888), referred to him as a "lion in the path" of critics with ethical concerns because of the erotic nature of so many of the anecdotes on which his stories were based. For James, the sexual impulse was "the wire that moves almost all Monsieur de Maupassant's puppets." Maupassant's early critics spoke also of his pessimism with regard to human nature and his tendency to represent human beings of all walks of life as pathetic creatures moved only by the basest instincts. Tolstoy in particular took issue with his representation of the working class. Others pointed to Flaubert's influence, or to the autobiographical aspects of Maupassant's work. In fact, for many early critics, his life held considerably more fascination than his work, with the result that biographies were for a long time more plentiful than critical studies.

Whatever the critical reception may have been, Maupassant appealed from the start to readers throughout the world, and his works have been widely translated. English translations of the stories did not respect the integrity of the original collections and appeared most often arranged as so-called complete works or selected stories. The earliest American edition of the complete works, published by the St. Dunstan Society in 1903, includes some sixty stories falsely attributed to Maupassant. Furthermore, fanciful translations make this edition highly unreliable. Fortunately, today's Anglophone has an excellent selection of trustworthy translations from which to choose.

Henri René Albert Guy de Maupassant, the first child of Laure Le Poittevin and Gustave de Maupassant, was born on 5 August 1850. Records show a discrepancy as to his birthplace (some scholars maintain it was Fécamp), but the official view, supported by his birth certificate, is that he first saw the light of day at the château de Miromesnil (near Dieppe, Normandy), rented for the occasion by his socially conscious mother, who found the modest town of Fécamp, where the couple lived, unsuitable for the birth of a child she felt certain was to be a genius. The household in which the young Maupassant was raised was not a happy one. Laure was difficult, prone to neuroses, and often ill-tempered, while Gustave sought relief in the arms of other women. The situation did not breed harmony, and the impressionable child witnessed frequent disputes, both verbal and physical, between his parents. When he was six years old, his mother gave birth to a second son, Hervé, who was somewhat dull-witted and who shared his mother's nervous constitution. In his later years, one of Maupassant's most haunting memories was his brother's mental collapse and subsequent internment. Hervé died in 1889.

When Maupassant was twelve years old, his parents separated. Placed in his mother's custody, he remained in frequent contact with his playboy father, treating him with a certain condescension, but feeling none of his mother's resentment toward him. Nevertheless, his cynicism with regard to marriage, an attitude that permeates his work, dates from this early age. Before separating, his parents had purchased a villa, Les Verguies, in Etretat. There Laure raised her two children, tutoring Guy at home with the help of a local vicar, l'abbé Aubourg. Her elder son, who was particularly sensitive to literature, reminded her of her brother Alfred Le Poittevin, a good friend of Flaubert and a poet in his own right, who had died prematurely in 1848. Thanks partly to this resemblance, Flaubert later took an interest in the young Maupassant.

Dividing his time between lessons at home and escapades on the beaches and cliffs of Etretat, Maupassant was scarcely a model student. Thus, in 1863, with a heavy heart, Laure enrolled him in a boarding school, the Institution ecclésiastique in Yvetot, not far from Etretat. However, the discipline and piety of a Catholic boarding school were inimical to the temperament of this robust, cynical thirteen-year-old, and after a few months of forced subservience, he began to incite the other students to mischief. In order to give vent to his anger and to relieve his boredom, he composed poetry, and he took pleasure in using this new weapon to satirize the "cloître solitaire" (solitary cloister) in which he felt imprisoned. One such poem, discovered by the adminis-

Maupassant, age seven

trators, brought upon him the ultimate punishment: expulsion. There followed a joyous reunion with his mother, who was not unhappy to have him at home once again.

The vigorous adolescent took advantage of his newly won freedom to court the opposite sex, losing his innocence at the age of sixteen, a fact that is not insignificant, since his apparently insatiable sexual appetite and his renowned promiscuity were to prove devastating to his health. During the same period he saved the English poet Algernon Charles Swinburne from drowning and was invited to dine with him and his companion, an Englishman named George Powell, in their chalet, the Chaumière de Dolmancé. The young Maupassant was deeply impressed by the perversity of these two eccentrics, who gave him, as a souvenir of their encounter, a mummified hand. Maupassant's first story, "La Main d'écorché" ("The Dead Hand," 1875), and its subsequent versions, were inspired by this acquisition.

The next phase of Maupassant's formal education took place at the lycée Corneille in Rouen, where the atmosphere of freedom and tolerance was beneficial to his developing literary talent. Continuing to compose poetry, he was quick to attract the attention of his instructors, and his mother further encouraged him by putting him in touch with the poet and dramatist Louis Bouilhet, who had been one of her childhood friends. During one of his visits to Bouilhet, Maupassant first met Flaubert, who subsequently invited him to his retreat at Croisset. If Bouilhet sought to refine Maupassant's talent as a poet,

Flaubert felt instinctively that the young man was meant to be a prose artist, and it was not long before their master-disciple relationship became firmly established. With Bouilhet's death in 1869, Flaubert's influence became predominant, although it would be some time before Maupassant abandoned his poetic aspirations.

The Franco-Prussian War, which broke out in July 1870, was further instrumental in forming the young writer. Maupassant, who had gone to Paris to study law, enlisted in the army immediately, so eager was he to participate in a victory he felt to be imminent. He was bitterly disappointed by the devastating outcome, and the civil war that followed nourished his pessimism, destroying the last of his beliefs in the power and grandeur of France. His experience was to bear fruit a decade later in "Boule de Suif" ("Ball-of-Tallow," 1880), the first of many war stories and the one that made him an overnight celebrity. In the intervening years he completed his "apprenticeship" in Paris by working first in the Ministère de la Marine (Ministry of the Navy) from 1872 to 1878, then, thanks to Flaubert's influence, in the Ministère de l'Instruction publique (Ministry of Public Education) from 1878 to 1882. During this period he came to know—and to despise—the tedious life of a civil servant, another vein that he was to exploit in his stories.

The monotony of his work was relieved by outdoor pursuits, particularly excursions in the country and canoe trips down the Seine, and by women, most often prostitutes and one-night stands picked up at his favorite dive, La Grenouillère, made famous by Pierre-Auguste Renoir's celebrated painting. One of his encounters was to prove fatal: the symptoms of first-stage syphilis appeared in 1877, and since there was in the nineteenth century no known cure for the disease, it followed its relentless course throughout the rest of his life, causing him migraine headaches, paralysis of the ocular muscle, hallucinations, and other symptoms, ending, when the infection progressed to the central nervous system and the brain, with madness. Flaubert warned his young friend of the danger of his excesses and exhorted him to work ("Il faut travailler plus que ça. . . . Trop de putains, trop de canotage, trop d'exercice!" [You must work harder. . . . Too many prostitutes, too much canoeing, too much exercise!]).

Maupassant *was* devoting a great deal of his time to writing, and he had turned to the theater, which allowed him to indulge his taste for farce. His first play, an obscene comedy entitled *A la feuille de rose. Maison turque* (Turkish Brothel), coauthored by his friend Robert Pinchon, was presented in 1877 and earned the disgust of Edmond de Goncourt, while Flaubert quite enjoyed its scatological humor. Subsequent dramatic efforts (*Histoire du vieux temps* [Story of the Old Days, presented 1879], *Une Répétition* [A Rehearsal], and *La Trahison de la comtesse de Rhune* [The Betrayal of the Countess of Rhune]) were published posthumously in his *Œuvres complètes* (1907-1910). Although they were more respectable than his first effort, it soon became apparent that Maupassant's talent as a playwright was limited.

Furthermore, his poetic endeavors still failed to impress Flaubert, although the latter persisted in encouraging his young friend and in trying to find a publisher for his work. One of his poems, "Au bord de l'eau" (At the Water's Side, 1876), concerns the dangers of excessive sensuality. Republished as "Une Fille" (A Prostitute) under the pseudonym of Guy de Valmont in 1879, the poem nearly caused judicial problems for him because of its allegedly pornographic content. Flaubert, who had himself undergone the ordeal of the trial of *Madame Bovary* (1857; translated, 1881), rallied to his disciple's cause and prevented the case from being heard in court. Nevertheless, the publicity that surrounded the case served Maupassant well at a time when the publisher Georges Charpentier was preparing his collected poetry for publication.

At the same time, Maupassant continued trying his hand at narrative prose, between 1875 and 1877 composing a philosophical tale, "Le Docteur Héraclius Gloss" (first published in the *Revue de Paris,* [1921]). Furthermore, he had been a regular visitor at Zola's residence at Médan, and had agreed to collaborate with several other young writers (among them Paul Alexis, Joris-Karl Huysmans, Henry Céard, and Léon Hennique) on a volume of collected stories that would be linked by a common theme: the war of 1870. The approach was to be neither patriotic nor antipatriotic, the goal being, in Maupassant's words, "de donner à nos récits une note juste sur la guerre" (to give in our stories an accurate account of the war). Although *Les Soirées de Médan* (Evenings in Médan, 1880), as they entitled the collection, was interpreted as a manifestation of adherence on the participants' part to Zola's naturalist credo, for Maupassant the collaboration was merely expedient, and he soon made his independence clear. In the meantime, however, he took full advantage of the fame that he acquired as soon as the collection appeared. The critics were unanimous in their praise of his contribution, "Boule de Suif," which was widely regarded as the best of the collection. The jubilant Flaubert hailed it as a masterpiece. With the publication of this single story, Maupassant's career was brilliantly launched.

Today "Boule de Suif" remains one of Maupassant's most famous stories. A tale of hypocrisy and betrayal, it was a stinging indictment of Rouen's "respectable" society, the upstanding citizens who made France's defeat by the Prussians inevitable. Using a moving vehicle as a setting (one of his favorite devices), Maupassant assembles a diverse society composed of nuns, aristocrats, bourgeois shopkeepers, and a republican activist in a coach together with the titular heroine, a corpulent prostitute. All are fleeing Rouen as the enemy approaches; but only the prostitute has valid reasons for her flight, the others being motivated by cowardice and greed. Initially disdainful of their traveling companion, the honorable company befriends her when they grow hungry, for she alone has brought provisions. She becomes even more valuable to them when, during a stopover in Tôtes, the Prussian officer occupying the hotel in which they lodge refuses to let them continue their journey until the prostitute has satisfied his lust. Indignant at the idea of giving herself to the enemy, Boule de Suif is finally won over by her fellow travelers through a carefully planned and slyly executed verbal seduction. The journey resumes in the final pages of the story, and the protagonist, her sacrifice forgotten, weeps softly as the others eat their lunches, shunning her once again, "comme si elle eût apportée une infection dans ses jupes" (as if she were carrying an infection under her skirts). This time she has neglected to pack food for the journey.

The stunning success of "Boule de Suif" results not only from its technical perfection and its realistic portrayal of a historical period by means of a single anecdote, but also from its sobering assessment of the causes of France's ignominious defeat in the war against the Prussians. In Maupassant's story the prostitute becomes a symbol of France herself, invaded and violated by the enemy with the full cooperation of her most "honorable" citizens. Ten years after the fact, the French were able to accept a harsh perspective on the war that they would have found unpalatable earlier.

A week after the publication of *Les Soirées de Médan, Des Vers* (Poetry, 1880) was published by Charpentier. Less than two weeks later, by a strange irony of fate, Flaubert succumbed to a cerebral hemorrhage on 8 May 1880. His role in the establishment of Maupassant's career had been substantial. Besides offering encouragement to his young friend and intervening on his behalf in securing publishers for his early work, the master had shared with the disciple his own philosophy of letters, insisting on the necessity of finding *le mot juste* (the precise word) to describe each concept and thing, as well as on the importance of accurate observation. Maupassant learned his lesson well, as his highly visual descriptions and his remarkable concision amply demonstrate. Flaubert further aided the apprentice Maupassant by introducing him into literary circles that included not only Zola but also Turgenev, Alphonse Daudet, Edmond de Goncourt, and Paul Bourget, and if some of these literati (most notably Goncourt) criticized Maupassant in their writings, their scorn was motivated more by jealousy (of his successes with women as well as with the public) than by any real lack of esteem.

By the end of May 1880, just weeks after Flaubert's death, Maupassant had become a regular contributor to a respected Paris newspaper, the *Gaulois*. His first publications were stories written in the 1870s and reworked for the occasion under the global title of *Les Dimanches d'un bourgeois de Paris* (The Sundays of a Parisian Bourgeois). They were linked by their central character, a minor government employee named Monsieur Patissot, who becomes for Maupassant the personification of stupidity. Maupassant's journalistic collaboration would soon be expanded to include the *Gil Blas* and the *Figaro*.

In the meantime he spent less and less time in the Ministry of Public Education, requesting—and obtaining—repeated medical leaves with the support of his physician. In fact, his health problems were very real, and he took advantage of his freedom to travel to Corsica, not only to be with his mother, who was ill, but because he hoped the climate would alleviate some of his own physical ailments as well. Although Maupassant received extensions of his leave until 1882, he had, for all intents and purposes, left the ministry by 1880.

In 1881 *La Maison Tellier* (Madame Tellier's Establishment), Maupassant's first collection of

Caricature of Maupassant by an unknown artist, 1884

stories, was published by Havard. Approximately half of the stories had appeared in print previously, in such periodicals as the *Bulletin Français*, the *Revue Politique et Littéraire*, and the *Nouvelle Revue*. Maupassant's collaboration with the journals of his day was to increase as his reputation grew, so that in later collections most if not all of the stories had been published in periodicals prior to being gathered in a volume. And, as would also be the case with most of the later volumes, Maupassant selected as his collection's title that of the story he wished to highlight. Here, as elsewhere, the chosen story was distinguished from the others in the collection by its greater length, a *nouvelle* (long story) rather than a conte. Critical reaction to *La Maison Tellier* was somewhat mixed, but sales were spectacular. Appealing to the public imagination by again focusing on the figure of the prostitute, Maupassant was both conforming to a current vogue (Huysmans, Zola, and Edmond de Goncourt were also exploiting this vein) and hoping for a success equal to the one brought to him by his first fictional whore. He was not disappointed.

A masterpiece of irony set, like "Boule de Suif," in Normandy, his native province, "La Maison Tellier" recounts the unanticipated two-day closing of a Fécamp brothel and the confusion and disarray of the disgruntled bourgeois customers who find a notice tacked to one of the entrances: "Fermé pour cause de première communion" (Closed because of First Communion). The story, based upon a playful juxtaposition of the house of ill-repute with the house of God, narrates the excursion of Madame Tellier and her employees to her niece's First Communion in a neighboring town, their emotional reaction to the religious service, which awakens in them dim memories of their own long-lost purity, and their willing, even joyful, return to their "professional" duties after the Mass. The Communion wine corresponds with the champagne served gratis to customers upon their return: "Ça n'est pas tous les jours fête!" (It's not every day that we have something to celebrate!) explains the radiant Madame Tellier.

Maupassant's audacity in narrowing the gap between the sacred and the profane, the bourgeois and the harlots, and his scarcely veiled suggestion that the latter are necessary to the former, was applauded by the critics and ensured the success of the story and of the collection to which it gave its name. As with most of Maupassant's collections, the stories brought together by this volume are unified neither in tone nor in subject. Indeed, in their variety they present a microcosm of Maupassant's fictional universe, for many of the subjects that were to preoccupy him throughout his creative life were already present here. "La Maison Tellier," with its ribald tone, is balanced by "Sur l'eau" ("On the River"), which has the disquieting, mysterious atmosphere of the fantastic tales for which Maupassant would later become famous. "Histoire d'une fille de ferme" ("Story of a Farm Girl") and "Le Papa de Simon" ("Simon's Papa") narrate the plight of the fatherless child, the first from the point of view of the mother, the second from that of the child. Both end on an optimistic note, with the discovery of a surrogate father. Four other tales, "Une Partie de campagne" ("A Country Excursion"), which features Parisian shopkeepers in a deeply moving tale that was later turned into a masterful film by Jean Renoir; "La Femme de Paul" ("Paul's Mistress"); "Au printemps" ("In the Spring"); and "En famille" ("A Family Affair") betray Maupassant's early cynicism with regard to love, marriage, and family, a cynicism that was to grow with the passing years.

Yet in spite of this apparent disparity, a common thread runs through many of the stories: suicide by drowning, or the temptation thereof, is evoked in four of them, and no fewer than seven present aquatic settings, whether it be the Seine, the unnamed river of "Le Papa de Simon," or the pond of "Histoire d'une fille de ferme." The frequent presence of water is characteristic of Maupassant's fictional universe in general and has been the subject of extended commentaries by several of his critics. The collection is interesting from a narratological viewpoint as well, for it serves as an illustration of Maupassant's storytelling technique at the beginning of his career. Only one of the stories, "Au printemps," makes use of a framing device, something that he was to exploit increasingly as the years went by.

Encouraged by the success of *La Maison Tellier*, Maupassant returned to a manuscript on which he had been working intermittently since 1877, that of his first novel, *Une Vie* (1883; translated as *A Woman's Life*, 1885). But once again he interrupted his writing, first to travel to Algeria as a reporter for the *Gaulois* (there is evidence that his anticolonialist sentiments developed during this period), then to continue to write stories for the periodical press. This second group of tales would be collected under the title *Mademoiselle Fifi* (1882). Seeking to exploit anew the basic thematics of "Boule de Suif," Maupassant chose to give prominence to a tale of war and prostitution, originally published under another of his pseudonyms, Maufrigneuse. However, the eponymic Mademoiselle Fifi is not, as one might expect, the prostitute, but rather a sadistic Prussian army officer who is so nicknamed because of his favorite expression, "fi, fi donc" (pooh!).

Like "Boule de Suif," "Mademoiselle Fifi" recounts the heroism of a harlot (here named Rachel), which serves as a striking contrast to the cowardice of her more respectable fellow citizens. And, like "La Maison Tellier," "Mademoiselle Fifi" is based upon a conjunction of religion and prostitution, for it is the village priest who protects Rachel by hiding her in the church belfry after she stabs the brutal Prussian officer to death when he makes insulting remarks about France. Maupassant had a special weakness for prostitutes, representing them in his fiction as victims of fate who seek—and find—their "morality" in a nonsexual sphere. Moreover, for an author as preoccupied with masks as was Maupassant, prostitutes were refreshingly candid members of a hopelessly hypocritical society.

Mademoiselle Fifi includes seven stories, all but one featuring women in central roles, and, as is the case with the first collection, Maupassant's cynicism with regard to male-female relationships is evident. Most of the heroines in this collection are adulterous, and the female sex in general is portrayed as insensitive ("Mots d'amour" ["Words of Love"]), perverse ("La Bûche" ["The Log"]), vain ("Marroca"), superstitious ("La Relique" ["The Relic"]), and naive ("Une Aventure parisienne" ["An Adventure in Paris"]). Yet this misogynistic perspective is balanced by the sensitive portrayal of a young woman who is ridiculed and ostracized because she had been sexually abused as a child ("Madame Baptiste").

Besides illustrating its author's compassion for society's victims, whether male or female, "Madame Baptiste" is notable as an example of the framed tale, in which a first narrator yields to a second and then, at the conclusion of the embedded tale, resumes the narration to achieve a satisfying closure. The links between frame and inner story often orient the reader's interpretation of the text. Moreover, the framing technique also gives the narrative an oral quality, for the embedded tale is generally presented as an oral narration. This in turn contributes to the ease and rapidity of the reading process. The critic Alain Buisine, observing that France's rail system was developing quickly during the second half of the nineteenth century and remarking on the large number of Maupassant's tales that take place in railroad carriages, referred to the short story, as practiced by Maupassant, as the "TGV de la narrativité" (the express train of narrativity).

The commercial success of *Mademoiselle Fifi* allowed Maupassant to have a chalet built in Etretat. Christened La Guillette (Little Guy) on the advice of his friend Hermine Lecomte du Noüy, the house served as a country residence for this increasingly affluent writer, who was thenceforth able to divide his time between the cliffs of his native Normandy and the glitter and excitement of life in the capital.

Maupassant's first novel, *Une Vie*, originally serialized in *Gil Blas*, was several years in the making, and his correspondence with his mother reveals that he had a great deal of trouble with the transitions. Incorporating tales he had published previously, Maupassant wove the narrative of a young Norman woman, Jeanne Le Pertuis des Vauds, who is in turn dominated by her father; her husband, Julien de la Mare; and her son, Paul (nicknamed Poulet). Her life is one of disillusionment: Julien betrays her, first with her maid and then with a neighbor; she learns at the bedside of her dying mother that the latter had been an adulteress; and her son, a good-for-nothing drifter who gets in touch with his mother only when he needs her financial support, fathers a child with a mistress who dies in childbirth. Even religion offers no solace, for the town's kindly old pastor is replaced by a fanatic young priest who finds relief for his own sexual frustrations by delivering thunderous sermons and exercising a cruel tyranny over his flock. In the novel's final scene, Jeanne, impoverished because of her son's excesses, has sold the family home and is moving to more modest lodgings. As she travels to her new house, which is far from her beloved sea, she holds her infant grandson on her lap. Maupassant gives her maid Rosalie the last word: "La vie, voyez-vous, ça n'est jamais si bon ni si mauvais qu'on croit" (Life, you see, is never as good or as bad as we think it is).

Although it was on the whole well received by the critics (apart from a few who objected to its bleak pessimism) and enjoyed an immense popular success, *Une Vie* is not regarded today as one of Maupassant's most felicitous novelistic efforts, and it is often compared unfavorably to *Madame Bovary*, with which it bears many affinities. Nevertheless, as his first sustained narrative, this novel offers many useful insights into Maupassant's developing attitudes. The reader senses his almost visceral love of his native province and of the sea, his equally visceral horror of maternity (as expressed by Julien), his fascination with the untamed beauty of Corsica (where Jeanne and Julien honeymoon), his anticlerical sentiments, his sympathy for the plight of a lonely woman (the fictional figure is said to have been inspired by his mother), and his pessimism with regard to the possibility of happiness in marriage. Today, the novel is taught rather frequently in women's studies courses, where it is valued for its perceived documentary realism.

If the perspective offered by *Une Vie* is decidedly somber, the tales that make up *Contes de la bécasse* (Stories of the Woodcock, 1883), his next collection, offered some relief from Maupassant's increasingly pessimistic Weltanschauung. Although the stories are introduced, in the tradition of Giovanni Boccaccio, as tales told in turn by members of an assembled group, in this case hunters (whence the title), this fiction is not sustained, and the stories differ widely in both narrative technique and subject. As with his first two collections, Maupassant simply assembled previously published stories, waiting until he had enough to make a volume before submitting them. There was no serious attempt at coherence, and his ends were purely mercenary.

However, during this period many of his stories centered on the Norman peasantry, and this focus is reflected in *Contes de la bécasse*. Some were inspired by man's passion for hunting; these are among the most playful ("Un Coq chanta" ["A Cock Crowed"] and "Farce normande" ["A Normandy Joke"]). Others adopt a lighthearted approach to serious subjects ("L'Aventure de Walter Schnaffs," which recounts the war of 1870 from the viewpoint of a cowardly Prussian soldier). On the whole, though, one discovers here Maupassant's deep understanding of the Norman temperament and his mastery of *le parler normand* (Norman speech), reproduced in the many dialogues of this collection. The sobering pieces in this collection drew their inspiration from the war ("La Folle" ["The Madwoman"]), from their author's fear of paternity ("Un Fils" ["A Son"]), of aging ("Menuet"), and of fear itself ("La Peur" ["Fear"]).

The years 1883 to 1885 were especially productive for Maupassant: in this brief period, four additional collections of stories appeared (*Clair de lune* [Moonlight, 1883]; *Miss Harriet* [1884]; *Les Sœurs Rondoli* [The Sisters Rondoli, 1884]; and *Yvette* [1884]), together with *Au soleil* (1884; translated as *African Wanderings*, 1903), his first travel journal. This period also saw the death of Turgenev, one of Maupassant's most ardent admirers, who had played an important role in promoting the Frenchman's work in his native Russia. Maupassant's extraordinary productivity during this time (he was contributing one to two stories weekly to newspapers, in addition to chronicles on various topics) is all the more remarkable when one considers that he was suffering from debilitating migraines that prevented him from working for hours, sometimes days, at a time. The progressive phases of his illness have been described by the Belgian François Tassart (among others), whom he hired as his valet de chambre in November 1883 and who was to remain with him until he was interned in Dr. Emile Blanche's sanitarium in 1892. (In fact, Tassart continued to visit him daily during his internment.) Tassart's two biographies of Maupassant (*Souvenirs sur Guy de Maupassant par François, son valet de chambre* [Memories of Guy de Maupassant by François, His Manservant, 1911] and *Nouveaux souvenirs intimes sur Guy de Maupassant* [New Intimate Memories of Guy de Maupassant, 1962]), while not entirely credible, offer many insights into the psyche of this prolific writer, whom Hippolyte Taine nicknamed "le taureau triste" (the sad bull).

Several of the stories in *Clair de lune* treat the subject of madness, for Maupassant's first serious doubts about his own sanity date from this period. "Conte de Noël" (Christmas Story) is a tale of possession and exorcism narrated by a country physician; "Mademoiselle Cocotte" traces the origin of a coachman's insanity, while the narrator of "Apparition" relates a terrifying encounter with the ghost of a friend's deceased wife. One of the tales, "La Légende du Mont Saint Michel," which recounts the legendary struggle between Saint Michael and Satan, appears to provide the symbolism for several of the others. In these stories man is presented as a participant in a battle against diabolical forces, whether they take the form of madness, or of a vicious monster (the hunter of "Le Loup" ["The White Wolf"] is likened to "un moine hanté du diable" [a monk haunted by the devil]), or of woman (for l'abbé Marignan of "Clair de lune," woman is "le tentateur qui avait entraîné le premier homme et qui continuait toujours son œuvre de damnation" [the tempter who led astray the first man and who would always continue her work of damnation]). The view of woman as temptress is balanced in *Clair de lune* by that of woman as victim: "L'Enfant" and "Le Pardon" ("Forgiveness") in particular bear witness to a profound sympathy with the plight of women.

This sympathy is further manifested in the title tale of the next collection, *Miss Harriet.* The heroine, a middle-aged English spinster who is spending the summer at a Norman inn, falls victim to the unintentionally flirtatious conduct of Léon Chenal, the story's narrator, a bored French artist who finds himself lodged in the same inn and becomes fascinated by her exalted love of nature and her deeply religious sensibility. Misunderstood by the innkeeper, who refers to her as "la démoniaque," hated by the townspeople, Miss Harriet is sensitive to the kindness shown her by Chenal, and, seeing his paintings of the region, she becomes convinced that he is a kindred spirit. Her brief, unrequited love for him drives her to despair, and she drowns herself in the inn's well.

This story is important for two reasons. In the first place, it serves as an example of one of Maupassant's many memorable portraits of the English. His youth in Etretat, a favorite vacation spot for visitors from across the Channel, provided him with ample opportunities to observe their idiosyncrasies and linguistic tics. He would continue his sketch—sometimes caricaturally, prompting James to complain about his "growl of anglophobia"—in "Découverte" ("Discovery," 1884), "Nos Anglais" ("Our Friends the English," 1885), and "L'Epave" ("The Wreck," 1886). Secondly, "Miss Harriet" illustrates his compassion for those who, by chance or design, lead celibate lives, a theme he also treated elsewhere ("Regret," "Clair de lune," and "Mademoiselle Perle"). There is some irony—perhaps poignancy would be a better word—in the fact that Maupassant was also a consummate cynic with regard to the possibility of finding "true love." Despite his legendary sexual prowess and countless mistresses, despite his fathering three children by the same woman (a spa employee named Joséphine Litzelmann), Maupassant never married and, with the exception of his mother, to whom he was deeply attached, never knew lasting love for a woman.

Among the stories in *Miss Harriet*, the best-known are "La Ficelle" ("The String," 1883), a Kafkaesque tale of innocence punished, and "Garçon, un bock!" ("Waiter, A Bock!"), a story often interpreted autobiographically, in which a downtrodden alcoholic explains that his despair originated when, as a child, he witnessed a fight between his parents. Perhaps the most revealing tale in the collection is "Idylle" (1884), which recounts the chance meeting, in a train carriage, between a hungry Italian laborer and a young wet nurse who has not given the breast in two days and suffers from an overabundance of milk. The undisguised sensuality of the nursing episode that ensues lends itself to a psychoanalytical interpretation.

Another story in this collection, "La Mère Sauvage" ("Mother Savage"), which concerns a Norman woman's revenge on the Prussians, provided the pretext for a secret admirer to write Maupassant a letter. Intrigued by her elegant style and weary of the high-society women he was forced to frequent, Maupassant welcomed this diversion, and he responded eagerly; there followed a correspondence of some months, which lasted until the death of the young woman. Her name—Maupassant was eventually able to pierce her anonymity, although it is doubtful that he ever met her—was Marie Bashkirtseff.

Another woman, Countess Emmanuella Potocka, occupied an important place in his sentimental life at about the same time. During this period (early 1884) *Au soleil*, Maupassant's first volume of travel memoirs, based upon his voyage to Africa, appeared. Two more collections, *Les Sœurs Rondoli* and *Yvette*, were published that year. In both title tales, the point of view is that of a disillusioned man-about-town who takes his pleasure where he finds it, most often in the company of women of easy virtue. "Les Sœurs Rondoli" tells of the narrator's amorous encounter with a sulky but obliging Italian woman, and his discovery, the following year, that she has an equally obliging younger sister who, encouraged by their mother, is eager to please the foreign visitor while at the same time helping to alleviate the family's budgetary problems. In a more somber register, "Yvette" (a reworking of "Yveline Samoris," published in the *Gaulois* [20 December 1882]) evokes the plight of a young woman who comes to realize that her mother is a courtesan and her apparently distinguished friends nothing but customers posing as aristocrats. The portrait of Yvette is drawn with great sensitivity. As with prostitutes and spinsters, young girls are often presented as victims in Maupassant's work, suggesting once again that the traditional characterization of the author as a complete misogynist needs to be qualified. Nevertheless, it is perhaps symptomatic of his growing cynicism that whereas in "Yveline Samoris" the young heroine succeeds in committing suicide upon learning the truth about her mother's "profession," Yvette makes only a half-hearted attempt to kill herself and in the end resigns herself—almost happily—to the necessity of following in her mother's footsteps.

In earlier years Maupassant turned out stories as quickly as he could, relying on his earnings to meet day-to-day expenses of Parisian life, haggling with his editors for every last franc. At this juncture, however, he began to show a preference for longer narratives (both "Yvette" and "Les Sœurs Rondoli" are, properly speaking, *nouvelles* rather than contes), a testimony to his financial independence as well as to his desire to realize a loftier professional ambition, that of becoming a respected novelist. This is not to say that he did not continue to write shorter narratives: indeed, in March 1885 Havard published a collection thrown somewhat hastily together and entitled, without explanation, *Contes du jour et de la nuit* (Day and Night Stories).

This collection resembles the others in that it offers a blend of the merely amusing and the deeply disquieting (whence perhaps the title). It differs from them in that all of its stories are brief, and that a greater geographical diversity is represented in the settings, at least half of the stories taking place outside of Normandy, either in Paris, in the south of France, or in Corsica. This shift in locus corresponds to the movement of Maupassant's life: although he escaped from the capital whenever he was able, traveling north to Etretat, or south to Cannes or Nice, or even to Algeria, enjoying as often as possible the pleasures of boating, his career forced him to lead a salon existence in Paris most of the year. He had not yet become the chronicler of high society, however, and his most memorable portraits of Parisian life were still situated in the milieu of the civil servants. "La Parure" ("The Diamond Necklace,"

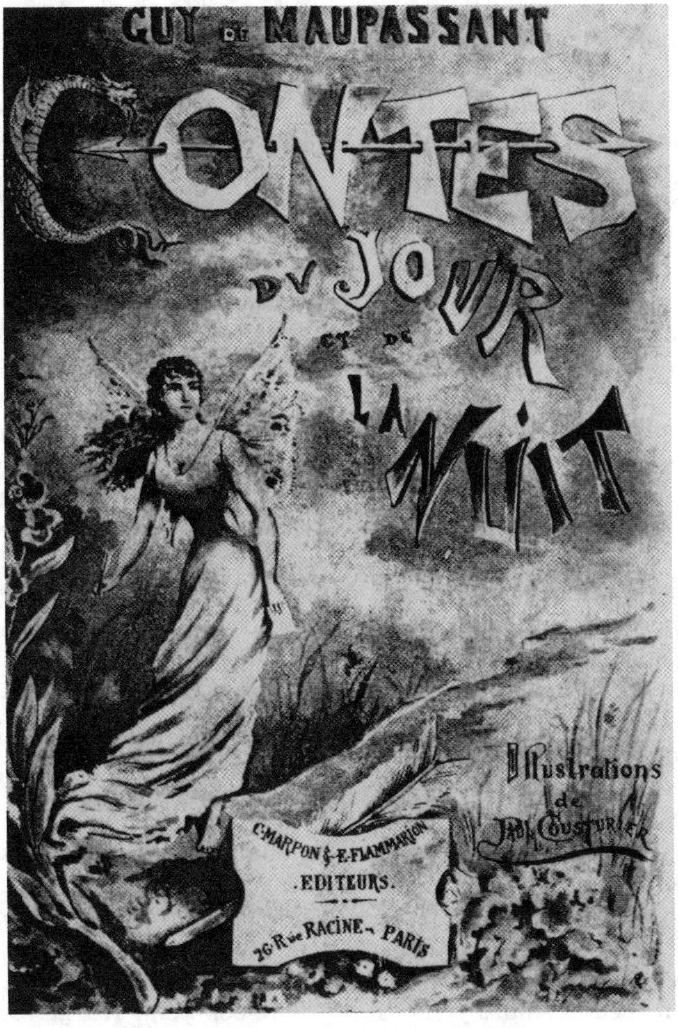

Cover for the first of two collections of Maupassant's short stories published in 1885

1884), one of Maupassant's best-known tales, famous for its whip-crack conclusion, is featured in this collection. The twist ending, later exploited by O. Henry, was in fact not typical of Maupassant's stories.

Maupassant was also gaining familiarity with the world of journalism, so it is not surprising that his second novel (which was to be his longest), announced by Havard in May 1885, covers the world of Paris journalism. As with *Une Vie*, the new novel, *Bel-Ami* (translated, 1891), had been serialized in *Gil Blas*. Drawing on current events (the rise of the large daily newspaper, the French incursion into Tunisia) for background, Maupassant painted a sordid picture of a city he had come to know and, in his Norman heart of hearts, despise. Gone are the loving descriptions of nature that characterize *Une Vie*; gone is the interest in provincial nobility. In what appears at first glance to be a classic Bildungsroman (although recent criticism has disputed this appellation), *Bel-Ami* recounts the adaptation of a creature to its milieu.

A handsome but destitute young army officer from the provinces, George Duroy is working as a government employee at the Gare du Nord when he chances upon an old army friend, Charles Forestier. The encounter is most fortuitous: Forestier finds him a job with the newspaper for which he works (cannily named the *Vie Française* [French Life]), and in just three years (the time span recorded by the novel), the uneducated, untalented, unscrupulous Duroy manages to rise through the ranks of the paper's hierarchy. An opportunist and a womanizer who accepts with pleasure the fitting nickname "Bel-Ami," bestowed on him by the daughter of one of his mistresses, Duroy owes his professional success to the women who fall prey to his charm.

He begins with Madame de Marelle, Madame Forestier's best friend, who introduces him to the newspaper's "inner circle" and slips coins into his pockets. From her he moves to Madame Forestier herself, an intelligent and independent woman who reluctantly agrees to marry him upon the death of her husband and who serves as his ghostwriter, as she had for Forestier. She too is associated with financial gain, not only because her talent allows him to remain on the staff of the *Vie Française*, but also because she inherits a large sum of money when one of her lovers dies. Her continued infidelity as much as his insatiable lust for power leads an increasingly cynical Duroy to seek reassurance of his virility in the arms of another.

His choice, Virginie Walter, the aging wife of the editor in chief who has never before been unfaithful to her husband, is foolishly sentimental, and Duroy finds her childish conduct irritating and embarrassing. Thus, although it proves to be both financially and professionally rewarding, the affair does nothing to restore Duroy's ailing ego. Abandoning her brutally, he plans and executes an artful seduction of her daughter, Suzanne. The novel's final scene features a symbolically deified Duroy at the altar of the Church of the Madeleine, exchanging wedding vows with Suzanne Walter and basking in his new power: he has just been named as André Walter's successor, editor in chief of the *Vie Française*. Lest the reader mistakenly assume that Duroy intends to be faithful to his young bride, Maupassant closes his novel with the description of a nostalgic Duroy reminiscing about Madame de Marelle.

Bel-Ami is a biting satire of Parisian society in general, and of the journalistic milieu in particular. The theme of Duroy's triumphant climb through the echelons of a fictitious—and highly disreputable—Paris daily newspaper allowed Maupassant to question the tremendous political power wielded by the press and to expose the abuse to which such power was susceptible. It further allowed him to criticize France's policy of colonial expansion, the taking of Tunisia being rather thinly disguised in the novel as "the Moroccan adventure." Finally, the financial wheeling and dealing of André Walter may be seen as an attack on the unscrupulous and increasingly powerful capitalists bred by a postindustrial society in which moral considerations were eclipsed by material ones. Money and women: nothing else counts in the world of *Bel-Ami*, a world that can be summed up by reference to a single metaphor, prostitution.

It is hardly surprising that the ambitious Duroy, who encounters many mirrors, real and symbolic, in his climb to the apex of his profession, feels the greatest affinity for a prostitute, sensing keenly that "ils étaient de même race, de même âme, et que son succès aurait des procédés audacieux du même ordre" (they were of the same race, shared the same soul, and that his success would have bold strategies of the same kind). In *Bel-Ami* the reduction of all activity to the venal bears testimony not only to Maupassant's contempt for the crassly commercial society in which he lived but also to his lack of esteem for the journalistic medium in which he was forced to publish.

Greeted with anger by those who felt personally targeted, *Bel-Ami* was nevertheless reviewed favorably by most critics. Moreover, despite Maupassant's fears that Victor Hugo's death would have a negative impact on sales, his novel was ultimately an immense commercial success. Maupassant had proven himself capable of *une œuvre de longue haleine* (a substantial work), for, although he constructed his second novel in much the same way as his first, incorporating stories and articles published previously, they are better integrated into the whole, the transitions are smoother, and the plot is better constructed and more coherent. If *Une Vie* records the descent of a female protagonist, *Bel-Ami* records the ascent of a male. With the exception of *Mont-Oriol* (1887; translated, 1891), which grants equal importance to male and female perspectives, all future novels would feature a masculine point of view.

Maupassant's health continued to deteriorate, and some disturbing new mental symptoms (a strange sensation of having a double, a nebulous sense of his own identity), together with continued physical suffering, led him to seek a cure at one of the popular thermal stations, Châtelguyon, in the Massif Central. Although the treatment was in the long run inefficacious, the experience did bear fruit in the writing of his next novel, *Mont-Oriol*. In the meantime, however, he continued to write stories, and three more collections appeared, *Monsieur Parent* (1885), *Toine* (1886), and *La Petite Roque* (1886). The first two, which appeared only a few weeks apart—*Monsieur Parent* put out by Ollendorff in December 1885, *Toine* by Marpon and Flammarion in January 1886 (Maupassant deliberately avoided submitting all his work to one publisher, so as to give himself a broadly based power over the Paris publishing industry)—are as disparate in their composition as the stories in *Contes du jour et de la nuit*.

Returning once again to the practice of naming his collection after the longest tale, Maupassant highlighted for the first collection the story of a doubtful paternity. In the second collection the title story concerns a Norman bon vivant who suffers a paralyzing stroke and is recruited by his wife for the job of hatching eggs, while the third collection begins with the story of a provincial mayor who rapes and murders a young girl. "Monsieur Parent" was in fact a revision of "Le Petit" ("The Little One," 1883). The subject of the illegitimate child had fascinated Maupassant from the earliest days of his career; he was to return to it repeatedly, with multiple variations on the same theme. Whether the product of a brief liaison ("Un Fils"), or the love child sent away to be raised by others ("L'Abandonné" ["The Abandoned One," 1884]), or the unsuspected son, raised by his mother ("Le Champ d'oliviers" ["The Olive Grove," 1890]), the child who is denied the influence of his father becomes an alien being, a terrifying mirror who serves as a reminder of the bestial coupling that produced him. The biological fathers of Maupassant's fictional universe are rarely imbued with paternal sentiments. Ironically, perhaps, the wronged husbands generally feel most strongly the bonds of paternity toward those they assume falsely to be their offspring. This is the case with Monsieur Parent, and Maupassant tells with great compassion the man's horrifying discovery that his beloved son is not his own, his anguish when the child goes to live with his mother, and the aimlessness of the life Parent leads after the separation.

With "Toine," Maupassant returned to the lighthearted tone of the Norman farce in what the critic Louis Forestier termed the fabliau tradition. However, as Forestier also remarked, beneath the comic surface one senses some of Maupassant's preoccupations: his fear of aging and of impotence (a theme he treated in another story in this collection, "Le Moyen de Roger" ["Roger's Method," 1885]), the anguish of frustrated paternity, and the inevitable unhappiness of married life. Both in *Toine* and in *Monsieur Parent*, by far the greatest number of stories feature women, be they prostitutes ("Le Lit 29" ["Bed No. 29," 1884], "L'Armoire" ["The Closet," 1884], "L'Ami Patience" ["Friend Patience," 1883]), adulterous wives ("La Chambre 11" ["Room No. 11," 1884], "L'Imprudence" [1885], "Monsieur Parent" [1885]), mothers ("La Mère aux monstres" ["The Mother of Monsters," 1883]), or defenseless young brides ("La Dot" ["The Dowry," 1884]).

At least two of the stories, "La Chevelure" ("A Woman's Hair," 1884) and "Un Fou" ("A Madman," 1885), are inspired by the fear of madness, a theme Maupassant was to treat with increasing intensity and frequency. In fact the number of stories that refer to madness in their titles ("Fou?" ["Mad?," 1883], "Un Fou?" ["A Madman?," 1884], "La Folle" ["The Madwoman," 1882], and "Un Fou") is in itself significant. "Un Fou," which is of particular interest, since it brings together many of Maupassant's favorite themes, describes the sadistic impulse of a high-court judge who, having sentenced countless criminals, becomes fascinated with the thin line that separates life from death. He succumbs to the temptation to kill, beginning with the mutilation of a defenseless goldfish, and "graduating" to the murder of a young boy. One finds here the post-mortem "exposure" of one who was believed to be virtuous (as in "Les Bijoux" ["The False Gems," 1883], *Une Vie*, "Le Testament" ["The Will," 1882] and *Pierre et Jean* [1888; translated as *The Two Brothers*, 1889]), a theme that may well have been inspired by Maupassant's fear of self-revelation through his fiction. Furthermore, the story describes the pleasure—distinctly erotic in nature—of killing, a theme that is also treated in the many hunting stories of Maupassant's corpus (for example, "Amour" ["Love," 1886], "Le Loup," "Farce normande," and "Un Coq chanta").

These two themes—that of the posthumous revelation and that of the link between sexuality and violence—are combined in the title tale of *La Petite Roque*. The protagonist of this story is a town mayor, Renardet, who, suffering from an imperious sexual hunger since the death of his wife, comes upon a young girl (la petite Roque—the little Roque child—of the title) bathing in a woodland pond and rapes her, "sans comprendre ce qu'il faisait" (without understanding what he was doing). Terrified by her screams, he closes his massive hands around her neck, "sans qu'il songeât à la tuer" (without meaning to kill her). Renardet, who must direct the investigation into the death of the child, writhes in the grip of fear and remorse, becoming prey to hallucina-

Cover for the first of two collections of Maupassant's short stories published in 1886

tions and eventually losing his mind. The tale ends when he leaps to his death after trying unsuccessfully to persuade the postman to return a letter of confession he has written to the examining magistrate in a moment of weakness.

This tale of a man driven to crime and then progressively dispossessed of his reason because of his irrepressible sexual instinct offers an interesting variation on a typically naturalistic subject, one that Zola treated nearly two decades earlier in *Thérèse Raquin* (1867; translated, 1881). But it is also possible that Maupassant's own obsessions—he was suffering terrifying hallucinations, a condition that resulted indirectly from his own insatiable carnal appetite—were finding expression in his fiction. Moreover, the interior/exterior opposition so frequently found in Maupassant's work is illustrated here, for Renardet's "exterior" (specifically, his exalted social position) masks his guilt, placing him beyond suspicion until his bizarre conduct leads to his downfall. Whatever the case, the reputedly objective observer was clearly developing a taste for psychological analysis.

"La Petite Roque," first published serially in *Gil Blas* (18-23 December 1885), appeared in the volume of the same name in May 1886. There was no real unity in this collection of previously published stories, which Maupassant assembled with customary negligence when he was not traveling or working on his new novel, *Mont-Oriol*.

Begun in July 1885, this third novel was more or less finished by April 1886 and was published serially by *Gil Blas* at the end of the year. It appeared in book form in January 1887. The writing of the novel, much of which took place in a rented villa, Le Bosquet (The Grove), in Antibes, was punctuated by a trip to southern Italy and by Mediterranean excursions on his newly acquired yacht, purchased with royalties from his second novel and appropriately christened *Bel-*

Ami. A novel of manners like *Une Vie* and *Bel-Ami, Mont-Oriol* is the only one of Maupassant's novels to derive its unity—and its title—from geography. There is no single character through which events are filtered, as is the case in all of Maupassant's other novels. Although the name of the thermal station is fictitious, the setting is not: Maupassant drew his inspiration from Châtelguyon, in Auvergne, the spa he had visited for a cure during the summer of 1883 and to which he returned again in July 1885 and July 1886.

Grounded in historical reality, the novel chronicles the discovery of mineralized springs in a small Auvergne town and the subsequent establishment of a thermal station by the wealthy Jewish businessman William Andermatt, who engages in intense and not altogether scrupulous negotiations with the wily, suspicious peasants in order to persuade them to sell him their land. Maupassant weaves a sentimental tale of love and betrayal against this backdrop of tough-minded financial maneuvering. Andermatt and his wife, Christiane, are staying at the neighboring spa of Enval when a boulder on the old peasant Oriol's property is dynamited, revealing a spring that inspires Andermatt to create a competing spa.

Concurrently, Christiane, who has come to the thermal establishment in search of a cure for infertility, meets Paul Brétigny, her brother's playboy friend—a character very much in the mold of Maupassant himself—who falls in love with her, seduces her, then leaves her for another when he learns that their affair has resulted in a pregnancy, "[étant] de la race des amants et non point de la race des pères" ([belonging] to the race of lovers and not at all to that of fathers). The normally shrewd Andermatt, naive where his personal life is involved, assumes the child is his own. The spa, ironically, has provided a setting for Christiane's "cure" in a way Andermatt would never have suspected.

Maupassant's correspondence reveals that he had a great deal of trouble with the sentimental passages, and although many of his critics welcomed the new, less cruelly objective narration, the author did not think highly of his creation. The critic Edward Sullivan agreed, finding *Mont-Oriol* the weakest of Maupassant's novels and lamenting the absence of irony and the inadequate integration between the financial and the sentimental plots. Nevertheless, the novel is not without interest for the modern reader. It has considerable documentary value because it exposes with remarkable accuracy the mechanism of a typical business venture of the time and because it paints a fairly precise—although cynical—picture of the state of the medical profession in the early 1880s. The descriptions of treatments that resemble torture and of vicious competition among the spa physicians, who are presented as incompetent charlatans interested only in financial gain, may seem exaggerated to the modern reader, but in fact they rang true to Maupassant's contemporaries. Despite remarkable advances in medical knowledge and technology in the second half of the century, which propelled physicians to the most respected levels of society, the nineteenth-century Frenchman, still surrounded by quacks and subjected to inefficacious and painful treatments, was understandably skeptical where medical science was concerned. With good reason the nineteenth century came to be known as the "age of heroic therapy."

In *Mont-Oriol,* Maupassant also gave expression to his preoccupation with the illegitimate child, this time from the viewpoint of the mother; related themes of the disgust inspired by the pregnant woman, the horror of paternity, and the inevitable disappointments of conjugal love were also treated, as was the sexual awakening of a young woman, here associated (as in *Une Vie*) with the magic of an aquatic setting. If, as several critics have noted, many of the characters are without substance, being drawn according to stereotypes of the day (the Jewish financier, the Don Juan, the dissipated former aristocrat, the avaricious peasant), his heavily caricaturized portraits of the spa physicians allowed Maupassant to give vent to his frustrations regarding his own disease, against which even the most respected physicians and the most elegant watering holes seemed powerless.

Indeed, Maupassant's deteriorating health had become by this time impossible to ignore, and both stories and novels betrayed his attempts to deal with his real-life drama. The definitive version of his most famous fantastic tale, "Le Horla" ("The Horla"), published for the first time in May 1887, just five months after the publication of *Mont-Oriol,* recounts the plight of a passive victim, an unwilling host to an invisible parasite that is slowly sapping his power and his life. It is a role with which Maupassant identified most keenly, and one can trace the development of his fear—and his authorial skill—by examining the three stages in the writing of this well-known story.

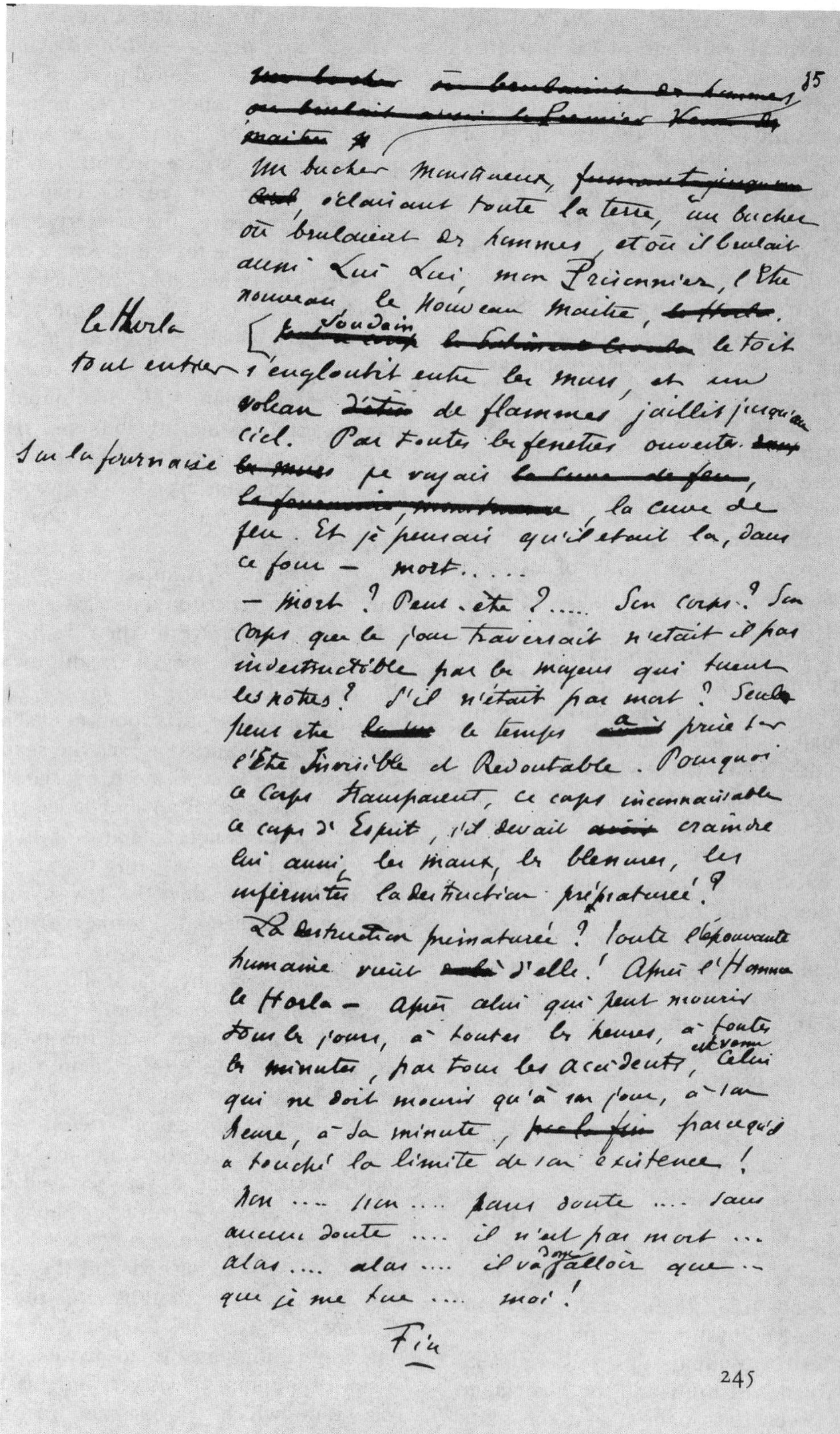

15

un bucher monstrueux, éclairant toute la terre, un bucher où brulaient des hommes, et où il brulait aussi Lui Lui, mon Prisonnier, l'Être nouveau le Nouveau maitre,

le Horla

Soudain le toit tout entier s'engloutit entre les murs, et un volcan de flammes jaillit jusqu'au ciel. Par toutes les fenêtres ouvertes sur la fournaise je voyais la cuve de feu. Et je pensais qu'il était là, dans ce four — mort....

— Mort? Peut-être?.... Son corps? Son corps que le jour traversait n'était-il pas indestructible par les moyens qui tuent les nôtres? S'il n'était pas mort? Seul peut-être le temps prise sur l'Être Invisible et Redoutable. Pourquoi ce corps transparent, ce corps inconnaissable ce corps d'Esprit, s'il devait craindre lui aussi, les maux, les blessures, les infirmités la destruction prématurée?

La destruction prématurée? Toute l'épouvante humaine vient d'elle! Après l'Homme le Horla — Après celui qui peut mourir tous les jours, à toutes les heures, à toutes les minutes, par tous les accidents, est venu Celui qui ne doit mourir qu'à son jour, à son heure, à sa minute, parce qu'il a touché la limite de son existence!

Non.... non.... sans doute.... sans aucun doute.... il n'est pas mort... alors.... alors.... il va donc falloir que... que je me tue.... moi!

Fin

245

Last page of the manuscript for the 1887 version of "Le Horla" (Bibliothèque Nationale)

In the original tale, "Lettre d'un fou" ("Letter from a Madman," 1885), a somewhat complacent philosopher-narrator commits himself to a mental hospital when an experiment involving "exciting" the senses results in a temporary inability to see his reflection in a looking glass. To the empty-mirror scene of this preliminary sketch, the author added in the first version of "Le Horla" (published in October 1886) the horror of being visited during the night by an invisible being that sucks his life from his lips. Certain "objective" phenomena appear to establish the reality of the mysterious being, who has preyed upon an entire population in Brazil, and the narrator speculates that perhaps man's successor on Earth has arrived. The tale is framed by comments from his physician, who is himself uncertain as to whether or not his patient is insane, leaving the reader in that doubt which the critic Tzvetan Todorov finds to be the sine qua non of the fantastic genre.

The definitive version of "Le Horla," nearly three times as long as the 1886 version, is presented as the diary of a madman; the same incidents are repeated, but in more detail, and many "minor" incidents round out the tale. Here, the fantastic has been "internalized" so to speak; there is virtually no doubt about the diarist's madness, which is attested not only by the events themselves, but by the highly emotional and agitated style of the narration. Moreover, no physician is present to guide the reader in his interpretation of the text, and the story ends with the narrator's attempt to kill the invisible "monster" by setting fire to his house, which he immediately judges to be futile: "Non . . . non . . . sans aucun doute, sans aucun doute . . . il n'est pas mort . . . Alors . . . alors . . . il va donc falloir que je me tue, moi!" (No . . . no . . . undoubtedly, undoubtedly . . . he's not dead . . . so . . . so . . . I'm going to have to kill myself!).

Maupassant predicted correctly that his own sanity would be questioned when this story appeared, but in point of fact, he was in full possession of his faculties during the writing of what has been considered a masterpiece of the fantastic genre. Although this story has a subtext that clearly reveals some of its author's most troubling obsessions, the role played by literary fashion must not be overlooked. The fantastic, introduced into France early in the century, when E. T. A. Hoffmann's works were translated into French, had been reinvigorated by Charles Baudelaire's translation of Edgar Allan Poe's work at midcentury. In Maupassant's rendition of the genre that Todorov dubbed "la mauvaise conscience de ce XIXe siècle positiviste" (the guilty conscience of the positivistic nineteenth century), late-nineteenth-century scientific thought must also be given its due. In particular, the idea of a successor to man who would prey upon him owes a great deal to Charles Darwin's theory of evolution by natural selection. Furthermore, in the 1887 version the narrator's niece is placed under hypnosis, an addition clearly inspired by Jean-Martin Charcot's experiments at La Salpêtrière.

In a more general way, the pathology of mental illness fascinated the nineteenth-century Frenchman, and Maupassant himself was irresistibly drawn to this subject. "Les fous m'attirent" (I am attracted to the insane), proclaims the narrator of "Madame Hermet," a story published just a few months before the definitive version of "Le Horla." The resounding praise of madness that follows ("Eux seuls peuvent être heureux sur la terre, car, pour eux, la Réalité n'existe plus" [They alone can be happy on Earth, because, for them, Reality no longer exists]) is belied by the story itself, which recounts the tormented suffering brought on by remorse. The subject of mental pathologies is treated in this negative register throughout Maupassant's work, whether he focuses on magnetism, hallucinations, phobias, or neuroses. Although it may appear somewhat speculative to draw a parallel between Maupassant's degenerating physical health and his preoccupation with insanity, the fact that the latter is most often figured as a "creature from beyond" (le hors-là) who literally eats away at the fiber of the human being does suggest a connection between the two phenomena. This was, after all, the period of the bacteriological revolution, when the discovery of microscopic organisms that could wreak havoc on the body gave new meaning to the concept of the invisible enemy.

Less than a month after "Le Horla" appeared, Maupassant was hard at work on his fourth novel, *Pierre et Jean*. Written during the summer of 1887 (a summer that also saw his first balloon ride and the birth of his third child to Joséphine Litzelmann), Maupassant's shortest novel (considered by most critics to be his best) was published in January 1888, the first of three major publications that year, the other two being a travel journal, *Sur l'eau* (translated as *Afloat*, 1889), and a volume of stories, *Le Rosier de Madame Husson* ("Madame Husson's May King").

Like "Le Horla," *Pierre et Jean* records a dispossession. The plot is deceptively simple: two brothers, Pierre and Jean Roland, having returned to the family home following their professional studies (Pierre, the elder, is a physician, whereas Jean has studied law), are about to embark upon their respective careers when Léon Maréchal, an old friend of the family, dies, naming Jean sole heir to his estate. Pierre broods at first about this inequity, then slowly comes to the realization that Jean is Maréchal's son. His moral indignation at the thought that his mother could have engaged in an extramarital affair is exacerbated by his jealousy of Jean, who has managed to awaken the interest of a pretty young widow, Madame Rosémilly, and who, thanks to his inheritance, is able to set himself up handsomely in a rented apartment.

The subject of this psychological novel—Maupassant's first—is the intense mental suffering of Pierre Roland, a suffering relieved only by communion with the maternal sea. Set in Le Havre, the novel makes extensive use of the sea as backdrop and as symbol, and the possibilities of the homophonic pair *mer/mère* (sea/mother) are richly exploited. The novel also records the progressive alienation of the legitimate son, who is eventually excluded from the family circle. Thus, although Maupassant's continuing preoccupation with the problem of illegitimacy is once again treated here, the perspective is quite different.

It has been said that Maupassant's own life inspired *Pierre et Jean,* that his skepticism with regard to feminine virtue led him to wonder whether his mother had taken lovers when it became obvious that her marriage to Gustave was doomed. Rumors had flown at one stage that Flaubert was the biological father of Maupassant, and although Maupassant scoffed at such an idea (indeed, it has been largely discredited), he may well have pondered the possibility that either he or his brother was the product of an extramarital affair. Whatever the case, the interest of this novel lies less in its treatment of the illegitimate son than in the overwhelming tyranny of obsession to which Pierre falls victim. Indeed, the Oedipal nature of the relationships between mother and both sons, together with a curious "doubling" of characters (for example, between Madame Roland and Madame Rosémilly), strongly suggests the usefulness of a psychoanalytical reading.

Because Ollendorff, Maupassant's publisher, judged *Pierre et Jean* too brief to be published in a volume by itself, Maupassant augmented it with a theoretical essay on the novel ("Le Roman" ["The Novel"]), which is known, somewhat misleadingly, as the preface to *Pierre et Jean.* Although the stereotype of Maupassant producing stories as easily as an apple tree produces fruit (an appropriate analogy, no doubt, for a Norman writer) carries with it the implication that he did not meditate on the exigencies of his art, the opposite is true, as his chronicles on Zola, Flaubert, and others amply demonstrate. Maupassant's essay begins with an attack on critics who approach the novel with preconceived notions rather than judging each work on its own terms. In Maupassant's view, the genre can encompass many forms. Readily confessing his immense debt to Bouilhet and Flaubert, he then outlines his objective technique.

In his view novice writers should describe the uniqueness of humble objects, for they can achieve originality through their personal vision. They should strive for objectivity even while realizing that their own experiences will necessarily color their descriptions and portrayal of character. Finally, they should give the illusion of reality without resorting to a pretentious or archaic style: "La langue française ... est une eau pure que les écrivains maniérés n'ont jamais pu et ne pourront jamais troubler" (The French language ... is a pure spring that mannered writers given to affectation have never been able and will never be able to trouble). Some critics have seen in this last imperative an attack on the Goncourts, who were known for their "style artiste" (artistic style) as well as for their virulent attacks on Maupassant in their *Journal.* But the essay also contains a more subtle criticism of Zola's naturalism, with its claim of absolute objectivity, and suggests that Maupassant wished to disassociate himself once and for all from the naturalist movement. With *Pierre et Jean* one can take the measure of his progress.

Maupassant's fourth novel was on the whole very well received by his contemporaries, and it remains a critical favorite today, its tightly constructed plot being seen as a vast improvement on previous efforts, where he appears to proceed by an accumulation of incidents. *Pierre et Jean* also met with great popular success: sales were large enough to allow the author to exchange his yacht for a much larger sailing vessel, which he promptly christened *Bel-Ami II,* and while sailing the Mediterranean on his new "floating palace," he composed *Sur l'eau.*

Frontispiece for the first edition of Maupassant's 1888 collection of short stories

Although it contains some descriptions of the cities and towns at which he dropped anchor, *Sur l'eau* is perhaps not a travel journal in the traditional sense, for by far the greatest portion of the work is given to reflections on various subjects, from the intoxicating pleasure of solitude to the slavery of marriage. In his prefatory comments Maupassant wrote, "En somme, j'ai vu de l'eau, du soleil, des nuages et des roches—je ne puis raconter autre chose—et j'ai pensé simplement, comme on pense quand le flot vous berce, vous engourdit et vous promène" (In summary, I saw water, sun, clouds and rocks—I can't tell about anything else—and I thought simple thoughts, the sort one thinks when one is rocked, made drowsy and transported by the movement of the water).

Maupassant claimed to have set down in this work his most intimate thoughts, a claim that some critics find suspect in view of the fact that most of the subjects had already been treated in chronicles. Whatever the case, there can be little doubt that the aquatic setting provided him with the distance and solitude necessary to assemble a work that Ernest Boyd, one of his biographers, described as a "prolonged, pathetic plaint of boredom, disillusionment, weariness, and pain."

Toward the end of 1888, *Le Rosier de Madame Husson* was published by Quantin. Forestier has remarked on the unusual homogeneity that marks this volume of short stories, both in subject (most of the stories focus on women, the couple, and love) and tone (most adopt a comical perspective). It is perhaps no accident that of the fourteen stories that make up this collection, eight were first published prior to 1885. Indeed, Maupassant, who was giving his attention to longer narratives, had just about emptied his current bag of stories and had to resort to using some published as far back as 1883 in order to complete this volume. However, even the later stories are characterized by a tone of amused detachment, and subjects that could well have been treated with more solemnity (for example, the corrupting power of money, which is the major theme of the title story, originally published in 1887) were rendered here with the good-natured humor of the confirmed cynic.

In his personal life, meanwhile, there was much distress. Hervé's mental condition was increasingly unstable, causing Maupassant considerable anxiety, and his own suffering was unremitting. This did not stop him from beginning work on a new novel, *Fort comme la mort* (1889; translated as *Strong as Death*, 1899), and traveling again to Africa, a trip that was to bear fruit in the writing of "Allouma," the lead story in one of the last collections that was to be published during his lifetime, *La Main gauche* (The Left Hand, 1889). The title for this volume evokes the expression "mariage de la main gauche" (left-hand marriage), which refers to common-law marriages, and, indeed, all but one of the stories feature extramarital liaisons.

Although a glance at the stories included in this volume reveals that the Norman vein has not been depleted ("Hautot père et fils" ["Hautot Senior and Hautot Junior," 1889], "Le Lapin" ["The Rabbit," 1887], and "Boitelle" [1889] are all set in Normandy), the mores of Parisian high society provide continuing inspiration ("Les Epingles" ["The Pins," 1888], "Le Rendez-vous" [1889]). However, perhaps the most interesting stories of this collection are the two set in Africa, "Allouma" (1889) and "Un Soir" ("One Evening," 1889), for both contain lengthy meditations on women.

The narrator of the first is captivated by the animal sensuality of the mysterious African woman Allouma, whose eyes, "allumés par le désir de séduire, par ce besoin de vaincre l'homme" (kindled by the desire to seduce, the need to conquer man), inflame passion in her beholder while revealing nothing of her soul. As the incarnation of the incomprehensible, she becomes a symbol of woman—so often the mysterious other in Maupassant's work—and of the indigenous population of her country, which cannot be tamed or understood by the "conquering" French colonists: "Jamais peut-être un peuple conquis par la force n'a su échapper aussi complètement à la domination réelle" (Never, perhaps, has a people conquered by force managed to escape real domination as thoroughly as this).

That Maupassant used the figure of a woman to express his anticolonial sentiments is highly significant. Moreover, for all of its apparent differences, the other story set in Africa, "Un Soir," also recounts the anguish of suspicion and the frustrating impenetrability of women, and, once again, reference is made to the eyes. Upon suspecting his mistress of infidelity, the protagonist attempts to discern the truth in her glance: "Ses yeux clairs et limpides—ah! les yeux des femmes!—semblaient pleins de vérité, mais je sentis vaguement, douloureusement, qu'ils étaient pleins de mensonge" (Her clear and limpid eyes—oh! the eyes of women!—seemed full of truth, but I sensed vaguely, painfully, that they were full of lies). The revenge he exacts upon a defenseless octopus forms the substance of this strange narrative.

Whereas in the early work, women are often portrayed either as victims or as "possessions" of men, the general shift in subject from peasant women and prostitutes to high-society women is accompanied by an increasing tendency to portray women as tormentors and men as victims. Maupassant's last two novels, *Fort comme la mort* and *Notre cœur* (1890; translated as *The Human Heart*, 1890), differ from previous works not only in the milieu they describe—that of the indolent rich—but also in the increasingly active role played by women, who, innocently or knowingly perfidious, cause untold suffering in their male admirers.

Maupassant began work on *Fort comme la mort* in the spring of 1888; a study of the manuscript reveals extensive corrections, suggesting that he had still not mastered his new, "sentimental" style. The rigorously indifferent persona he projected in the early works was clearly more "natural" to him; what is more, his illness impeded his progress, and he was unable to meet even his self-imposed deadlines. Despite these difficulties, he managed to complete the novel in about eight months. *Fort comme la mort* appeared in serialized form in the *Revue Illustrée* between February and May 1889 and was published in book form by Ollendorff shortly thereafter. Although it is not highly regarded today, Maupassant's fifth novel was hailed at the time of its appearance as the first work that exposed a chink in the armor of its author's celebrated indifference.

The principal theme, the pain of aging, is treated with compassion and sensitivity. The main character, Olivier Bertin, is a salon artist whose specialty is portraiture. The novel describes his love affair with one of his subjects, the Parisian socialite Any de Guilleroy, their mutual pain at the ravages of aging, which includes for Bertin a frustrating artistic sterility, and Bertin's gradual realization that he has fallen in love with Any's daughter, Annette, who appears to him like a younger version of her mother. The anguish of this unrequited antumnal love is described with particular poignancy, as is that of Bertin's waning talent, and critics have been quick to point to the well-documented decline in Maupassant's creative imagination as a source for this novel. Sullivan goes so far as to suggest that the novel itself, by its very weaknesses and by a "confusion of method," bears witness to this decline.

Maupassant's early novels are rigorously objective. With *Pierre et Jean,* his first psychological novel, he retained the objective method to the extent possible, making ample use of gesture, dialogue, and interior monologue to expose his characters' thoughts, and religiously avoiding overt identification with one or another of his characters. In his last two novels, however—both of which feature the creative artist in a milieu that is in a sense foreign to him, Parisian high society—the distance between Maupassant and his characters has been bridged, and it takes little imagination to recognize many characteristics of the author in Olivier Bertin or André Mariolle (protagonist of *Notre cœur*).

It is as if the task of writing a psychological novel focused on the Parisian aristocracy (reputedly inspired by Paul Bourget) could not be carried out without adopting an "alien" perspective, that of the artist. Whereas Maupassant felt at ease in the worlds he had described previously—those of the peasants, the petty functionaries, the clientele of the spa—the aristocratic milieu remained foreign to him, despite the many hours he spent in high society. Unfortunately, in his attempt to combine the psychological approach with the objective in an analysis of this milieu, Maupassant was not entirely successful, although both novels have much to recommend them.

By choosing an artist as protagonist, Maupassant was following in the footsteps of many nineteenth-century French authors, among them Balzac, Edmond and Jules de Goncourt, Huysmans, and Zola. More significant, however, is his decision to highlight the period of his hero's decline, for in so doing he was able to express his anxieties regarding the value of his art and the impending demise of his talent. Moreover, by making his artist a bachelor, he was able to portray convincingly the unhappiness of the older man, who, having shunned marriage in a spirit of fierce independence, finds that his solitude weighs heavily upon him in his declining years.

The irony is that Bertin has not managed to avoid the ultimately destructive company of women. And despite the rather sympathetic feminine portraits found in *Fort comme la mort* (indeed, the descriptions of Any's suffering—although tinged with irony—are poignant), one cannot ignore the impression that Bertin's artistic sterility, while attributed primarily to age, also results at least in part from the negative influence of the opposite sex. If he originally owed his success as a portrait artist entirely to his female subjects, who inspired him by their beauty, the torture inflicted upon him by Any and Annette, however innocent, leads first to the death of his creative powers, then to his biological death.

This theme is further developed in *Notre cœur,* the last of Maupassant's completed novels. Only one collection of stories, *L'Inutile Beauté* (Useless Beauty, 1890), separates the two novels, and the title story also features the destruction of the male ego by a high-society woman. The heroine of *Notre cœur,* Michèle de Burne, brings to perfection the femme-fatale type in Maupassant's fictional universe. Cold, artificial, and incapable of real love, she nevertheless inspires love in others, and she feeds hungrily upon the attention of her suitors.

The novel details the enslavement of one such suitor, the hapless André Mariolle, a talented young man with a tendency to dilettantism, who definitively abandons all artistic aspirations when he falls in love with Madame de Burne. Although she eventually yields to his amorous demands, her unsatisfying love for him ("J'aime sèchement, mais j'aime" [I love without passion, but I love], she tells him) is dwarfed by her self-love, and he retreats in pain to the country, where he finds a young servant girl, Elisabeth, who is able to soothe his wounded ego with the simplicity of her love. In the end he returns to his Paris socialite, but he takes Elisabeth along for comfort.

Michèle de Burne reigns over a salon attended by a novelist (Lamarthe), a musician (Massival), a philosopher (Maltry), and (on one occasion) a sculptor (Prédolé). Only Prédolé proves resistant to her charms: all of the others have succumbed to the tyranny of her beauty, have allowed themselves to be "possessed" by her, and have suffered the anguish of unrequited love. Her effect upon them has been decisive: Massival

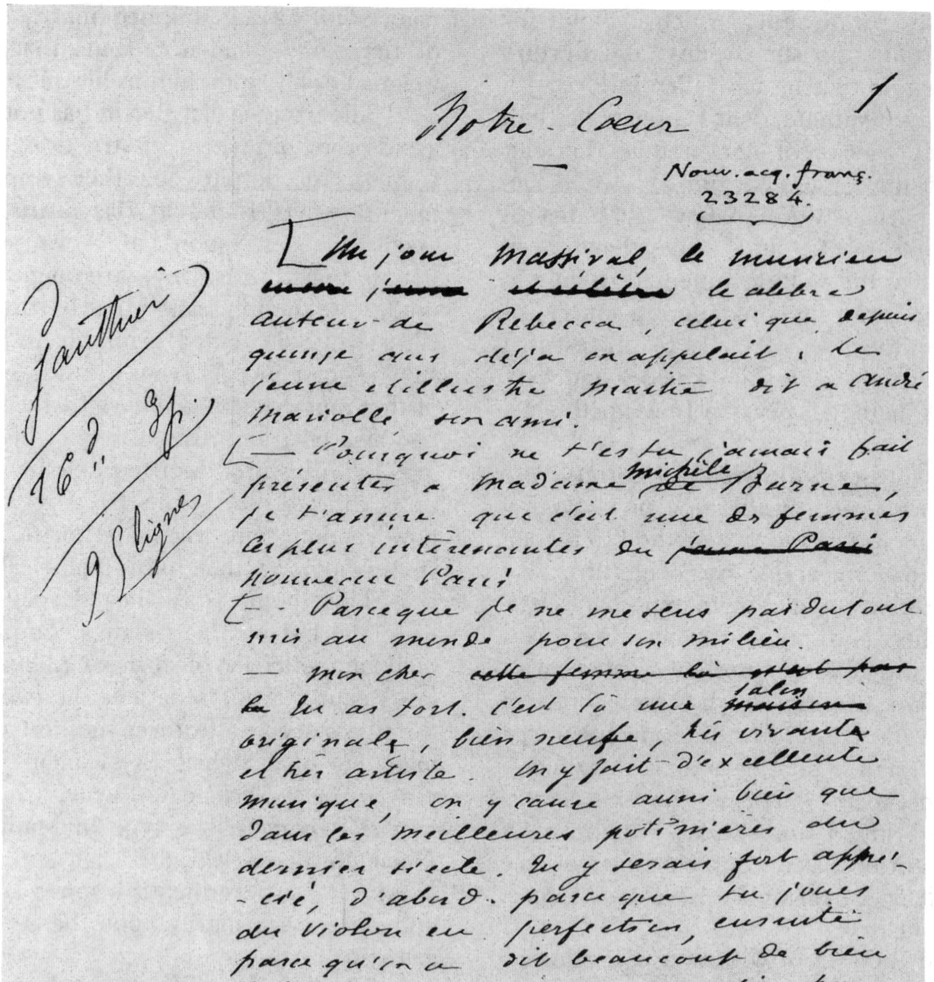

Notre-Cœur 1

Nouv. acq. franç. 23284.

Gauthier 16d. Ep. 9 lignes

Un jour Massival, le musicien le célèbre auteur de Rebecca, celui que depuis quinze ans déjà on appelait : le jeune illustre maître dit à André Mariolle son ami.
— Pourquoi ne t'es-tu jamais fait présenter à Madame Michèle de Burne, je t'assure que c'est une des femmes les plus intéressantes du nouveau Paris
— Parce que je ne me sens pas du tout né pour son milieu.
— Mon cher tu as tort. C'est là un salon original, bien neuf, très vivant et très artiste. On y fait d'excellente musique, on y cause aussi bien que dans les meilleures potinières du dernier siècle. Tu y serais fort apprécié, d'abord parce que tu joues du violon en perfection, ensuite parce qu'on a dit beaucoup de bien de toi dans la maison ; enfin parce que tu passes pour n'être pas banal et ne point prodiguer les visites.
Flatté mais résistant encore, supposant d'ailleurs que cette démarche pressante n'était point ignorée de la jeune femme, Mariolle fit un « Peuh ! je n'y tiens guère » où le dédain voulu se mêlait au consentement acquis déjà.
Massival reprit
— Veux-tu que je te présente un de ces jours. Tu la connais d'ailleurs par nous tous qui sommes de son intimité, car nous parlons d'elle

273

First page of the manuscript for Maupassant's last novel (Bibliothèque Nationale) "avait subi cette espèce d'arrêt qui semble frapper la plupart des artistes contemporains comme une paralysie précoce" (had suffered the kind of creative blockage that seems to strike most contemporary artists like a premature paralysis).

Lamarthe regains his objectivity and uses his talent as a form of revenge against this cold socialite and her ilk, devoting his novels to the lucid, cynical description of "cette race nouvelle de femmes" (this new breed of women) of which Michèle de Burne is the archetype. For his part, Mariolle has exchanged all aesthetic ambitions for the unique goal of winning her heart: "Elle a tout remplacé pour moi, car je n'aspire plus à rien, je n'ai plus besoin, envie ni souci de rien" (She has replaced everything for me, for I no longer aspire to anything, need anything, want or care about anything). The novel records Mariolle's wretched slavery to her and to the superficial world of which she is a symbol.

Some critics have noted that Mariolle and Lamarthe represent two aspects of Maupassant, the man and the novelist, and that Prédolé is the ideal for which he strove in vain, the artist "[qui] n'aime qu'une chose, son art, ne pense qu'à cela, ne vit que pour cela . . . [et] ne s'inquiète guère des femmes" ([who] loves only one thing, his art, thinks only of that, lives only for that . . . [and] hardly worries about women). While this is certainly true, it is significant that Maupassant chose to emphasize the plight of Mariolle—of all his characters, the one most completely destroyed, dispossessed of the creative impulse, by his contact with a woman. "Il n'y avait plus rien dans cet homme, rien qu'Elle. Il était à elle plus qu'elle-même. Et elle était contente" (There was no longer anything in this man, anything but Her. He belonged to her more than she belonged to herself. And she was happy).

Indeed, Maupassant tells the reader that Mariolle belongs to Michèle more than a burning house belongs to the fire, and this heroine is associated not with the aquatic element, as is the case with Maupassant's early heroines, but with fire. Her role as a heartless *allumeuse* (tease, but in the sense of one who inflames desire in others) is underlined not only by the anglophonic resonances of her name, Burne (Maupassant knew English and had traveled to England in 1886), but by other references to fire in the novel. Consumed by his love for this woman, Mariolle no longer exists except in relationship to her. With *Notre cœur*, the sun was setting upon Maupassant's creative life, and the intense despair he felt is reflected in the hopelessness of the situation depicted in his last completed novel.

While Maupassant was putting the finishing touches on *Notre cœur*, he composed "L'Inutile Beauté." The "useless beauty" of the story's title is a countess who, after bearing seven children in eleven years for her possessive husband, throws off the mantle of repeated pregnancies. She plants a seed of doubt in her husband's head by suggesting that one of her children is not his, thereby dispossessing him of his confidence and peace of mind for six years, until she reveals that she has lied. Exasperated at first, her husband suddenly sees her in a new light, as an ideal woman, one "[qui] n'était plus seulement une femme destinée à perpétuer sa race" ([who] was no longer only a woman destined to perpetuate her race). Thus she, like Michèle de Burne (who bears no children), incarnates the "modern" woman, a "useless beauty" who has in a sense thwarted the designs of Divine Providence.

Considering Maupassant's obsessive preoccupation with the illegitimate son and the horror of pregnancy, as expressed in *Une Vie* and *Mont-Oriol*, it is perhaps easy to understand why the woman who refuses to submit to the laws of biological reproduction would be presented as an ideal. The last—and no doubt one of the most chilling—of Maupassant's stories about illegitimacy appears in the same collection. "Le Champ d'oliviers" features a priest who is robbed of his tranquillity when his previously unknown illegitimate son, "sordide coureur de routes" (a sordid vagabond), comes to haunt him after his mother's death. A Christ figure who is forced to accept the responsibility for producing a child who appears as the incarnation of vice, the priest takes his own life. The collection includes another tale of dispossession recounted in the fantastic mode, "Qui sait?" ("Who Knows?," 1890). The narrator of this tale, returning home one night to see all of his possessions leaving his house under their own power, commits himself to an asylum.

L'Inutile Beauté is made up exclusively of stories that first appeared in 1889 or 1890. The three tales just summarized, considered among the finest of Maupassant's entire production, thus accurately reflect his bleak vision at the close of his career, a vision brought into even sharper focus when one considers the nostalgia for the carefree days of rowing on the Seine evoked in "Mouche" ("Fly," 1890), another story in this collection. Plagued by his worsening health and distraught over the death of Hervé in November 1889, Maupassant was overwhelmed with fears for the future. In particular, he was haunted by the terrifying insanity that preceded Hervé's internment, and by his brother's ominous words: as he was led away by the doctors, Hervé shouted to Guy, who had brought him to the asylum on the pretext of showing him a piece of property for sale, "Ah! Guy! Misérable! Tu me fais enfermer! C'est toi qui est fou, tu m'entends! C'est toi le fou de la famille!" (Oh, Guy, you wretch! You're having me locked up! You're the one who's crazy, do you understand! You're the crazy one in the family!).

In the year following the June 1890 publication of *Notre cœur*, Maupassant tried his hand at two additional novels, one, "L'Ame étrangère" (The Foreign Soul), in the tradition of *Fort comme la mort* and *Notre cœur*, which he abandoned rather quickly, and the other, "L'Angélus," which was to have taken as its subject the Prussian occupation of Normandy, and which remained unfinished not for lack of inspiration, but because he was slowly overcome by a general paralysis that prevented him from writing. Despite their fragmentary state, these unfinished works are valuable to the Maupassant scholar for several reasons. One detects an eleventh-hour realization on Maupassant's part that he had reached an impasse with the high-society psychological novel. The return to the war of 1870, a Norman setting, and an objective technique brings the reader full circle.

Indeed, much in "L'Angélus" is reminiscent of "Boule de Suif," and critics who have examined the fragments are convinced that Maupassant, having "found himself" once again after his unfortunate forays into then-fashionable literary forms, had a masterpiece in the making. But "L'Angélus" also provides insights into the sources of the theme of dispossession, which seems to have been ubiquitous in the later fiction. The novel's heroine, a provincial countess on the eve of giving birth to her second child, sees her home invaded by brutal Prussian soldiers who proceed to beat her into submission, maiming her fetus. Born crippled, her son is compared to Christ, for, like him, he has received "de l'impitoyable destinée un triste sort" (a sad fate from pitiless destiny). A violent diatribe against the sadistic Divinity that could permit such cruelty and injustice was to have been included in the novel, echoing similar sentiments uttered by other characters throughout Maupassant's fiction (as in "Moiron" [1887]), but with particular vehemence in the last works. If Maupassant's suffering heroes are often portrayed as Christ figures, the figure of God the Father is always presented as malevolent.

As the summer of 1891 approached, Maupassant was again seized with his old wanderlust. Tassart, who followed him through the south of France, takes note in his journal of his master's repeated consultations with physicians in a desperate attempt to arrest the progress of his illness. He also notes, not without alarm, his master's repeated sexual encounters, and the exhaustion that followed them. One woman in particular, to whom he refers as "la dame en gris" (the woman in gray) and whom biographers have identified either as Marie Kahn or the androgynous Gisèle d'Estoc, seems to have pursued him during this year, prompting Henri Troyat, a recent biographer, to write, "Homme de proie dans sa jeunesse, il est devenu la victime des femmes de proie dans son âge mûr" (Preying upon women in his youth, he became their prey in his later years). One can trace the same progression in his fictional universe.

Maupassant made an unsuccessful attempt at taking his life on the night of 1-2 January 1892. On 7 January he was interned at Dr. Blanche's mental hospital in Passy, near his beloved Seine. For the next eighteen months, he knew a terrifying succession of hallucinations, seizures, convulsions, and attacks of delirium. He died on 6 July 1893, at the age of forty-two, of third-stage syphilis. Fragments of his two unfinished novels were found among his papers; these, together with *La Paix du ménage* (1893; translated as *Peace at Home—at any Price*, 1941), a two-act comedy adapted from the short story "Au bord du lit" ("Beside the Bed," 1883) in 1888, and two collections of stories, *Le Père Milon* (Old Milon, 1899) and *Le Colporteur* (The Peddler, 1900), were published posthumously.

Since 1970, thanks largely to the structuralist interest in narratology, there has been a growing appreciation of the extraordinary complexity of the short-story form, and Maupassant, as one of its most successful practitioners, has been rehabilitated, so to speak. His works have received the imprimatur of the French literary establishment, publication in the prestigious Pléiade edition. Two volumes of stories (*Contes et nouvelles*) appeared in 1974 and 1979. The publication of a volume devoted to the novels (*Romans*) in 1987 is

The last known photograph of Maupassant, 1891

probably even more significant, since, with the sole exception of *Pierre et Jean,* which was the object of a series of scholarly articles in the 1960s, his novels, although popular during his lifetime, were until recently not deemed original enough to merit scholarly scrutiny. Despite this evidence of a growing respect for his novelistic accomplishments, the judgment of posterity still seems to favor his short fiction.

Eschewing the representation of narrowly focused social and political problems, Maupassant captured in his art the timeless joys and tragedies of human existence, and his characters, as recognizable today as they were one hundred years ago, have withstood the test of time. The photographic appeal of his narratives continues to attract playwrights and filmmakers, and many of his stories have been adapted for screen and stage. Maupassant, always a popular favorite, is no longer regarded as facile, a writer to be read in one's youth and then put aside for more "serious" authors, but a worthy object of study in his own right. Despite his refusal to accept the honor of membership in the prestigious Académie Française, his place in what Stanley Jackson has termed "the aristocracy of letters" is secure.

Letters:

Correspondance, 3 volumes, edited by Jacques Suffel (Evreux: Cercle du Bibliophile, 1973).

Bibliographies:

Edward D. Sullivan and Francis Steegmuller, "Supplément à la bibliographie de Guy de Maupassant," *Revue d'Histoire Littéraire de la France,* 49 (October-December 1949): 370-375;

André Vial, *Guy de Maupassant et l'art du roman* (Paris: Nizet, 1954), pp. 617-627;

Gérard Délaisement, *Maupassant journaliste et chroniqueur, suivi d'une bibliographie générale de l'œuvre de Guy de Maupassant* (Paris: Albin Michel, 1956);

Artine Artinian, *Maupassant Criticism in France, 1880-1940* (New York: Russell & Russell, 1969);

Robert Artinian and Artine Artinian, *Maupassant Criticism: A Centennial Bibliography, 1880-1979* (London: McFarland, 1982).

Biographies:

Hermine Lecomte du Nouy, *Amitié amoureuse* (Paris: Calmann-Lévy, 1896);

Edouard Maynial, *La Vie et l'œuvre de Guy de Maupassant* (Paris: Mercure de France, 1906);

François Tassart, *Souvenirs sur Guy de Maupassant par François, son valet de chambre* (Paris: Plon, 1911);

Ernest Boyd, *Guy de Maupassant* (New York: Knopf, 1926);

Georges Normandy, *Maupassant* (Paris: Rasmussen, 1926);

Normandy, *Maupassant intime* (Paris: Albin Michel, 1927);

Normandy, *La Fin de Maupassant* (Paris: Albin Michel, 1927);

Pierre Borel, *Le Destin tragique de Guy de Maupassant* (Paris: Editions de France, 1927);

Stanley Jackson, *Guy de Maupassant* (London: Duckworth, 1938);

Paul Morand, *Vie de Maupassant* (Paris: Flammarion, 1942);

Borel, *Maupassant et l'androgyne* (Paris: Editions du Livre Moderne, 1944);
Francis Steegmuller, *Maupassant: A Lion in the Path* (New York: Random House, 1949);
Albert-Marie Schmidt, *Maupassant par lui-même* (Paris: Editions du Seuil, 1962);
Tassart, *Nouveaux souvenirs intimes sur Guy de Maupassant,* edited by Pierre Cogny (Paris: Nizet, 1962);
Armand Lanoux, *Maupassant le bel ami* (Paris: Fayard, 1967);
Michael Lerner, *Maupassant* (New York: George Braziller, 1975);
Henri Troyat, *Maupassant* (Paris: Flammarion, 1989).

References:

Marie-Claire Bancquart, *Boule de suif et autres contes normands* (Paris: Garnier, 1971);
Bancquart, *Maupassant conteur fantastique* (Paris: Minard, 1976);
Micheline Besnard-Cousodon, *Etude thématique et structurale de l'œuvre de Maupassant: Le piège* (Paris: Nizet, 1973);
Philippe Bonnefis, *Comme Maupassant* (Lille: Presses Universitaires de Lille, 1981);
Charles Castella, *Structures romanesques et vision sociale chez Maupassant* (Lausanne: Editions de l'Age d'Homme, 1972);
Mary Donaldson-Evans, *A Woman's Revenge: The Chronology of Dispossession in Maupassant's Fiction* (Lexington, Ky.: French Forum, 1986);
John Dugan, *Illusion and Reality* (The Hague: Mouton, 1973);
A. J. Greimas, *Maupassant: Sémiotique du texte* (Paris: Seuil, 1976);
Trevor A. Harris, *Maupassant in the Hall of Mirrors* (New York: St. Martin's Press, 1990);
Henry James, *Partial Portraits* (London: Macmillan, 1888);
Jacques Lecarme and Bruno Vercier, eds., *Maupassant miroir de la nouvelle* (Saint-Denis: Presses Universitaires de Vincennes, 1988);
Robert Lethbridge, *Maupassant: "Pierre et Jean"* (London: Grant & Cutler, 1984);
Christopher Lloyd, *Maupassant: "Bel-Ami"* (London: Grant & Cutler, 1988);
Anne Marmot Raim, *La Communication non-verbale chez Maupassant* (Paris: Nizet, 1986);
Nafissa A.-F. Schasch, *Guy de Maupassant et le fantastique ténébreux* (Paris: Nizet, 1983);
Edward Sullivan, *Maupassant the Novelist* (Princeton: Princeton University Press, 1954);
Sullivan, *Maupassant: The Short Stories* (Great Neck, N.Y.: Barron's Educational Series, 1962);
Knud Togeby, *L'Œuvre de Maupassant* (Paris: Presses Universitaires de France, 1954);
Leo Tolstoy, *Guy de Maupassant* (London: Brotherhood, 1898);
André Vial, *Maupassant et l'art du roman* (Paris: Nizet, 1954);
Kurt Willi, *Déterminisme et liberté chez Guy de Maupassant* (Zurich: Juris Druck und Verlag, 1972).

Papers:

Maupassant's papers are at the Bibliothèque Nationale, Paris, the Pierpont Morgan Library, New York, and in private collections.

Octave Mirbeau

(16 February 1848 - 16 February 1917)

Aleksandra Gruzinska
Arizona State University

Octave Mirbeau, circa 1895

BOOKS: *Le Comédien* (Paris: Brunox, 1882);

Maîtres modernes. Le Salon de 1885 (Paris: Baschet, 1885);

Lettres de ma chaumière (Paris: Laurent, 1885); republished in part as *Contes de la chaumière* (Paris: Charpentier, 1894);

Le Pour et le contre (Paris: Léon Vanier, 1887);

Le Calvaire (Paris: Ollendorff, 1887); translated by Louis Rich as *Calvary* (New York: Lieber & Lewis, 1922);

L'Abbé Jules (Paris: Ollendorff, 1888);

Sébastien Roch (Paris: Charpentier, 1890);

Les Mauvais Bergers, pièce en 5 actes et en prose (Paris: Fasquelle, 1898);

L'Epidémie, pièce en 1 acte et en prose (Paris: Fasquelle, 1898);

Le Jardin des supplices (Paris: Fasquelle, 1899); translated by Alvah C. Bessie as *Torture Garden* (New York: Claude Kendall, 1931);

Le Journal d'une femme de chambre (Paris: Fasquelle, 1900); translated by William Faro as *Celestine: Being the Diary of a Chambermaid* (New York: Faro, 1930);

Vieux ménages, pièce en 1 acte et en prose (Paris: Fasquelle, 1901);

Les Vingt et un Jours d'un neurasthénique (Paris: Fasquelle, 1902);

Le Portefeuille, comédie en 1 acte et en prose (Paris: Fasquelle, 1902);

Les Affaires sont les affaires, comédie en 3 actes et en prose (Paris: Fasquelle, 1903);

Farces et moralités (Paris: Fasquelle, 1904)—includes *L'Epidémie, Vieux ménages, Le Portefeuille, Les Amants, Scrupules, Interview*;

Dans l'antichambre, histoire d'une minute (Paris: A. Romagnol, 1905);

La 628-E-8 (Paris: Fasquelle, 1907);

Le Foyer, pièce en 3 actes et en prose, by Mirbeau and Thadée Natanson (Paris: Fasquelle, 1908);

Dingo (Paris: Fasquelle, 1913);

La Vache tachetée (Paris: Flammarion, 1918);

La Pipe de cidre (Paris: Flammarion, 1919);

Chez l'illustre écrivain (Paris: Flammarion, 1919);

Un Homme sensible (Paris: Flammarion, 1919);

Un Gentilhomme (Paris: Flammarion, 1920);

Les Mémoires de mon ami (Paris: Flammarion, 1920);

Les Souvenirs d'un pauvre diable (Paris: Flammarion, 1921);

Aristide Maillol (Liège: Aux Armes de France, Société des Dilettantes, 1921);

Le Petit Gardeur de vaches (Paris: Flammarion, 1922).

Editions and Collections: *Théâtre I* (Paris: Flammarion, 1921)—includes *Vieux ménages, Les Affaires sont les affaires, L'Epidémie*;

Théâtre II (Paris: Flammarion, 1922)—includes *Interview, Le Portefeuille, Les Mauvais Bergers, Scrupules*;
Théâtre III (Paris: Flammarion, 1922)—includes *Le Foyer, Les Amants*;
Des Artistes, first series: 1885-1896 (Paris: Flammarion, 1922);
Des Artistes, second series: 1897-1912 (Paris: Flammarion, 1924);
Gens de théâtre (Paris: Flammarion, 1924);
Les Ecrivains, first series: 1884-1894 (Paris: Flammarion, 1925);
Les Ecrivains, second series: 1895-1910 (Paris: Flammarion, 1926);
Les Grimaces et quelques autres chroniques (Paris: Flammarion, 1927);
Œuvres illustrées, 10 volumes, edited, with an introduction, by Roland Dorgelès (Paris: Editions Nationales, 1934-1936);
Théâtre (Paris: Editions Nationales, 1935)—includes *Les Mauvais Bergers, Les Affaires sont les affaires, Le Foyer*;
La Mort de Balzac (Paris: Lérot, 1989);
Sur la statue de Zola (Caen: L'Echoppe, 1989);
Dans le ciel, edited by Pierre Michel and Jean-François Nivet (Caen: L'Echoppe, 1990);
Combats pour l'enfant, edited by Michel (Vauchrétien: Ivan Davy, 1990);
Contes cruels, 2 volumes, edited by Michel and Nivet (Paris: Séguier, 1990);
Combats politiques, edited by Michel and Nivet (Paris: Séguier, 1990);
Notes sur l'art, edited by Michel and Nivet (Caen: L'Echoppe, 1990);
Sac au dos, edited by Michel and Nivet (Caen: L'Echoppe, 1991);
Lettres de l'Inde, edited by Michel and Nivet (Caen: L'Echoppe, 1991);
L'Affaire Dreyfus, edited by Michel and Nivet (Paris: Séguier, 1991).

PLAY PRODUCTIONS: *Les Mauvais Bergers*, Paris, Théâtre de la Renaissance, 14 December 1897;
L'Epidémie, Paris, Théâtre Antoine, 29 April 1898;
Les Amants, Paris, Théâtre du Grand-Guignol, July 1901;
Vieux ménages, Paris, Théâtre du Grand-Guignol, 19 November 1901;
Interview, Paris, Théâtre du Grand-Guignol, 1 February 1902;
Le Portefeuille, Paris, Théâtre de la Renaissance-Gémier, 19 February 1902;
Scrupules, Paris, Théâtre du Grand-Guignol, May 1902;
Les Affaires sont les affaires, Paris, Comédie-Française, 20 April 1903;
Le Foyer, by Mirbeau and Thadée Natanson, Paris, Comédie-Française, 7 December 1908.

OTHER: *Claude Monet. Auguste Rodin*, preface by Mirbeau (Paris: Galerie Georges Petit, 1889);
Jean Grave, *La Société mourante et l'anarchie*, preface by Mirbeau (Paris: Stock, 1891);
Dessins de Rodin, preface by Mirbeau (Paris: Goupil, 1897);
Francis de Croisset, *Les Nuits de quinze ans*, preface by Mirbeau (Paris: Ollendorff, 1898);
L'Hommage des artistes à Picquart, preface by Mirbeau (Paris: Société Libre d'Edition des Gens de Lettres, 1899);
Louis Lamarque (Eugène Montfort), *Un An de caserne*, preface by Mirbeau (Paris: Stock, 1901);
Jean Lombard, *L'Agonie*, preface by Mirbeau (Paris: Ollendorff, 1901);
Jules Huret, *Tout yeux, tout oreilles*, preface by Mirbeau (Paris: Fasquelle, 1901);
Sacha Guitry, *Petite Hollande*, preface by Mirbeau (Paris: Stock, 1908);
Marguerite Audoux, *Marie Claire*, preface by Mirbeau (Paris: Fasquelle, 1910);
Léon Werth, *La Maison blanche*, preface by Mirbeau (Paris: Fasquelle, 1913);
Renoir, preface by Mirbeau (Paris: Bernheim-Jeune, 1913);
Cézanne, preface by Mirbeau (Paris: Bernheim-Jeune, 1914);
Albert Adès and Albert Josipovici, *Le Livre de Goha le simple*, preface by Mirbeau (Paris: Calmann-Lévy, 1919).

Best known for his controversial novels and plays, Octave Mirbeau remains to be rediscovered as a short-fiction writer and art critic. He championed the causes of unknown artists who were destined to become giants in their fields: first and foremost Auguste Rodin, Claude Monet, and Camille Pissarro. He also wrote in favor of the painters Vincent van Gogh, Paul Gauguin, Auguste Renoir, Edgar Degas, Paul Cézanne, Pierre Bonnard, Edouard Vuillard, and Maurice Utrillo; the sculptors Camille Claudel and Aristide Maillol; and the musicians César Franck, Claude Debussy, and Richard Wagner. As a journalist he espoused their causes very early in his prolific career, during which he wrote more than a thousand articles between 1874 and 1917, sometimes under the pseudonyms of Daniel René, Henry Lys, and Jean Maure. The directors of the *Gaulois* and the *Figaro*, the *France* and the *Journal* eagerly displayed his name on their front pages. Because Mirbeau differed politically from many of them and wished to increase freedom of expression, he founded *Grimaces* and *Paris-Midi, Paris-Minuit*. The press afforded him an opportunity to exert a curious influence on the public, one worthy of a truly committed writer.

Octave-Marie-Henri Mirbeau was born into a financially comfortable middle-class family on 16 February 1848 in Trévières. His grandfather Louis-Amable Mirbeau was a widower with four children when he married Louise-Catherine Adélaïde Charpentier. The oldest of their eight children, Louis-Amable, became a *prêtre libre*, a cleric not attached to a parish. Before he died on 26 March 1867 in the arms, so to speak, of his nineteen-year-old nephew Octave, he had tried to instill in him the bourgeois ideal of hard work. Instead, he seems to have inspired Mirbeau's terrifying and tormented priest in *L'Abbé Jules* (1888).

Mirbeau's father, Ladislas-François, was born in Regmalard (now spelled Rémalard) in Normandy. Unlike his ancestors, who practiced law, he became an *officier de santé*. The title commonly designated physicians who studied and practiced medicine but had no formal degree. After marrying Eugénie-Augustine Duboscq, the daughter of a lawyer, he settled in Trévières, in the northeastern Calvados department of Normandy. In September 1849 he took the family back to Regmalard, where Octave grew up with his older sister, Marie, and his younger sister, Berthe-Marie.

As an elected official (a council member and later an adjunct to the mayor), Ladislas-François dreamed of sending his only son to the well-known Jesuit school in Vannes, Brittany. In letters to Alfred Bansard des Bois, Mirbeau called his four years with the Jesuits (12 October 1859 - 9 June 1863) a living hell. They culminated in a mysterious dismissal, presumably because of Octave's poor scholastic record. One may suspect, however, other causes of a more delicate nature, reflected in *Sébastien Roch* (1890). Octave continued his studies at various boarding schools or *pensions* (in Rennes [1863] and in Caen [1865]). During this uphill battle for scholastic success he failed exams twice before receiving his baccalaureate diploma in 1866.

Like his father, Octave considered becoming a physician, but he soon lost enthusiasm for medicine and switched to law on 14 November 1866. He worked for the honorable "Maître Robbe," a lawyer and a friend of the family. Nevertheless, neither medicine nor law appealed to Mirbeau, yet the latter afforded him the opportunity to take several trips to Paris in April and May of 1867. He saw the World Exposition, went to the theater and opera, met Parisian women, and caught a glimpse of the elegant Princess de Murat. These distractions contributed, no doubt, to his failure of his first exam in 1867. In April 1869 the family recalled young Mirbeau, now deeply in debt, to Regmalard, from where he confided to des Bois: "Consider me dead and buried!"

On 8 July 1870 Mirbeau's forty-five-year-old mother died unexpectedly. To des Bois, Octave wrote tenderly about her, and his distress seems sincere. Yet, as characters, mothers remain noticeably absent from Mirbeau's works, and on the rare occasions when one is present, she seems ineffective, greedy, or harsh, and sometimes cold, as in *L'Abbé Jules*.

The Franco-Prussian War of 1870 eventually saved Mirbeau from becoming a lawyer. During the lottery draft of 1869, he picked the number fifty-two out of ninety-eight. His father resorted to a rather common practice among financially comfortable families and paid a man to take Octave's place. With the declaration of war, however, Mirbeau was called to serve in the Forty-ninth Regiment, stationed near the Orne River. On 31 July he was promoted to *sous-lieutenant* and later to lieutenant. Like many of his companions, undernourished and exhausted, he became ill and wandered from one infirmary to another before obtaining permission to seek medical care, first in Le Mans, then in Alençon, where his general granted him a sick leave.

When he resumed his military duties he was still sick. After he had experienced the horrors of war and the cruelty of men, his calvary intensified when he was falsely accused of desertion. The trauma and humiliation of an eight-month-long investigation ended in an acquittal on 12 September 1871. Besides compassion for the unfortunate and the suffering, the war taught him to dislike authorities fiercely, particularly the military. These feelings occupy an important position in his fiction.

Mirbeau in his study, mid 1890s

At twenty-three he was ready for political and literary battles. His family supported the monarchists, yet he saw himself as a son of the Revolution, politically in harmony with the eighteenth-century Enlightenment. The years immediately following the Franco-Prussian War were not yet an appropriate time for Mirbeau to show his true feelings. A long and bitter apprenticeship awaited him in the world of Legitimists, Bonapartists, and the partisans of moral order before he finally was able to express his radical self in support of anarchism and peace.

In 1872 Dugué de la Fauconnerie became editor of the Bonapartist paper *Ordre* (founded on 1 October 1871) and hired Mirbeau as his secretary. He soon wrote theater reviews and, beginning in October 1876, contributed columns (about forty bear his name), some of which criticize Camille Saint-Saëns, defend Wagner, and praise the poet Léon Dierx. These early essays are characterized by imprecations and irony, humor and wit, which later became his trademark. On 16 December 1876 he reported in a lively manner a curious incident somewhat unflattering to the actress Alice Regnault, who had lost her part in a revival of the play by Alexandre Dumas *père*, *La Reine Margot* (1847), and had thrown a script at the director during rehearsals at the Théâtre du Palais Royal.

Before leaving the *Ordre* in 1877, Mirbeau accompanied de la Fauconnerie on a campaign after which the latter easily won in the elections of 16 February 1876. Mirbeau took careful notes and later used them for a novel that features an astute politician running for office, *Un Gentilhomme* (A Gentleman, 1920). The time was propitious for consolidating friendships. He played a small part in Guy de Maupassant's *A la feuille de rose: Maison turque* (Turkish Brothel, 1875) at a private gathering and met Gustave Flaubert and Ivan Turgenev. His friends and acquaintances included Maupassant, Dierx, Philippe-Auguste de Villiers de l'Isle-Adam, Léon Hennique, Paul Alexis, and other writers who surrounded Emile Zola. Mirbeau wrote to Edmond de Goncourt to express admiration for his works. The guest list at the literary dinner Chez Trapp included his name and Joris-Karl Huysmans's.

During the government of Marie-Edmé-Patrice de MacMahon and Albert de Broglie (May 1877), Gaston de Saint-Paul became prefect of Foix, in the Ariège (Pyrenees), and nominated Mirbeau as his *chef de cabinet* (private secretary) on 27 May 1877. The latter's talent as a pamphleteer, reputation as a fighter, and sharp pen served to promote the short-lived government of moral order and the Bonapartists. From March 1877 until January 1879, he was editor of the conservative *Ariégeois*, where his controversial contributions culminated in a duel with Jules Grégoire, which Mirbeau later fictionalized in the story "Le Duel de Cassaire et de Pescaire" in *Lettres de ma chaumière* (Letters from My Thatched Cottage, 1885).

In 1879 Mirbeau served as secretary to Arthur Meyer, director of the *Gaulois*, who made him a regular contributor to the columns "Tout-Paris" and "Paris déshabillé." Meyer sent him to Madrid to report on the marriage of King Alphonso XII to Maria Christina de Habsburg-Lorraine. Mirbeau later went to Murcia for a first-hand look at its disastrous floods. He remained at the *Gaulois* until 8 January 1881, speaking out against the evils of what would later become some of the hallmarks of fin-de-siècle society—its decadence, neurasthenia, and addiction to morphine.

The political events of 1877 absorbed much of Mirbeau's energy. Because he was far from Paris, he did not contribute to *Les Soirées de Médan* (Evenings in Médan, 1880), an anthology that included works by major naturalist writers. His absence, although regrettable, helped Mirbeau to avoid being labeled a naturalist without losing any friends. He remained somewhat outside the naturalist school, never becoming a follower of Zola, probably because of his fierce independence. During this period he began his association with the *Illustration* (December 1880 - March 1881) and *Paris-Journal* (April 1881- April 1882), signing for this reactionary newspaper some thirty-three articles on politics under the pseudonym Daniel René. One entitled "L'Anarchie" foreshadows Mirbeau's future political orientation. He gradually introduced themes that became his trademark: he favored a government that guaranteed *les libertés fondamentales* (basic freedoms), promoted peace rather than narrow patriotism, and denounced the behavior of politicians. His accounts of current events were polemical in tone and contained such rhetorical devices as: false naïveté, humor, irony, affectations (*les grimaces*), imaginary dialogues, and false interviews, which conveyed a lively and thundering tone to his prose.

When Meyer took over *Paris-Journal* in 1882, Mirbeau sent him short stories, including "La Chambre close" (The Closed Room, 9 May 1882). "La Chanson de Carmen" (Carmen's Song, 21 August 1882) was Mirbeau's first contribution to the *Figaro*. Influenced by Jules-Amédée Barbey d'Aurevilly (greatly admired by Mirbeau) and Edgar Allan Poe, it borders on the supernatural and the fantastic. Carmen is a humble girl who marries a wealthy man. Soon after, a strange obsession takes hold of the husband, and he becomes irritated by a certain tune that Carmen frequently sings. After the obsession drives him to kill her, he discovers that death did not destroy the exasperating tune, which now dwells hauntingly in his mind.

Encouraged by Francis Magnard, Mirbeau wrote "Le Comédien" (The Actor, 26 October 1882). The article provoked an outrage among Parisian actors, who stormed the headquarters of the *Figaro*, demanding satisfaction. Several duels followed. Paris was in an uproar, with many taking stands either for or against "Le Comédien." The paper withdrew its support of Mirbeau, and he immediately resigned.

With Paul Hervieu and Grosclaude as collaborators, he became editor in chief of *Paris-Midi, Paris-Minuit* (15 January 1883 - 18 April 1883), then of *Grimaces* (21 July 1883 - January 1884). The defiant tone of the latter provoked readers and succeeded in attracting attention. Mirbeau's first editorial, "Ode au choléra," created another sensation. He invoked the dreadful disease upon Paris and France to rid them of corrupt politicians. Other editorials, anti-Semitic in tone, later haunted him when he became a battling Dreyfusard in the 1890s. At the peak of his journalistic career he dabbled in the stock market, but when the Union Générale collapsed on 19 January 1882, Mirbeau was plagued by debts. In December 1883 he left Paris for Brittany.

The year 1885 proved to be eventful for the anarchist movement in France and for Mirbeau, who became one of its staunchest supporters. He no doubt had read Pyotr Kropotkin's "Paroles d'un révolté" (A Revolutionary's Words, 1885) and ardently admired Leo Tolstoy, author of *Ma Religion* (My Religion, 1885). In that year he also scored a significant victory. At thirty-seven, Mirbeau finally published his first collection of short stories. *Lettres de ma chaumière* was composed in the village of Audierne, near Finistère, where he had fled in December 1883 to get away from his vindictive mistress, a Parisian beauty bearing the biblical name of Judith. He probably had met her as early as 1880 or 1881. As a result of her treatment, he endured great emotional suffering. Judith pursued him in

Brittany before finally loosening her grip on Mirbeau, who had truly submitted to "l'alcoolisme de l'amour," or a druglike addiction to love. Mirbeau's letters to his friend Hervieu hardly provide enough information about this mysterious woman, who inspired him to create Juliette, the heroine of his first autobiographical novel. Judith is probably to blame for his less-than-kind portrayal of women, often treated by Mirbeau as beautiful but cruel tormentors with angelic names.

Lettres de ma chaumière brings to mind Alphonse Daudet's *Lettres de mon moulin* (1869; translated as *Letters from My Mill*, 1880). The twenty-one stories in Mirbeau's collection, however, resemble less Daudet's than those of Maupassant and are dedicated to various writers as expressions of friendship, admiration, or simply as indications of stylistic affinities. This in no way diminishes Mirbeau's originality in portraying the wretchedness of the human condition and social injustice. Like Honoré de Balzac, he often draws comparisons between animals and people. His protagonists are neighbors, mostly simple folk, whom he met in Audierne. They speak their local dialect and stroll through the countryside of Brittany, one of Mirbeau's privileged places.

Lettres de ma chaumière inaugurated an extraordinary literary career encompassing short stories, novels, plays, and music and art criticism. Mirbeau's farsightedness and originality were often overlooked by the public, but his friends—Monet, Rodin, and Stéphane Mallarmé, to name a few—admired him. Their faith in his talent and rhetorical expertise was such that when all else failed, they deferred to him to promote talented newcomers. Nonetheless, the short stories passed almost unnoticed in the press. By 1885 the ardent, outspoken pamphleteer had made some enemies, a fact that explains some of the critical silence and the many pseudonyms he used.

Having recovered his emotional and financial equilibrium, Mirbeau returned to the *Gaulois* and stayed there until 1886. In October 1884 the *France* (and the *Matin*) published his articles on various painters (Pierre Puvis de Chavannes, Degas, Renoir, Pissarro, and Félicien Rops) and the writers Zola, Henri Becque, and Barbey d'Aurevilly. His best friends, Monet and Rodin, continued to enjoy great visibility in the press, thanks to Mirbeau's articles.

In the fall of 1884 Mirbeau's contacts increased through Regnault, the actress whom he had treated somewhat lightly in the *Ordre*. Having retired from the stage, the rich widow of Jules Louis Renard (not to be confused with the author) was writing for the *Gaulois*, signing her articles "Mitaine de Soie" (Silk Glove). Apparently Meyer asked Mirbeau to edit one of her pieces. This may have prompted their relationship. He married her in 1887, but not without first confronting Sibylle Mirabeau, Countess de Martel, granddaughter of the revolutionary Honoré-Gabriel Riqueti, Comte de Mirabeau. She was also a contributor to the *Gaulois* and a prolific writer (with an eye on Mirbeau) who wrote under the pseudonym Gyp. Her novel *Le Druide* (1885), meaning Druid or Gallic, is a roman à clef in which Gyp fictionalized her conflict with Mirbeau.

In July 1886, in the company of Regnault, he traveled to Noirmoutier, in Brittany, and wrote his first novel. The scandal that followed the publication of *Le Calvaire* (1887; translated as *Calvary*, 1922) assured its financial success. Thanks to Paul Bourget, then Mirbeau's friend, Juliette Adam had agreed to serialize *Le Calvaire* in the *Nouvelle Revue*. After reading the second chapter, she feared that what she considered to be its unpatriotic tone might alienate her conservative readers and decided to omit it. The controversy sharpened the appetite of the Parisians, who eagerly awaited the untruncated version.

Le Calvaire is a confession in which three artists, Charles Martel (a poet), Jean Mintié (a writer), and Lirat (a sculptor), sacrifice their talent for the love of Juliette Roux. The narrator, Mintié, painstakingly describes the suffering and degradation he has endured at the hands of this frivolous and selfish woman. Like Mirbeau, Jean comes from Normandy and a family of lawyers. He loses his mother at the tender age of twelve in the first chapter. The second chapter, which caused all the furor, gave the book its reputation as a war novel. Jean's misfortunes during the Franco-Prussian War resemble Mirbeau's. For him, however, the war ends in an embrace. Having just killed an enemy soldier against his will, probably by a reflex due to his military training, Jean feels repelled by his action. In a moment of revolt, he kisses the Prussian on the mouth, still full of blood. Jean's gesture betrays deep compassion for, and solidarity with, all victims of war and suffering, including the enemy. It nonetheless shocked Mirbeau's contemporaries.

With only a modest volume to his credit and the war experience behind him, Jean goes to Paris in search of literary glory. He develops a sin-

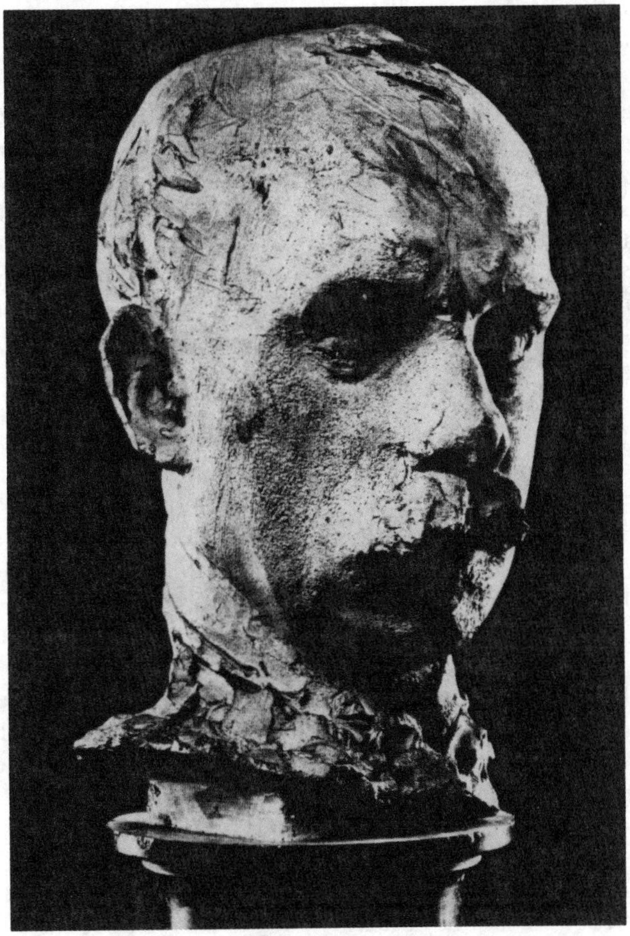

Bust of Mirbeau by Auguste Rodin (Musée Rodin)

cere admiration for the sculptor Lirat (possibly modeled after Degas), in whose studio he first sees Juliette Roux. He falls in love and immediately surrounds her in his mind with a halo of innocence, yet she has just ruined Charles Malterre and now awaits a new victim. Disregarding Lirat's warnings, Jean decides to live with Juliette. What follows is a litany of Juliette's infidelities, her sexual orgies, and Jean's torment. Although he submits to her every whim, the relationship disintegrates and Juliette finds a new victim in Lirat. The sculptor's betrayal of friendship saves Jean. Surprised, shocked, and in despair, he dons working clothes and leaves Paris, not unlike Mirbeau, who once fled to Audierne to escape Judith.

Juliette has many traits attributed to the cruel woman, or "la Belle Dame sans merci." Like a vampire, she feeds on her lovers, drains their energy, and leaves them panting and helpless. Juliette's portrait, however, keeps changing. Born out of the imagination of the male protagonists and their emotions, this beautiful femme fatale, a courtesan and a fallen idol, forever attracts new victims, yet remains mysterious, for she rarely speaks, if at all, in her own voice. Her beauty and cruelty attract and inspire the artists. Indeed, Jean's love for Juliette leads to his rebirth as an artist. For those who approach her, Juliette is at once the impassive speaker in Charles Baudelaire's "La Beauté" and the seductive "angel or siren" to whom the same poet addressed his "Hymne à la beauté"—that is, both a goddess and a courtesan who inflicts torment and brings inspiration.

Mirbeau and Alice were married on 25 May 1887 at Westminster, England. Because she was a Protestant, no religious ceremony took place, and the details of the marriage contract remain unknown. Alice was born Augustine Alexandrine Toulet on 5 February 1849 in Paris. Her family origins were modest. She married Renard, whose death left her caring alone for a son. Once widowed, she turned to the stage and performed at the Bouffes Parisiennes and the Théâtre de

Cluny and scored some success at the Palais Royal and the Gymnase for her great beauty rather than her talent.

She authored two novels (sometimes erroneously attributed to Mirbeau), *Mademoiselle Pomme* (1886) and *La Famille Carmettes* (The Carmettes Family, 1888). Alice shared Mirbeau's passion for painting and, thanks to a timely intervention by Rodin, had a picture accepted for the 1886 exposition. She had a reputation for being wealthy and owned considerable real estate in the suburbs of Paris. During the thirty years of their marriage, she efficiently managed the household and finances and surrounded Mirbeau with a certain well-being and comfort. In so doing she may have alienated some of Mirbeau's financially poor but artistically rich friends, Pissarro in particular.

In June 1887 the newlyweds returned to Paris. In July they left for Kérisper, Brittany, where Mirbeau wrote his second novel in beautiful natural surroundings. The subject and its treatment shocked some of his contemporaries. Hippolyte Taine and Maupassant admired it, and Mallarmé called *L'Abbé Jules* "une œuvre magistrale" (a masterly work).

As the first-person narrator, Albert Dervelle recalls a discussion during dinner involving the imminent return to Viantais of his Uncle Jules. He was eleven years old at the time. Later in the evening the Dervelles share the news with Judge Robin; the stiff Mrs. Robin; Reverend Sortais, a parish priest; and Mayor Servières and his charming wife, all very conservative people who lead uneventful lives.

In a lengthy retrospective that includes personal recollections and those of other people, Albert, now speaking in the third person, re-creates his uncle's life. Albert's father remembers his brother's cruel pranks and fits of irrational and violent behavior (not unlike those of his brutal and drinking father). Without any previous signs of a religious calling, the brother surprises the family by choosing the priesthood (and celibacy). Ahead of him lies a long road paved with suffering, struggles, and relapses caused by the overwhelming temptations of the flesh. Moreover, in spite of repeated efforts to suppress his urge for violence and tyranny, he often fails, with serious consequences for future promotions.

During his first Mass as an ordained priest, he makes a public confession and reveals past crimes that both move and scandalize all Viantais. Yet his memory, intelligence, and competence attract the attention of the local bishop, who later makes him his secretary. Jules uses this promotion to terrorize other priests and to isolate the bishop from their influence. He attempts to rape a peasant woman, writes a reactionary pastoral letter, and publicly insults the *grand vicaire*.

Having often absolved the repentant sinner, the bishop regretfully relieves Jules of his post. With his customary weakness he bestows on him the rectorship of Randonnais. In spite of this generosity, Jules steals two of his gold coins to fulfill a dream and acquire a personal collection of books. Shortly after, in a gesture of sublime charity, he gives the coins to a wretched beggar woman with two children. Ten years later he abandons the rectorship in Randonnais and leaves for Paris. After six years of silence, Albert's father receives the news that Jules is coming home to Viantais.

Interwoven in Jules's story and in contrast with it is the life of the Trinitarian Brother Pamphile, who, like Jules, nurtures a dream and wants to rebuild the thirteenth-century monastery of Reno to its former glory. In order to raise the necessary funds, he undertakes a truly epic and humiliating beggar's tour, characterized by arduous work, which carries him to distant places in and out of France. The money he raises pays for the services of dishonest architects and suppliers who take advantage of the old dreamer. When, in his turn, Jules tries to extort money from Brother Pamphile for his personal library, the monk, indifferent to threats, refuses. On the memorable day when the bishop dismisses Jules, the latter pays Brother Pamphile a second visit with more honorable intentions, only to find him dead. In another sublime and unselfish gesture, he buries Pamphile's decaying body.

On the day when Jules returns to Viantais, the Dervelles give him their very best room and invite friends for a welcoming dinner. This only angers him, and he instantly moves to a hotel, breaking all contacts with his relatives. Because Mrs. Dervelle suspects that her brother-in-law is rich, she keeps an eye on the inheritance. Her attempts to renew contact with him fail for two years. She finally conceives the idea of entrusting her son's education to Jules, who, to everyone's surprise, accepts. The lessons take place at Les Capucins, Jules's property outside Viantais, which now houses his library. The first thing on the agenda of Albert's education is to discard his old books. The mentor tells him to learn from nature and follow his natural instincts. Under his guidance thirteen-year-old Albert begins to read Lucretius, Benedict de Spinoza, George Sand, and Blaise Pascal, rebels who either loved nature or defended controversial ideas.

Jules is called one day to give last rites to a peasant girl. Finding her dead on arrival, he forgoes the ceremony. This sign of irreverence and disregard for tradition and customs shocks the Viantais, who do not know that Jules is weak, sick, and about to die. The Dervelles assist him devotedly (and selfishly) in his last days. Only after his death do they discover that Jules has bequeathed all his wealth to the first parish priest who dares to defrock himself. Finally, to fulfill a last wish, they burn his mysterious trunk, from which, as from Pandora's box, the fire unleashes erotic symbols of breasts, thighs, and phalli, which have so tormented him all his life.

Reginald Carr perceived *L'Abbé Jules* as a novel of revolt, in which an individual fights against the middle-class values forced upon him and pays dearly for his actions. There is a vague sentiment of anarchism in Jules, who defies all those who repress nature in the individual. Labels such as anticlerical, scabrous, and obscene, used by some of Mirbeau's contemporaries to describe *L'Abbé Jules*, do not do the novel justice. Albert Dervelle's (and Mirbeau's) compassionate portrayal of an unfortunate priest who made a wrong choice as a young man invites dialogue on such subjects as celibacy, vocation, and preparation for priesthood.

Mirbeau dedicated his next novel to Edmond de Goncourt. *Sébastien Roch* begins in 1862, when an ambitious provincial *quincaillier* (hardware dealer) from the village of Pervenchères in the department of Orne (Normandy), Joseph-Hippolyte-Elphège Roch, conceives the bold idea of sending his eleven-year-old son to a well-known Jesuit school (in Vannes, Brittany), which accepts mainly sons of nobility. In his mind such an education can lead to good business connections, and this far outweighs any considerations of his son's happiness or survival in the rigorous ambience of the school. Dominated by this ambitious, aggressive, and energetic father, the shy Sébastien knows no other maternal affection than that of Mme Lecautel, an intelligent and sensitive neighbor. About the same age as Sébastien, her precocious daughter, Marguerite, feels attracted to the boy and is sorry to see him go to school. On their way to Vannes, Sébastien and M. Roch meet one of the Jesuit fathers, who assures M. Roch that the charming Sébastien will be loved by his teachers. These are ominous words.

Almost immediately the boys tease Sébastien about his name, his accent, and his family origins. The strict code of conduct and daily routine, punctuated by the clock, further increase his unhappiness, and he makes an unsuccessful attempt to escape. On the positive side, Sébastien meets a boy from the lower classes, Bolorec, and makes friends with him. The sensitive Sébastien, endowed with a predominantly peaceful disposition, sees no end to his disappointments. Be it rote memorization of barbarian (Latin) verbs or lessons on the violent history of Brittany, he loses enthusiasm and his work suffers. As a consequence he is often disciplined and condemned to bread, water, and isolation. To this long list of negatives, his classmate Guy de Kerval adds humiliation when he retracts an invitation he had extended, because his aristocratic parents disapprove of Sébastien. The hero finally revolts, fights back, and at the end of the year reaps two awards.

Three years in Vannes make Sébastien less open. On the other hand, he becomes more passionate about music, art, and poetry, with a special admiration for Victor Hugo's poem "Pour les pauvres" (For the poor). Having grown delicately handsome, almost feminine, he attracts the attention of Father de Kern. Sébastien's very modest academic success in Vannes contrasts with his father's success when the latter is elected mayor of Pervenchères.

Father de Kern's interest in Sébastien develops into a strange attraction. Having gained his confidence, he invites him to his room and seduces him, revealing the true nature of his feelings. This "crime d'une âme d'enfant" (crime against an innocent child's soul) overwhelms Sébastien. Surprised by the reaction, Father de Kern wastes no time in confessing and absolving the boy so he will remain silent.

Instead of a detailed account of the seduction, the narrator uses a line of dots, and leaves it to the reader to reconstruct the traumatic moment. This discreet procedure seems to indicate a clear desire on Mirbeau's part to avoid sensationalizing the novel in order to emphasize compassion and understanding for young victims of sexual crimes, such as Mirbeau himself might have witnessed in Vannes.

The remaining chapters of part 1 and those of part 2 show the effects of the trauma on Sébastien, who is immediately dismissed, along

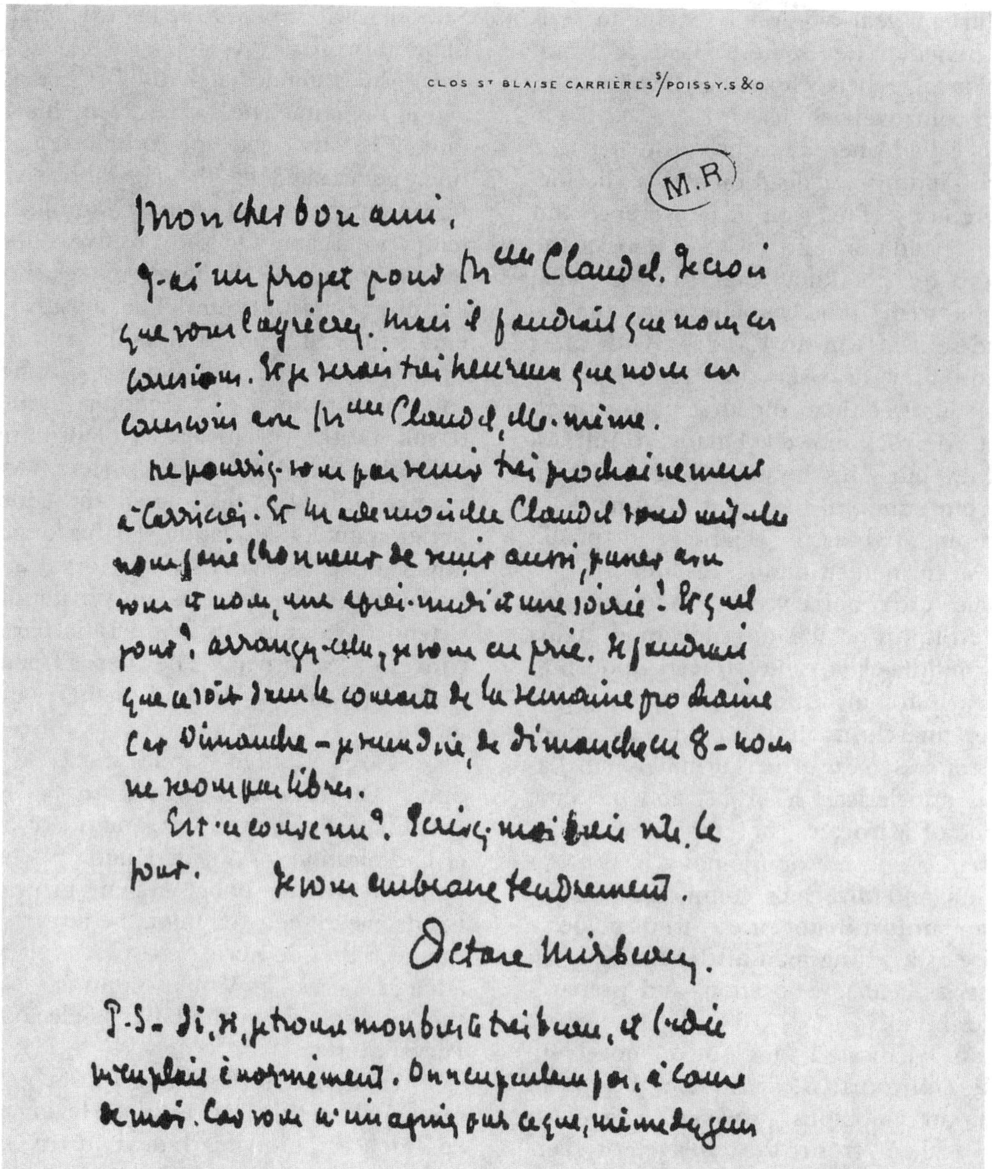

CLOS St BLAISE CARRIÈRES S/POISSY. S &O

M.R

Mon cher bon ami,

J'ai un projet pour Mlle Claudel. Je crois que vous l'agréerez. Mais il faudrait que nous en causions. Et je serais très heureux que nous en causions avec Mlle Claudel, elle-même.

Ne pourriez-vous pas venir très prochainement à Carrières. Et Mademoiselle Claudel voudrait-elle nous faire l'honneur de venir aussi, passer avec vous et nous, une après-midi et une soirée ! Et quel jour ? arrangez-cela, je vous en prie. Il faudrait que ce soit dans le courant de la semaine prochaine car dimanche – prochain, le dimanche 8 – nous ne serons pas libres.

Est-ce convenu ? Écrivez-moi bien vite le jour. Je vous embrasse tendrement.

Octave Mirbeau.

P.S. – Si, il je trouve mon buste très beau, et l'idée m'en plaît énormément. On ne s'occupe pas, à cause de moi. Car vous n'imaginez pas ce que, même des gens

Letter from Mirbeau to Auguste Rodin concerning Camille Claudel (Musée Rodin)

with Bolorec, for reasons shrouded in mystery. He cannot turn to his father for compassion. Indeed, deeply disappointed and humiliated by his son's dismissal, M. Roch takes him home only after all attempts to keep him in Vannes, including bribery, prove useless.

In part 2, written as a diary, Sébastien reflects on the once-familiar surroundings, his family and friends, among whom he feels vaguely unhappy and isolated. On 18 January 1869 he draws the wrong number during the lottery conscription. Rather than let his son join the army, M. Roch pays a man to take Sébastien's place. Marguerite's affection, their intimate encounters, and her sexual advances bring back the past, which prevents Sébastien from fully sharing her love. Her entreaties no doubt seem less attractive than the very seductive voice of Father de Kern, which keeps haunting him.

At the onset of the Franco-Prussian War, he joins the army. By a happy coincidence, he and Bolorec serve in the same division, a joyful reunion for the two friends who fight side by side, until Sébastien is killed at the tender age of nineteen. Rather than abandon his dead friend, Bolorec picks him up, drapes his body over his shoulders, and carries it away from the battlefield. Sébastien and Bolorec may well represent two different aspects of Mirbeau. The sensitive Sébastien, who seems unable to shed his past, dies during the war, while the more resilient Bolorec survives and continues to fight, not unlike Mirbeau, who fought literary battles.

With the publication of his first three novels, all somewhat autobiographical, Mirbeau's literary fortune seemed assured. During the next decade or so he lost several good friends and admirers. Mallarmé died in 1898, Becque in 1899, Edmond de Goncourt in 1896, and in 1901 another dear friend, his dog Dingo. But this was also to be a very productive decade, starting with Mirbeau's collaboration at the *Journal* in 1891 and his support for Remy de Gourmont, who had lost his post at the Bibliothèque Nationale for writing "Le Joujou patriotisme" (The Toy Patriotism). Jean Grave called on him to testify at his trial, and Mirbeau prefaced his book *La Société mourante et l'anarchie* (The Dying Society and Anarchy, 1891). In 1894 he defended the anarchist intellectuals Félix Fénéon, Elisée Reclus, and Laurent Tailhade, and in 1895 Oscar Wilde. Nor did he forget his painter and sculptor friends: Mirbeau wrote prefaces to help raise money for Gauguin, and to promote the art of Monet, Rodin, and Pissarro, as well as that of Félix Vallotton, Renoir, Cézanne, and Maillol. Mallarmé recommended Maurice Maeterlinck to Mirbeau, and the latter's article on *La Princesse Maleine* (1889) turned the unknown writer into an overnight success. Mirbeau admiringly wrote also about Knut Hamsun (*La Faim*, 1890; translated as *Hunger*) and prefaced Marguerite Audoux's *Marie Claire* (1910).

Beginning with Zola's "J'accuse" (*Aurore*, 13 January 1898), the Dreyfus Affair exploded and transformed much of France into a battleground. Mirbeau fought in the ranks of the Dreyfusards, on the side of the persecuted and the accused, and staunchly supported Zola, who had intervened on the side of Dreyfus. A former friend, Bourget, now seen as an enemy, fought on the opposite side. Dedicated to all men who shape a nation's destiny, including government leaders and teachers, *Le Jardin des supplices* (1899; translated as *Torture Garden*, 1931) is a portrait, done partly through allegory and metaphor, of the infested political atmosphere of the 1890s. The novel provides three samples of torture gardens: a Parisian literary salon; an entire century, from the Reign of Terror (1794) to the fin de siècle; and a Chinese museum, which introduces the themes of love and the Orient.

The work is in the form of a confession, divided into three uneven parts. The first of its two narrators appears only in the "Frontispiece" and introduces the reader to the Parisian literary salon of a well-known writer (probably Bourget), where scientists and men of letters discuss the problem of the criminal instinct, which they feel dominates humanity. The illustrious writer suggests, among vigorous protests, that women do not share this criminal instinct. The others feel that if there is inequality between the genders, women show a marked superiority over men in criminal inventiveness. A guest, unknown to the others, proposes to prove it. As the second narrator, he takes over and reads from a prepared manuscript the story of a personal adventure.

"On a Mission" is a long flashback to the Reign of Terror. The narrator recalls some of his crooked and corrupt ancestors, who practiced the art of doing others in and whose education further reinforced low moral principles. Following in their footsteps, he has become a debauched boulevardier and has just lost an election to a more corrupt adversary. An influential government official and former friend proposes a temporary exile on a scientific mission in Ceylon. En route on a ship, he meets a beautiful Englishwoman, Clara, bound for her native China, who appears as the antidote to corruption. Having fallen in love with Clara, he follows her to China. Her love, however, has more stings than sweetness, so he leaves, then returns after a painful two-year separation.

Clara takes the repentant lover to a Chinese museum. Only a few hours in length, the visit forms nonetheless the longest part of the novel and is filled with an orgy of spectacles of torture, set against a background of exotic flora and fauna, which are intended to enhance the suffering of the victims and the art of the torturers. When the museum closes, an unconscious Clara collapses into her lover's arms, exhausted by the intensely sadistic pleasures human suffering has produced.

The novel concludes with part 2, but not the story. The narrator-protagonist survives the visit, escapes from Clara, and returns to Paris. He has literary aspirations, frequents literary circles, and has just finished reading his manuscript before a distinguished audience, as one learns in the "Frontispiece," which opens the novel but also gives the conclusion to the story. More than an introduction, the "Frontispiece" is the main gate to the true garden of tortures, which encompasses the entire world and includes miniature torture gardens similar to the literary gathering of intellectuals in Paris. Tolstoy and Wilde admired the book. From then on Mirbeau adopted a new approach to the novel. Under his hand, the form acquired an episodic and picaresque character, and its architecture, if any, became harder to recognize.

Mirbeau's career as a playwright began in 1897. Concerning conflicts between workers and the industrial establishment, *Les Mauvais Bergers* opened at the Théâtre de la Renaissance on 14 December 1897. The part of the courageous, struggling, and compassionate Madeleine was played by Sarah Bernhardt, to whom Mirbeau devoted an admiring article, very different in tone from "Le Comédien," which had so angered actors in 1882. Several one-act plays followed, some staged by the pioneering producer André Antoine. On 20 April 1903 *Les Affaires sont les affaires* (Business is Business) opened at the Comédie-Française, scoring a resounding success and establishing Mirbeau's reputation as a playwright.

Its main character, Lechat, a successful entrepreneur with political ambitions, was first seen in "Agronomie," a short story from *Lettres de ma chaumière*. He dominates his family and keeps an eye on the property of ruined noblemen, buying it at bottom prices. He is about to marry his daughter to a nobleman's son. The "ungrateful," "selfish," and certainly unhappy Germaine foils her father's plan by running away with a poor engineer of her choice, naively hoping that she and her future husband may both earn a living. Another blow follows when Lechat's son dies in a car accident. As the body is brought in, he prepares to mourn him, but not without first confounding his enemies and consolidating a profitable financial deal.

Le Foyer, written in collaboration with Thadée Natanson, became the object of a court battle between Mirbeau and the administration (Jules Claretie in this case) of the Comédie-Française. Mirbeau won a small victory, and the Comédie-Française staged *Le Foyer* on 7 December 1908. The points of contention concerned the portrayal of the main character, an aristocrat and distinguished member of the Académie Française. Baron J. G. Courtin makes personal use of funds appropriated for a public charity (an orphanage) entrusted to his care. The play did not surpass the success of *Les Affaires sont les affaires*, but it afforded Mirbeau the occasion to take trips to Berlin and Vienna, where it was later successfully performed.

According to Françoise Cachin, Mirbeau was now often seen at the offices of the *Revue Blanche*. He found there a certain tone of anarchism and irreverence that must have pleased him. Between January and June of 1900 the editors of the *Revue Blanche* published as a serial *Le Journal d'une femme de chambre* (translated as *Celestine: Being the Diary of a Chambermaid*, 1930), his most popular and best-known novel.

Alice and Octave had often complained about the difficulties of hiring and keeping domestic help. They suddenly saw their difficulties multiply after the novel appeared. Mirbeau wrote to Eugène Montfort that his publisher had added extra exclamation points everywhere, an indication of the spirit in which the book was received. In his private notes, Robert de Montesquiou (whose judgment in such matters is, however, suspect) called it "un bouquin salaud" (a dirty book) and compared the diary's putative author, Célestine, to the Marquis de Sade's Justine. Next to Mirbeau, Sade seemed a "compassionate" philosopher.

"The stormy, ferocious, truculent and admirable novel," as it was later called, drew a resounding success, and its sales in 1900 were brisk, with more than one hundred thousand copies sold in one year. A stage adaptation in 1931 and two film versions, one by Jean Renoir (1946), the other by Luis Buñuel (1964), attest to its enduring popularity.

Dedicated to Jules Huret, the novel includes a note by Mirbeau, who claims that he is only the editor. This well-known device for denying authorship and thus responsibility, while nevertheless proclaiming oneself as author, fooled neither contemporaries nor critics. Written as a diary divided into seventeen long episodes, it mostly refers to Célestine R. . .'s frequent changes in employment, either because her service displeases her masters or she tires of their sexual advances. Not that Célestine is prudish! As the daughter of a fisherman from Brittany, she experienced love and rape at a tender age. As a chambermaid with many years of service to her credit, she accepts a position with the financially comfortable Lanlaires in the little town of Mesnil-Roy, in Normandy.

On 21 September (probably supposed to be 1898), after some years with the Lanlaires, she begins her diary, in which she unloads feelings of resentment, frustration, and humiliation experienced on the job. The diary is good therapy, keeping her mentally fit and allowing her to laugh at present and past masters. Her service with the Lanlaires coincides with two political events, its beginning with Alfred Dreyfus's exile to Devil's Island, and its end with his return to France on 1 July 1899 (an event at which Mirbeau was present). She stops writing as soon as she marries Joseph, the Lanlaires' gardener, and moves up the social ladder.

As Mirbeau's most attractive character, Célestine is intelligent, perspicacious, and usually polite, though insolent on occasion. By comparison with provincial folk, she seems elegant and refined. Quick to learn, she appraises Mme Lanlaire as someone whose decisions count, then flirts with the husband to make her mistress jealous. Célestine dislikes Mme Lanlaire because she keeps her busy, treats her with reserve, and abstains from spicy gossip and intimate confessions. By this point Célestine has acquired a strong taste for them. Whenever Mme Lanlaire's reserve annoys her, she consults the past. Like Pandora's box, it unleashes a steady flow of memories about loquacious and corrupt mistresses and masters.

The Lanlaires' neighbor, Captain Mauger, finds Célestine appetizing and covets her as his servant and mistress. The husky Joseph, who supports religion and tyranny while railing at the republic and the Jews, also has an eye on her. In this uneventful existence, the rape of little Clara briefly dissipates the boredom of provincial life. Célestine suspects Joseph, but crime only makes him look more attractive. He soon admits that she makes his blood curdle and asks her to join him in Brittany, where he plans to buy a café. She gladly chooses marriage to Joseph over double-duty service as maid and mistress to Captain Mauger.

In the last entry in her diary, 10 November (probably supposed to be 1899), the Lanlaires' silver was to be polished, but they find it missing. By intuition, Célestine immediately blames Joseph. He, on the contrary, plays more than ever the role of exemplary servant and encourages her to imitate Mme Lanlaire, the perfect mistress in Joseph's eyes. For once, Célestine heeds the advice. Both servants score a bittersweet victory as they see their disconsolate masters weep over Célestine's and Joseph's departure.

As one reads, this basic and incidental structure is not easily discernible, interwoven as it is with multiple flashbacks. Amid her frustrations, Célestine vents her feelings by recalling former masters who by far surpass the dishonesty and corruption of the Lanlaires. She finds provincial life boring, which adds to her misery, and no matter how humiliating service in Paris may have been, it now seems more attractive—another reason to dwell on the past. The flow of flashbacks gives the diary a chaotic rhythm and affords a picture of fin-de-siècle morals, as seen through the eyes of a representative of the lower classes. Célestine literally and symbolically takes off her masters' clothes and reveals their hidden vices and dirty linen. Even Bourget makes an appearance, to explain why he considers chambermaids unworthy of his interest. Mirbeau, whose interest in the lower classes remained strong, cultivates in the book a savory style, marked by an impression of spontaneity. But, like Dante's *Divine Comedy*, it is a descent into hell. However attractive and humorous it may seem, it too is a garden of tortures nonetheless.

Les Vingt et un Jours d'un neurasthénique (Twenty-one Days of a Neurasthenic) appeared in 1902. Its title implies a certain [dis]unity. Twenty-one days fill twenty-three chapters and feature the daily activities of the inhabitants of a resort town in the Pyrenees. The narrator (probably based on Mirbeau himself, who spent three weeks in Luchon during July 1897) makes various acquaintances and friends, who become the protagonists. The episodes include the typical Mirbelian fare of incidents of human baseness, aggressiveness, and hypocrisy, often related to politics, medicine, and law. Mirbeau's readings of Friedrich Nietzsche perhaps explain the book's morose ambience and reflections of neurasthenia, a disorder with which both Alice and Octave were afflicted.

Success had turned Mirbeau into a rather wealthy man with a taste for exotic luxuries and an eye for new inventions. The latest to attract his attention was the automobile. He bought one of the first built by Fernand Charron, to whom he dedicated *La 628-E-8* (1907). The bizarre title suggests a mystery novel. In reality, it was the car registration of Mirbeau's Charron. As the very first novel about the automobile, *La 628-E-8* marked a new departure in fictional subject matter. Car, driver (Brochette), and passenger (Mirbeau) give unity to the otherwise episodic trip, which begins and ends at the Franco-German border. The text blends types of discourse, including narrative and literary and art criticism. The road signs whiz by as the car

Mirbeau in his later years (drawing from Norman L. Kleeblatt, ed., The Dreyfus Affair: Art, Truth, and Justice, *1987)*

moves through France, the Rhineland, Belgium, and Holland, where inevitably it arouses admiration. Varied landscapes and cultural artifacts speed by, leaving the travelers barely enough time to recover from physical and mental fatigue. This distorts their perception of reality, and, very soon, the trip acquires a meandering psychological dimension, reflecting Mirbeau's mental landscapes—he who travels, in Montaigne-like fashion, "un peu à travers moi-même" (a little inside myself).

One of these mental landscapes provoked a scandal. The section on Balzac centers on his death, and specifically on the role Evelina Hanska de Balzac played at that critical moment. In Mirbeau's version, Mme Hanska appears as the unfaithful wife, who enjoys the friendship of the fashionable portrait painter Jean Gigoux, while her ailing husband dies with only a hired woman at his bedside. Gigoux's "oral" testimony (the man did know Balzac's wife intimately) incriminates Mme Hanska even more than Hugo's account in *Choses vues* (Things Seen, 1887). On 6 November 1907 the *Temps* published lengthy excerpts from this part of Mirbeau's book. Immediately, the Countess Mniszek, Hanska's daughter by a previous marriage, protested against the novelist's portrayal of her mother. Out of compassion for this eighty-year-old woman, Mirbeau eliminated the offensive chapter. A few copies escaped the mutilation (Raymond Poincaré's is at the Bibliothèque Jacques Doucet in Paris), but the Balzac episode never appeared in the place intended for it, right after and in contrast with a section on Bourget's women. A later edition reproduced the Balzac chapter in the appendix. Mirbeau's Evelina Hanska, though a historical figure, shares with Juliette, Clara, and Célestine many traits, including those of cruelty and insensitivity, with which Mirbeau endowed the majority of his female characters.

Octave and Alice were plagued by health problems, she by severe migraines, he by neurasthenia and depression. The dynamic Mirbeau slowly withered away physically, yet still led an active, though no longer frenetic, life. He was elected to and participated in the deliberations of the Académie Goncourt, which began to function in 1903 and awarded France's most coveted literary prize. He helped elect Elémir Bourges and Jules Renard. In 1907 he wrote a series of provocative articles on hospitals and physicians for the *Matin.*

Mirbeau's enthusiasm for nature remained undiminished, as did his passion for growing exotic flowers and raising rare birds. He made it a point to include nature in his works as a consolation for the shortcomings of human beings. For his last novel, written when he was so weak that Léon Werth had to help out with the manuscript, he chose as the protagonist a friend from the animal world. He dedicated *Dingo* (1913) to Dr. Albert Robin, his devoted physician.

Either from Australia or Africa, Dingo, a dog, arrives at Ponteilles-en-Barcis by mail, in a crate as big as a child's casket. In spite of the dog's inborn ferociousness, his master (probably intended to be read as Mirbeau) showers him with affection. Dingo shows himself worthy of it, for his qualities shine in the first six chapters. He obviously dislikes the rich, the bourgeois, and the military; he ferrets out every psychological, social, and literary pedantism and hypocrisy. On the other hand, he likes the simple folk, such as the gardener Piscot, and the underprivileged, on whom he bestows his friendship.

Beginning in chapter 7, Dingo creates havoc in the vicinity, killing the neighbors' chickens and sheep. One day he tries to teach Miche, a female cat and the object of his affection, the pleasures of hunting and killing. She, however, has nothing to learn from Dingo and is far more advanced and "civilized." She scorns Dingo's brutality and swiftness in killing. A voyeur by preference (like Clara and Célestine), Miche derives pleasure by watching her victims slowly agonize under her playful paws. She is mysterious and impenetrable like Juliette, cruel and sadistic like Clara, and supple, mischievous, and very much at ease in Paris, like Célestine. Transposed into the animal kingdom, the battle of the sexes remains extremely intense. The attraction between male and female is electrifying, and frustration and lack of understanding are aggravated by the fact that Miche belongs to a different species.

Mirbeau resorts to old techniques here, including those of *Lettres de ma chaumière*. The narrator mingles with the neighbors, learns what makes them tick, records their accents, and then draws their portraits from nature, like the Impressionists, not always to their liking: Théophile Lagniaud, the radical mayor of Ponteilles-en-Bracis (based on Cormeilles-en-Vexin); a local policeman, Jaulin, who kills his old mother; the once beautiful Irma Pouillaut, now a retired milkwoman; and Coquereux, condemned by the courts for accidentally killing a little girl, then raping her. Their stories serve to expose the courts and lawyers, as well as the military, all of whom are tormentors in this miniature garden of tortures. After Ponteilles, Dingo adjusts poorly to Paris for lack of space and prefers the forest of Fontainebleau. Yet, when his new mistress becomes ill, the fierce dog shows exemplary devotion and stays at her bed for three long weeks before eventually dying himself. He is buried under a venerable oak tree.

During thirty years of marriage Alice and Octave searched for the ideal place to live; most of their residences were close to Paris. They filled their homes with works of art. Mirbeau sought shelter in the countryside from his literary and political battles: in Les Damps, near Pont-de-l'Arche (Eure), in 1889; in Carrières-sous-Poissy in 1893; in a château in Cormeilles-en-Vexin in 1904; and finally, in 1908, in their dream house in Cheverchement, near Triel-sur-Seine. They also kept a pied-à-terre in Paris, residing first at 3, boulevard Delessert (1897), then at 68, rue du Bois de Boulogne (1901). By 1912 Mirbeau had grown too weak to commute between Triel and Paris and so moved his Parisian pied-à-terre to 139, avenue Longchamp, then to the rue Beaujon, across from his devoted physician Robin. He died there on 16 February 1917 at the age of sixty-nine.

Mirbeau's bust by Rodin dominates the author's grave in the cemetery of Passy in Paris. The tombstone bears an inscription from *Lettres de ma chaumière*: "Ne hais personne, pas même le méchant. Plains-le, car il ne connaîtra jamais la seule jouissance qui console de vivre: faire le bien" (Hate no one, not even the evildoer. Pity him, for he will never know the only true pleasure that consoles the living: to do good).

On 19 February 1917 there appeared the "Testament politique d'Octave Mirbeau," delivered by Alice to the *Petit Parisien,* a right-wing, prowar paper. Its patriotic tone surprised, shocked, and deeply chagrined friends and admirers. Those who saw in Mirbeau a fierce pacifist felt betrayed and blamed Alice and her ally, Gustave Hervé, whom Mirbeau had once admired for his antimilitary stance. Hervé, however, had since become a staunch advocate of *la guerre à outrance* (war at any cost). He and Alice were blamed for taking advantage of Mirbeau's illness and guiding his pen. The preface to *Le Livre de Goha le simple* (1919), dated 25 October 1916

Mirbeau, one year before his death

and written four months before his death, is perhaps a truer testament.

In 1918 Mirbeau's house in Cheverchement was given to the Société des Gens de Lettres. His valuable art collection was auctioned in 1919. Alice died in 1931, leaving the estate to the Académie des Sciences in Paris, now the depository of a rich collection of Mirbelian documents. Posterity buried in silence the once-powerful man of letters. However, Pierre Michel and Jean-François Nivet (a devoted Mirbelian scholar for more than twenty years) broke the silence with a monumental, thousand-page biography, *Octave Mirbeau: L'Imprécateur au cœur fidèle* (1990). It should restore to the nineteenth-century French Don Quixote a prominent place in the history of literature.

Letters:

Correspondance avec Auguste Rodin, edited by Jean-François Nivet (Paris: Lérot, 1988);

Lettres à Alfred Bansard des Bois (mars 1862 - octobre 1874), edited by Pierre Michel (Paris: Limon, Montpellier, 1989);

Correspondance avec Camille Pissarro, edited by Michel and Nivet (Paris: Lérot, 1990);

Correspondance avec Claude Monet, edited by Michel and Nivet (Paris: Lérot, 1990);

"Lettres d'Octave Mirbeau à Emile Zola," edited by Michel and Nivet, *Cahiers Naturalistes*, 64 (1990): 7-46.

Biographies:

Edmond Pilon, *Octave Mirbeau* (Paris: Bibliothèque Internationale d'Edition, 1903);

Martin Schwartz, *Octave Mirbeau: Vie et œuvre* (The Hague: Mouton, 1966);

Pierre Michel and Jean-François Nivet, *Octave Mirbeau: L'Imprécateur au cœur fidèle* (Paris: Séguier, 1990).

References:

Françoise Cachin, "Un Défenseur oublié de l'art moderne," *Œil*, 90 (June 1962): 50-55, 75;

Cahiers d'Aujourd'hui, special number on Mirbeau, 9 (1922);

Reginald Carr, *Anarchism in France: The Case of Octave Mirbeau* (Montreal: McGill-Queen's University Press, 1977);

Léon Deffoux, *Le Naturalisme* (Paris: Œuvres Représentatives, 1927);

Marc Elder, *Deux essais: Octave Mirbeau, Romain Rolland* (Paris: Crès, 1914);

Europe, special number on Mirbeau, 458 (June 1977);

Emile Faguet, "*Le Portefeuille* d'Octave Mirbeau," *Journal des Débats* (12 June 1905);

Ernest Gaubert, "L'Œuvre et la morale d'Octave Mirbeau," *Mercure de France*, 93 (1 October 1911): 510-532;

Remy de Gourmont, "Octave Mirbeau," *Promenades littéraires*, first series (Paris: Mercure de France, 1904), pp. 69-78;

Aleksandra Gruzinska, "Octave Mirbeau Antimilitariste," *Nineteenth-Century French Studies*, 4 (Spring 1976): 394-403;

Gruzinska, "Octave Mirbeau's Madame Hanska in *La Mort de Balzac*," *Nineteenth-Century French Studies*, 15 (Spring 1987): 302-314;

Jean-Maurienne, *Les Tribulations de la Société des Amis d'Octave Mirbeau* (Paris: Société Française d'Imprimerie et de Librairie, 1939);

Léopold Lacour, "Le Théâtre d'Octave Mirbeau," *Revue de Paris*, 3 (15 May 1903): 432-448;

Jules Lemaître, "*Les Mauvais Bergers* d'Octave Mirbeau," *Revue des Deux Mondes*, 145 (1 January 1898): 208-211;

Pierre Michel, "Mirbeau et Zola: Entre mepris et veneration," *Cahiers Naturalistes*, 62 (1988): 47-77;

Michel, "Les 'Palinodies' d'Octave Mirbeau? A propos de Mirbeau et de Daudet," *Cahiers Naturalistes*, 62 (1988): 116-126;

Eugène Montfort, "Visages d'hier et d'aujourd'hui, Octave Mirbeau," *Candide*, 290 (3 October 1929): 6;

Jean-François Nivet, "Mirbeau journaliste," Ph.D. dissertation, University of Lyons, 1987;

Nivet, "Octave Mirbeau et l'affaire Dreyfus," *Cahiers Naturalistes*, 64 (1990): 79-101;

Maxime Revon, *Octave Mirbeau: Son œuvre* (Paris: La Nouvelle Revue Critique, 1924);

Camille de Sainte-Croix, "Octave Mirbeau: *Le Journal d'une femme de chambre*," *Revue Blanche*, no. 23 (September 1900): 72-76;

Laurent Tailhade, "Mirbeau," *Œuvre* (17 February 1917);

Sylvie Thieblement, "La Vie d'un mécène au regard accusateur," Ph.D. dissertation, University of Nancy, 1986;

Léon Werth, "Octave Mirbeau," *Cahiers d'Aujourd'hui*, first series 4 (April 1913): 176-182;

Robert E. Ziegler, "Hunting the Peacock: The Pursuit of Non-reflective Experience in Mirbeau's *Le Jardin des supplices*," *Nineteenth-Century French Studies*, 12-13 (Summer-Fall 1984): 162-174.

Papers:

Mirbeau's manuscripts are located at the Bibliothèque de l'Institut (Académie des Sciences), Bibliothèque Nationale, Bibliothèque de l'Arsenal, and Bibliothèque Jacques Doucet, all in Paris.

Rachilde
(Marguerite Eymery Vallette)

(11 February 1860 - 4 April 1953)

Melanie C. Hawthorne
Texas A&M University

SELECTED BOOKS: *Monsieur de la Nouveauté* (Paris: Dentu, 1880);

La Femme du 199ᵉ (Périgueux: Dupont, 1881);

Monsieur Vénus (Brussels: Brancart, 1884; revised edition, Paris: Brossier, 1889); translated by Madeleine Boyd as *Monsieur Vénus* (New York: Covici, Friede, 1929);

Histoires bêtes pour amuser les petits enfants d'esprit (Paris: Brissy, 1884);

Queue de poisson (Brussels: Brancart, 1885);

Nono (Paris: Monnier, 1885);

La Virginité de Diane (Paris: Monnier, 1886);

A mort (Paris: Monnier, 1886);

La Marquise de Sade (Paris: Monnier, 1887);

Le Tiroir de Mimi-Corail (Paris: Monnier, 1887);

Madame Adonis (Paris: Monnier, 1888);

L'Homme roux (Paris: Librairie Illustrée, 1888);

Minette (Paris: Librairie Française et Internationale, 1889);

Le Mordu (Paris: Brossier, 1889);

Théâtre (Paris: Savine, 1891);

La Sanglante Ironie (Paris: Genonceaux, 1891);

L'Animale (Paris: H. Simonis Empis, 1893);

Le Démon de l'absurde (Paris: Mercure de France, 1893);

La Princesse des Ténèbres (Paris: Calmann-Lévy, 1896);

Les Hors nature (Paris: Mercure de France, 1897);

L'Heure sexuelle (Paris: Mercure de France, 1898);

La Tour d'amour (Paris: Mercure de France, 1899);

La Jongleuse (Paris: Mercure de France, 1900); translated, with an introduction, by Melanie C. Hawthorne as *The Juggler* (New Brunswick, N.J. & London: Rutgers University Press, 1990);

Contes et nouvelles (Paris: Mercure de France, 1900);

L'Imitation de la mort (Paris: Mercure de France, 1903);

Le Dessous (Paris: Mercure de France, 1904);

Le Meneur de louves (Paris: Mercure de France, 1905);

Son printemps (Paris: Mercure de France, 1912);

La Délivrance (Paris: Mercure de France, 1915);

La Terre qui rit (Paris: Maison du Livre, 1917);

Dans le puits ou La vie inférieure (Paris: Mercure de France, 1918);

La Découverte de l'Amérique (Geneva: Kundig, 1919);

La Maison vierge (Paris: Ferenczi, 1920);

Les Rageac (Paris: Flammarion, 1921);

La Souris japonaise (Paris: Flammarion, 1921);

Le Grand Saigneur (Paris: Flammarion, 1922);

L'Hôtel du Grand Veneur (Paris: Ferenczi, 1922);

Le Parc du mystère, by Rachilde and Francisco de Homem-Christo (Paris: Flammarion, 1923);

Le Château des deux amants (Paris: Flammarion, 1923);

Au seuil de l'enfer, by Rachilde and Homem-Christo (Paris: Flammarion, 1924);

La Haine amoureuse (Paris: Flammarion, 1924);

Le Théâtre des bêtes (Paris: Les Arts et le Livre, 1926);

Refaire l'amour (Paris: Ferenczi, 1927);

Alfred Jarry ou Le surmâle de lettres (Paris: Grasset, 1928);

Madame de Lydone, assassin (Paris: Ferenczi, 1928);

Le Prisonnier, by Rachilde and André David (Paris: Editions de France, 1928);

Pourquoi je ne suis pas féministe (Paris: Editions de France, 1928);

Portraits d'hommes (Paris: Mornay, 1929);

Le Val sans retour, by Rachilde and Jean-Joë Lauzach (Paris: Fayard, 1929);

La Femme aux mains d'ivoire (Paris: Editions des Portiques, 1929);

L'Homme aux bras de feu (Paris: Ferenczi, 1930);

Les Voluptés imprévues (Paris: Ferenczi, 1931);

Notre-Dame des rats (Paris: Querelle, 1931);

L'Amazone rouge (Paris: Lemerre, 1931);

Rachilde, circa 1890, in a photograph inscribed to her husband, Alfred Vallette

Jeux d'artifices (Paris: Ferenczi, 1932);
Mon étrange plaisir (Paris: Baudinière, 1934);
La Femme Dieu (Paris: Ferenczi, 1934);
L'Aérophage, by Rachilde and Lauzach (Paris: Les Ecrivains Associés, 1935);
L'Autre Crime (Paris: Mercure de France, 1937);
Les Accords perdus (Paris: Editions Corymbes, 1937);
Pour la lumière (Paris: Fayard, 1938);
La Fille inconnue (Paris: Imprimerie La Technique du Livre, 1938);
L'Anneau de Saturne (Paris: Ferenczi, 1939);
Face à la peur (Paris: Mercure de France, 1942);
Roman d'un homme sérieux (Paris: Mercure de France, 1942);
Duvet d'ange (Paris: Messein, 1943);
Survie (Paris: Messein, 1945);
Quand j'étais jeune (Paris: Mercure de France, 1947);
A l'auberge de l'Aigle (Rheims: A l'Ecart, 1977).

PLAY PRODUCTIONS: *La Voix du sang*, Paris, Théâtre d'Art, 10 November 1890;
Madame la Mort, Paris, Théâtre d'Art, 20 March 1891;
Le Vendeur de soleil, Paris, Théâtre de la Rive Gauche, June 1894.

OTHER: F. A. Cazals, *Le Jardin des ronces*, preface by Rachilde (Paris: Editions de la Plume, 1902);
Marie Huot, *Le Missel de Notre-Dame des Solitudes*, preface by Rachilde (Paris: Sansot, 1908);
Alfred Machard, *Petits romans parisiens; Souris l'Arpète*, preface by Rachilde (Paris: Mercure de France, 1914);
André David, *L'Escalier de velours*, preface by Rachilde (Paris: Flammarion, 1922);
Lucien Aressy, *La Dernière Bohème. Verlaine et son milieu*, preface by Rachilde (Paris: Jouve, 1923);

Jean Rogissart, *Au chant de la grive et du coq*, preface by Rachilde (Mézières: Editions de la Grive, 1930);

Claude Kamme, *Le Message des jours*, preface by Rachilde (Paris, 1934).

The name of Rachilde has long been associated with those of minor decadent writers and symbolists of the last two decades of the nineteenth century. She is also known for her work with the *Mercure de France*, one of the foremost literary journals, which she cofounded with her husband, Alfred Vallette, and to which she regularly contributed reviews of fiction, as well as her own original work. Her name has also been linked to that of the writer Alfred Jarry, one of her closest friends, whom she supported financially and emotionally in a variety of ways. Although she was immensely successful at the beginning of her career, her reputation has since been relegated to that of "supporting role" status, and there has been little attempt until recently to assess her literary career in any serious fashion. Her oeuvre is considerable, however, and in addition to novels she wrote plays, literary criticism, memoirs, and poetry. Her last books were published in the 1940s, making the scope of her work extend far beyond turn-of-the-century decadence. Although much of it is hastily written, occasionally trite or repetitive, and frequently uneven in accomplishment, much of it is innovative and entertaining, registering important social and literary currents in ways that have all too often been overlooked.

Born on 11 February 1860 at the family home of Le Cros, just outside Périgueux in provincial France, Marguerite Eymery was the first and only child of Joseph Eymery, the illegitimate son of a marquis and a career army officer, and Gabrielle Feytaud Eymery, the daughter of a newspaper editor of old Périgourdin stock. Many details surrounding Rachilde's background remain obscure, but what is known suggests an emotionally troubled household. Joseph, whom Rachilde described as a Don Juan, had originally been paying court to Gabrielle's mother before transferring his attentions to the daughter. Gabrielle's parents had hoped for something better for her—after all, she had been presented at the court of Emperor Napoleon III, while Joseph was illegitimate. The marriage was supposedly a love match, but Gabrielle was quickly disillusioned, refusing further conjugal relations with her husband after the birth of their daughter some fifteen months after their marriage. Yet she remained emotionally attached to her husband, and when he left the family to follow the call of duty in the Franco-Prussian War, Gabrielle was inconsolable, convinced he would never return. It is all too easy to see in these family anecdotes reflections of the mental instability that would cause Gabrielle to end her days in an asylum and her daughter to seek early independence.

As a soldier by profession and a stoic by temperament, Joseph had little in common with his wife's family. He had no tolerance or respect for what he called "scribblers," and since Gabrielle's family traced their literary ancestry back to the sixteenth-century author Brantôme, their very sense of family identity and tradition must have been antipathetic to him. His interest in a family was to have a son, someone who would share his disdain for words and his love of hunting. He was to be disappointed on all counts.

Rachilde's early childhood was a solitary one. Her early care was provided by a nurse rather than her mother, her father rejected her because she was not a boy, and the family was constantly being uprooted as they moved from garrison to garrison. Later, life was more settled at the family home of Le Cros, but the Gothic atmosphere of the run-down, overgrown house only stimulated Rachilde's active imagination further. Her education was neglected, being provided by a series of governesses and curates who made little impression. Rachilde amused herself by reading whatever caught her eye in her grandfather's library, to which she had unlimited, unsupervised access. She thus made the acquaintance of Voltaire and the marquis de Sade and discovered the joys of literature as well as a thing or two about life. Writing became her own outlet, at first in secret and later more openly. When her parents engaged her at fourteen to an officer of her father's acquaintance, her rebellious nature, her vague mysticism, and her self-expression through writing fused into one strategy. A recurring apparition of a drowned man threatening to silence her prompted both her writing and a series of events that Rachilde described at different moments as accidents and as suicide attempts, bizarre behavior for a good bourgeois daughter.

This adolescent revolt had two interrelated consequences: the engagement was eventually called off, and Rachilde turned more frequently to writing. She began to publish her stories in local newspapers, at first anonymously, and eventually under the pseudonym by which she came to be known. The acquisition of this name, too,

Rachilde, 1887 (engraving after a drawing by E. Langlois)

came about through a typical blend of fancy and pragmatism, the strands of which have become impossible to disentangle. Her family was much given to spiritism, a fad then sweeping the country. The teenage Marguerite Eymery claimed that she had been contacted during a séance by a sixteenth-century Swedish gentleman by the name of Rachilde, who dictated stories to her. It was the perfect response to her parents' disapproval: it turned their own gullibility against them and legitimated her writing by giving it the authority of an external (male) source. The name Rachilde stuck and gradually became the only name by which the author was known. Whether or not Rachilde was conscious of it when she invented the name, it turned out to have a welcome flexibility, for at first readers could assume it was a man's (last) name, while later it could be perceived as a single female-marked name analogous to "Colette." It thus preserved a gender ambiguity and avoided the question of patronymics (no one was quite sure whether it was a last or a first name).

After publishing short stories in local newspapers, Rachilde began to set her sights on a more national reputation, which inevitably involved breaking into the Paris literary circles. She persuaded her mother, who kept an apartment in the capital, to take her there for a few seasons, and used the time to make connections. It was hard work, but Rachilde possessed the tenacity, ambition, and stamina necessary to launch her career, and worked to develop her talent. A cousin who edited a commercial fashion newspaper for women gave her the entrée she needed, introducing her to Sarah Bernhardt, who obtained for her a preface from Arsène Houssaye, which was the bait needed to persuade a publisher to accept a novel in volume form. By the time the fashion newspaper folded, Rachilde had made the literary contacts she needed to continue independently, and in 1881, when she reached the age of majority, she moved definitively to the capital.

Her chance to make a name for herself came in 1884, when she published *Monsieur Vénus* (translated, 1929). Wisely, Rachilde published this work in Brussels, a choice that had two advantages: the novel was morally dubious and liable to prosecution, and thus publication abroad provided some protection; but at the same time the whiff of scandal was precisely what was needed to interest an otherwise indifferent public in the work of this still-unknown writer. The strategy, whether planned or not, worked like a charm. Upon publication the book was immediately banned in Belgium and sold like hotcakes in France. Rachilde was an overnight sensation, and her "coauthor," Francis Talman, consigned to oblivion. (He was another shield in case of prosecution but contributed almost nothing to the writing; subsequent editions of the work dropped his name entirely.)

The novel was undoubtedly successful: it was widely displayed in shop windows, and everyone seemed to have heard of it. It opened some doors and closed others to its author, the gains far outweighing the losses in this respect. But the success was mingled with a certain amount of misapprehension: no one could decide whether the novel was innocuous or pornographic (or possibly both). The French authorities considered prosecuting, but were hampered by the fact that they did not actually understand it; they tried to enlist the author's help in clarifying certain passages, but for some reason the author seemed reluctant to cooperate.

The debate about *Monsieur Vénus* continues today, with readers unable to decide whether it is radically subversive or merely a conventional and even reactionary narrative borrowing the accoutrements of subversion in order to capitalize on fashion. The plot concerns a privileged heiress, Raoule de Vénérande, who falls in love with a flower maker, Jacques Silvert. Raoule treats Jacques as a man of her time and class would treat his mistress, with the result that Jacques adopts an increasingly feminine role. The relationship begins to go awry when Raoule marries Jacques, who acts the part of the wife so well that he makes advances to Raoule's friend the Baron de Raittolbe. Raoule uses this pretext to arrange a duel, in which Jacques, somewhat paradoxically under the circumstances, participates as the male defender; Raoule also arranges for him to be killed. After his death Raoule becomes a recluse, worshiping a wax model of him that incorporates relics of his body as though he were a martyr. In many respects, then, the novel relies on heterosexual romance and the conventions of marriage and monogamy, reinforcing traditional elements of gender roles. On the other hand, it can be read as challenging those roles, as well as those of class, and as playing with their different permutations in such a way as to reveal and destabilize the underlying social construction of those roles.

Jennifer Birkett finds the novel's images "ludicrous" and asserts that the text "scarcely justifies more than one reading." She sees Raoule "forced back into the role of victim. Everything she invents for herself is recuperated for men's pleasure." In contrast to this reading, Dorothy Kelly welcomes the way the novel deconstructs gender: "The decadent, upside-down world turns itself around so many times that one loses one's bearings and after a while notices only the artificial machine of reversal, the artificial nature of gender identity itself." While it may be impossible to decide upon one single correct reading of the novel, one must concede that the novel's ambiguity gives it continued interest and relevance today. With the increasing importance of gender as a philosophical category, the novel can no longer be dismissed as a mere blip on the chart of decadence. This realization has spurred the reappraisal of Rachilde as a writer with something to offer modern readers.

In the years following the publication of *Monsieur Vénus*, Rachilde proceeded to experiment in her fictional laboratory, varying the sexual proclivities of her heroines in an attempt to examine love and sexuality in a new way. They include the rather pathetic figure of Mary Barbe, the eponymous heroine of *La Marquise de Sade* (1887), as well as the counterpart to *Monsieur Vénus*, *Madame Adonis* (1888), a novel that plays with the dramatic theme of doubles and mistaken identity. This series of heroines culminates in *La Jongleuse* (1900; translated as *The Juggler*, 1990), in which Rachilde presents cerebral sexuality in its purest form through the character Eliante Donalger.

Eliante's love object is a Greek amphora, the rival to a medical student (Léon Reille) for Eliante's affections. Léon tries to persuade Eliante to accept his advances, while she offers instead her young niece Missy. The surprise ending—involving Rachilde's favorite devices, substitution and confused identity—echoes *Monsieur Vénus* in its refusal of simple interpretation. Is

Woodcut illustrations by Gustave Alaux for the 1925 edition of La Jongleuse

Eliante's death a sign that her ideals are impossible, or is her suicide a moral victory? Whatever the verdict, the novel is among Rachilde's most accomplished creations, combining carefully structured dramatic action with comic relief and suspense. The novel takes its place in a long tradition of French meditations on love; it encapsulates the preoccupations of its own time; and it also points the way for future modernist novels.

During this period of prolific production (she published nineteen works between *Monsieur Vénus* in 1884 and *La Jongleuse* in 1900), Rachilde's personal life also underwent many changes. Her success in 1884 earned her wide popularity, and she found herself among the literary avant-garde. She met Alfred Vallette, whom she married in 1889, and together they founded the *Mercure de France*, one of the foremost reviews in France for several decades. Rachilde contributed some of her own works and became a regular reviewer of fiction. She also ran a literary salon, and in 1890 began combining these responsibilities with those of motherhood, when her only daughter, Gabrielle, was born. (Gabrielle would marry the nephew of the poet Paul Fort; she died in 1984.)

In addition, Rachilde branched out in other directions: she continued to write short stories, but also launched herself in the theater, having several plays produced during the 1890s. Through her connections to the theatrical world she was able to promote the work of Alfred Jarry, helping him, for example, to get his play *Ubu roi* (translated as *Ubu Rex*, 1968) performed in 1896. The friendship with Jarry lasted until his death, and was an important source of mutual inspiration and influence that has been insufficiently studied.

Rachilde continued to publish in the years immediately preceding World War I, though at a slightly slower rate (four publications between 1901 and 1914), as well as after the war, but her popularity was beginning to wane. The role of Germany in the war intensified her strong anti-German sentiments (formed as early as 1870), and left her at odds with modern movements that she perceived (rightly or wrongly) as being Germanic in origin. This was the case, for example, with surrealism, many of whose early proponents were not French: for instance, Rachilde thought of Guillaume Apollinaire, who used the word *surrealism* in 1918, before the movement itself was launched, as a foreigner when compared to a true Frenchman, such as Jarry. Her antipathy was overdetermined, moreover, for, in addition to her xenophobia, she harbored profeminine feelings, and surrealism was inhospitable to women such as Rachilde because of its male chauvinism. Surrealism accepted women as muse figures, but women as active agents (writers, artists) were marginalized by the movement, and indeed it could be argued that surrealism was part of a larger modern reaction to women that underlay the angst of modernism and the rise of fascism.

Although Rachilde as a literary figure was obscured by the dominance of surrealism in the interwar period, she continued to write (it was her only source of income). She was far from being out of touch with modern literary developments, moreover. She had exerted an important influence on the futurist F. T. Marinetti earlier in the century, and was also connected to the circle of expatriate British and American writers living in Paris in the first half of the twentieth century through her friendship with Natalie Clifford Barney. In the interwar years she again wrote prolifically (thirty works—some coauthored—of prose, poetry, and literary criticism between 1919 and 1938).

In her fiction she continued to examine the question of women and their place in society through the creation of unusual heroines, such as Madame de Lydone (from the novel of that title, 1928), a woman who perceives herself as something of an anachronism in modern society, but who turns that position of marginalization into a position of power. In such heroines Rachilde both registers her own situation as a woman who has lived too long (long enough to see her reputation decline) and explores the situation of many French women who had experienced new freedoms in the twentieth century, only to discover that their presence produced a hostile reaction. Although Rachilde claimed that she was not a feminist, and wrote a short book to this effect, *Pourquoi je ne suis pas féministe* (Why I Am Not a Feminist, 1928), the personal freedoms that she had insisted upon all her life both for herself and for her fictional heroines cannot be denied. Rachilde also turned at this time to coauthored work, helping several young men to establish their literary reputations, and to works of criticism and memoirs (among these, her 1928 book on Jarry remains one of the best sources of firsthand information about him).

In 1935 Vallette died at the age of seventy-eight, leaving Rachilde without an important

Eve Francis, Maurice Verne, Rapoport fils, *and Rachilde at a midnight supper, Christmas 1920*

source of support and stability in her life. This circumstance, combined with the advent of yet another war a few years later, led to serious personal difficulties. Her only source of income had been her writing, and as this was interrupted by war, by failing health and eyesight, and by the gradual defection of her audience, her situation became more and more precarious. It is a strange phenomenon that World War II seems to have created a significant rupture in the history of (French) women's literature. Up to this point, many women writers were known, even if only marginally, but during the postwar period, when surrealism, existentialism, and the absurd dominated the literary scene, the memory of their existence seems to have been erased. Only recently has this tradition begun to be remembered.

Rachilde published little after World War II: some poetry (*Survie* [Survival, 1945]) and memoirs (*Quand j'étais jeune* [When I Was Young, 1947]), but no more fiction. When she died after a fall in 1953, she was all but forgotten. She rated a brief obituary in the *Monde* (and even this managed to get her date of birth wrong) and a tribute in the *Mercure de France*, but nothing like the state funeral accorded Colette the following year. Rachilde owes her rediscovery to the second wave of the women's movement and the interest it stimulated in women writers during the 1970s (when several of her novels were republished), and to the renewed interest in decadence and modernism on the part of a society once again confronting its "fin de siècle."

Letters:

Auriant, "Neuf lettres inédites de Rachilde au père Ubu," *Bayou*, 20 (1956): 42-51;

Pierre Lambert, "Trois lettres de Rachilde à J.-K. Huysmans," *Bulletin de la Société J.-K. Huysmans*, 41 (1961): 250-254;

Michel Sanouillet, *Francis Picabia et "391"* (Paris: E. Losfeld, 1966);

Organographes du Cymbalum Pataphysicum, 18 (1982): 1-51;

Will L. McLendon, "Autour d'une lettre inédite de Rachilde à Huysmans," *Bulletin de la Société J.-K. Huysmans*, 77 (1983): 21-24.

Bibliographies:

"Eléments d'approche d'une bibliographie périgourdine de Rachilde (1877-1883)" and "Bi-

Rachilde in her salon, 1930 (photograph by Harlingue-Viollet)

bliographie postérieure à 1879," *Organographes du Cymbalum Pataphysicum*, 19-20 (4 April 1983): 109-120, 121-148;

Melanie C. Hawthorne, "Rachilde," in *Critical Bibliography of French Literature: The Nineteenth Century* (Syracuse, N.Y.: Syracuse University Press, 1993), pp. 78-84.

Biographies:

Ernest Gaubert, *Rachilde* (Paris: Sansot, 1907);

André David, *Rachilde, homme de lettres* (Paris: La Nouvelle Revue Critique, 1924);

Claude Dauphiné, *Rachilde: Femme de lettres, 1900* (Périgueux: P. Fanlac, 1985);

Auriant, *Souvenirs sur Madame Rachilde* (Rheims: A l'Ecart, 1989);

Dauphiné, *Rachilde* (Paris: Mercure de France, 1991).

References:

Joseph Ageorges, "Rachilde," in his *Critique de sympathie: Portraits littéraires* (Lyons & Paris: E. Vitte, 1909), pp. 126-128;

Natalie Barney, "Rachilde," in her *Aventures de l'esprit* (Paris: Edmond-Paul frères, 1929);

Maurice Barrès, "Mademoiselle Baudelaire," *Chroniques* (February 1887): 77-79;

Jules Bertaut, *La Littérature féminine d'aujourd'hui* (Paris: Librairie des Annales Politiques et Littéraires, 1909);

Micheline Besnard-Coursodon, "*Monsieur Vénus, Madame Adonis:* Sexe et discours," *Littérature*, 54 (May 1984): 121-127;

Jennifer Birkett, *The Sins of the Fathers: Decadence in France, 1870-1914* (London: Quartet, 1986);

Françoise Cachin, "*Monsieur Vénus* et l'ange de Sodome. L'Androgyne au temps de Gustave

Moreau," *Nouvelle Revue de Psychanalyse*, 7 (Spring 1973): 63-69;

Henriette Charasson, "Rachilde," *Revue de Hollande*, 4 (1917): 977-985;

Marcel Coulon, "L'Imagination de Rachilde," *Mercure de France*, 142 (15 August - 15 September 1920): 545-569;

Claude Dauphiné, "Rachilde et Colette: De l'animal aux Belles Lettres," *Bulletin de l'Association Guillaume Budé*, 2 (1989): 204-210;

Dauphiné, "Sade, Rachilde et Freud: Lecture de *La Marquise de Sade*," *Bulletin de l'Association des Professeurs de Lettres*, 17 (1981): 55-59;

Dauphiné, "La Vision médiévale de Rachilde dans *Le Meneur de louves*," in *Mélanges Jean Larmat: Regards sur le moyen-âge et la Renaissance*, edited by Maurice Accarie (Paris: Les Belles-Lettres, 1982), pp. 489-492;

Lucienne Frappier-Mazur, "Marginal Canons: Rewriting the Erotic," *Yale French Studies*, 75 (1988): 112-128;

Marie Thérèse Gaddala, "Nos amies les bêtes: De Colette à Rachilde," in her *Ceux que j'aime . . . : De Maurice Barrès à Paul Morand* (Paris: Figuière, 1927), pp. 160-167;

Remy de Gourmont, "Rachilde," in his *Le Livre des masques* (Paris: Mercure de France, 1895);

Melanie C. Hawthorne, "Monsieur Vénus: A Critique of Gender Roles," *Nineteenth-Century French Studies*, 16, nos. 1 & 2 (1987-1988): 162-179;

Hawthorne, "Rachilde," in *French Women Writers*, edited by Eva Sartori and Dorothy Zimmerman (New York: Greenwood, 1991), pp. 346-356;

Hawthorne, "The Social Construction of Sexuality in Three Novels by Rachilde," *Michigan Romance Studies*, 9 (1989): 49-59;

Alfred Jarry, "Ce que c'est que les ténèbres," in his *Œuvres complètes*, volume 2 (Paris: Gallimard, 1987), pp. 432-435;

Gustave Kahn, "La Littérature des jeunes et son orientation actuelle," *Revue*, 37 (1 April 1901): 36-51;

Dorothy Kelly, *Fictional Gardens: Role and Representation in Nineteenth-Century French Narrative* (Lincoln: University of Nebraska Press, 1989);

Jean Lorrain, "Mademoiselle Salamandre," in his *Dans l'oratoire* (Paris: C. Dalou, 1888), pp. 204-215;

Camille Mauclair, "Eloge de la luxure," *Mercure de France*, 8, no. 41 (May 1893): 43-50;

Will L. McLendon, "Huysmans, Rachilde et le roman de 'mœurs parisiennes,'" *Bulletin de la Société J.-K. Huysmans*, 77 (1985): 21-24;

Francis de Miomandre, "Rachilde, Princesse des Ténèbres," *Art Moderne*, 13 & 14 (1903): 117-119, 125-127;

Organographes du Cymbalum Pataphysicum, 19-20 (4 April 1983);

Léo Paillet, "Rachilde," in his *Dans la ménagerie littéraire* (Paris: Baudinière, 1925), pp. 149-161;

Gaston Picard, "Rachilde," *Larousse Mensuel*, 467 (July 1953);

Noël Santon, *La Poésie de Rachilde* (Paris: Le Rouge et le Noir, 1928);

Jennifer Waelti-Walters, *Feminist Novelists of the Belle Epoque: Love as a Lifestyle* (Bloomington: Indiana University Press, 1990);

Robert E. Ziegler, "Fantasies of Partial Selves in Rachilde's *Le Démon de l'absurde*," *Nineteenth-Century French Studies*, 19, no. 1 (1990): 122-131;

Ziegler, "The Suicide of 'La Comédienne' in Rachilde's *La Jongleuse*," *Continental, Latin-American and Francophone Women Writers: Selected Papers from Wichita State University Conference on Foreign Literature, 1984-1985* (Lanham, Md.: University Presses of America, 1987), pp. 55-61.

Papers:

The Harry Ransom Humanities Research Center, University of Texas at Austin, the Bibliothèque Nationale, Paris, and the Fonds Jacques Doucet, Paris, have holdings of Rachilde's manuscripts.

Marcel Schwob

(23 August 1867 - 26 February 1905)

Robert Ziegler
Montana Tech

BOOKS: *Etude sur l'argot français*, by Schwob and Georges Guieyesse (Paris: Emile Bouillon, 1889);

Le Jargon des Coquillards en 1455 (Paris: Emile Bouillon, 1890);

Cœur double (Paris: Ollendorff, 1891); selections translated, with an introduction, by Iain White in *The King in the Golden Mask and Other Writings by Marcel Schwob* (Manchester, U.K.: Carcanet, 1982);

Le Roi au masque d'or (Paris: Ollendorff, 1892); selections translated in *The King in the Golden Mask and Other Writings by Marcel Schwob*;

Mimes (Paris: Mercure de France, 1893); translated by A. Lenalie (Portland, Maine: Thomas B. Mosher, 1901);

Le Livre de Monelle (Paris: Le Chailley, 1894); translated by William Brown Meloney as *The Book of Monelle* (Indianapolis: Bobbs-Merrill, 1929);

Annabella et Giovanni (Paris: Mercure de France, 1895);

La Croisade des enfants (Paris: Mercure de France, 1896); translated by John L. Foley as *The Children's Crusade* (Portland, Maine: Thomas B. Mosher, 1923);

Spicilège (Paris: Mercure de France, 1896);

Vies imaginaires (Paris: Charpentier et Fasquelle, 1896); translated by Lorimer Hammond as *Imaginary Lives* (New York: Boni & Liveright, 1924);

La Porte des rêves (Paris: Les Bibliophiles Indépendants, 1899);

La Légende de Serlon de Wilton, abbé de l'Aumône (Paris: Editions de la Vogue, 1899);

Mœurs des diurnales: Traité du journalisme, as Loyson-Bridet (Paris: Mercure de France, 1903);

La Lampe de Psyché (Paris: Mercure de France, 1903);

Notes pour le commentaire (Paris: Champion, 1904);

François Villon: Rédactions et notes (Paris: Dumoulin, 1912).

Collection: *Les Œuvres complètes de Marcel Schwob*, 10 volumes, edited by Pierre Champion (Paris: Bernouard, 1927-1930).

OTHER: Rachilde, *Le Démon de l'absurde*, preface by Schwob (Paris: Mercure de France, 1893);

Robert Louis Stevenson, *Le Dynamiteur*, preface by Schwob (Paris: Plon, 1894);

Georges Courteline, *Messieurs les Ronds-de-cuir*, preface by Schwob (Paris: Flammarion, 1895);

Gustave Flaubert, *La Légende de Saint-Julien l'Hospitalier*, preface by Schwob (Paris: Ferroud, 1895);

Henry Bataille, *La Chambre blanche*, preface by Schwob (Paris: Mercure de France, 1895);

Théophile Gautier, *La Chaîne d'or*, preface by Schwob (Paris: Ferroud, 1896);

Emilie Lalou [Pierre Nahor], *Hiésous*, preface by Schwob (Paris: Ollendorff, 1903);

Le Parnasse satyrique du XVe siècle: Anthologie de pièces libres, edited by Schwob (Paris: Welter, 1905);

Le Petit et le Grand Testament de François Villon, edited by Schwob (Paris: Champion, 1905).

TRANSLATIONS: Wilhelm Richter, *Les Jeux des Grecs et des Romains*, translated by Schwob and Auguste Bréal (Paris: Emile Bouillon, 1891);

Daniel Defoe, *Moll Flanders* (Paris: Ollendorff, 1895);

William Shakespeare, *La Tragique Histoire de Hamlet, Prince de Danemark*, translated by Schwob and Eugène Morand (Paris: Charpentier et Fasquelle, 1900);

Francis Marion Crawford, *Francesca da Rimini* (Paris: Fasquelle, 1902);

Charles Whibley, *Rabelais en Angleterre* (Paris, 1904).

From disciple Pierre Champion to critic George Trembley, those who have chronicled the

Marcel Schwob, circa 1899

life of Marcel Schwob often acknowledge the impulse to create a purely fictional portrait of the author, one modeled on his theory of the art of biography. According to Champion, what should be written of Schwob is an imaginary life, and this view is playfully implemented by Trembley in the introduction to his *Marcel Schwob: Faussaire de la nature* (1969). There is no certainty, Trembley states, as to the date and place of birth of Marcel Schwob, but documents suggest he was linked to the fifteenth-century band of Coquillards, in whose argot he was fluent. Others claim he had an unhealthy interest in little girls and prostitutes, but add that this passion was tinged with so much piety and pity that the crimes imputed to him were often indistinguishable from acts of kindness. Still others insist on having seen Schwob in Paris, in the midst of a small group of men of letters, dreaming of a comfortable chair at the Collège de France or aspiring to membership in the Académie Française. But such a supposition seems hardly plausible. As Trembley states, "Le valétudinaire qui mourut un dimanche de février 1905 dans un modeste appartement de la rue Saint-Louis-en-l'Ile, emporté par la plus banale des grippes, n'est assurément pas Marcel Schwob" (The valetudinarian who, on a Sunday in February 1905, died of a common flu in a modest apartment on the rue Saint-Louis-en-l'Ile is assuredly not Marcel Schwob).

The incongruence between the historical reality of Schwob, the man, with his penchant for painstaking archival research, and the self-fictionalizer, who projected himself into his imaginary lives, has long disconcerted critics, prompting efforts to reconcile the author's creativity and erudition. Vincent O'Sullivan's early dismissal of Schwob as an imitator, a "derivative" writer who "had to be started by something he admired," has since given way to a recognition that, as André Billy said, if Schwob has been unjustly forgotten, "il est tout entier à redécouvrir" (he remains entirely to be rediscovered). The trend toward a more positive reassessment of Schwob's place in history has been marked by the appearance of several new editions of his major works, among them *Vies imaginaires* (1896; translated as *Imaginary Lives*, 1924) by Gallimard in 1957, *Le Livre de Monelle* (1894; translated as *The Book of Monelle*, 1929) and *Spicilège* (1896) by Mercure de France in 1959 and 1960 respectively, and *Le Roi au masque d'or* (1892; partially translated as *The King in the Golden Mask*, 1982) in the 10/18 collection "Fin de Siècles," edited by Hubert Juin.

Among those who have undertaken to reevaluate Schwob's writings, there is now consensus that his ability to combine his talents as artist and scholar is what enabled him to achieve success in the form he came closest to perfecting: the conte. These critics no longer believe that Schwob's accomplishments as medievalist and linguist inhibited his creativity, but that they rather served as a springboard to his resurrection of the historical figures with whom he most closely identified. As Christian Berg puts it, "Pour Schwob, la bibliothèque n'est pas de *l'écrit*, mais du *à vivre*" (For Schwob, the library does not consist of something written, but of something to be lived).

Mayer-André-Marcel Schwob was born on 23 August 1867 in Chaville, a small town not far from Paris. Shortly before the birth of his second son, Schwob's father, Georges, returned from Egypt, where he had been attached to the foreign affairs ministry of the Egyptian viceroy. In Chaville he resumed work as a newspaperman before moving to Tours in 1870 and there taking over the editorial responsibilities of the *Républicain Indre-et-Loire*. Already at age three the precocious Marcel had learned to speak both German and English, when his father acquired the liberal paper *Phare de la Loire* and relocated with his family, this time to Nantes, where Schwob would spend the remainder of his childhood.

Schwob's mother, née Mathilde Cahun, was a descendant of the Kaims and counted among her ancestors both laborers and rabbis. Having come from a family steeped in Jewish tradition, Mathilde is described by Champion as a rather severe and authoritarian figure, "quelque peu tyrannique dans son amour pour ses enfants" (somewhat tyrannical in her love for her children). Yet she also provided Marcel with all the educational opportunities that personal sacrifice would allow, seeing to it that her son profited from the presence in the household of English governesses and German tutors, with the result that he distinguished himself in his early school years by winning academic prizes, particularly in languages. Still, the young Schwob's interests were not exclusively academic, as he proved to be an avid reader of Edgar Allan Poe and enjoyed playing games of pirates with his sister Maggie. Even in his reading, Schwob demonstrated what would develop into an enduring tendency to live vicariously through the adventures he discovered in books. "Quand j'étais enfant," as Schwob wrote in *Il Libro della mia memoria* (in *Œuvres complètes*, volume two [1927]), "je m'enfermais au grenier pour lire un voyage au Pôle Nord, en mangeant un morceau de pain trempé dans un verre d'eau. Probablement j'avais bien mangé, mais je me figurais mieux prendre part à la misère de mes héros" (When I was a child, I would lock myself in the attic, and, while eating a piece of bread soaked in water, I would read of a voyage to the North Pole. I had probably eaten well, but I imagined I could better share that way in the misery of my heroes).

In late 1881 Schwob enrolled in the lycée Louis-le-Grand in Paris and took up residence with his maternal uncle Léon, who for several years had served as an assistant conservator of the Bibliothèque Mazarine. Along with teaching Schwob a theory of translation that stressed capturing the essence of the thought over the exactitude of the word, Léon Cahun, himself the author of several historical fictions, assuredly influenced his young charge as much by the rigorousness of his research as by the subjects of his tales of violence and warfare, set in remote places and ancient times.

Between 1883 and 1886 Schwob began his first literary endeavors, including a translation of Catullus and a novel set in ancient Rome, whose heroine, Poupa, is described by John Alden Green as a "child-like and very dreamy young girl, prototypic of the eleven creatures whose stories are told in the second part of *Le Livre de Monelle*." During this time Schwob became familiar with the writing of Charles Baudelaire, Poe, and Joris-Karl Huysmans, authors who were beginning to leave their imprint on the fin-de-siècle generation. He also read widely in Arthur Schopenhauer, whose influence is apparent in the two long poems Schwob undertook on the legends of Faust and Prometheus. In 1885 Georges Schwob, likely disenchanted by his son's literary predilections and lack of accomplishment in school, persuaded Marcel to volunteer for army duty. But while his service with the 35th artillery regiment in Vannes apparently did little to curb the young man's wayward behavior, his experience in Brittany was used to provide the setting for several of the tales included in his inaugural collection, *Cœur double* (Double Heart, 1891).

Upon his return to civilian life, Schwob suffered the disappointment of being refused at the Ecole Normale but did obtain his licentiate in November 1888, and the following year began his association with the noted philologist Michel Bréal, then a professor at the Sorbonne. Under the latter's tutelage, Schwob collaborated with his

Marguérite Moreno, whom Schwob married in 1900 (from John Alden Green, ed., Marcel Schwob: Correspondance inédite, *1985)*

friend Georges Guieyesse on a study of French argot, which, following his coauthor's suicide in May 1889, was published later that year. Prefigurative of Schwob's scholarly orientation in general and of his fascination with the language of the underworld in particular, *Etude sur l'argot français* characterizes argot as a self-conscious, artificial system of linguistic deformations intended to mystify the noninitiate. Argot, as Champion says, was the "secret door" that gave Schwob access to the works of François Villon, toward whom much of Schwob's scholarly activity would thenceforth be directed. Indeed, Schwob's comprehensive research on Villon was utilized and acknowledged by Gaston Paris in his 1903 volume on the medieval poet.

Published at the beginning of his most prolific years, Schwob's first collection, *Cœur double*, shows evidence of his continuing interest in "la pègre" (the underworld) and of his affinity for the Breton countryside, with which he had grown familiar during his army duty. As would be the case with most of his subsequent collections, Schwob wrote a preface to *Cœur double* that was intended to give a philosophical framework upon which the tales were to be organized. Reprinted in *Spicilège* as "La Terreur et la pitié" (Terror and Pity), the preface purports to trace the individual's spiritual evolution from experiences of terror occasioned by superstition, a belief in the supernatural, and uncanny chains of circumstances, to self-induced terror, resulting from an experimentation with opium or from obsessional love. It is through the subject's ability to empathize that he first discovers himself in others and, having recognized in them his own suffering and fear, purges himself of all human and superhuman terrors, leaving him with only a sense of pity.

The second half of the collection, "La Légende des gueux" (The Beggars' Legend), examines the same Aristotelian catharsis of potentially harmful passions. Beginning in prehistory, in the age of polished stone, moving on to ancient Rome, the Middle Ages, and then through the succeeding centuries, the tales are set in periods that mark off different stages in the development of literature. The privileged form, as Schwob envisioned it, would thenceforth be "le roman d'aventures" (the novel of adventure). No longer would man be determined by the naturalists' investigations; instead, he would be able to give free rein to his own imagination. Similarly, "le domaine de l'art est la liberté" (the domain of art is liberty), its function being to record the coincidence of a character's moment of internal crisis and an upheaval occurring in the external world, which together constitute the "adventure."

Green and others have commented on the somewhat pedantic nature of Schwob's preface, but many of the tales thematically anticipate later concerns. It is out of pity that Monelle and her epigone will appear in the night to offer their solace to writers such as Thomas De Quincey, Fyodor Dostoyevski, and Schwob's narrator himself. Similarly, as Monelle's sisters, girls of indeterminate age, will embody the entire range of human emotion, from the petulant self-centeredness of "L'Egoïste" to the devoted self-abnegation of "La Sacrifiée," so the artless child characters of *Cœur double* will challenge with their innocence the murderous ideologues of "La Terreur future" (The Future Terror). Forcing them to question their own values and convictions, the children compel a recognition that individual human lives are more important than collective systematic bloodshed so that, at the end, the revolutionaries' eyes are opened, and "la pitié descendit en eux" (pity descended into them).

Overall, the critical reception of Schwob's first book was favorable, as the collection appeared in two separate editions in 1891 alone. Jules Renard, a colleague and friend of Schwob, saluted the author "dont le nom est un aboiement" (whose name is a bark) and recommended the text with the cryptic observation "que tous ceux qui *doivent* lire *Cœur double* le liront" (all those who *must* read *Cœur double* will read it). Henri Bérenger, in a January 1892 article in the *Ermitage,* ascribed to Schwob "le don des visionnaires et l'érudition la plus vaste" (the gift of visionaries and the broadest erudition) and qualified him as a modern-day Denis Diderot, perhaps less spontaneous, but more of an artist.

After having initially been rejected by Lecène et Oudin, Schwob's second collection, *Le Roi au masque d'or,* was published by Ollendorff in November 1892. More than the preceding volume, *Le Roi au masque d'or* attests to the author's enduring fascination with the themes of masking, impersonation, and the transformational power of fiction. The inflexibility of a character in his attachment to his self-image, the confusion of the subject's self with a facade first assumed out of expediency, and the reconversion of a public persona into a privately ratified identity are issues broached by Schwob in these stories, which anticipate the oppositional Sartrean concepts of "pour-soi" (being for oneself) and "pour-autrui" (being for others). These tales pose the question of whether identity is a dynamic, collaborative construct, or whether others' petrifying gaze or the contemplation of self in a mirror gives a factitious sense of continuity and permanency that experience works to destabilize.

The title story tells of a king masked in gold who lives in a palace where mirrors are forbidden. Surrounded by jesters wearing masks of hilarity, women with masks of innocence and purity, and priests with masks of a sober expression, the king lives among those whose essence has been made visible. But when challenged by a blind beggar to recognize that sightlessness and uncertainty are superior to illusory convictions, the king takes off his mask, exposing his face to a young girl, who flees in horror from the sight of the king revealed to be a leper. After ordering the unmasking of the members of his court—the priests with their sleepy eyes and comic expressions, the jesters with faces ravaged by insomnia and worry, and the women with faces that were themselves masks congealed by boredom, stupidity, and ugliness—the king puts out his eyes and sets out in search of "la cité des Misérables."

On his way he encounters a girl and, hearing the sound of bells, mistakes his fellow sufferer for a shepherdess with her flock. She agrees to take him to his destination, but before arriving the king dies, healed of his disfigurement and cleansed of his illness by his own blood, free at last, as the beggar observes, to remove all his masks, "d'or, de lèpre et de chair" (of gold, leprosy and flesh). It is not coincidental, as Michel Viegnes has remarked, that the king, whose identity has taken on the metallic changelessness of his mask, first discovers himself in the flowing water of a river, "image héraclitéenne du devenir et du temps" (Heraclitean image of time and of becoming). Indeed, as the mask does not cover the true face beneath it, meanings can never reliably be circumscribed, and metamorphosis is what betokens an ever-receding referent, since, as Schwob says, "tout en ce monde n'est que signes, et signes de signes" (in this world, everything is only signs, and signs of signs).

Along with the quest for self-consistency that, in Schwob, always seems to end in failure, there is also the threat of the actor's imprisonment in his role, a misfortune befalling the two fourteenth-century gamblers and vagrants in "La Peste" (The Plague). Arrested for having allegedly taken part in a rebellion against the pope, the men, in order to escape torture and induce their jailers to set them free, decide to counterfeit themselves as victims of the plague that is ravaging the countryside. But the mask they don ends up adhering to their faces, as they succumb to the disease in the course of the night and, like the king, obtain deliverance only at the cost of their own lives.

The ubiquity of the "routiers" (highwaymen) and "faux-visages" (false-faces) that people Schwob's stories shows his tendency to link the assumption of disguises to the pursuit of a life of change and dereliction. Champion relates a conversation between Schwob and the Dutch philologist W. G. C. Byvanck, in which the former, when asked what mythical figure best embodied the literary spirit of the era, answered:

> "La figure d'Ahasvérus, du Juif-Errant, du voyageur sans trêve qui a rencontré l'Idéal sur son chemin mais qui lui a tourné le dos, parce qu'il ne le reconnaissait point dans la forme où il se

présentait à lui; et il s'est mis à marcher, furieux contre lui-même, poussé par la folie d'une espérance vaine, et il marche toujours"

(The figure of Ahasuerus, the Wandering Jew, the relentless traveler who encountered the Ideal in his path, but didn't recognize it in the form in which it appeared to him; and he began to walk, furious with himself, driven by the madness of a vain hope, and he is walking still).

Schwob's best-known book, *Le Livre de Monelle,* was inspired, according to Champion and others, by Schwob's relationship with an uneducated prostitute known only as Louise, a frail and ingenuous creature with chestnut hair and laughing eyes. Projecting onto this uncomplicated figure his nostalgia for the childhood denied him by his precociousness and scholarly upbringing, Schwob idealized the one he referred to by the affectionate diminutive "la petite Vise." The unfathomability of the child's mind was what impressed the cerebral author, whose works prominently feature child characters, from Maïe in "Le Pays bleu" (The Blue Land) to the young martyrs in *La Croisade des enfants* (1896; translated as *The Children's Crusade,* 1923).

In addition to the child's capacity for surprise, which had intrigued Baudelaire, Schwob focuses on the impermanence of childhood, which he associates with the fugitive status of the criminals and outcasts he also catalogues in his stories: "hommes primitifs . . . dont l'ignorance et la simplicité s'apparentent à celles des enfants" (primitive men . . . whose ignorance and simplicity are related to those of children). Green has adduced convincing evidence that the death of Louise in December 1893 could hardly have served as the motivating force behind Schwob's writing of *Monelle,* since much of the book had already appeared as discrete stories prior to that time. Still, there is little doubt that Schwob's relationship with the illiterate Louise and the devastation he felt in the aftermath of her death helped to crystallize certain ideas about childhood that then found expression in his volume.

Le Livre de Monelle consists of three distinct and seemingly independent sections: "Les Paroles de Monelle" (Monelle's Words), "Les Sœurs de Monelle" (Monelle's Sisters), and "Monelle." The first, a body of disconnected and engimatic pronouncements, summarizes Monelle's philosophy, in which wisdom is paradoxically achieved through its renunciation. Designated as a prostitute, Monelle herself is like a mask, having no identity except for the one assumed when she adapts herself to those to whom she brings her "pity" and consolation. Trembley relates the little prostitute's self-dispossession and sympathetic mimesis to Schwob's description, in the preface to *Cœur double,* of the path that leads from selfishness to charity, from terror to pity, and from self to others—one that requires, as Schwob said, "l'expansion de sa propre vie à l'expansion de la vie de tous" (the expansion of one's own life to the expansion of the life of all).

Monelle's lessons, which presuppose that they themselves will be transcended, stress the changeable over the ossified, simultaneity over continuity, play over work, and lies over truth. In the same way that Schwob had been drawn to Louise for her ability to live in the present, so Monelle counsels the writer against attempting to arrest time's passage: "Sois heureux avec le moment. Tout bonheur qui dure est malheur. N'attarde pas le moment: tu laisseras une agonie. Vois: tout moment est un berceau et un cercueil: que toute vie et toute mort te semblent étranges et nouvelles" (Be happy with the moment. All happiness that lasts is unhappiness. Do not delay the moment: you will leave behind you a death agony. See: each moment is a cradle and a coffin: let each life and each death seem strange and new to you).

Without any teleological significance, Monelle's message is anti-Socratic: "Ne te connais pas toi-même" (Know not thyself), she advises, lest self-knowledge preclude self-renewal. Like Ahasuerus, Monelle's disciples must always continue to move forward, but unlike him, they are enjoined not to grieve over an ideal that they had once failed to recognize. Memory and remorse are what paralyze the one who is tempted to look backward, surrendering to an impulse that will change him "en statue de larmes pétrifiées" (into a statue of petrified tears). Rather than being nihilistic, as Wesley Goddard has claimed, Monelle's teachings warn against a loss of self in the nothingness of past regrets and future hopes, and prescribe instead a coincidence of self with the sole reality that can be apprehended in the here and now.

Monelle's sisters, whom she describes as various avatars of herself, have also embarked on the fruitless search for an identity that eludes them, retracing the same itinerary from selfishness to altruism that Schwob had charted in *Cœur double.* "L'Egoïste" (The Selfish One) runs away from the orphanage where she reports having been abused by "Mademoiselle," beaten, and locked up inside a spider-infested broom closet. But her selfishness prevents her from crediting the reality of others, and she accuses the ship's boy who has helped her escape of egoism when circumstances inconvenience her, and of deceit when he tells her things she would rather not hear.

"La Voluptueuse" (The Sensual One) enjoys playing games of make-believe, dreaming that she is the wife whom the sadistic Blackbeard murdered. Similar to the author's, her evasion is a purely imaginary one, modeled on the fairy tales and legends she has read, but the masochistic fantasy of her own execution remains unrealizable, since neither the story she enacts nor the conditions of the game allow it to be borne out. Many of Schwob's stories contain a cautionary message about the danger or frustration inherent in projecting one's own life into another's. Either a failure of imagination may abbreviate the voyage, returning the individual to his point of departure, or else the individual identifies so strongly with a literary character that "authorial" control over the fantasy is lost, and the subject is unable to recover the self that he has abandoned. Selfishness is what characterizes those who ask that reality fulfill their text-based fantasies, or who dismiss as untruth the experience that shows their beloved fictions as mystifications.

Having heard stories of an enchanted land filled with hummingbirds, breadfruit, and fireflies, Bargette ("La Déçue" [The Disappointed One]), a lockkeeper's daughter, dreams of running away to the South, but when she arrives in the Midi, she finds none of the features she had imagined in a paradise of sunshine and accuses not her own credulity, but the duplicity of those who have taken her.

Cice's ("L'Exaucée" [The Fulfilled One]) fantasy is to become a new Cinderella, but the royal carriage that passes before her is a hearse from which emanate the effluvia of a corpse. Morgane, "L'Insensible" (The Insensitive One), never having found her own reflection, departs on a journey, remembering the mirror that had foretold of Snow White's beheading. Yet she discovers her image in a plate filled with blood as an incarnation of the figure of Salome, joining thereby a familiar trope found in many examples of decadent art. Only those whose quest is on another's behalf enter into a self-authored legend, like the woodsman's daughter ("La Sauvage" [The Wild One]), who rescues the green girl and runs away from an adult identity, and Lilly ("La Sacrifiée" [The Sacrificed One]), who looks for the magical herb that will cure her sister's paralysis and, her mission completed, is delivered from earth by the fairy queen who makes the sick whole.

It is Monelle whose fictions heal the disease of adulthood, freeing inmates from their jail of self-knowledge, and who vanishes in death so that she may reappear to lead her followers to the white kingdom. Her disciples are the children who retain the prerogative of playful self-reinvention, and to whom lies are just opportunities to exercise the freedom that comes with improvisation. To her listener she can only suggest oxymoronically that he "learn ignorance" and cultivate illusion, since obeying her precepts means they must be rejected, so that Monelle does not become a "philosophy." By abandoning her band of childlike followers, he accedes to the wisdom she preaches, as change and renewal are the keys to her realm, not the corruption of things seen as permanent: "Toutes choses sont fugitives; mais Monelle est la plus fugitive.... Oublie-moi et je te serai rendue" (All things are ephemeral, and Monelle the most ephemeral.... Forget me, and I will be returned to you).

Along with publishing *Mimes* (1893; translated, 1901), a collection of tableaux set in ancient Greece, Schwob remained active in his scholarly work during these years, presenting a paper (*Annabella et Giovanni* [1895]) on John Ford's *'Tis Pity She's a Whore* (1633), translating Daniel Defoe's *Moll Flanders* (1722), and expanding his circle of literary acquaintances to include Paul Claudel and Alfred Jarry, whose *Ubu roi* (1896; translated as *Ubu Rex*, 1968) contains a dedication to Schwob. In early 1895 Schwob first met Marguérite Moreno, an actress at the Théâtre Français whom he would eventually marry, and to whom the author wrote the impassioned and often lyrical love letters compiled by Champion in the final volume of the *Œuvres complètes*.

Yet at the end of the same year, Schwob underwent the first in a series of operations for an illness whose nature has remained undisclosed, a "mal assez mystérieux" (rather mysterious ailment), Champion remarked, that affected him "dans sa dignité d'homme" (in his male dignity). Still, in the initial stages of his sickness, Schwob's creativity remained largely unimpaired, and in 1896 Mercure de France published the first edition of *La Croisade des enfants*, Schwob's adaptation of the medieval legend of the child pilgrims who set off for Jerusalem, only to perish in a storm at sea. Heralded by Remy de Gourmont as

Schwob, Léon Daudet, and W. G. C. Byvanck

"un petit livre miraculeux" (a miraculous little book), Schwob's text was later set to music and performed at the Concert Colonne in 1905.

The year 1896 also marked the appearance of Schwob's last major collection of tales, *Vies imaginaires*, whose preface, "L'Art de la biographie" (The Art of Biography), represents a synthesis of Schwob's views on the apparently conflicting demands of scholarship and historical research with the artist's recourse to subjectivism and invention. As the pity of the prostitute Monelle had allowed an expansion of her own life to an expansion of the life of all, the biographer's art does not conflate its subject with the social collectivity it may have affected, but rather adds to man's knowledge by focusing on a historical figure's unique characteristics. Refining further the theories of James Boswell and John Aubrey, Schwob renounces "general ideas," affirming that the biographer's role is to render his subject's idiosyncrasies, even if doing so requires that he renounce a concern for historical truth.

The function of biography is different from that of history, its emphasis not on the impact of military victories, literary masterpieces, or scientific discoveries, but on the details that particularize its subjects, revealing them as different from everyone else. Readers partake in pleasurable guesswork about the reasons for the habits of figures from the past: Samuel Johnson's tendency to carry the dried peel of an orange in his pockets, Aristotle's wearing over his stomach a small leather bag filled with hot oil. As attention to accuracy may inhibit the biographer in the exercise of his creativity, so his subjects need not be great men, according to Schwob: "Aux yeux du peintre le portrait d'un homme inconnu par Cranach a autant de valeur que le portrait d'Erasme"

(In the eyes of the painter, Cranach's portrait of an unknown man has as much value as the portrait of Erasmus).

Odd facts gleaned from the lives of both the forgotten and the famous activate the imagination in this collection, prompting author and characters to abandon the document in favor of the adventure born of conjecture. Thus, literature should not be viewed as a substitute for life, but as a springboard to the reverie arising from what is unknown and awaiting discovery. For Lucretius, reading serves as an impetus rather than as a barrier to action, and the wisdom contained in Epicurus's treaty cannot explain away his love for an African woman. Preferring experience to understanding, he drinks the potion his lover prepares: "Et tout aussitôt sa raison disparut, et il oublia tous les mots grecs du rouleau de papyrus. Et pour la première fois, étant fou, il connut l'amour; et dans la nuit, ayant été empoisonné, il connut la mort" (And immediately his reason fled, and he forgot all the Greek words on the papyrus scroll. And for the first time, being mad, he experienced love; and in the night, having been poisoned, he also knew death).

Familiar with the lore of notorious pirates, Major Stede Bonnet tries to be like them, outfitting a ship with cutlasses, cannons, grappling irons, and barrels of rum. But after his ship is commandeered by the genuine Blackbeard, he is apprehended and made to stand trial, convicted of "[une] trop grande application à la littérature" (applying himself too greatly to literature), and then hanged from a gallows in Charlestown. These stories often reflect on a pattern of action that must have appealed to the author, the impulse to learn ignorance, as Monelle had counseled, and to forsake the library for the world—like Petronius, "qui désapprit entièrement l'art d'écrire, sitôt qu'il vécut de la vie qu'il avait imaginée" (who entirely unlearned the art of writing, as soon as he lived the life he had imagined). Yet as the narrator leaves Monelle's wandering band, preferring suffering, love, and creation, Schwob's works attest, by his having written them, to his refusal to become his own character.

As Schwob's deteriorating health prevented him from setting out on any new textual voyages, he began as compensation to travel more extensively in the final few years of his life—first to England, where he wed Marguérite in September 1900, and then to Jersey, where he described worsening condition in letters to his new wife. In the following year Schwob undertook an arduous voyage to Samoa, a pilgrimage to the grave of Robert Louis Stevenson, with whom Schwob had corresponded. Long an admirer of Stevenson's powerful evocation of the buccaneers who appear in similar guise in his own tales, Schwob often spoke of the affinity he felt for the author of *Treasure Island* (1883), and already in 1894 had written a preface to the French-language translation of *The Dynamiter* and an essay on the novelist that appears in *Spicilège*, a collection of essays.

Schwob's letters give a detailed account of his harrowing five-month voyage on board *La Ville de la Ciotat*, which left him debilitated and exhausted, resolved, as he wrote to Marguerite, never to go away again. Back in Paris the brilliant "conteur" of the mid 1890s found himself unable to derive any inspiration from his journey and contented himself instead with work on a translation of *Macbeth* and on a satire on journalism, *Mœurs des diurnales*, written in the style of François Rabelais and published under the pseudonym Loyson-Bridet in 1903.

In the last two years of his life, Schwob, whose inability to remain long at a single address seemed to parallel the peripatetic careers of his characters, finally fixed himself with his wife and Chinese servant, Ting, in an old house on the rue Saint-Louis-en-l'Isle. There he assembled some of his previous works into a volume he entitled *La Lampe de Psyché* (1903) and made plans for subsequent projects that he was never to complete. Following a trip to Italy in 1904 to visit Francis Marion Crawford, whose *Francesca da Rimini* he had translated two years before, Schwob returned to Paris, where, in failing health, he feverishly continued his research on Villon, sketched out a project for a critical study of Charles Dickens, and finished the last few texts included in the final volume of his *Œuvres complètes*. On 13 February 1905 Schwob wrote a letter to Marguérite in which he complained of a flu that had left him prostrate, yet his wife was unable to return to his side before he passed away on 26 February.

As Champion commented, at the time of Schwob's death at the age of thirty-seven, "son cycle imaginatif était terminé depuis dix ans peut-être" (his cycle of imaginative works had already been finished for perhaps ten years). Yet if his reputation has been maintained to some degree until this day, it is based on the fiction he authored during his tragically foreshortened career. Some critics have denigrated Schwob for his indulgence in tales of violence and perversion and, like Mario Praz, have dismissed him as an-

Sarah Bernhardt in two scenes from Hamlet, *1899. Schwob and Eugène Morand translated the Shakespeare drama into French for this great actress.*

other minor fin de siècle figure, even while conceding that his "art is much superior to that of many of the Decadents." Others have commented on the universality of Schwob's settings and themes, praising his economy of diction and polished style. Some scholars, moreover, have called attention to certain modern writers' indebtedness to Schwob, among them André Gide, whose *Les Nourritures terrestres* (1897; translated as *The Fruits of the Earth*, 1949) demonstrates a remarkable thematic parallel with *Monelle*, and the Argentine novelist Jorge Luis Borges, whose *Historia Universal de la Infamia* (1958; translated as *The Universal History of Infamy*) is widely regarded as having been influenced by *Vies imaginaires*.

Yet Schwob's problematizing of the question of authorial identity, his recourse to fiction as an instrument of self-transformation and renewal, anticipate present-day literary concerns. With the reprinting of his major works in more popular editions and the emergence of serious critical interest in his long-neglected writings, one might hope that Schwob, like his character Monelle, might for a time have been forgotten in preparation for contemporary readers' recovery of his message.

Letters:

Marcel Schwob: *Correspondance inédite*, edited by John Alden Green (Geneva: Droz, 1985).

Biography:

Pierre Champion, *Marcel Schwob et son temps* (Paris: Bernard Grasset, 1927).

References:

Christian Berg, "Un Réalisme irréel," *Quinzaine Littéraire*, 299 (1979): 5-6;

W. G. C. Byvanck, *Un Hollandais à Paris en 1891* (Paris: Perrin, 1892);

Wesley Goddard, "Marcel Schwob (1867-1905), conteur et critique littéraire," Ph.D. dissertation, University of Paris, 1950;

Remy de Gourmont, *Nouveaux masques* (Paris: Mercure de France, 1898);

John Alden Green, "The Literary Career of Marcel Schwob (1867-1905)," Ph.D. dissertation, University of Washington, 1960;

Hubert Juin, "Les Masques de Schwob," *Quinzaine Littéraire*, 299 (1979): 6;

Monique Jutrin, *Marcel Schwob: "Cœur double"* (Lausanne: Editions de l'Aire, 1982);

Marguérite Moreno, *Souvenirs de ma vie* (Paris: Editions de Flore, 1948);

Vincent O'Sullivan, "Two Lives," *Dublin Magazine* (January-March 1928): 33-44;

Mario Praz, *The Romantic Agony*, translated by Angus Davidson (New York: Meridian, 1956);

S. A. Rhodes, "Marcel Schwob and André Gide: A Literary Affinity," *Romanic Review*, 22 (January-March 1931): 28-37;

George Trembley, *Marcel Schwob: Faussaire de la nature* (Geneva: Droz, 1969);

Louise Trudel, "L'Enfance dans les contes de Marcel Schwob," *Revue de l'Université d'Ottawa*, 38 (October-December 1968): 561-587;

Michel Viegnes, "Mythes, symboles et révélation dans *Le Roi au masque d'or* de Marcel Schwob," *Symposium*, 40 (Spring 1986): 71-82;

Robert Ziegler, "Marcel Schwob and the Fin-de-Siècle Flight from Time," *French Review*, 56 (April 1983): 688-695.

Papers:

Many of Schwob's manuscripts are in the Marcel Schwob Memorial Collection at Brigham Young University.

Jules Vallès (Louis-Jules Vallez)

(11 June 1832 - 14 February 1885)

Robin Orr Bodkin

BOOKS: *L'Argent*, anonymous (Paris: Ledoyen, 1857; revised edition, Paris: Livre-Club Diderot, 1969);

Jean Delbenne, anonymous (Paris: Dubuisson, 1865; revised edition, Paris: Livre-Club Diderot, 1969);

Les Réfractaires (Paris: Achille Faure, 1865; revised edition, Paris: Mornay, 1930; revised edition, Paris: Les Editeurs Français Réunis, 1955; revised edition, Paris: Livre-Club Diderot, 1969);

La Rue (Paris: Achille Faure, 1866; revised edition, Paris: Les Editeurs Français Réunis, 1969; revised edition, Paris: Livre-Club Diderot, 1969);

Jacques Vingtras, as Jean La Rue (Paris: Charpentier, 1879); republished as *Jacques Vingtras: L'Enfant* (Paris: Charpentier, 1881; revised edition, Paris: Quentin, 1884); republished as *L'Enfant* (Paris: Mornay, 1920); republished as *Jacques Vingtras I: L'Enfant* (Paris: Les Editeurs Français Réunis, 1950);

Les Enfants du peuple (Paris: Administration du journal *La Lanterne*, Lemer, 1879);

Jacques Vingtras: Le Bachelier (Paris: Charpentier, 1881); republished as *Le Bachelier* (Paris: Mornay, 1921); republished as *Jacques Vingtras II: Le Bachelier* (Paris: Les Editeurs Français Réunis, 1950);

La Rue à Londres (Paris: Charpentier, 1884; revised edition, Paris: Fasquelle, 1914; revised edition, Paris: Les Editeurs Français Réunis, 1951; revised edition, Paris: Livre-Club Diderot, 1969);

Jacques Vingtras: L'Insurgé: 1871 (Paris: Charpentier, 1886); republished as *L'Insurgé* (Paris: Mornay, 1923); republished as *Jacques Vingtras: L'Insurgé* (Paris: Nouvelle Librairie de France, 1950); republished as *Jacques Vingtras III: L'Insurgé* (Paris: Les Editeurs Français Réunis, 1950); translated by Sandy Pe-

Jules Vallès

trey as *The Insurrectionist* (Englewood Cliffs, N.J.: Prentice-Hall, 1971);

Mazas (Paris: L'Estampe Originale, 1894);

Les Blouses: La famine à Buzançais: 1847 (Paris: Edouard-Joseph, 1919); republished as *Les Blouses* (Paris: Les Editeurs Français Réunis, 1957; revised edition, Paris: Livre-Club Diderot, 1969);

Des Mots (Paris: Edouard-Joseph, 1920; revised edition, Paris: Lérot, 1986);

Les Souvenirs d'un étudiant pauvre, edited by Bernard Lecache (Paris: Gallimard, 1930; revised edition, Paris: Livre-Club Diderot, 1969; revised edition, Paris: Les Editeurs Français Réunis, 1972);

Le Tableau de Paris, edited by Lecache (Paris: Gallimard, 1932; revised edition, Paris: Delphes, 1944); edited by Marie-Claire Bancquart (Paris: Les Editeurs Français Réunis, 1971);

Un Gentilhomme (Paris: Gallimard, 1932; revised edition, Paris: Les Editeurs Français Réunis, 1957; revised edition, Paris: Livre-Club Diderot, 1969);

Le Cri du peuple: 1848-1871 (Paris: Les Editeurs Français Réunis, 1953; revised edition, Paris: Livre-Club Diderot, 1969);

Le Testament d'un blagueur (Paris: Livre-Club Diderot, 1969);

Pierre Moras (Paris: Livre-Club Diderot, 1969);

Le Candidat des pauvres (Paris: Livre-Club Diderot, 1969; revised edition, Paris: Les Editeurs Français Réunis, 1972);

La Dompteuse (Paris: Livre-Club Diderot, 1969);

Littérature et révolution (Paris: Les Editeurs Français Réunis, 1969);

La Commune de Paris (Paris: Les Editeurs Français Réunis, 1970).

Collections: *Les Œuvres de Jules Vallès*, 15 volumes, edited by Lucien Scheler (Paris: Les Editeurs Français Réunis, 1950-1972);

L'Œuvre de Jules Vallès, edited, with an introduction, by Gaston Gille (Paris: Le Club Français du Livre, 1953);

Jules Vallès: Œuvres complètes, 4 volumes, edited by Scheler and Marie-Claire Bancquart (Paris: Livre-Club Diderot, 1969-1970);

Jules Vallès: Œuvres, 2 volumes, edited by Roger Bellet (Paris: Gallimard, Bibliothèque de la Pléiade, 1975-1990).

OTHER: André Lemoyne, *Les Charmeuses*, preface by Vallès (Paris: Firmin-Didot, 1867);

Alphonse Legros, *Histoire du Bonhomme Misère*, introduction by Vallès (London: R. Guenaut, 1877);

Benoît Malon, *Le Nouveau Parti*, preface by Vallès (Paris: Derveaux, 1881);

Emile Bergerat, *Chroniques de l'homme masqué*, preface by Vallès (Paris: Marpon et Flammarion, 1882);

Auguste Lançon, *Les Animaux chez eux*, contributions by Vallès and others (Paris: L. Baschet, 1882);

Lucien-Victor Meunier, *Les Clameurs du pavé*, preface by Vallès (Paris: Baillière et Messager, 1884);

Jean-Baptiste Clément, *Chansons*, preface by Vallès (Paris: G. Robert, 1885);

Eugène Pottier, *Chants révolutionnaires*, foreword by Vallès (Paris: Bureau du comité Pottier, 1885);

Séverine, *Notes d'une frondeuse: De la Boulange à Panama*, preface by Vallès (Paris: Simonis Empis, 1894).

Long before Albert Camus's *L'Homme révolté* (1951; translated as *The Rebel*, 1953), Jules Vallès, through the example of his life and literature, articulated boldly and firmly a revolutionary "non." His "non! à un monde mal fait" (no! to a poorly made world) and its attendant revolt were the foundation upon which he constructed what is considered by most modern critics his masterpiece, the *Jacques Vingtras* trilogy. These three thinly veiled autobiographical novels (*Jacques Vingtras*: *L'Enfant* [1879], *Jacques Vingtras: Le Bachelier* [1881], and *Jacques Vingtras: L'Insurgé: 1871* [1886; translated as *The Insurrectionist*, 1971]—the titles referring to the hero, respectively, as child, graduate, and insurrectionist) first appeared in either epistolary or journalistic form during one of the most politically turbulent periods in nineteenth-century French history. In fact, from 1848 to 1885, Paris, which certainly provides the gravitational pull (if not the center) for all three novels, was a seething cauldron of political activism. For the poor and oppressed it was a climate of violence. Vallès was unequivocally and uniquely attuned to the cry of the people (*Le Cri du peuple* [1953]) and the teeming life boiling out of the Parisian street (*La Rue* [1866]). Both of these terms became titles to which he returned time and again as a means of mobilizing his creative energies. He filled his three most widely known novels with eyewitness accounts of the events leading up to and continuing through the Commune of 1871, that "glorious harbinger" of the proletariat's victory over the bourgeoisie, according to Karl Marx. But beyond this historical import, the process of writing, compiling, and rewriting the trilogy became not only a demonstration of Vallès's will to pursue political involvement but a creative method as well. As in the case of Camus's rebel, the luxury of standing on the sidelines of an evolving modern society either as a nonpartisan or as a Romantic solipsist was no longer an option. At odds with his time, Vallès stood, therefore, in mid-nineteenth-century France like a sentinel blessed with a stentorian voice and a vigorous pen committed to signaling the complacencies of the past, but above all pointing to the beauties of the risks ahead.

Unlike Camus grappling with the existential absurdity of the twentieth century, Vallès wielded his pen not so much against the conditions of life itself as against the specific servitudes, miseries, and injustices perpetrated by a political regime. Napoleon III and the establishment in 1852 of the Second Empire bore most of the brunt of his criticism. Under the pressure of sweeping social change, not just in France but throughout Europe as a whole, the emperor and his administration recognized the need for reform and liberalization but more often than not resorted to repression as the preferred way of governing. The resultant human tragedies (child abuse, an educational crisis, the ravages of poverty and unemployment, homelessness, the suppression of free speech and the press, the warehousing of people in the workplace and in prisons, and the eternal opposition of labor and capital—concerns that make Vallès's writings seem very timely today) came surging to the fore in the writings of the *réfractaire* (rebel or reactionary), as he liked to call himself. Vallès's lived revolt, then, against the world into which he was cast was transposed in his best works as a type of social realism. His *tranches de vie* (slices of life) certainly brought a nod of recognition from some of his more widely known contemporaries, such as Théodore de Banville, Alphonse Daudet, Emile Zola, Paul Alexis, and Edmond and Jules de Goncourt. But it was apparent that they were reluctant to share center stage with this dissident who obviously stood behind his militant political program—a program advocating the overthrow of all established institutions as well as embracing the uncertainty of a new era.

Throughout his fifty-two turbulent years, certainly in his more introspective moments, Vallès attempted to isolate the source of his fiercely independent nature. Though three geographical areas—the provinces, Paris, and London—framed the major events of his life, he returned time and again to his provincial origins as the only substantial means of deciphering his behavior. Born Louis-Jules Vallez in the small village of Puy-en-Velay in the former province of Auvergne on 11 June 1832, he often remarked that he came from a strange race of people, "dont les fils portent tous au cœur un besoin terrible de liberté et même l'instinct de révolte" (all of whose sons carry within their hearts an intense need for freedom and even the instinct for revolt). Indeed, from his early childhood he was taught that the people of Auvergne had descended from one of the most powerful yet civilized tribes of ancient Gaul—the Arverni. This tribe had rallied around a young warrior by the name of Vercingétorix in 52 B.C. to struggle against the invading armies of Julius Caesar. Ultimately, such valor and determination became the wellspring of legendary deeds for all who came from this region.

As an adult Vallès could point with pride to this lineage and, no doubt, consider it as a possible explanation for the intensity of his political and ideological convictions. However, as a young lad with an active imagination seeking escape from the domestic squabbles of his working-class parents marooned in the provinces of nineteenth-century France, the leap was not too great to picture himself fighting alongside the legendary chieftain. Together with such an imaginary playmate, he probably waged many successful battles for freedom and justice. These two concepts frequently surfaced within the Vallès household and were often left hanging in its depressed air, less as banners to uphold than as signs of their absence.

While the intense need for freedom was the birthright of every *Auvergnat*, it was much more for young Jules. What began, then, as a heritage and intensified into a diversionary response to familial conflict ended by significantly shaping the course of his life. From this angle Vallès seemed destined to become an unwavering voice for the common good, rebuking political tyranny and social inequity. Yet, to sketch Vallès lashing out with an imaginary companion at abstract foes à la Don Quixote would critically misrepresent the import of his provincial origins; it would lay the foundation for nothing more than a budding romanticist's quest of empty ideality. In fact Vallès grappled early on with the warring contraries of a homo duplex. At almost every turn his youthful idealism ran up against insurmountable odds, not to mention the pessimism created in his home life, and was invariably forced to knuckle under. As a result the harsh realities in and around Puy-en-Velay gave an ironic and subsequently skeptical twist to his outlook on life.

Both sides of his family sprang from the hardy peasant stock of the Haute-Loire region. Just to survive, the Vallezes and the Pascals (Jules's mother's family) had for generations been accustomed to riveting themselves to a small plot of mountainous terrain from sunrise to sunset. This kind of pragmatism—or, more accurately, the will to survive—finally drove Jean-Louis Vallez, Jules's father, to break the stifling and deadly cycle of his farming ancestry. His ambition, wrought in the smithy of minimal results for maximum effort, compelled him to undertake one of the most daring adventures of his historical moment—climbing the social ladder. As Stendhal's *Le Rouge et le noir* (1830; translated as *The Red and the Black*, 1913) so poignantly dramatizes, the avenues for social mobility during this era, although publicly promoted, were rather limited.

Despite these circumstances Jean-Louis set out to make the transition from merely surviving to becoming a professional educator. In 1829, three years after receiving his baccalaureate, he married Julie Pascal, of similar background and aspiration. In the course of the next decade, she gave birth to his seven children, only two of whom, Jules and Marie-Louise (born in 1835), survived. Significantly, the *s/z* separation between father and son took place when the family name was erroneously recorded as *Vallès* on Jules's birth certificate. Instinctively, Jean-Louis signed the document *Vallez* without noting the official misspelling. This gap widened and became all the more symbolic, particularly during the first sixteen years of Jules's life, as his father tenaciously held to his dream of securing a permanent teaching position. After eight years, first as an instructor at the departmental school for deaf-mutes in Puy and then minimally upward to the Collège Royal, Jean-Louis packed the Vallezes off to nearby Saint-Etienne. There, in 1840, Jean-Louis settled into one of the lowest-ranking positions in the secondary school system. As his father labored in obscurity, Jules began to distinguish himself in Greek, Latin, and rhetoric. Paradoxically, the same colleagues who vilified the father for his incompetence embraced the son as a promising classicist.

In 1845, after failing the oral component of the *agrégation* (he eventually succeeded in the summer of 1846), Jean-Louis accepted a post at the Collège Royal of Nantes. The long journey by carriage to Orléans and then by steamboat down the Loire to the bustling western port proved especially eye-opening to his teenage son. Never before had his parents' limitations (his father's idiosyncratic quest for self-importance amid the cold indifference of academe, his mother's greed and pretention) appeared so evident. But above all what was brought into clear focus as Jules left behind his rural birthplace was the realization that he could abide neither his parents' outlook nor their system of values much longer. Lurking just beneath his veneer of conformity was a bitter rebellion waiting for the right moment to explode.

Meanwhile, once established in Nantes, he continued down the road to academic success, ultimately grabbing first prize in rhetoric and Latin in 1848. However, when news of the overthrow of Louis-Philippe's constitutional monarchy came singing over the telegraph on 25 February 1848, Vallès and two of his friends, Charles-Louis Chassin and Evariste Mangin, went down into the public square to celebrate. They planted "freedom trees" in support of a Second Republic that, they hoped, would be founded on the aggressive socialism flowering in France during the late 1840s—the socialism of thinkers such as Charles Fourier, Louis Blanqui, Louis Blanc, and Pierre-Joseph Proudhon, among the more influential. For this young man of sixteen, such a gesture marked the opening of the floodgates of his rebellion. It was only a matter of months before Jules Vallès began to distance himself openly from his family, but above all from his father.

The desire to escape from his father and family, to flee Nantes, crystallized when his revolutionary exuberance was unmercifully crushed as well as proven pathetically naive. Just four months after the joyous events of February, during the so-called June Days (23-26 June), the newly elected Assembly ordered Gen. Louis Eugène Cavaignac to implement a swift and bloody repression of the radical elements of the original overthrow. This brief civil war of 1848—launched in Paris mostly against an amorphous army of impoverished students, artisans, and unemployed workers—killed more than fifteen hundred "rebels," with thousands more arrested and ultimately exiled to Algeria. The injustice of this tragic episode shattered Vallès. In the wake of his disillusionment, a rage against all figures of authority—parents, professors, the state—began to burn deep within his consciousness as well as demand expression. This rage, accompanied by a sense of defeat, would later echo as a leitmotiv throughout his principal works.

In August of that same year, primarily as a concession to his father's insistence (which had become less and less influential, given his political awakening), he took the *baccalauréat* examinations and failed. One month later, still reluctantly attempting to follow through with his father's master plan, he was off to Paris to brush up his skills at the lycée Bonaparte before another try at the dreaded exam. Fully aware that his son was slipping out of his grasp, Jean-Louis made a desperate attempt in February 1849 to bring him under control. Writing to Mme Voilquin, a family friend living in Paris, he implored her to contact Jules and make every effort to impress upon him the importance for an eventual academic career of obtaining his credentials before the age of twenty-two. Whatever she may have said fell on deaf ears. The aura of Paris, its vitality, its promise of opportunity, and its politics had taken hold. Not only did Vallès fail the examinations twice again in 1850 (at Rennes in April and August), but he was again unsuccessful in 1851.

These failures, along with the rumors filtering back to Nantes that his son had plunged headlong into the left-wing politics of Paris (attending Jules Michelet's courses at the Collège de France, then rioting in the streets when the government closed the classes because of Michelet's subversive rhetoric in March 1851), had Jean-Louis shaking in his boots—not so much out of concern for his son, but for his own future and the pending decision on his tenure at the Collège Royal. Finally, with the reports of his son's efforts to organize an armed resistance in response to Napoleon III's coup d'état on 2 December 1851—that *coup de maillet* (hammer blow) leading to the Second Empire and the suppression of an entire generation—he was pushed to wit's end. He felt he had no other choice than to authorize official intervention.

After summoning his son back to Nantes, he had him institutionalized under the care of Dr. Bauchet on 31 December at the St. Jacques asylum "on grounds of insanity complicated by suicidal tendencies." Jules managed, however, to leak out a cry for help. He convinced one of the infirmary nurses to mail a quickly scrawled note directly to his fellow *lycéens* Arthur Ranc and Arthur Arnould in the Latin Quarter. Jean-Louis never could have anticipated the response of his son's newfound friends, nor their political acumen. Arnould, in particular, rose to the occasion, warning Jules's father by return mail that if he did not free his son immediately the scandal would be exposed to the public. Furthermore, he made clear that he would convince his father, a renowned professor of literature at the University of Poitiers, to bring his considerable influence to bear upon a certain tenure decision at the Collège Royal of Nantes. Jean-Louis acquiesced.

Miraculously, on 2 March 1852 Jules was pronounced cured and then released by the same Dr. Bauchet who had just recently diagnosed him as severely disturbed. Apparently Vallès suffered no aftereffects of his "illness" or his stay at the asylum, for seven weeks later he was at the University of Poitiers, where in early May he at long last passed the baccalaureate, under the tutelage of Professor Arnould. Within the next month the young graduate left for Paris to make his way, never seriously looking back again. Although enduring almost nine years of exile (September 1871 to July 1880) in Belgium, Switzerland, and England for his participation in the revolution of

1871, the rest of his life would revolve around the "City of Light."

Little did Vallès realize that his sense of victimization (whether at the hands of his parents, his teachers, or societal authority at large) had only just begun. Once on his own in the capital city, amid its booming commercialism, he had to face the fact that his degree was nonmarketable. Without sufficient funds he quickly gravitated to the bohemian life of the Left Bank. But it was hardly the version extolled in some earlier works of the Romantic period; it was in fact an existence framed by misery and abject poverty. This period of floundering from 1852 to 1857 —attempts at law school in 1853, an assassination plot against Napoleon III in June of the same year, itinerant tutoring at the Testu boardinghouse in 1854, secretarial work for Gustave Planche in 1855, and, finally, fighting duels in 1856—marked the leanest years of his life and only succeeded in exacerbating his indignation. That is, while acknowledging these experiences as an inevitable part of forging a new life, he came to view his uncertainty and hypersensitivity as those of an *écorché vif* (someone skinned alive).

What he did learn, however, during this rocky apprenticeship was that the process of writing had become the most effective way of calming his rage, which flared against all those who would build walls around human freedom. It would seem that, as a way of earning his keep, the most logical application of his classical formation would have been the teaching profession. And yet, having seen what his father had been through, he vowed to undertake it only as a last resort. Thus, putting pen to paper to stave off poverty not only provided Vallès with a more acceptable use of his baccalaureate, but it came to fulfill a deeper need as well. Hardly romanticizing his chosen vocation, he prostituted himself in the beginning, scribbling down almost anything that paid: jingles, dictionary entries, pamphlets, tour guides, and even newspaper articles. Gradually he found his niche as a militant journalist, a journalistic *garde-chiourme* (overseer), weighing in heavily against all forms of human servility, particularly those created by Napoleon III and his repressive regime. Under Vallès's pen, the lived discontinuity and explosive immediacy of journalism became a tool of emancipation. It appealed, therefore, to both his need for freedom as well as his righteous indignation at the sight of the poor and dispossessed—that "great federation of pain"—shuffling along the modern boulevards only recently created by Baron Georges-Eugène Haussmann.

While it is often impossible to identify such turning points with certainty, most of his biographers have selected his father's death in 1857 to mark that moment when his career gathered steam and set off on a discernible course. From this point on he survived from day to day by contributing to or heading up liberal dailies that often lasted no longer than a few months. All the while he began producing longer, more creative expressions of his revolutionary outlook in public lectures, a play, feuilletons, and novels. Throughout the rest of his years, only on two occasions did he detour slightly from his writing vocation. In 1860, under the yoke of financial exigency, he tried being a civil servant at the Vaugirard town hall in the XV$^{i\text{'}eme}$ arrondissement, and then in the spring of 1863 he became what he had promised never to become—a teacher, at the Collège de Caen. Predictably, his teaching career did not last long, for the following September he returned to Paris. Thenceforth, his commitment to the power and process of writing would never waver again.

He began to steer his career onto a collision course with the historical events underpinning as well as leading to the Paris Commune (1871). During the maelstrom of this civil upheaval, Vallès managed to consubstantiate, certainly for himself but especially for others, the acts of revolt, revolution, and writing. As a result of his involvement and the polemical voice he gave it in his publications, he was exiled for almost nine years, living in constant fear, mostly in London. Throughout this period his writing not only allowed him to survive financially and psychologically, but it prepared his triumphant return to Paris. When he stepped off the train from Brussels at 7:40 P.M. on 13 July 1880 after amnesty for all Communards had been granted, this intransigent rebel knew that he was about to take Paris again. This time it would not be via the storm of insurrection, not by fighting in the streets as in 1871, cowering behind cobblestone barricades against superior forces, but outwardly in the bookshops and kiosks; in short, in the hearts and minds of a reading populace.

With his resuscitated journalistic voice and his *Jacques Vingtras* trilogy, he would show how his personal revolt against a "poorly made world" had emerged (*L'Enfant*), evolved (*Le Bachelier*), and then exploded (*L'Insurgé*) with that of his entire generation. Virtually writing himself into the grave, he died five years later, on 14 February

Caricature of Vallès as a dog dragging a pot, by André Gill

1885, exhausted but proud to have remained true to himself and his principles. Two days after his death tens of thousands followed his funeral procession to Père Lachaise cemetery. Eugène Pottier, the author of the *Internationale*, eulogized him as "the candidate of misery, the deputy of the slain." That same day Vallès's newspaper (the one he had resurrected upon his return from exile), the *Cri du Peuple*, its borders in black, declared in bold type that "la Révolution vient de perdre un soldat, la littérature un maître. Jules Vallès est mort" (The Revolution has just lost a soldier, and literature a master. Jules Vallès is dead).

Perhaps this unique combination in Vallès of an impassioned journalist with a classically educated man, a serious social critic of the exploitation of the masses and an activist committed to "liberté sans rivages" (freedom without limits), led him to chart new stylistic terrain in the realm of the narrative. Whatever the case, the "presentational" or thoroughly modern quality of his novels offended, if not confounded, those colleagues who emerged as proponents of realism or the closely related naturalist movement. The extraordinary freedom and fullness of the Vallesian narrative—a narrative whose originality springs from the discontinuity of its sequences and their temporal indeterminacy; the nervous discourse of his dialogues; the conflation of author, narrator, and narratee; the pictorial economy; the irony; the humor; the onomatopoeic transpositions; and the shifting semantic levels, to list but a few of the most outstanding stylistic features (features that seem closer to what the contemporary reader has come to accept as an enhanced verisimilitude)—produced a less than favorable reaction, particularly from Zola and his naturalist *école de Médan* (Médan School).

As a counterpoint, Vallès ridiculed as pretentious their intent to portray lived reality "in all its details." Moreover, he felt that their prose tended to bog down into a ponderous, excessively linear exposition spilling over with pseudoscientific documentation. In short, it was hardly a "natural" way of conveying a sense of lived reality and was therefore misleading. Out of frustration Zola, particularly through the polemics of his disciple Alexis, went so far as to exhort Vallès to put politics aside and not let it get in the way of his creative genius. The implication was that it muddled his writing. Thus, whether from the perspective of his sociopolitical *engagement* or that of his stylistic innovations used to (re)produce it, Vallès was a rebel; however, he was without question a rebel *with* a cause.

It is, therefore, certain that the Vallesian "non"—this revolt into literary style, this revolution leading to a creative process that sutured political history to the production of literature—made him a perennial outsider. Shortly after Vallès's death, one of the most influential critics of his day, Ferdinand Brunetière, opened his postmortem in the 1 March 1885 edition of the prestigious *Revue des Deux Mondes* with the following observation: "C'est d'un vilain homme que je vais parler" (I shall speak of a disagreeable man). Indeed, if ever there existed in nineteenth-century French letters a journalist or novelist seemingly irremediably marked by misfortune while simultaneously advancing toward fame, it was Vallès. As if singled out by a hideous sign or a grotesque tattoo that compelled others to avoid his singularity, he had to learn to live and write in the midst of a conspiracy of silence. When discussing this phenomenon with respect to Edgar Allan Poe as well as speculating on its diabolical origin, Charles Baudelaire simply called it *le guignon* (bad luck), which writes itself in large letters across the forehead of its prey.

Certainly few writers were more systematically ignored or officially ostracized than this man apparently with "le diable au corps" (the devil in his soul), to use his words. The fines and public admonishments endured by several of the most celebrated writers of the period, such as Baudelaire for his *Fleurs du mal* (1857; translated as *Flowers of Evil*, 1909) and Gustave Flaubert for *Madame Bovary* (1857; translated, 1881), were minimal when compared to the official pursuit of Vallès. He was perceived as a loose cannon rolling about the decks of the Second Empire, the Commune, and the Third Republic. Although it was not uncommon to use a pen name in the nineteenth century, for Vallès it quickly became a requirement. He often had to resort to pseudonyms such as Asvell (an anagram of his surname), Max, Z, Jean Max, Un Réfractaire, Jean La Rue, or Jacques Vingtras just to get his work considered for publication.

After the success of Honoré de Balzac, Henry Murger, and Eugène Sue with the *roman-feuilleton* (serial novel), the sequential publication of a novel in a successful newspaper emerged for budding writers after 1850 as the least expensive and most expeditious way into print. When Vallès came calling as a journalist or novelist, the fears, of course, were that if his name became affixed to that particular press or publishing house, then the conservative readership would either flee in droves, insist upon retractions, force imprisonment (Vallès was first imprisoned at Mazas in 1853 and then twice at Sainte-Pélagie in 1868), shut down the business altogether, or all of the above. In this regard his reputation preceded him, making the recourse to pseudonyms all the more necessary.

Understandably, he chose not to sign his first major publication, *L'Argent* (Money, 1857), but indicated it was "par un homme de lettres devenu homme de bourse" (by a former man of letters turned stockbroker). Although more a pamphlet than a novel, this text was hardly original, for the bulk of it had been provided by a certain Saucebel. As a wealthy industrialist with inside connections to a potential publisher, Saucebel had hired Vallès to compose "in prose and verse" publicity brochures for his fertilizer company. While fascinated by his raw energy, the entrepreneur recognized not only that his young writer aspired to much more than generating interest in manure, but also that he had had a run of bad luck in his efforts to become a published author. Apparently with the sincere intent of providing an entry into this arena, Saucebel had an associate pass on to Vallès a highly technical manual concerning the *Bourse* (stock market) and the acquisition of capital, with the understanding that he would spruce it up and bolster or amplify it where needed. With such an opportunity Saucebel assumed that the young man could now make his own way.

True to form, Vallès threw himself enthusiastically into the task, absorbing as much information as he could tolerate. He frequented the stock market, sensing its pulsing rhythms. He rubbed shoulders with the power brokers, the rich, and the influential. Many nights were spent intently studying Proudhon's 1852 *Manuel du spéculateur à la Bourse* (The Stock Market Speculator's Handbook). And he even feigned swallowing François Guizot's infamous directive "Enrichissez-vous!" (Get rich!) as a viable response to being born under the sign of poverty and political exclusion. He appeared to be unfaithful to his true inclinations especially in his most significant contribution to the text, an introductory letter addressed to Jules Mirès, a legendary rags-to-riches financier. That is, while replacing the cry of "Vive la révolution!" (Long live the revolution!) with "Vive l'argent!" (Long live money!), the "anonymous author," the future *candidat des pauvres* (poor man's candidate), seemed to celebrate and aspire to Mirès's miraculous ascendance from virtual obscurity to enormous wealth.

Those true inclinations, however, were visible through the author's sarcasm and irony. While, as a "former" man of letters, the *bachelier* confessed profusely to seeing the error of his ways and promised that in the future he would worship only at the modern temple of true value, represented by the stock exchange and its quest of material wealth, so caustic were the vitriol and irony that those in the cafés who had read Vallès or heard him hold forth extemporaneously on the same subject were hardly fooled. Consequently, despite the succès de scandale of *L'Argent*, and in spite of his controversial run of related articles splashing across the financial pages of the *Figaro* shortly thereafter, the militant writer continued to run afoul of the established journalistic and literary community. Later, in *Insurgé*, he would typify this ongoing antagonism by recalling Emile de Girardin's initial refusal to take him in as a contributor to the *Presse*: "Il nous faut des disciplinés, bons pour la tactique et la manœuvre, jamais vous ne vous y astreindrez, jamais!" (We have to have disciplined people, good tacticians and followers; you'll never tie yourself down to that, never!). Paradoxically, after being censured himself, Girardin eventually hired Vallès with the understanding that "Bouledogue, on va vous déchaîner! Vous ferez la chronique le dimanche. . . . Et qu'on vous entende aboyer, n'est-ce pas?" (Bulldog, we are going to unchain you! You'll write the lead article for Sunday's paper. . . . Make sure people hear you bark, understand?).

After Vallès had waged this kind of battle for more than a decade, struggling to make a marketable name, caricatures of him began to appear frequently in the Parisian dailies. One, sketched by his friend and associate André Gill, portrayed him as a ferocious dog clattering through the streets of Paris with a tin pot tied to his tail, chasing angrily after a funeral procession. Despite this unflattering image, Vallès no doubt roared with laughter at the situational irony. He was nonetheless relentless in his efforts to be heard and read, even going so far as to try to establish his own newspapers. The titles, of course, were emblematic—the *Rue* (the first version in June 1867), *Journal de Sainte-Pélagie* (while in prison in 1868), the *Peuple* (February 1869), the *Réfractaire* (May 1869). When he managed in 1871 to put together the *Cri du Peuple*, which would emerge as the voice of the Commune, he fell victim once again to the caricaturist's scrutiny. This time, fist clenched, sleeves rolled, he was a disheveled worker or peasant with hobnail boots striding aggressively about the boulevards designed by Haussmann, gesticulating and vituperating at the top of his lungs for no apparent reason while the passersby scurried on, hoping to avoid any contact.

From the fictional case of François-René de Chateaubriand's René to the real one of the young seer from Charleville, Arthur Rimbaud, the plight of the fated writer or other sensitive soul victimized by society was a common thread in the evolution of French Romantic and post-Romantic thought. In 1852 Murger, in his *Scènes de la vie de bohème* (translated as *Bohemian Life*, 1899), had tried to paint a faithful portrait of this experience. However, for Vallès this portrait was too saccharine, too bourgeois, and thus a gross misrepresentation. In fact "murgérisme," to employ his term, had not advanced much beyond the *mal du siècle* (sickness of the century) of the early Romantics; it seemed nothing more than a carefree apprenticeship before being sanctified by the bourgeois establishment. The scenes of camaraderie, the raucous life in Parisian cafés, or excessive self-indulgence (all the while dashing off a few lines that effortlessly found their way to a publisher) were not painful at all.

Upon returning from Murger's funeral on 1 February 1861, Vallès finally recognized his true calling. Rather than seek his entry as a Romantic *révolté* turned bourgeois *égayeur* (pleaser), he concluded that his apparent weakness was indeed his strength. Thenceforth, he would turn his victimization on its head. Rather than avoid or refuse it, he would embrace it. The true misery, poverty, and dislocation—the other side of the Murger coin—would become his focus. According to Roger Bellet, perhaps the most accomplished Vallesian scholar to date, it was precisely with this "revelation" that the trilogy was born. Ultimately he envisioned this project as long-term and in Balzacian dimensions, covering that generation irremediably influenced by the brief and bloody civil war of 1848. Although the title and scope would change over the years ("Histoire de vingt ans," "Histoire d'une génération," and finally *Jacques Vingtras*), it would be a sociohistorical mosaic giving expression and dignity to a sector of Parisian life often ignored or forgotten altogether.

His initial efforts in this regard produced only small journalistic compositions that, in spite of their brutally realistic portraits, remained very much within the wake of Romantic thought. Still searching for the right title and scorching tone, he penned an article entitled "Les Réfractaires" that exploded onto the front page of the *Figaro* on 14 July 1861. According to Bellet, this publication not only marked the beginning of Vallès's arrival but enabled him to determine the direction he would explore for the rest of his career. Four years later he gathered together various articles in this vein, most of which had been published in the *Figaro*, some from as far back as 1857, and without regard to chronology or continuity arranged them into nine chapters. The result was the first fiction to bear his name, *Les Réfractaires*. Although he had false starts, such as the excessively Romantic novella *Jean Delbenne* (1865), *Les Réfractaires* held that voice and tone with which Vallès would feel most comfortable. So successful was the book that thereafter critics such as Charles-Augustin Sainte-Beuve simply addressed him as the "reactionary."

As a series of unforgettable portraits, this novel relates encounters with marginal literary figures of the Second Empire, including Planche, Armand le Bailly, Eugène Cressot, Fontan Crusoé, and Vallès himself, as well as mythical ones, such as *Le Bachelier géant* (The Giant Graduate). No ranks exist among these outsiders, for they are sworn to freedom, refusing any request "to take a number" in their daily lives. Not unlike the nephew in Denis Diderot's *Le Neveu de Rameau* (1823; translated as *Rameau's Nephew*, 1897), these reactionaries confront the reader, making him squirm in the face of some of the injustices and hypocrisies sanctioned by received thought, particularly that found in canonical literature. In this context the chapter "Victimes du livre" plays a central role. Throughout the trilogy, Vallès returns to and explores in greater detail this phenomenon of an increasingly better-educated proletariat.

Deconstructing (long before Jacques Derrida) the moral and ideological impact of reading books (what better or more diverse examples than *René*, the works of George Gordon, Lord Byron, and *Madame Bovary*), he indicates that instead of accepting insipid truisms he seeks the source of moral impropriety in the written word: " 'Cherchez la femme,' disait un juge. . . . C'est le volume que je cherche moi, le chapitre, la page, le mot" ("Look for the woman," some judge used to say. . . . As for me, it is the volume for which I search, the chapter, the page, the word). Implicit in the interplay of anger, irony, and humor that brings the suffering of these educational victims to life is a serious indictment of society and its educational process. Indeed, the day of reckoning, the day of *L'Insurgé*, seems close at hand. Thus, in this curious gallery of irregulars, pariahs, and mountebanks, Vallès takes a major step toward legitimizing his reputation as an author with whom the literary establishment would have to contend.

Surely, Vallès had arrived, or so it seemed. Just seven months later, in June 1866, he launched his second signed novel, *La Rue*. Not one to abandon a good strategy, he hastily collected those short, circumstantial articles that had been seen mostly in the *Evénement* and the *Epoque* from April 1865 to March 1866. He arranged them in chronological order and divided them into six parts: "La Rue," "Souvenirs," "Les Saltimbanques," "Londres," "La Servitude," and "La Mort" (The Street, Memories, The Acrobats, London, Servitude, and Death).

Originally conceived under the rubric "Servitude et Liberté," *La Rue* was, therefore, more than a mere title for Vallès. It was a powerful symbol charged with all the horror and ecstasy of the modern urban jungle. It was the proving ground for the *réfractaires*. Like the many articles, like the three newspapers (1867, 1870, and 1879) to which he gave this title, it was comparable to the legendary phoenix continually transmuting death into life. More specifically, the Parisian street, with all its conflicting forces, was a marvelous but tragic arena in which to play out the exile of a militant writer seeking to be heard under an oppressive regime. Simultaneously imposing estrangement and community, the street welcomes and digests all, even the most extreme and violent of reactionaries. Within their labyrinthic twists and turns, Paris and the streets of the Second Empire gave to all, albeit precariously, an identity and acceptance. Vallès, as a "naturalized Parisian" as he called himself, never ceased to be amazed by the incessant parade of the strange and monstrous creatures he found in the city, in contrast to the familiarity of his provincial hometown.

The sights, sounds, and smells evoked in *La Rue* are decidedly carnivalesque and give a sense of freedom and spontaneity. But the enumeration of poor people, cripples, acrobats, strongmen, boxers, bearded ladies, clowns, and jugglers—while once again demonstrating Vallès's unique curiosity and gift of observation—betrays his strong identification with those exiled to society's periphery. Curiously, although he would denounce Baudelaire at his death in 1867 as too bourgeois and too hypocritical, there is a focus in *La Rue* not unlike that of the "Parisian Prowler," that prose poet of the *Spleen de Paris* (1869; translated as *Poems in Prose*, 1909). In the prose poem "Les Foules" (Crowds), Baudelaire, like the Vallesian streetwalker, intimates that to descend into the urban street is to bathe in the multitudes; but, paradoxically, it is also to wash oneself in solitude. It is to risk one's identity for the chance of securing a fragile moment of solidarity with others in an ambience devoid of the hierarchies of wealth, power, and knowledge.

Bellet suggests that Vallès's identification with the poor and marginal stemmed from the quotidian insecurity and discontinuity of their lives. As a young writer trying to "make it," constantly working under the pressures of censorship, of an editor who might cut or suppress some of his copy, Vallès felt closer to those who had already been beaten or never had a chance in the beginning. Certainly this is a strange posture to assume for someone trying to build on a recent success. And yet the doubts about his writing are pervasive in *La Rue*: "Je ne puis écrire dix lignes sans éprouver . . . l'indicible douleur du vaincu!" (I cannot write ten lines without feeling . . . the indescribable pain of someone who has been defeated!). What could be seen as another expression of Romantic defeatism in the face of inevitable challenge is in *La Rue* a serious, realistic effort to come to grips with the arena, the modern urban battlefield where Vallès, the writer, would surely have daily defeats but victories as well. It is only in the harsh glare of such an arena that the graduate with no marketable skills and without political clout in a burgeoning capitalistic economy might learn to transform himself into the insurrectionist.

La Rue hardly created the same stir as its predecessor. Several factors contributed to this lackluster response. As a freshly published author who had received considerable public acclaim, Vallès was not only competing with himself in the bookstalls, but the novelty of his talent was already widely publicized in the literary cafés. In addition, shortly before the publication of *La Rue*, he had written a scathing article (26 March 1866) for Girardin's *Liberté* against a well-known, recently deceased military official, Gen. Joseph Vantini Yousouf. According to Vallès, Yousouf shamelessly paid his soldiers extra if they cut the ears off anyone of Arabic descent killed while fighting in the Algerian campaign of 1844. Thereafter, the *Liberté* was officially forced to retract this article as well as demand the resignation of its author. Thus, from this point of view *La Rue* was, perhaps, rapidly put together in desperation. That is, in spite of a decade of writing and publishing on almost a daily basis to carve out a foothold, the reactionary was fully cognizant that his days were numbered. He knew that he would soon feel the sting of rejection and humiliation, that he would be thrown back to the street again.

Given the options, one might anticipate a conciliatory gesture, especially as Vallès approached middle age with little more than his controversial reputation and his convictions intact. Sometimes when opportunity has all but disappeared, it is not uncommon to see the rebel fold his tent in order to put food on his table. To seek comfort by compromising one's principles or to wrap oneself in the security of past accomplishments is a much easier road to follow. But in the case of Vallès quite the contrary is true. Most critics confirm that his literary and journalistic production from this point until his death at the age of fifty-two not only continued virtually unabated but built to a veritable crescendo. Gaston Gille, the most thorough of Vallès's biographers, divides these years 1867 to 1885 into three increasingly intensified periods: 1) that of the "insurrectionist," from June 1867 to the collapse of the Commune and Vallès's escape to London in October 1871; 2) that of the "proscribed," from October 1871 to the granting of amnesty by the Third Republic to all exiles on 10 July 1880; and 3) that of the "repatriate," from Vallès's return to Paris just three days later, on 13 July 1880, to his last hours in February 1885 at 77 boulevard Saint-Michel.

To a significant degree, any attempt to track the life and works associated with the first

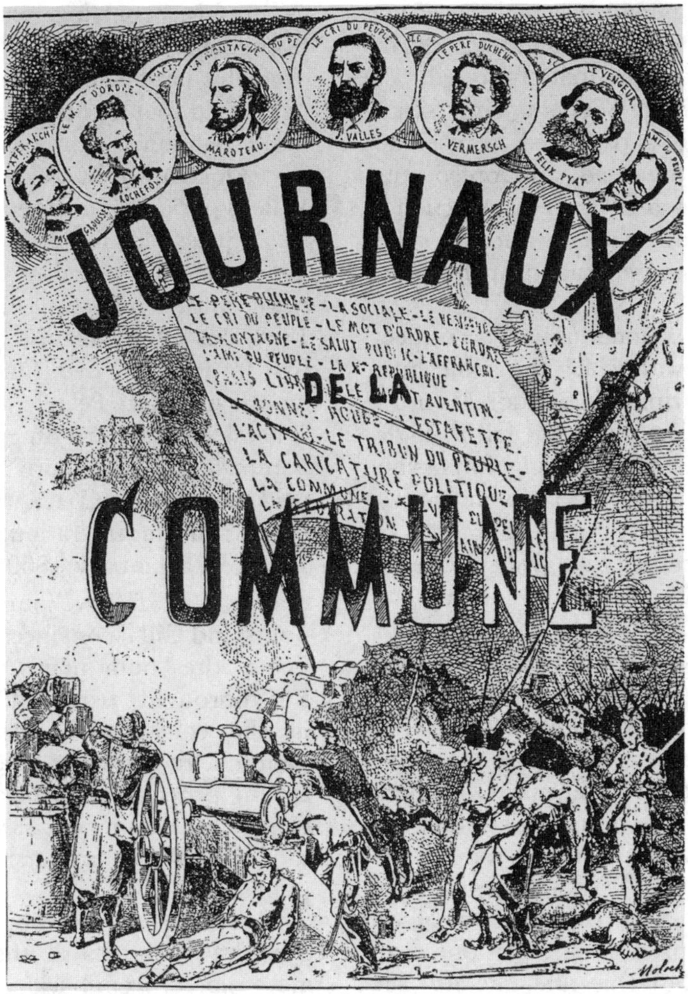

Lithograph by Moloch depicting the editors of periodicals during the Paris Commune. Vallès is pictured at top center.

period, that of the "insurrectionist," must fall short. While obviously brief in comparison to the other two, it is not only the most densely packed moment vis-à-vis people, places, and events, but unquestionably the most resounding. Moreover, all of the above components seem to converge and then accelerate in the symbol that Vallès and his writing became as the explosion of the Commune approached. At times Vallès's personal history appears to merge seamlessly with that of the extraordinary social transformation taking place around him. What happened prior to the establishment of the Commune (26 March 1871) and during its two-month run is written in and through the unique role played by Vallès as an eyewitness, participant, and chronicler.

In terms of the sentimental education—that coming of age of a defeated generation—depicted in the trilogy, the period of the "insurrectionist" is the final stage as opposed to the first. It is that stage where revolt, rather than establishing a protective distance through pathetic Romantic posturing or impractical ideality, transmutes itself into action, into a consciously pursued insurrection. Specifically, it is that moment in 1871 when the socially oppressed and excluded of 1848, fatally marked by birth, finally turned on their bourgeois oppressors with the intent of settling accounts long overdue. Thus, the period of the "insurrectionist" shows Vallès shoulder to shoulder with the working-class people. His insight into their condition clearly substantiates the view that, although they may have started disadvantaged, a conspiracy of sociopolitical forces was required to compel them to accept such a plight. From this angle some are born poor and are therefore destined, if they remain passive, to be victimized by the rich and powerful. But this period comprises much more than the democratic/autocratic and labor/capital struggles that had been building in France from at least 1830 (if not the Revolution of 1789). It is marked additionally by the bloody crackdown that followed, *La Semaine sanglante* (Bloody Week), during which Vallès and all who had participated were either summarily executed, deported, or forced into exile. In short, this period of open insurrection is that historical moment when a society splits apart, losing at least one generation in the process.

But what about this tumultuous swirl of people, places, and events with which the name Jules Vallès was affiliated during this period? Even the most global consideration could not fail to highlight its appearance in a seemingly impossible number of journalistic and novelistic endeavors. Following the sincere but truculent advice of Girardin—who had observed that given all the official hostility to his work, he should start his own paper—Vallès took the offensive. Instead of reinventing himself with pseudonyms, instead of retreating or disappearing after every controversial publication, he would try to build a large readership that would produce second thoughts in even the most zealous of official censors. In these four short years he founded and directed seven different newspapers (some, of course, were short-lived) and contributed to at least ten others. Each of his own papers was decidedly more socialistic in orientation than its predecessor. Just one year after the novel with the same title, the *Rue* hit the streets in June 1867. It was followed by the *Journal de Sainte-Pélagie* (January 1869), the *Peuple* (February 1869), the *Réfractaire* (May 1869), the *Corsaire* (November 1869), the *Cri du Peuple* (February 1871), and then the *Drapeau* (March 1871).

In addition to this journalistic flurry, Vallès managed to publish in feuilleton *Un Gentilhomme* (September to October 1869), *Le Testament d'un blagueur* (October to December 1869), and *Pierre Moras* (November 1869 to January 1870). Of the three, *Le Testament d'un blagueur*, with its autobiographical frame, would play the most central role in the trilogy. Borrowing directly from *Le Testament*, Vallès would later recast in *L'Enfant* the dialectical model pitting a young man's quest for freedom against his sense of exile brought on by the sociocultural demands to conform. But what these three serials revealed above all was that Vallès's larger Balzacian project "to compose the history of twenty years" (1848 to 1868) or the "history of his generation" was coming into clearer focus. Consequently, the Commune would serve as a catalyst enabling him eventually to translate his personal history into a collectivized one. However, this larger undertaking that became the trilogy would require his exile in London before coming to fruition.

One can only touch on the major events of Vallès's period of insurgency as well as on the notable figures encountered, for both were enormously complex and peripatetic. When he was twice imprisoned for subversive journalism in 1868, his pleas against police brutality earned first a fine of five hundred francs and one month at Sainte-Pélagie. Then, for "excitation à la haine et au mépris du gouvernement" (provocation of hatred and scorn for the government), he paid two thousand francs and spent two more months in incarceration, from late November 1868 to 28 January 1869. Upon his release, several of his fellow journalists—Auguste Passedouet and Gill—convinced him to run for local office as the "poor man's candidate." He did and was thoroughly trounced. The ridicule expressed in the conservative press was merciless. Undaunted, five months later he traveled to Waterloo to prepare an article for Pierre Larousse's *Grand Dictionnaire universel du XIXe siècle*. Deemed too politically controversial, this article was never published.

Amid the mounting tensions between the conservative forces of the government and the more liberal republican factions, an event occurred on 10 January 1870 that pushed Vallès and his socialist colleagues into the Paris streets to voice their protest. A young liberal journalist, Victor Noir, was murdered by Pierre Bonaparte, a first cousin of the emperor as well as a longstanding opponent of any kind of social reform. Vallès and his radical compatriots saw their fate bound tightly to this tragedy. In their desperation only one recourse remained. The moment of the Commune, the moment of open rebellion, was close at hand. With Louis-Napoleon's declaration of war against Otto von Bismarck's Prussia on 19 July 1870, with the subsequent capitulation of Sedan on 2 September and the four-month siege of Paris that followed, history provided the necessary impetus for the revolt to begin.

When news of Louis-Napoleon's capture reached Paris on 4 September 1870, Vallès and his fellow reactionaries filled the streets again, demanding the proclamation of the Third Republic. The imperial officials gave little resistance, and a provisional government took over, immediately charged with the continuation of the war against the Prussian invaders. Thus France experienced one of the most bloodless revolutions in its history. But this was truly the calm before the storm.

The widespread need for reform and redirection pulled Vallès, in spite of himself, into the role of a leader. Preferring to remain on the outside and agitate, he suddenly found himself involved with the newly formed Comité Central Républicain (Central Republican Committee). He embraced more and more the concept of a commune; and last but not least this outsider paradoxically joined a strictly hierarchical organization as head of the 191st battalion of the National Guard. On the night of 31 October, Vallès, along with thirty of his men, committed one of those acts that would help shape his legend as a Communard. He took over the town hall at Villette and held it until the next morning as a demonstration of protest. "In the name of the revolution" he was designated mayor of the arrondissement. He promptly turned over to his men all the available food (some herring) and money (twelve hundred francs). The provisional government blew the incident out of proportion, condemning it in the press as a flagrant act of sedition. Vallès consequently went into hiding. But he quickly resurfaced in a long letter printed in Blanqui's 7 November edition of the *Patrie en Danger*, defending himself admirably and pointing out the irony of feeding the neighborhood militia with a few fish as well as paying them a few pennies for their vigilance. But beyond the rhetorical import of his clever rebuttal, Vallès was now recognized everywhere, and not just in the streets, as one of the directing forces of the revolutionary movement. As Girardin had advised, he had definitely taken to the offensive and had begun to create a powerful following.

By January 1871 it was apparent that Paris could not hold. The Prussians were at the doorstep, about to overrun the city. When the provisional government decided not to resist, an armistice was signed on 28 January, with the proviso that elections be held as soon as possible to appoint a national assembly willing to forge a lasting peace settlement. Once held, these elections showed a more than two-to-one majority in favor of the monarchists. Essentially, the elections turned on the question of whether one should end the war with a negotiated peace, which was the prevailing view of the monarchists, or fight to the bitter end, which was that of the republicans. Paris voted heavily in favor of the republicans. Although he ran and was not elected, Vallès received strong support, with more than thirty thousand votes—obviously much better than his first attempt.

As an outspoken critic of the former emperor's foreign policy as well as Prussian militarism, Adolphe Thiers was selected as "chief of the executive power of the French republic." For Vallès, Thiers was a veritable "wolf in sheep's clothing." He was that same unscrupulous, conservative politician who had recommended to King Louis-Philippe that he leave Paris and return with fifty thousand soldiers in order to crush the insurrectionists in the 1848 civil uprising. Vallès feared more of the same was on the horizon. The agreement that Thiers negotiated with Bismarck, which was ratified on 1 March 1871 and signed in May, came at great expense: five billion francs of indemnity and the annexation of Alsace and most of Lorraine. But perhaps more telling, the German army was allowed to stage a victory parade along the Champs-Elysées in a predominantly republican Paris that had overwhelmingly voted for continuing the war. After launching his new paper, the *Cri du Peuple*, in late February with the sole intent of "saving Paris," Vallès not only hammered hard in his editorials on the dishonorable peace Thiers had fashioned but especially pointed out the insidious plan behind the victory march. That is, Vallès realized that Thiers had treacherously betrayed the Parisian populace.

With the Prussian forces mobilized in the most visible section of the city, Thiers had hoped to provoke a violent repression and thus eliminate his troublesome revolutionary detractors. On the eve of the parade, Vallès's lead article exhorted his faithful to proceed with calm, to recognize that the bourgeoisie was trying to do them in at the hands of the Prussians. Three days later, on 4 March, when it was quite certain that his readers (more than sixty thousand copies) had taken his advice to heart, had restrained themselves, he congratulated them in an article entitled "Bravo Paris."

Unfortunately, when Thiers's first plan failed, he decided on a more aggressive approach. On 18 March, realizing that the National Guard far outnumbered the regular army, and that in the case of civil conflict the former would probably side with the revolutionaries, he tried to seize their cannons, which were at Montmartre. He failed again. This time, however, hostilities could not be avoided. Two of Thiers's generals

(Claude Martin Lecomte and Clément Thomas) who had given the order to fire on the crowds beginning to gather were captured and executed by the revolutionary guard. Upon hearing the outcome, Thiers, along with the administrative personnel of the Third Republic, fled to Versailles, where they would spend the next two months plotting their return. With this incident the insurrection of the Paris Commune was under way.

On 21 March the *Cri du Peuple*, which had been suspended since 12 March, reappeared, selling more than one hundred thousand copies. In one quick stroke it had emerged as the official voice of the Commune. Assuredly, Vallès felt a sense of accomplishment, if not exhilaration, finding himself no longer exiled but at the center of the events that would unfold over the next two months. Indeed, as editor in chief of a suddenly successful daily with a socialist slant, he had a triple role to play. He was fully aware that he would contribute not only as an architect of the political developments in the weeks to come, but as a participant and commentator as well.

Just one week into the Commune, on 26 March he accepted a candidacy for official office from the XV[ieme] arrondissement and was this time elected. At last he would be heard and, he hoped, would manage to effectuate meaningful social change. He plunged wholeheartedly into the political process of municipal self-governing in the days that followed. He listened; he debated; he speechified, admonished, and finally voted. Among his fellow socialists, Vallès's political tendencies were more moderate than radical. Neither Blanquist (that is, not a follower of Blanqui) nor Jacobin, he was reluctant to embrace any kind of "ism" and therefore often defended opinions not necessarily his own simply to avoid falling into the trap of doctrinaire thinking. It was perhaps for this reason that as the end drew near—the inevitable retaliation of Versailles—he chose to pursue his political experiment to its only respectable conclusion. And on 21 May, rather than seek escape, he presided over the last session of the Commune. He was fully cognizant that at that very moment Thiers's forces were entering the city and beginning their street-by-street push to retake it. As the session concluded, he descended again into the familiar haunts of the Parisian streets he knew and loved so well. Assuredly it was a defeat, but this last gesture was filled with the quiet and orderly dignity that comes from remaining true to one's principles.

In the ensuing "Bloody Week" (21 May to 28 May), he wandered across the city, visiting the makeshift barricades set up to defend against the more powerful artillery of the regular forces. Despite the odds, he did his best to communicate solidarity with those who shared his commitment. Yet he still watched in horror the burning of the Tuileries Palace and the Hôtel de Ville (City Hall) at the hands of his more radical constituents. As Thiers's juggernaut gained momentum, everywhere Vallès turned the folly of defeat spread uncontrollably with all its destruction and violence. He was shocked and finally compelled to intervene when it appeared that the Communards were going to blow up the Panthéon. Ironically, he would later be condemned to death (4 July 1872) in absentia for supposedly promoting the very burning and looting against which he attempted to intercede.

After seeing many of his closest allies fall at the last defensible barricade at Belleville, Vallès heard the cry: "Perdus! Sauve qui peut!" (We've lost! Every man for himself!). At that moment he knew more than ever that he wanted to live. He knew that in order to tell the story of the twenty thousand to thirty thousand slaughtered by the *Versaillais* (soldiers of the government, headquartered at Versailles) during these seven days, he would have to survive. Slowly, without drawing too much attention, he slipped away. Disguised as a "Doctor Jolyen," he embarked upon a voyage that would lead to Brussels and ultimately to London for the next nine years. In the weeks immediately following his disappearance, the conservative press tore into him with a passion, reporting his "execution" and his "cowardly death" on at least two different occasions (in the *Moniteur du Peuple* and in the *Constitution*). Thus, at this point he was doubly exiled; for, as a stranger in a foreign land, he was exiled from his generation as well as from himself. Throughout this historical moment no other figure seemed to generate in France the same hostility or the same lust for vengeance.

Before these last violent days of his "insurgency," Vallès often remarked that every great writer has but one essential story to tell. Balzac, for example, had discovered within himself the common thread from which he wove his works in all their uniqueness and complexity. If the Commune, then, helped identify and refine Vallès's story, it was his exile—that period of the "proscribed," to quote Gaston Gille—that brought it to the fore. Given a choice, he probably would have stayed in Brussels, where at least his exile would not have been linguistic. However, because of the Belgian laws of extradition, especially concerning fugitive Communards, he had to push on to London, arriving in late October 1871.

Far from constituting an interruption to his career, the next eight years and nine months revolved around little more than the act of writing. The quantity of his correspondence alone was phenomenal. To sketch only a tiny list, his most frequent correspondents included Gill, Arthur Arnould, Hector Malot, Aurélien Scholl, Zola, and many editors. Obviously, the physical location of London, coupled with his monolingualism, necessitated cultivating an army of intermediaries in Paris who could marshal his words into print. Initially, the risk was too great for the older publishers with whom he had an established reputation. The gaping wound of "Bloody Week" had not yet healed. Vallès, therefore, was forced to employ tactics that had served him so well in the past. Proscribed literally and linguistically, he began to reinvent himself by publishing articles under pseudonyms. In addition he wrote a play, *La Commune de Paris*, at the end of 1872, which, in spite of his efforts to have it performed in Lausanne, was not produced. He even started an illustrated gazette in November 1874, the *Coming P.*, which unfortunately folded after several issues.

Yet beyond these activities and others, Vallès began to look with ambivalence at the long trek toward reestablishing himself. He had been down this road before with *L'Argent* when he was struggling to build his reputation under the Second Empire. He had no intention of sacrificing either the knowledge gained in that twenty-year battle or the time it had required. Finally, something clicked; perhaps it was the death in 1875 of Jeanne-Marie, a daughter he fathered with a Belgian woman teaching in London. Whatever the specific motivation, he knew at last that it was time to set in motion his "grande machine romanesque" (grand novel machine). It was time to write that sequence of novels he had envisioned as early as Murger's funeral in 1861. In his correspondence from 1874 to 1878 with his most trustworthy Parisian confidants, Scholl and Malot, he tried out several titles while continuing to insist on a broad historical perspective. Their less than enthusiastic response for a work of such magnitude drove him to recast it. Gradually, with their cajoling, he narrowed the scope to three loosely autobiographical volumes whose narratives would follow one another more or less chronologically. Through the principal character of Jacques Vingtras, Vallès would rewrite his life from birth up to (and including) the events of 1871, while using as a backdrop the beloved "history of his generation." *Jacques Vingtras I* would cover 1832 to 1848; *Jacques Vingtras II*, 1850 to approximately 1857; and *Jacques Vingtras III*, 1860-1862 through May 1871.

The work began in earnest in February 1876. But it was only after tireless negotiations by Malot that *Jacques Vingtras* appeared in feuilleton with the *Siècle* in 1878. Vallès, or "La Chaussade" as the serial was signed, had thus reemerged. He reasserted himself if for no other reason than to respond to the protests that grew louder with each successive installment. This literary cacophony prompted the publisher Georges Charpentier to purchase the publishing rights and put it into print under the same title in May 1879. This time, instead of "La Chaussade," Vallès decided on "Jean La Rue," a pen name that had proved particularly successful for him during his exile. Only after the amnesty would Charpentier risk a second edition in 1881, with the new title *Jacques Vingtras: L'Enfant*, finally signed Jules Vallès. Ironically, the "proscribed" would not have a chance to review his own novel until the third edition was published with Quentin and after he had returned to Paris.

Critics have often pointed to the dedication of each volume of the trilogy as a key to unlocking the specific text. *L'Enfant* is dedicated in part: "A TOUS CEUX qui crevèrent d'ennui au collège ou . . . qui, pendant leur enfance, furent tyrannisés par leurs maîtres ou rossés par leurs parents" (To all those who died of boredom in school or . . . who, during their childhood, were tyrannized by their teachers or brutalized by their parents). The binary opposition signaled by the dedication (the constraints of adulthood opposing the childhood wish for unbridled freedom) structures the entire novel. Even the titles of the first and last chapters reveal dramatically this ordering device. The first, "Ma Mère," establishes the maternal force that pervades the novel and continues to inculcate repressive values in the child, even in the mother's absence. The last chapter, "Délivrance," is a desperate expression of the child's (now young man's) efforts to free himself, whether by the self-destructive act of a duel or by an escape to Paris.

Although no dates are given, *L'Enfant* traces the moral and psychological development of

Séverine (Caroline Rémy), Vallès's devoted friend and assistant during the last five years of his life

Jacques from his birth in 1832 in Puy-en-Velay to his student days in Paris at the age of sixteen, where he fulfills not his goals but those of his parents. They want him to pass the baccalaureate exam and consequently feel obliged at the end of his secondary education to send him to Paris for special tutoring. In its broadest strokes this novel sketches a common evolution in the emerging industrial society of nineteenth-century France. The migration of peasant or working-class people from their bucolic place of birth to the large city is a common frame for many of the "realistic" novels of this era.

L'Enfant deals only with the triad of mother, father, and son. On the surface the locales that buoy the narrative (of twenty-five chapters, three are devoted to Puy, nine to Saint-Etienne, four to Nantes, and four to Paris) represent the Vingtras/Vallez family breaking through social barriers as the father advances within the academic hierarchy. Each new post from Puy to Nantes apparently marks another successful step. But the narrator—sometimes as Jacques the submissive but perplexed child, sometimes as his skeptical, sardonic adult persona, and sometimes both simultaneously—insists on showing the destructive side of the quest. He continually subverts the educational myth driving the parental value scheme. Not only is Jacques unnecessarily neglected as his father gives less and less time to parenthood, but he must endure the emotional and psychological fallout when the father fails professionally. As a *pion* (hack teacher), the father is disliked and humiliated by both his students and colleagues. Jacques is, then, ironically driven to excel in each new school not because he necessarily accepts his father's unmitigated belief in the power of books, but because he wants to compensate for his father's intellectual shortcomings.

Often indicating that he prefers the life of his peasant cousins, who seem much more open than the academics revered by his father, Jacques achieves success nonetheless according to their institutionalized values. From Jacques's vantage point, his father's allegiance to a classical education represents an uninvestigated intellectual posture as well as a hidden political agenda. That is, the sanctification of the past for its own sake condones and perpetuates social iniquity; and to worship it blindly leads to such mind-sets as "no need for change: things have always been that way." Their relationship turns, then, on an emotional codependency in which Jacques defends his father (ultimately in a duel), who continues to reject his son as his professional milieu rejects him. Victimized by the very books that were originally embraced for their liberating or socially mobilizing potential, the father, therefore, ends by victimizing his students, but more importantly his own son.

The mother fares far worse, for she is a sociocultural victim who applies her limited view to everything. Despite her best intentions to provide for her family, she dominates them. She incarcerates the household, wrapping it in the unquestioned logic of platitudinous thought. Many of her ideas about child psychology and education are quite humorous, but disastrously misleading. Jacques is spanked once a day for good measure. He is forced to wear gaudy costumes she finds stylish. The inevitable result is that he feels doubly exiled. He is told to sit up and eat all of his onions even though he cannot stomach them. When such stupidity seems incongruous even to her, she tidies it up with the justification "Voilà, ça t'apprendra" (There, that'll teach you).

Neither strictly autobiographical nor completely fictive, *L'Enfant* re-creates Vallès's childhood while interpreting it through the eyes of an adult. In this regard its narrative is a complex weaving of past and present, of innocence and disillusionment, of spontaneity and critical distance. As protagonist and narrator, Jacques not only is caught up in the events described, but also critically evaluates them. On the one hand, the chase after the father's career from town to town, institution to institution, seems exciting as well as liberating. On the other, Jacques wrestles with the mixed message as to what entails true success. The questions "Where are we going next?" and "What are we looking for?," although never formulated, are certainly implicit in his thoughts. Furthermore, he notes the breakdown in family unity and communication as his father's professional obligations become more demanding. Finally, he feels that unique sequestration his father has experienced passing through life as if it were a deferral of any enduring sense of self or accomplishment.

Small wonder that *L'Enfant* translates an abhorrence for the educational institutions of mid-nineteenth-century France, particularly those exacting a slavish devotion to the past, to corporal punishment, to rote learning, and to student passivity. Far ahead of its time, Vallès's *L'Enfant* outlines a very modern educational dilemma. That is, shall education be the process of pursuing truths wherever they may lead in order to break free from sociocultural limitation, or shall it be content with privileging patterns from the past and those citizens who have by birth a head start? Jacques fails to discover an acceptable response. His rejection of the traditional answers embodied in his father and mother and his subsequent pursuit of something more socially equitable serve as the foundation upon which the next two volumes of the trilogy are constructed.

From as early as its sequential appearance in the *Siècle, L'Enfant* created an uproar with its negative portrayal of childhood and the family. Although he had scheduled *Jacques Vingtras II*, the editor, Philippe Jourde, canceled the sequel in December 1878, fearing for his publication. But on this occasion Vallès did not have to go begging. In January 1879 Sigismond Lacroix, an ardent admirer of the exiled writer, founded a socialist daily, the *Révolution Française*. He could think of no better way to inaugurate his paper than with a controversial feuilleton such as the one he anticipated in *Vingtras II*. The series ran under the title *Mémoires d'un révolté* from January to May and was signed with the now transparent "Jean La Rue." More important, however, was the fact that Lacroix asked Vallès to contribute two articles a week to the editorial pages of the paper and to contemplate a long-term engagement as a foreign correspondent, if not as a coeditor stationed abroad. Vallès jumped at the offer, for he sensed that it signaled the turning point in his exile. Not only could he chase poverty from his door temporarily, but he now had the means to reinsert his voice directly into the dialogues of the Parisian political arena. Without a doubt he had his agenda at the ready, with "complete amnesty for the exiled Communards" at the very top. The *Révolution Française* lasted only until June before being fined out of existence, but it did manage to bring the debate about amnesty to the forefront.

Despite the loss of this forum, that same month of June proved particularly gratifying for Vallès. Lemer published *Les Enfants du peuple*, a disparate collection of articles written between 1867 and 1870. This came on the heels of the May release of *L'Enfant*. Additionally, after seeing the name Vallès or "Jean La Rue" virtually at every turn, Charpentier traveled to London at the end of the month to set up a contract for *Vingtras II* as well as *La Rue à Londres*. The latter was a series of portraits about London and its people reminiscent of the 1866 novel *La Rue*. Neither of these texts would appear in print until after the repatriation. But in the literary climate of Paris in the summer of 1879, it was more than apparent that the exiled Communard had become a force with which to be reckoned.

Vallès's campaign to return to Paris advanced by another stage when he moved to Brussels in August 1879, with the express intent of bringing back his old weekly newspaper, the *Rue*. Presumably, he could direct from closer range the major salvos needed to break once and for all the conspiracy of silence that had surrounded his name since the Commune. At long last, on 29 November the editor in chief was at the helm again. Unfortunately, the team of young journalists who needed firsthand attention from their leader was assembled many kilometers to the southwest, in Paris. At great personal expense to Vallès, the paper struggled for a month but never got off the ground. In part to recoup the debt, Vallès quickly put together two serial works. The first, *Le Candidat des pauvres*, appeared in Tony Révillon's *Journal à un Sou* from December 1879 to February 1880. With his larger project always in mind, Vallès designed this series to fill the chronological gap (1857 to 1862) separating *Vingtras II* and *Vingtras III*. The second, *Les Blouses*, started in Georges Clemenceau's paper, the *Justice*, in June 1880 but was discontinued shortly thereafter. This series chronicled the famine and peasant revolt at Buzançais in 1847. Once again with the larger view as a guiding principle, "the chronicler of his generation" had intended to explore the pervasive unrest in the working class leading up to the revolution of 1848.

No sooner was the amnesty approved in July 1880 than Vallès was back in Paris. The "repatriate" had returned to play out that last intense phase of his life. Heart brimming and head spinning with projects, he set at once to tying the trilogy together into a "perfect ensemble." Juggling an extraordinary number of writing projects (articles in the *Vie Moderne* and the *Citoyen de Paris*, a preface for Benoît Malon's *Le Nouveau Parti* [1881], and a new serial, *La Dompteuse*), he reworked the original feuilleton *Mémoires* into *Jacques Vingtras: Le Bachelier*, all the while fleshing out *Vingtras III*. Thus, by the spring of 1881, he had the third volume of the trilogy well under way and two books selling side by side, his new novel, *Le Bachelier*, along with the second edition of *L'Enfant*.

If in its broadest sense *L'Enfant* demythologizes childhood, then *Le Bachelier* sets its sights on the educational system and its product—"the graduate." The dedication reads: "A ceux qui, nourris de grec et de latin, sont morts de faim" (To those who, nourished on Greek and Latin, died of hunger). Indeed, the novel begins with Jacques arriving in Paris around 1848 with his *peau d'âne* (diploma) in hand, bubbling with optimism, ready to sculpt his fame and fortune. Thirty-three chapters later it ends on a somber note. After attending his father's funeral—he was worn out prematurely by years of teaching—Jacques comes to a painful conclusion. Having tried throughout the novel to convert his classical formation into gainful employment and having been thwarted at every turn, he finds that he has no other recourse than to follow in his father's footsteps. In order to survive in the most elemental way, he is forced to hire on as a *pion*. He is broken down by socioeconomic forces beyond his control and compelled to shoulder the educational mantle that had finally crushed his father.

"Sacré lâche!" (Damn coward!) are the last two words of the novel, uttered by a fellow *bachelier* upon hearing of Jacques's capitulation. Beyond their irony, these two words provide insight into the novel as a whole as well as the ultimate role of the experience it reflects in the making of an insurrectionist. On one level they translate the defeat and disillusionment experienced by Jacques and all those who were similarly "nourished." Significantly, Jacques as a protagonist struggles throughout the novel to avoid the academic servitude that broke his father. From this first point of view, then, the epithet "Sacré lâche!" stresses the bankruptcy of the diploma as well as the institution that created it.

Vallès not only shows the baccalaureate unmarketable in the emerging profit-driven economy of nineteenth-century France but paints it as a source of an increasingly marginalized social class—an intellectual bohemia. Rather than give a quaint Romantic portrait à la Murger he bores in on the conscious tyranny of the system. This process of victimization is poignantly brought to the fore when Monsieur Bonardel in a job interview asks Jacques what skills he possesses: "Que savez-vous faire?" (What do you know how to do?). Jacques's reaction is quite comical on the one hand, for he cannot respond, feeling that he has not had adequate time to prepare for such a "simple" question. But on the other, he pitifully stammers: "Je suis bachelier" (I'm a graduate). Bonardel repeats the question, indicating that Jacques's first response has no value.

On another level, "Sacré lâche!" is an expression of brooding defiance. It communicates an angry denunciation of the process in question as well as a hope that, despite the solitude and misery, will maintain the search for something better. Thus, at the conclusion of *Le Bachelier,* Vallès indicates that for the moment Jacques will servilely bide his time, "manger à ta gamelle" (eat at the bourgeois mess) in order to survive. But there is also the implication that somewhere in the future the *bachelier* will rise up, transform himself into an insurgent, and demand his just dues. Furthermore, at that moment no one should be in the least surprised to see marching behind him "un drapeau, avec des milliers de rebelles" (a banner with thousands of rebels in support).

In this context the second volume of the trilogy picks up and develops the narrative momentum with which the first concludes. Hardly a lull before the storm of the Commune, it sets the vast sociopolitical stage upon which *Vingtras III* is erected. Historically, *Le Bachelier* covers then that long transition between the revolution of 1848 and that of 1871 without actually linking to either one. From beginning to end, Jacques passes through a sentimental education retracing the Icarian curve of many a Romantic hero. However, unlike his predecessors, for whom suicide was a possible release, he ends by seeking a more practical answer. Over the course of the novel, he studies the sources of his defeat and humiliation and begins the transformation of his emotional response into a course of action, if not a call to arms.

As in *L'Enfant,* Vallès only loosely connected the facts and chronology of a specified period of his life in order to construct the thirty-three chapters of his narrative. Particularly revealing in this regard are the beginning and ending, which are more symbolic than factual. The disillusionment that Jacques experiences as he unsuccessfully seeks employment as a *bachelier* is predicated on having already received the degree before the novel begins. Vallès transposes, then, the fact that although distinguished in rhetoric and Latin, not only did he fail his examinations repeatedly, he did not pass them until May 1852, six months after the December 1851 coup d'etat. This very coup is situated not at the beginning, but midway through the novel. Another glaring inconsistency is the silence with which Vallès surrounds his two-month stay in a mental asylum. Lastly, the novel concludes on Jacques's vigil the night before his father's funeral, coupled with his bitter decision to become a teacher. These two moments are, therefore, conflated, because Jean-Louis Vallez died in 1857 and it was not until the winter of 1862-1863 that his son accepted a post at the Collège de Caen.

With *Le Bachelier* behind him, Vallès turned to the three principal activities that would consume him and his final days: 1) an expanded journalistic involvement, with contributions to *Gil-Blas,* the *Réveil,* the *France,* and the *Matin* as well as the editorship of his resuscitated *Cri du Peuple* (October 1883); 2) the final touches on *La Rue à Londres* (1884), a volume of collected articles on the street scenes of London, offering, especially, another view of the Communard's exile; and 3) *L'Insurgé.* Associated with this last frenzy of writing was Caroline Rémy, called Séverine, or his "belle camarade," as Vallès often addressed her. He had befriended this beautiful young blonde in Brussels, along with her constant companion, Dr. Guebhard, in April 1880. Little did he realize at that time that she would end by serving as his secretary, disciple, nurse, and collaborator.

Gradually over the next few years, what he did realize, specifically as he settled back into Parisian life, was that his long struggle to get his word out was about to come to a close. Along with his failing health (diabetes not diagnosed until February 1884), his triple role of editor, journalist, and creative writer had exhausted him. And more and more Séverine was there, willing and thoroughly capable of assuming the responsibilities of the "insurrectionist." When she later reflected on the early stages of their relationship she noted with pride that "nous fîmes alors—entre 1881 et 1883—la campagne du *Réveil* . . . les *Tableaux de Paris* dans *Gil-Blas,* lesquels furent continués dans *La France,* puis la première partie de *L'Insurgé* qui parut dans la revue de Mme Adam et *La Rue à Londres*" (We managed to do then—between 1881 and 1883—the *Réveil* campaign . . . the *Tableaux de Paris* in *Gil-Blas,* which were continued in the *France,* then the first part of *L'Insurgé,* which appeared in Mrs. Adam's review, and *La Rue à Londres*).

Indeed, most of the literary output of this period was accomplished by Vallès and Séverine together. Tragically, however, only fourteen of the thirty-five chapters of *L'Insurgé* ran in Adam's journal in April 1882; and although other portions were later published in the January 1884 edition of the *Cri du peuple,* Vallès died

Caricature of Vallès in 1880 (from Max Gallo, Jules Vallès ou la révolte d'une vie, *1988)*

on 14 February 1885, before seeing the final version in print. Faithful as only a fellow *réfractaire* could be, Séverine persevered and brought the text into its final form, which Charpentier published in May 1886. Despite her diligence and, by this time, Vallès's substantial following, the Parisian press all but ignored the release.

Jacques's "non," this emerging revolt that serves as the dynamic as well as the internal linkage of the trilogy, is pushed to its third and final stage in *L'Insurgé*. Having taken on his family and his schools, Jacques now does battle with his society. As with the other two volumes of the trilogy, the dedication points to the balance of power, the victims and their torturers: "AUX MORTS DE 1871. A tous ceux qui, victimes de l'injustice sociale, prirent les armes contre un monde mal fait et formèrent, sous le drapeau de la Commune, la grande fédération des douleurs" (TO THE DEAD OF 1871. To all those who, victims of social injustice, took up arms against a poorly made world and formed, under the banner of the Commune, the great federation of pain).

A personal reality feverishly lived, an impassioned indictment of all forms of social tyranny, and an unrelenting commitment to political action—all three combine in *L'Insurgé* to fulfill Vallès's desire to be the historian, if not the greatest novelist, of the Paris Commune. There is of course much more, for the novel is Vallès's supreme act of redemption. It is his crowning effort to redeem all those of his generation (the "48ers") unconsciously brutalized by their parents and teachers, who were simply passing on received thought without questioning it. From this point of view *L'Insurgé* is the counterpart and the response to the questions posed by *Vingtras I* and *Vingtras II*. It is ultimately a resolution and a lasting commemoration of the sacrifices of a generation of true believers, many of whom Vallès saw perish on the barricades or at the hands of executioners during "Bloody Week."

The novel treats, not without chronological fits and starts, that period of Vallès's life from 1862 through May 1871. The narrative begins with Jacques's days as a tutor in Caen and ends on the barricades just before the complete collapse of the Commune. Of the thirty-five chapters given to this development, the first seventeen are devoted to Jacques's emergence as a radical journalist and orator from 1862 to the fall of Sedan in September 1870. Whereas Vallès actually began his journalistic career with an anodyne title "Le Dimanche d'un jeune homme pauvre" (The Sunday of a Poor Young Man), Jacques springs fully clad with *Les Réfractaires*. All of this emphasizes that as an "insurrectionist," he has learned to take the offensive. He has learned to prevail as a controversial journalist unafraid to speak his mind rather than flounder hopelessly, as in *Le Bachelier*. The second half of the novel documents in kaleidoscopic fashion the fall of the Second Empire, the declaration of the Third Republic, and the Commune—all in eighteen chapters. The first six of these deal specifically with the transfer of power to the Republic, the next six treat the seated Commune, and the last six focus intensely on the desperate fighting between 21 and 28 May.

Thus, the events of the Commune become the subject, object, and conclusion of this novel. Convinced that he has lived a unique historical moment, Vallès endeavors to reconstruct it in epochal strokes without idealizing it. Indeed, as chapters speed by, accelerated by the narrative's attempt to overtake the experience (the prison stay at Sainte-Pélagie, the elections of 1869, Victor Noir's murder and funeral procession, Jacques as a military leader, the Villette affair, and then the Commune), the novel seems to plunge brutally toward closure, if not self-destruction.

Yet nothing could be further from Vallès's intent than to dead-end in an irreversible defeat. In fact, he subverts the old saw that "revolutions devour their children." In this context, to attempt to change the society, "to dare," is not suicidal, but the fullest expression of hope. Just as Jacques turns certain death into survival by slipping away from the barricades disguised as an ambulance driver, the failure of the Commune is for Vallès a symbolic awakening to a new era. It is an era characterized by a sober, pragmatic view of the sociopolitical forces (and not those of a Romantic destiny) that conspire to impede the pursuit of freedom. But above all it is a modern era forced to confront harsh realities such as child abuse, the failure of educational institutions, unemployment, and poverty. Given his modernity, his *question sociale* as he phrased it, Vallès speaks directly and frankly (and in a style not without abundant humor and irony) to the contemporary reader.

One of the most celebrated writers in the twentieth century who has given voice to this very modern relationship between literature and revolt is Camus. In an article titled "L'Artiste et son temps" (and which reproduces his speech four days after receiving the Nobel Prize on 14 December 1957), he shows that from the mid nineteenth century the artist in Western civilization has increasingly run the risk of becoming nothing more than a perpetrator of a *luxe mensonger* (deceitful luxury). Whether through the heresy of "idealism" (art for art's sake) or that of "realism," more and more artists have progressively cut themselves off from the complex weaving of events that shape a people and their quest for freedom. But Camus also maintains that there has been throughout this evolution a singular race of brave sentinels willing to commit themselves and their art to that frighteningly complex task of fighting for the freedom of all those unable to do so for themselves. With his massive production, and particularly his trilogy, Vallès not only ranks among the restless soldiers in the eternal struggle for social justice, but among its literary masters as well. It seems fitting that the icy conspiracy of silence that has long surrounded his name has finally begun to thaw and that now he may assume his rightful place alongside those singular *révoltés* of whom Camus spoke.

Letters:

Jacques Vingtras IV: Le Proscrit: Correspondance avec Arthur Arnould, preface by Lucien Scheler (Paris: Les Editeurs Français Réunis, 1950; enlarged, 1973);

Correspondance avec Hector Malot: 1862-1884, preface and notes by Marie-Claire Bancquart (Paris: Les Editeurs Français Réunis, 1968);

"Une Correspondance Vallès-Zola; Echos d'une correspondance Zola-Tourguéneff (1865-1879)," *Europe*, 470-472 (June-August 1968): 171-181;

Vallès (Jules)-Séverine: Correspondance, preface and notes by Scheler (Paris: Les Editeurs Français Réunis, 1972);

"Autour de la correspondance de Jules Vallès avec Jules Levallois," *Europe*, 616-617 (August-September 1980): 168-183.

Bibliographies:

Gaston Gille, *Jules Vallès, sources, bibliographie, iconographie vallésiennes: Essai critique* (Paris: Jouve, 1941);

Germaine Frigot, *Jules Vallès, bibliographie* (Paris: Bibliothèque de la Ville de Paris, Mairie de Paris—Direction des Affaires Culturelles, 1985).

Biographies:

Jean Richepin, *Les Etapes d'un réfractaire: Jules Vallès* (Paris: Lacroix-Verboeckhoven, 1872);

Léon Séché, *Portraits à l'encre: Jules Vallès, sa vie et son œuvre: Documents nouveaux et inédits avec un portrait dessiné à la plume* (Paris: Revue Illustrée de Bretagne et d'Anjou, 1886);

Alexandre Zévaès, *Jules Vallès: Son œuvre, portrait et autographe* (Paris: Nouvelle Revue Critique, 1932);

Ulysse Rouchon, *La Vie bruyante de Jules Vallès*, 3 volumes (Saint-Etienne: Editions de la Région Illustrée, 1935-1939);

Gaston Gille, *Jules Vallès, 1832-1885: Ses révoltes, sa maïtrise, son prestige* (Paris: Jouve, 1941);

Michel-Leon Hirsh, *Jules Vallès l'insurgé: Essai biographique* (Paris: Méridien, 1949);

Marie-Claire Bancquart, *Jules Vallès* (Paris: Seghers, 1971);

Max Gallo, *Jules Vallès ou la révolte d'une vie* (Paris: Robert Laffont, 1988).

References:

Frans Amelinckx, "Découverte de soi et altérité dans *Le Bachelier* de Jules Vallès," *Revue d'Etudes Vallésiennes*, 2 (October 1985): 83-90;

Roger Bellet, *Jules Vallès, journaliste du Second Empire, de la Commune de Paris et de la IIIe République (1857-1885)* (Paris: Les Editeurs Français Réunis, 1977); republished as *Jules Vallès, journalisme et révolution, 1857-1885* (Paris: Lérot, 1987);

Philippe Bonnefis, *Vallès: Du bon usage de la lame et de l'aiguille* (Lausanne: L'Age d'Homme, 1982);

Paul Bourget, "Jules Vallès," in his *Etudes et portraits (1885)* (Paris: Lemerre, 1889), pp. 155-170;

Colloque Jules Vallès (Lyons: Presses Universitaires de Lyon, 1976);

Gérard Delfau, *Jules Vallès: L'exil à Londres (1871-1880)* (Paris: Bordas, 1971);

Europe, issue on Vallès, 144 (December 1957);

Europe, issue on Vallès, 470-472 (June-August 1968);

Exposition. Choisy-le-Roi (Val de Marne), Centre Culturel Communal (October 1971);

Paul Gerbod, *La Vie quotidienne dans les lycées et collèges au XIXe siècle* (Paris: Hachette, 1968);

Hi Sook Hwang, "La Vision du peuple chez Jules Vallès," *Modern Language Studies*, 15 (Fall 1985): 313-328;

Philippe Lejeune, "Techniques de narration dans le récit d'enfance," in *Colloque Jules Vallès* (Lyons: Presses Universitaires de Lyon, 1976), pp. 51-74;

Caryl Lloyd, "The Politics of Privacy in the Works of Jules Vallès," *French Review*, 58 (May 1985): 835-842;

Pierre Pillu, "L'Autoportrait chez Vallès," *Revues d'Etudes Vallésiennes*, 2 (October 1985): 91-100;

William Serman, *La Commune de Paris* (Paris: Fayard, 1986);

Charles J. Stivale, *Œuvre de sentiment, œuvre de combat: La trilogie de Jules Vallès* (Lyons: Presses Universitaires de Lyon, 1988);

Geoffrey Strickland, "Maupassant, Zola, Jules Vallès and the Paris Commune of 1871," *Journal of European Studies*, 52 (December 1983): 298-307;

Jean-François Tétu, "Aspects de l'idéologie de la révolte chez Jules Vallès," in *Colloque Jules Vallès* (Lyons: Presses Universitaires de Lyon, 1976), pp. 91-106;

Gretchen Van Slyke, "Militancy in the Making: The Example of *Le Bachelier*," *Stanford French Review*, 11 (Fall 1987): 331-344.

Papers:

Vallès's manuscripts of *Le Bachelier, L'Insurgé*, and *La Rue à Londres* are located at the Bibliothèque Nationale in Paris.

Jules Verne

(8 February 1828 - 24 March 1905)

Arthur B. Evans
DePauw University

BOOKS: *Cinq semaines en ballon, voyage de découvertes en Afrique* (Paris: Hetzel, 1863); translated by William Lackland as *Five Weeks in a Balloon* (New York: D. Appleton, 1869; London: Chapman & Hall, 1870);

Voyage au centre de la Terre: Trajet direct en 97 heures (Paris: Hetzel, 1864); translated as *A Journey to the Center of the Earth* (London: Griffith & Farran, 1872; New York: Scribner, Armstrong, 1874);

Les Aventures du capitaine Hatteras, 2 volumes (Paris: Hetzel, 1864-1865); translated as *At the North Pole* [volume 1] and *The Desert of Ice* [volume 2] (Philadelphia: Porter & Coates, 1874);

De la Terre à la lune (Paris: Hetzel, 1865); translated by J. K. Hoyt as *From the Earth to the Moon* (Newark, N.J.: Newark Printing and Publishing, 1869);

Les Enfants du capitaine Grant, 3 volumes (Paris: Hetzel, 1867-1868); translated as *In Search of the Castaways* (Philadelphia: Lippincott, 1873);

Géographie illustrée de la France et de ses colonies (Paris: Hetzel, 1867);

Vingt mille lieues sous les mers, 2 volumes (Paris: Hetzel, 1869-1870); translated by L. Mercier as *Twenty Thousand Leagues Under the Sea* (London: Sampson Low, Marston / Boston: George M. Smith, 1873);

Découverte de la Terre (Paris: Hetzel, 1870);

Autour de la lune (Paris: Hetzel, 1870); translated by Mercier and E. E. King as *Round the Moon* (London: Sampson Low, Marston, 1876; New York: George Munro, 1878);

Une Ville flottante, suivi des Forceurs du blocus (Paris: Hetzel, 1871); translated as *A Floating City, and the Blockade Runners* (London: Sampson Low, Marston / New York: Scribner, Armstrong, 1874);

Aventures de trois Russes et de trois Anglais (Paris: Hetzel, 1872); translated as *Meridiana* (London: Sampson Low, Marston, 1873; New York: Scribner, Armstrong, 1874);

Le Pays des fourrures (Paris: Hetzel, 1873); translated by N. D'Anvers as *The Fur Country* (London: Sampson Low, Marston / Boston: J. R. Osgood, 1874);

Le Tour du monde en quatre-vingts jours (Paris: Hetzel, 1873); translated by G. M. Towle as *A Tour of the World in Eighty Days* (Boston: J. R. Osgood, 1873); translated by Mercier as *Around the World in Eighty Days* (London: Sampson Low, Marston, 1874; New York: George Munro, 1877);

Le Docteur Ox; Maître Zacharius; Un Hivernage dans les glaces; Un Drame dans les airs (Paris: Hetzel, 1874); translated as *Dr. Ox's Experiment, and Other Stories* (London: Sampson Low, Marston, 1874);

L'Ile mystérieuse, 3 volumes (Paris: Hetzel, 1874-1875); translated by W. H. G. Kingston as *The Mysterious Island,* 3 volumes (London: Sampson Low, Marston, 1875; New York: Scribner, Armstrong, 1875-1876);

Le Chancellor (Paris: Hetzel, 1875); translated by E. E. Frewer as *The Survivors of the Chancellor* (London: Sampson Low, Marston, 1875);

Michel Strogoff, Moscou-Irkoutsk (Paris: Hetzel, 1876); translated by Kingston as *Michel Strogoff, The Courier of the Czar* (London: Sampson Low, Marston / New York: Scribner, Armstrong, 1877);

Hector Servadac: Voyages et aventures à travers le monde solaire (Paris: Hetzel, 1877); translated as *Hector Servadac: Travels and Adventures Through the Solar System* (New York: George Munro, 1877);

Les Indes noires (Paris: Hetzel, 1877); translated by Kingston as *The Child of the Cavern* (London: Sampson Low, Marston, 1877);

Un Capitaine de quinze ans (Paris: Hetzel, 1878); translated as *Dick Sand; or, A Captain at Fifteen* (New York: George Munro, 1878);

Histoire des grands voyages et des grands voyageurs: Découverte de la Terre [volume 1], *Les Grands Navigateurs du XVIII*^{eme} *siècle* [volume 2], and *Les Voyageurs du XIX*^{eme} *siècle* [volume 3]

Jules Verne (photographs by Nadar)

(Paris: Hetzel, 1878-1880); translated by D. Leigh as *The Exploration of the World: Famous Travels and Travellers* [volume 1], *The Great Navigators of the 18th Century* [volume 2], and *The Exploration of the World* [volume 3] (New York: Scribners, 1879);

Les Cinq Cents Millions de la Bégum, suivi de Les Révoltés de la "Bounty" (Paris: Hetzel, 1879); translated as *The 500 Millions of the Begum* (New York: George Munro, 1879); translated by Kingston as *The Begum's Fortune* (Philadelphia: Lippincott, 1879-1880);

Les Tribulations d'un Chinois en Chine (Paris: Hetzel, 1879); translated as *The Tribulations of a Chinaman in China* (New York: George Munro, 1879);

La Maison à vapeur: Voyage à travers l'Inde septentrionale (Paris: Hetzel, 1880); translated as *The Steam House: or, A Trip Across Northern India* (New York: George Munro, 1880-1881);

La Jangada: Huit cents lieues sur l'Amazone (Paris: Hetzel, 1881); translated by W. J. Gordon as *The Giant Raft* (London: Sampson Low, Marston, 1881-1882);

Le Rayon vert, suivi de Dix heures de chasse (Paris: Hetzel, 1882); translated by M. de Hauteville as *The Green Ray* (London: Sampson Low, Marston, 1883);

L'Ecole des Robinsons (Paris: Hetzel, 1882); translated as *Robinson's School* (New York: George Munro, 1883);

Kéraban-le-Têtu (Paris: Hetzel, 1883); translated by J. Cotterell as *The Headstrong Turk* (New York: George Munro, 1883);

L'Etoile du Sud: Le pays des diamants (Paris: Hetzel, 1884); translated as *The Vanished Diamond: A Tale of South Africa* (London: Sampson Low, Marston, 1885); translated as *The Southern Star* (New York: George Munro, 1885);

L'Archipel en feu (Paris: Hetzel, 1884); translated as *The Archipelago on Fire* (New York: George Munro, 1885; London: Sampson Low, Marston, 1886);

Mathias Sandorf (Paris: Hetzel, 1885); translated (New York: George Munro, 1885; London: Sampson Low, Marston, 1886);

L'Epave du Cynthia (Paris: Hetzel, 1885); translated as *The Waif of the "Cynthia"* (New York: George Munro, 1886);

Un Billet de loterie, suivi de Fritt-Flacc (Paris: Hetzel, 1886); *Un Billet de loterie* translated by L. E. Kendall as *Ticket No. "9672"* (New York: George Munro, 1886); *Fritt-Flacc* translated as "Dr. Trifulgas: A Fantastic Tale," *Strand Magazine*, 4 (July-December 1892);

Robur-le-conquérant (Paris: Hetzel, 1886); translated as *The Clipper of the Clouds* (London: Sampson Low, Marston, 1887); translated as *Robur the Conqueror* (New York: George Munro, 1887);

Nord contre Sud (Paris: Hetzel, 1887); translated by Kendall as *Texar's Vengeance, or North Versus South* (New York: George Munro, 1887);

Le Chemin de France, suivi de Gil Braltar (Paris: Hetzel, 1887); translated as *The Flight to France; or, The Memoirs of a Dragoon* (London: Sampson Low, Marston / New York: F. F. Lovell, 1888);

Deux ans de vacances (Paris: Hetzel, 1888); translated as *Adrift in the Pacific* (London: Sampson Low, Marston, 1889);

Famille-sans-nom (Paris: Hetzel, 1889); translated as *A Family Without a Name* (New York: J. W. Lovell, 1889; London: Sampson Low, Marston, 1891);

Sans dessus dessous (Paris: Hetzel, 1889); translated as *Topsy-Turvy* (New York: J. S. Ogilvie, 1890);

César Cascabel (Paris: Hetzel, 1890); translated by A. Estroclet as *Caesar Cascabel* (New York, Cassell: 1890; London: Sampson Low, Marston, 1891);

Mistress Branican (Paris: Hetzel, 1891); translated by Estroclet (New York: Cassell, 1891; London: Sampson Low, Marston, 1892);

Le Château des Carpathes (Paris: Hetzel, 1892); translated as *The Castle of the Carpathians* (London: Sampson Low, Marston, 1893; New York: Merriam, 1894);

Claudius Bombarnac (Paris: Hetzel, 1892); translated (London: Sampson Low, Marston, 1894);

P'tit-Bonhomme (Paris: Hetzel, 1893); translated as *Foundling Mick* (London: Sampson Low, Marston, 1895);

Mirifiques aventures de Maître Antifer (Paris: Hetzel, 1894); translated as *Captain Antifer* (London: Sampson Low, Marston / New York: R. F. Fenno, 1895);

L'Ile à hélice (Paris: Hetzel, 1895); translated by Gordon as *Floating Island* (London: Sampson Low, Marston, 1896; New York: W. L. Allison, 1900);

Face au drapeau (Paris: Hetzel, 1896); translated by C. Hoey as *For the Flag* (London: Sampson Low, Marston, 1897);

Clovis Dardentor (Paris: Hetzel, 1896); translated (London: Sampson Low, Marston, 1897);

Le Sphinx des glaces (Paris: Hetzel, 1897); translated by Hoey as *An Antarctic Mystery* (London: Sampson Low, Marston, 1898; Philadelphia: Lippincott, 1899);

Le Superbe Orénoque (Paris: Hetzel, 1898);

Le Testament d'un excentrique (Paris: Hetzel, 1899); translated as *The Will of an Eccentric* (London: Sampson Low, Marston, 1900);

Seconde patrie (Paris: Hetzel, 1900); translated as *Their Island Home* [volume 1] and *The Castaways of the Flag* [volume 2] (London: Sampson Low, Marston, 1923);

Le Village aérien (Paris: Hetzel, 1901); translated by I. O. Evans as *The Village in the Treetops* (London: Arco / New York: Ace, 1964);

Les Histoires de Jean-Marie Cabidoulin (Paris: Hetzel, 1901); translated by Evans as *The Sea Serpent: The Yarns of Jean Marie Cabidoulin* (London: Arco, 1967; Westport, Conn.: Associated Booksellers, 1970);

Les Frères Kip (Paris: Hetzel, 1902);

Bourses de voyage (Paris: Hetzel, 1903);

Un Drame en Livonie (Paris: Hetzel, 1904); translated by Evans as *A Drama in Livonia* (London: Arco, 1967);

Maître du monde (Paris: Hetzel, 1904); translated as *The Master of the World* (London: Sampson Low, Marston / Philadelphia: Lippincott, 1914);

L'Invasion de la mer (Paris: Hetzel, 1905);

Le Phare au bout du monde (Paris: Hetzel, 1905); translated as *The Lighthouse at the Edge of the World* (London: Sampson Low, Marston, 1923);

Le Volcan d'or (Paris: Hetzel, 1906); translated by Evans as *The Golden Volcano: The Claim on the Forty Mile Creek* [volume 1] and *Flood and Famine* [volume 2] (London: Arco / Westport, Conn.: Associated Booksellers, 1962);

L'Agence Thompson and Co. (Paris: Hetzel, 1907); translated by Evans as *The Thompson Travel Agency: Package Holiday* [volume 1] and *End of the Journey* [volume 2] (London: Arco, 1965);

La Chasse au météore (Paris: Hetzel, 1908); translated by F. Lawton as *The Chase of the Golden Meteor* (London: Grant Richards, 1909);

Le Pilote du Danube (Paris: Hetzel, 1908); translated by Evans as *The Danube Pilot* (London: Arco, 1967; Westport, Conn.: Associated Booksellers, 1970);

Les Naufragés du "Jonathan" (Paris: Hetzel, 1909); translated by Evans as *The Survivors of the Jonathan: The Masterless Man* [volume 1] and *The Unwilling Dictator* [volume 2] (Westport, Conn.: Associated Booksellers, 1962);

Le Secret de Wilhelm Storitz (Paris: Hetzel, 1910); translated by Evans as *The Secret of Wilhelm Storitz* (Westport, Conn.: Associated Booksellers, 1963);

Hier et demain (Paris: Hetzel, 1910)—includes "La Famille Raton," "M. Ré-Dièze et Mlle Mi-Bémol," "La Destinée de Jean Morénas," "Le Humbug," "Au XXIXeme siècle: La journée d'un journaliste américain en 2889," and "L'Eternel Adam"; translated by Evans as *Yesterday and Tomorrow* (London: Arco, 1965);

L'Etonnante Aventure de la mission Barsac (Paris: Hachette, 1919); translated by Evans as *The Barsac Mission: Into the Niger Bend* [volume 1] and *The City in the Sahara* [volume 2] (Westport, Conn.: Associated Booksellers, 1960).

Editions and Collections: *Voyages extraordinaires* (Paris: Hetzel, 1863-1910);

Extraordinary Voyages (London: Sampson Low, Marston, 1874-1923);

Works of Jules Verne, edited by Charles F. Horne (New York: Vincent Parke, 1911);

Voyages extraordinaires (Paris: Hachette, "Collection Hetzel," 1914-1934);

Voyages extraordinaires (Paris: Hachette, "Bibliothèque Verte," 1924-);

The Novels of Jules Verne, edited by H. C. Harwood (London: Gollancz, 1929);

Works of Jules Verne, edited by I. O. Evans (London: Arco, 1961-1967);

Voyages extraordinaires (Paris: Livre de Poche, 1966-1968);

Œuvres complètes de Jules Verne (Lausanne: Editions Rencontre, 1966-1971);

Voyages extraordinaires (Paris: Michel de l'Ormeraie, 1976-1984);

Voyages extraordinaires (Paris: Hachette, "Intégrales Jules Verne," 1977-1989);

The Best of Jules Verne, edited by Alan K. Russell (Secaucus, N.J.: Castle, 1978);

Histoires inattendues, edited by Francis Lacassin (Paris: UGE, "10/18," 1978);

Textes oubliés, edited by Lacassin (Paris: UGE, "10/18," 1979);

Jules Verne: Classic Science Fiction, edited by Russell (Secaucus, N.J.: Castle, 1981);

The Works of Jules Verne, edited by Claire Boss (New York: Avenel, 1983);

Poésies inédites, edited by Christian Robin (Paris: Le Cherche Midi, 1989);

Voyage à reculons en Angleterre et en Ecosse (Paris: Le Cherche Midi, 1989).

PLAY PRODUCTIONS: *Les Pailles rompues*, Paris, Théâtre Historique, 12 June 1850;

Le Colin-Maillard, by Verne and Michel Carré, music by Aristide Hignard, Paris, Théâtre Lyrique, 21 April 1853;

Les Compagnons de la Marjolaine, by Verne and Carré, music by Hignard, Paris, Théâtre Lyrique, 6 June 1855;

Monsieur de Chimpanzé, by Verne and Carré, music by Hignard, Paris, Bouffes-Parisiennes, 8 February 1858;

L'Auberge des Ardennes, by Verne and Carré, music by Hignard, Paris, Théâtre Lyrique, 1 September 1860;

Onze jours de siège, by Verne and Charles Wallut, Paris, Théâtre du Vaudeville, 1 June 1861;

Un Neveu d'Amérique, ou les Deux Frontignac, Paris, Théâtre Cluny, 17 April 1873;

Le Tour du monde en quatre-vingts jours, by Verne and Adolphe d'Ennery, music by Debillemont, Paris, Théâtre de la Porte-Saint-Martin, November 1874;

Le Docteur Ox, by Verne and Philippe Gille, music by Jacques Offenbach, Paris, Théâtre des Variétes, 14 April 1877;

Les Enfants du capitaine Grant, by Verne and d'Ennery, music by Debillemont, Paris, Théâtre de la Porte-Saint-Martin, 26 December 1878;

Michel Strogoff, by Verne and d'Ennery, Paris, Théâtre de Châtelet, 17 November 1880;

Voyage à travers l'impossible, by Verne and d'Ennery, Paris, Théâtre de la Porte-Saint-Martin, 25 November 1882;

Kéraban-le-Têtu, Paris, La Gaîté-Lyrique, 3 September 1883;

Mathias Sandorf, by Verne, William Busnach, and Georges Maurens, Paris, Théâtre de l'Ambigu, 27 November 1887.

OTHER: Robert Cromie, *A Plunge into Space*, preface by Verne (London: F. Warne, 1891).

Jules Verne is arguably one of the most misunderstood writers of the entire French literary tradition. Although ranked as the fifth most-translated author of all time (behind Lenin, Agatha Christie, Walt Disney, and the Bible—according to a UNESCO poll), Verne and his *Vo-*

Honorine Verne, the author's wife, in her early forties

yages extraordinaires (1863-1910; translated as *Extraordinary Voyages*, 1874-1923) have, until very recently, been persistently denied any literary recognition in France. And in America, where everyone has heard of him but nobody actually reads his novels anymore, Verne has become an unstudied yet ubiquitous cultural icon—"The Father of Science Fiction," "The Seer of the Space Age," and "The Inventor of the Nautilus." But neither in his homeland nor in most countries around the world have Verne and his works been treated for what they truly are: in the history of literature, Verne's *Voyages extraordinaires* constitutes the birth of a unique, hybridized form of novel. This new brand of fiction, a forerunner of what would eventually evolve into the genre called science fiction, could be described as "scientifically didactic Industrial Age epic" or, more simply—as the author himself chose to label it—the *roman scientifique* (scientific novel). By any name, it represents the first successful attempt to incorporate science into literature.

Verne's personal reputation and literary status from his earliest work to the present day make a fascinating and bewildering saga. He has been acclaimed by some of the greatest writers of France, such as George Sand, Alexandre Dumas *père*, Théophile Gautier, Stéphane Mallarmé, Guillaume Apollinaire, Jean Cocteau, Jean-Paul Sartre, Blaise Cendrars, Raymond Roussel, Michel Foucault, and Michel Butor, yet he was denied admission into the Académie Française, and his works remained for nearly a century taboo in the French classroom (the publishers of the prestigious Pléiade editions—in some respects the litmus test of literary respectability in France—continue to refuse to publish the collected works of Verne). Record-breaking sales of his early works suddenly made Verne an international celebrity, yet his later masterpieces were left unsold and unwanted. He was idolized by several generations, yet he led a life of self-imposed solitude and secrecy. And, although beloved of Hollywood movie moguls and Disneyland tourists, Verne continues to be thoroughly unknown as a historian, a geographer, a social critic, and an early environmentalist.

As Verne methodically churned out novel after novel from 1863 to 1905, the true nature of his works was often masked by the dazzling success of his earliest fictions, which fired the positivistic imaginations of his late-nineteenth-century reading public. He quickly became (quite literally) a legend in his own time: his novels sold by the millions, theatrical adaptations of his works played to sellout crowds, and his luxury-edition red and gold volumes became a standard Christmas gift in millions of Second Empire and Third Republic bourgeois homes. But many personal myths also began to cling to his name: that he was really a Polish Jew named Olchewitz; that ghostwriters actually composed his novels for him; that he had personally visited all the foreign countries depicted in his works; that he had never set foot outside of France; that he was a scientist, an engineer, or an inventor; and that he was a visionary who could accurately predict the future, among many others.

Most of these gossipy misconceptions about him and his new brand of literature—sometimes the inadvertent result of his publisher's commercially pragmatic marketing practices—originated in France during Verne's lifetime. But they rapidly spread and took root in England, Russia, America, and many other countries where his (most often watered-down) translations enjoyed unprecedented success. Sometimes the poor quality of the translations, coupled with sensationalistic journalism and sketchy biographical data, served to nourish these myths. As a result, Verne's image as a writer of futuristic science fiction and adolescent adventure stories became more and more culturally entrenched. And for several generations after his death, Verne continued to be what these popular beliefs had made of him, and most readers worldwide remembered him as such. Once his meteorlike commercial success came to an end, Verne and his unique works became classified as a curious footnote in the history of paraliterature. He was revered as a twofold grandfather figure for both science fiction and children's literature; he was hailed as a famous and popular writer; but he was meticulously kept on the far margins of the French literary canon.

Then an amazing turnabout took place in France during the late 1960s and early 1970s. With the advent of structuralism and postmodern literary criticism, Verne's texts were resuscitated, stripped of their popular mythology, and scrutinized as fictional narrative. And, in the revealing light of such linguistic, sociohistorical, epistemological, psychoanalytical, and semiotic analyses, a new Jules Verne emerged: an author whose vision and imagination and whose style and complexity constituted perfect terrain for advanced literary analysis. Suddenly Verne and his *Voyages extraordinaires* were (once again, one hundred years later) the rage of Paris. Reprints of his novels appeared from a variety of prestigious French publishing houses; university dissertations and theses began to analyze his works; detailed studies of his life and writings multiplied on booksellers' shelves; respected literary journals began to publish articles about him; literary critics, for the first time, placed Verne "in a first-rank position in the history of French literature," according to Marc Angenot; and the cities of Nantes and Amiens—the author's birthplace and later residence, respectively—even fought (in court!) over the ownership rights of Verne's original manuscript collection.

Outside of France, this Vernian vogue took a bit longer to catch on. But catch on it eventually did. With the growing academic respectability of science fiction and the sudden popularity of "new" French literary critics such as Roland Barthes, Foucault, and Jacques Lacan on Western campuses, the study of Verne increased as well. For example, after nearly a half century of virtually no serious Anglo-American literary criticism on Verne, the period from 1975 to 1990 witnessed no fewer than two biographies, seven monographs, one primary and secondary bibliography, and dozens of scholarly articles in a wide variety of academic journals on this prolific French author who was for so long deemed unworthy of critical attention. And the Verne renaissance continues even today.

What then was the true story behind the highly publicized yet enigmatic life of this author? How did he come to write this series of sixty-four novels using a new narrative format (the *roman scientifique*), novels that ingeniously blend scientific knowledge with literary discourse? Where did he get his ideas? To what extent did his life reflect his fiction, and vice versa? How much did his publisher and *père spirituel* Pierre-Jules Hetzel influence his young protégé's novelistic craft? And why, during the final twenty years of his life, did Verne (and his works) suddenly change character—becoming adamantly antiscience, antiprogress, and antitechnology—as the latter novels of the *Voyages extraordinaires* demonstrate so vividly?

Verne was born on 8 February 1828 to a middle-class family in the western port city of Nantes. His mother, Sophie (née Allotte de la Fuye), was the daughter of a prominent Nantes family of shipowners. His father, Pierre Verne, was a lawyer and the son of a Provins magistrate. Jules had three sisters—Anna, Mathilde, and Marie—and one brother, Paul, who eventually became a naval engineer and helped his older brother from time to time with the mechanical details of his imaginary technological marvels.

As a child and young man, Jules was a good student. He repeatedly won awards for meritorious performance in geography, music, and Greek and Latin during his years in primary and secondary school, and he passed his *baccalauréat* easily in 1846. But he especially loved the sea. The small shipyard docks of nearby Ile Feydeau and the bustling Nantes harbor itself, where merchandise-laden freighters arrived from around the world, never failed to spark his youthful imagination with visions of far-off lands and exotic peoples. And he also loved machines. Reminiscing about those formative years when interviewed by a British journalist in 1894, Verne confided: "While I was quite a lad, I used to adore watching machines at work. My father had a country-house at Chantenay, at the mouth of the Loire, and near the government factory at Indret. I never went to Chantenay without entering the factory and standing for hours watching the machines. . . . This penchant has remained with me all my life, and today I have still as much pleasure in watching a steam-engine or a fine locomotive at work as I have in contemplating a picture by Raphael or Corregio."

Intending that his son follow in his footsteps as an attorney, Pierre sent Jules to Paris in 1848 to study law. The correspondence between father and son during the next ten years indicates that Jules took his studies seriously—completing his law degree in just two years—but that he also had found a new vocation, literature: "C'est vraiment un plaisir par trop incompris à Nantes que celui d'être au courant de la littérature. . . . Il y a des études profondes à faire sur le genre présent et surtout le genre à venir" (It's really a pleasure all too misunderstood in Nantes to be in the midst of the literary world. . . . There are serious studies to be done on the present genre[s] and especially that of the future [1848]). "Je puis faire un bon littérateur et ne serai qu'un mauvais avocat, ne voyant dans toutes choses que le côté comique et la forme artistique, et ne prenant pas la réalité sérieuse des objets" (I can be a good writer, whereas I would always be a bad lawyer, seeing only the comic side and artistic form in everything and never appreciating the serious reality of objects [1851]). "La littérature avant tout, puisque là seulement je puis réussir puisque mon esprit est invariablement fixé sur ce point!" (Literature above all! There alone can I succeed, for my mind is focused uniquely on this goal! [1851]).

Inspired by the likes of Victor Hugo, Alfred de Vigny, and Gautier, and introduced (via family contacts on his mother's side) into several high-society Parisian literary circles, the young Romantic Verne began to write. He composed poetry and penned several short stories: *Les Premiers Navires de la marine mexicaine* (The First Ships of the Mexican Navy, 1851), *Un Voyage en ballon* (A Balloon Trip, 1851), *Martin Paz, nouvelle historique* (Martin Paz, Historical Short Story, 1851), *Maître Zacharius* (Master Zacharius, 1854), and *Un Hivernage dans les glaces* (Wintering in the Ice, 1855). He also wrote plays, some of which were performed in local theaters: *Les Pailles rompues* (Broken Straws, 1850), *Le Colin-Maillard* (Blind Man's Bluff, 1853), and *Les Compagnons de la Marjolaine* (The Marjolaine's Companions, 1855). Verne even became close friends with the very popular Dumas *père* and Dumas *fils* and, through the former's intervention, managed to become the secretary of the Théâtre Lyrique in 1852.

As he continued to compose his plays and poetry—and sell an occasional short story or essay to supplement his meager income—Verne was steadily obsessed with the idea of becoming a recognized French dramatist—a dream that was never to materialize, at least not as he had imagined it would. And many years were to pass before Verne would reluctantly decide to abandon his theatrical aspirations and redirect those energies toward scientifically didactic adventure stories. During those difficult years of 1850 to 1862, and prior to his fateful meeting with Hetzel, Verne spent more and more of his time writing lucrative short stories and scientific/historical articles for popular periodical journals such as the

Professor Aronnax in Vingt mille lieues sous les mers. *Verne served as the model for this illustration by Edouard Riou for the original edition.*

Musée des Familles. This activity, while fascinating for Verne, required long days in the Bibliothèque Nationale gathering the necessary documentation, poring over reference works of geography and world history, and carefully reading a variety of popular science magazines. And although this continual research might appear laborious, Verne seemed to revel in it, saying: "Je travaille beaucoup maintenant . . . je suis fort souvent à la bibliothèque qui m'offre d'inépuisables ressources" (I'm working a lot now . . . I am very often at the library, which offers me endless resources). "Je travaille du matin au soir, ne sortant que dans les circonstances indispensables, mais tout ce labeur m'amuse à un point extraordinaire" (I work from morning till night, going out only when it's absolutely necessary, but all this labor amuses me to an extraordinary degree).

During these extended work sessions at the Bibliothèque Nationale (where he could also stay warm, for his garret apartment was not well heated), Verne first conceived of the possibility of writing a wholly new type of novel, what he first called a *roman de la science* (novel of science). This new form would fully incorporate the large amounts of factual material that he was accumulating in his library research, as well as that gleaned from essays in the *Musée des Familles* and other journals. It would combine scientific discovery, action and adventure, history and geography, and be patterned on the novels and tales of Sir Walter Scott, James Fenimore Cooper, and Edgar Allan Poe—the latter's works had been translated in 1856 by Charles Baudelaire and collectively called *Histoires extraordinaires* (Extraordinary Stories), a title of some significance when one considers the title eventually chosen for Verne's own series of novels.

In 1857 Verne married Honorine Morel (née de Viane), a twenty-six-year-old widow with two daughters. Taking advantage of his new father-in-law's contacts in Paris and a monetary wedding gift from his own father, Verne reluctantly decided to discontinue his work at the Théâtre Lyrique and assumed a full-time job as *agent de change* (stockbroker) at the Paris Exchange with the firm Eggly & Cie. He spent his early mornings at home writing (at a desk with two drawers—one for his plays, the other for his scientific essays) and most of his days at the Bourse doing business and associating with other young financiers who had interests similar to his own. One such acquaintance, Félix Duquesnel, said of him during this period: "[Verne] réussissait plus de bons mots que d'affaires . . . prompt à la riposte, gouailleur, narquois, sceptique en toutes choses, une seule exceptée: de son origine bretonne, il garda toute sa vie la mentalité catholique" (Verne did better with his witticisms than he did with business . . . quick at answering back, mocking, sarcastic, and skeptical in every respect but one: from his Breton background he retained a Catholic mentality that stayed with him all his life).

When not writing or at the stock exchange, Verne spent his time either with his old theater friends—dubbed years earlier the "Onze-Sans-Femmes" ("Eleven Without Wives," but most of whom were married by this time)—or at the Bibliothèque Nationale, collecting scientific and historical tidbits and copying them onto notecards for future use, a habit he would continue throughout his life. As at least one biographer has noted, the long weekend sessions he spent in the reading rooms of the library may well have been also partly motivated by a simple desire for peace and quiet: in 1861 Verne's son Michel was born and greatly annoyed his father with his incessant crying. But whatever the case may have been, his long-contemplated ideas for a *roman de la science* soon crystallized into a rough draft of what would later be titled *Cinq semaines en ballon* (1863; translated as *Five Weeks in a Balloon*, 1869)—the first novel of the *Voyages extraordinaires*. The inspiration for this story of an intrepid trio of Englishmen and their balloon flight across the then largely unexplored continent of Africa was the culmination of a variety of different circumstances, both in Verne's life and in the events taking place during this historical period in France.

First, owing to a violent dispute with the editor in chief of the *Musée des Familles* in 1856, Verne no longer contributed articles and short stories to this journal. Increasingly determined, however, to expand his short narratives into a full-length scientific novel, Verne discussed his idea for a *roman de la science* with his friends, with his colleagues, and with three individuals in particular: Jacques Arago (famous explorer and brother to the respected physicist and astronomer François Arago), Henri Garcet (Verne's cousin, a mathematician, who would eventually help him with the complex trajectories of his moon novels), and Félix Tournachon, known to most Parisians by his popular pseudonym "Nadar." The influence of Nadar during this period was decisive. Widely recognized as a famous photographer, daredevil balloonist, and cofounder of the Société d'encouragement pour la locomotion au moyen d'appareils plus lourds que l'air (Society for the Encouragement of Air Travel via Heavier-than-Air Vehicles)—of which Verne eventually became secretary, later incorporating many of the society's precepts into his novel *Robur-le-conquérant* (1886; translated as *The Clipper of the Clouds*, 1887)—Nadar quickly initiated Verne into the mysteries of air travel. He also brought Verne into his own circle of friends, including such noted engineers and scientists as Jacques Babinet (inventor of the hygrometer) and Ponton d'Amécourt (engineer of one of the earliest scale-model helicopters). The many theoretical discussions among Nadar and his friends ultimately provided Verne with the technical knowledge that enabled him to write his first *roman scientifique*, complementing as it did his own rapidly growing geographical and historical erudition. The friendship between Nadar and Verne would last throughout their lives: as a tribute to his friend, Verne even used an anagram of Nadar's name for one of his heroes in *De la Terre à la lune* (1865; translated as *From the Earth to the Moon*, 1869)—Michel Ardan—a character whose actions are modeled on Nadar's own legendary exploits.

A second influencing factor on the author had to do with current events: stories both about balloon travel—real (Nadar) and fictional (Poe's *Hans Pfall* [1835; translated, 1856], for example)—and about African explorers were becoming very popular in France during the late 1850s and early 1860s. Daily newspaper accounts of the exotic discoveries of Heinrich Barth, Sir Richard Francis Burton, John Speke, and James Augustus Grant soon generated a large following of avid French readers who shared their ongoing adventures on the "dark continent." There is no doubt that Verne, conscientious as he was about staying abreast of such developments, saw in these travelogues (and the public's response to them) the ideal scenario for his first scientific adventure novel.

In September 1862 Verne was introduced to Hetzel through a friend of both the publisher and Dumas *père*. Verne promptly asked Hetzel if he would consider reviewing for publication his manuscript tentatively titled "Un Voyage en l'air" (An Air Voyage)—a manuscript that, according to his wife, the author had very nearly destroyed a few weeks earlier after his rejection by another publishing house. Hetzel agreed to the request, seeing in this narrative the potential for an ideal "fit" with his newly established family-oriented periodical, the *Magasin d'Education et de Récréation*. A few days later Verne and Hetzel began what would prove to be a highly successful author-publisher collaboration, lasting for more than forty years and resulting in more than sixty *romans scientifiques*. Shortly after the publication and immediate commercial success of Verne's first novel, retitled *Cinq semaines en ballon*, Hetzel offered the young writer a ten-year contract for at least two novels per year of the same sort. Soon after, Verne quit his job at the stock exchange and began to write full time.

It is important, when considering both the subsequent novels of the *Voyages extraordinaires* and the corresponding growth of Verne's paraliterary reputation, to understand how these works were originally marketed by Hetzel. Beginning in 1866 with Verne's tale of arctic exploration, *Les Aventures du capitaine Hatteras* (translated as *At the North Pole* and *The Desert of Ice*, 1874), Hetzel decided (for commercial purposes) to group Verne's novels into a series, and the *Voyages extraordinaires* were officially born. And at least one of Verne's novels from this series—he often completed three or more per year—had to be first published (in feuilleton [serial] format) in the bimonthly *Magasin d'Education et de Récréation*, to appear later in hardcover format. By reading the publisher's preface to the first volume of this encyclopedic journal, one can discern three important points: the parent-and-child public to whom the *Magasin* was principally addressed, the goals that it sought to achieve, and (more crucially) those ideological and pedagogical parameters within which Verne was required to tailor his narratives:

> Il s'agit pour nous de constituer un enseignement de famille dans le vrai sens du mot, un enseignement sérieux et attrayant à la fois, qui plaise aux parents et profite aux enfants. Education, récréation—sont à nos yeux deux termes qui rejoignent. L'instructif doit se présenter sous une forme qui provoque l'intérêt: sans cela il rebute et dégoûte de l'instruction; l'amusement doit cacher une réalité morale, c'est-à-dire utile: sans cela il passe au futile, et vide les têtes au lieu de les remplir.
>
> Là devra être l'unité de notre œuvre, qui pourra, si elle réussit, contribuer à augmenter la masse des connaissances et d'idées saines, la masse de bons sentiments, d'esprit, de raison et de goût qui forme ce qu'on pourrait appeler le capital moral de la jeunesse intellectuelle de la France.
>
> (We are trying to create a journal for the entire family that is educational in the truest sense of the word; one that is both serious and entertaining, one that would be of interest to parents and of profit to children. Education and recreation—these two terms, in our opinion, should complement one another. Instruction should be presented in a manner so as to incite real interest; otherwise, it tends to be too off-putting and disheartening. Entertainment should contain a moral lesson; otherwise, it tends to be pointless and empties heads instead of filling them.
>
> This will be the unity of our journal, which, if it succeeds, will contribute to the acquisition of knowledge, healthy ideas and emotions, reason, wit, and good taste by those who constitute, one might say, the moral stock of our educated youth of France.)

The overtly didactic intent of the *Magasin d'Education et de Récréation*—as well as its companion series (for hardcover publication of individual titles), *Bibliothèque d'Education et de Récréation*—is clear indeed. Responding to a perceived lack of science education in France's predominantly Catholic-controlled public schools and an overall decline in the moral fabric of the bourgeois children of the Second Empire, Hetzel deliberately marketed his publications to address this social need. As a result, although providing Verne with a relatively lucrative publishing outlet for his *romans scientifiques* and serving as both literary mentor and a kind of personal adviser to the young author, Hetzel also acted as Verne's prime censor. He required the author to conform to strict house rules in all matters of pedagogy, morality, and political ideology in the *Voyages extraordinaires*—limitations that at one point caused Verne to complain bitterly to Hetzel about "le milieu assez restreint où je suis condamné de me

Illustrations by Riou for the original edition of Vingt mille lieues sous les mers, *depicting the giant squid*

mouvoir" (the rather restricted environment that I'm condemned to move around in).

Emulating the commercial success of Hetzel's family journal in France, a similar feuilleton-type periodical in Great Britain, the *Boy's Own Paper*—marketed primarily for young men—began to publish the first English translations of Verne's works. The results were a mixed blessing. Verne's translated narratives enjoyed an instant and lasting popularity among the youthful readers of the *Boy's Own Paper*. But the translations themselves were invariably hurried and amateurish—slapdash bowdlerizations that summarily deleted most of the science, altered the plots as well as the names of the characters, and emphasized only the most sensationalistic parts of the original texts. Thus, Verne's (or, more precisely, Hetzel's) English connection with the *Boy's Own Paper* not only exacerbated the growing tendency among French literary scholars to categorize Verne as an author fit only for adolescents, but it also popularized maimed translations of Verne's narratives that severely undermined the integrity of the author's original texts. Further, it was most often these early hackneyed British translations that were (and, unfortunately, still are) reprinted and marketed with great commercial success throughout America.

Following Verne's historic meeting with Hetzel, the remainder of his life and works can be divided into two distinct periods: 1862-1886, what might be termed Verne's "Hetzel period," when he wrote the majority of his most celebrated *Voyages extraordinaires*, became relatively wealthy, and began to collaborate on various stage adaptations of his works for Parisian theaters; and 1886-1905, a period that witnessed a growing pessimism in the author's outlook and the presence of a variety of antiscience, proenvironment, and social themes in his works (thus marking a drastic departure from his earlier positivist leanings). To these divisions in Verne's career can be added a period (1905-1919), when, following Verne's death, his posthumous works were edited (and sometimes substantially rewritten) by his son Michel.

In 1864 Verne published *Voyage au centre de la Terre* (translated as *A Journey to the Center of the Earth*, 1872), which would prove to be one of his most popular extraordinary voyages. Mixing elements of geologic pedagogy, subterranean adventure, and a kind of "rites of passage" initiation for its young protagonist, Axel, this novel tells how the obstinate but warmhearted German professor Lidenbrock discovers an ancient manuscript written in code by the medieval explorer Arne Saknussemm. This cryptogram (a favorite device of Verne's), when finally deciphered, reveals how he had managed to journey to the center of Earth. Lidenbrock, his reluctant nephew Axel, and a taciturn but loyal Icelandic guide named Hans follow the path marked by their predecessor, enter the crater of an extinct volcano, descend into Earth, and eventually discover a subterranean world. The original source of this story was undoubtedly the many "hollow Earth" theories circulating in France during this period, as well as growing public interest in the sciences of geology (scientific debates about inner-Earth's true composition, the invention of the first seismograph in 1855), of paleontology (the impact of Baron Georges Cuvier's theories, newly discovered dinosaur fossils), and of evolution (the controversial transformist theories of Jean de Lamarck, Charles Darwin, and others).

Narrated in the first person by the impressionable and romantic young Axel, the novel, with its discursive structure, manages to maintain an even balance between Lidenbrock's detailed scientific exposés as he instructs his nephew during their journey and the latter's poetic reveries. This delicate intertwining of fact with fantasy, mathematics with myth, and didacticism with daydreaming constitutes the core of Verne's narrative recipe for the vast majority of his *Voyages extraordinaires* during this period. In 1978, in a precedent-setting decision that amply reflected Verne's new status in French letters, France's Ministry of Education placed *Voyage au centre de la Terre* on the *agrégation* reading list within the French university system, precipitating a rush of undergraduate and graduate studies of this and other Vernian novels and (finally) consecrating a place for them within the university literary canon.

Verne's famous *De la Terre à la lune*—along with its 1870 sequel, *Autour de la lune* (translated as *Round the Moon*, 1876)—was the first "realistic" (that is, scientifically plausible) manned moon voyage in Western literature. Breaking with the often utopian "imaginary voyages" of the past—for example, those of Lucian, William Godwin, Savinien de Cyrano de Bergerac, Johannes Kepler, and Bernard Le Bovier de Fontenelle—Verne based his extrapolative tale on the lessons of modern astronomy and astrophysics. Many of his stunning predictions in these two novels were to prove true one hundred years later during America's Apollo program: the launching location selected (not far from Cape Canaveral, Florida), the initial velocity necessary for escaping Earth's gravity, the composition of the spacecraft itself (aluminum) as well as its height and weight, the mathematical trajectories necessary for a rendezvous with the moon, and even the space vessel's reentry and splashdown in the Pacific (less than three miles from Apollo's). And if Verne's greatest—albeit historically understandable—error was to launch his "space-bullet" using a gigantic cannon, such a strategy was a logical extension of the other major focus of these novels: a biting (albeit quite humorous) satire of Yankee competitiveness and post-Civil War weapons technology.

Following the publication of his first "circumnavigatory quest" novel in 1867, *Les Enfants du capitaine Grant* (translated as *In Search of the Castaways*, 1873), wherein a group of British children circle the world to find their castaway father—and the laborious completion of a Hetzel-mandated *Géographie illustrée de la France et de ses colonies* (Illustrated Geography of France and Its Colonies, 1867)—Verne moved his family to the northern coast town of Le Crotoy in 1868. He purchased his first yacht, which he dubbed the *Saint-Michel* after his son. And, during his frequent voyages on the Somme and along the coast of France—ensconced in the yacht's ample cabin with its portable library—he began revising a manuscript first sketched out several years earlier and tentatively called "Un Voyage sous les eaux" (An Underwater Voyage). A year later, in early 1869, Verne put the finishing touches on his first novel of the sea, *Vingt mille lieues sous les mers* (1869-1870; translated as *Twenty Thousand Leagues Under the Sea*, 1873).

The sheer imaginative power of *Vingt mille lieues sous les mers*, the brooding and enigmatic genius of Nemo, and the "dream machine" character of the *Nautilus* itself (named after Robert Fulton's experimental craft of 1797) have made it perhaps the most memorable of all Verne's *Voyages extraordinaires*. Originally, however, the idea for this one came to Verne from a letter (dated

1865) written to him by one of his earliest admirers—George Sand:

> Je vous remercie, Monsieur, de vos . . . deux saisissants ouvrages. . . . Je n'ai qu'un chagrin, en ce qui les concerne, c'est de les avoir finis et de n'en avoir pas une douzaine à lire. J'espère que vous nous conduirez bientôt dans les profondeurs de la mer et que vous ferez voyager vos personnages dans ces appareils de plongeurs que votre science et votre imagination peuvent se permettre de perfectionner.
>
> (Thank you, dear Sir, for your . . . two thrilling novels. . . . I have only one regret about them, that I have finished reading them and I don't have a dozen more to read. I hope that you will soon lead us into the depths of the sea and that you will have your characters travel in those diving machines that your science and your imagination are capable of perfecting.)

Also interesting—particularly in the context of Hollywood's later interpretive treatment of this novel—is the fact that Hetzel originally requested that Nemo be portrayed as a sworn enemy of the slave trade, thereby providing a clear ideological justification for his merciless attacks on certain seagoing vessels (versus the revenge motive in Disney's *20,000 Leagues Under the Sea* [1954]). Verne, on the contrary, at first wanted Nemo to be a Pole and his implacable hatred to be directed against the Russian czar (in a direct reference to the bloody Russian suppression of Poland in 1863). But Hetzel was deeply concerned with the possible diplomatic ramifications of such a plot line and the likelihood of the book being banned. Both author and publisher, however, eventually reached a compromise. It was decided that Nemo's exact motives would remain intriguingly obscure (at least until the conclusion of *L'Ile mystérieuse* [1874-1875; translated as *The Mysterious Island,* 1875]): he would be portrayed as the champion of liberty and the avenger of the oppressed. Incidentally, the portrait of Professor Aronnax in the original illustrated version of *Vingt mille lieues sous les mers* was that of (a beardless) Verne himself at age forty-one.

During the summer of 1870 Verne received the Légion d'honneur (ironically, one of the last official acts of a corrupt government that the author despised). At the start of the short-lived Franco-Prussian War, Verne moved his family to Amiens to stay with his wife's relatives, joined the Le Crotoy home guard, and patrolled the Somme with the *Saint-Michel* (specially fitted with a small cannon on its bow). After the ensuing German occupation and the Paris Commune, Verne himself moved permanently to Amiens. Located halfway between Paris and Le Crotoy, Amiens was a quiet town and an ideal pied-à-terre for writing, for quick trips to Le Crotoy, and for his theater interests in the nearby capital. Verne spent the remaining thirty-three years of his life in Amiens.

In 1873 Verne published his most commercially successful novel, *Le Tour du monde en quatre-vingts jours* (translated as *Around the World in Eighty Days,* 1874). The idea for this, his second "circumnavigation" narrative, came from two sources: a travel article in the popular journal *Magasin Pittoresque* a few years before (following the opening of the Suez Canal); and Poe's *Three Sundays in a Week* (1841; translated, 1859). On a wager, the imperturbable Englishman Phileas Fogg and his servant Passepartout set out to circle the globe in eighty days, experiencing along the way a variety of adventures ranging from the rescue of an Indian princess to a shoot-out in the Old West. The surprise ending of *Le Tour du monde en quatre-vingts jours* was rendered all the more effective because of the initial published format of the work: a suspense-filled serial in the Parisian newspaper *Temps* (6 November - 22 December 1872), which nearly tripled its circulation during this period.

The hardcover novel quickly set new sales records both in France and abroad: more than a half-million copies during the first year alone. Verne's growing celebrity correspondingly soared. The following year he was elected to the Académie d'Amiens, his *Voyages extraordinaires* were "officially" recognized by the Académie Française, and an extravagant stage adaptation of *Le Tour du monde en quatre-vingts jours* (with Adolphe D'Ennery)—complete with live elephants, serpents, and exotic regalia—proved to be a resounding success and would play uninterrupted at the Théâtre du Châtelet for a record-breaking fifty years. Verne's theatrical ambitions were finally satisfied. Three years later, in 1877, the author worked with Jacques Offenbach to bring his lighthearted farce *Le Docteur Ox* (1874; translated as *Dr. Ox's Experiment,* 1874) to the stage. Verne then teamed up twice again with D'Ennery for successful theater productions of his *Les Enfants du capitaine Grant* in 1878 and, two years later, of his popular Russian epic *Michel Strogoff* (1876; translated as *Michel Strogoff, The Courier of the Czar,* 1877).

Verne at age fifty

In 1877 Verne successively purchased two more yachts (dubbed the *Saint-Michel II* and the *Saint-Michel III* respectively), and, during the years following, he sailed to ever more distant ports of call: southern Spain, Algeria, Scotland, Denmark, Norway and Sweden, Italy, the Baltic, and Ireland, among other destinations. Not surprisingly, many of these locales found their way, sooner or later, into the settings of his subsequent *Voyages extraordinaires*: the coal mines of Scotland in *Les Indes noires* (1877; translated as *The Child of the Cavern*, 1877), northern Algeria in *Hector Servadac* (1877; translated, 1877), the Adriatic islands in *Mathias Sandorf* (1885; translated, 1885), and an orphanage in Ireland in *P'tit-Bonhomme* (1893; translated as *Foundling Mick*, 1895), among others. On one such voyage to Rome, Verne was invited to a private audience with Pope Leo XIII. And almost wherever he docked, he was met with cheering crowds of admirers—an indication of his well-established international celebrity.

In 1879 Verne published a curious novel that, in retrospect, seems to foreshadow certain changes after 1886 in his overall views concerning science, technology, and human values: *Les Cinq Cents Millions de la Bégum* (translated as *The Begum's Fortune*, 1879-1880). The only combination utopia/dystopia in the *Voyages extraordinaires*, this narrative tells the story of a huge inheritance received by two (highly symbolic) individuals—Dr. Sarrasin of France and Herr Schultze of Germany—from a long-lost and fabulously wealthy raja of India related to them by marriage. Each proceeds to build the city of his dreams in the wilds of the American Northwest: Sarrasin, a modern utopian village (based on the principles of his medical specialty, hygiene), and Schultze, a Dantesque fortresslike factory for the production of cannons and high-tech armaments (for sale to the expansionist industrialized nations of the world).

Incarnating French attitudes toward Germany during the postwar years of the 1870s and announcing certain events of the early twentieth century, Herr Schultze is Verne's first truly evil scientist. His vision of nature and man is focused uniquely on relationships of force, as dictated by cold, analytical logic. Identifiably Nietzschean in his evolutionary beliefs (and evoking a kind of scientific social Darwinism), Herr Schultze is fanatically devoted to the extermination of the weaker elements of the human race and to the rise of a new ruling class of technological supermen. Although he is defeated in the end (by the deus-ex-machina intervention of Providence), the dark portrait of Herr Schultze in this tale nevertheless underscores what would eventually become three of Verne's most passionate beliefs: first, that science in the hands of evil men becomes evil; second, that the raw power of technology breeds moral corruption; and three, that only the wrath of God can limit such excesses.

The latter half of Verne's novelistic production from 1886 to 1905, although varied, very often reflects this change of focus: a slow but steady metamorphosis away from the overall optimism of a positivistic and Saint-Simonian socialist worldview, to be replaced by an outlook that is generally pessimistic, cynical, and antiscience. As might be expected, the scientific pedagogy in these texts becomes less central: it is severely abridged, watered down, or cut out altogether. Motifs of environmental protection, human morality, and social responsibility are more frequent. Humor tends either to disappear entirely, or is recentered in irony or acidic satire. And the scientists themselves are increasingly portrayed as crazed megalomaniacs who use their technological lore for purposes of world domination or unlimited wealth.

The underlying reasons for this palpable change of tone in Verne's later works can be traced to certain events in the author's life as well as in the social fabric of late-nineteenth-century France. For example, during a time when he was experiencing serious problems with his rebellious son Michel (repeated bankruptcies, costly amorous escapades, divorce from his first wife, difficulties with the law), Verne began to have serious financial worries of his own, and even was forced to sell the *Saint-Michel.* He also had to cope with the successive deaths of three individuals who were very close to him: his longtime mistress, Mme Duchêne, in 1885; his editor and friend Hetzel in 1886; and his own mother in 1887. Furthermore, an important event in Verne's life that is still cloaked in mystery took place on 9 March 1886: he was attacked at gunpoint by his mentally disturbed nephew Gaston and shot in the lower leg. Lodged in the bone of his ankle, the bullet could not be removed, and he remained partially crippled for the rest of his life. In a 21 December 1886 letter to Hetzel *fils*, Verne confided: "Du reste, je suis entré dans la série noire de ma vie" (For the rest, I have entered the black part of my life). And, a few years later, he disclosed his feelings to his brother Paul, saying: "Il n'y a encore que ces distractions intellectuelles qui vaillent la peine d'être prises.... Mon caractère est profondément altéré et j'ai reçu des coups dont je ne me relèverai jamais" (There remain only these intellectual distractions that are worth bothering with.... My personality is deeply changed, and I have received blows from which I'll never recover).

This growing pessimism in Verne's private life had its counterpart in the French social climate of the 1880s and 1890s as well. A severe long-term economic crisis from 1882 to 1895—provoked in part by agricultural disasters, a depressed manufacturing industry, skyrocketing unemployment, and a series of bank failures—coupled with ongoing political strife (the Boulangiste movement and the fall from power of Jules Ferry) created in the French public a general mood of disillusionment and frustration with the government's positivist policies of the past. Not coincidentally, during this turbulent period Verne began to serve as an elected official for the city of Amiens, a role that put him into daily confrontation with such matters, as he and his fellow councilmen grappled with the local impact of these difficult issues.

Other international developments during this period undoubtedly colored Verne's outlook as well: the late-nineteenth-century rise of modern capitalistic imperialism—intensifying the hegemonic power of banks, profit-conscious investors, and moneylenders in government policy and decisionmaking—and the frenetic rivalry among the industrialized nations of the Western world to colonize (and exploit) a greater and greater number of Third World countries in Africa, the Far East, Indonesia, and the South Seas. Finally, this period also saw the birth of the modern military-industrial complex—where the advances in scientific technology were unilaterally applied to the production of ever-more-lethal weapon systems, where national military budgets soared as France

Verne's home in Amiens

and other industrialized nations sought to consolidate their geostrategic holdings with ironclad warships, machine guns, poison-gas canisters, and new long-range artillery. Whether such international developments directly affected the composition of Verne's later *Voyages extraordinaires* is a moot point. But the author was undeniably a witness to, and very conscious of, these profound transformations in the overall tenor of his times. And the ideological texture of his novels from this period of 1886 to 1905 does indeed change dramatically.

A striking example of these changes can be seen in the later volumes of Verne's cycle novels: those narratives that incorporate characters from or continue the storyline of earlier works. Such serials would eventually include the trilogy of *De la Terre à la lune*, *Autour de la lune*, and *Sans dessus dessous* (1889; translated as *Topsy-Turvy*, 1890); the trilogy of *Les Enfants du capitaine Grant*, *Vingt mille lieues sous les mers*, and *L'Ile mystérieuse*; and the two-novel series of *Robur-le-conquérant* and *Maître du monde* (1904; translated as *The Master of the World*, 1914).

This practice of "recycling" always took as its point of departure only those novels that enjoyed an initially substantial commercial success. One interesting characteristic of these sequels—and one that aptly reflects the profound differences between the Verne of 1863-1886 and the Verne of 1886-1905—is that they invariably highlight some form of *reversal* when compared to their precursors.

For example, in the first trilogy the amazing feats of ballistic engineering by Barbicane's "Gun-Club" become (quite literally) earthshaking when, instead of heroically "shooting" a manned capsule around the moon, they seek to alter the angle of Earth's axis with a gigantic cannon blast. Totally indifferent to the catastrophic environmental and human damage that would result from such a project, they hope to melt Earth's polar ice cap in order to uncover vast mineral wealth for themselves and the United States. Barbicane and company not only fail in this ambitious enterprise (because of a providential lightning bolt) but actually become caricatures of their former selves as Verne ferociously satirizes their blatant social irresponsibility and positivistic hubris.

In the second trilogy the conclusion of *Les Enfants du capitaine Grant* features a villain named Ayrton who is purposely abandoned on a deserted South Pacific island for his crimes. But he is later discovered, rescued, and reformed by Cyrus Smith and the other industrious castaways of *L'Ile mystérieuse*. The latter eventually chance upon their hidden island benefactor: Captain Nemo in his famed *Nautilus*. And they are able to recognize him immediately because—in a delightful, and quite typical, Vernian self-reference—they had read a certain well-known book entitled *Vingt mille lieues sous les mers*! Ayrton the criminal antihero is rehabilitated and becomes a legitimate hero; Nemo, the adventurous, powerful, and rebellious wanderer of the seas in *Vingt mille lieues sous les mers*, becomes a repentant old man on his deathbed, confessing his criminal past; and even the miraculous *Nautilus* itself is pathetically imprisoned in a sea cave—doomed nevermore to sail the open sea or explore its mysterious depths.

In the third series Robur the Conqueror, in his helicopterlike airship, *Albatros*—Robur, symbol of man's transcendence above and conquest of nature—degenerates into an insane megalomaniac who, threatening global terrorism from his high-tech inventions, demands to be "Master of the World." Similar to Herr Schultze, Robur is also stopped only by divine intervention (again, a lightning bolt). But what is important to note is that these latter volumes of this series of novels in the *Voyages extraordinaires* clearly reflect Verne's own ideological turnabout as he appears deliberately to undermine the scientific and moral assumptions upon which his earlier (and best-known) works were built.

Many other post-1886 novels of the *Voyages extraordinaires* tend to target, either as their primary focus or as an adjacent theme, a wide range of social and environmental issues: the oppression of the Québécois in Canada in *Famille-sans-nom* (1889; translated as *A Family Without a Name*, 1889); ignorance and superstition in *Le Château des Carpathes* (1892; translated as *The Castle of the Carpathians*, 1893); the intolerable living conditions in orphanages in *P'tit-Bonhomme*; the plague of partisan politics and the ongoing destruction of Polynesian island cultures in *L'Ile à hélice* (1895; translated as *Floating Island*; 1896); the imminent extinction of whales in *Le Sphinx des glaces* (1897; translated as *An Antarctic Mystery*, 1898); the environmental damage caused by the oil industry in *Le Testament d'un excentrique* (1899; translated as *The Will of an Eccentric*, 1900); and the slaughter of elephants for their ivory in *Le Village aérien* (1901; translated as *The Village in the Treetops*, 1964), among many others.

During his final years, despite increasingly poor health (arthritis, cataracts, diabetes, and severe gastrointestinal problems), the death of his brother Paul in 1897, and annoying family squabbles, Verne continued diligently to churn out two to three novels per year. But it soon became evident that the sales of his *Voyages extraordinaires* were beginning to slip badly. Although sales of reprints and translations of his earlier works still numbered in the millions, his later works were selling only in the mere thousands. And many of his final novels—*Le Superbe Orénoque* (The Superb Orinoco River, 1898), *Les Frères Kip* (The Kip Brothers, 1902), *Bourses de voyage* (Travel Scholarships, 1903), and *L'Invasion de la mer* (The Invasion of the Sea, 1905)—did not even sell out their first printings. Furthermore—a telling commentary—they remain untranslated into English even today.

Although somewhat disheartened by the declining sales of his works, Verne refused to become overly upset: "Vous me dites que le public ne veut plus lire. Je crois qu'il lit beaucoup, au contraire, mais il lit des milliers de journaux qui le gavent de romans-feuilletons et ce doit être une des raisons qui rendent si mauvaise la vente des volumes. Je le regrette bien pour les quelques ouvrages que j'ai encore à faire et qui, dans ma pensée, compléteront la peinture de la Terre sous la forme du roman. Mais je ne me décourage pas et je travaille beaucoup" (You say that the public does not want to read anymore. On the contrary, I believe that it reads much, but that it reads thousands of newspapers that stuff it with serials—and that must be one of the reasons for the poor sales. I regret this, especially for those few works that I still have to do and that, to my mind, will complete this portrait of Earth in the form of novels. But I do not get discouraged, and I am working hard).

Many foreign journalists visited Amiens from 1894 to 1905 to interview the legendary Jules Verne—who now seemed more popular outside of France than within—and their testimonies provide a rare and revealing glimpse into the author's private life. When asked about his work habits, Verne replied: "My method of work? Well, until recently, I invariably rose at five and made a point of doing three hours' writing before breakfast. The great bulk of my work was always done in this time, and though I would sit down for a couple of hours later in the day, my stories have really nearly all been written when most folks are sleeping."

When asked about his reading preferences, he replied: "To give you an idea of my reading, I come here every day after lunch and immediately set to work to read through 15 different papers, always the same 15, and I can tell you that very little escapes my attention. When I see something of interest, down it goes. Then I read the reviews, such as the *Revue Bleue*, the *Revue Rose*, the *Revue des Deux Mondes*, *Cosmos*, Tissandier's *La Nature*, Flammarion's *L'Astronomie*. I also read through the bulletins of the scientific societies, and especially those of the Geographical Society, for geography is my passion and my study. I have all of Reclus's works—I have a great admiration for Elisée Reclus—and the whole of Arago. I also read and reread . . . the collection known as *Le Tour du Monde*, which is a series of stories of travel."

And, finally, when asked about his literary status, Verne confessed, "Je ne compte pas dans la littérature française" (I don't count in French literature), a statement that evoked the following reaction from his British interviewer: "Who was it

Frontispiece by Riou for the 1882 double edition of two of Verne's popular novels

who spoke thus, with drooping head, and with a ring of sadness in his cheerful voice? Some writer of cheap but popular *feuilletons* for the halfpenny press, some man of letters who has never made a scruple of stating that he looks upon his pen as a money-getting implement? No! Strange, monstrous as it will appear, it was none other than Jules Verne. Yes, THE Jules Verne . . . who has delighted us all the world over for so many years."

With a drawer full of nearly completed manuscripts in his desk, Verne fell seriously ill in early 1905, a few weeks after his seventy-seventh birthday. Lucid until the end, he told his wife Honorine to gather the family around him, and he died quietly on 24 March 1905. He was buried on 28 March in the cemetery of La Madeleine in Amiens. Two years later an elaborate sculpture depicting the author rising from his tomb and engraved with the words "Vers l'immortalité et l'éternelle jeunesse" (Toward immortality and eternal youth) was placed over his grave. In 1926 the American publisher Hugo Gernsback used a representation of Verne's tomb as a logo for his *Amazing Stories*: the first literary magazine featuring Verne-like tales of "scientifiction"—a term coined by Gernsback, later changed to "science fiction."

In early May of 1905 Verne's son Michel, as executor of his father's estate, published in the Parisian newspapers *Figaro* and *Temps* (later to become the *Monde* in 1944) a complete list of his father's works left in manuscript: eight novels, sixteen plays, four short stories, an untitled novel, and a chronicle called *Voyage à reculons en Angleterre et en Ecosse* (Voyage Backward to England and Scotland, 1989). Hetzel *fils* immediately contracted to publish seven of the novels (the eighth being too incomplete): *Le Phare au bout du monde* (1905; translated as *The Lighthouse at the Edge of the World*, 1923), *Le Volcan d'or* (1906; translated as *The Golden Volcano: The Claim on the Forty Mile Creek* and *Flood and Famine*, 1962), *L'Agence Thompson and Co.* (1907; translated as *The Thompson Travel Agency: Package Holiday* and *End of the Journey*, 1965), *La Chasse au météore* (1908; translated as *The Chase of the Golden Meteor*, 1909), *Le Pilote du Danube* (1908; translated as *The Danube Pilot*, 1967), *Les Naufragés du "Jonathan"* (1909; translated as *The Survivors of the Jonathan*: *The Masterless Man* and *The Unwilling Dictator*, 1962), and *Le Secret de Wilhelm Storitz* (1910; translated as *The Secret of Wilhelm Storitz*, 1963). The short stories were grouped into a collection titled *Hier et demain* (1910; translated as *Yesterday and Tomorrow*, 1965). The final posthumous novel, completed by Michel from his father's notes, was published many years later by Hachette (who bought the rights to Verne's works from Hetzel *fils* in 1914) as *L'Etonnante Aventure de la mission Barsac* (1919; translated as *The Barsac Mission: Into the Niger Bend* and *The City in the Sahara*, 1960).

Recently, these posthumous novels of the *Voyages extraordinaires* have become the topic of some controversy among Verne critics: how much and in what ways did Michel Verne alter these texts prior to their publication? After close inspection of Verne's surviving manuscripts of these works (currently housed in the Centre Jules Verne in Nantes), it now appears certain that Michel's hand in the composition of Verne's final *Voyages extraordinaires* was much greater than had been previously recognized. Michel, who frequently assisted and collaborated with his father

Verne, age seventy-six

during the latter's final years (and increasingly so as Jules's health began to fail), is now known to have been the principal author not only of the posthumous *L'Etonnante Aventure de la mission Barsac* but also of several other texts normally credited exclusively to Jules: the short stories "L'Eternel Adam" ("Eternal Adam"), "Au XXIXeme siècle: La journée d'un journaliste américain en 2889" ("In the Twenty-ninth Century: A Day in the Life of an American Journalist in 2889")—both published in *Hier et demain*—and "Un Express de l'avenir" ("An Express of the Future," first published in English in the *Strand*, 1895), as well as large portions of *L'Agence Thompson and Co.* and *Les Naufragés du "Jonathan."*

In 1985 the Université de Picardie and the Société Jules Verne sponsored an international conference in Amiens on Verne and his *Voyages extraordinaires*—one of many such conferences on Verne since the sesquicentennial of his birth was celebrated in 1978. The theme of the gathering was "Modernités de Jules Verne"—a richly symbolic indication of how the author's "extraordinary" visions and novelistic innovations continue to warrant the epithet "modern." In the words of Jean Chesneaux, a prominent Verne scholar: "Si Jules Verne reste présent parmi nous . . . c'est qu'il apporte sur la modernité un témoignage puissant, original, irremplaçable. Cet homme du XIXe siècle a chanté les pouvoirs illimités de la science et de la technique. . . . Il a été un patriote loyal et convaincu de la modernité dont son œuvre voulait être l'épopée. . . . Mais ce même homme du XIXe siècle avait déjà pressenti ce qui ne s'est que très lentement dégagé dans son œuvre . . . à savoir tout ce que le prodigieux Bond en Avant des sociétés industrielles renfermait de perversions et de périls" (If Jules Verne is still present among us . . . it is because he brings to the notion of modernity a commentary that is powerful, original, and irreplaceable. This man of the nineteenth century celebrated the limitless powers of science and technology.... He was a loyal and confirmed partisan of a modernity of which his works intended to be an epic portrayal.... But this same man of the nineteenth century already had a premonition that surfaced only very slowly in his works ... an awareness of the perils and perversions implicit in this prodigious Leap Forward by industrialized societies).

Letters:

Mario Turiello, "Lettre de Jules Verne à un jeune Italien," *Bulletin de la Société Jules Verne*, 1 (1936): 158-161;

"Jules Verne: 63 lettres," *Bulletin de la Société Jules Verne*, 11-13 (1938): 47-129;

A. Parménie, "Huit lettres de Jules Verne à son éditeur P.-J. Hetzel," *Arts et Lettres*, 15 (1949): 102-107;

A. Parménie and C. Bonnier de la Chapelle, *Histoire d'un éditeur et de ses auteurs, P.-J. Hetzel (Stahl)* (Paris: Albin Michel, 1953);

"Quelques lettres," *Livres de France*, 6 (May-June 1955): 13-15;

"Lettre à Nadar," *Arc*, 29 (1966): 83;

De Balzac à Jules Verne, un grand éditeur du XIXe siècle: P.-J. Hetzel, Catalogue de la Bibliothèque Nationale (Paris, 1966);

André Bottin, "Lettres inédites de Jules Verne au lieutenant colonel Hennebert," *Bulletin de la Société Jules Verne*, 17 (1971): 36-44;

"Sept lettres à sa famille et à divers correspondants," in *Jules Verne*, edited by P.-A. Touttain (Paris: Cahiers de l'Herne, 1974), pp. 63-70;

"Deux lettres à Louis-Jules Hetzel," in *Jules Verne*, pp. 73-74;

"Lettres à Nadar," in *Jules Verne*, pp. 76-80;

"Lettre à Paul, à propos de Turpin," in *Jules Verne*, pp. 81-82;

"Deux lettres inédites," *Bulletin de la Société Jules Verne*, 48 (1978): 253-254;

"Correspondance," *Bulletin de la Société Jules Verne*, 49 (1979): 31-34;

"Correspondance avec Fernando Ricci," *Europe*, 613 (1980): 137-138;

"Correspondance avec Mario Turiello," *Europe*, 613 (1980): 108-135;

"Lettres diverses," *Europe*, 613 (1980): 143-151;

"Trente-six lettres inédites," *Bulletin de la Société Jules Verne*, 68 (1983): 4-50;

"Spécial Lettres No. 2," *Bulletin de la Société Jules Verne*, 69 (1984): 3-25;

"Spécial Lettres No. 3," *Bulletin de la Société Jules Verne*, 78 (1986): 3-52;

"Spécial Lettres No. 4," *Bulletin de la Société Jules Verne*, 83 (1987): 4-27;

"Spécial Lettres No. 5," *Bulletin de la Société Jules Verne*, 88 (1988): 8-18;

"Spécial Lettres No. 6," *Bulletin de la Société Jules Verne*, 94 (1990): 10-33.

Interviews:

R. H. Sherard, "Jules Verne at Home: His Own Account of His Life and Work," *McClure's*, 2 (January 1894): 115-124; translated into French by W. Butcher as "Jules Verne chez lui: Sa propre version de sa vie et de son œuvre," *Bulletin de la Société Jules Verne*, 95 (1990): 20-30;

Marie A. Belloc, "Jules Verne at Home," *Strand*, 9 (February 1895): 206-213; translated into French as "Jules Verne chez lui," in *Textes oubliés*, edited by Francis Lacassin (Paris: UGE, "10/18," 1979), pp. 355-366;

Edmondo De Amicis, "A Visit to Jules Verne and Victorien Sardou," *Chautauquan*, 24 (March 1897): 701-707;

Gordon Jones, "Jules Verne at Home," *Temple Bar*, 129 (June 1904): 664-671.

Bibliographies:

Mark R. Hillegas, "A Bibliography of Secondary Materials on Jules Verne," *Extrapolation*, 2 (December 1960): 5-16;

François d'Argent and P.-A. Touttain, "Orientation bibliographique," in *Jules Verne*, edited by Touttain (Paris: Cahiers de l'Herne, 1974), pp. 348-361;

François Raymond and Daniel Compère, *Le Développement des études sur Jules Verne* (Paris: Minard, 1976);

Piero Gondolo della Riva, *Bibliographie analytique de toutes les œuvres de Jules Verne* (Paris: Société Jules Verne, 1977);

Jean-Michel Margot, *Bibliographie documentaire sur Jules Verne* (Ostermundigen, Switzerland: Margot, 1978; revised, 1982, 1989);

Edward Gallagher, Judith Mistichelli, and John Van Eerde, *Jules Verne: A Primary and Secondary Bibliography* (Boston: G. K. Hall, 1980);

Edward and Judith Myers, *A Bibliography of First Printings of the Writings of Jules Verne in the English Language* (New Hartford, Conn.: Country Lane, 1989).

Biographies:

Charles Lemire, *Jules Verne* (Paris: Berger-Levrault, 1908);

Marguerite Allotte de la Fuye, *Jules Verne, sa vie, son œuvre* (Paris: Simon Kra, 1928); translated by Erik de Mauny as *Jules Verne* (London: Staples, 1954);

Kenneth Allot, *Jules Verne* (London: Crescent, 1940);

Jean Jules-Verne, *Jules Verne* (Paris: Hachette, 1973); translated by R. Greaves as *Jules Verne: A Biography* (New York: Taplinger, 1976);

Jules Verne, "Souvenirs d'enfance et de jeunesse," in *Jules Verne*, edited by P.-A. Touttain (Paris: Cahiers de l'Herne, 1974), pp. 57-62; translated as "The Story of My Boyhood," *Youth's Companion* (9 April 1891): 211;

Marc Soriano, *Jules Verne* (Paris: Julliard, 1978);

Charles-Noël Martin, *La Vie et l'œuvre de Jules Verne* (Paris: Michel de l'Ormeraie, 1978).

References:

Peter Aberger, "The Portrayal of Blacks in Jules Verne's *Voyages extraordinaires*," *French Review*, 53 (1979): 199-206;

Marc Angenot, "Jules Verne and French Literary Criticism, I," *Science-Fiction Studies*, 1 (1973): 33-37;

Angenot, "Jules Verne and French Literary Criticism, II," *Science-Fiction Studies*, 1 (1973): 46-49;

Angenot, "Jules Verne: The Last Happy Utopianist," in *Science Fiction: A Critical Guide*, edited by Patrick Parrinder (New York: Longman, 1979), pp. 18-32;

Arc, issue on Verne, 29 (1966);

Roland Barthes, "Nautilus et Bateau ivre," in *Mythologies* (Paris: Seuil, 1957), pp. 90-92; translated by A. Lavers as "The Nautilus and the Drunken Boat," in *Mythologies* (New York: Hill & Wang, 1972), pp. 65-67;

Barthes, "Par où commencer?," *Poétique*, 1 (1970): 3-9;

Kenneth Berri, "Les *Cinq Cents Millions de la Bégum* ou la technologie de la fable," *Stanford French Review*, 3 (1979): 29-40;

Ray Bradbury, "The Ardent Blasphemers," foreword to *Twenty Thousand Leagues Under the Sea*, translated by A. Bonner (New York: Bantam, 1962), pp. 1-12;

Jean-Jacques Bridenne, *La Littérature française d'imagination scientifique* (Lausanne: Dassonville, 1950);

Alain Buisine, "Repères, marques, gisements: A propos de la robinsonnade vernienne," *Revue des Lettres Modernes*, 523-529 (April-June 1978): 113-139;

William Butcher, "Le Sens de *L'Eternel Adam*," *Bulletin de la Société Jules Verne*, 58 (1981): 73-81;

Butcher, *Verne's Journey to the Center of the Self* (London: Macmillan, 1990);

Michel Butor, "Le Point suprême et l'âge d'or à travers quelques œuvres de Jules Verne," *Arts et Lettres*, 15 (1949): 3-31; reprinted in his *Répertoire I* (Paris: Editions de Minuit, 1960), pp. 130-162;

Ross Chambers, "Cultural and Ideological Determinations in Narrative: A Note on Jules Verne's *Cinq Cents Millions de la Bégum*," *Esprit Créateur*, 21 (Fall 1981): 69-78;

Jean Chesneaux, *Une Lecture politique de Jules Verne* (Paris: Maspero, 1971); translated as *The Political and Social Ideas of Jules Verne* (London: Thames & Hudson, 1972);

Daniel Compère, *Approche de l'île chez Jules Verne* (Paris: Lettres Modernes, 1977);

Compère, "Le Bas des pages," *Bulletin de la Société Jules Verne*, 68 (1983): 147-153;

Compère, "Poétique de la carte," *Bulletin de la Société Jules Verne*, 50 (1979): 69-74;

Compère, *Un Voyage imaginaire de Jules Verne: Voyage au centre de la terre* (Paris: Lettres Modernes, 1977);

Peter Costello, *Jules Verne: Inventor of Science Fiction* (London: Hodder & Stoughton, 1978);

Ghislain de Diesbach, *Le Tour de Jules Verne en quatre-vingts livres* (Paris: Julliard, 1969);

René Escaich, *Voyage au monde de Jules Verne* (Paris: Editions Plantin, 1955);

Europe, issue on Verne, 33 (1955);

Europe, issue on Verne, 595-596 (1978);

Arthur B. Evans, "The Extraordinary Libraries of Jules Verne," *Esprit Créateur*, 28 (1988): 75-86;

Evans, *Jules Verne Rediscovered: Didacticism and the Scientific Novel* (Westport, Conn.: Greenwood, 1988);

Evans, "Science Fiction vs. Scientific Fiction in France: From Jules Verne to J.-H. Rosny aîné," *Science-Fiction Studies*, 15 (1988): 1-11;

I. O. Evans, *Jules Verne and His Works* (London: Arco, 1965);

Bernard Frank, *Jules Verne et ses voyages* (Paris: Flammarion, 1941);

Verne's tomb in Amiens

Peter Haining, *The Jules Verne Companion* (London: Souvenir, 1978);

Marie-Hélène Huet, *L'Histoire des Voyages extraordinaires* (Paris: Minard, 1973);

Jules Verne et les sciences humaines (Paris: UGE, "10/18," 1979)—papers given at a conference at the Centre Culturel de Cerisy-la-Salle, 1978;

Jules Verne—filiations, rencontres, influences, Colloque d'Amiens II (Paris: Minard, 1980)—papers given at a conference in Amiens, 1978;

Livres de France, issue on Verne, 5 (1955);

Pierre Macherey, "Jules Verne ou le récit en défaut," in his *Pour une théorie de la production littéraire* (Paris: Maspero, 1966), pp. 183-266; translated by G. Wall as "The Faulty Narrative," in *A Theory of Literary Production* (London: Routledge & Kegan Paul, 1978), pp. 159-240;

Magazine Littéraire, issue on Verne, 119 (December 1976);

Andrew Martin, "Chez Jules: Nutrition and Cognition in the Novels of Jules Verne," *French Studies*, 37 (January 1983): 47-58;

Martin, "The Entropy of Balzacian Tropes in the Scientific Fictions of Jules Verne," *Modern Language Review*, 77 (January 1982): 51-62;

Martin, *The Knowledge of Ignorance from Cervantes to Jules Verne* (Cambridge: Cambridge University Press, 1985);

Martin, *The Mask of the Prophet* (Oxford: Clarendon, 1990);

Charles-Noël Martin, *La Vie et l'œuvre de Jules Verne* (Paris: Michel de l'Ormeraie, 1976);

Walter J. Miller, *The Annotated Jules Verne: From the Earth to the Moon* (New York: Crowell, 1978);

Miller, *The Annotated Jules Verne: Twenty Thousand*

Leagues Under the Sea (New York: Crowell, 1976);
Modernités de Jules Verne (Paris: Presses Universitaires de France, 1988)—papers given at a conference in Amiens sponsored by the Université de Picardie, 1985;
Marcel Moré, *Nouvelles explorations de Jules Verne* (Paris: NRF, 1963);
Moré, *Le Très Curieux Jules Verne* (Paris: NRF, 1960);
Nouvelles recherches sur Jules Verne et le voyage, Colloque d'Amiens I (Paris: Minard, 1978)—papers given at a conference in Amiens, 1976;
Jean-Pierre Picot, "Parodie et tragédie de la régression dans quelques œuvres de Jules Verne," *Romantisme*, 27 (1980): 109-128;
François Raymond, ed., *Jules Verne 1: Le Tour du monde* (Paris: Minard, 1976);
Raymond, ed., *Jules Verne 2: L'Ecriture vernienne* (Paris: Minard, 1978);
Raymond, ed., *Jules Verne 3: Machines et imaginaire* (Paris: Minard, 1980);
Raymond, ed., *Jules Verne 4: Texte, image, spectacle* (Paris: Minard, 1983);
Raymond, ed., *Jules Verne 5: Emergences du fantastique* (Paris: Minard, 1987);
Christian Robin, *Un Monde connu et inconnu* (Nantes: Centre Universitaire de Recherches Verniennes, 1978);
Marilyn Gaddis Rose, "Two Misogynist Novels: A Feminist Reading of Jules Verne and Villiers de l'Isle-Adam," *Nineteenth-Century French Studies*, 9 (Fall/Winter 1980-1981): 117-123;
Mark Rose, "Filling the Void: Verne, Wells and Lem," *Science-Fiction Studies*, 8 (1981): 121-142;
Rose, "Jules Verne: Journey to the Center of Science Fiction," in *Coordinates: Placing Science Fiction*, edited by George E. Slusser (Carbondale: Southern Illinois University Press, 1983), pp. 31-41;
Michel Serres, *Jouvences sur Jules Verne* (Paris: Editions de Minuit, 1974);
Serres, "Le Savoir, la guerre, et le sacrifice," *Critique*, 367 (December 1977): 1067-1077;
Darko Suvin, "Communication in Quantified Space: The Utopian Liberalism of Jules Verne's Fiction," in his *Metamorphoses of Science Fiction* (New Haven: Yale University Press, 1979), pp. 147-163;
Simone Vierne, *Jules Verne* (Paris: Ballard, 1986);
Vierne, *Jules Verne et le roman initiatique* (Paris: Sirac, 1973);
André Winandy, "The Twilight Zone: Image and Reality in Jules Verne's *Strange Journeys*," *Yale French Studies*, 43 (1969): 101-110.

Papers:

The most important collection of Verne manuscripts and letters (in addition to those in the Bibliothèque Nationale) is located at the Centre Jules Verne in Nantes. Also in Nantes are the Musée Jules Verne and the Centre Universitaire de Recherches Verniennes. Another extensive collection of Verne materials is located in the archives of the Société Jules Verne, Amiens.

Jean-Marie Mathias Philippe-Auguste, Comte de Villiers de l'Isle-Adam

(7 November 1838 - 18 August 1889)

John Blaise Anzalone
Skidmore College

BOOKS: *Deux essais de poésie* (Paris: L. Tinterlin, 1858);
Premières poésies (Lyons: N. Scheuring, 1859);
Isis (Paris: Dentu, 1862);
Elën (Paris: Poupart-Davyl, 1865);
Morgane (St. Brieuc: Guyon Francisque, 1866); revised as *Le Prétendant* (Paris: Corti, 1965);
La Révolte (Paris: Lemerre, 1870); translated by Theresa Barkley as *The Revolt* (London: Duckworth, 1901);
Le Nouveau Monde (Paris: Richard, 1880);
Maison Gambade, père et fils, Srs (Paris: La Comédie Humaine, 1882);
Contes cruels (Paris: Calmann-Lévy, 1883); translated by Robert Baldick as *Cruel Tales* (London: Oxford University Press, 1966);
L'Eve future (Paris: Brunhoff, 1886); translated by Marilyn Gaddis Rose as *Eve of the Future Eden* (Lawrence, Kans.: Coronado, 1981); translated by Robert Martin Adams as *Tomorrow's Eve* (Urbana, Chicago & London; University of Illinois Press, 1982);
Akëdysséril (Paris: Brunhoff, 1886);
L'Amour suprême (Paris: Brunhoff, 1886);
Tribulat Bonhomet (Paris: Tresse et Stock, 1887);
Histoires insolites (Paris: Quantin, 1888);
Nouveaux contes cruels (Paris: Librairie Illustrée, 1888);
Chez les passants (Paris: Comptoir d'Edition, 1890);
Axël (Paris: Quantin, 1890); translated by June Guicharnaud (Englewood Cliffs, N.J.: Prentice-Hall, 1970); translated by Marilyn Gaddis Rose (Dublin: Dolmen, 1970);
L'Evasion (Paris: Tresse et Stock, 1891); translated by Mrs. Barkley as *The Escape* (London: Duckworth, 1901);
Nouveaux contes cruels et Propos d'au delà (Paris: Calmann-Lévy, 1893);
Trois portraits de femmes (Paris: Bernard, 1929);
Reliques (Paris: Corti, 1954);
Nouvelles reliques (Paris: Corti, 1968);

Philippe-Auguste, Comte de Villiers de l'Isle-Adam (photograph by Nadar)

Sonnet (Paris: Fata Morgana, 1990).
Collections: *Œuvres complètes*, 11 volumes (Paris: Mercure de France, 1914-1931);
Œuvres complètes, 2 volumes, edited by Alan Raitt and Pierre-Georges Castex, with Jean-Marie Bellefroid (Paris: Gallimard, Bibliothèque de la Pléiade, 1986).

PLAY PRODUCTIONS: *La Révolte*, Paris, Théâtre du Vaudeville, May 1870;

Le Nouveau Monde, Paris, Théâtre des Nations, February 1883;
Axël, Paris, Théâtre de Montparnasse, April 1894;
Elën, Paris, Théâtre-Libre, 1895.

Acknowledged, even lionized, during his own lifetime by an elite circle of writers for his genius, his spellbinding talents as a storyteller, and his resistance to positivist lessons of progress, Philippe-Auguste, Comte de Villiers de l'Isle-Adam sank into relative obscurity in the early twentieth century. In many respects he was the victim of his own colorful life: the heir to a resounding noble name, but poor almost to the point of abjection, aggressive in his rejection of the materialist, bourgeois ethos of his society, Villiers closely incarnated the Romantic myth of the *poète maudit*. During the 1880s he attained an almost legendary status with the young symbolist poets, and with good cause. Alone among his generation of writers, Villiers enjoyed a personal relationship with Charles Baudelaire. In 1869 he visited Richard Wagner in Triebschen, where he read to the great composer his play *La Révolte* (1870; translated as *The Revolt*, 1901). He had long championed Wagnerism and the new music in France. At Stéphane Mallarmé's Tuesday gatherings in the rue de Rome, he alone spoke on equal terms with the master poet. In short he could claim a matchless personal prestige. But when he died of cancer in 1889, in a hospice for the indigent, his great promise seemed unfulfilled. Times were changing, and his star was beginning to fade.

His works had appeared in such small editions, or were scattered among so many different and sometimes ephemeral journals, that even in his own lifetime they were known to only a handful of enthusiasts. After his death, twenty-five years would pass before the appearance of the first volumes of his collected works. And as the memory of his vibrant and compelling presence faded in the minds of contemporaries, Villiers seemed fated to join that rather crowded club of marginal eccentrics for which the late nineteenth century in France is deservedly famous.

Several factors have been involved in Villiers's return to view and attaining the prominent place in fin de siècle letters he now commands. Fittingly for a writer who was both a traditionalist in his adherence to vanished institutions and a visionary in the breathless sweep of his imagination, Villiers's rehabilitation was initiated by traditional literary historians, thanks to whom the facts of his biography and his bibliography have at last been separated from the legends. They have been joined by a new generation of critics and theorists, who, by sweeping aside canonical literary hierarchies, have been better able to focus on some of the most disquieting and singular aspects of his works.

Villiers was born in St. Brieuc, Brittany, on 7 November 1838, the heir to a name of ancient nobility, but the scion of a family already burdened by material hardship and mental eccentricity. Though he probably descended from a minor branch of the Villiers family, he never wavered in the conviction that he was the latest member of the legendary Villiers de l'Isle-Adam line, among whom could be counted the founder of the Order of the Knights of Malta and a marshal of France. His fierce attachment to the splendor of the Villiers name and his rejection of its social destitution after the Revolution of 1789 formed the cornerstone for a poetics of nobility and race: in the fallen world into which he came, only one activity held the promise of redemption—literature.

It seems indeed that from a very early age, and despite a quirky and uneven schooling, Villiers destined himself for literary greatness. An only child, he was supported in this ambition by his indulgent family: his father, Marquis Joseph-Toussaint, penniless and obsessed by buried treasure and fabulous wealth; his retiring mother, Marie-Françoise Le Nepvou de Carfort; and his maternal aunt and godmother, Marie-Félix Daniel de Kérinou, whose small fortune provided for a time the only material stability the family would ever experience. As the artistically inclined Villiers reached the end of a sheltered, provincial childhood, the promise of literature grew more immediate. In the late 1850s the small family progressively relocated to the capital to facilitate the marquis's frequent, harebrained moneymaking schemes. But the move had the additional effect of introducing the gifted son—the family's great hope for future distinction—to the Paris literary milieu, to the cafés and theaters he would restlessly haunt for much of his life. As the decade drew to a close, Villiers's earliest works began to appear in print.

Some thirty years later, the *Contes cruels* (1883; translated as *Cruel Tales*, 1966) and *L'Eve future* (1886; translated as *Tomorrow's Eve*, 1982) consolidated Villiers's reputation as a prose writer of unusual range and gifts, thereby initiating a partial view of him that persists even today. But he

Drawing of Villiers de l'Isle-Adam at age twenty by Lemercier de Neuville
(from Contes cruels nouveaux, nouveaux contes cruels, *1968)*

was by predilection a playwright, who dreamed of a vast, poetic theater that would revolutionize the French stage. It is thus important to emphasize that his earliest writerly projects were predominantly poetic and dramatic in nature. He had plotted plays of epic proportion based on the Faust and Don Juan legends; he had also practiced music and verse before coming to Paris, and it was with poetry that his career began.

The *Premières poésies* (First Poems, 1859), despite Villiers's subsequent disclaimers, were clearly intended to make his mark in the literary world. They appeared in an ambitious, elaborately printed volume that would demonstrate his affiliations with Alphonse de Lamartine, Victor Hugo, Alfred de Musset, and Alfred de Vigny. Considering his preoccupation with his lineage, it is no exaggeration to claim that this first significant publication represents an attempt to establish for himself a place in the genealogy of romanticism. The attempt fell short. *Premières poésies* is an undistinguished collection of derivative juvenile verse that displays little beyond its author's espousal of the themes and attitudes of the literature of the early nineteenth century. By 1859 Romantic poetry and theater were, of course, entirely outdated: different aesthetic criteria had come into play and would be crucial in the eventual critical or public success of a writer. But Villiers was especially attracted to the strains of romanticism that implied revolt and rejection, so that, even after he abandoned poetry as unsuited to his particular genius, he clung stubbornly to a Romantic rhetoric that signaled his rejection of the modern society that had already dispossessed and disowned the Villiers de l'Isle-Adams.

In effect a paradigm began to take shape at this time that drove Villiers's lifelong indictment of what Léon Daudet called "le stupide dix-neuvième siècle" (the stupid nineteenth century). It consists of a distinctly personal fusion of Romantic ideology, idealist philosophy, and occult doctrine, all of which came together during the 1860s to reinforce Villiers's native, superstitious Catholicism. From his first novel, *Isis* (1862), to his first plays, *Elën* (1865) and *Morgane* (1866), all of Villiers's literary output during this decade bears the stamp of this heterogeneous fusion. It colors his first short stories. It accounts for the impression of genius he created personally, as well as the incomprehension his writing regularly generated among noninitiates.

By late 1859 Villiers began frequenting the salon of Count Hyacinthe du Pontavice de Heussey, a distant Breton cousin, with whom he engaged in lengthy philosophical disputes. Pontavice's utilitarian socialism was the perfect foil for Villiers's aristocratic antipositivism. In *Isis*, Villiers turned to the sketchy knowledge of occultism and Hegelianism he by then possessed in order to rebut Pontavice's belief in progress. The novel that appeared in 1862, in an edition of only one hundred copies, was the first and only installment of a projected seven-volume work of speculative metaphysics. Villiers was not one to shun unorthodox literary undertakings; here he had set himself the task of using literature to prove to materialists such as his cousin that the realities of the spirit were all the more exigent for being trampled by a heedless society. The use of literature as an ideological weapon, a fundamental aspect of Villiers's writerly psychology, began here.

Isis often seems like a compilation of the disparate occultist and philosophical readings Villiers was hastily assimilating for his attack on contemporary materialism. He pays so little attention to plot, and so much to sonorous cadences, that *Isis* is perhaps more aptly described as a prose poem. His passion for ideas, however, leads him to accumulate poetic passages in interminable, abstruse discussions about the nature of reality that are often simply baffling in a work purporting to be a novel. But *Isis* is redeemed, and becomes an intimation of the great works of Villiers's maturity, by the lyric creation of a female magus named Tullia Fabriana, the first in a series of strong, even dominant, female characters that inhabit his writings and provide one of their most salient and singular features.

Tullia Fabriana, a Florentine princess of great beauty and powerful intellect, lives in ascetic isolation in her castle, where she languishes in the knowledge that the world of 1788 holds little interest for her. Her study of secret, occult doctrine has, however, revealed to her that transcendent power can be attained through the mystical union of souls. To this end she undertakes to seduce the young count Wilhelm de Strally d'Anthas, with whom she will plot to take over the kingdom of Naples. The seduction, essentially a prelude to the plot of subsequent installments, barely begins as the first volume draws to a close. But by introducing the idea, common in occultist doctrine, of a hierogamy, or sacred marriage, Villiers adds a compelling human dimension to Tullia's situation that is a welcome corrective to the novel's intellectual giddiness.

Indeed, the single most important trait that relates *Isis* to the two Romantic dramas that follow it consists of the quest for transcendence by an elite couple, before whom "les forces réunies de l'or et de l'amour tomberaient positivement" (the combined forces of gold and love would positively fail). In these early works, the initiator is always the woman. In contrast with her, the men seem weak, immature, indecisive. In *Isis*, Wilhelm de Strally is clearly to be molded to suit Tullia's project. In *Elën* the young student leader Samuel Wissler falls prey to the charms of the countess Elën, a femme fatale whose identity as a rich courtesan hides a profound thirst for the Absolute that Samuel is unable to satisfy. In *Morgane* the adventurer Morgane de Poleastro forms a conspiratorial political alliance with the rebel Sergius d'Albamah. Their plot to conquer the throne of the Two Sicilies is thwarted, and they realize too late that it has also cost them an ideal love. In the quest for a perfect couple that is the common theme of all three works, the bitter lesson seems to be that spiritual aspirations and material fulfillment can never coexist.

Villiers de l'Isle-Adam had high hopes for these first plays. His ambition was to rival Hugo with a resounding success in the theater that would bring him fortune by trumpeting his name across literary Paris. But in fact, like *Isis*, the works were quite simply unknown to the public of the 1860s. These too were published in extremely small editions, intended as actors' scripts, or as introductions to theatrical agents, and were never republished during Villiers's lifetime. Although he subsequently revised *Morgane* quite brilliantly under the title *Le Prétendant* and wrote four other plays, the fame and fortune he sought in the theater were to elude him entirely.

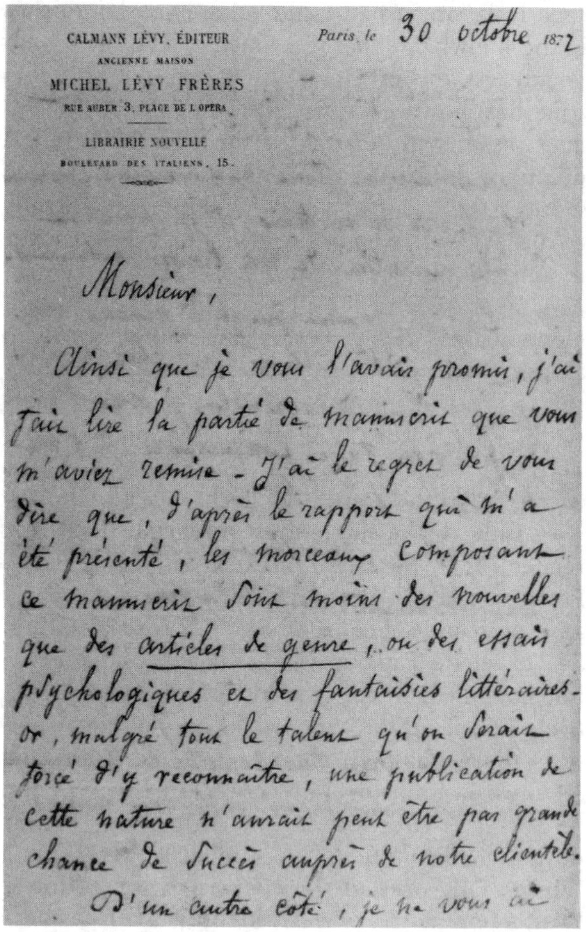

CALMANN LÉVY, ÉDITEUR
ANCIENNE MAISON
MICHEL LÉVY FRÈRES
RUE AUBER 3, PLACE DE L'OPÉRA
LIBRAIRIE NOUVELLE
BOULEVARD DES ITALIENS, 15.

Paris, le 30 octobre 1872

Monsieur,

Ainsi que je vous l'avais promis, j'ai fait lire la partie de manuscrit que vous m'aviez remise - J'ai le regret de vous dire que, d'après le rapport qui m'a été présenté, les morceaux composant ce manuscrit sont moins des nouvelles que des articles de genre, ou des essais psychologiques et des fantaisies littéraires. Or, malgré tout le talent qu'on serait forcé d'y reconnaître, une publication de cette nature n'aurait peut être pas grande chance de succès auprès de notre clientèle.

D'un autre côté, je ne vous ai

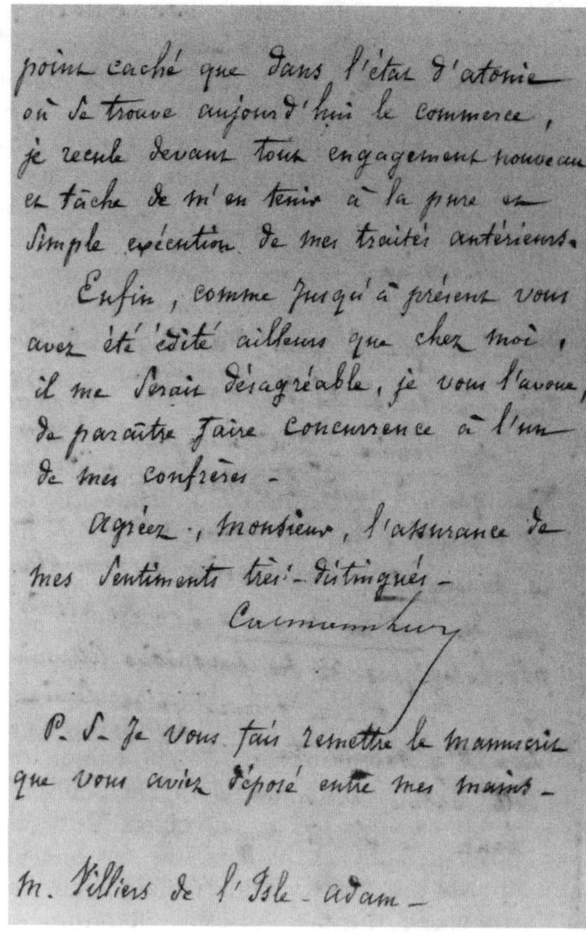

point caché que dans l'état d'atonie où se trouve aujourd'hui le commerce, je recule devant tout engagement nouveau et tâche de m'en tenir à la pure et simple exécution de mes traités antérieurs.

Enfin, comme jusqu'à présent vous avez été édité ailleurs que chez moi, il me serait désagréable, je vous l'avoue, de paraître faire concurrence à l'un de mes confrères -

Agréez, Monsieur, l'assurance de mes sentiments très-distingués -

Calmann Lévy

P. S. Je vous fais remettre le manuscrit que vous aviez déposé entre mes mains -

M. Villiers de l'Isle-Adam -

Letter to Villiers de l'Isle-Adam from the publisher Calmann Lévy, refusing to publish a volume of Villiers's articles. Eleven years later Lévy published Villiers's Contes cruels *(from* Contes cruels nouveaux, nouveaux contes cruels, *1968).*

By the mid 1860s Villiers was thus in the paradoxical position of having written two plays, a novel, and a collection of poetry that warranted him a reputation for genius in poetic circles, even as he was virtually unknown to the general reading public. Certainly his friends in the literary world helped soften this near-total lack of general recognition. Théodore de Banville, for example, had conferred extravagant praise on *Isis.* And by 1864 Villiers had met the man who would be his closest and best friend. Mallarmé, years later, in the solemnly beautiful lecture he wrote as a tribute to his dead comrade, vividly recalled the dazzling impression Villiers made on those he met. But most crucial to his career as a writer was his friendship with Baudelaire, whom he probably met at the Brasserie des Martyrs in 1860, and with whom he remained in regular contact for several years. As Alan W. Raitt has claimed, "There can be no doubt that Baudelaire altered the whole course of Villiers's life"—and in many subtle ways. *Les Fleurs du mal* (1857; translated as *Flowers of Evil,* 1909), of course, as well as the elder poet's unconditional enthusiasm for Edgar Allan Poe and Wagner, did much to redirect Villiers's aesthetic preferences away from an exclusive allegiance to the Romantics and closer to the modern spirit of bizarre beauty that Baudelaire heralded. From contact with the works of Poe in Baudelaire's translations, Villiers was drawn to the short story. And Baudelaire's enthusiasm for Wagner found a ready reply in the musically gifted Villiers. There is little doubt that these exciting new models prompted Villiers to attempt his first tales in the late 1860s.

But there were other, imperious reasons for Villiers to extend his writerly range in an attempt to live by his pen. Material woes were beginning to dog the family. In March 1864 the marquis de Villiers de l'Isle-Adam declared bankruptcy in Paris. Later that year Villiers set out to Lyons in search of a rich heiress to marry, the first of several such attempts to secure a fortune. All would fail, and increasingly they took on tragicomic overtones that are reflected in his later works. But the search for a more stable financial situation had become a very pressing matter indeed. Thus it was that in 1867 Villiers cofounded the *Revue des Lettres et des Arts* as a way of securing a regular outlet for his writing. Though only twenty-five weekly issues appeared, the *Revue* was notable for its publication of the new Parnassian writing. Most important, it was there that Villiers published his first two tales, *Claire Lenoir* and *L'Intersigne* (The Sign).

Claire Lenoir is recounted by Dr. Tribulat Bonhomet, a brilliantly satirical creation who represents the self-sufficient debility and spiritual opacity of the century for Villiers. The story pits the modern materialist doctor Bonhomet against the Hegelian idealist Césaire Lenoir and his Christian wife, Claire. In an irony characteristic of the work, Claire suffers from a severe vision problem, but it is Bonhomet's blindness that Villiers emphasizes by his use of the fantastic in the tale's conclusion. During her death agony, Claire has a horrible vision; immediately after her demise, Bonhomet examines her and observes on her retina the image of her lover, beheaded by a savage with the face of Césaire. For all his arrogance, Bonhomet has encountered a phenomenon that his scientific knowledge is powerless to understand. The story has been termed a Menippean satire, in which Villiers for the first time wields heavy irony and sarcastic humor in the destruction of positivist certainties.

L'Intersigne, on the other hand, is a tightly crafted tale of the supernatural. A young man suffering from a "spleen héréditaire" tries to find repose by visiting his friend Abbé Maucombe, a country priest. That night he has frightening visions foretelling the abbé's imminent death. The pacing, the seeming monomania of the narrator, and the hallucinations of which he is victim all point to Poe's influence, but the story is also faithful to Villiers's preoccupations with metaphysics and spiritual realities. The premonitions of the priest's death cannot be explained rationally, and the reader, like the narrator, must look elsewhere to interpret the cryptic message of the sign encoded in the story's title.

Claire Lenoir and *L'Intersigne* were followed in 1869 by a third tale, *Azraël* (later revised as *L'Annonciateur*), published in the journal *Liberté*. Dedicated to Wagner, it is a retelling of a biblical legend of the angel of death in Parnassian style. Its heavily ornate, symphonic prose, reminiscent of Gustave Flaubert's *Salammbô* (1862; translated, 1885), recurs in some of Villiers's later tales, and is an important element in his stylistic repertory. That repertory was essentially complete by the time *Azraël* appeared, but Villiers was not in Paris to celebrate its publication. Thanks to clever negotiating, he had traveled to Germany with his friends Catulle Mendès and Judith Gautier, ostensibly as newspaper correspondents to the Munich Exposition Universelle (the first World's Fair), but in fact so that they could visit Wagner. This was a great moment for Villiers, who was himself an unusually talented musician, singer, and composer. He revered Wagner as the initiator of a great synthesis in the art of dramatic musical composition. The lessons of Wagnerism were no idle matter of enthusiasm for Villiers. They would deeply mark his attempts to write the drama he hoped would transform the French stage. Perhaps he even began work on that play, to be called *Axël*, around the time of his visit to the composer. But while in Triebschen, he read to Wagner his latest play, *La Révolte*, a very different work from anything he had produced until then.

The difficulty of having his Romantic dramas seriously considered for production led him to try a different tack by writing a play situated in the bourgeois drawing rooms of his contemporaries. *La Révolte* involves only two characters, the banker Felix and Elisabeth, his young associate and wife. One night Felix returns home to discover Elisabeth ready to leave him. Calmly she tells him that she can no longer share the exclusively materialist life he leads, that she aspires to a deeper fulfillment. He listens in utter incomprehension, and faints when she actually walks out the door. But soon Elisabeth returns, a broken woman. Three years of life with Felix have made her incapable of acting on her dream of a different life. Worse, her very ability to dream has been destroyed.

Beneath its contemporary setting, then, *La Révolte* conceals a tragic allegory of modern spiritual distress, as Villiers once indicated in a sarcastic rejoinder by describing Elisabeth as a "Prométhée femelle dont le foie est dévoré par une oie" (a female Prometheus whose liver is devoured by a goose). But for once the high hopes he had for a play seemed justified. The reading at Wagner's had encouraged him, and in early 1870 a provocative article by Alexandre Dumas *fils* prompted the Théâtre du Vaudeville to stage

La Révolte. It ran for five performances. The bourgeois public was not at all flattered by Villiers's portrayal of Felix's antipathetic response to the lofty concerns of his heroine. Years before Henrik Ibsen would triumph on the Paris stage with *A Doll's House* (1879), Villiers's thesis that a woman might deem middle-class material comfort an obstacle to inner truth provoked little but scorn.

Again Villiers saw his hopes for overnight success dashed because of an uncomprehending public. But now the luxury of waiting for another chance at theatrical fortune was out of the question. The 1870s would be, in Raitt's apt description, Villiers's "years of darkness." The social upheaval of the Franco-Prussian War and the Paris Commune, followed by the death in August 1871 of Tante Kérinou, left the family nearly destitute. At times over the next ten years, Villiers would support himself in abject "jobs" such as that of a boxing sparring partner or "cured madman" in the waiting room of an alienist. He did not abandon writing extensive compositions for his poetic theater-to-be, but even as he published the first installments of *Axël* in 1872 in the *Renaissance Littéraire et Artistique* and wrote *Le Nouveau Monde* (The New World, 1880), he had to resort increasingly to writing tales for any journals that would pay, however poorly, for his copy. By late 1877 he had accumulated enough stories to propose a volume of them to the firm of Calmann-Lévy, but the publisher turned him down with a letter of rejection that suggests his uncertainty about where to situate Villiers's writing in both commercial and literary terms.

Throughout the 1870s Villiers wrote extensively, producing an immense family genealogy, two plays, a novel, and dozens of short stories. Parts of major works appeared sporadically in newspapers, yet nothing had been published in book form since *La Révolte* in 1870. Villiers seemed at times to have disappeared almost entirely from view. Only an improved commercial climate finally led Calmann-Lévy to accept an anthology of short stories for publication in February 1883 under the title *Contes cruels*. The acceptance came none too soon. Villiers had had a son, Victor, in 1881 by Marie Dantine, the illiterate charwoman he would live with until his death. He also had to support his increasingly demented father. A book contract was nothing short of a godsend. This landmark collection of twenty-eight short pieces had cost Villiers years of tremendous effort; he sold it outright to the publisher for a mere 375 francs. But at last a book of his tales was available to a readership increasingly interested in what he had to say.

The most striking feature of the *Contes cruels* on first view is their remarkable diversity. Mordant satires of the venality and cupidity of contemporary society such as "Les Demoiselles de Bienfilatre" ("The Erring Sisters") and "Virginie et Paul" are followed by a haunting tale of the supernatural, "Véra," and a sinister evocation of pathological mania, "Le Convive des dernières fêtes" ("The Eleventh Hour Guest"). Prose poems give way to scientific fantasies, detailing inventions such as "La Machine à gloire" ("The Machine for Fame") or "L'Appareil pour l'analyse chimique du dernier soupir" ("The Instrument for the Chemical Analysis of the Last Breath").

Villiers was in full possession of his multifaceted genius in these tales, many of which had been revised extensively over the years. By turns he is the satirist, the social critic, the poet, the visionary, and the spellbinder, each story taking the narrative stage with equal persuasiveness and success. Faced with such jarring changes of tonal register and style, the reader may well experience a kind of disorientation. And indeed shock was what Villiers specifically intended to produce. The cruelty emphasized in the title, experienced by many of the characters, is perhaps most subtly exerted upon the reader, whose convictions about reality are constantly tested and challenged.

In the same month of February 1883 the staging of *Le Nouveau Monde* ended in perhaps the greatest fiasco of Villiers's career. But his final setback in the theater occurred just as the *Contes cruels* launched his reputation as a prose writer unlike anyone else then at work in France. The stories made it easier for him to place his copy, and in the six years from their appearance until his death, Villiers would take maximum advantage of his newfound celebrity. To judge by the praise Joris-Karl Huysmans lavished on the *Contes cruels* in *A Rebours* (1884; translated as *Against the Grain*, 1922) by giving the volume a prominent place in the library of his character des Esseintes, its violent mood swings sent an electrical jolt through a new readership.

A specific polarity carries the charge of these stories, and of most of Villiers's writing in his final years. It consists of a current alternating between idealistic longing and grinding satire, a current that Villiers succinctly defined in dedicating his 1886 novel *L'Eve future* "aux rêveurs, aux

Caricature of Villiers de l'Isle-Adam by Coll-Toc for Les Hommes d'Aujourd'hui *(1886), which featured a tribute by Paul Verlaine*

railleurs" (to dreamers, to deriders). Inspired by his failed arranged marriage to an English heiress in 1874, the work had appeared in earlier versions, in installments in different journals from 1880 through 1885. It tells of what transpires when, to repay a moral debt, the scientist-inventor Edison undertakes to rescue his friend Lord Celian Ewald from that most drastic of fictional disasters, a love affair with the wrong woman. Alicia Clary possesses a sublime, perfect body, but the soul of a bourgeois goddess. Edison reveals to the suicidal Ewald that for years he has been working on the timeless problem of what to do with woman, and now he has the answer, albeit at the experimental stage: simply do without her. He proposes to create for Ewald the perfect replica of Alicia in the form of an android named Hadaly. All Ewald will have to do for the experiment to work is to believe in the animated Hadaly. Unable to distinguish her from Alicia, Ewald falls in love with the robot and resolves to live in seclusion with her on his estate in Scotland. But the novel ends with a catastrophic shipwreck that destroys Hadaly forever.

This disquieting, prescient, and utterly original novel moves quickly and deeply into what can only be called controlled delirium. Never had Villiers sustained both abstract complexity and visionary lyricism so thoroughly. *L'Eve future* confronts with breathtaking focus central taboos and ambivalences of the decadent period that are perhaps just as pressing today. Questions of gender, sexuality, and desire, questions about the power and limits of machines and science over human capacity to think and experience the real, are all raised with the express purpose of disturbing the reader. Villiers states as much in a letter to Jean Marras, calling the work "un livre vengeur, brillant, qui glace et force toutes les citadelles du rêve" (a brilliant, vengeful book that chills and forces the very citadel of dreams). In *L'Eve future* the android replaces the female partner in the perfect couple that had obsessed Villiers since *Isis* and *La Révolte*. But by creating her, the scientist Edison and the nostalgic lover Ewald also attempt a hybrid combination that places positivism in the service of romanticism, a transcendence of opposites that seems to work until the book's deus ex machina conclusion. This strangely moving novel is one of Villiers's greatest and most personal works, all of which abound in similar leaps toward the unattainable, in the refusal of human imperfections and, in the end, of life itself. Such is the lesson of Villiers's posthumous dramatic masterwork, *Axël*.

From 1886 to 1888 he brought out several new collections of tales, including *L'Amour suprême* (1886), *Tribulat Bonhomet* (1887), a volume entirely devoted to the character Villiers called the grotesque "archétype de (ce) siècle" (archetype of [this]century), and the *Nouveaux contes cruels* (1888). But most of his energy was devoted to *Axël*, a work he had been meditating, writing, and revising for nearly twenty years. That energy was now waning fast. His harsh life had aged him prematurely; from 1886 on, his health declined steadily. Mallarmé had to arrange for a subscription among Villiers's friends to support him in his distress. At last, in the summer of 1889 his intestinal cancer forced him into a hospice. There he died, on 18 August, after an in extremis marriage to Marie Dantine that finally legitimized his beloved son, Totor.

Thanks to the solicitous intervention of Huysmans, *Axël* was published in 1890. The play has been called Villiers's literary testament; it quickly became the bible of the young symbolist generation. Few works proclaim with such bitter conviction, born of harsh experience, the pessimism that emerges in the play's extraordinary conclusion. Sara de Maupers and Axël d'Auërsperg have rejected initiation—she into Catholic vows, he into occult apprenticeship with his teacher, the magus Maître Janus—in order to pursue a treasure hidden by Axël's father during the Napoleonic wars. They discover one another and fall in love in the burial crypt of Axël's castle, where Sara has come on Easter morning, following a clue that enables her to discover the treasure. With limitless wealth literally at their feet, the young lovers realize that the world can only corrupt the perfect union they now share, and they

Villiers de l'Isle-Adam in his later years (portrait by Guth; from Contes cruels nouveaux, nouveaux contes cruels, *1968)*

commit suicide before life can imprison them in its illusions.

By their suicides Axël and Sara refuse to acknowledge the Creation so as to avoid the degradation of the spirit, which is not of the world. Their renunciation of the treasure and of life represents a total break with a world that has been recognized as false and fallen; it provoked scandalized reactions among Villiers's inner circle, and rightly so. Although Villiers intended to revise *Axël* so as to give it a more orthodox conclusion, the play's power derives specifically from the defiant gesture of renunciation by its protagonists. The end of *Axël* proposes, in effect, a rigorously anti-Christian message that underscores the many intellectual temptations Villiers's work as a whole conveys. As Henri Roujon, one of his earliest biographers, so aptly noted, Villiers "avait gardé tant bien que mal la foi bretonne de son

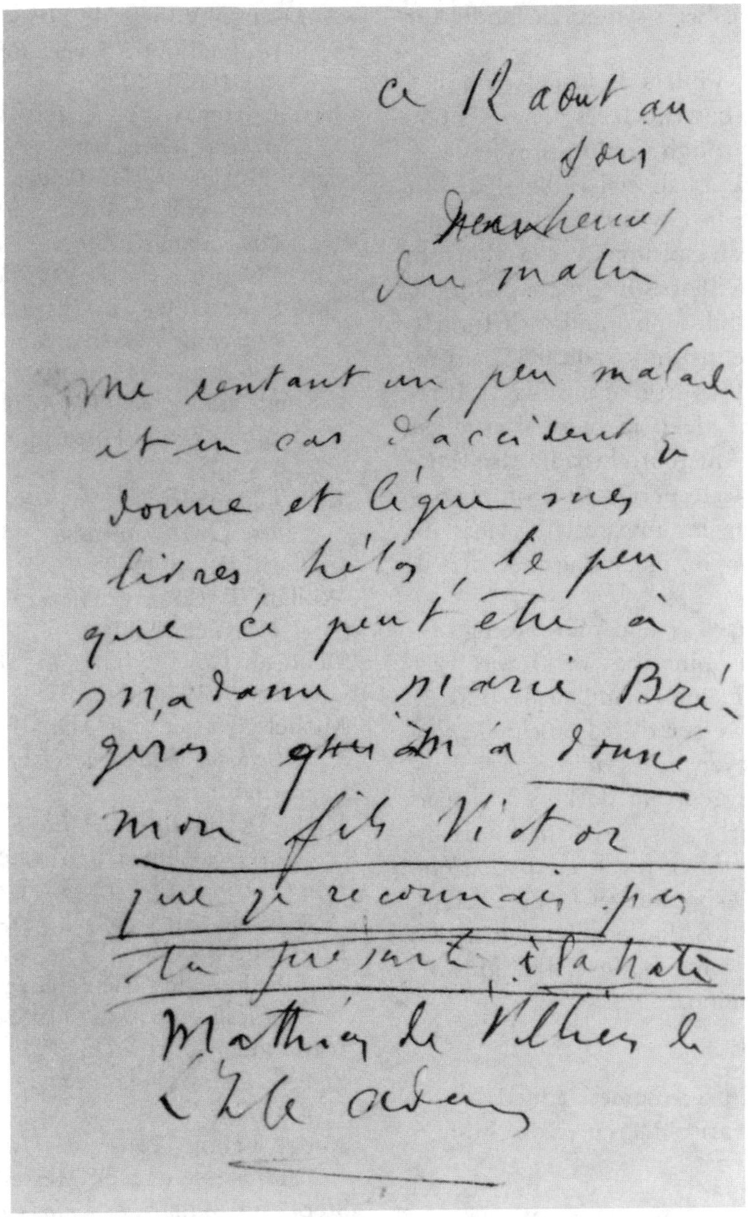
ce 12 août au soir
Neuf heures,
du matin

Me sentant un peu malade et en cas d'accident je donne et lègue mes livres, hélas, le peu que ce peut être à madame Marie Brégeras qui m'a donné mon fils Victor que je reconnais par la présente, à la hâte.
Mathias de Villiers de l'Isle Adam

Will written by Villiers de l'Isle-Adam six days before his death (from Contes cruels nouveaux, nouveaux contes cruels, *1968)*

enfance, non sans laisser des lambeaux de dogme à tous les buissons de l'hérésie" (more or less kept the Breton faith of his childhood, but not without leaving shreds of dogma on all the thorns of heresy).

Villiers's belief in a transcendent spirituality appears in its fullest form in *Axël*, through the symbolic character of Maître Janus. The magus has arranged for the meeting and the suicide of these last surviving members of two ancient noble families in order to create "un signe nouveau" (a new sign). In a profound sense, that sign is dual. Suicide is typically associated with despair; here, as a consequence of philosophic idealism, it does seem to point to the integral nihilism that literary history has identified as Villiers de l'Isle-Adam's legacy. At the same time, the triumph of transcendence allows for a positive reading of the suicide. What Axël and Sara achieve by rejecting the treasure is a form of mastery. They conquer the "double illusion of gold and love" that the narrator of *Isis* identifies as the obstacle to spiritual fulfillment. By their mystical union of opposites, Axël and Sara celebrate a sacred marriage that their death consecrates as a symbol, a model for spiritual salvation.

Ultimately then, Villiers de l'Isle-Adam, like the legendary Janus, has two faces. There is one that sees the world through tired eyes, filled with bitterness and regret, as an evil to be fled. But there is a second, the face of a visionary, seeking a world where human spirituality can flourish. To view in this light Villiers's fascination with the occult, with idealist philosophy, and with futuristic science is to realize just how radical was his rejection of rationalist discourse, of positivism. It reminds readers of the deep ideological conflicts his writing inscribes, which are broadly also those of the entire fin de siècle period. It prompts one to see his rich legacy in unexpected places: in 'pataphysics, for example, or among the surrealists.

Certainly Villiers was uncompromising, exclusive, arrogant: for him the world was ever "peuplé d'êtres qui, même au milieu de flots de lumière, ne peuvent cesser d'être obscurs" (peopled by beings who even in the midst of streaming light cannot emerge from darkness). But as so many of his works show, he never relinquished a profound thirst for what in *Axël* he called "la Lumière, l'Espérance et la Vie" (Light, Hope and Life), and it is that passion that makes his works, however strange, however flawed, worthy of continued attention.

Letters:

Correspondance générale, 2 volumes, edited by Joseph Bollery (Paris: Mercure de France, 1962).

Bibliography:

Joseph Bollery, *Biblio-iconographie de Villiers de l'Isle-Adam* (Paris: Mercure de France, 1936).

Biographies:

R. du Pontavice de Heussey, *Villiers de l'Isle-Adam* (Paris: Savine, 1893);

E. de Rougemont, *Villiers de l'Isle-Adam* (Paris: Mercure de France, 1910);

Alan W. Raitt, *The Life of Villiers de l'Isle-Adam* (Oxford: Clarendon, 1981).

References:

John Anzalone, "Golden Cylinders: Inscription and Intertext in *L'Eve future*," *Esprit Créateur*, 26 (Summer 1986): 38-47;

Anzalone, "Villiers de l'Isle-Adam and the Gnostic Tradition," *French Review*, 57, no. 1 (October 1983): 20-27;

Jacques-Henry Bornecque, *Villiers de l'Isle-Adam, créateur et visionnaire* (Paris: Nizet, 1974);

Peter Bürgisser, *La Double Illusion de l'or et de l'amour chez Villiers de l'Isle-Adam* (Bern: Peter Lang, 1969);

Pierre-Georges Castex, "Villiers de l'Isle-Adam et sa cruauté," in his *Le Conte fantastique en France de Nodier à Maupassant* (Paris: Corti, 1962), pp. 345-364;

Castex, *Villiers de l'Isle-Adam, 1838-1889* (Paris: Bibliothèque Historique de la Ville de Paris, 1989);

Ross Chambers, "L'Ange et l'automate," *Archives des Lettres Modernes*, 128 (Paris: Minard, 1971), pp. 3-80;

William T. Conroy, *Villiers de l'Isle-Adam* (Boston: Twayne, 1978);

Deborah Coyningham, *Le Silence éloquent* (Paris: Corti, 1975);

Michel Crouzet and Alan W. Raitt, eds., *Actes du Colloque Villiers de l'Isle-Adam* (Paris: SEDES, 1990);

Jean Decottignies, *Villiers le taciturne* (Lille: Presses Universitaires de Lille, 1983);

Emile Drougard, "Le Vrai Sens d'*Axël*," *Grande Revue* (April 1931): 262-284;

Rodolphe Gasché, "The Stelliferous Fold: On Villiers de l'Isle-Adam's *L'Eve future*," *Studies in Romanticism*, 22 (1983): 293-327;

Jean-Paul Gourévitch, *Villiers de l'Isle-Adam ou l'Univers de la transgression* (Paris: Seghers, 1971);

André Lebois, *Villiers de l'Isle-Adam, révélateur du verbe* (Neuchâtel: Messeiller, 1952);

Stéphane Mallarmé, *Villiers de l'Isle-Adam* (Paris: Librairie de l'Art Indépendant, 1890);

Alain Néry, *Les Idées politiques et sociales de Villiers de l'Isle-Adam* (Paris: Diffusion Université Culture, 1984);

Jacques Noiray, *Le Romancier et la machine*, volume 2: *Jules Verne et Villiers de l'Isle-Adam* (Paris: Corti, 1982);

Gwenhaël Ponnau, "Science, sagesse et folie dans les contes et dans *L'Eve future* de Villiers de l'Isle-Adam," in *Trois figures de l'imaginaire littéraire* (Paris: Les Belles Lettres, 1982);

Julia Przybós, "La Foi du récit: Etude sur *Véra* de Villiers de l'Isle-Adam," *French Review*, 53, no. 3 (February 1980): 369-377;

Alan W. Raitt, *Villiers de l'Isle-Adam et le mouvement symboliste* (Paris: Corti, 1965);

Marilyn Gaddis Rose, "Two Misogynist Novels: A Feminist Reading of Jules Verne and Villiers de l'Isle-Adam," *Nineteenth-Century French Studies*, 9, nos. 1 & 2 (Fall/Winter 1980-1981): 117-123;

Henri Roujon, *La Galerie des bustes* (Paris: Rueff, 1909).

Papers:

Many of Villiers's papers are in private collections. Some manuscripts are located at the Bibliothèque Nationale, Paris, and at the Bibliothèque Municipale de La Rochelle.

Emile Zola

(2 April 1840 - 29 September 1902)

Philip Walker
University of California, Santa Barbara

SELECTED BOOKS: *Contes à Ninon* (Paris: Librairie Internationale, 1864); translated by Edward Vizetelly as *Stories for Ninon* (London: Heinemann, 1895);

La Confession de Claude (Paris: Librairie Internationale, 1865); translated by George D. Cox as *Claude's Confession* (Philadelphia: T. B. Peterson & Bros., 1882);

Mes haines: Causeries littéraires et artistiques (Paris: Achille Faure, 1866);

Le Vœu d'une morte (Paris: Imprimerie Dubuisson, 1866); translated by Comte C. S. de Soissons as *A Dead Woman's Wish* (London: Greening, 1902);

Mon salon (Paris: Librairie Centrale, 1866);

Edouard Manet: Etude biographique et critique (Paris: E. Dentu, 1867);

Les Mystères de Marseille, roman historique contemporain, 3 volumes (Marseilles: Imprimerie Arnaud, 1867-1868); translated by Cox as *The Mysteries of Marseille: A Love Story* (Philadelphia: T. B. Peterson & Bros., 1882);

Thérèse Raquin (Paris: Librairie Internationale, 1867); translated by John Stirling (Philadelphia: T. B. Peterson & Bros., 1881);

Madeleine Férat (Paris: Librairie Internationale, 1868); translated by Stirling as *Magdalen Ferat* (Philadelphia: T. B. Peterson & Bros., 1880);

La Fortune des Rougon (Paris: Librairie Internationale, A. Lacroix, Verboeckhoven, 1871); translated by Stirling as *The Rougon-Macquart Family* (Philadelphia: T. B. Peterson & Bros., 1879);

La Curée (Paris: Librairie Internationale, A. Lacroix, Verboeckhoven, 1871); translated by Stirling as *In the Whirlpool (La Curée)* (Philadelphia: T. B. Peterson & Bros., 1879);

Le Ventre de Paris (Paris: Charpentier, 1873); translated by Stirling as *The Markets of Paris (Le Ventre de Paris)* (Philadelphia: T. B. Peterson & Bros., 1879);

Thérèse Raquin, drame en quatre actes (Paris: Charpentier, 1873); translated by Alexander Teixeira de Mattos and George Moore (London, 1891);

La Conquête de Plassans (Paris: Charpentier, 1874); translated by Stirling as *The Conquest of Plassans: A Tale of Provincial Life* (Philadelphia: T. B. Peterson & Bros., 1879);

Nouveaux contes à Ninon (Paris: Librairie Internationale, J. Hetzel & A. Lacroix, 1874);

Les Héritiers Rabourdin, comédie en trois actes (Paris: Charpentier, 1874); translated by Teixeira de Mattos as *The Heirs of Rabourdin* (London: Henry, 1894);

La Faute de l'abbé Mouret (Paris: Charpentier, 1875); translated by Stirling as *The Abbé's Temptation; or, La Faute de l'abbé Mouret* (Philadelphia: T. B. Peterson & Bros., 1879);

Emile Zola (photograph by Nadar)

Son Excellence Eugène Rougon (Paris: Charpentier, 1876); translated by Stirling as *Clorinda, or the Rise and Reign of His Excellency Eugène Rougon, the Man of Progress, Three Times Minister* (Philadelphia: T. B. Peterson & Bros., 1880);

L'Assommoir (Paris: Charpentier, 1877); translated by Edward Binsse as *Gervaise (L'Assommoir): The Natural and Social Life of a Family under the Second Empire* (New York: G. W. Carleton, 1879);

Une Page d'amour (Paris: Charpentier, 1878); translated by Mary Neal Sherwood as *Hélène, a Love Episode* (Philadelphia: T. B. Peterson & Bros., 1878);

Théâtre: Thérèse Raquin, Les Héritiers Rabourdin, Le Bouton de rose (Paris: Charpentier, 1878);

Nana (Paris: Charpentier, 1880); translated by Stirling as *Nana: Sequel to L'Assommoir* (Philadelphia: T. B. Peterson & Bros., 1880);

Le Roman expérimental (Paris: Charpentier, 1880); translated by Belle M. Sherman as *The Experimental Novel, and Other Essays* (New York: Cassell, 1893);

Le Naturalisme au théâtre: Les théories et les exemples (Paris: Charpentier, 1881);

Documents littéraires: Etudes et portraits (Paris: Charpentier, 1881);

Nos auteurs dramatiques (Paris: Charpentier, 1881);

Une Campagne (Paris: Charpentier, 1882);

Pot-Bouille (Paris: Charpentier, 1882); translated by Stirling (Philadelphia: T. B. Peterson & Bros., 1882);

Le Capitaine Burle; Comment on meurt; Pour une nuit d'amour; Aux champs; La Fête à Coqueville; L'Inondation (Paris: Charpentier, 1882);

Au Bonheur des Dames (Paris: Charpentier, 1883); translated by Stirling as *The Ladies' Paradise; or, The Bonheur des Dames* (Philadelphia: T. B. Peterson & Bros., 1883);

La Joie de vivre (Paris: Charpentier, 1884); translated by Stirling as *Joys of Life* (Philadelphia: T. B. Peterson & Bros., 1884);

Naïs Micoulin; Nantas; La Mort d'Olivier Bécaille; Madame Neigeon; Les Coquillages de M. Chabre; Jacques Damour (Paris: Charpentier, 1884);

Germinal (Paris: Charpentier, 1885); translated by Carlynne (Chicago & New York: Belford Clarke, 1885);

L'Œuvre (Paris: Charpentier, 1886); translated as *His Masterpiece? (L'Œuvre); or, Claude Lantier's Struggle for Fame: A Realistic Novel* (London: Vizetelly, 1886);

La Terre (Paris: Charpentier, 1887); translated as *The Soil: A Realistic Novel* (London: Vizetelly, 1888);

Renée, pièce en cinq actes (Paris: Charpentier, 1887);

Le Rêve (Paris: Charpentier, 1888); translated by Cox as *The Dream* (Philadelphia: T. B. Peterson & Bros., 1888);

La Bête humaine (Paris: Charpentier, 1890); translated by Count Edgar de Valcourt Vermont as *Human Brutes* (Chicago: Laird & Lee, 1890);

L'Argent (Paris: Charpentier, 1891); translated by Max Maury as *Money (L'Argent)* (Chicago: Laird & Lee, 1891);

La Débâcle (Paris: Charpentier & Fasquelle, 1892); translated by Ernest A. Vizetelly as *The Downfall: A Story of the Horrors of War* (London: Chatto & Windus, 1892);

Le Docteur Pascal (Paris: Charpentier & Fasquelle, 1893); translated by Ernest A. Vizetelly as *Doctor Pascal; or, Life and Heredity* (London: Chatto & Windus, 1893);

Les Trois Villes. Lourdes (Paris: Charpentier & Fasquelle, 1894); translated by Ernest A. Vizetelly as *Lourdes* (London: Chatto & Windus, 1894);

Les Trois Villes. Rome (Paris: Charpentier & Fasquelle, 1896); translated by Ernest A. Vizetelly as *Rome* (London: Chatto & Windus, 1896);

Messidor. Drame lyrique en quatre actes et cinq tableaux (Paris: Fasquelle, 1897);

Nouvelle campagne (Paris: Fasquelle, 1897);

Les Trois Villes. Paris (Paris: Fasquelle, 1898); translated by Ernest A. Vizetelly as *Paris* (London: Chatto & Windus, 1900);

Les Quatre Evangiles. Fécondité (Paris: Fasquelle, 1899); translated by Ernest A. Vizetelly as *Fruitfulness (Fécondité)* (London: Chatto & Windus, 1900);

La Vérité en marche (Paris: Fasquelle, 1901);

Les Quatre Evangiles. Travail (Paris: Fasquelle, 1901); translated by Ernest A. Vizetelly as *Work (Travail)* (London: Chatto & Windus, 1901);

L'Ouragan, drame lyrique en quatre actes, poème d'Emile Zola, musique d'Alfred Bruneau (Paris: Fasquelle, 1901);

Les Quatre Evangiles. Vérité (Paris: Fasquelle, 1903); translated by Ernest A. Vizetelly as *Truth (Vérité)* (London: Chatto & Windus, 1903);

L'Enfant roi, comédie lyrique en cinq actes, livret d'Emile Zola, musique d'Alfred Bruneau (Paris: Charpentier & Fasquelle, 1905).

Editions and Collections: *Her Two Husbands, and Other Novelettes*, translated by George D. Cox (Philadelphia: T. B. Peterson & Bros., 1883);

The Jolly Parisiennes, and Other Novelettes, translated by Cox (Philadelphia: T. B. Peterson & Bros., 1888);

The Attack on the Mill, and Other Sketches of War, with an Essay on the Short Stories of M. Zola by Edmund Gosse (London: Heinemann, 1892);

Stories for Ninon (Contes à Ninon et Nouveaux contes à Ninon), 2 volumes, translated by Edward Vizetelly (London: Heinemann, 1895);

Short Stories, by Emile Zola, translated by William Forster Apthorp (Boston: Copeland & Day, 1895);

The Dreyfus Case: Four Letters to France (London & New York: J. Lane, 1898);

Poèmes lyriques (Paris: Fasquelle, 1921);

Two Novelettes: Shell-fish and For a Night of Love (New York: Zolaian Society of America, 1926);

Les Œuvres complètes, 50 volumes, edited by Maurice Leblond (Paris: Bernouard, 1928-1929);

The Attack on the Mill, and Four Seasons of Love (Cupernham, U.K.: Little Blue Book, 1929);

Stories from Emile Zola, translated by Lafcadio Hearn (London: Allen, 1935);

Mes voyages: Lourdes, Rome. Journaux inédits, edited by René Ternois (Paris: Fasquelle, 1959);

Salons, edited by F. W. J. Hemmings and Robert J. Niess (Geneva: Droz, 1959);

Les Rougon-Macquart: Histoire naturelle et sociale d'une famille sous le Second Empire, 5 volumes, edited by Armand Lanoux and Henri Mitterand (Paris: Gallimard, 1960-1967);

Œuvres complètes, 15 volumes, edited by Mitterand (Paris: Cercle du Livre Précieux, 1966-1970);

Contes et nouvelles, edited by Roger Ripoll and Sylvie Luneau (Paris: Gallimard, 1976);

La Fabrique de Germinal: Dossier préparatoire de l'œuvre, edited by Colette Becker, with a preface by Claude Duchet (Paris: SEDES, 1986);

Carnets d'enquêtes: Une ethnographie inédite de la France, edited by Mitterand (Paris: Plon, 1987);

Un Homme à vendre: Ebauche inédite d'un projet de comédie satirique, edited by James B. Sanders (London, Ontario: University of Western Ontario, 1988);

Germinal: Drame inédit en 5 actes et 12 tableaux précédé du scénario de la pièce également inédite, edited by James B. Sanders (Longueuil, Quebec: Editions du Préambule, 1988).

PLAY PRODUCTIONS: *Madeleine*, Paris, Théâtre-Libre, 9 May 1869;

Thérèse Raquin, Paris, Théâtre de la Renaissance, 11 July 1873;

Les Héritiers Rabourdin, Paris, Théâtre Cluny, 3 November 1874;

Le Bouton de rose, Paris, Palais Royal, 6 May 1878;

Renée, Paris, Théâtre du Vaudeville, 16 April 1887;

Messidor, libretto by Zola, music by Alfred Bruneau, Paris, Académie Nationale de Musique, 19 February 1897;

L'Ouragan, libretto by Zola, music by Bruneau, 29 April 1901;

L'Enfant roi, libretto by Zola, music by Bruneau, Paris, Théâtre National de l'Opéra-Comique, 3 March 1905;

Lazare, libretto by Zola, music by Bruneau, Washington, D.C., Saint Matthew's Cathedral, 17 October 1986.

OTHER: William Busnach and Octave Gastineau, *L'Assommoir, drame en cinq actes et huit tableaux*, preface by Zola (Paris: Charpentier, 1881);

Busnach, *Trois pièces tirées des romans et précédés chacune d'une préface d'Emile Zola. L'Assommoir. Nana. Pot-Bouille*, prefaces by Zola (Paris: Charpentier, 1884);

August Strindberg, *Père*, "lettre-préface" by Zola (Paris: Nielsson, 1888);

Charles Chincholle, *Mémoires de Paris*, preface by Zola (Paris: Librairie Moderne, 1889);

Leo Tolstoy, *L'Argent et le travail*, translated by Halpérine Kaminsky, preface by Zola (Paris: Marpon & Flammarion, 1891);

Anonymous, *Le Roman d'un inverti-né*, preface by Zola, in *Tares et poisons: Perversion et perversité sexuelles*, by Dr. Laupts [Dr. Georges Saint-Paul] (Paris: Georges Carré, 1896).

Emile Zola is one of the most important nineteenth-century French novelists, along with Stendhal, Victor Hugo, Honoré de Balzac, and Gustave Flaubert. *Les Rougon-Macquart* (1871-1893; translated as *The Rougon-Macquarts*, 1896-1900), the series of twenty novels that Zola published between 1870 and 1893, is a major monument of French fiction, and several of the individual works in it, above all *L'Assommoir* (1877; translated as *Gervaise (L'Assommoir): The Natural and Social Life of a Family under the Second Empire*, 1879), *Nana* (1880; translated as *Nana: Sequel to L'Assommoir*, 1880), *Germinal* (1885; translated, 1885), and *La Terre* (1887; translated as *The Soil: A Realistic Novel*, 1888), are generally regarded as masterpieces of world literature. Zola also wrote short stories, plays, and opera librettos and had already established himself by the age of thirty as one of France's leading literary, drama, and art critics and social and political journalists.

As an art critic, he was among the first to recognize the genius of Edouard Manet and the Impressionists and to promote them in the public press. He also was an early champion of Auguste Rodin. What is more important for Zola's literary fame, however, is that he has always been the writer whose name is most closely associated with the naturalist movement in literature. He popularized the terms "naturalist" and "naturalistic" in their literary sense, led the tumultuous press campaign that assured the triumph of naturalism in the late 1870s and early 1880s, and remained its main champion and theorist to the end of his life. He tirelessly promoted, moreover, his own image of himself as a naturalistic writer, succeeding so well that even today the discovery of his volcanic lyrical and epic genius and other non- (or supra-) naturalistic qualities still frequently comes as a surprise.

Zola was also one of the leading defenders of Capt. Alfred Dreyfus, a Jewish army officer wrongly accused by his superiors in 1894 of spying for Germany. They persisted in treating him as guilty even after they knew that he was innocent. The resultant *affaire* grew into a major national political crisis, pitting the French liberal republican left against the militaristic, nationalistic, authoritarian right; anticlericals against right-wing Catholics; proponents of racial tolerance against anti-Semites. Thanks in part to Zola's courageous efforts on his behalf, not only was Dreyfus brought back from Devil's Island in 1899 and, seven years later, completely exonerated, but the course of French history was

Zola at age twenty-five

changed in favor of the liberal humanitarian ideals that Zola had championed.

The full extent of Zola's cultural, political, and social impact has yet to be gauged. He was one of the principal fathers of the modern novel, including the modern American novel, which he helped shape indirectly through the works of Hamlin Garland, Stephen Crane, Frank Norris, and other American disciples. His naturalist theories contributed to the evolution of the theater and the cinema, and at least sixty individual films have been based on his novels, beginning with Ferdinand Zecca's *Les Victimes de l'alcoolisme* (The Victims of Alcoholism, 1902). Zola's influence on other areas of modern culture has been less systematically investigated and, in any case, would be hard to measure; but it has by no means been negligible and has been exerted in areas as different as town planning and secular religious thought.

Many of his contemporaries were shocked by what struck them as crude or obscene in his choice of subject matter, not to mention his political liberalism, anticlericalism, and satirical portrayals of the middle class. Many retaliated, such as the ultrabourgeois critic Ferdinand Brunetière, by concocting the myth that Zola was a bad artist. In 1883 his fiction was denounced in the British House of Commons as "only fit for swine," and his English publisher, Henry Vizetelly, was heavily fined for bringing out translations of *Nana, Pot-Bouille* (1882; translated, 1882), and *La Terre.* Later, Zola's very prominence in the literary world made him the target of younger writers eager to take his place in the sun. Many, including the symbolists, had more in common with him than they realized. Yet he was for decades treated as the whipping boy for everything of which the late-nineteenth- and early-twentieth-century avant-gardes disapproved. (This was not, however, without poetic justice, for he had treated Hugo in much the same way.) Zola's courageous defense of Dreyfus deepened the hatred that many right-wing readers had already harbored for him. On the other hand, his literary genius was never without admirers, including such discerning readers as the great French poet Stéphane Mallarmé; and Zola's role in the Dreyfus Affair, while condemned by many people, also made him a hero in the eyes of millions of others all around the globe.

Emile-Edouard-Charles-Antoine Zola was born in Paris on 2 April 1840. On his father's side, he was descended from a family of soldiers who had served in the army of the ancient Republic of Venice for generations. His father, Francesco Zola (originally Zolla, meaning in Italian "a clod of earth"), started out in the military, but his real interests were mathematics and engineering. After the Revolution of 1830, he settled permanently in France. Commissioned to build the dams and canal necessary to provide the Provençal city of Aix with an adequate water supply, he moved there with his pretty wife, the former Emilie Aubert (the daughter of a French glazier and occasional housepainter), and Emile in 1843. However, in March 1847, only three months after the first pickax struck the earth, Francesco came down with pleurisy and died, leaving his wife and son little more than shares in the Canal Company and debts of more than ninety thousand francs.

Because of the shady maneuvers of a principal stockholder plotting to take it over at a reduced price, the company went bankrupt, and Emilie, caught up in interminable futile lawsuits, was left with no income. The family's fortunes steadily worsened. They moved a total of five times in ten years, always to cheaper quarters, ending up in two sordid rooms on a street inhabited only by poor working-class people. Although she and her aged parents did everything possible to shield Emile from the effects of these misfortunes, the boy was affected by them as he grew older. They help explain his lifelong compassion for the poor, his longing for social justice, his rejection of what usually passes for charity, and his hatred of middle-class hypocrisy, cupidity, and pride. His fictionalized portrayals of Aix, the Plassans of his novels, teem with scheming, avaricious middle-class characters reminiscent of those who had stolen his mother's and his inheritance.

In many respects, however, Zola's childhood years in Aix were among the best of his life. After his First Communion, in 1852, he was enrolled as a scholarship student at the town's official preparatory school, the Collège Bourbon (now the lycée d'Aix). Poorly prepared, he started out at the bottom of his class, but soon his work improved, and almost every year won him prizes in Latin, history, French narration, and science. He, Paul Cézanne (the future great painter), and another schoolmate, Baptistin Baille, made frequent excursions into the countryside—reflected in Cézanne's idyllic Provençal landscapes and portrayals of bathers as well as in some of the most delightful pages of Zola's novels. During these jaunts Zola acquired that pagan love of nature and respect for the forces of life that pervade his writings. Together with these two inseparable companions, he also discovered Hugo and Alfred de Musset, whose verses they would often take along with them in their pockets or game bags. Zola was already trying his hand at writing, composing a long novel about the Crusades as well as narratives and dialogues in verse. He was also dreaming of composing an epic poem, tentatively titled "La Chaîne des êtres" (The Great Chain of Being) or "La Genèse" (Genesis), recounting the whole history of creation, past, present, and future. The project—conceived when modern geology and biology were in their infancy, rapidly evolving, torn by violently competing hypotheses—was, of course, far too ambitious. But even though it was unachievable in its original form, Zola would never really abandon it. It would grow through a series of metamorphoses and combinations with other projects into the three great series of novels that were to be his major works.

His grandmother Aubert died in the fall of 1857. Once again, the boy, temperamentally somber, nervous, high-strung, terrified even by thunder, had to face the awful reality of death, which would turn, as the years passed, into one of his most obsessive literary themes. Then misfortune struck another blow. The family's increasingly desperate financial situation forced them to move to Paris, where Emilie would be in a better position to try to enlist the support of her husband's powerful friends. She managed, with help from one of them, to obtain a scholarship for Emile at the lycée Saint-Louis. Starting out in the science section, he did his best to compete with the Parisian students, who were much better prepared, but he was homesick and disoriented. Instead of paying attention in class, he furtively read Hugo, Alphonse de Lamartine, Jules Michelet, and his other favorite authors, finished a comedy, scribbled down poems and short stories, and composed long letters to Cézanne and Baille.

At the beginning of his second academic year in Paris, he almost died from what was probably typhoid fever. After he returned to school, it was much the same as the year before. In June 1859 he applied for the baccalaureate exam, the one great hurdle that any French student intending to go on to an institution of higher learning had to pass. He did extremely well on the writtens and breezed through the scientific part of the orals. But he failed in literature, partly because of a disagreement with his examiner regarding an interpretation of one of Jean de La Fontaine's fables. At the end of November, he took the exam again, in Marseilles, but this time did not even make it through the writtens.

Since the door to the higher professions was now tightly shut to him, he was forced to accept a job, obtained for him by one of his father's friends, as a copy clerk in the Excise Office, on the Paris docks. But he hated it, finding it boring, poorly paid, without any possibility of promotion, and, worst of all, dehumanizing. In June 1860 he quit. About nineteen months went by during which he was mostly unemployed. His interrupted bourgeois education had taught him nothing of practical worth. He was timid, thin, hungry, and shabbily dressed. He pawned everything he could and borrowed money from his friends. Sometimes he was reduced to catching a sparrow on the roof outside his window and roasting it on the end of a curtain rod, and occasion-

Portrait of Zola by Edouard Manet, 1868 (Musée du Louvre)

ally he did not eat at all. Along with digestive troubles, he felt unbearable pressure on his chest and coughed up blood. Years later, when he would describe the pains of hunger experienced by Gervaise, the working-class heroine of *L'Assommoir*, he would be able to do so with unmatched precision and vividness.

During this same grim period, from the autumn of 1859 through January 1862, he remained, however, deeply engaged in activities central to his artistic formation, consciously or unconsciously laying the foundations of his major works. He browsed for hours at the bookstalls along the Seine and followed the *Siècle* and other left-wing publications. He read Dante, William Shakespeare, André Chénier, George Sand, Charles-Augustin Sainte-Beuve, and Michel Eyquem de Montaigne, along with his old favorites. Above all, he took advantage of his enforced leisure to write, consciously imitating his Romantic heroes but groping for new, more original themes and forms, and trying to forge his own personal vision of reality. He not only wanted to construct, like God the Creator, his own unique fictional world; he accepted the Romantic conception of the poet as a prophet in the tradition of Jesus and the Old Testament prophets, and he aspired to follow in their footsteps.

It is important to remember, if one wishes to understand Zola and his literary achievement, that the intellectual and spiritual crisis brought on by the eighteenth-century Enlightenment, the French Revolution, and the rise of modern science was at its peak in France during his lifetime. Zola's Paris, like the Roman Empire in the first century, was a boiling caldron of philosophical and religious ideas. Like thousands of other thoughtful mid-nineteenth-century Frenchmen, the young writer spent hours wrestling with the great eternal questions about the nature of reality, the problem of evil, and the meaning of life. At certain moments he confessed that he was still a Christian. But what he retained of his boyhood beliefs had mostly dissolved into a vague, unstable Romantic Christianity, which he soon largely abandoned in its turn. Yet even as many of his Christian beliefs faded away, he acquired most of the secular values that would inspire him from then on.

These were, above all, life, nature, love, truth, science, progress, the nineteenth century, justice, work, power, and humanity. Drawn largely from the secular French culture of his day and thenceforth always at the core of his thought, they would dictate the main underlying themes of his writings. He would end up by sacralizing and even—in his last, utopian works—deifying some of them. During this initial stage of his career, he was already constructing around several of them, especially love, the first of the succession of "new faiths" that would spring, one after the other, from his powerful, creative imagination and find expression in his writings. For example, *Paolo*, a long poem composed in 1860, the year he turned twenty, was motivated, as he wrote Cézanne, by a desire to exalt Platonic love, make it more attractive than carnal love, and demonstrate that in their skeptical century love could itself serve as a faith, instilling faith in God and in the immortality of the soul. "Religion," another poem composed during this same formative period, concludes with the divine revelation that carnal as well as spiritual love is the divine flame that rules the universe.

He also now began to develop the general aesthetic doctrines that would undergird his later, specifically naturalistic theories. What he wanted and would always want more than anything else was nothing less than literary immortality. As he would exclaim years later, in 1878: "Eh! bon Dieu! quel courage aurions-nous à la besogne, si les plus humbles entre nous ne se berçaient pas du rêve de vivre dans les siècles?" (Good God! Where would we get the courage to go on working if the lowliest of us did not harbor the dream of living on throughout the centuries?). These aesthetic doctrines grew essentially out of his meditations on the problem of how he could achieve this audacious goal. His chief method was to seek to gather from literary history what all the great poets of the past had in common, thus providing himself with the model that he himself would have to follow to become in his turn immortal. He already suspected what some of the most general conclusions would be: for example, that every age has its own particular poetry and that the writer who finds it will be justly famous; or that even as one portrays the peculiar historical realities of one's own epoch and treats the new themes it offers, one must bring out what is eternal in mankind if one wishes one's works to survive. Zola would continue for many years afterward to meditate on the same problem, inserting his various conclusions here and there in his critical writings. Taken all together, they amount to a surprisingly comprehensive, systematic, and permanently valuable guide to the paths that lead to lasting literary fame.

His artistic formation was also affected during this time by an incident in his personal life, a miserably unsuccessful attempt to redeem a poor young prostitute named Berthe through applying to her his idealistic, Romantic doctrine, inspired by Hugo and others, of the redemptive power of pure love. What started out as a noble experiment ended up as sheer debauchery. Disillusioned, he loathed himself as much as her. Yet although the experiment was a failure, it was salutary both for his moral development and his formation as a realistic writer, for it helped him wean himself from romanticism and arrive at a truer conception of reality. The redemptive lover would become one of his stock characters, the most famous being Goujet, Gervaise's Christ-like lover in *L'Assommoir*, but except in his last, highly utopian novels, the redemptive process would always abort, just as it had with Berthe.

This first, impoverished stage of Zola's career ended in early 1862, when, through the good offices of another friend of his father's, he was hired as a clerk at Hachette's publishing house. Its brilliant, liberal founder and head, Louis Hachette, was the editor and publisher of Maximilien Littré, Michelet, Sainte-Beuve, Emile Deschanel, Hippolyte Taine, and other influential authors. At first Hachette employed Zola in the shipping department, wrapping books, but shortly afterward, recognizing his talent, put him in charge of publicity. In doing so Hachette not only profited the firm, whose sales promptly soared, but he did the young writer an enormous favor, for he was now in the best possible position to study the workings of the literary marketplace and to obtain a foothold in it. Michelet, Sainte-Beuve, and Taine promptly became his friends, and he made hundreds of other valuable contacts. Among other things, he took account of the capital importance of journalism in the contemporary world, and soon he was writing for pe-

Paul Alexis reading to Zola, 1869 (painting by Paul Cézanne; Bibliothèque Nationale)

riodicals, partly to add to his meager income, partly to exploit the leverage that being a journalist gave him.

Along with the rapidly growing number of his articles, he successfully submitted to the editors with whom he was in correspondence some of his short stories and, toward the end of March 1864, observed that he had enough of them to make up a small book. He managed not long afterward to get them published under the title *Contes à Ninon* (1864; translated as *Stories for Ninon*, 1895). The style, modeled on his Romantic and classical readings, is for the most part emotional, mincing, affected, and precious, but there are some good pages. The following year he published his first novel, based on his affair with Berthe, *La Confession de Claude* (1865; translated as *Claude's Confession*, 1882). The style is barer, more sober and realistic than that of *Contes à Ninon*, but still very derivative, reminiscent of Musset in particular. Yet most of the reviewers, while expressing some reservations as to the subject, warmly praised the book. Others reacted with just the sort of indignation for which Zola, now a skillful publicist, had been hoping. They accused him of depicting shameful and degrading love, of purveying filth, of "hideous realism." He boasted to a friend that people now feared and insulted him, that he was now classified among those writers whom the public reads with horror.

Zola had by then given up his project for an epic poem recounting the whole history of Earth, including human civilization. The vision of natural history behind it, largely based on the German philosopher Immanuel Kant and the French naturalist Georges Cuvier, continued to evolve in his mind, becoming increasingly pantheistic. From then on he would conceive of nature as animated by a single soul in which everything shared, and he liked to imagine that the universe, far from having been completed by God in six days, was still creating itself. With each new major catastrophe, he maintained, the shape of the Earth changed. New species, including Homo sapiens, appeared, only to be replaced by others. But even though mankind would disappear in its turn, all creatures, he posited, would, as parts of the great whole, be present to admire the universe in its final state of perfection. Driven by his prophetic urge, he inserted into the *Salut Public* of Lyons (14 October 1865) several paragraphs proposing this vision as a new philosophical and religious faith. *Les Rougon-Macquart* would contain many reflections of it, along with most of his other, partly contradictory, philosophical and religious ideas.

As he continued to progress through his mid and late twenties, he was also developing the essential elements of his literary naturalism. He was more certain than ever that the main thrust of his age was in the direction of science. He was increasingly convinced that the art of his age, to be original, had to participate in the great modern quest for scientific knowledge. Furthermore, he also sensed that one kind of lasting fame comes from an artist's having imposed a new and enduring literary formula, become the chief figure of a movement, attracted followers, or created the archetypes of an era. He was certain that the right literary formula for his own era involved precisely that marriage of art and science. Thanks largely to Taine, he became an enthusiastic admirer of Flaubert, Stendhal, and Balzac. He discovered Edmond and Jules de Goncourt, Charles Dickens, William Makepeace Thackeray, Edgar Allan Poe, and Nathaniel Hawthorne. He became aware of Charles Darwin, whose *On the Origin of Species* (1859) had appeared in French translation in 1862. Zola's new heroes, especially Balzac, Stendhal, Flaubert, and the Goncourts, exemplified all the qualities that he admired. More and more he was attracted to realism, but he also valued artistic personality. He concluded that the really important thing, if one wished to achieve immortal fame, was to be a genius, to possess a powerful temperament. "Une œuvre d'art," he wrote in the essay "Proudhon et Courbet," first published in two installments in the 26 July and 31 August 1865 issues of the *Salut Public*, "est un coin de la création vu à travers un tempérament" (A work of art is a corner of creation seen through a temperament).

In January 1866 he left Hachette in order to devote himself exclusively to his journalism and creative writing. He could often be observed meeting with a group of young revolutionary artists, including several of the future impressionists, at the Café Guerbois, the cradle of modern art. Antoine Guillemet, Frédéric Bazille, and Ignace Fantin-Latour almost always came. Cézanne, Camille Pissarro, and Claude Monet showed up occasionally. James Whistler and Edgar Degas dropped in every once in a while. They were all dead set against the state-supported artistic tradition and looking for a new way to paint. On the occasion of that year's official exhibition, or Salon, Zola published a series of articles in the *Evénement* vigorously promoting Manet, whom these young painters all admired. He also had good things to say about some of them. At the same time, he saucily attacked the current art establishment. The resultant uproar so frightened the newspaper's publisher, the mighty press lord Henri de Villemessant, that he hired another art critic to express the traditional point of view and forced Zola to cut short his series. But Zola had triumphantly accomplished his purpose of helping to put Manet and the new school he admired on the map while adroitly publicizing some of his own aesthetic views.

That same year, 1866, he published *Mes haines* (My Hates), his first volume of collected essays, mostly on art and literature. He also published *Mon salon* (My Salon), a collection of his art essays. He wrote a potboiler novel, *Le Vœu d'une morte* (translated as *A Dead Woman's Wish*, 1902). This was followed, in 1867, by another potboiler, *Les Mystères de Marseille* (translated as *The Mysteries of Marseille: A Love Story*, 1882), and, on a more serious level, by a long brochure on Manet, *Edouard Manet: Etude biographique et critique* (Edouard Manet: A Biographical and Critical Study), which the grateful painter included in his famous portrait of Zola.

Furthermore, Zola published that same year *Thérèse Raquin* (translated, 1881), the novel that he rightly regarded as the major work of his youth. It recounts the murder of a husband by his wife's lover, and the lovers' destruction by their own remorse. Still one of Zola's most widely read books, it is a first-rate horror story with a concrete, colorful style and a beauty of form reminiscent of the great classics. For literary historians, it is, moreover, noteworthy as Zola's first attempt to apply his new naturalist literary ideal, that is to say, to write a novel that would be a treatise of moral anatomy, a compilation of human facts, and an experimental philosophy of the passions. In the preface to the second edition, which came out in May 1868, he declared that, in analyzing the two lovers, Thérèse and Laurent, he had simply performed on two living bodies the sort of analytical operations that surgeons perform on cadavers. In the same historically important preface, he used the term "naturalist" for the first time to designate the group of contemporary writers, in-

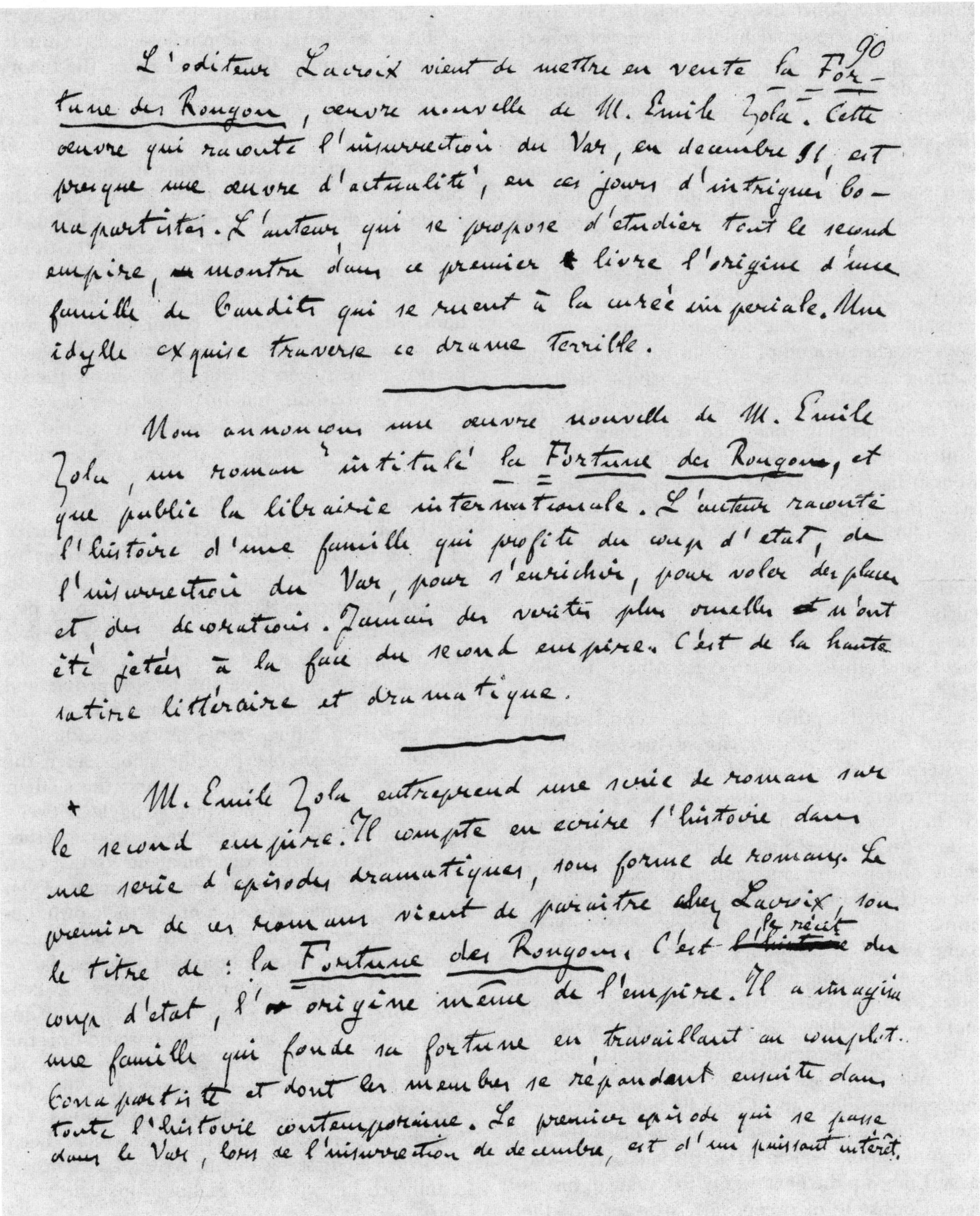

L'éditeur Lacroix vient de mettre en vente la Fortune des Rougon, oeuvre nouvelle de M. Emile Zola. Cette oeuvre qui raconte l'insurrection du Var, en décembre 51, est presque une oeuvre d'actualité, en ces jours d'intrigues bonapartistes. L'auteur qui se propose d'étudier tout le second empire, montre dans ce premier livre l'origine d'une famille de bandits qui se ruent à la curée impériale. Une idylle exquise traverse ce drame terrible.

Nous annonçons une oeuvre nouvelle de M. Emile Zola, un roman intitulé la Fortune des Rougon, et que publie la librairie internationale. L'auteur raconte l'histoire d'une famille qui profite du coup d'état, de l'insurrection du Var, pour s'enrichir, pour voler des places et des décorations. Jamais des vérités plus cruelles n'ont été jetées à la face du second empire. C'est de la haute satire littéraire et dramatique.

+ M. Emile Zola entreprend une série de roman sur le second empire. Il compte en écrire l'histoire dans une série d'épisodes dramatiques, sous forme de romans. Le premier de ces romans vient de paraître chez Lacroix, sous le titre de : la Fortune des Rougon. C'est le récit du coup d'état, l'origine même de l'empire. Il a imaginé une famille qui fonde sa fortune en travaillant au complot bonapartiste et dont les membres se répandent ensuite dans toute l'histoire contemporaine. Le premier épisode qui se passe dans le Var, lors de l'insurrection de décembre, est d'un puissant intérêt.

Publicity notices by Zola for La Fortune des Rougon, *his first* Rougon-Macquart *novel (Bibliothèque Nationale)* cluding the Goncourts, to which he belonged. Some critics were scandalized by the novel, considerably increasing sales. One even called it "une flaque de boue et de sang" (a puddle of mud and blood), to which Zola responded that truth, like fire, purifies everything. But those commentators whose opinions really mattered to him, Taine and Sainte-Beuve, perhaps the most respected French literary critic of the day, were impressed by it.

Zola's next novel, *Madeleine Férat* (1868; translated as *Magdalen Ferat*, 1880), has to do with a woman happily married until her former lover—a close friend of her husband, who knows nothing about their relationship—suddenly shows up after an absence of many years. Zola was principally concerned with illustrating a contemporary physiological theory that once a woman has given herself to a man she is his forever. It is likely, the theory maintains, that even her child by another man will resemble her original lover. *Madeleine Férat* is not one of Zola's best works, but it has some good scenes and sold fairly well, partly because the public prosecutor was shocked by certain allegedly immoral passages and threatened to sue Albert Lacroix, Zola's publisher.

The author, then in his late twenties, rightly sensed that the time was ripe at last to write his masterpiece, *Les Rougon-Macquart*. He had done nearly everything a beginning writer should do. He had discovered his main values and themes, found his guiding literary principles, mastered the essentials of his craft, gotten to know the reading public, gained knowledge of the world and human nature, tested his powers, and made his name known to the critics and the public. Especially since joining in 1868 the staff of the *Tribune*, a top liberal republican weekly, he had, moreover, developed an extraordinarily powerful style—warm, passionate, and torrential, but at the same time clear and concise, with an enormous range. Throughout 1868 he spent every moment that he could working on his plans for his magnum opus, which, as it turned out, would largely take up the next twenty-five years of his career. Consisting of twenty novels (instead of the ten he had originally foreseen), the series, whose themes would revolve around all his main values, would concentrate primarily on life: life's irrepressible power, which had fascinated him ever since his boyhood in Aix, and life rushing on, overcoming all obstacles, forever renewing itself.

On one level the whole multivolume work would be an encyclopedic physiological treatise illustrating, through fictional examples, the theory of heredity of Dr. Prosper Lucas, a well-known scientific authority of Zola's day. On another level the series would depict the eternal spectacle of life continuing and renewing itself on the social, cultural, and historical plane, as seen through the frame of the Second Empire (1852-1870). It would evoke what Zola correctly saw as the dominant traits of his age—its energy, impatience, democratic fevers, social mobility, unbridled ambitions, dazzling rewards, confusions, nervous tensions, and murderous competition. It would portray a vast society caught up not just in the Industrial Revolution, but in the whole process of world destruction and renewal. It would, in short, narrate the birth of modern mass civilization.

But, in accordance with Zola's deeper aesthetics, it would also portray, reflected in the mirror of a particular century, the enduring traits of nature—above all, human nature. It would portray society: the everlasting nature of crowd psychology; the general nature of war, economic class struggle, and social change; the eternal relationships between people and places, people and things; the various roles of sex and money; and such enduring human types as the stockbroker, the banker, the shopkeeper, the labor leader, the prostitute, the priest, the artist, and the soldier. It would evoke the unending struggle between birth and death. It would also, among other things, include dozens of animals in its vast cast, along with hundreds of human characters. Even the settings would take on a life of their own, becoming characters in their turn—mines, slums, middle-class apartment houses, churches, factories, banks, farms, department stores, a Provençal town, and the whole city of Paris. In doing so, they would also come to stand for the whole eternal setting of man, much as the various "stations" of medieval mystery plays did. Indeed, Zola's ultimate objective in writing *Les Rougon-Macquart* was still, just as it had been when he had first set out to write "La Genèse," to embrace the whole of reality in a single work of art.

He would accomplish this mostly through his skillful use of countless frames, including, most notably, not only the Second Empire, but also the history of one large, extended family group, the Rougons and Macquarts, all descended from a single ancestor. He wanted to por-

The boulevard Montmartre, Paris, circa 1865 (engraving by Morin). At extreme right is Lacroix-Verboeckhoven, publisher of Zola's first two Rougon-Macquart *novels.*

tray, as he jotted down in his notes, a family that rushes in pursuit of all the good things the future promises at the outset of a century of liberty and truths, then stumbles and falls in its headlong race because of the troubled gleams of the moment, the fatal convulsions attending the birth of a world.

Lacroix had agreed in early 1869 to publish this project. A contract was drawn up, assuring Zola a meager but adequate income of five hundred francs a month, and he soon started to work on the initial volume, *La Fortune des Rougon* (1871; translated as *The Rougon-Macquart Family*, 1879). On 2 April 1870 he turned thirty. That June, he married the woman with whom he had been living for more than five years, Gabrielle Eléonore Alexandrine Meley, a former seamstress. As before, he divided his time between his creative writing and his journalism. On 19 July 1870 France declared war on Prussia. Like most other members of the extreme left, he regarded this as the final proof of the criminal folly of the emperor Napoleon III, and he would have been imprisoned for saying so if the news of the disastrous French defeat at Wissembourg, in August, had not prevented him from being brought to trial. After the fall of the empire and just before the Prussian siege of Paris began in September 1870, Alexandrine, his mother, and he fled, first to Marseilles, then to Bordeaux, seat of the Government of National Defense.

Together with an old friend he founded a short-lived newspaper, the *Marseillaise*, served as the private secretary of a government minister, and, after the war, became a parliamentary correspondent for the new National Assembly. His terse, colorful, and passionate dispatches (republished by Henri Mitterand in his edition of Zola's complete works, 1966-1970) are among the most interesting, but least well known, of Zola's nonfictional writings. Back in Paris in March 1871, he witnessed the civil war of the Commune that same year and the horrible carnage brought about by its fall. But by then his personal life had pretty much resumed its prewar course. His circle of close acquaintances included, or would soon include, his illustrious fellow authors Flaubert, Edmond de Goncourt, Alphonse Daudet, Guy de Maupassant, and Ivan Turgenev. Meanwhile, the *Siècle*, the biggest newspaper in France at that time, had, after a long interruption caused by the war, finished serializing *La Fortune des Rougon* in March 1871. (Almost all of Zola's novels were printed in installments in newspapers before coming out in book form.) The novel started appearing in bookshops that October.

Set in Plassans, a small Provençal town modeled on Aix, it tells the story of the origins of the Rougon-Macquart family in the marriage and affair of a rich, eccentric old peasant woman, Adélaïde Fouque. It also contains a satirical account of the rise to wealth and power of her ambitious, unscrupulous son, Pierre Rougon. It includes an epic account of a republican insurrection in Provence caused by Louis-Napoleon's coup d'état on 2 December 1851. It features a charming love idyll, modeled on the Roman poet Ovid's tale of Pyramus and Thisbe, involving Adélaïde's grandson Silvère Mouret and Miette, a beautiful orphan girl. The critics paid little attention; the book market was in a slump, and the novel fell far short of attaining the commercial success for which Zola had hoped. But the great poet Théophile Gautier hailed its author as a new master. Flaubert wrote Zola that he was overwhelmed by its power.

While doing his best to promote this first novel of the series, Zola composed the last four chapters of the second one, *La Curée* (1871; translated as *In the Whirlpool (La Curée)*, 1879). The *Cloche* had to discontinue its publication after the public prosecutor, responding to charges of immorality, threatened to seize the paper if it went on printing it. The novel concerns the corrupt high society of Paris during the Second Empire and traces the progress of Pierre's youngest son, Aristide Rougon (known as Saccard), as he ruthlessly amasses a colossal fortune. It also concerns Aristide's effeminate, vicious son, Maxime, and his incestuous affair with his stepmother, Renée, by far the most interesting character. *La Curée* is a splendid piece of work. However, it too sold poorly when it first came out, one of the reasons being that Lacroix was about to go bankrupt and could not provide the usual publicity. Fortunately, an adventurous young publisher, Georges Charpentier, came to Zola's rescue and brought out his books from then on, becoming one of his staunchest friends.

The third novel, *Le Ventre de Paris* (1873; translated as *The Markets of Paris (Le Ventre de Paris)*, 1879), was a logical sequel to *La Curée*. After having depicted the shady, thriving world of high finance during the Second Empire, Zola now portrayed the complacent, materialistic middle class of shopkeepers and small traders. He developed the theme of the eternal war between the haves and the have-nots of this world. One of the central characters is Lise Quenu, a prosperous pork butcher's wife, descended from the illegitimate side of the family, the Macquarts. At first she harbors, then—to restore her peace of mind—betrays to the authorities her naive, idealistic, republican brother-in-law, Florent. The novel's setting, the picturesque central food market of Paris, is the object of powerful descriptions stylistically recalling Impressionist paintings. On the symbolic level, it stands, just as Zola intended it to, for the belly—the belly of Paris, the belly of humanity, and, by extension, the belly of the empire, the bovine French middle class secretly supporting the empire, because the empire supplies its mash day and night. The novel was a great success; the critics seemed to have rediscovered Zola.

The next novel, *La Conquête de Plassans* (1874; translated as *The Conquest of Plassans: A Tale of Provincial Life*, 1879), the fourth of the series, sharply contrasts with *Le Ventre de Paris* in some ways, just as it complements it in others. Having portrayed the Parisian middle class, Zola turned back to the provincial middle class. Having indulged in an orgy of description giving full rein to his love of color, crowds, vast panoramas, and elaborate metaphors and symbols, he felt the need of writing a soberly styled novel of psychological analysis placed in a restricted setting. *La Conquête de Plassans* is a gruesome horror story recounting the briefly successful struggle, shortly after Napoleon III's coup d'état, of a brutal, ambitious priest to win Plassans over to the empire. It sold poorly, but the great critic Brunetière, who would grow later into one of Zola's harshest critics, praised its exact, true-to-life qualities. Flaubert found it even better than *Le Ventre de Paris*.

Zola still dreamed of conquering the stage, but he never became the truly successful dramatist that he wanted to be. In 1873 his theatrical version of *Thérèse Raquin* had only a brief run. Another of his plays, composed the following year, *Les Héritiers Rabourdin* (The Rabourdin Heirs), inspired by Ben Jonson's *Volpone* (1606), was applauded by the first-night audience but torn apart by the critics, and it folded after only a few performances. Starting in April 1874, Flaubert, Edmond de Goncourt, Turgenev, Daudet, and Zola began to meet once a month for an elaborate gourmet dinner that, since they had all suf-

Zola in 1876 (photograph by Carjat)

fered the indignity of having their plays hissed, they dubbed the "Dinner of the Hissed Authors." Zola would also dine periodically with a group of his young admirers and disciples, occasionally joined by Cézanne or some other friend from Aix.

La Faute de l'abbé Mouret (1875; translated as *The Abbé's Temptation; or, La Faute de l'abbé Mouret*, 1879), the fifth volume in the Rougon-Macquart series, is also, like its predecessor, set in Provence, and its hero is also a priest, the young Serge Mouret, Adélaïde's great-grandson. He is highly strung, intensely devout, and otherworldly. On one level the novel is an anticlerical demonstration of the dangers of clerical celibacy. On another level it is a development of the theme of the conflict between Catholicism and the revived pagan cult of nature, life, and eros, which had become a major feature of nineteenth-century French secular religious thought, including Zola's. The second of the three parts is a modern—and very pagan—variation on the biblical story of Adam and Eve, set in Paradou, a vast, ruined Provençal garden, the natural paradise of the eighteenth-century philosophers. The book, only superficially naturalistic, has rightly been called the first great symbolist novel. Taine wrote Zola that it was in style and proportions an intoxicating poem rather than a novel, and that it reminded him of a Persian poem and certain passages in Indian epics. Before 1875 was over, *La Faute de l'abbé Mouret* had already gone through four editions, and it has always been one of Zola's most popular novels.

The sixth volume of the series, *Son Excellence Eugène Rougon* (1876; translated as *Clorinda, or the Rise and Reign of His Excellency Eugène Rougon, the Man of Progress, Three Times Minister*, 1880), transports the reader back to Paris. A political novel, its hero is Pierre and Félicité Rougon's oldest son, Eugène, whose overriding motive is to dominate and manipulate other men. While almost totally ignored by the public, the novel has enduring value as a psychological study of raw political ambition. Zola portrays in it the sort of people he knew and hated, and once again he is at his satirical best—cruel, cold-eyed, a would-be modern Juvenal.

One of the reasons why this novel was neglected was that the immense scandal caused by the serialization, starting in April 1876, of his next one, *L'Assommoir*, exploded shortly after *Son Excellence Eugène Rougon* appeared. This totally distracted the public's attention. *L'Assommoir*, Zola's first great international success, has lost none of its power more than a century after it was written. In its own day it was also one of the most controversial of Zola's works. Its impact has always been due in part to its sociological subject: the working class, or more exactly, the working class of mid-nineteenth-century Paris, as it really was. When Zola wrote *L'Assommoir* in the 1870s, the modern French industrial proletariat was still being born. The French bourgeoisie eyed it with a mixture of curiosity, contempt, guilt, and fear. Hugo and other Romantics had written novels about the suffering of the poor of their day, but their depictions had been sentimental and, by realistic standards, quite false. Zola, who knew the Parisian working class as well as any other author of his time, made no attempt to idealize it. On the contrary, he was the first major French author to portray it comprehensively in all its degradation.

The plot, a simple curve, is not complex. It has to do with the modest rise and terrible fall of the book's heroïne, the laundress Gervaise Macquart. Having accompanied her lover, Lantier, to Paris, she and their two young sons, Etienne and Claude, are abandoned by him. She marries a zinc worker, Coupeau; has another child, Nana; works hard; acquires a small laundry; but loses everything after Coupeau, crippled by a fall from a roof, turns to drink, dragging her down with him. The novel explores in detail the hellish world in which she has been trapped, the crowded streets, tenements, taverns, factories, slaughterhouses, and hospitals. It shows the promiscuity, squalor, drunkenness, hunger, and prostitution of the slums. It depicts the brutality with which the poor all too often treat each other and the indifference of society to their plight. It deliberately questions the doctrine of a Divine Providence protecting widows and orphans.

Zola does not hesitate to describe vividly the scene in which Gervaise discovers her drunken husband sprawled in the midst of his vomit in their bed. Zola goes on to show her taking refuge in the bed of their boarder, her former lover, Lantier, while her little daughter, Nana, the future prostitute, curiously watches. Nor does Zola spare his readers any of the details of Gervaise's decline, ending in her slow, agonizing death from starvation. This sort of thing was too much for thousands of Zola's contemporaries, many of whom did not really approve of lower-class subject matter anyway. The novel struck many commentators as dirty, crude, and pornographic. Even Hugo, the author of *Les Misérables* (1862), joined in the chorus of blame, calling it a bad book that showed, as if wantonly, the hideous sores of the privation and degradation to which the poor had been reduced. In fact both Hugo and Zola had the same humanitarian objectives, but they disagreed as to how to achieve them.

However, horrible as the novel's details seem, it also has undeniable beauty: its epic sweep; the power of its character descriptions; its panoramas of working-class life; its cleanly arching plot; its language, drawn from the colorful, poetic slang of the Parisian lower class itself; its infernal imagery; and its complex, omnipresent, dreamlike symbolism. Mallarmé, one of the fathers of modern poetry, called it, in a letter to Zola, a truly great work, worthy of an epoch in which truth had become the popular form of beauty. The hubbub caused by *L'Assommoir* astonished everyone, including Zola himself. It inspired parodies, caricatures, songs, pamphlets, and brochures. Even the Parisian working people, whom some critics accused Zola of libeling, purchased more than forty thousand copies of a cheap, popular illustrated edition in the course of 1878 alone. Ironically, this novel about the poor made Zola a rich as well as famous man. Thanks to earlier profits, he had been able in April 1877 to move to an elegant apartment, which he and Alexandrine sumptuously furnished, on the rue de Boulogne. In 1878 the golden torrent flooding in from *L'Assommoir* made it possible for the couple to acquire a second residence, a little farmhouse at Médan, in the Seine valley, about twenty-five miles from Paris. It was to be a perfect second home. He would gradually enlarge it, building a tower and making other improvements until it assumed baronial proportions.

L'Assommoir had come out in book form in January 1877. On 16 April, at the Restaurant Trapp, Maupassant, Henry Céard, Joris-Karl Huysmans, and other young naturalists held a banquet at which they lauded Flaubert, Zola, and Edmond de Goncourt as the masters of modern literature. The premier of William Busnach and Octave Gastineau's adaptation of *L'Assommoir* took place at the Ambigu Theater on 28 May 1878. It was a smash hit, with 250 performances in Paris and several tours in the French provinces and abroad.

Meanwhile the press campaign that Zola was directing to consolidate the victory of naturalism was well under way. In fact it was only the continuation of the efforts that he had been making for years to impose his literary views. In 1877 he dashed off seventy articles; in 1878, sixty-nine; in 1879, around a hundred. The most famous, "Le Roman expérimental" (translated as "The Experimental Novel," in *The Experimental Novel, and Other Essays*, 1894), was first published in the Saint Petersburg literary review *Messager de l'Europe* (September 1879). It was then republished in the *Voltaire* between 16 and 20 October 1879. In it, Zola identifies naturalism with the experimental scientific method proposed by Claude Bernard, one of the founders of modern scientific medicine, in his widely read *Introduction à l'étude de la médecine expérimentale* (1865; translated as *An Introduction to the Study of Experimental Medicine*, 1927).

Zola accepted Bernard's scientific determinism and underlying assumption that the only kind of knowledge available to man was scientific knowledge. He even went so far as to proclaim that naturalist novelists were themselves experimental scientists and that the results of the "experiments" they conducted on their human guinea pigs had scientific value. The merit of this pretension, made in the heat of battle, has been debated. Some late-twentieth-century critics have tended to take it more seriously than earlier commentators. In any case Zola, contrary to what many readers, including some eminent critics, have supposed, was not describing in "Le Roman expérimental" his actual novelistic practice. He was, rather, constructing a regulatory ideal, which he admitted that he and his generation, at least, would never fully attain. He was expressing the nineteenth-century reverie of a world in which all human activities—including literature, politics, and even religion—would be ruled by science. He was also complying with the principle, drawn from his larger aesthetic, that one way to achieve immortal fame is to capture and exploit the forces of one's own age. Literary movements, he believed, are not made by anyone. Each movement comes in its own time, but glory attends the writer who dominates it and leaves his mark upon it.

While firing off these journalistic salvos, Zola was, as always, working hard at his creative writing. Between 1876 and 1880 he churned out fifteen short stories, including at least one masterpiece in the genre, "L'Attaque du moulin" (translated as "The Miller's Daughter" in *The Mysteries of Marseille*, 1882; retranslated as "The Attack on the Mill," 1892), concerning the Franco-Prussian War. It first appeared in a collection of stories, *Les Soirées de Médan* (Evenings in Médan, 1880), published by him and five of the younger naturalists as a symbol of their friendship and common literary tendencies.

Above all, Zola was still at work on *Les Rougon-Macquart*. The eighth novel in the series, *Une Page d'amour* (translated as *Hélène, a Love Episode*, 1878), came out in 1878. Set in the elegant Parisian suburb of Passy, it is first and foremost a tender psychological study of a good, pure-hearted woman, Hélène Grandjean (another Rougon-Macquart family member), and her violent but short-lived passion for Dr. Henri Duberle, a respected, essentially decent, married man. Then, in 1880 came *Nana*. In writing it Zola plunged once again into the infernal regions of the Second Empire, this time the Parisian demimonde, the world of imperial gallantry, Jacques Offenbach's music, the cancan, masks, backstage corridors, racehorses, and fast women. Modeled on several real-life courtesans, Nana, Gervaise's daughter, reappears in the novel as one of the great whores of literature, her rise and fall paralleling that of the empire. But the novel is not only her story and the stories of the men whom she destroys. It is, as Zola intended it to be, the "poem" of male carnal appetite, and it is an apocalyptic warning of the consequences of social injustice. Nana, as Zola portrays her, is not only a naturalistic embodiment of Venus; she is, to use one of the images Zola applies to her in the text, a golden fly that rises from the dunghills of society to enter the windows of palaces and infect their inhabitants. Descriptions of her horrible death from smallpox alternate with evocations of the beginning of the Franco-Prussian War and of the Second Empire's fall. The scandal caused by this novel surpassed the one over *L'Assommoir*. The

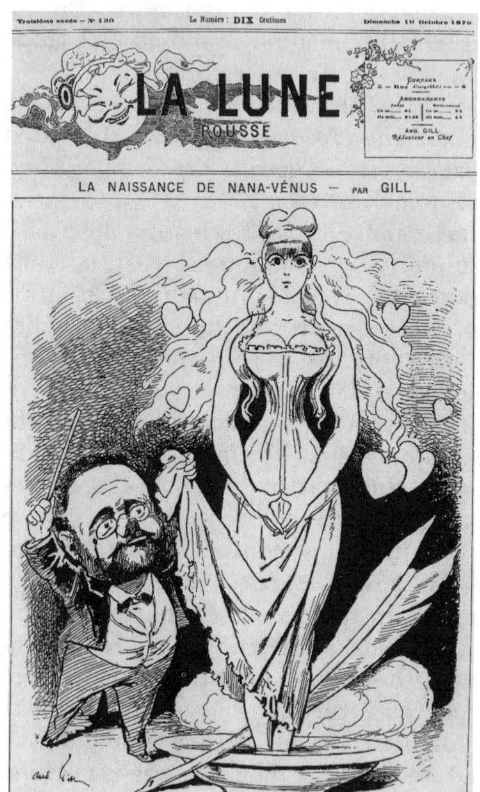

Three caricatures of Zola by André Gill from 1877 (top), 1878 (bottom left), and 1879

first edition, consisting of fifty-five thousand copies, was gobbled up in no time at all, and, before the year was over, ninety printings had already been sold out. Edmond de Goncourt, increasingly jealous of Zola, played down his achievement, but Flaubert was ecstatic, more convinced than ever that Zola was a man of genius.

But if 1880 was the year of one of Zola's greatest literary triumphs, it was also a year of multiple bereavements. His friend Louis Duranty, an older writer who had been one of the leaders of the realist school in the 1850s, died that April. A month later a telegram arrived from Maupassant announcing Flaubert's death. In October, Zola's mother died. Zola tried to drown himself with work, but he was continuously haunted by the specter of death. He was more than ever aware of the sadness of life, the universality of pain—an awareness reinforced by the growing French cult of the pessimistic German philosopher Arthur Schopenhauer. Zola and Alexandrine, who shared his necrophobia, kept a light burning all night in their bedroom, and sometimes, troubled by the thought of death, he would suddenly leap out from under the covers and stand quaking beside the bed in a state of indescribable terror.

In October 1882 he had a nervous breakdown. His suffering was aggravated by the spiritual and intellectual anarchy reigning within him, the endless tug-of-war between religious doubt and the desire for faith, between the chaotic multitude of pessimistic and optimistic ideas competing in his head. He longed vainly for the comfort of the old religion and mumbled prayers despite his skepticism. When he was caught up in conversation or engaged in his literary press campaign, which he went on waging until the fall of 1881 (when he largely gave up journalism), he would become dogmatic—ever the prophet. He would loudly recite his creed that naturalism was the very agent of the nineteenth century, or he would exhort his contemporaries to have faith in humanity, in their century, in science, in progress, in life. But when the conversation ended or the pen had fallen from his hand, he would sink back into black doubt and despair. Nearly all the fiction that he would write from then on, including *Germinal* and the other great masterpieces of the 1880s and early 1890s, would reflect, along with his acute consciousness of evil and metaphysical and religious anguish, his intensified quest for a redemptive vision of reality.

Toward the middle of 1880, he started planning a novel about the ideas of suffering and goodness, and after his mother died, he included the death of a mother among the major episodes. Then he put the whole project aside, because the subject had grown too painful. Instead, he wrote *Pot-Bouille*, a dryly satirical novel on the theme of middle-class licentiousness. Centered on Octave Mouret, a darkly handsome, ambitious young man with the morals of an alley cat, it is set in a luxurious Paris apartment house that turns out to be a den of iniquity. It lays bare with a classical simplicity of style the depravity hidden under its residents' hypocritically virtuous exteriors, stressing above all the theme of the immoral use of sex for pleasure and profit. The critics, indignant bourgeois all, generally damned it. The public appeared to agree, and sales were modest.

Zola's next novel, *Au Bonheur des Dames* (1883; translated as *The Ladies' Paradise; or, The Bonheur des Dames*, 1883), has a fascinating historical theme: the rise of modern big business at the expense of many small, traditional merchants. The hero is again Octave Mouret, and the plot concerns his successful efforts to make his department store, Au Bonheur des Dames, ever more prosperous. The love interest is supplied by the story of Octave's relationship with one of his employees, Denise Baudu. As Zola commented in his plot outline, the whole story resides in a twofold movement: Octave making his fortune from women—exploiting them and speculating on their coquettishness—and at the end, when he triumphs, finding himself conquered by a woman. Once again, as in all of the earlier Rougon-Macquart series, there emerges a comprehensive, marvelously colorful, realistic, and, at the same time, poetic portrayal of a milieu. Most critics received the novel fairly well, but it has never been one of Zola's most popular works.

After finishing it he started working again on the project that he had dropped not long after his mother's death, the novel on the themes of suffering and goodness. Titled *La Joie de vivre* (1884; translated as *Joys of Life*, 1884), it is set in a small, grim, remote Norman fishing village slowly crumbling into the sea, and it is by far the most philosophical, autobiographical, and confessional of the first twelve Rougon-Macquart novels. As he composed it, Zola was obsessed with the question "Is life worth living?" The answer that the book provides, insofar as it does so at all, is ambiguous. One does not know whether the title is meant to be ironic or not. The principal male character, Lazare Chanteau, reflects, among other things, the neurotic, superstitious,

Zola on a haystack at Médan

skeptical, pessimistic, death-obsessed side of Zola. The principal female character, Lazare's orphaned cousin, Pauline Quenu, embodies qualities that Zola admired but was far from wholly possessing: the spirit of charity, patience, forgiveness, and, above all, the marvelous capacity to see life as it is, with all its horrors, and still love it passionately. *La Joie de vivre* is, in its own curious fashion, a great book, perhaps even, as Henri Guillemin has suggested, a masterpiece, but its appeal has always, understandably, been limited to a small public.

Germinal, its successor, came out in book form in February 1885, a few days after the last installment of the serialized version, begun in November 1884, had appeared in the Paris daily *Gil Blas*. Like *L'Assommoir* and *Nana*, this new novel was at once a smashing worldwide success, eliciting high praise, mingled with shouts of outrage, from the critics and the vast reading public alike. It is essentially a sequel to *L'Assommoir*, but whereas *L'Assommoir* takes up the private life of the workers, *Germinal* focuses on their social and political role. In it, Zola, carrying on in the tradition of Hesiod and Homer, wrote the great epic of the birth and awakening of the modern industrial proletariat and its first movements of revolt against social and economic injustice. The dramatic frame is an unsuccessful strike in a giant coal mine near Valenciennes, in the north of France. The main-viewpoint character is Gervaise's son Etienne Lantier, the strikers' leader and the hero of the primary subplot, a dark love idyll; but the true central character is a collective one, the whole community of miners. Whereas only a few decades before the novel was written such characters would have been considered fit only for low farce, Zola managed to transform them into great tragic heroes, as moving in their misfortunes as Homer's Hector or Sophocles' Oedipus.

The novel, the first great work of literature to recount a strike, has everything that it takes to make a superb epic, above all love and war, gods, monsters, and even a descent into the underworld. The struggle between capital and labor is a modern form of warfare just as capable of entrancing a wide modern public as the Trojan War was of appealing to the ancient Greeks. The mines in which much of the action takes place are transformed by Zola's eye into Dantesque visions of hell. As in the old epics, everything is alive; objects are turned into monsters. The big mining company is transformed metaphorically into a mysterious, evil, all-devouring god. The strikers are presented as a force of nature. Multiple parallels with events and characters from the book of Genesis, and from Greek tales of the creation and the wars between the gods, intensify the impression that one is witnessing, in the titanic struggle recounted in the novel, the birth of a world.

The more one reflects on the novel, the more one may be struck, moreover, by its powerful, yet hidden, art, including its *savant* background music composed mostly of natural sounds—howling winds, a miner's cough, the panting of mine pumps, the noise of picks, the roar of crowds, the herdlike clatter of feet—and its masterful use of color (mostly red and black), reminiscent in some ways of Cézanne, in others of Vincent van Gogh (who fervently admired Zola). Along with the historical themes, there are extended metaphorical developments dominated by man-animal comparisons and the figurative equation of the mines first with hell, then with a womb, and of the strike with a great storm, and of the miners and the revolutionary ideas planted in their heads with germinating seeds. The title recalls, among other things, the month of Germinal in the French Revolution calendar as well as a famous revolt that took place in Paris during the revolutionary period. Thoroughly documented and intensely realistic, the novel is, nevertheless, a terrifying nightmare in which everything has, or at least may have, symbolic meanings.

Like dreams, it lends itself to multiple possible interpretations—many wildly conflicting, none perfect. To be sure, a certain part of the novel's message is perfectly clear—its condemnation of what generally passes as bourgeois charity, for example, or its refusal to blame any one class for the evils of the system. As Zola insisted, *Germinal* is a cry for pity and justice for the oppressed of this Earth. But answers to many of the more philosophical and religious questions that it poses are not given, only suggested—questions regarding, for instance, the possibility of social progress, the conflict between Marxism and Darwinism, the necessity of revolutionary violence, or the nature of reality. Read in one kind of light, the novel may seem, as it did to many of Zola's contemporaries, to express Zola's more pessimistic or skeptical side. Read in another light, it may appear to reflect one or another of the optimistic visions of man, nature, God, and history competing for predominance in his mind. Or it may symptomize the confusion of his philosophical and religious thought. The reader is left free to choose among the possible interpretations planted by Zola in the text or to supply his or her own—as indeed most critics have. Marxists, anarchists, socialists, Darwinists, Schopenhauerians, and Catholics can—and have—read into it illustrations of their own philosophies.

Zola's next novel was *L'Œuvre* (1886; translated as *His Masterpiece? (L'Œuvre); or, Claude Lantier's Struggle for Fame: A Realistic Novel*, 1886). Centered on the painter Claude Lantier, another of Gervaise's sons, the novel has as its subject the birth of modern art. Here, Zola minutely reconstructs in barely fictionalized form the avant-garde art world in which he had spent many hours in his youth—the world of Manet, Cézanne, Monet, Pissarro, and others. It is also about Zola's own painful, never-ending struggle to create and the drama of artistic creation in general. Claude is a genius who nevertheless fails to achieve his obsessive goal of embracing the whole of nature in a single work and loses track of reality in the process. In the end he hangs himself in front of his incomplete painting. Although modeled on several historical artists, including, Manet, Cézanne, and Zola himself, he is first and foremost a fictional creation born largely of Zola's own self-doubts, personal fantasies, and myths. It was long thought that the reason why Cézanne seems to have stopped corresponding with Zola shortly after this novel appeared was that, like most of the other painters reflected in it, he was offended by it. Recent critics have, however, questioned this, finding no hard proof. Although not one of Zola's most popular works, *L'Œuvre* has always strongly appealed to many readers, including, of course, art historians who approach it as a roman à clef.

By the time Zola's next novel, *La Terre*, appeared, a reaction to naturalism, which had begun several years earlier, was rapidly gaining strength in the younger generation. Even some of those writers, including Maupassant and Huysmans, who had fought alongside Zola in his campaign to promote naturalism, were now heading off in new directions. Zola's own fame, however, continued to grow, and it was clear that he had lost none of his creative power. *La Terre* was another blockbuster, and it has remained one of Zola's most popular and highly regarded novels. On the sociohistorical level, it is a detailed, comprehensive, realistic study of the French peasantry. The dramatic frame is a variation on the story of King Lear transposed into the peasant world. It has to do mainly with the sufferings and violent murder of an old peasant, Fouan, who foolishly divides his farm among his greedy, selfish children while he is still alive. To some extent the novel is also a chapter in the life of Jean Macquart, Gervaise's brother, now married to one of Fouan's daughters and one of the principal observers of the old man's tragedy. But, first and foremost, *La Terre*, as its title implies, is about Earth, a vast prose poem celebrating the Great Mother, supremely indifferent to the sufferings of the human insects laboring on her surface as she calmly pursues her mysterious, far-off goal. The novel is full of wonderful descriptions capturing the rhythms of peasant life, the round of the seasons, the rituals of seed time and harvest, the coupling of bulls and cows, the lovemaking of men and women, and the agony of birth and death. As in *Germinal*, the last chapter ends with the word "terre" (earth).

While some critics immediately sensed the work's greatness, many others, even as they devoured the latest installment in the *Gil Blas*, were rudely shocked. Everything, no matter how earthy, revolting, or horrible, is recounted in Homeric detail. The widely respected novelist Anatole France accused Zola of trying to exploit a perverted popular taste for obscenity in fiction. A group of five younger writers, Paul Bonnetain, J.-H. Rosny, Lucien Descaves, Paul Margueritte, and Gustave Guiches, took advantage of the occasion to fire off a long, indignant, and highly scurrilous attack directed not only at the novel but also at Zola. Accusing him of moral depravity, they violently rejected him as their literary master. This document, the work for which some of these writers are now chiefly remembered, was published in the *Figaro* (18 August 1887) under the title "*La Terre*. A Emile Zola," but it was immediately baptized "Le Manifeste des cinq" (The Manifesto of the Five). It created an enormous stir, partly because rumor had it that its authors had been egged on by Daudet and Edmond de Goncourt, whose jealousy of Zola had by then grown into an obsession.

Undaunted, Zola kept on writing, turning out the remaining novels of the series at the rate of about one every year, just as he had with the earlier ones. *Le Rêve* (1888; translated as *The Dream*, 1888) strongly contrasts with *La Terre*. It recounts the love story of a beautiful, pale, very pious girl (naturally, another Rougon-Macquart family member) who dreams of love, realizes her dream, and then dies. The setting is dominated by a giant cathedral next to which she grows up and in which she is married. She expires in her handsome groom's arms just as they are leaving it after the wedding ceremony.

That same year, Zola took on a mistress, Jeanne Rozerot, a good-looking, placid, twenty-year-old woman whom his wife had engaged to help with the mending and sewing. He was nearly fifty and still childless. Within a few weeks after their liaison began, Jeanne became pregnant. In the fall of 1889 she gave birth to a baby girl, whom they named Denise. Barely more than a year later, a second child was born, this time a boy, Jacques. Alexandrine had been kept in the dark, but shortly after Jacques's birth, an anonymous "well-wisher" apprised her of the truth, and for months her and Zola's life was sheer hell. Yet it soon became apparent to both of them that, while they could not be happy together, they could not be happy apart either. Finally, still heartbroken but calmer, she accepted the situation and even became fond of the children. After Zola's death, she permitted them to assume the Zola name.

Meanwhile, the final Rougon-Macquart volumes continued to pour out. The seventeenth, *La Bête humaine* (1890; translated as *Human Brutes*, 1890), is a black, gruesome, powerful crime story in a railroad setting. Its hero, the engineer Jacques Lantier, Etienne and Claude's brother, is a homicidal maniac whose blood lust is combined with a sexual urge. The locomotive is made to symbolize, among other things, both the forces of "progress" and the atavistic passions that lurk in the depths of man. One of the best of the many movies inspired by Zola's fiction is based on it—Jean Renoir's 1938 film of the same name, starring Jean Gabin as Jacques.

The eighteenth volume, *L'Argent* (1891; translated as *Money (L'Argent)*, 1891), takes the reader into the world of banking and the stock exchange. It climaxes with the crash of the shares of a major bank in which thousands of innocents have invested. Its hero is the speculator and robber baron Aristide Rougon, already encountered in *La Curée*.

The nineteenth volume, *La Débâcle* (1892; translated as *The Downfall: A Story of the Horrors of War*, 1892), portrays the Franco-Prussian War, the fall of the Second Empire, and the civil war of the Paris Commune. Its central characters are two soldiers, Jean Macquart and his companion and friend Maurice Levasseur. The story devel-

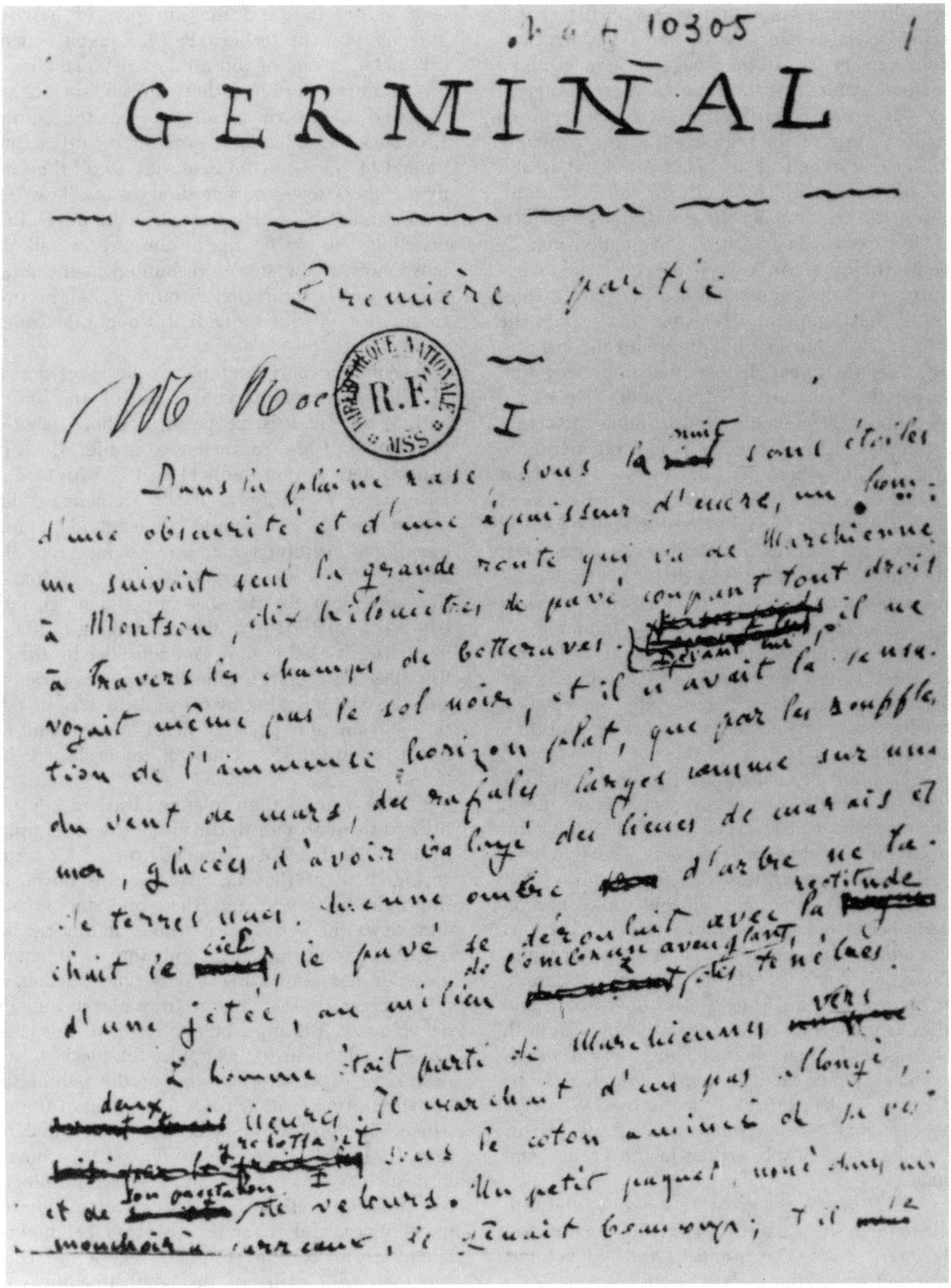

First page of the manuscript for one of Zola's Rougon-Macquart *novels (Bibliothèque Nationale)*

ops, through a succession of spectacular battle scenes, a Darwinian view of war as an atrocious but necessary part of the struggle for survival, an essential element of the process whereby eternal life perpetuates, purifies, and renews itself. *La Débâcle* is one of the most realistic and conscientiously researched of all Zola's novels. It is also one of those in which his gift for storytelling, his genius for bringing out the full drama of history, and his extraordinary poetic imagination may be seen at their best. As he wrote the concluding paragraphs, he was haunted by his personal memories of the Commune. He evokes once again the flames of the burning buildings and the crimson night sky that, years before, had impressed him during the insurrection's final hours. He elaborates upon these motifs, transforming them into a complex symbol of death and regeneration. Paris burning becomes, in his eye, the field plowed up once again so that from the renewed and purified soil might spring the idyll of a new golden age. Even as the blazing sun goes down and the city burns, it seems that a new day is already dawning: "C'était le rajeunissement certain de l'éternelle nature, de l'éternelle humanité, le renouveau promis à qui espère et travaille" (It was the certain rejuvenation of an everlasting nature, of an imperishable humanity, the renewal promised to him who keeps on working and does not despair).

Edmond de Goncourt was incapable of finding in it a single page of any true literary merit, but the reviews were largely favorable. One compared Zola to the greatest poets who had ever lived. That October, less than four months after the novel had come out, 150,000 copies had already been sold, not counting those in the foreign editions. (It was by then customary for translations of Zola's novels into English, Spanish, Portuguese, Italian, Dutch, Danish, Russian, and other languages to come out simultaneously with the original French edition.) The American novelist Henry James thought that *La Débâcle* was one of Zola's works most likely to survive. Whatever the case may be, it remains one of the two or three best war novels written in the French language.

La Débâcle is the great, resounding, epical finale to the historical study underlying the Rougon-Macquart series. The twentieth and last volume, more autobiographical, lyrical, and prophetic, *Le Docteur Pascal* (1893; translated as *Doctor Pascal; or, Life and Heredity*, 1893), concludes the underlying physiological study with its emphasis on the laws of heredity and the interplay of heredity and environment. Its hero, Pascal Rougon, a medical doctor, is one of those many fictional characters scattered here and there throughout the series who are clearly mouthpieces of the author. Like Zola, Pascal has kept a minute record, accompanied by his own commentaries, of all the family members' lives and hereditary traits. This "scientific treasure" is reproduced in the novel, thus enabling Zola to tie up in the process all the loose ends of the stories recounted in the series and to proffer indirectly, through Pascal, his own summaries of the individual Rougon-Macquart novels.

Zola had also intended *Le Docteur Pascal* to be the philosophical conclusion of the series, and, in a sense, it is, proposing a whole religious philosophy of life. According to it, life, which he equates here as repeatedly elsewhere with God, is movement. Heredity is the movement of life passed on. If one could understand it well enough to manipulate it, one could create the world. Work is the movement of life. History is the movement of life writ large. The gigantic labor of humanity, its stubborn clinging to life, is its excuse, its redemption. One must live for the effort that life requires. One must live in order to add one stone to the far-off and mysterious edifice, and the only peace of heart one can find on Earth lies in the joy of having accomplished this task.

These and other related ideas, mostly expressed through Pascal, constitute the philosophical message that Zola intended to give his series at the moment that he planned this novel, as shown in his notes. Yet when one stands back and views the series as a whole, it quickly becomes apparent that this is only one of the many more or less conflicting philosophies, or quasi-religious creeds, that emerge from it or its individual volumes. It is impossible to reconcile this vitalism logically with, for example, the black, brutal pessimism of *La Bête humaine* or the pantheistic eroticism of *La Faute de l'abbé Mouret*, according to which salvation is to be achieved through making love. *Les Rougon-Macquart* and many of the novels in it, such as *Germinal*, remain essentially ambiguous philosophically. The products of an age of metaphysical and religious crisis and heightened scientific activity, they resonate, like a vast echo chamber, with many of the conflicting ideas of their epoch. Their documentary, photographic realism masks the absence in them of any solid, coherent, stable vision of reality.

Zola at work in his study at Médan

What is more important for the average reader, *Le Docteur Pascal* is also a love story about Pascal's passionate relationship with his young niece, Clotilde. As Zola wrote it, he was undoubtedly thinking of his own liaison with Jeanne Rozerot. He dedicated the novel, however, to his wife and the memory of his mother. The novel—and the series—ends with a vision of Clotilde nursing their baby son and dreaming that he is the new messiah for which the world is waiting. The final image is that of the infant holding up, as he sucks, a little arm in the air, "tout droit, dressé comme un drapeau d'appel à la vie" (straight up, raised like a flag hailing life). Significantly, the last word of the novel—and the series—is "vie" (life).

The two series of novels that occupied most of the rest of Zola's career are sequels to *Les Rougon-Macquart*. The first, *Les Trois Villes* (The Three Cities, 1894-1898), is a trilogy. It carries on, in late-nineteenth-century settings, the themes, already treated in *Les Rougon-Macquart*, of progress and of world destruction and renewal. In particular, it reflects Zola's old fascination with religious change, and it depicts what seemed to him and many of his contemporaries to be the inexorable decline of traditional religion and his and his contemporaries' attempt to find or create a new one to take its place. Its hero is a spiritually troubled priest, Pierre Froment, who, as Zola's disciple and early biographer Paul Alexis was among the first to point out, is still another fictional avatar of Zola himself.

In the first novel of the trilogy, *Lourdes* (1894; translated, 1894), Pierre makes a pilgrimage to the famous Catholic shrine of Lourdes in the hope that the Holy Virgin will cure him of his doubts, but to no avail. In the second novel, *Rome* (1896; translated, 1896), he goes to the Holy City to try to obtain the pope's approval of his book advocating a new Christian socialist social order, but he is again unsuccessful. In the third novel, *Paris* (1898; translated, 1900), he returns to Paris, the capital of the new world that is being born out of the ruins of the collapsing old world, reigned over by Rome. Although his Catholicism by now has completely crumbled, he nevertheless devotes himself to works of charity while desperately seeking a new faith. In the end he embraces the "new religion of science" that he has forged for himself. He also sheds his frock, marries, and devotes himself to helping his chemist brother in his lab.

Many critics have considered *Lourdes* to be one of Zola's best novels, and it has certainly been one of his dozen or so most popular ones. The other two novels contain powerful passages, including many masterful descriptions of the cities in which they are set. Few if any novelists have portrayed so well the psychology of metaphysical anguish or of the divided soul. Nevertheless, when Zola wrote *Les Trois Villes,* he had clearly passed his prime. He repeats old themes and scenes and tends to theologize. The symbolism is obvious. *Germinal* and more than one of Zola's other earlier novels are, like most truly great, enduring works of literature, magic mirrors in which each reader sees himself or herself and his or her own reality reflected. *Les Trois Villes* has little of that wonderful ambiguity, that enduring capacity to inspire and welcome new and different interpretations.

This is even truer of Zola's last fictional series, *Les Quatre Evangiles* (The Four Gospels, 1899-1903). He had originally planned to include in it only three novels, but expanded the number to four in order to reinforce the parallel he wanted to set between his "gospels" and the four Gospels of the New Testament. For the same reason, he named the hero of each of the novels after one of the four New Testament evangelists: Matthieu, Marc, Luc, and Jean. (They are all Pierre Froment's sons.) Although Zola retains in *Les Quatre Evangiles* many of his realistic mannerisms, he is no longer primarily concerned with depicting historical reality. The stories that he narrates in these novels, or would have narrated (he died before he could write his fourth "gospel"), all take place mostly in the future—the mythical twentieth century of his Romantic and humanitarian reveries. He confessed that after a lifetime of recording reality, he had earned the right to dream, but he went on to insist, paradoxically, that the dreams that he was communicating to his readers in his "gospels" were authorized by science. Like many other nineteenth-century intellectuals, he claimed that his own philosophical and religious ideas had a scientific basis, while accusing those he disagreed with of being unscientific.

Fécondité (1899; translated as *Fruitfulness (Fécondité),* 1900), the first of these four novels, proclaims that the ever-expanding force of life is the driving force of progress. Less a novel than a long prose poem, it is the gospel of Venus, queen of seeds and immortal hope. On the other hand, *Travail* (1901; translated as *Work (Travail),* 1901), in which he prophetically portrays the final triumph of socialism over capitalism after a terrible world war, deifies work. It proclaims work the world's salvation, health, joy, and sovereign peace, the sole truth, the only master and god. Its blueprint of an ideal socialist community, Beauclair, influenced the utopian architect Tony Garnier and, through Garnier, the great twentieth-century town planner Le Corbusier. The novel also went so far as to propose a complete new religion of work, with prayers, rites, and a messianic leader (Luc Froment), whose life parallels Christ's. *Vérité,* posthumously published in 1903 (translated as *Truth (Vérité),* 1903), depicts a better world brought about by the triumph of scientific truth, represented by the schoolteacher Marc Froment, over the forces of darkness, above all the Roman Catholic Church.

In writing these final "gospels," Zola pursued more single-mindedly than ever his ambition, going back to his youth, to be the prophet for which the world was waiting. Yet it is significant that what he came up with was not one, but several logically rather inconsistent works, each with a different deity or supreme value, each with a different new messiah, each with a different vision of the world's future and the path to social salvation. Was it that, unable to achieve his goal of finding a truly satisfactory new faith, he had, in his despair, taken refuge in fictional faiths—faiths that were not so much the fruit of faith as of a willing suspension of disbelief? In any case there can be little doubt that Zola was indeed a new prophet after all, in his own odd, paradoxical way. Strangely enough, these curious books were studied all over France in turn-of-the-century working-class night schools. The power of Zola's intellectual influence was further attested to by a poll taken in 1979 of fourteen hundred Parisian university students, in which Zola's name was put down more frequently than any other in response to the question as to which author had influenced the respondent the most.

During this final period of Zola's life, while he was engaged in writing *Les Trois Villes* and *Les Quatre Evangiles,* most of the events occurred that constituted the Dreyfus Affair, that terrible miscarriage of justice that divided French society into two violently opposed camps. The main details are well known. On 22 December 1894 Capt. Alfred Dreyfus, a Jewish officer in the French army, was convicted by a court-martial of having sold military secrets to Germany. He was

Cinq Centimes

JEUDI 13 JANVIER 1898

ERNEST VAUGHAN

L'AURORE

Littéraire, Artistique, Sociale

J'Accuse...!

LETTRE AU PRÉSIDENT DE LA RÉPUBLIQUE

Par ÉMILE ZOLA

LETTRE

A M. FÉLIX FAURE

Président de la République

Monsieur le Président,

First page of the article in which Zola defended Capt. Alfred Dreyfus, who had been court-martialed and convicted of espionage degraded in a public ceremony and sent to Devil's Island. When evidence was discovered proving that the real criminal was Maj. Ferdinand Walsin-Esterhazy, not Dreyfus, the army, which feared that its prestige was at stake, refused Dreyfus a new trial. There can be little doubt that the anti-Semitism that was then very widespread in France was one of the other factors leading to this decision.

At first Zola paid scant attention to the affair, but finally, convinced by his conversations with Dreyfus's defenders that the man was innocent, he decided to intervene. He had already fired off a few articles and pamphlets on behalf of Dreyfus when, on 11 January 1898, a court-martial, to the dismay of many, acquitted Esterhazy. Persuaded that a direct challenge to the government and military authorities was now necessary to keep Dreyfus's case alive, he published in the Parisian newspaper *Aurore* two days later, on 13 January, an instantly world-famous open letter to the president of the Republic. The title was chosen by the editor, Georges Clemenceau: "J'accuse. . . !" (translated as "To M. Félix Faure" in *The Dreyfus Case: Four Letters to France*, 1898). Calculated to make a libel suit inevitable, the letter accused various high officers as well as the officers of Esterhazy's court-martial of intentionally concealing the truth or of giving in to the promptings of others. There was a tremendous uproar, and France was shaken from top to bottom.

In a celebrated trial, conducted by a biased judge, Zola was found guilty and sentenced to a year in prison and a fine of three thousand francs. He promptly appealed, and on 2 April 1898 the proceedings were quashed. A second trial took place on 18 July at Versailles, but, on the advice of his lawyer and friends, as concerned as ever with keeping the case alive, he fled to England without waiting for the result. The verdict this time would have been without appeal. He remained in England, writing *Fécondité*, until 4 June 1899, when, having heard that there was to be a review of the first Dreyfus trial, he returned to Paris. During Zola's exile Col. Hubert Henry, one of the chief behind-the-scenes plotters in the affair, had committed suicide, and Esterhazy had fled and confessed. The Cour de Cassation ordered a new trial for Dreyfus, which resulted in the curious verdict of guilty with extenuating circumstances. The French president pardoned him on 19 September 1899, but he would not be completely exonerated until 1906. Thus Zola, who died in 1902, never had the satisfaction of witnessing the final happy conclusion to this sad episode of French history.

On Sunday, 28 September 1902, Alexandrine and he left Médan to take up their autumn and winter quarters on the Rue de Bruxelles. It was chilly, so a fire was lit in their bedroom. It burned badly, and the room filled with carbon monoxide while they slept. The next morning one of the servants, after knocking repeatedly on their bedroom door, became frightened, broke it down, and found Alexandrine lying unconscious and Zola dead. There is a strong possibility, based on a deathbed confession, that the chimney had been deliberately blocked by workmen repairing the roof of a neighboring house. But this has never been proven. (The Dreyfus Affair had made for Zola many irreconcilable enemies.) On Sunday, 5 October 1902, there was a gigantic public funeral. A delegation of miners marched in the long procession, shouting rhythmically, "Germinal! Germinal!" One of the eulogists, Anatole France, the same literary colleague who had so severely condemned *La Terre*, now called Zola "un moment de la conscience humaine" (which means both "a moment of the conscience of man" and "a moment of man's consciousness"). On the night of 4 June 1908, Zola's coffin was solemnly removed from its tomb in the Montmartre Cemetery and transported to the Paris Panthéon, the resting place of some of France's greatest heroes. After a second funeral, his remains were placed, not far from Voltaire's and Jean-Jacques Rousseau's sarcophagi, in the crypt below. They are still there today, sharing a small vault with Hugo's.

When one tries to size up Zola, it quickly becomes apparent that one of his chief traits both as a man and as an artist was his extraordinary commitment to his values, not the least of which were truth and justice. It also becomes evident how faithfully he complied with the principles of the universal theory of art that he had developed in his lifelong meditations on how to achieve his highest goal: lasting fame. This theory is, indeed, a far better key to the understanding and appreciation of Zola's achievement than his naturalism, which is only a special application of it to a particular set of historical circumstances.

Over the years he had distinguished between several varieties of lasting fame. There was the sort that, as he noted in an 1877 essay on Alexandre Dumas *fils*, sprang from having fought valiantly and effectively in the cause of truth. There was the sort that issued from formal perfection. There was the kind acquired by writers whose works had gone out of favor but who remained, like George Sand or François-René de Chateaubriand, striking, memorable figures who had left an indelible mark on their times. There was the immortality that came from possessing an extraordinary imagination. There was the kind that had its source in the artistic reflection of a powerful temperament, the spectacle of a powerful personality—a Shakespeare, a Balzac, a Hugo—at grips with nature, bending it to his will, imprinting his personality upon it, breathing into it his own life. There was the lasting fame that resulted from an artist's having captured, expressed, and perpetuated the life of a whole society, civilization, moment in history. There was the glory of having created, like Shakespeare or Balzac, a world of one's own that could be set against the divine creation. There was, as Zola had also remarked, the glory of having, like Balzac, imposed a new and enduring literary formula, of having become the chief figure of a movement, attracted followers, created the archetypes of an entire era. Zola, lashed on by his obsessive fear of death and fierce ambition to survive the grave, had obviously done his best to attain every one of these different varieties of enduring fame.

Now that more than a century has passed since he wrote his best works, the true nature of his fiction is also becoming clearer. During much of the early twentieth century, Zola was relegated to a kind of critical limbo. The public at large continued to devour him, but literary critics who had good things to say about his writings were few and far between. On 17 July 1932 André Gide noted in his *Journal* that he considered the discredit of Zola at that time as a monstrous injustice that said little for the literary critics of the day. Since around 1950, however, Zola has been the object of a new critical reevaluation. Between 1952 and 1980 alone, more than twenty-six hundred new books and articles about him were published. His works lend themselves extraordinarily well to most of the new critical approaches that have flourished since the middle of the twentieth century. The old myths and prejudices that blinded many earlier critics have been largely dispelled. The habit, which Zola himself encouraged, of judging his works primarily in the context of his naturalist theories or, worse, of confounding his theory and practice, has been discarded by most serious students of his art. In particular, no serious modern critic would repeat the mistake, commonly made by the older ones, of interpreting his fiction solely or even predominantly in the light of "Le Roman expérimental."

There is general agreement that a much better guide is to be found, for example, in Zola's remark in a letter addressed to his friend Céard on 22 March 1885, just after the publication of *Germinal*: "Nous mentons tous plus ou moins, mais quelle est la mécanique et la mentalité de mon mensonge? Or—c'est ici que je m'abuse peut-être—je crois encore que je mens pour mon compte dans le sens de la vérité. J'ai l'hypertrophie du détail vrai, le saut dans les étoiles sur le tremplin de l'observation exacte. La vérité monte d'un coup d'aile jusqu'au symbole" (We all lie more or less, but what are the mechanics and mentality of our lies? Now—and I may be fooling myself in this respect—I still believe that, in my case, I lie in the direction of truth. I have an excessive love for true detail, the leap toward the stars from the springboard of exact observation. Truth mounts with a single stroke of its wing all the way up to symbol).

All in all, the new critical approaches that have emerged during the last half of the twentieth century, with their emphasis on close textual analysis, have afforded the public a better understanding of the character of Zola's fiction and the sources of its great lasting power. Modern readers have, among other things, a far better conception of the great poet in Zola, and also of the complex, ambiguous, essentially operatic structure of his works. At the same time, respect for Zola's more scientific qualities has also been growing. The theory of heredity that he incorporated into *Les Rougon-Macquart* has been surpassed, but it has been shown that Zola was a far better scholar and scientist in many other respects (for example, in history, economics, and crowd psychology) than was once supposed. As his great English biographer F. W. J. Hemmings has pointed out, he "was the first of those who raised sociology to the dignity of art."

It has also become apparent that the overall structure of Zola's fiction largely resulted from the interplay of two opposing forces, one centripetal, the other centrifugal. On the one hand, he loved the aesthetic ideas of unity, clarity, and simplicity. On the other hand, he wanted to burst through the bounds of the novel, to absorb and transform in his fiction all the traditional literary genres: the realistic novel, tragedy, comedy, farce, melodrama, epic, idyll, biography, history, scientific dissertation, and other forms. He wanted to be realistic and visionary, satirical, lyri-

Zola with his mistress Jeanne Rozerot and their children, Denise and Jacques

cal, scientific, and prophetic, all in the same works. He wanted his fiction to portray him, to incarnate him, to be "ma chair," "mon sang" (my flesh, my blood), as he liked to say, with all his protean qualities, violent inconsistencies, warring personalities—the scientist, the dreamer, the romantic, the positivist, the optimist, the pessimist, the visionary prophet and would-be new messiah, the dogmatic theorist, the timid self-doubter. He wanted, just as he had when he was planning "La Genèse" or "La Chaîne des êtres," to see and say everything, to put the whole of limitless reality into a single work. He wanted to give full expression to his radical skepticism, his leaps of faith, the eternal war going on within him between religious hope and despair. He wanted his novels to reflect his centerless, chaotic vision of reality, the host of more or less nebulous, tentative, unstable, shifting metaphysical and religious credos warring within him, each struggling for full expression—hence his tendency to group his novels together into series rather than independent works. This enabled him to combine works incorporating different genres and different sides of himself and of his thought into larger unities better reflecting his full diversity. This resulted in the many barely disguised autobiographical features of his fiction, the host of characters embodying this or that side of his personality. He made heavy use of techniques of ambiguity—dreamlike symbols, for example, capable of assuming multiple meanings, or free indirect discourse (in which one does not know whether the author is citing his own ideas or merely those of a character). He built frames within frames, complex synecdochic structures, in which everything—a character, a setting, an action—represents the larger whole of which it is a part: the working class, the priesthood, capital, humanity, or life.

Moreover, modern criticism has discovered the great extent to which Zola incorporated into his fiction biblical and classical Greco-Roman myths, perhaps hoping thereby to impart to his own work something of their enduring, timeless qualities. The presence of great eternal archetypes in Zola's fiction undoubtedly adds to its power, along with its realism, its rich ambiguities, its nightmarish qualities, its psychological and social truth, its concern with the great problems of modern life, and indeed of all life everywhere. So do his fascination with the machine and the birth of modern mass culture; his visionary and prophetic qualities; his rhythmic, operatic structures; his background music; and his impressionistic or expressionistic qualities reminiscent of Monet, Cézanne, and Van Gogh.

Zola is still, many decades after his death, a marvelously timely author. The world he depicted is still here. His best works, such as *Germinal*, treat problems that have lost none of their urgency. They are as terrifying as they were when they first appeared. Even his style, marvelously virile, colorful, and powerful, has aged little. While the reputations of many of the leading literary figures of his day—Paul Bourget, for example, or Anatole France—have faded, Zola's has been growing ever brighter.

Letters:

Correspondance, 2 volumes (Paris: Fasquelle, 1907-1908);

Correspondance, 2 volumes, edited by Maurice Le Blond (Paris: Bernouard, 1928-1929);

Dix-neuf lettres de Stéphane Mallarmé, edited by Léon Deffoux (Paris: La Centaine, 1929);

Paul Cézanne: Correspondance, edited by John Rewald (Paris: Grasset, 1937);

Emile Zola's Letters to J. Van Santen Kolff, edited by Robert J. Niess (St. Louis: Washington University Press, 1940);

Lettres inédites de Louis Desprez à Emile Zola, edited by Guy Robert (Paris: Les Belles Lettres, 1952);

J.-K. Huysmans: Lettres inédites à Emile Zola, edited by Pierre Lambert, with an introduction by Pierre Cogny (Geneva: Droz, 1953);

Henry Céard: Lettres inédites à Emile Zola, edited by Colin A. Burns (Paris: Nizet, 1958);

Emile Zola: Lettres inédites à Henry Céard, edited by Albert J. Salvan (Providence, R.I.: Brown University Press, 1959);

"Correspondance," in *Œuvres complètes*, volume 14, edited by Henri Mitterand (Paris: Cercle du Livre Précieux, 1970), pp. 1181-1542;

Naturalisme pas mort: Lettres inédites de Paul Alexis à Emile Zola, 1871-1902, edited by Bard H. Bakker (Toronto: University of Toronto Press, 1971);

Correspondance, 11 volumes, edited by Bakker (Montreal: Presses de l'Université de Montréal, 1978-);

Trente années d'amitié: Lettres de l'éditeur Georges Charpentier à Emile Zola, edited by Colette Becker (Paris: Presses Universitaires de France, 1980).

Interview:

Jules Huret, *Enquête sur l'évolution littéraire* (Paris: Charpentier, 1891).

Bibliographies:

F. W. J. Hemmings, "Zola par delà la Manche et l'Atlantique (essai bibliographique)," in *Cahiers Naturalistes*, no. 23 (Paris: Fasquelle, 1963): 299-312;

Henri Mitterand and Halina Suwala, *Emile Zola journaliste: Bibliographie chronologique et analytique des articles d'Emile Zola (1859-1881)* (Paris: Les Belles Lettres, 1968);

Léon Lipschutz, *Une Bibliographie dreyfusienne: Essai de bibliographie thématique et analytique de l'affaire Dreyfus* (Paris: Fasquelle, 1970);

David Baguley, *Les Œuvres de Zola traduites en anglais (1878-1968)*, in *Cahiers Naturalistes*, no. 40 (Paris: Fasquelle, 1970): 195-209;

Roger Ripoll, *Emile Zola journaliste: Bibliographie chronologique et analytique. II. (Le Sémaphore de Marseille, 1871-1877)* (Paris: Les Belles Lettres, 1972);

Clive R. Thomson, *Index des Cahiers Naturalistes (années 1955-1974, numéros 1 à 48)*, in *Cahiers Naturalistes*, no. 49 (Paris: Fasquelle, 1975): 191-233;

Baguley, *Bibliographie de la critique sur Emile Zola: 1864-1970* (Toronto & Buffalo: University of Toronto Press, 1976);

Baguley, *Bibliographie de la critique sur Emile Zola: 1971-1980* (Toronto, Buffalo & London: University of Toronto Press, 1982);

Brian Nelson, *Emile Zola: A Selective Analytical Bibliography* (London: Grant & Cutler, 1982);

Dolorès Signori and Dorothy Spiers, *Emile Zola dans la presse parisienne, 1880-1902* (Toronto: Research Program on Zola and Naturalism, University of Toronto, 1985);

Signori and Spiers, *Entretiens avec Emile Zola* (Ottawa: University of Ottawa Press, 1990).

Biographies:

Fernand Xau, *Emile Zola* (Paris: Marpon et Flammarion, 1880);

Paul Alexis, *Emile Zola: Notes d'un ami* (Paris: Charpentier, 1882);

Ernest Seillière, *Emile Zola* (Paris: Grasset, 1923);

Matthew Josephson, *Zola et son temps* (New York: Macaulay, 1928);

Denise Le Blond-Zola, *Emile Zola raconté par sa fille* (Paris: Fasquelle, 1931);

Henri Barbusse, *Zola* (Paris: Gallimard, 1932);

Zola near the end of his life

Armand Lanoux, *Bonjour, Monsieur Zola* (Paris: Amiot-Dumont, 1954);

Henri Mitterand, *Zola journaliste de l'affaire Manet à l'affaire Dreyfus* (Paris: Armand Colin, 1962);

Elliott M. Grant, *Emile Zola* (New York: Twayne, 1966);

F. W. J. Hemmings, *Emile Zola* (Oxford: Clarendon, 1966);

Hemmings, *The Life and Times of Emile Zola* (London: Elek / New York: Scribners, 1977);

Graham King, *Garden of Zola: Emile Zola and His Novels for English Readers* (London: Barrie & Jenkins / New York: Barnes & Noble, 1978);

Joanna Richardson, *Zola* (London: Weidenfeld & Nicolson / New York: St. Martin's Press, 1978);

Bettina Knapp, *Emile Zola* (New York: Ungar, 1980);

Philip Walker, *Zola* (London: Routledge & Kegan Paul, 1985).

References:

David Baguley, *Naturalist Fiction: The Entropic Vision* (Cambridge: Cambridge University Press, 1990);

Baguley, ed., *Critical Essays on Emile Zola* (Boston: G. K. Hall, 1986);

Colette Becker, ed., *Les Critiques de notre temps et Zola* (Paris: Garnier frères, 1972);

David F. Bell, *Models of Power: Politics and Economics in Zola's "Rougon-Macquart"* (Lincoln & London: University of Nebraska Press, 1988);

Jean Borie, *Zola et les mythes, ou de la nausée au salut* (Paris: Editions du Seuil, 1971);

Patrick Brady, *"L'Œuvre" d'Emile Zola: Roman sur les arts, manifeste, autobiographie, roman à clef* (Geneva: Droz, 1976);

Calvin S. Brown, *Repetition in Zola's Novels* (Athens: University of Georgia Press, 1963);

Cahiers Naturalistes (Paris: Société des Amis d'Emile Zola & Editions Fasquelle, 1955-);

Lawson A. Carter, *Zola and the Theatre* (New Haven, Conn.: Yale University Press, 1963);

Auguste Dezalay, *L'Opéra des Rougon-Macquart: Essai de rhythmologie* (Paris: Klincksieck, 1983);

Jacques Dubois, *"L'Assommoir" de Zola: Société, discours, idéologie* (Paris: Larousse, 1973);

Esprit Créateur, issue on "Zola et le naturalisme," 25 (Winter 1985);

Neide de Faria, *Structures et unité dans "Les Rougon-Macquart" (La poétique du cycle)* (Paris: Nizet, 1977);

Marcel Girard, "L'Univers de *Germinal*," *Revue des Sciences Humaines*, 69 (1953): 59-76;

Jean-Max Guieu, *Le Théâtre lyrique d'Emile Zola* (Paris: Fischbacher, 1983);

Guieu and Alison Hilton, eds., *Emile Zola and the Arts* (Washington, D.C.: Georgetown University Press, 1988);

Philippe Hamon, *Le Personnel du roman: Le système des personnages dans "Les Rougon-Macquart" d'Emile Zola* (Geneva: Droz, 1983);

Chantal Jennings, *L'Eros et la femme chez Zola* (Paris: Klincksieck, 1977);

Lewis Kamm, *The Object in Zola's "Rougon-Macquart"* (Madrid: José Porrúa Turanzas, 1978);

John C. Lapp, *Zola before the "Rougon-Macquart"* (Toronto: University of Toronto Press, 1964);

Robert Lethbridge and Terry Keefe, eds., *Zola and the Craft of Fiction (Essays in Honour of*

F. W. J. Hemmings) (Leicester: Leicester University Press, 1990);

Harry Levin, *The Gates of Horn* (New York: Oxford University Press, 1966);

J. H. Matthews, *Les Deux Zola: Science et personnalité dans l'expression* (Geneva: Droz, 1957);

Henri Mitterand, *Le Discours du roman* (Paris: Presses Universitaires de France, 1980);

Mitterand, *Le Regard et le signe: Poétique du roman réaliste et naturaliste* (Paris: Presses Universitaires de France, 1987);

Mitterand, *Zola et le naturalisme* (Paris: Presses Universitaires de France, 1986);

Robert J. Niess, *Zola, Cézanne, and Manet: A Study of "L'Œuvre"* (Ann Arbor: University of Michigan Press, 1968);

Alain Pagès, *Le Naturalisme* (Paris: Presses Universitaires de France, 1989);

Présence de Zola (Paris: Fasquelle, 1953);

Roger Ripoll, *Réalité et mythe chez Zola*, 2 volumes (Lille: Atelier Reproduction des Thèses, l'Université de Lille III / Paris: Champion, 1981);

Guy Robert, *Emile Zola: Principes et caractères généraux de son œuvre* (Paris: Les Belles Lettres, 1952);

Robert, *"La Terre" d'Emile Zola: Etude historique et critique* (Paris: Les Belles Lettres, 1952);

Naomi Schor, *Zola's Crowds* (Baltimore & London: Johns Hopkins University Press, 1978);

Michel Serres, *Feux et signaux de brume: Zola* (Paris: Grasset, 1975);

Halina Suwala, *Naissance d'une doctrine; Formation des idées littéraires et esthétiques de Zola (1859-1865)* (Warsaw: Wydawnictwa Uniwersyitetu Warsawskiego, 1976);

Philip Walker, *"Germinal" and Zola's Philosophical and Religious Thought* (Amsterdam & Philadelphia: John Benjamins, 1984);

Walker, "Prophetic Myths in Zola," *PMLA*, 74 (1959): 444-452;

Angus Wilson, *Emile Zola: An Introductory Study of His Novels* (London: Secker & Warburg, 1964);

Yale French Studies, issue on Zola, no. 42 (1969).

Papers:

Of the two principal collections of Zola's manuscripts, the larger, containing material on *Les Rougon-Macquart* and *Les Quatre Evangiles*, is at the Bibliothèque Nationale, Paris. The second, including material on *Les Trois Villes*, is at the Bibliothèque d'Aix-en-Provence. The manuscript of *Nana* is in the Pierpont Morgan collection, New York. Part of Zola's preparatory notes for *Le Docteur Pascal* is at the Bodmer Library, Geneva. The Research Program on Zola and Naturalism at the University of Toronto possesses a large assortment of Zola's letters and manuscripts. Other letters are at Brown and Harvard universities. The University of California at Santa Barbara has a microfilm collection of Zola's preparatory notes for *Germinal* and other *Rougon-Macquart* novels.

Checklist of Further Readings

The following list includes books in English and French that deal with literary history in France in the nineteenth century, the genre of the novel during that period or as a whole, pertinent themes and problems in literary history, or more than one French fiction writer between 1860 and the end of the century, whether analytically in discrete chapters or synthetically. Many of these studies reflect or constitute the most up-to-date scholarship in the area. The reader wishing to pursue further studies can consult, in addition to the annual *MLA International Bibliography*, the following major listings: Otto Klapp, *Bibliographie der französischen Literaturwissenschaft* (Frankfurt: Klosterman, 1960-), not annotated but very thorough and particularly good for European criticism; the bibliography in *Revue d'Histoire Littéraire de la France*, edited by René Rancœur (formerly a rubric of each issue, now printed as issue number 3 of each volume); and *Critical Bibliography of French Literature: The Nineteenth Century*, 2 volumes (Syracuse, N.Y.: Syracuse University Press, 1993), a major annotated bibliography that completes the series begun by David C. Cabeen in 1947.

Anderson, R. D. *France, 1870-1914: Politics and Society*. London: Henley / Boston: Routledge & Kegan Paul, 1977.

Apter, Emily. *Feminizing the Fetish: Psychoanalysis and Narrative Obsession in Turn-of-the-Century France*. Ithaca, N.Y.: Cornell University Press, 1991.

Baguley, David. *Naturalist Fiction: The Entropic Vision*. New York: Cambridge University Press, 1990.

Bancquart, Marie-Claire. *Images littéraires du Paris "fin-de-siècle."* Paris: Editions de la Différence, 1979.

Bernheimer, Charles. *Figures of Ill Repute: Representing Prostitution in Nineteenth-Century France*. Cambridge, Mass.: Harvard University Press, 1989.

Bessière, Jean, ed. *Roman, réalités, réalismes*. Paris: Presses Universitaires de France, 1989.

Bethlenfalvay, Marina. *Les Visages de l'enfant dans la littérature française du XIXe siècle*. Geneva: Droz, 1979.

Birkett, Jennifer. *The Sins of the Fathers: Decadence in France, 1870-1914*. London & New York: Quartet, 1986.

Bredin, Jean-Denis. *The Affair: The Case of Alfred Dreyfus*. Translated by Jeffrey Mehlman. New York: Braziller, 1986.

Brombert, Victor. *The Intellectual Hero: Studies in the French Novel, 1880-1955*. Philadelphia & New York: Lippincott, 1961.

Burns, Michael. *Dreyfus: A Family Affair, 1789-1945*. New York: HarperCollins, 1991.

Cailliet, Emile. *The Themes of Magic in Nineteenth-Century French Fiction*. Translated by Lorraine Havens. Philadelphia: Porcupine Press, 1980.

Chambers, Ross. *Mélancolie et opposition: Les débuts du modernisme en France*. Paris: José Corti, 1987.

Charvet, P. E. *A Literary History of France*, volume 5 [i.e., 6]: *The Nineteenth and Twentieth Centuries, 1870-1940*. London: Ernest Benn / New York: Barnes & Noble, 1967.

Citti, Pierre. *Contre la décadence: Histoire de l'imagination française dans le roman, 1890-1914*. Paris: Presses Universitaires de France, 1987.

Clark, Priscilla Parkhurst. *Literary France: The Making of a Culture*. Berkeley: University of California Press, 1987.

Cruickshank, John, ed. *French Literature and Its Background*, volume 5: *The Late Nineteenth Century*. London, Oxford & New York: Oxford University Press, 1969.

Dakyns, Janine R. *The Middle Ages in French Literature, 1851-1900*. London: Oxford University Press, 1973.

Elwitt, Sanford. *The Making of the Third Republic: Class and Politics in France, 1868-1884*. Baton Rouge & London: Louisiana State University Press, 1975.

Furst, Lilian R. *Counterparts: The Dynamics of Franco-German Literary Relationships, 1770-1895*. Detroit: Wayne State University Press, 1977.

Gooch, G. P. *The Second Empire*. London: Longmans, Green, 1960.

Graña, César. *Bohemian Versus Bourgeois: French Society and the French Man of Letters in the Nineteenth Century*. New York & London: Basic Books, 1964.

Griffiths, Richard. *The Reactionary Revolution: The Catholic Revival in French Literature, 1870-1914*. New York: Ungar, 1965.

Haig, Stirling. *The Madame Bovary Blues: The Pursuit of Illusion in Nineteenth-Century French Fiction*. Baton Rouge & London: Louisiana State University Press, 1987.

Hartman, Elwood. *French Literary Wagnerism*. New York & London: Garland, 1988.

Hicks, John, and Robert Tucker, eds. *Revolution and Reaction: The Paris Commune 1871*. Amherst: University of Massachusetts Press, 1973.

Houston, John Porter. *Fictional Technique in France, 1802-1927: An Introduction*. Baton Rouge & London: Louisiana State University Press, 1972.

Johnson, Douglas. *France and the Dreyfus Affair*. London: Blandford, 1966.

Jones, Louisa E. *Sad Clowns and Pale Pierrots: Literature and the Popular Comic Arts in 19th-Century France*. Lexington, Ky.: French Forum, 1984.

Kelly, Dorothy. *Fictional Genders: Role and Representation in Nineteenth-Century French Narrative*. Lincoln: University of Nebraska Press, 1989.

Kleeblatt, Norman L., ed. *The Dreyfus Affair: Art, Truth, and Justice*. Berkeley: University of California Press, 1987.

Leroy, Géraldi, ed. *Les Ecrivains et l'Affaire Dreyfus*. Paris: Presses Universitaires de France, 1983.

Locke, Robert R. *French Legitimists and the Politics of Moral Order in the Early Third Republic*. Princeton: Princeton University Press, 1974.

Marguèze-Pouey, Louis. *Le Mouvement décadent en France*. Paris: Presses Universitaires de France, 1986.

Martin, Andrew. *The Knowledge of Ignorance: From Genesis to Jules Verne*. Cambridge: Cambridge University Press, 1985.

McLendon, Will L., ed. *L'Hénaurme Siècle*. Heidelberg: Carl Winter Universitäts-Verlag, 1984.

Mitchell, Robert L., ed. *Pre-Text/Text/Context: Essays on Nineteenth-Century French Literature*. Columbus: Ohio State University Press, 1980.

Muray, Philippe. *Le 19e siècle à travers les âges*. Paris: Denoël, 1984.

Neubauer, John. *The Fin-de-Siècle Culture of Adolescence*. New Haven: Yale University Press, 1992.

Noiray, Jacques. *Le Romancier et la machine: L'image de la machine dans le roman français (1850-1900)*, 2 volumes. Paris: José Corti, 1981.

Pasco, Allan H. *Novel Configurations: A Study of French Fiction*. Birmingham, Ala.: Summa, 1987.

Petrey, Sandy. *Realism and Revolution: Balzac, Stendhal, Zola and the Performances of History*. Ithaca, N.Y.: Cornell University Press, 1989.

Pierrot, Jean. *The Decadent Imagination, 1880-1900*. Translated by Derek Cottman. Chicago & London: University of Chicago Press, 1981.

Pouilliart, Raymond. *Le Romantisme*. III: *1870-1896*. Paris: Arthaud, 1968.

Praz, Mario. *La Chair, la mort et le Diable dans la littérature du XIXe siècle: Le romantisme noir*. Paris: Denoël, 1977.

Raitt, A. W. *Life and Letters in France: The Nineteenth Century*. New York: Scribners, 1965.

Ridge, George Ross. *The Hero in French Decadent Literature*. Athens: University of Georgia Press, 1961.

Sagnes, Guy. *L'Ennui dans la littérature française de Flaubert à Laforgue (1848-1884)*. Paris: Armand Colin, 1969.

Saurat, Denis. *Modern French Literature, 1870-1940*. Port Washington, N.Y.: Kennikat Press, 1971.

Schneider, Marcel. *Histoire de la littérature fantastique en France*. Paris: Fayard, 1985.

Scott, Malcolm. *The Struggle for the Soul of the French Novel: French Catholic and Realist Novelists, 1850-1970*. Washington, D.C.: Catholic University Press, 1990.

Seager, Frederic H. *The Boulanger Affair: Political Crossroads of France, 1886-1889*. Ithaca, N.Y.: Cornell University Press, 1969.

Snyder, Louis L. *The Dreyfus Case: A Documentary History*. New Brunswick, N.J.: Rutgers University Press, 1973.

Spackman, Barbara. *Decadent Genealogies: The Rhetoric of Sickness from Baudelaire to D'Annunzio*. Ithaca, N.Y.: Cornell University Press, 1989.

Sutton, Michael. *Nationalism, Positivism and Catholicism: The Politics of Charles Maurras and the French Catholics, 1890-1914*. Cambridge: Cambridge University Press, 1982.

Terdiman, Richard. *The Dialectics of Isolation: Self and Society in the French Novel from the Realists to Proust*. New Haven: Yale University Press, 1976.

Todorov, Tzvetan. *The Fantastic: A Structural Approach to a Literary Genre*. Translated by Richard Howard. Cleveland: Case Western Reserve University Press, 1973.

Van Tieghem, Philippe. *Petite histoire des grandes doctrines littéraires en France*. Paris: Presses Universitaires de France, 1960.

Williams, Roger L. *The Horror of Life*. Chicago: University of Chicago Press, 1980.

Contributors

John Blaise Anzalone	*Skidmore College*
B. F. Bart	*University of Pittsburgh*
Robin Orr Bodkin	*Keswick, Virginia*
Catharine Savage Brosman	*Tulane University*
John E. Coombes	*University of Essex*
Terence Dawson	*National University of Singapore*
Mary Donaldson-Evans	*University of Delaware*
Arthur B. Evans	*DePauw University*
John A. Fleming	*University of Toronto*
Aleksandra Gruzinska	*Arizona State University*
Alec G. Hargreaves	*Loughborough University, England*
Melanie C. Hawthorne	*Texas A&M University*
Leonard R. Koos	*Mary Washington College*
Robert Lethbridge	*Cambridge University*
Roy Jay Nelson	*University of Michigan*
E. J. Richards	*Tulane University*
Murray Sachs	*Brandeis University*
Philip Walker	*University of California, Santa Barbara*
Robert Ziegler	*Montana Tech*

Cumulative Index

Dictionary of Literary Biography, Volumes 1-123
Dictionary of Literary Biography Yearbook, 1980-1991
Dictionary of Literary Biography Documentary Series, Volumes 1-10

Cumulative Index

DLB before number: *Dictionary of Literary Biography,* Volumes 1-123
Y before number: *Dictionary of Literary Biography Yearbook,* 1980-1991
DS before number: *Dictionary of Literary Biography Documentary Series,* Volumes 1-10

A

B

C

D

E

F

G

H

I

J

K

L

M

N

O

P

Q

R

S

T

U

V

W

Y

Z

ISBN 0-8103-7600-8
90000
9 780810 376007

8878

(Continued from front endsheets)

80: *Restoration and Eighteenth-Century Dramatists,* First Series, edited by Paula R. Backscheider (1989)

81: *Austrian Fiction Writers, 1875-1913,* edited by James Hardin and Donald G. Daviau (1989)

82: *Chicano Writers,* First Series, edited by Francisco A. Lomelí and Carl R. Shirley (1989)

83: *French Novelists Since 1960,* edited by Catharine Savage Brosman (1989)

84: *Restoration and Eighteenth-Century Dramatists,* Second Series, edited by Paula R. Backscheider (1989)

85: *Austrian Fiction Writers After 1914,* edited by James Hardin and Donald G. Daviau (1989)

86: *American Short-Story Writers, 1910-1945,* First Series, edited by Bobby Ellen Kimbel (1989)

87: *British Mystery and Thriller Writers Since 1940,* First Series, edited by Bernard Benstock and Thomas F. Staley (1989)

88: *Canadian Writers, 1920-1959,* Second Series, edited by W. H. New (1989)

89: *Restoration and Eighteenth-Century Dramatists,* Third Series, edited by Paula R. Backscheider (1989)

90: *German Writers in the Age of Goethe, 1789-1832,* edited by James Hardin and Christoph E. Schweitzer (1989)

91: *American Magazine Journalists, 1900-1960,* First Series, edited by Sam G. Riley (1990)

92: *Canadian Writers, 1890-1920,* edited by W. H. New (1990)

93: *British Romantic Poets, 1789-1832,* First Series, edited by John R. Greenfield (1990)

94: *German Writers in the Age of Goethe: Sturm und Drang to Classicism,* edited by James Hardin and Christoph E. Schweitzer (1990)

95: *Eighteenth-Century British Poets,* First Series, edited by John Sitter (1990)

96: *British Romantic Poets, 1789-1832,* Second Series, edited by John R. Greenfield (1990)

97: *German Writers from the Enlightenment to Sturm und Drang, 1720-1764,* edited by James Hardin and Christoph E. Schweitzer (1990)

98: *Modern British Essayists,* First Series, edited by Robert Beum (1990)

99: *Canadian Writers Before 1890,* edited by W. H. New (1990)

100: *Modern British Essayists,* Second Series, edited by Robert Beum (1990)

101: *British Prose Writers, 1660-1800,* First Series, edited by Donald T. Siebert (1991)

102: *American Short-Story Writers, 1910-1945,* Second Series, edited by Bobby Ellen Kimbel (1991)

103: *American Literary Biographers,* First Series, edited by Steven Serafin (1991)

104: *British Prose Writers, 1660-1800,* Second Series, edited by Donald T. Siebert (1991)

105: *American Poets Since World War II,* Second Series, edited by R. S. Gwynn (1991)

106: *British Literary Publishing Houses, 1820-1880,* edited by Patricia J. Anderson and Jonathan Rose (1991)

107: *British Romantic Prose Writers, 1789-1832,* First Series, edited by John R. Greenfield (1991)

108: *Twentieth-Century Spanish Poets,* First Series, edited by Michael L. Perna (1991)

109: *Eighteenth-Century British Poets,* Second Series, edited by John Sitter (1991)

110: *British Romantic Prose Writers, 1789-1832,* Second Series, edited by John R. Greenfield (1991)

111: *American Literary Biographers,* Second Series, edited by Steven Serafin (1991)

112: *British Literary Publishing Houses, 1881-1965,* edited by Jonathan Rose and Patricia J. Anderson (1991)

113: *Modern Latin-American Fiction Writers,* First Series, edited by William Luis (1992)

114: *Twentieth-Century Italian Poets,* First Series, edited by Giovanna Wedel De Stasio, Glauco Cambon, and Antonio Illiano (1992)

115: *Medieval Philosophers,* edited by Jeremiah Hackett (1992)

116: *British Romantic Novelists, 1789-1832,* edited by Bradford K. Mudge (1992)

117: *Twentieth-Century Caribbean and Black African Writers,* First Series, edited by Bernth Lindfors and Reinhard Sander (1992)